A history
of
archaeological
thought

BRUCE G. TRIGGER

A history of archaeological thought

PUBLISHED BY THE PRESS SYNDICATE OF THE UNIVERSITY OF CAMBRIDGE
The Pitt Building, Trumpington Street, Cambridge, United Kingdom

CAMBRIDGE UNIVERSITY PRESS
The Edinburgh Building, Cambridge CB2 2RU, UK
40 West 20th Street, New York, NY 10011–4211, USA
477 Williamstown Road, Port Melbourne, VIC 3207, Australia
Ruiz de Alarcón 13, 28014 Madrid, Spain
Dock House, The Waterfront, Cape Town 8001, South Africa

http://www.cambridge.org

First published 1989
Eleventh printing 2005

Printed in the United Kingdom at the University Press, Cambridge

British Library Cataloguing in Publication data
Trigger, Bruce G. (Bruce Graham), 1937–
A history of archaeological thought
1. Archaeology to 1988
I. Title
930.1'09

Library of Congress Cataloguing in Publication data
Trigger, Bruce G.
A history of archaeological thought/Bruce G. Trigger
p. cm.
Bibliography
Includes index.
ISBN 0 521 32878 0 (hardback) ISBN 0 521 33812 2 (paperback)
1. Archaeology – History.
2. Archaeology – Philosophy – History.
I. Title
CC100.T75 1989
930.1 – dc19 88-16926 CIP

ISBN 0 521 32878 0 hardback
ISBN 0 521 33818 2 paperback

CE

To Barbara

CONTENTS

ILLUSTRATIONS

PREFACE

This study is a combined product of book-learning, archaeological experience, and oral tradition. It grew out of a course on the 'History of Archaeological Theory' that I have taught annually since 1975. Since I began the course, I intended to write a book on this subject. My first efforts resulted in the original essays published in *Time and Traditions* (Trigger 1978a) and *Gordon Childe: Revolutions in Archaeology* (Trigger 1980a). While I continued to write papers on various aspects of the history of archaeology (see especially Trigger 1980b, 1981a, 1984a, 1984e, 1985a, 1985c, 1986b), for various reasons two more attempts in the early 1980s to begin this book came to nothing. One of the reasons was my feeling that the time was not yet propitious. Then, in the spring of 1986, I made a third attempt and found that the book was 'writing itself'. I believe that this change reflects my growing satisfaction with current developments in archaeological interpretation. Many archaeologists, not only in the West but apparently also in the Soviet Union, are expressing concern about what they perceive as the theoretical fragmentation of their discipline. On the contrary, I believe that current developments are helping archaeologists to transcend the limitations of narrowly focused sectarian approaches and resulting in more holistic and fruitful interpretations of archaeological data. There is also growing realism in assessing the limitations of archaeological data at the same time that there is greater flexibility in seeking ways to overcome these limitations. These developments draw upon past as well as present archaeological accomplishments. It is therefore a useful time to review archaeological thinking from a historical perspective.

A brief statement of my own theoretical position is in order. I have always regarded a materialist outlook as being more productive of an understanding of human behaviour than any other approach. Intelligently applied, it in no way diminishes an appreciation of the unique characteristics of the human mind, while it facilitates the insertion of social science theory into a broader biological understanding of human origins and behaviour. Yet I have never found that ecological determinism, neo-evolutionary theory, or cultural materialism provide satisfactory explanations of the full range of variation found in human behaviour or of the various complexities of concrete sequences of cultural change. Throughout my career I have sought to reconcile a materialist approach with efforts to account for the historical diversity that characterizes the archaeological record. This has fostered my growing appreciation of historical materialism, to which I was initially attracted by my efforts to understand the past rather than as a result of dogmatic political convictions. In particular, I have found Gordon Childe's historically and contextually oriented Marxism to be infinitely preferable to the more deterministic forms of evolutionary Marxism or the flirting with idealism that characterizes much so-called neo-Marxism.

While this book has been written as a unit, I have drawn to varying degrees upon my previous writings. The outline of the study of the history of archaeology in the bibliographical essay for chapter one is based heavily on Trigger (1985a). Many of the ideas used to structure chapters four and five were developed in Trigger (1978a) and (1984a), while the sections dealing with Childe in chapters five and seven are based on Trigger (1980a) and more particularly Trigger (1984b) and (1986c). Chapter six is based in part on Trigger (1984c), although the views that I have expressed about Soviet archaeology in that paper have been considerably modified. Chapter nine makes use of ideas developed in Trigger (1982a, 1984e, 1985b, 1985d, 1988). Some of the references cited in chapter six were located by Rosemarie Bernard in the course of writing her McGill undergraduate honours thesis 'Marxist Archaeologies: A History of their Development in the U.S.S.R., Europe, and the Americas' (1985). I am also grateful to Peter Timmins for his advice in drafting the section of chapter nine dealing with site-formation processes. For factual information and bibliographical assistance I thank Chen Chun, Margaret Deith, Brian Fagan, Norman Hammond, Fumiko Ikawa-Smith, June Kelley, Philip Kohl, Isabel McBryde, Mary Mason, Valerie Pinsky, Neil Silberman, Robert Vogel, Alexander von Gernet, Michael Woloch, and Alison Wylie, as well as many other colleagues around the world who have sent me reprints of their papers.

Preface

The history of archaeology is not a new subject. Hence anyone writing a general study is standing on the shoulders of his predecessors. Because of that, wherever it has seemed appropriate to do so, I have cited authoritative secondary sources rather than extended an already mammoth bibliography with references to still more primary sources that are impossible to obtain in most libraries. I have, however, whenever possible, examined these primary sources and where discrepancies have been found I have abandoned defective secondary ones or drawn attention to their shortcomings. Where old and inaccessible works are easily available in reprinted form (and in English translation), I have cited the latter, adding the date of the original in square brackets.

Research for this book was greatly assisted by a sabbatical leave from McGill University and a Canada Council Leave Fellowship in 1976–7, while some further work was done during another sabbatical leave when I held a Social Sciences and Humanities Research Council of Canada Leave Fellowship in 1983. I wish to thank both undergraduate and graduate students who have taken 'History of Archaeological Theory' for their many contributions to the development of the ideas expounded in this book. I also thank my daughters, Isabel and Rosalyn, for help with word-processing and encouraging maximum clarity of expression. Finally I dedicate this book to my wife, Barbara.

CHAPTER 1

The relevance of archaeological history

Though there exists one major academic industry . . . telling the social scientists . . . how they can turn themselves into genuine scientists, there exists another, with at least as flourishing an output, putatively establishing that the study of man and society cannot be scientific.

ERNEST GELLNER, *Relativism and the Social Sciences* (1985), p. 120

Since the 1950s archaeology, especially in North America and Western Europe, has shifted from a seemingly complacent culture-historical orthodoxy to ambitious theoretical innovations. The latter, far from producing an anticipated new consensus, have led to growing disagreement about the goals of the discipline and how these goals can be achieved (Dunnell 1983: 535). Increasing numbers of archaeologists, following in the wake of historians and sociologists, have abandoned positivist certainty and begun to entertain doubts about the objectivity of their research. They see social factors as determining not only the questions that they ask but also the answers that they judge to be convincing. Extreme versions of this view deny that archaeologists can offer interpretations of their data that are other than a reflection of the transient values of the societies in which they live. Yet, if archaeology cannot produce some kind of cumulative understanding of the past and a commentary that is at least partially independent of specific historical contexts, what scientific, as opposed to political, psychological, or aesthetic, justification can be offered for doing archaeological research?

This book examines the relations between archaeology and its social milieu from a historical perspective. Such an approach provides a comparative viewpoint from which problems of subjectivity, objectivity, and the gradual accumulation of knowledge can be assessed. In recent years a growing number of archaeologists have come to agree with the philosopher and archaeologist R. G.

Collingwood (1939: 132) that 'no historical problem should be studied without studying . . . the history of historical thought about it' (Dunnell 1984: 490). Historical investigations of archaeological interpretation have multiplied and more sophisticated methodologies have been adopted (Trigger 1985a). This approach is not, however, without its critics. Michael Schiffer (1976: 193) has asserted that graduate courses should cease to be 'histories of thought' and instead should systematically expound and articulate current theories. His position embodies the view that the truth or falseness of theoretical formulations is independent of social influences and hence of history but can be determined by applying scientifically valid procedures of evaluation to adequate bodies of data. Taken to an extreme, this view implies that the history and philosophy of archaeology are totally unrelated to each other. Ironically, historical analysis provides a privileged viewpoint from which the respective merits of these opposing positions can be evaluated.

The following chapters will survey the main ideas that have influenced the interpretation of archaeological data, especially during the last 200 years. I will examine in detail some of the social factors that have helped to shape the ideas that have structured this work and the reciprocal impact that archaeological interpretations have had on other disciplines and on society. To do this it is necessary to compare the way in which archaeological thought has developed in various parts of the world. It is impossible in a single volume to examine every archaeological theory or even every regional archaeological tradition. I hope, however, that by concentrating on a limited number of significant developments it will be possible to learn something about the major factors that have shaped archaeological interpretation. Following L. R. Binford (1981), a distinction will be drawn between an internal dialogue, by which archaeologists have sought to develop methods for inferring human behaviour from archaeological data, and an external dialogue, in which they use these findings to address general issues concerning human behaviour and history. While I do not claim that these two levels of discourse are clearly separable, the internal dialogue embraces the distinctive concerns of archaeology as a discipline, while the external one constitutes archaeology's contribution to the social sciences. This is, however, a distinction that has only recently become clear to most archaeologists.

The public reaction to archaeological findings indicates the need to view the history of archaeology in a broad social context. The popular image of archaeology is of an esoteric discipline that has no relevance for the needs or concerns of the present. Ernest Hooton (1938: 218) once described archaeologists as being viewed as 'the senile playboys of science rooting in the rubbish heaps of antiquity'. Yet for almost 200 years a widespread concern for the broader implications of archaeological discoveries has contradicted this image of archaeology. No one would deny the romantic fascination aroused by spectacular archaeological finds, such as those by Austen Layard at Nimrud or Heinrich Schliemann at Troy in the nineteenth century, and the more recent discoveries of the tomb of Tutankhamen, the Palace of Minos, the life-size ceramic army of the Chinese Emperor Qin Shihuangdi, and several million-years-old fossil hominids in East Africa. This does not, however, explain the intense public interest in the controversies that have surrounded the interpretation of many more routine archaeological findings, the attention that diverse political, social, and religious movements throughout the world have paid to archaeological research, and efforts by various totalitarian regimes to control the interpretation of archaeological data. During the second half of the nineteenth century, archaeology was looked to for support by both sides in the debate about whether evolutionism or the book of Genesis provided a more reliable account of human origins. As recently as the 1970s a government-employed archaeologist found his position no longer tenable when he refused to cast doubt on the evidence that stone ruins in Central Africa were built by the ancestors of the modern Bantu.

My adoption of a historical perspective does not mean that I claim any privileged status for such an approach with respect to objectivity. Historical interpretations are notoriously subjective, to the extent that many historians have viewed them as merely expressions of personal opinion. It is also recognized that, because of the abundance of historical data, evidence can be marshalled to 'prove' almost anything. There may be some truth in William McNeill's (1986: 164) argument that, even if historical interpretation is a form of myth-making, the myths help to guide public action and are a human substitute for instinct. If this is so, it follows that they are subject to the operation of the social equivalent of natural selection and hence may more closely approximate reality over long periods of time. This, however, is a tenuous basis on which to base our hopes for the objectivity of historical interpretations.

I do not claim that the historical study presented here is any more objective than are the interpretations of archaeological or ethnological data that it examines. I believe, however, as do many others who study the history of archaeology, that a historical approach offers a special vantage point from which the changing relations between archaeological interpretation and its social and cultural milieu can be examined. The time perspective provides a different basis for studying the ties between archaeology and society than do philosophical or sociological approaches. In particular it permits the researcher to identify subjective factors by observing how and under what circumstances interpretations of the archaeological record have changed. Although this does not eliminate the bias of the observer, or the possibility that these biases will influence the interpretation of archaeological data, it almost certainly increases the chances of gaining more rounded insights into what has happened in the past.

Approaches to the history of archaeology

The need for a more systematic study of the history of archaeological interpretation is indicated by serious disagreements about the nature and significance of that history. A major controversy centres on the role played by explanation in the study of archaeological data over the last two centuries. G. R. Willey and J. A. Sabloff organized their *A History of American Archaeology* (1974, 1980) in terms of four successive periods: Speculative, Classificatory–Descriptive, Classificatory–Historical, and Explanatory, the last of which began in 1960. This scheme implies that archaeology in the western hemisphere experienced a long gestation during which descriptive and classificatory objectives predominated, prior to developing significant theories to explain its data. Yet, as the British historian E. H. Carr (1967: 3–35) has reminded us, the mere characterization of data as being relevant or irrelevant, which occurs even in the most descriptive historical studies, implies the existence of some kind of theoretical framework. It can further be argued in opposition to the idea of a neutral observational language, that not even the simplest fact can be constituted independently of a theoretical context (Wylie

1982: 42). In the past most of these frameworks were not formulated explicitly or even consciously by archaeologists. Today, especially in the context of American archaeology, many theoretical propositions are systematically elaborated. Yet it is surely misleading to restrict the status of theory to the self-conscious formulations of recent decades. Moreover, a close examination of the history of archaeological interpretation suggests that earlier theories were not always as implicit or disjointed as they are often believed to have been.

Others accept that archaeologists employed theories in the past but maintain that until recently there was not enough consistency in this process for these theories to have constituted what Thomas Kuhn has called a research paradigm. Kuhn (1970: 10) has defined a paradigm as an accepted canon of scientific practice, including laws, theory, applications, and instrumentation, that provides a model for a 'particular coherent tradition of scientific research'. Such a tradition is sustained by a 'scientific community' and is propagated in journals and textbooks that are controlled by that community. D. L. Clarke (1968: xiii) described archaeology as an 'undisciplined empirical discipline' and suggested that its theoretical development, at least until very recent times, must be regarded as being in a pre-paradigmatic state. Until the 1960s, archaeological theory remained a 'disconnected bundle of inadequate subtheories' that had not been structured within a comprehensive system. He also implied that only approaches that are recognized internationally can qualify as paradigms (ibid. 153–5). Yet detailed studies of earlier phases in the development of archaeology are revealing much more comprehensive and internally consistent formulations than were hitherto believed to have existed. This is especially true of studies that respect the integrity of the past and judge the work done in terms of the ideas of the period rather than modern standards (Meltzer 1983; Grayson 1983, 1986).

Some archaeologists combine Kuhn's idea of scientific revolutions with an evolutionary view of the development of their discipline. They maintain that successive phases in the development of archaeological theory display enough internal consistency to qualify as paradigms and that the replacement of one paradigm by another constitutes a scientific revolution (Sterud 1973). According to this view, successive innovators, such as Christian Thomsen, Oscar Montelius, Gordon Childe, and Lewis Binford, recognized major anomalies and inadequacies in conventional interpretations of archaeological data and shaped new paradigms that significantly changed the direction of archaeological research. These paradigms not only altered the significance that was accorded to archaeological data but also determined what kinds of problems were and were not regarded as important.

Yet archaeologists do not agree about the actual sequence of major paradigms that are supposed to have characterized the development of archaeology (Schwartz 1967; essays in Fitting 1973). This may partly reflect a lack of clarity in Kuhn's conception of a paradigm (Meltzer 1979). Some critics have assumed that a discipline may be characterized simultaneously by a number of functionally different types of paradigms. These may be only loosely related to one another and may alter at different rates to produce an overall pattern of change that is gradual rather than abrupt. Margaret Masterman (1970) has differentiated three main types of paradigm: metaphysical, relating to the world view of a group of scientists; sociological, that define what is accepted; and construct, that supply the tools and methods for solving problems. No one of these types alone constitutes 'the' paradigm of a particular era. Kuhn has also been accused of ignoring the importance of competition and mobility between rival 'schools' for bringing about change in a discipline (Barnes 1974: 95). It may also be that, because of the complexity of their subject-matter, the social sciences have more such schools and competing paradigms than do the natural sciences and perhaps because of this individual paradigms tend to coexist and replace one another relatively slowly (Binford and Sabloff 1982).

An alternative view, which is more in accord with these critiques of Kuhn and with Stephen Toulmin's (1970) thesis that sciences do not experience revolutions but rather gradual changes or progressions, holds that the history of archaeology has involved a cumulative growth of knowledge about the past from early times to the present (Casson 1939; Heizer 1962a; Willey and Sabloff 1974; Meltzer 1979). It is maintained that, although various phases in this development may be delineated arbitrarily, archaeology changes in a gradual fashion, with no radical breaks or sudden transformations (Daniel 1975: 374–6). Some archaeologists view the development of their discipline as following a course that is unilinear and inevitable. The data base is seen as continuously expanding and new interpretations are treated as the gradual elaboration, refinement, and modification of an existing corpus of theory. This view does not, however, take account of the frequent failure of archaeologists to develop their ideas in a systematic fashion. For example, while nineteenth-century naturalists with archaeological interests, such as Japetus Streenstrup (Morlot 1861: 300) and William Buckland (Dawkins 1874: 281–4) carried out experiments to determine how faunal remains were introduced into sites, research of this sort did not become routine in archaeology until the 1970s (Binford 1977, 1981).

A third view treats the development of archaeological theory as a process that is non-linear and frequently unpredictable. Changes are viewed as caused not so much by new archaeological data as by novel ideas about human behaviour that are formulated elsewhere in the social sciences and may reflect social values that exhibit fluctuations in popularity. Because of this, archaeological interpretation does not change in a linear fashion, with data being construed ever more comprehensively and satisfactorily. Instead, changing perceptions of human behaviour can radically alter archaeological interpretations, rendering information that previously seemed important of relatively little interest (Piggott 1950, 1968, 1976; Daniel 1950; Hunter 1975). This view accords with Kuhn's (1970: 103) observation that shifting paradigms not only select new issues as being important but also deflect attention from problems that otherwise might have been thought worthy of further study. This view, unlike the evolutionary ones, does not regard it as certain that most changes in theoretical orientation result in the forward movement of archaeological research.

Some archaeologists doubt that the interests and concepts of their discipline change significantly from one period to another. Bryony Orme (1973: 490) maintains that the archaeological interpretations offered in the past were more like those of the present than is commonly believed and that archaeological preoccupations have changed little. A remarkable antiquity can be demonstrated for some ideas that are commonly believed to be modern. Archaeologists argued that growing population densities led to the adoption of more labour-intensive forms of food production long before they rediscovered this idea in the work of Ester Boserup (Smith and Young 1972). As early as 1673, the British statesman William Temple had adumbrated this theory with his observation that high population densities force people to work hard (Slotkin 1965: 110–11). In 1843 the Swedish archaeologist Sven Nilsson (1868: lxvii) argued that increasing population had brought about a shift from pastoralism to agriculture in prehistoric Scandinavia. This concept was also implicit in the 'oasis' theory of the origin of food production, as expounded by Raphael Pumpelly (1908: 65–6) and adopted by Harold Peake and H. J. Fleure (1927) and by Gordon Childe (1928). They proposed that postglacial desiccation in the Near East had compelled people to cluster around surviving sources of water, where they had to innovate in order to feed higher population densities. Yet, while ideas persist and recur in the history of archaeology, this does not mean that there is nothing new in the interpretation of archaeological data. Such ideas must be examined in relation to the different conceptual frameworks of which they were a part at each period. It is from these frameworks that these concepts derive their significance to the discipline and, as the frameworks change, their significance does also. According undue importance to particular ideas and not paying enough attention to their changing context will lead archaeologists to underestimate the amount of significant change that has characterized the development of archaeological interpretation.

Many archaeologists note that one of the principal characteristics of archaeological interpretation has been its regional diversity. David Clarke (1979: 28, 84) and Leo Klejn (1977) have both treated the history of archaeology as one of regional schools. Clarke maintained that archaeology had only recently begun to cease being a series of divergent traditions, each with its own locally esteemed body of theory and preferred form of description, interpretation, and explanation. It is clear that there have been, and still are, regional traditions in archaeological interpretation (Daniel 1981b; Evans *et al.* 1981: 11–70; Trigger and Glover 1981–2). What has not yet been studied adequately is the nature of their divergences. To what degree do they represent irreconcilable differences in the understanding of human behaviour, differences in the questions being asked, or the same basic ideas being studied under the guise of different terminologies? Cultural differences are important. Yet, on closer inspection, most interpretations by archaeologists working within different national traditions can be assigned to a limited number of general orientations. Elsewhere I have identified three types: colonialist, nationalist, and imperialist or world-oriented

(Trigger 1984a). These have replicated themselves in the archaeology of countries that are geographically remote from one another and the archaeology of a particular nation may switch from one type to another as its political circumstances change. Such approaches to archaeological interpretation will be examined in detail in later chapters.

Yet studies of regional traditions, with a few notable exceptions (Bernal 1980; Chakrabarti 1982), have failed to take account of the vast intellectual exchange that has characterized the development of archaeology in all parts of the world during the nineteenth and twentieth centuries. This is dramatically illustrated by the early study of shell mounds. Reports of the pioneering studies by Danish scholars, who began their work in the 1840s, stimulated a large number of investigations of shell heaps along the Atlantic and later the Pacific coasts of North America in the latter half of the nineteenth century (Trigger 1986a). When the American zoologist Edward Morse went to teach in Japan, after analysing material from shell mounds along the coast of Maine for the Harvard University archaeologist Jeffries Wyman, he discovered and excavated in 1877 a large Mesolithic shell deposit at Omori, near Tokyo. Some of his zoology students dug another shell mound by themselves and it was not long before Japanese archaeologists who had studied in Europe established the study of the Mesolithic Jomon culture on a professional basis (Ikawa-Smith 1982). The Scandinavian studies also stimulated the early investigation of shell mounds in Brazil (Ihering 1895) and Southeast Asia (Earl 1863). Even the ideologically opposed archaeological traditions of Western Europe and the Soviet Union have significantly influenced each other, despite decades when scientific contact of any sort was very difficult and even dangerous. For all these reasons it seems unwise to over-estimate the independence or theoretical distinctiveness of these regional archaeologies.

Less attention has been paid to the effects of disciplinary specialization within archaeology on the ways in which archaeological data are interpreted (Rouse 1972: 1–25). Yet differing orientations along these lines may account for as many differences as do regional traditions. Classical archaeology, Egyptology, and Assyriology have been strongly committed to studying epigraphy and art history within a historical framework (Bietak 1979). Medieval archaeology has developed as an investigation of material remains that com-

1 Important movements in archaeology an

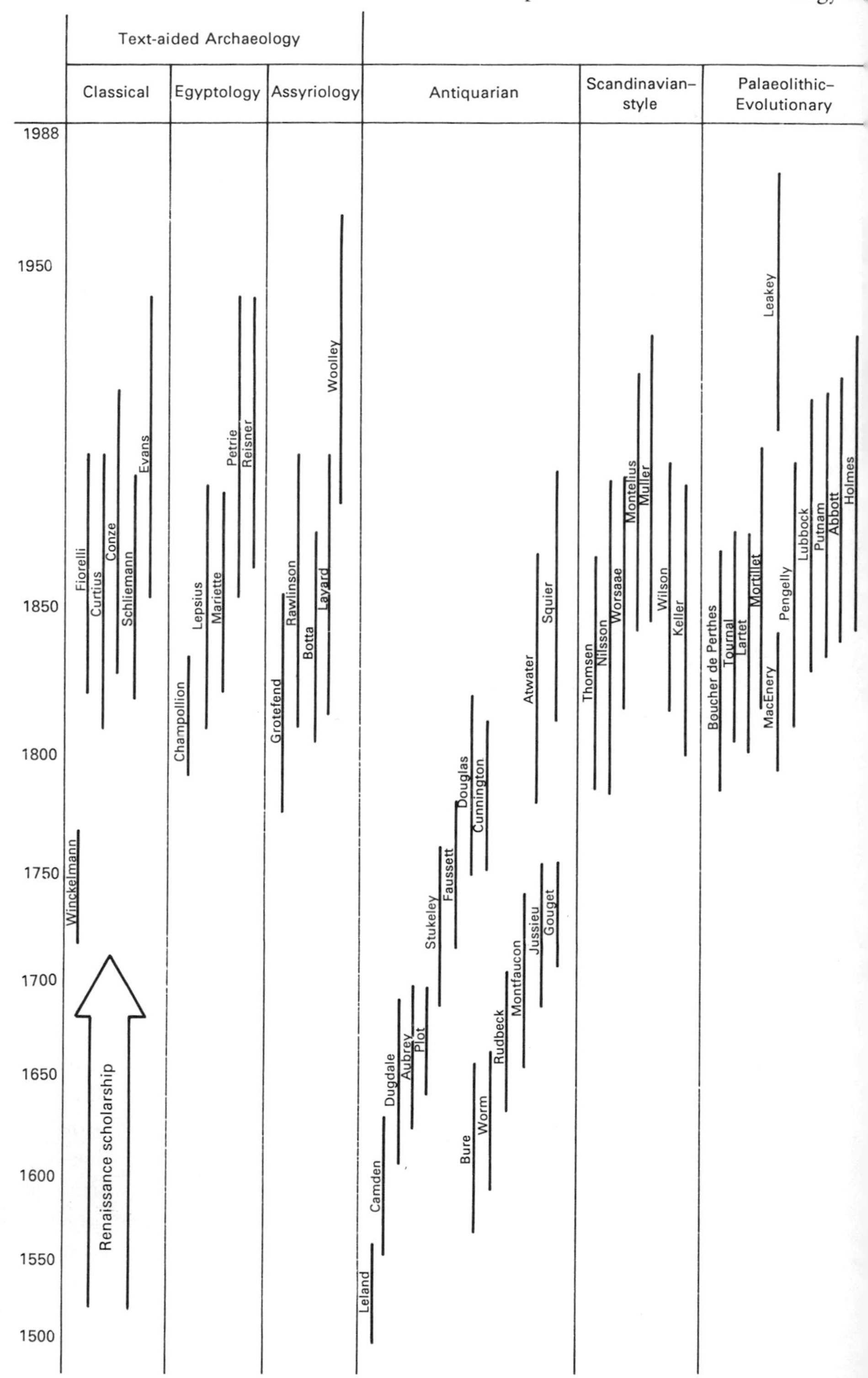

ne major figures associated with them

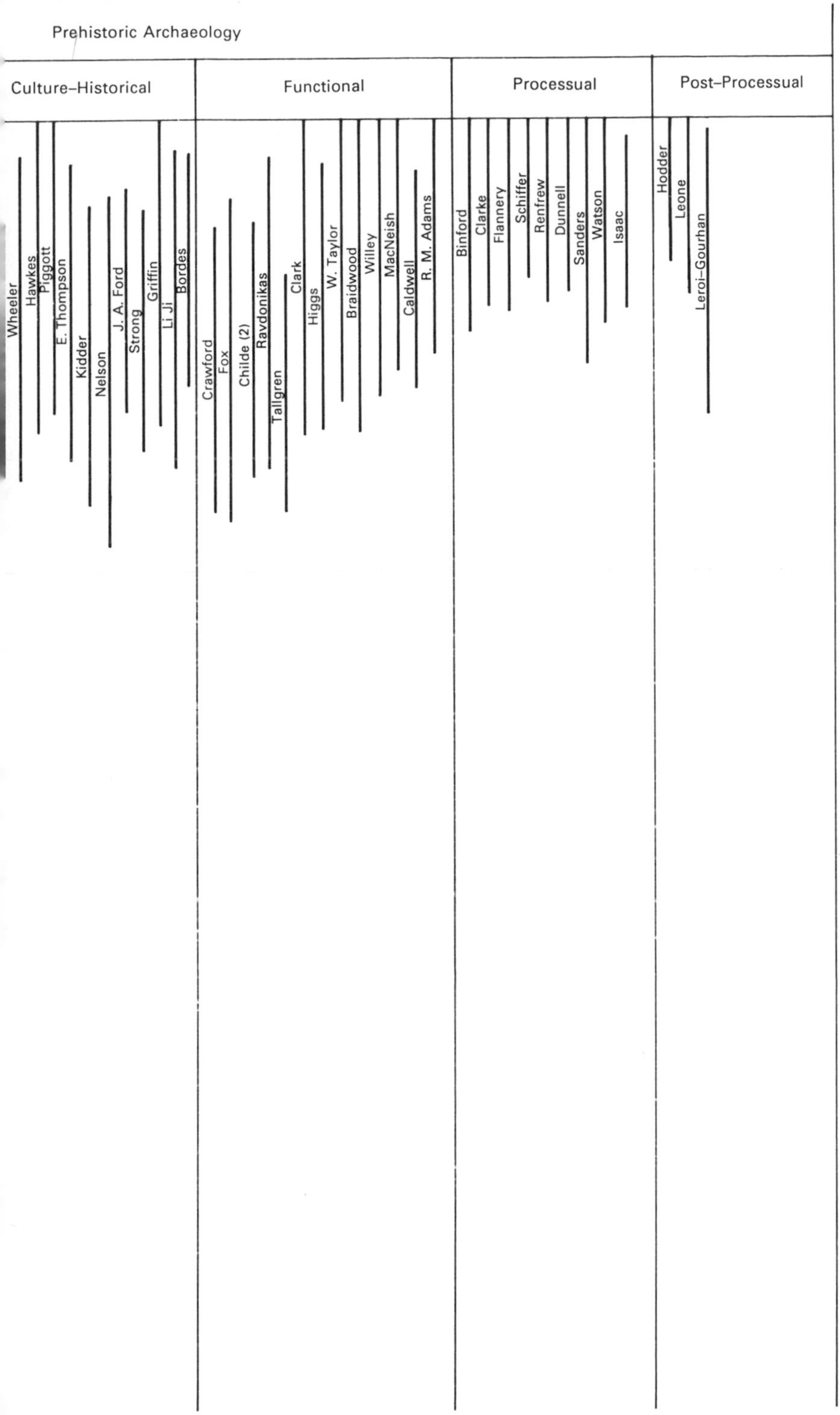

Prehistoric Archaeology

Culture–Historical

Wheeler
Hawkes
Piggott
E. Thompson
Kidder
Nelson
J. A. Ford
Strong
Griffin
Li Ji
Bordes

Functional

Crawford
Fox
Childe (2)
Ravdonikas
Tallgren
Clark
Higgs
W. Taylor
Braidwood
Willey
MacNeish
Caldwell
R. M. Adams

Processual

Binford
Clarke
Flannery
Schiffer
Renfrew
Dunnell
Sanders
Watson
Isaac

Post–Processual

Hodder
Leone
Leroi–Gourhan

plements research based on written records (M. Thompson 1967; D. M. Wilson 1976; Barley 1977). Palaeolithic archaeology developed alongside historical geology and palaeontology and has maintained close ties with these disciplines, while the study of later prehistoric periods frequently combines data from numerous other sources with archaeological findings. These include linguistics, folklore, physical anthropology, and comparative ethnology (D. McCall 1964; Trigger 1968a; Jennings 1979). Yet, while several of these types of archaeology have developed in considerable intellectual isolation from each other over long periods and have been further estranged as a result of the balkanization of their respective jargons, historical connections, sporadic interaction, and common methodological interests have been sufficient for all of them to share numerous interpretative concepts.

In an effort to avoid at least some of the problems outlined above, the present study will not survey trends in archaeological interpretation from a specifically chronological, geographical, or sub-disciplinary perspective (Schuyler 1971). Instead it will investigate a number of interpretative trends in roughly the chronological order in which they originated. These trends frequently overlapped and interacted with each other, both temporally and geographically, and the work of many individual archaeologists reflects several trends, either at different stages of their careers or in some combination. This approach allows a historical study to take account of changing styles of archaeological interpretation which cannot be fitted into clearly defined chronological or geographical pigeonholes but which reflect waves of innovation that have transformed archaeology.

The environment of archaeology

No one denies that archaeological research is influenced by many different kinds of factors. At present the most controversial of these is the social context in which archaeologists live and work. Very few archaeologists, including those who favour a positivistic view of scientific research, would deny that the questions archaeologists ask are influenced at least to some degree by this milieu. Yet positivists maintain that, so long as adequate data are available and these data are analysed using proper scientific methods, the validity of the resulting conclusions is independent of the prejudices or beliefs of the investigator. Other archaeologists believe that, because their discipline's findings concerning the past are consciously or unconsciously seen to have implications for the present or about human nature generally, changing social conditions influence not only the questions archaeologists ask but also the answers that they are predisposed to find acceptable.

David Clarke (1979: 85) had these external factors in mind when he described archaeology as an adaptive system 'related internally to its changing content and externally to the spirit of the times'. Elsewhere he wrote: 'Through exposure to life in general, to educational processes and to the changing contemporary systems of belief we acquire a general philosophy and an archaeological philosophy in particular – a partly conscious and partly subconscious system of beliefs, concepts, values and principles, both realistic and metaphysical' (ibid. 25). Still earlier Collingwood (1939: 114) had observed that every archaeological problem 'ultimately arises out of "real" life . . . we study history in order to see more clearly into the situation in which we are called upon to act'.

In recent years archaeology has been powerfully influenced by the attacks that relativists have launched against the concept of science as a rational and objective enterprise. These attacks have their roots in the anti-positivism of the para-Marxist Frankfurt School, as represented most recently in the writings of Jürgen Habermas (1971) and Herbert Marcuse (1964). These scholars stress that social conditions influence both what data are regarded as important and how they are interpreted (Kolakowski 1978c: 341–95). Their views have been strengthened by Kuhn's paradigmatic concept, by the arguments of the sociologist Barry Barnes (1974, 1977) that scientific knowledge is not different in kind from any other forms of cultural belief, and by the anarchistic claims of the American philosopher of science Paul Feyerabend (1975) that, because objective criteria for evaluating theories do not exist, science should not be fettered by rigid rules and that personal preferences and aesthetic tastes should be relied on to evaluate rival theories. Ideas of this sort have attracted a considerable following in recent years among self-styled critical archaeologists, especially in Britain and the United States. While some argue that in the long run greater awareness of social biases will promote more objectivity (Leone 1982), others maintain that even basic archaeological data are mental constructs and hence are not independent of the social milieu in which they are utilized (Gallay 1986: 55–61). The more extreme formulations ignore the qualifications of Habermas and Barnes that 'knowledge arises out of our encounters with reality and is continually subject to feedback-correction from these encounters' (Barnes 1977: 10). Instead, they conclude that archaeological interpretations are determined entirely by their social context rather than by any objective evidence. Thus statements about the past cannot be evaluated by any criteria other than the internal coherence of any particular study 'which can only be criticised in terms of internal conceptual relations and not in terms of externally imposed standards or criteria for "measuring" or "determining" truth or falsity' (Miller and Tilley 1984: 151). A broad spectrum of alternatives separates those hyper-positivistic archaeologists who believe that only the quality of archaeological data and of analytical techniques determines the value of archaeological interpretations and the hyper-relativists who are inclined to accord archaeological data no role, but instead explain archaeological interpretations entirely in terms of the social and cultural loyalties of the researcher.

While the influences that societies exert on archaeological interpretations are potentially very diverse, the development of archaeology has corresponded temporally with the rise to power of the middle classes in Western society. Although many of the early patrons of classical archaeology belonged to the aristocracy, since Ciriaco de' Pizzicolli in the fifteenth century archaeologists have been predominantly members of the middle class: civil servants, clergymen, merchants, country squires, and, with increasing professionalization, university teachers. In addition, much of the public interest in archaeological findings has been found among the educated middle classes, including sometimes political leaders. All branches of scientific investigations that have developed since the seventeenth century have done so under the aegis of the middle classes. Yet archaeology and history are readily intelligible disciplines and their findings have strong implications concerning human nature and why modern societies have come to be as they are (Levine 1986). This transparent relevance for current political, economic, and social issues makes relations between archaeology and society especially complex and important. It therefore seems reasonable to examine archaeology as an expression of the ideology of the middle classes and to try to discover to what extent changes in archaeological interpretation reflect the altering fortunes of that group.

This is not to claim that the middle classes are a unitary phenomenon. The bourgeoisie of the Ancien Régime, composed largely of clerics, professionals, and royal administrators, has to be distinguished from the entrepreneurial bourgeoisie of the Industrial Revolution (Darnton 1984: 113). The interests and degree of development of the middle classes also have varied greatly from one country to another and within each country they have been divided into various strata, while individuals who prefer either more radical or more conservative options are found in each stratum. It is also evident that archaeology has not been associated with the whole middle class but only with that part of it, largely composed of professionals, which is inclined to be interested in scholarship (Kristiansen 1981; Levine 1986).

Relations between interests and ideas are contextually mediated by a large number of factors. Archaeologists therefore cannot expect to establish a one-to-one correspondence between specific archaeological interpretations and particular class interests. Instead they must analyse the ideas influencing archaeological interpretations as tools with which social groups seek to achieve their goals in particular situations. Among these goals are to enhance the group's self-confidence by making its success appear natural, predestined, and inevitable, to inspire and justify collective action, and to disguise collective interests as altruism (Barnes 1974: 16); in short, to provide groups and whole societies with mythical charters (McNeill 1986). Without denying the significance of individual psychological traits and cultural traditions, the relations between archaeology and the middle classes provide an important focus for examining the relationship between archaeology and society.

Most professional archaeologists also believe their discipline to be significantly influenced by a large number of other internal and external factors. All but the most radical relativists agree that one of these is the archaeological data base. Archaeological data have been accumulating continuously for several centuries and new data are traditionally held to constitute a test of earlier interpretations. Yet what data are collected and by what methods are influenced by every archaeologist's sense of what is significant, which in turn reflects his or her theoretical presuppositions. This creates a reciprocal relationship between data collection and interpretation that leaves both open to social influences. Moreover, the data recovered in the past are often neither adequate nor appropriate to solve the problems that are considered important at a later time. This is not simply because archaeologists were unfamiliar with techniques that became important later and therefore failed to preserve charcoal for radiocarbon dating or soil samples for phytolith analysis, although such gaps in documentation can be extremely limiting. New perspectives frequently open up whole new lines of investigation. For example, Grahame Clark's (1954) interest in the economy of the Mesolithic period led him to ask questions that simply could not be answered using data collected when the main interest of Mesolithic studies was typological (Clark 1932). Likewise, the development of an interest in settlement archaeology revolutionized archaeological site surveys (Willey 1953) and provided a stronger impetus for the recording and analysis of intrasite distributions of features and artifacts (Millon *et al.* 1973). Hence, while archaeological data are being collected constantly, the results are not necessarily as cumulative as many archaeologists believe. Indeed, archaeologists often seem to build more on what their predecessors concluded about the past than on the evidence on which these conclusions were based.

What archaeologists can study is also influenced by the resources that are made available for archaeological research, the institutional contexts in which research is carried out, and the kinds of investigations societies or governments are prepared to let archaeologists undertake. To obtain support archaeologists must please their sponsors, whether these be wealthy patrons (Hinsley 1985), colleagues and politicians managing the allocation of public funds (Patterson 1986a), or the general public. There may also be social restrictions on excavating certain kinds of sites, such as cemeteries or religious localities (Rosen 1980). In these ways considerable constraint may be exerted on the research archaeologists do and how they interpret their finds.

Until the twentieth century, few archaeologists were educated in the discipline. Instead they brought to archaeology a variety of skills and viewpoints acquired in many different fields and avocations. All of them had studied a curriculum in which classical and biblical material was emphasized. Basic principles derived from a widespread interest in numismatics played an important role in the development of typology and seriation by Christian Thomsen, John Evans, and other early archaeologists (McKay 1976). In the nineteenth century a growing number who took up the study of archaeology had been educated in the physical and biological sciences. Even now it is claimed that significant differences can be noted in the work done by professional archaeologists whose early training was in the humanities or natural sciences (Chapman 1979: 121). More recently, a large number of prehistoric archaeologists have been trained in anthropology or history departments, depending on local preferences. The role played by particularly successful teachers or charismatic archaeologists as exemplars in shaping the practice of archaeology on a national and an international scale is also significant. Younger archaeologists may strike off in new directions and pioneer novel techniques of analysis or interpretation in order to try to establish a reputation for themselves. This phenomenon is particularly common during periods of rapid growth and a broadening range of employment opportunities.

Archaeological interpretation has also been influenced by developments in the physical and biological sciences. Until recent decades, when collaborative research involving archaeologists and natural scientists became routine, with rare exceptions the flow of information between these disciplines was unidirectional, with archaeologists being the recipients. Hence research in the natural sciences was only fortuitously related to the needs of archaeologists, although from time to time discoveries were made that were of tremendous importance for archaeology. The development of radiocarbon and other geochronometric dating techniques after World War II provided archaeologists for the first time with a universally applicable chronology and one that allowed the duration as well as the relative order of archaeological manifestations to be determined. Pollen analysis has provided valuable new insights into prehistoric climatic and environmental changes, while trace-element analysis has added an important dimension to the study of the prehistoric movement of certain kinds of goods. Innovations derived from the physical and biological sciences have generally been incorporated into archaeological research throughout the world rapidly and with little resistance. The main obstacle to their spread is the lack of funds and trained scientific personnel in smaller and poorer countries, a factor that probably creates more disparity between the archaeology of rich and poor countries than any other. Yet even now, when more physical and biological research is being undertaken specifically to solve archaeological problems, discoveries in these fields remain some of the least predictable happenings that influence archaeological interpretation.

The proliferation of electronic forms of data processing has revolutionized archaeological analysis no less than did radiocarbon dating. It is now possible to correlate in a routine fashion vast amounts of data, which in the past only an exceptional archaeologist, such as W. M. F. Petrie, would have attempted to analyse (Kendall 1969, 1971). This allows archaeologists to use the abundant data at their disposal to search for more detailed patterning in the archaeological record and to test more complex hypotheses (Hodson *et al.* 1971; Doran and Hodson 1975; Hodder 1978; Orton 1980; Sabloff 1981). New theoretical orientations have been encouraged by specific developments of a mathematical nature. General systems theory (Flannery 1968; Steiger 1971; Laszlo 1972a; Berlinski 1976) and catastrophe theory (Thom 1975; Renfrew 1978; Renfrew and Cooke 1979; Saunders 1980) are both mathematical approaches to the study of change, even if their strictly mathematical aspects have been emphasized less than the underlying concepts in applying them to archaeological problems.

The interpretation of archaeological data has also been significantly affected by the changing theories of human behaviour espoused by the social sciences. It has been especially influenced by concepts derived from ethnology and history, the two disciplines with which archaeology has maintained the closest ties. Theoretical concepts derived from geography, sociology, economics, and political science have also influenced archaeology, either directly or through anthropology and history. Yet, inasmuch as all these disciplines have been shaped by many of the same social movements that have influenced archaeology, it is often difficult to distinguish social science influences on archaeology from those of society at large.

The interpretation of archaeological data is also significantly influenced by established beliefs about what has been learned from the archaeological record. It often happens that specific interpretations of the past are uncritically accommodated to changing general views, rather than carefully scrutinized and assessed, even when these interpretations were formulated in accordance with a general view that has been rejected. For example, when R. S. MacNeish (1952) used pottery seriations to demonstrate that local development explained the origin of the Northern Iroquoian cultures of eastern North America better than did migration, he continued to accept small-scale migrations as accounting for the origins of a few specific groups. He and other archaeologists forgot that these micro-migrations were not based on sound archaeological evidence but had been part of the larger-scale migrationary theorizing that MacNeish himself had disproved. In this fashion specific views about the past can persist and influence archaeological interpretation long after the reasoning that led to their formulation has been discredited and abandoned (Trigger 1978b).

Archaeological interpretation

Archaeology is a social science in the sense that it tries to explain what has happened to specific groups of human beings in the past and to generalize about processes of cultural change. Yet, unlike ethnologists, geographers, sociologists, political scientists, and economists, archaeologists cannot observe the behaviour of the people they are studying and, unlike historians, most of them do not have direct access to the thoughts of these people as they are recorded in written texts. Instead archaeologists must infer human behaviour and ideas from the material remains of what human beings have made and used and of their physical impact on the environment. The interpretation of archaeological data depends upon an understanding of how human beings behave at the present time and particularly of how this behaviour is reflected in material culture. Archaeologists must also invoke uniformitarian principles in order to use an understanding of modern geological and biological processes to infer how such processes have helped to shape the archaeological record. Yet they are far from agreed how such understandings can be applied legitimately and comprehensively to derive an understanding of past human behaviour from their data (Binford 1967a, 1981; Gibbon 1984; Gallay 1986).

Archaeologists have begun to follow the example of philosophers of science (Nagel 1961) and other social-science disciplines in classifying their theories or generalizations into high, middle, and

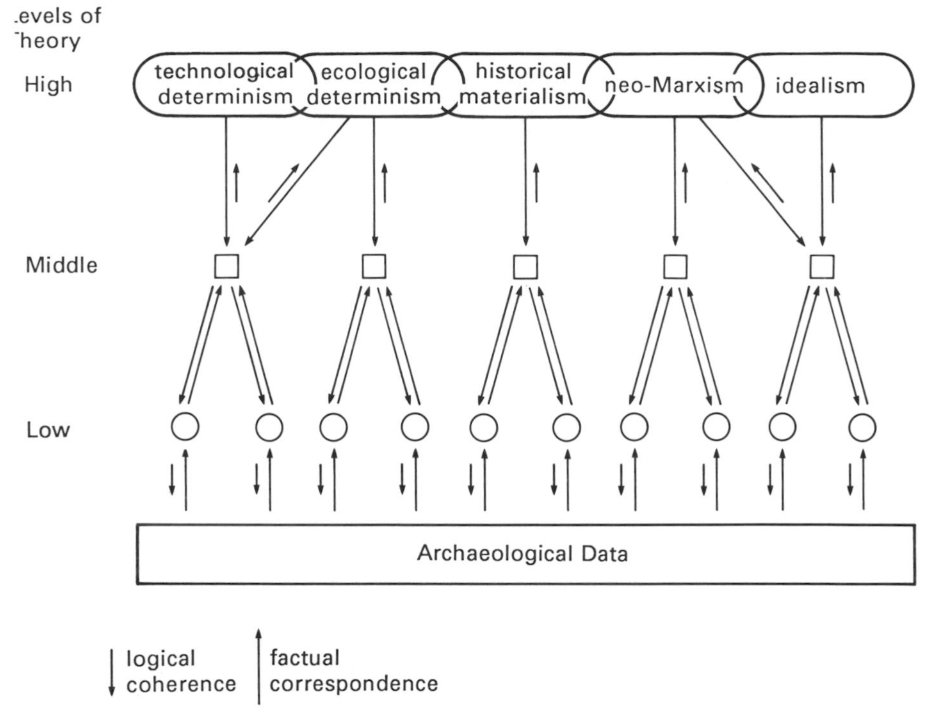

2 Relationships between levels of generalizations

low categories (Klejn 1977; Raab and Goodyear 1984). This scheme facilitates a more systematic understanding of the nature of archaeological theory and of the processes of reasoning that characterize the discipline.

Low-level theories have been described as empirical research with generalizations (Klejn 1977: 2). These appear to be the same as Ernest Nagel's (1961: 79–105) experimental laws, of which he gives as an example the proposition that all female whales suckle their young. Such generalizations are normally based on regularities that are repeatedly observed and which can be refuted by the observation of contrary cases. The vast majority of generalizations on which further archaeological interpretations are based are empirical ones of this sort. They include most typological classifications of artifacts; the identifications of specific archaeological cultures; the demonstration by means of stratification, seriation, or radiocarbon dating that one archaeological manifestation dates earlier, or later, than another; and the observation that in an individual culture all humans are buried in a particular position accompanied by specific types of artifacts. These generalizations are based on observations that specific attributes or artifact types occur repeatedly in a particular association with each other, correlate with a specific geographical locality, or date to a certain period. The dimensions of such generalizations are the classical ones of space, time, and form (Spaulding 1960; Gardin 1980: 62–97). Archaeologists also may assume that specific types of projectile points served particular functions and that each archaeological culture was associated with a specific people. These inferences, which refer to human behaviour, differ substantially from generalizations which are based on empirical observations of correlations between two or more categories of archaeologically tangible data. In many instances the behavioural assumptions turn out to be incorrect, unproved, or misleading. Because of the nature of archaeological data, low-level generalizations never refer to human behaviour. From the point of view of such behaviour, they are regularities to be explained rather than explanations in their own right.

Middle-level theories have been defined as generalizations that attempt to account for the regularities that occur between two or more sets of variables in multiple instances (Raab and Goodyear 1984). Social-science generalizations should have cross-cultural validity and also make some reference to human behaviour. In addition they must be sufficiently specific that they can be tested by applying them to particular sets of data. An example of a middle-level anthropological generalization is Ester Boserup's (1965) proposition that among agricultural economies population pressure leads to situations that require more labour for each unit of food produced in order to derive more food from each unit of arable land. This theory would be archaeologically testable if archaeologists could establish reliable measures of absolute or relative changes in population, the labour intensiveness and productivity of specific agricultural regimes, and a sufficiently precise chronology to specify the temporal relationship between changes in population and food production. Doing this would require elaborating what Lewis

Binford (1981) calls middle-range theory, which attempts to use ethnographical data to establish valid relationships between archaeologically observable phenomena and archaeologically unobservable human behaviour. Although 'middle-level' and 'middle-range' theories are not identical, in that middle-level theory can refer exclusively to human behaviour, while middle-range ones must refer both to human behaviour and archaeologically observable traits, all of Binford's middle-range theory can be regarded as a type of middle-level theory. Middle-range theory is vital for the testing of all middle-level theory relating to archaeological data.

High-level, or general theories, which Marvin Harris (1979: 26–7) calls 'research strategies' and David Clarke (1979: 25–30) labelled 'controlling models', have been defined as abstract rules that explain the relationships among the theoretical propositions that are relevant for understanding major categories of phenomena. Darwinian evolutionism and more recently the synthetic theory of biological evolution, which combines Darwinian principles with genetics, are examples of general theories relating to the biological sciences. In the human domain, general theories refer exclusively to human behaviour; hence there are no theoretical formulations at this level that pertain specifically to archaeology rather than to the social sciences in general. There are also no general theories that have ever been as universally accepted by social scientists as the synthetic theory of evolution has been by biologists. Examples of rival high-level theories that currently influence archaeological research are Marxism (or historical materialism), cultural materialism, and cultural ecology. These are all materialist approaches and hence overlap to varying degrees. Although idealist approaches, such as were inherent in Boasian anthropology earlier in the twentieth century, are less elegantly articulated than are their materialist counterparts, this orientation still inspires much of the work that is done in the social sciences (Coe 1981; Conrad 1981). Because these bodies of theory attempt to interrelate concepts rather than to account for specific observations they cannot be confirmed or falsified directly (Harris 1979: 76). In that respect they resemble religious dogmas or creeds. Their credibility can, however, be influenced by the repeated success or failure of middle-level theories that are logically dependent on them.

Yet such indirect testing is not a simple matter. While many middle-range theories may have significance for distinguishing between materialist and non-materialist modes of explanation, social scientists exhibit much ingenuity in dismissing results that do not agree with their presuppositions as exceptions and even in reinterpreting them as unexpected confirmation of what they believe. Given the complexity of human behaviour, there is considerable scope for such mental gymnastics. It is even more difficult for archaeologists to distinguish among the three materialist positions listed above. Because of the indirectness of tests, the rise and fall in the popularity of specific high-level generalizations seems to be influenced more by social processes than by the scientific examination of logically related middle-level theories. Between 1850 and 1945 a strong emphasis was placed on biological, and more specifically racial, explanations of variations in human behaviour. Scientific demonstrations that explanations of this sort did not hold in specific instances were inadequate to undermine the widespread faith of scholars in the general validity of a racist approach (Harris 1968: 80–107). Yet racial theories were almost totally abandoned as a scientific explanation of human behaviour following the military defeat of Nazi Germany in 1945 and the consequent revelation of the full extent of its racist-inspired atrocities.

Ideally it should be possible to establish a logically coherent relationship among high, middle, and low levels of theory and a correspondence between middle- and low-level generalizations and observable data. In recent years American archaeologists have fiercely debated whether middle-level theory should be derived deductively as a coherent set of interrelated concepts from high-level theories or may also be constructed inductively from data and low-level generalizations. Those who support the deductive approach argue that explanations of human behaviour, as opposed to empirical generalizations about it, can only be based on covering laws stated as hypotheses and tested against independent sets of data (Watson *et al.* 1971: 3–19; Binford 1972: 111). Those who favour a deductive approach seek to establish explicit, logical connections between high- and middle-level theory. Generally, however, they underestimate the tenuous, complex, and intractable nature of the relationship between these two levels. On the other hand, hyper-inductivists tend to view general theory as an ultimate goal that can be considered only after a large corpus of reliable generalizations has been established at the low and middle levels (M. Salmon 1982: 33–4; Gibbon 1984: 35–70; Gallay 1986: 117–21). Yet, because numerous implicit assumptions about the nature of human behaviour colour what is believed to be a sound explanation of archaeological data, high-level concepts can be ignored only at the risk that implicit ones unwittingly will distort archaeological interpretations. Most successful scientific theory-building involves a combination of both approaches. In the first instance, explanations can be formulated either inductively or deductively. Yet, however they are formulated, their status as scientific theories depends both on their logical coherence, internally and with other accepted explanations of human behaviour, and on establishing a satisfactory correspondence between them and any logically related empirical generalizations, and finally with an adequate corpus of factual evidence (Lowther 1962).

Archaeologists also disagree about the formal nature of the generalizations that they seek to elaborate. In modern American archaeology, as within the positivist tradition generally, it is assumed that all laws must be universal in nature. This means that they provide statements about relations between variables that are assumed to hold true regardless of the temporal period, region of the world, or specific cultures that are being studied. These generalizations vary in scale from major assumptions about historical processes to regularities dealing with relatively trivial aspects of human behaviour (M. Salmon 1982: 8–30). This approach is exemplified by formalist economics, which maintains that the rules used to explain the economic behaviour of Western societies explain the behaviour of all human beings. Such an approach accounts for significant variations in human behaviour in different societies by viewing them as the results of novel combinations and permutations of a fixed set of interacting variables (Burling 1962; Cancian 1966; Cook 1966). Universal generalizations are frequently interpreted as reflecting an invariant human nature.

Other archaeologists maintain that general laws of this sort concerning human nature are relatively few in number. A much larger number of generalizations applies only to societies that share the same or closely related modes of production. This position is similar in its general orientation to that of the economic substantivists. In contrast to the position adopted by the formalists, substantivists maintain that the rules, as well as the forms, of economic behaviour are fundamentally altered by evolutionary processes (Polanyi 1944, 1966; Polanyi *et al.* 1957; Dalton 1961). The substantivist approach implies that novel properties can and do emerge as a result of sociocultural change and that human nature can be transformed as a consequence of it (Childe 1947a). This distinction between universal generalizations and more restricted ones may not be as far-reaching or absolute as its proponents maintain. Some generalizations that apply only to specific types of societies can be rewritten in the form of universal generalizations, while universal ones may be reformulated, usually in greater detail, so that they apply specifically to a particular class of society. Yet those who stress the importance of restricted generalizations argue that all or most of them cannot be transformed into universal generalizations without a severe loss in content and significance (Trigger 1982a).

The third type of generalization is specific to an individual culture or to a single group of historically related cultures. An example would be the definition of the canons that governed ancient Egyptian or classical Greek art (Childe 1947a: 43–9; Montané 1980: 130–6). This kind of generalization is potentially very important inasmuch as most cultural patterning is probably of this sort. Yet no convincing way has been found to move beyond speculation in interpreting the meaning of such patterning in the archaeological record in situations where supplementary historical documentation or ethnographic data are not available. Where they are not, such regularities remain at the level of empirical generalizations.

Challenge

A final question is whether a historical study can measure progress in the interpretation of archaeological data. Are steady advances being made towards a more objective and comprehensive understanding of archaeological findings, as many archaeologists assume? Or is the interpretation of such data largely a matter of fashion and the accomplishments of a later period not necessarily more comprehensive or objective than those of an earlier one? In examining the successive patterns that have influenced the interpretation of archaeological data, I shall attempt to determine to what extent an understanding of human history and behaviour has been irreversibly altered as a result of archaeological activity. Yet it is likely that the social influences that have shaped a scientific tradition in the past are revealed more easily after social conditions have changed, while current influences are much harder to recognize. This makes present interpretations of archaeological data generally appear to be more objective than those of the past. Hence, by themselves historical observations do not necessarily distinguish objective progress from changing culturally shared fantasies. To do that, historical investigators must seek to discover to what extent this irreversibility has been assured not only by the logical appeal of archaeological interpretations but also by their continuing factual correspondence with a growing data base. If this can be done, we may hope to learn something about the objectivity or subjectivity of archaeological interpretations; to what extent archaeology can be more than the past relived in the present, in the sense Collingwood defined that process; the degree to which any sort of understanding is communicable from one age or culture to another; and the extent to which an understanding of the history of archaeology can influence archaeological interpretation.

To do justice to these topics, I will seek to avoid writing a history of archaeological interpretation that is unduly presentistic and strive to understand the intellectual history of each major trend in its social context. In order to keep this book within reasonable limits, however, I refer more to works that have contributed to the long-term development of archaeological interpretation than to unsuccessful and repetitious studies or to the many publications that have mainly added to our factual knowledge of the remains of the past. In his survey of the history of the interpretation of Stonehenge, Chippindale (1983) has shown that works of these latter sorts constitute the bulk of archaeological literature.

CHAPTER 2

Classical archaeology and antiquarianism

Knowing the past is as astonishing a performance as knowing the stars.

GEORGE KUBLER, *The Shape of Time* (1962), p. 19

Some recent treatments of the history of archaeology have suggested that the current concern with explanation is a modern development (Willey and Sabloff 1980: 9–10). It is alleged that prior to the 1960s there was no established body of theory. Instead each scholar was free to build his discipline anew on the basis of his own ideas. Yet general beliefs about human origins and development that are potentially testable using archaeological data long antedate any recognizable discipline of archaeology. It is concepts such as these that either implicitly or explicitly constituted the earliest high-level theories that gave purpose and direction to the collection and study of archaeological data. Hence archaeology, no more than any other scientific discipline, passed through a stage in which data were collected entirely for their own sake or in the hope that in the future enough would be known for serious questions to be asked. From the time when archaeological data became an object of serious study, scholars examined them in the hope that they would shed light on problems that were significant from a philosophical, historical, or scientific point of view.

The ancient world

All human groups appear to have some curiosity about the past. For much of human history, however, this interest has been satisfied by myths and legends concerning the creation of the world and of humanity, and by traditions chronicling the adventures of individual ethnic groups. Among tribal peoples these accounts frequently refer to a continuing supernatural realm and serve as a mythical charter for present-day social and political relations, as is the case with the Australian Aborigine concept of dream-time (Isaacs 1980). In other cases oral traditions claim to preserve accurate accounts of human activities over many generations (Vansina 1985).

A different approach developed in those early civilizations where written records provided a chronological framework and information about what had happened in the past that was independent of human memory. Even so, the compiling of annals did not give rise to the writing of detailed histories of the past or narratives of current events either in the Mediterranean region or in China until after 500 B.C. (Van Seters 1983; Redford 1986). Moreover, the development of history as a literary genre did not ensure the concurrent growth of a disciplined interest in the material remains of earlier times.

Artifacts from an unknown past have been collected by at least some tribal societies. Projectile points, stone pipes, and native copper tools made thousands of years earlier are found in Iroquoian sites of the fifteenth and sixteenth centuries A.D. in eastern North America. These objects must have been discovered in the course of everyday activities and kept by the Iroquoians (Tuck 1971: 134), just as 'thunderstones' (stone celts) and 'elf-bolts' (stone projectile points) were collected by European peasants in the medieval period (European stone celts were also sold to goldsmiths who used them for burnishing [Heizer 1962a: 63]). While we have no direct record of how the Iroquoians regarded these finds, they may have treated them as charms, as they are said to have done various types of peculiarly shaped stones, which they believed belonged to spirits who had lost them in the woods (Thwaites 1896–1901, 33: 211). In many cultures such artifacts were believed to have a supernatural rather than a human origin and were credited with magical powers, which may have been the main reason they were collected.

The remains of the past were also used in the religious observances of the early civilizations. In the sixteenth century the Aztecs performed rituals at regular intervals in the ruins of Teotihuacan, a city that had been inhabited in the first millennium A.D. and which was believed to be where the gods had re-established the cosmic order at the beginning of the most recent cycle of existence (Heyden 1981). They also included much older Olmec figurines, as well as valuable goods from many parts of their empire in the ritual deposits that were periodically buried in the walls of their Great Temple in

Tenochtitlan (Matos 1984). Yet to identify such activities as archaeology, even 'indigenous archaeology', is to dilute the meaning of the word beyond useful limits.

In later stages of the ancient civilizations artifacts came to be valued both as the relics of specific rulers or periods of national greatness and as sources of information about the past. In Egypt, conscious archaism was already displayed in the construction of royal tombs beginning in the Twelfth Dynasty (1991–1786 B.C.) (Edwards 1985: 210–17). In the Eighteenth Dynasty (1552–1305 B.C.) scribes left graffiti to record their visits to ancient and abandoned monuments, while a fragmentary predynastic palette has been found inscribed with the name of Queen Tiye (1405–1367 B.C.). In the Nineteenth Dynasty (1305–1186 B.C.), Khaemwese, a son of Ramesses II whose fame as a sage and magician was to last into Greco-Roman times, carefully studied the cults associated with ancient monuments near the capital city of Memphis as a basis for restoring these observances (Kitchen 1982: 103–9) and by the Saite Period (664–525 B.C.) knowledge of Old Kingdom relief carving was sufficiently detailed for an attempted stylistic revival (W. Smith 1958: 246–52). A collection of ancient Babylonian artifacts, including inscriptions, amassed by Bel-Shalti-Nannar, a daughter of King Nabonidus, in the sixth century B.C. has been described as the first known museum of antiquities (Woolley 1950: 152–4). This growing interest in the physical remains of the past was part of a heightened preoccupation with former times among the literate classes. Such interests had a strong religious component. It was believed that the gods or a series of culture heroes had established civilization in a perfect form at the beginning of time. Later generations of human beings had failed to maintain this ideal form. The monuments as well as the written records of the past therefore constituted tangible links to eras that were closer to the time of creation and hence were the means by which the sacred prototype of civilization could be more nearly approximated. Because of their greater proximity to the cosmic drama of creation these artifacts were probably also thought to be endowed with unusual supernatural power.

In the classical civilizations of Greece and Rome the production of substantial narrative histories based on written records and oral traditions, as well as an interest in ancient religious practices, local customs, and civil institutions, were accompanied only by a sporadic interest in the physical remains of the past. The Greek historian Thucydides noted that some of the graves dug up on Delos, when that island was purified in the fifth century B.C., belonged to Carians, since they contained armour and weapons resembling those of the Carians of his day. In his opinion this confirmed a tradition that Carians had once lived on the island (Casson 1939: 71). In his *Description of Greece*, written in the second century A.D., the physician Pausanias systematically described the public buildings, art works, rites, and customs of different regions of that country, together with the historical traditions associated with them. Yet, while he briefly described the celebrated Bronze Age ruins at Tiryns and Mycenae, for him and other classical writers of guide books, ruined buildings were 'hardly worth mentioning' (Levi 1979, 1: 3). The Greeks and Romans preserved valued relics of the past as votive offerings in their temples and graves were sometimes opened to recover the relics of 'heroes'. In support of literary evidence that the warriors of the Homeric age had all used bronze weapons, Pausanias noted that the blade of the alleged spear of Achilles in the temple of Athena at Phaselis was made of bronze (Levi 1979, 2: 17). Yet such historical inferences are notable for their rarity. Ancient bronzes and pottery vessels that were accidentally unearthed or plundered by dealers sold for high prices to wealthy art collectors (Wace 1949). Nevertheless, scholars made no effort to recover such artifacts in a systematic fashion, nor, despite some classicists' claims to the contrary (Weiss 1969: 2), did these artifacts become a special focus of study. There was absolutely no awareness that the material remains of the past could be used to test the numerous conflicting philosophical speculations about human origins and the general outlines of human history that characterized classical civilization.

Si-ma Qien, the first great Chinese historian, who wrote in the second century B.C., visited ancient ruins and examined relics of the past as well as texts when compiling material for the *Shi Ji*, his influential account of ancient Chinese history. The systematic study of the past was valued by Confucian scholars as a guide to moral behaviour and, by stressing a common heritage going back at least to the Xia Dynasty (2205–1766 B.C.), it played a powerful role in unifying Chinese cultural and political life (Wang 1985). Yet for almost a millennium Chinese historians continued to base their books on written records, while bronze vessels, jade carvings, and other ancient works of art only were collected as curiosities or heirlooms, as they were in the classical civilizations of the Mediterranean region.

While a few scholars of the ancient world occasionally used artifacts to supplement what could be learned about the past from written records, they did not develop specific techniques for recovering or studying such artifacts and utterly failed to establish a tradition of such research. Nothing resembling a discipline of archaeology can be said to have existed in any of these civilizations. Although philosophers replaced religious beliefs with various static, cyclical, and even evolutionary explanations for the origins of human beings and civilization, these remained purely speculative.

The medieval paradigm of history

In medieval Europe prehistoric tumuli and megalithic monuments were objects of local interest and priests occasionally recorded the folk tales that surrounded them. Few of these monuments escaped plundering by lords or peasants who believed them to contain treasure (Klindt-Jensen 1975: 9). Ancient buildings were also plundered in search of building material, holy relics,and treasure (Kendrick 1950: 18; Sklenář 1983: 16–18). The only certain knowledge of past times was thought to be what was recorded in the Bible, the surviving histories of Greece and Rome, and historical records incorporating traditions going back into the Dark Ages. On this basis a medieval Christian view of the past was evolved that in certain ways has continued to influence the interpretation of archaeological data to the present. This view can be summarized in terms of six propositions:

1 The world was thought to be of recent, supernatural origin and unlikely to last more than a few thousand years. Rabbinical authorities estimated that it had been created about 3700 B.C., while Pope Clement VIII dated the creation to 5199 B.C. and as late as the seventeenth century Archbishop James Ussher was to set it at 4004 B.C. (Harris 1968: 86). These dates, which were computed from biblical genealogies, agreed that the world was only a few thousand years old. It was also believed that the present world would end with the return of Christ. Although the precise timing of this event was unknown, the earth was generally believed to be in its last days (Slotkin 1965: 36–7).

3 Merlin erecting Stonehenge, from a fourteenth-century British manuscript

2 The physical world was in an advanced state of degeneration and most natural changes represented the decay of God's original creation. Since the earth was intended to endure for only a few thousand years there was little need for divine provision to counteract depletions resulting from natural processes and human exploitation of its resources. The biblical documentation of greater human longevity in ancient times provided a warrant for believing that human beings as well as the environment had been deteriorating physically and intellectually since their creation. The decay and impoverishment of the physical world also bore witness to humanity of the transience of all material things (Slotkin 1965: 37; Toulmin and Goodfield 1966: 75–6).
3 Humanity was created by God in the Garden of Eden, which was located in the Near East, and spread from there to other parts of the world, first after the expulsion of the original humans from the Garden of Eden and again following Noah's flood. The second dispersal was hastened by the differentiation of languages, which was imposed on humanity as divine retribution for their presumption in building the Tower of Babel. The centre of world history long remained in the Near East, where the Bible chronicled the development of Judaism and from where Christianity was carried to Europe. Scholars sought to link Northern and Western Europe to the recorded history of the Near East and the classical world by constructing fanciful pedigrees that identified biblical personages or individuals known from other historical accounts as the founders of European nations or early kings in that region (Kendrick 1950: 3). These claims, which were often based on folk etymologies, had the Goths descended from Gog, one of Noah's grandsons (Klindt-Jensen 1975: 10), and Brutus, a Trojan prince, becoming the first king of Britain after he defeated a race of giants who had previously lived there. Pagan deities were often interpreted as deified mortals who could be identified with minor biblical figures or their descendants (Kendrick 1950: 82). Continuing links were sought with the Near East, such as the claim first made by the monks of Glastonbury in A.D. 1184 that Joseph of Arimathea had brought the Holy Grail there in A.D. 63 (Kendrick 1950: 15).
4 It was believed to be natural for standards of human conduct to degenerate. The Bible affirmed that Adam and his descendants had been farmers and herdsmen and that iron working had been

practised in the Near East only a few generations later. The earliest humans shared in God's revelation of himself to Adam. Knowledge of God and his wishes was subsequently maintained and elaborated through successive divine revelations made to Hebrew patriarchs and prophets. These, together with the revelations contained in the New Testament, became the property of the Christian Church, which henceforth was responsible for upholding standards of human conduct. On the other hand, groups who had moved away from the Near East and failed to have their faith renewed by divine revelation or Christian teaching, tended to degenerate into polytheism, idolatry, and immorality. The theory of degeneration was also used to account for the primitive technologies of hunter–gatherers and tribal agriculturalists when they were encountered by Europeans. When applied to the spheres of technology and material culture, the concept of degeneration found itself in competition with the alternative view, promoted by Roman historians such as Cornelius Tacitus, that material prosperity encouraged moral depravity. Medieval scholars were primarily concerned with explaining moral and spiritual rather than technological progress and decay.

5 The history of the world was interpreted as a succession of unique events. Christianity encouraged a historical view of human affairs in the sense that world history was seen as a series of happenings that had cosmic significance. These events were interpreted as the results of God's predetermined interventions, the final one of which would terminate the struggle between good and evil. There was therefore no sense that change or progress was intrinsic to human history or that human beings, unaided by God, were capable of achieving anything of historical significance (Kendrick 1950: 3; Toulmin and Goodfield 1966: 56). Between God's interventions, human affairs continued in a static or cyclical fashion.

6 Finally, medieval scholars were even less conscious of historical changes in material culture than ancient Greek and Roman ones had been. A few popes and emperors, such as Charlemagne and Frederick Barbarossa, collected ancient gems and coins, reused elements of Roman architecture, and imitated Roman sculpture (Weiss 1969: 3–15). Yet, in general, there was no explicit awareness that in classical and biblical times human beings wore clothes or lived in houses that were significantly different from those of the

> Middle Ages. When statues of pagan deities were discovered, they were often destroyed or mutilated as objects of devil worship or indecency (Sklenář 1983: 15). Almost universally, biblical times were viewed as culturally, socially, and intellectually identical to those of medieval Europe.

During the Middle Ages an interest in the material remains of the past was even more restricted than it had been in classical times; being largely limited to the collection and preservation of holy relics. This did not encourage the development of a systematic study of the material remains of the past. Yet the view of the past that was held at this time formed the conceptual basis on which the study of archaeology was to develop in Europe as social conditions changed.

Development of historical archaeology

By the fourteenth century A.D., the rapid social and economic changes that marked the end of feudalism in northern Italy led scholars to try to justify political innovations by demonstrating that there were precedents for them in earlier times. Renaissance intellectuals turned to the surviving literature of the classical era to provide a glorious past for the emerging Italian city states and to justify the increasing secularization of Italian culture (Slotkin 1965: x). Their views generally reflected the interests of the rising nobility and bourgeoisie upon whose patronage they depended. While the use of historical precedents to justify innovation had its roots in medieval thinking the expanding search for these precedents slowly led to a realization that contemporary social and cultural life did not resemble that of classical antiquity. As a result of growing familiarity with the historical and literary texts of ancient Greece and Rome, which had remained unknown or unstudied in Western Europe since the fall of the Roman Empire, scholars came to realize that the past was separate from the present and different from it, that each period in the past had to be understood on its own terms, and that the past should not be judged by the standards of the present (Rowe 1965). The cultural achievements of ancient Greece and Rome were interpreted as evidence of cultural degeneration since that time, which in turn reinforced the traditional Christian view of human history. The aim of Renaissance scholars was to understand and try to emulate as best they could the glorious achievements of antiquity. At first there was little belief that in their present degenerate state human beings could ever hope to excel those achievements. Only in its possession of a religion based on divine revelation could the modern age be viewed as unambiguously superior to ancient times.

The appreciation of classical antiquity was not restricted to literature but rapidly extended into the fields of art and architecture. These were of particular concern to the Italian nobility and wealthy merchants, who were rivalling each other as patrons of the arts. Gothic styles were rejected and an effort was made to emulate the art and architecture of ancient Rome. This development gradually made it clear that not only the written word but also material objects surviving from the past could be important sources of information about classical civilization.

Both currents of interest are expressed in the work of Cyriacus of Ancona (Ciriaco de' Pizzicolli, A.D. 1391–1452), whose research entitles him to be considered the first archaeologist. He was an Italian merchant who travelled extensively in Greece and the eastern Mediterranean over a period of 25 years, often specifically in order to collect data about ancient monuments. In the course of his travels he copied hundreds of inscriptions, made drawings of monuments, and collected books, coins, and works of art. His chief interest, however, was public inscriptions. While his six volumes of commentaries on these inscriptions were destroyed in a fire in 1514, some of his other works survive (Casson 1939: 93–9; Weiss 1969: 137–42).

By the late fifteenth century, popes, such as Paul II and Alexander VI, cardinals, and other members of the Italian nobility were collecting and displaying ancient works of art. They also began to sponsor the systematic search for and recovery of such objects (Taylor 1948: 9–10). As early as 1462 Pope Pius II passed a law to preserve ancient buildings in the papal states and in 1471 Sixtus IV forbade the export of stone blocks or statues from his domains (Weiss 1969: 99–100). For a long time there was no excavation in the modern sense but merely digging in search of objects that had aesthetic and commercial value. The excavations that began at the well-preserved Roman sites of Herculaneum and Pompeii in the first half of the eighteenth century were treasure hunts of this sort, although a desire to recover statues and other works of art gradually came to be accompanied by an interest in Roman domestic architecture. There was, however,

4 Digging at Herculaneum, 1782

little concern for understanding the context in which finds were made. The owners of the land under which Pompeii was buried rented the right to entrepreneurs to dig there by the cubic yard (Leppmann 1968).

An interest in classical antiquity gradually spread throughout the rest of Europe. In due course members of the nobility became avid collectors of Greek and Roman art, which their agents purchased for them in the Mediterranean region. Early in the seventeenth century Charles I , the Duke of Buckingham, and the Earl of Arundel were friendly rivals in importing such works into England. In 1734 a group of English gentlemen who had travelled in Italy formed a Society of Dilettanti in London to encourage a taste for classical art. Over the next 80 years this society sponsored archaeological research in the Aegean region (Casson 1939: 202–5). Classical inscriptions, monuments, and works of art found in England, France, West Germany, and other lands that had been part of the Roman Empire were being studied systematically by local antiquarians, such as William Camden (1551–1623) in England, as early as the sixteenth century. Yet the great monetary value placed on high-quality works of art tended to restrict the investigation of such material and of the classical archaeology of the Mediterranean region to the nobility or those scholars who enjoyed their patronage (Casson 1939: 141).

The establishment of art history as a distinct branch of classical studies was the work of the German scholar Johann Winckelmann (1717–68). His *Geschichte der Kunst des Altertums* (*History of Ancient Art*) (1764) and other writings provided the first periodization of Greek and Roman sculptural styles, as well as meticulous descriptions of individual works and discussions of factors influencing the development of classical art, such as climate, social conditions, and craftsmanship. He also attempted to define ideal, and in his opinion eternally valid, standards of artistic beauty. Winckelmann's work shaped the future development of classical studies, which until modern times have continued to be based on the dual investigation of written documents and art history. Written records were viewed as providing an indispensable account of the history and development of thought of ancient Greece and Rome. Art history, while depending upon written records to provide the chronological and contextual data required to study changes in art styles, extended the study of the past into a sphere of material culture that could not be systematically investigated using only literary sources. While it was not an independent discipline, art history, as a properly constituted branch of classical studies, did more than illustrate what was already understood from written records.

Classical studies provided a model for the development of Egyptology and Assyriology. In the late eighteenth century almost nothing was known about the ancient civilizations of Egypt and the Near East except what had been recorded about them in the Bible and by the ancient Greeks and Romans. Their scripts could not be read and their writings and works of art were unstudied and largely remained buried in the ground. The systematic investigation of ancient Egypt began with observations by the French scholars who accompanied Napoleon Bonaparte's invasion of Egypt in 1798–9 and produced the multi-volume *Description de l'Egypte* beginning in 1809. Another result of this military campaign was the accidental discovery of the Rosetta Stone, a bilingual inscription that played a major role in Jean-François Champollion's (1790–1832) decipherment of the ancient Egyptian scripts, which began to produce substantial results by 1822. Egyptologists, such as Champollion and Karl Lepsius (1810–84), visited Egypt recording temples, tombs, and the monumental inscriptions associated with them. Using these inscriptions, it was possible to produce a chronology and skeletal history of ancient Egypt, in terms of which Egyptologists could study the development of Egyptian art and architecture. At the same time adventurers, including the circus performer and strong man Giovanni Belzoni and the agents of the French Consul-General Bernardino Drovetti, were locked in fierce competition to acquire major collections of Egyptian art works for public display in France and Britain (Fagan 1975). Their plundering of ancient Egyptian tombs and temples was halted only after the French Egyptologist Auguste Mariette (1821–81), who was appointed Conservator of Egyptian Monuments in 1858, took steps to stop all unauthorized work. Even his own excavations were designed to acquire material for a national collection rather than to record the circumstances in which it was found.

Although reports of cuneiform inscriptions reached Europe as early as 1602, the first successful attempt to translate such writing was made by Georg Grotefend (1775–1853) in 1802. It was not until 1849 that Henry Rawlinson (1810–95) succeeded in publishing a thorough study of the Old Persian version of the long trilingual text that the Achaemenid king Darius I (reigned 522–486 B.C.) had carved on a cliff at Bisitun in Iran. By 1857 he and other scholars had deciphered the version of the text that was composed in the older Babylonian language, thereby providing the means to unravel the history of ancient Babylonia and Assyria. Sporadic digging in search of treasure in Iraq gave way in the 1840s to Paul-Emile Botta's (1802–70) excavations in the ruins of Nineveh and Khorsabad and Austen Layard's (1817–94) at Nimrud and Kuyunjik. These excavations of elaborate neo-Assyrian palaces yielded vast amounts of ancient sculpture and textual material. The latter aroused great interest because some of them paralleled early stories in the Bible. Eventually, as for Egypt, an outline chronology was established for Mesopotamian civilization that allowed scholars to study changes in the styles of art and monumental architecture from the earliest stages of writing onward.

The development of Egyptology and Assyriology in the course of the nineteenth century added 3,000 years of history to two areas of the world that were of particular interest in terms of biblical studies, but for which no direct documentation had been available. Both disciplines modelled themselves on classical studies. They relied on written records to supply chronology, historical data, and information about the beliefs and values of the past, but also were concerned with the development of art and monumental architecture as revealed by archaeology. Both Egyptology and Assyriology depended even more heavily on archaeology than classical studies did, since the vast majority of texts they studied had to be dug out of the ground. Thus, while the investigation of art history continued to depend on written records for the chronological ordering of its data, the extension of this method to earlier periods made a growing number of archaeologists more aware of the extent to which archaeologically recovered objects constituted important sources of information about human achievement. To this degree the development of classical archaeology, which began in the Renaissance, helped to point the way towards a more purely archaeological study of prehistoric times. Nevertheless, classical archaeologists, such as D. G. Hogarth (1899: vi), continued to regard prehistoric archaeology as greatly inferior to the archaeological study of periods that can be illuminated by written texts.

5 Layard's reconstruction of an Assyrian palace, from *Monuments of Nineveh*, 1853

In China, as we have already noted, the writing of history had emerged as a significant literary genre with the work of Si-ma Qien early in the Han Dynasty. In the Song Dynasty (A.D. 960–1279) a new interest in antiquity was stimulated by the unearthing of bronze vessels of the Shang Dynasty, following a displacement in the course of the Yellow River. These vessels formed the nucleus of an imperial collection of antiquities still preserved in Beijing (Elisseeff 1986: 37–9). Song scholars began to publish detailed descriptions and studies of ancient bronze and jade objects, especially ones bearing inscriptions. The earliest surviving work of this sort, *Kaogutu* by Lu Dalin, describes in words and line drawings 210 bronze and 13 jade artifacts dating from the Shang to the Han Dynasties which were kept in the Imperial collection and in 30 private ones. The inscriptions on these objects were studied as sources of information about ancient epigraphy and historical matters and the artifacts themselves were minutely categorized in an effort to acquire information about early forms of rituals and other aspects of culture that was not supplied by ancient texts. Inscriptions, decorative motifs, and the general shapes of objects were also used as criteria for dating them and assuring their authenticity and in due course scholars were able to assign dates to vessels on the basis of formal criteria only. Although traditional antiquarianism suffered a severe decline after the Song Dynasty, systematic studies of this sort revived in the late Qing Dynasty (A.D. 1644–1911) and are viewed as providing an indigenous basis for the development of archaeology in modern China. This included early studies of inscriptions on Shang oracle bones that were unearthed at Anyang beginning in 1898 (Chang 1981). Until the 1920s, however, Chinese scholars made no effort to recover data by carrying out excavations, and antiquarianism remained a branch of traditional historiography rather than developing into a discipline in its own right, as classical studies, Egyptology, and Assyriology had done in the West.

In Japan, during the prosperous Tokugawa period (A.D. 1603–1868) gentleman-scholars of the samurai (warrior) and merchant classes collected and described ancient artifacts and recorded burial mounds and other ancient monuments as data relating to local and national history. By the end of the Tokugawa period these scholars were engaged in careful surveys of sites and artifacts even in areas that were remote from the urban centres of learning where such

6 Shang cast bronze ritual vessel, illustrated with rubbing of inscriptions and their transcription into conventional characters, from twelfth-century A.D. catalogue *Bogutu*

studies had begun (Ikawa-Smith 1982). Michael Hoffman (1974) has suggested that these activities were a response to European influence but this is by no means certain. It is possible that in Japan, as in China and Italy, an interest in material remains of the past developed as an extension of historical studies beyond the use of written texts.

On the other hand, systematic antiquarianism did not develop in India prior to the colonial period. Despite impressive intellectual achievements in other fields, Indian civilization did not evolve a strong tradition of historical studies (Chakrabarti 1982), perhaps because the Hindu religion directed efforts to understand the meaning of life and of historical events more towards cosmology (Pande 1985). Antiquarianism also failed to develop in the Near East, where Islamic peoples lived in the midst of impressive monuments of antiquity. Yet in that region there was a strong interest in history and efforts had been made to explain history in naturalistic terms, especially by Abu Zayd Abd ar-Rahman ibn Khaldun (A.D. 1332–1406), that modern historians judge to have been in advance of historical research anywhere else in the world (Masry 1981). The failure of antiquarianism to develop in the Arab world may be attributed to its rejection of pagan pre-Islamic civilizations and their works as an Age of Ignorance, to a tendency to view many features of Islamic history as cyclical, and to a religiously based disdain for works of art that involved the portrayal of human forms. India and the Arab world indicate the highly particularistic factors that must be taken into account in explaining the origins of archaeological research in any specific culture.

Nevertheless the parallels between Europe, China, and Japan suggest that, where traditions of historiography are well established, the chances are good that studies of written documents will come to be supplemented by systematic research on palaeography and art history. The much more extensive and systematic development of such studies in Europe, although they began there later than in China, can at least partly be attributed to the particular importance that medieval Christian thought attached to schemes of human history as a basis for understanding the human condition. The rediscovery of classical antiquity was seen as providing information about the glorious past of Italy, which received little attention in traditional biblical accounts, while the study of Egypt and Mesopotamia in the nineteenth century was largely motivated by a desire to know more about civilizations that had featured prominently in the Old Testament. A sense of the discontinuity and diversity of origins of European civilization encouraged research that relied ever more heavily on archaeology as a source of textual data as well as artifacts. This situation, which contrasted with the greater continuity in Chinese and Japanese history, may have helped to stimulate the development of archaeology as a major source of information about the literate civilizations of ancient times.

Antiquarianism in Northern Europe

Yet what did the development of text-aided archaeology signify for most of Central and Northern Europe, where historical records usually did not antedate the Roman period and in some areas began only after A.D. 1000? As long as people believed that the world had been created about 4000 B.C. and that the Bible provided a reliable chronicle of events in the Near East for the whole of human history, relatively little appeared to lie beyond the purview of written records or folk traditions. In the course of the Middle Ages chroniclers, who were often priests, had constructed a colourful picture of the remote past for each of the peoples of Europe. These accounts were based on legends and sheer invention as well as documents. In an uncritical climate of scholarship even written records were often successfully forged (Sklenář 1983: 14). English scholars proudly claimed that Arthur and before him King Brutus had conquered much of the world (Kendrick 1950: 36–7). Individual chronicles were frequently composed to support or oppose particular ruling groups. For example, Geoffrey of Monmouth, who wrote in the twelfth century, stressed England's earlier British, rather than its Anglo-Saxon past in order to please his Norman masters (ibid. 4). Prehistoric monuments were sometimes mentioned in these chronicles. Geoffrey of Monmouth associated Stonehenge with Arthurian legend, while in Germany megalithic graves and tumuli were often ascribed to the Huns, who had invaded Europe in the fifth century A.D. (Sklenář 1983: 16).

The stirrings of patriotism in Northern Europe, which led to the Reformation, stimulated a new and more secular interest in the history of these countries that was already evident by the sixteenth century. This patriotism was especially strong among the urban middle class, whose growing prosperity, whether based on royal service or professional training, was linked to the decline of feudalism and the development of national states. In England the Tudor dynasty was glorified by renewed historical studies of Arthurian legends that reflected the family's British, as opposed to narrowly English, origins. There was also a marked increase of interest in the history of England before the Norman Conquest as scholars combed early records in an attempt to prove that Protestantism, rather than engaging in innovation, was restoring elements of true Christianity that had been destroyed or distorted by Roman Catholicism (Kendrick 1950: 115).

Yet T. D. Kendrick (1950) has interpreted the growth of historical scholarship in England during the sixteenth century as a slow triumph of Renaissance over medieval thought. Historians, such as Polydore Vergil, rejected the uncritical approach of medieval chroniclers and sought to base their work on reliable documentary sources. This involved denying the historicity of many national legends that could not sustain careful comparison with the historical records of other countries (ibid. 38).

In England already by the fifteenth century John Rous (1411–91) and William of Worcester (1415–82) were aware that the past had been materially different from the present. William was working on a description of Britain that involved measuring and describing old buildings (Kendrick 1950: 18–33). This concern with the material remains of the past was strengthened by the destruction of the monasteries in the reign of Henry VIII. The dismantling of these familiar landmarks and the dispersal of their libraries spurred scholars to record what was being destroyed as well as monuments of the more remote past. In this way the study of physical remains began to supplement that of written records and oral traditions, giving rise to a new tradition of antiquarian, as distinguished from purely historical, scholarship. These leisured, although not rich, antiquarians were drawn from the professional and administrative middle class, which was expanding and prospering under the more centralized rule of the Tudors (Casson 1939: 143). For these patriotic Englishmen local antiquities were an acceptable substitute for those of Italy and Greece. They visited monuments dating from the medieval, Roman, and prehistoric periods and described them as part of county topographies and histories. They also recorded the local legends and traditions relating to these sites. In addition, some antiquarians made collections of local (as well as exotic) curiosities. John Twyne, who died in 1581, collected Romano-British coins, pottery, and glass, as well as studying earthworks and megaliths (Kendrick 1950: 105). A more varied and extensive, but less archaeological, collection of curiosities by the royal gardener John Tradescant was to become the nucleus of the Ashmolean Museum, established at Oxford in 1675. Hitherto collections containing antiquities had consisted either of church relics or the family heirlooms of the nobility.

At first no clear distinction was drawn between curiosities that were of natural and those that were of human origin. Scholars, as well as uneducated people, believed stone celts to be thunderstones (a view endorsed by the Roman naturalist Pliny [Slotkin 1965: x]) and stone projectile points to be elf-bolts, while in Poland and Central Europe it was thought that pottery vessels grew spontaneously in the earth (Abramowicz 1981; Sklenář 1983: 16). In a world unaware of biological evolution, it was not self-evident that a prehistoric celt was man-made while a fossil ammonoid was a natural formation. Most of these curios were found accidentally by farmers and manual labourers and there was as yet no tradition of excavating for prehistoric remains.

John Leland (1503–52) was appointed King's Antiquary in 1533. He played an important role in rescuing books following the dispersal of monastic libraries. He also toured England and Wales recording place-names and genealogies as well as objects of antiquarian interest, including the visible remains of prehistoric sites. Although he was only vaguely aware even of major changes in architectural styles in medieval times, his great innovation was his desire to travel to see things rather than simply to read about them (Kendrick 1950: 45–64). William Camden, the author of the first comprehensive topographical survey of England, concentrated mainly on Roman and early medieval remains. His *Britannia*, first published in 1586, was to go through many posthumous editions. Camden was also a founding member, in 1572, of the Society of Antiquaries, a London-based association for the preservation and study of national antiquities. This society was suppressed by James I in 1604, presumably because the Scottish-born monarch feared that it was encouraging English nationalism and hence opposition to his rule (Taylor 1948:

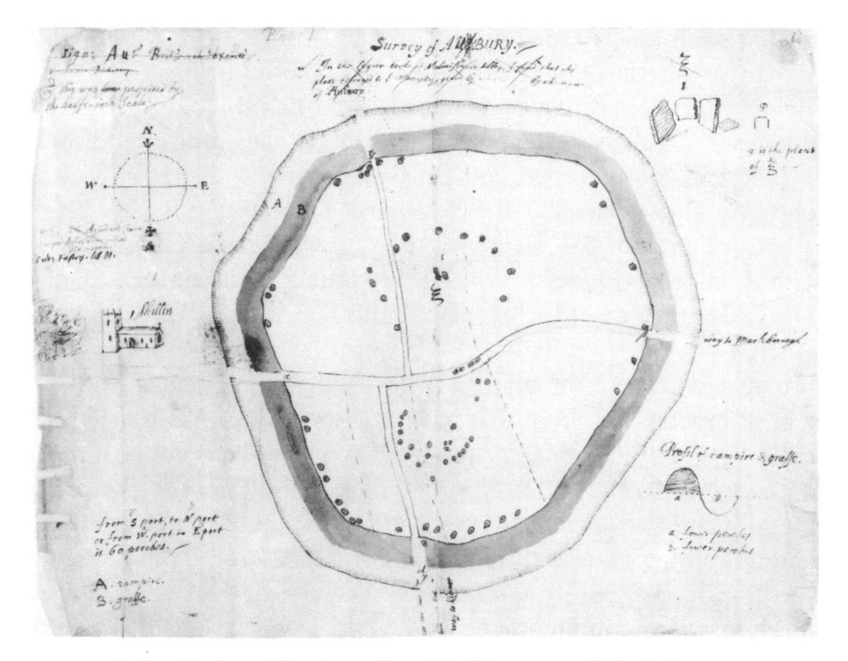

7 Aubrey's plan of Avebury, from his ***Monumenta Britannica***, *c*. 1675

10; Joan Evans 1956: 14). John Aubrey (1626–97), the most famous of the seventeenth-century English antiquarians, worked mainly in Wiltshire. He prepared descriptions of Stonehenge and Avebury, arguing that these great prehistoric monuments were probably druidical temples (Hunter 1975). The research of these early antiquarians was continued by a succession of historians and topographers, most of whom worked at the county level. They did little deliberate digging and had no sense of chronology apart from what was known from written records. Like classical archaeologists, they sought to explain ancient monuments by associating them with peoples mentioned in historical accounts. This meant that what we now recognize as prehistoric remains were generally ascribed quite arbitrarily either to the Britons, whom the Romans encountered when they first invaded England, or to the Saxons and Danes, who had invaded Britain after the fall of the Roman Empire.

Systematic antiquarian research developed somewhat later in Scandinavia than in England, as part of the political and military rivalry that followed the separation of Sweden and Denmark in 1523.

Renaissance historians soon became as fascinated with their respective national heritages as were those in England. They were encouraged by Kings Christian IV of Denmark (reigned 1588–1648) and Gustavus II Adolphus of Sweden (reigned 1611–32) to draw from historical records and folklore a picture of primordial greatness and valour that was flattering to their respective nations. This interest quickly extended to the study of ancient monuments. Royal patronage enabled leading antiquaries to record these monuments in a thorough and systematic fashion. Johan Bure (1568–1652), a Swedish civil servant, and Ole Worm (1588–1654), a Danish medical doctor, documented large numbers of rune stones. The inscriptions on these stones, which dated from the late Iron Age, permitted a classical archaeological approach to late prehistoric and early historical times. These antiquaries also collected information about much older megalithic tombs and rock drawings. Bure and Worm learned from each other despite the tense political relations between their countries and their own commitment to promoting patriotic sentiments (Klindt-Jensen 1975: 14–21). Some of their work was carried out by means of questionnaires that were distributed nationwide. Museums were also established in which humanly fabricated objects and natural curiosities were assembled. In Denmark one of the first of these was Worm's own museum which became the basis for the Kunstkammer, or Royal Collection, that was opened to the public in the 1680s. In Sweden an Antiquaries College was established at Uppsala in 1666 in order to pursue antiquarian research and national laws were passed to protect ancient monuments. These required the surrender of valuable finds to the king in return for a reward. Olof Rudbeck (1630–1702) trenched and drew vertical sections of Viking-age tumuli at Old Uppsala, and in this way he determined the relative age of the burials within individual mounds. He also believed that the thickness of sod accumulated above a grave could be used to indicate to the nearest century how much time had elapsed since a burial had been placed in it (Klindt-Jensen 1975: 29–31). Unfortunately, antiquarian research tended to languish in Sweden and Denmark as the political ambitions of these states and their economies faltered toward the end of the seventeenth century.

A similar, although less intense, interest in the physical remains of the past developed throughout Western and Central Europe. In medieval France, Roman and prehistoric ruins alike were ascribed to

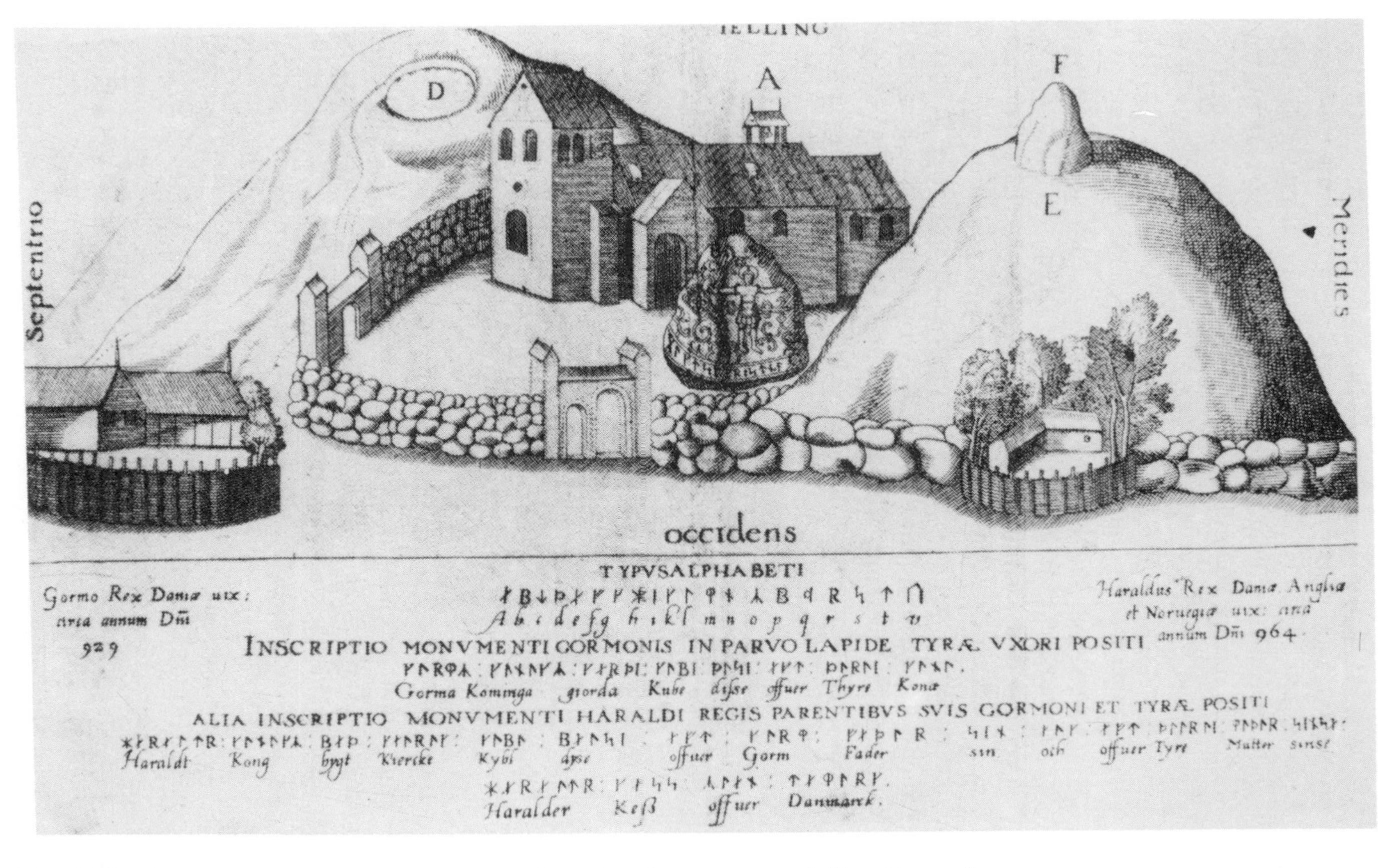

8 Engraving of tumuli and rune stones at Jelling, Denmark, 1591

heroes, such as Charlemagne and Roland, and to local saints. With the Renaissance, Roman antiquities were soon identified for what they were and Francis I (reigned 1515–47) and Henri IV (reigned 1589–1610) built up substantial collections of local and imported classical marble statues and bronzes. Much scholarship was concentrated on Roman inscriptions, while for a long time pre-Roman antiquities were little valued. Only in the eighteenth century did an interest develop in the earlier Celtic inhabitants of France and their origins. This led to the excavation of some prehistoric monuments. In the latter part of the eighteenth century a growing desire to demonstrate the cultural achievements of the Celts, who were recognized as the ancestors of the French, encouraged the study of pre-Roman times to develop independently of classical archaeology. This movement, which continued into the nineteenth century, was linked to growing nationalism. Like early English studies of pre-Roman remains, it encouraged more fanciful speculation than sober investigations and ultimately contributed little to the development of archaeology (Laming-Emperaire 1964).

In Germany the rediscovery in 1451 of the Roman historian Cornelius Tacitus' (*c.* A.D. 56–120) *Germania*, which contained a detailed description of the customs of the ancient Germans, led scholars to use classical sources rather than medieval legends to study their early history. This trend laid the basis for the first general historical study of ancient Germany, Philip Klüver's *Germaniae Antiquae* (Ancient Germany), published in 1616 (Sklenář 1983: 24–5). As happened elsewhere, this research led to a growing interest in the material remains of the past. The excavation of barrows at Marzahna in Saxony in 1587 was one of the first in Europe that sought to answer a specific question (whether the vessels found in such structures were manufactured or formed naturally) rather than to find treasure or enrich a collection (ibid. 38). A few efforts were also made to classify megaliths and funerary vessels according to shape and use (ibid. 33).

Analogous developments occurred in Hungary and the Slavic countries. Political figures, churchmen, and scholars incorporated archaeological finds into their collections of curiosities. In some princes' collections local discoveries considered to have artistic merit were displayed alongside statues and painted vessels imported from Italy and Greece. Some digging was carried out to recover artifacts and occasionally laws were passed to protect antiquities and secure new finds for national collections (Sklenář 1983: 32–3). While archaeological discoveries were often fancifully associated with historically known peoples, no system was devised for dating prehistoric artifacts anywhere in Europe. Indeed, in the absence of written inscriptions, it was not even clear which finds dated prior to earliest written records in any particular area and which did not.

Recognition of stone tools

The sixteenth and seventeenth centuries marked the beginning of worldwide Western European exploration and colonization. Mariners started encountering large numbers of hunter–gatherers and tribal agriculturalists in the Americas, Africa, and the Pacific. Descriptions of these peoples and their customs circulated in Europe and collections of their tools and clothing were brought back as curiosities. At first the discovery of groups who did not know how to work metal and whose cultures abounded with practices that were contrary to Christian teaching seemed to confirm the traditional medieval view that those who had wandered farthest from the Near East and lost contact with God's continuing revelation had degenerated both morally and technologically. Gradually, however, an awareness of these people and their tools gave rise to an alternative view, which drew a parallel between modern 'primitive' peoples and prehistoric Europeans. Yet it took a long time for this comparison to be generally accepted and even longer for all of its implications to be worked out.

The first step in this process was the realization by scholars that the stone tools being found in Europe had been manufactured by human beings and were not of natural or supernatural origin. Until the late seventeenth century crystals, animal fossils, stone tools, and other distinctively shaped stone objects were all classified as fossils. In 1669 Nicolaus Steno (1638–86) compared fossil and modern mollusc shells and concluded that they resembled each other more closely than either did inorganic crystals. Hence he argued that fossil shells were the remains of once living animals. Ethnographic analogies played a similar role in establishing the human origin of stone tools (Grayson 1983: 5). The possibility that people had once lived in Europe who did not know the use of metal tools was implicitly raised early in the sixteenth century by Pietro Martire d'Anghiera when he compared the native peoples of the West Indies with classical traditions of a primordial Golden Age (Hodgen 1964: 371).

The Italian geologist Georgius Agricola (1490–1555) expressed the opinion that stone tools were probably of human origin (Heizer 1962a: 62); while Michel Mercati (1541–93), who was Superintendent of the Vatican Botanical Gardens and physician to Pope Clement VII, suggested in his *Metallotheca* that, before the use of iron, stone tools might have been 'beaten out of the hardest flints, to be used for the madness of war' ([1717] Heizer 1962a: 65). He cited biblical and classical attestations of the use of stone tools and was familiar with ethnographic specimens from the New World that had been sent as presents to the Vatican. Ulisse Aldrovandi (1522–1605) also argued that stone tools were human fabrications in his *Museum Metallicum*, published in 1648. In 1655 the Frenchman Isaac de la Peyrère, one of the first writers to challenge the biblical account of the creation of humanity, identified thunderstones with his 'pre-Adamite' race, which he claimed had existed prior to the creation of the first Hebrew, which was described in the Book of Genesis.

In Britain increasing knowledge of the native peoples of the New World resulted in a growing conviction that stone tools were made by human beings. In 1656 the antiquarian William Dugdale (1605–86) attributed such tools to the ancient Britons, asserting that they had used them before they learned how to work brass or iron. Robert Plot (1640–96), Dugdale's son-in-law and the Keeper of the Ashmolean Museum, shared this opinion to the extent that in 1686 he wrote that the ancient Britons had used mostly stone rather than iron tools and that one might learn how prehistoric stone tools had been hafted by comparing them with North American Indian ones that could be observed in their wooden mounts. In 1699 his assistant Edward Lhwyd drew specific comparisons between elf-arrows and chipped flint arrowheads made by the Indians of New England. Similar views were entertained by the Scottish antiquarian Sir Robert Sibbald as early as 1684. Around 1766 Bishop Charles Lyttelton speculated that stone tools must have been made before any metal ones were available and therefore that they dated from some time prior to the Roman conquest (Slotkin 1965: 223). A decade later the writer Samuel Johnson ([1775] 1970: 56) compared British stone arrowheads with tools made by the modern inhabitants of the Pacific

Islands and concluded that the former had been manufactured by a nation that did not know the use of iron. By the eighteenth century such observations had encouraged a growing realization in the United Kingdom that antiquities could be a source of information about the past as well as curiosities worthy of being recorded in county topographies.

In France in 1719 Dom Bernard de Montfaucon (1655–1741), who 24 years earlier had published an account of the excavation of a megalithic stone tomb containing polished stone axes, ascribed such tombs to a nation that had no knowledge of iron. In reaching this conclusion he was influenced by knowledge of archaeological research in England and Scandinavia (Laming-Emperaire 1964: 94). Five years later the French scholar Antoine de Jussieu (1686–1758) drew some detailed comparisons between European stone tools and ethnographic specimens brought from New France and the Caribbean. He stated that 'the people of France, Germany, and other Northern countries who, but for the discovery of iron, would have much resemblance to the savages of today, had no less need than they – before using iron – to cut wood, to remove bark, to split branches, to kill wild animals, to hunt for their food and to defend themselves against their enemies' ([1723] Heizer 1962a: 69). In 1738 Kilian Stobeus, Professor of Natural History at the University of Lund, argued that flint implements antedated metal ones in Scandinavia and compared them with ethnographic specimens from Louisiana, an opinion echoed in 1763 by the Danish scholar Erik Pontoppidan (Klindt-Jensen 1975: 35–9). As late as 1655, as distinguished an antiquarian as Ole Worm had continued to think it likely that polished stone axes were of celestial origin rather than fossilized iron tools or stone ones, even though he had ethnographic examples of stone tools from the New World in his collection (ibid. 23). Nevertheless, by the seventeenth century both the human fabrication of stone tools and their considerable antiquity in Europe were widely accepted.

Yet a growing realization that stone tools had probably been used prior to metal ones in Europe and elsewhere did not necessitate the adoption of an evolutionary perspective (cf. Rodden 1981: 63), since stone tools could be seen in use alongside metal ones in the contemporary world. Noting that according to the Bible iron working was practised from early times, Mercati argued that knowledge of metallurgy must have been lost by nations that migrated into areas where iron ore was not found ([1717] Heizer 1962a: 66). Similar degenerationist views were widely held. Other antiquarians maintained that stone tools were used at the same time as metal ones by communities or nations that were too poor to own metal. As late as 1857 it was argued in opposition to the theory that stone tools antedated metal ones that stone tools must be imitations of metal originals (O'Laverty 1857; 'Trevelyan' 1857). Without adequate chronological controls and any archaeological data from many parts of the world, it remained possible that iron working and lack of such knowledge had existed side by side throughout most of human history. Prior to the nineteenth century there was no factual evidence to make an evolutionary view of human history more plausible than a degenerationist one. The strong religious sanctions enjoined by the degenerationist position also made many antiquarians reluctant to challenge it.

The Enlightenment paradigm

The development of an evolutionary view of the past was encouraged far less by a growing body of archaeological evidence than by a gradual transformation in thought that began during the seventeenth century in northwestern Europe, the region which was rapidly emerging as the economic hub of a new world economy (Wallerstein 1974; Delâge 1985). This view was based on rapidly increasing confidence in the ability of human beings to excel and to develop both economically and culturally. Early in the century the English philosopher and statesman Francis Bacon protested against the idea that the culture of classical antiquity was superior to that of modern times. A similar theme was echoed in France in the late seventeenth-century Quarrel between the Ancients and the Moderns, in which the 'moderns' argued that the human talents were not declining and hence present-day Europeans could hope to produce works that equalled or surpassed those of the ancient Greeks or Romans (Laming-Emperaire 1964: 64–6). While Raleigh and many other Elizabethan writers had continued to believe, in the medieval fashion, that the world was hastening toward its end, by the second half of the seventeenth century many Western Europeans were confident about the future (Toulmin and Goodfield 1966:

108–10). The reasons for this growing optimism included the scientific revolutions of the sixteenth and seventeenth centuries, as manifested above all in the work of Galileo and Newton, the application of scientific discoveries to the advancement of technology, and a widespread appreciation of the literary creations of English writers in the reign of Elizabeth I and of French ones under Louis XIV. Especially among the middle classes, these developments encouraged a growing faith in progress and a belief that to a large degree human beings were masters of their own destiny. They also inclined Western Europeans to regard the ways of life of the technologically less advanced peoples that they were encountering in various parts of the world as survivals of a primordial human condition rather than as products of degeneration.

Neither the Renaissance discovery that the past had been different from the present nor the realization that technological development was occurring in Western Europe led directly to the conclusion that progress was a general theme of human history. In the seventeenth century successive historical periods were viewed as a series of kaleidoscope variations on themes that were grounded in a fixed human nature, rather than as constituting a developmental sequence worthy of study in its own right (Toulmin and Goodfield 1966: 113–14). The Italian philosopher Giambattista Vico (1668–1774) viewed history as having cyclical characteristics and argued that all human societies evolve through similar stages of development and decay that reflect the uniform actions of providence. He prudently stressed, however, that this view of human history as governed by strict laws did not apply to the Hebrews, whose progress was divinely guided. Although he was not an evolutionist, his views helped to encourage a belief that history could be understood in terms of regularities analogous to those being proposed for the natural sciences (ibid. 125–9).

An evolutionary view of human history that was sufficiently comprehensive to challenge the medieval formulation not only on specific points but also in its entirety was formulated by the Enlightenment philosophy of the eighteenth century. This movement began in France, where it is associated with leading philosophers, such as Montesquieu, Turgot, Voltaire, and Condorcet, but it also flourished in Scotland in the school of so-called 'primitivist' thinkers, which included John Locke, William Robertson, John Millar, Adam

Ferguson, and the eccentric James Burnett, who as Lord Monboddo remains notorious for his claim that human beings and orangutans belong to a single species (Bryson 1945; Schneider 1967).

The philosophers of the Enlightenment combined a more naturalistic understanding of social processes with a firm belief in progress to produce an integrated set of concepts that purported to explain social change. They also created a methodology that they believed enabled them to study the general course of human development from earliest times. In England and the Netherlands, where political power was already in the hands of the mercantile middle class, intellectual activity was directed towards assessing the practical political and economic significance of this change. The continuing weakness of the French middle class in the face of Bourbon autocracy appears to have encouraged French intellectuals to engage in broader speculations about the nature of progress. The great impact that these ideas had on scholars in Edinburgh reflected not only the close cultural ties between France and Scotland but also the greater power and prosperity suddenly acquired by the Scottish middle class following Union with England in 1707.

The following are the most important tenets of the Enlightenment that were to become the basis of popular evolutionary thinking among the European middle classes:

1 Psychic unity. All human groups were believed to possess essentially the same kind and level of intelligence and to share the same basic emotions, although individuals within groups differed from one another in these features. Because of this there was no biological barrier to the degree to which any race or nationality could benefit from new knowledge or contribute to its advancement. All groups were equally perfectable. In its most ethnocentric form this constituted a belief that all human beings were capable of benefitting from European civilization. Yet it also implied that an advanced technological civilization was not destined to remain the exclusive possession of Europeans. Cultural differences were generally either ascribed to climatic and other environmental influences or dismissed as historical accidents (Slotkin 1965: 423).
2 Cultural progress as the dominant feature of human history. Change was believed to occur continuously rather than episodically and was ascribed to natural rather than supernatural causes.

The main motivation for progress was thought to be the desire of human beings to improve their condition, principally by gaining greater control over nature (Slotkin 1965: 441). Many Enlightenment philosophers regarded progress as inevitable, or even as a law of nature, while others thought of it as something to be hoped for (ibid. 357–91; Harris 1968: 37–9).

3 Progress characterizes not only technological development but all aspects of human life, including social organization, politics, morality, and religious beliefs. Changes in all of these spheres of human behaviour were viewed as occurring concomitantly and as following, in a general fashion, a single line of development. As a result of similar ways of thinking, human beings at the same level of development tended to devise uniform solutions to their problems and hence their ways of life evolved along parallel lines (Slotkin 1965: 445). Cultural change was frequently conceptualized in terms of a universal series of stages. Europeans were viewed as having evolved through all of these stages, while technologically more primitive societies had passed only through the first ones.

4 Progress perfects human nature, not by changing it but by progressively eliminating ignorance, passion, and superstition (Toulmin and Goodfield 1966: 115–23). The new evolutionary view of cultural change did not negate either the traditional Christian or the Cartesian notion of a fixed and immutable human nature. Yet human nature as it was now conceived was far removed from the medieval preoccupation with sinfulness and individual dependence on divine grace as the only means of achieving salvation.

5 Progress results from the exercise of rational thought to improve the human condition. In this fashion human beings gradually acquired greater ability to control their environment, which in turn generated the wealth and leisure needed to support the creation of more complex societies and the development of a more profound and objective understanding of humanity and the universe. The exercise of reason had long been regarded as the crucial feature distinguishing human beings from animals. Most Enlightenment philosophers also viewed cultural progress teleologically, as humanity's realization of the plans of a benevolent deity. A faith that benevolent laws guided human development

was long to outlive a belief in God among those who studied human societies.

The Scottish philosopher Dugald Stewart labelled the methodology that Enlightenment philosophers used to trace the development of human institutions 'theoretic' or 'conjectural' history (Slotkin 1965: 460). This involved the comparative study of living peoples whose cultures were judged to be at different levels of complexity and arranging these cultures to form a logical, usually unilinear, sequence from simple to complex. These studies were based largely on ethnographic data derived from accounts by explorers and missionaries working in different parts of the world. Despite disagreement about details, such as whether agricultural or pastoral economies had evolved first, it was believed that these sequences could be regarded as historical ones and used to examine the development of all kinds of social institutions. In the writings of the historian William Robertson and others, the apparently similar sequences of cultures in the eastern hemisphere and the Americas were interpreted as proof of the general validity of the principle of psychic unity and of the belief that human beings at the same stage of development would respond to the same problems in the same way (Harris 1968: 34–5).

It is generally acknowledged that a cultural-evolutionary perspective was widely accepted for explaining human history long before the publication of Darwin's *On the Origin of Species*. Glyn Daniel (1976: 41) doubts the importance of Enlightenment philosophy for the development of archaeology since Enlightenment scholars, with few exceptions (see Harris 1968: 34), ignored archaeological data in their own writings. That they did so is scarcely surprising since, in the absence of any established means for dating prehistoric materials, archaeology had little to contribute to their discussions of cultural evolution. This does not mean, however, that the writings of the Enlightenment did not influence the thinking of antiquarians. On the contrary, their advocacy of an evolutionary view of human development from primitive beginnings encouraged a more holistic understanding of prehistoric times.

In particular the Enlightenment encouraged renewed interest in the materialistic and evolutionary views of cultural development that had been expounded by the Roman Epicurean philosopher

Titus Lucretius Carus (98–55 B.C.) in his poem *De Rerum Natura* (On the Nature of Things). He argued that the earliest implements were hands, nails, and teeth, as well as stones and pieces of wood. Only later were tools made of bronze and then of iron. While his scheme was supported by various classical writings that referred to a period when bronze tools and weapons had not yet been replaced by iron ones, it was based largely on evolutionary speculations, which postulated that the world and all living species had developed as a result of irreducible and eternal particles of matter, which he called atoms, combining in ever more complex ways. Neither Lucretius nor any other Roman scholar sought to prove his theory and it remained only one of many speculative schemes known to the Romans. A popular alternative postulated the moral degeneration of humanity through successive ages of gold, silver, bronze, and iron.

Early in the eighteenth century French scholars were familiar both with the ideas of Lucretius and with the growing evidence that stone tools had once been used throughout Europe. They were also familiar with classical and biblical texts which suggested that bronze tools had been used prior to iron ones. In 1734 Nicolas Mahudel read a paper to the Academie des Inscriptions in Paris, in which he cited Mercati and set out the idea of three successive ages of stone, bronze, and iron as a plausible account of human development. Bernard de Montfaucon and many other scholars repeated this idea throughout the eighteenth century. In 1758 Antoine-Yves Goguet (1716–58) supported the Three-Age theory in a book that was translated into English three years later with the title *The Origin of Laws, Arts, and Sciences, and their Progress among the Most Ancient Nations*. He believed that modern 'savages set before us a striking picture of the ignorance of the ancient world, and the practices of primitive times' ([1761] Heizer 1962a: 14). Yet to square this evolutionary view with the biblical assertion that iron working had been invented before the flood, he claimed, like Mercati and some other contemporary evolutionists, that this process had to be reinvented after 'that dreadful calamity deprived the greatest part of mankind of this, as well as of other arts'. Glyn Daniel (1976: 40) correctly warned against exaggerating the influence that the Three-Age theory exerted on antiquarian thought during the eighteenth century. Yet, as an interest in cultural progress grew more pervasive, the Three-Age theory gained in popular esteem. In Denmark this idea was expounded by the historian P. F. Suhm in his History of Norway, Denmark, and Holstein (1776) and by the antiquarian Skuli Thorlacius (1802), as well as by L. S. Vedel Simonsen in his textbook of Danish history published in 1813. Yet, despite a growing number of supporters, the Three-Age theory remained as speculative and unproved as it had been in the days of Lucretius. By comparison, the observation that sometime in the remote past at least some Europeans had made and used stone tools was far more widely accepted.

Scientific antiquarianism

The study of prehistoric antiquities was also influenced by the general development of scientific methodology, which in turn was intimately related to the growing ability of Europeans to manipulate their environment technologically. The philosopher René Descartes (1596–1650), as part of his efforts to account for all natural phenomena in terms of a single system of mechanical principles, expounded the idea that the laws governing nature were universal and eternal. God was viewed as existing apart from the universe, which he had created as a machine that was capable of functioning without further intervention (Toulmin and Goodfield 1966: 80–4). Descartes' views, together with Francis Bacon's emphasis on inductive methodology and the exclusion of negative cases, produced a new spirit of scientific inquiry that was reflected in the importance that the Royal Society of London, founded by Charles II in 1660, placed on observation, classification, and experimentation. The members of the Royal Society rejected the authority that medieval scholars had assigned to the learned works of antiquity as the ultimate sources of scientific knowledge and devoted themselves to studying things rather than what had been written about them. Yet even some of these researchers were pleased when they thought they found their most recent discoveries anticipated in the great scientific writings of ancient times. Antiquarians were elected fellows of the Royal Society and their work was encouraged and published by the society, except when Isaac Newton was its president between 1703 and 1727. Although Newton was a great physical scientist, his interests in human history were decidedly mystical and medieval in character.

Members of the Royal Society provided accurate and detailed descriptions of archaeological finds. They identified animal bones from archaeological sites and sought to determine how tools had been made and used. They also tried to work out how large stones might have been moved and monuments constructed in ancient times. The kinds of research that the Royal Society encouraged are exemplified by the early work of William Stukeley (1687–1765). Like Camden before him (Daniel 1967: 37), he realized that the geometrical crop marks that farmers had noted in various parts of England since the medieval period (and which they had interpreted as supernatural phenomena) outlined the buried foundations of vanished structures (Piggott 1985: 52). He grouped together as types monuments of similar form, such as linear earthworks or different kinds of burial mounds, in hopes of interpreting them in the light of the meagre historical evidence that was available. Stuart Piggott (1985: 67) has noted that Stukeley was one of the first British antiquarians to recognize the possibility of a lengthy pre-Roman occupation, during which distinctive types of prehistoric monuments had been constructed at different times and different peoples might have successively occupied southern England. Even this, however, was suggested by Julius Caesar's documentation of a Belgic invasion of southeastern England shortly before the Roman conquest. At the

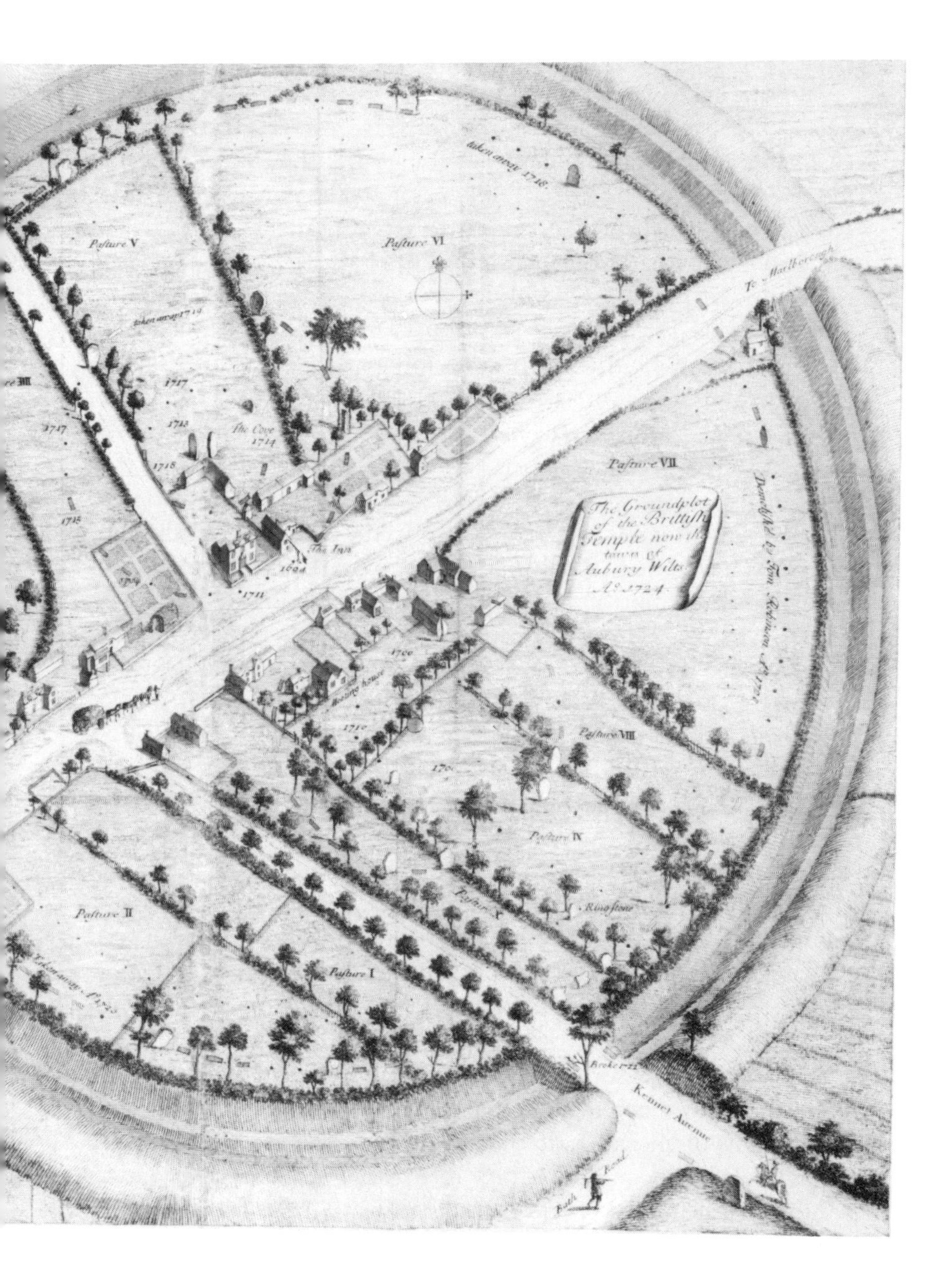

9 Stukeley's view of Avebury, published in *Abury*, 1743

same time, Stukeley and other antiquarians took the first steps towards trying to ascertain relative dates for archaeological finds for which there were no historical records. He observed construction layers in barrows and argued that Silbury Hill, the largest artificial mound in Europe, had been built prior to the construction of a Roman road, which curved abruptly to avoid it (Daniel 1967: 122–3). He also noted that Roman roads cut through Bronze Age disc ('Druid') barrows in several places (Piggott 1985: 67) and used the presence of bluestone chips in some burial mounds near Stonehenge to infer that these burials were contemporary with the building of the temple (Marsden 1974: 5). In 1758 his daughter Anna dated the White Horse cut in the chalk at Uffington, and which had been thought to be a Saxon memorial, to the pre-Roman period on the basis of its stylistic similarity to horses portrayed on pre-Roman British coins (Piggott 1985: 142). In 1720 the astronomer Edmund Halley estimated that Stonehenge might be 2,000 or 3,000 years old, following an examination of the depth of weathering of its stones; while a later comparison of relative weathering convinced Stukeley that Avebury was much older than Stonehenge (Lynch and Lynch 1968: 52). In Denmark Erik Pontoppidan carefully excavated a megalithic tomb on the grounds of a royal palace in northwest Sjaelland, the main Danish island, in 1744. He reported on the structure and the finds it contained in the first volume of the *Proceedings of the Danish Royal Society*, concluding that cremation burials found near the top of the mound dated from a more recent era than the stone chamber below them and the mound itself (Klindt-Jensen 1975: 35–6). When three megalithic tombs opened in 1776 were found to contain stone and bronze artifacts but not iron ones, O. Hoegh-Guldberg, the excavator, assumed that they were very ancient (ibid. 42–3).

Studies of these sorts helped to advance the investigation of prehistoric times by encouraging more accurate observations and descriptions of ancient artifacts and monuments, more disciplined thought about them, and efforts to date a few of them in either relative or calendrical terms. Although this research was too fragmentary and the results too disconnected to constitute a discipline of prehistoric archaeology, it helped to lay the groundwork for the eventual development of such a discipline. Noting similar trends in the antiquarian researches of the eighteenth century in continental

Europe, Karel Sklenář (1983: 59) observed that 'the very fact that archaeologists in Central Europe preferred analytical description of the facts to the formation of a synthetic picture of the past' shows how small was the contribution that the new scientific approach made to the development of a better knowledge of prehistory. This statement cannot be applied to England and Scandinavia, where antiquarians were making substantial progress in conceptualizing the problems confronting the study of prehistoric times and tentative steps were being taken to resolve these problems.

Antiquarianism and romanticism

The growing influence of cultural-evolutionary thought during the eighteenth century spawned a conservative reaction that at that time had even greater influence on antiquarian research than did evolutionism. In 1724 the French Jesuit missionary Joseph-François Lafitau (1685–1740), who had worked among the Indians of Canada, published his *Moeurs des sauvages ameriquains comparées aux moeurs des premiers temps*. Although this book has often been described as an early contribution to evolutionary anthropology, Lafitau argued that the religions and customs of the Amerindians and the ancient Greeks and Romans resembled each other because both were corrupt and distorted versions of the true religion and morality that God had revealed to Adam and his descendants in the Near East. These views, which revived the doctrine of degeneration, were similar to those held by Stukeley, who in later life was obsessed by the belief that the religion of the ancient Druids was a relatively pure survival of primordial monotheism and therefore closely akin to Christianity. Stukeley associated all of the major prehistoric monuments in Britain with the Druids and based extravagant interpretations of them on this premise. His writings were directed against the Deists, who believed that reasonable people could apprehend God without the help of revelation, a view that had much in common with the Enlightenment.

Stukeley's thinking also reflected a growing trend towards romanticism. This intellectual movement, which began in the late eighteenth century, was anticipated in the back-to-nature philosophy of Jean-Jacques Rousseau. Although he believed in the importance of reason, he emphasized emotion and sensibility as important aspects of human behaviour. He also stressed the inherent goodness of human beings and attributed greed and envy to the corrupting influences and artificiality of civilization. In Germany and England romanticism flourished in part as a revolt against French cultural domination and the literary and artistic restrictions of neo-classicism. In its championing of strong emotions, romanticism mingled a preoccupation with horror and evil with a delight in natural beauty. Romantically inclined individuals developed a strong interest in ruined abbeys, graves, and other symbols of death and decay, including human skeletons grinning 'a ghastly smile' (Marsden 1974: 18). They also treated 'primitive' or 'natural' societies and the 'spirit' of European nations as preserved in their monuments and folk traditions, especially those of the medieval period, as the ideal inspiration for arts and letters (K. Clark 1962: 66). In this fashion romanticism became closely linked to nationalism. It appealed to the more conservative members of the middle class, who identified neo-classicism with the values of the aristocracy and equated rationalism with atheism and political radicalism. Significantly, the Society of Antiquaries of London, which was founded in 1717 and received its charter in 1751, was far more interested in medieval England than in Roman or prehistoric Britain (Piggott 1985: 43–4). The romantic movement was strengthened in conservative circles in the years following the French revolution, when the Enlightenment was denounced for encouraging popular liberty and republicanism. In the conservative restoration that followed the defeat of Napoleon Bonaparte, a concerted effort was made to suppress Enlightenment ideas in Central and Western Europe.

The late eighteenth century has been viewed as a period of intellectual decline in historical and antiquarian studies in Britain (Piggott 1985: 108, 115–17, 154–5). Yet, romanticism appears to have been instrumental in encouraging a growing emphasis on excavation, and especially the excavation of graves, that contributed to the development of antiquarianism in the later part of the eighteenth century. Between 1757 and 1773 the Reverend Bryan Faussett (1720–76) excavated more than 750 Anglo-Saxon burial mounds in southeastern England. James Douglas (1753–1819), in his *Nenia Britannica, or Sepulchral History of Great Britain*, which was published in parts between 1786 and 1793 and based on a massive compilation of information derived from barrow excavations throughout Britain, assumed that graves containing only stone artifacts were earlier than those that also contained metal ones (Lynch and Lynch 1968: 48). Some of the best work done during this period was by William Cunnington (1754–1810) and his wealthy patron Sir Richard Colt Hoare. They surveyed a large area in Wiltshire, locating ancient village sites and earthworks and excavating 379 barrows. They recorded their observations carefully, divided barrows into five types, and employed stratigraphy to distinguish between primary and secondary interments. They used coins to date some barrows from the historical period and, like Douglas, thought it possible that graves containing only stone artifacts might be earlier than prehistoric burials accompanied by metal ones. Yet, despite these tentative advances, they were unable to demonstrate to 'which of the successive inhabitants' of Britain various classes of monuments were to be ascribed or even whether they were the work of more than one people. Moreover, Cunnington could not discover enough regularity in types of grave goods associated with particular barrow styles to implement the antiquary Thomas Leman's suggestion that stone, bronze, and iron weapons could be used to distinguish three successive ages (Chippindale 1983: 123). Thus, in Glyn Daniel's (1950: 31) words, they 'failed to find any way of breaking down the apparent contemporaneity of pre-Roman remains'. Even at the most elementary level, there were always antiquarians prepared to argue that graves containing only stone tools were not necessarily older than the rest but merely belonged to ruder tribes or poorer social groups. As yet there was no satisfactory rebuttal for this claim.

The New World

The first historical questions that Europeans asked about the native inhabitants of North and South America were who they were and from where they had come. Between the sixteenth and eighteenth centuries scholars speculated that the Indians might be descended from Iberians, Carthaginians, Israelites, Canaanites, and Tartars. Still more imaginative writers claimed that they came from the vanished continent of Atlantis. Most of these speculations reflected the pretensions or biases of particular groups of settlers. Some early Spanish colonists denied that the Indians had souls, which meant they were not human beings. They sought to be free to exploit them as they could animals. The Spanish Crown, however, wanted recognition from the Church that the Indians had souls, since that allowed the Spanish government to assert its right to govern them and to curb the independence of its colonists. When the Roman Catholic Church proclaimed native people to be human beings, it also meant that Christians were required to recognize that they were descended from Adam and Eve and hence had originated, like other peoples, in the Near East (Hanke 1959).

Some of the leaders of the seventeenth-century Massachusetts Bay Colony liked to think of their own colonists as constituting a New Israel and the Indians as Canaanites, whose possessions God was delivering into their hands as he had given Palestine to the ancient Hebrews. This was interpreted as giving the Puritans the right to seize land and enslave the Indians. As recently as 1783, Ezra Stiles, the President of Yale University, was promoting the idea that the Indians of New England were literally descended from Canaanites who had fled from Palestine at the time of Joshua's invasion, as recorded in the Bible (Haven 1856: 27–8).

Over time, however, there was growing support for the theory, first expounded in 1589 by the Jesuit priest José de Acosta in his *Historia natural y moral de las Indias* that the Indians had crossed the Bering Strait as wandering hunters from Siberia (Pagden 1982: 193–7). Although Acosta believed that the Indians had lost all knowledge of sedentary life in the course of their migrations, later proto-evolutionists saw in America evidence of what the childhood of all humanity had been like. In the late sixteenth century it was being suggested that in ancient times the native inhabitants of Britain had been as primitive as the modern Indians of Virginia (Kendrick 1950: 123). On the other hand, degenerationists viewed native cultures as the corrupt remnants of the divinely revealed patriarchal way of life described in the Book of Genesis and also saw amongst them evidence of the half-remembered teachings of early Christian missionaries. In the seventeenth century the technological inferiority and alleged cultural degeneracy of native American cultures by comparison with European ones were interpreted in theological terms as manifestations of divine displeasure (Vaughan 1982). During the next century some leading European scholars advanced the more naturalistic argument that the New World was climatically inferior to Europe and Asia and that this accounted for the inferiority of its indigenous cultures as well as of its plant and animal life (Haven 1856: 94).

In Mexico and Peru archaeological monuments were frequently effaced or destroyed during the sixteenth and seventeenth centuries in an attempt to eliminate the memories native people had of their pre-Christian past (Bernal 1980: 37–9). A particular effort was made to destroy symbols of Aztec sovereignty and national identity. Only a small number of European travellers discussed the great pre-Hispanic monuments of Mexico and Peru prior to the nineteenth century.

Before the late eighteenth century almost no notice was taken of prehistoric remains in North America apart from occasional references to rock carvings and rock paintings which were usually thought to be the work of modern native peoples. Few collections of artifacts recovered from the ground were assembled in North America and the excavation of sites was rarely attempted. Among the exceptions is a splendid collection of polished stone tools from the late Archaic period found near Trois-Rivières, in Quebec, in 1700 and preserved in a convent from that time to the present (Ribes 1966). Equally exceptional were Thomas Jefferson's carefully reported excavation of an Indian burial mound in Virginia in 1784 (Heizer 1959: 218–21) and the alleged exploration of a burial mound in Kansas a decade earlier (Blakeslee 1987). Throughout this period a pervasive ethnocentrism caused Europeans to doubt that anything significant could be learned about the history of peoples whom they viewed as savages fit only to be swept aside, or in rare cases assimilated, by the advance of European civilization. Because of the paucity of archaeological data, most discussions of native history had to be based on oral traditions (often garbled in transmission and not understood in their cultural context), comparative ethnology, and physical resemblances. A notable exception to this was the naturalist and explorer William Bartram, who in 1789 used contemporary ceremonial structures belonging to the Creek Indians of the southeastern United States as a basis for interpreting prehistoric mound sites in that region. Ian Brown (n.d.) has pointed out that this is one of the earliest known examples of the employment of the direct historical approach to interpret archaeological remains in North America.

The impasse of antiquarianism

In North America no less than in Europe antiquarians who were interested in what are now recognized to be prehistoric remains looked to written records and oral traditions to provide a historical context for their finds no less than did classical archaeologists. Yet in the case of prehistoric remains there were no adequate written records. In his book on the antiquities of the island of Anglesey published in 1723 the Reverend Henry Rowlands noted that 'in these inextricable recesses of antiquity we must borrow other lights to guide us through, or content ourselves to be without any' (Daniel 1967: 43). He went on to declare that 'analogy of ancient names and words, a rational coherence and congruity of things, and plain natural inferences and deductions grounded thereon, are the best authorities we can rely upon in this subject, when more warrantable relations and records are altogether silent in the matter'. Generally the explanation of a monument consisted of trying to identify what people or individual mentioned in ancient records had constructed it and for what purpose. This approach left Camden to speculate whether Silbury Hill had been erected by the Saxons or the Romans and whether it had served to commemorate soldiers slain in a battle or was erected as a boundary survey marker. While Stukeley demonstrated stratigraphically that this mound was older than the nearby Roman road, his conclusion that it was the tomb of the British king Chyndonax, the founder of Avebury, was a mere flight of fantasy (Joan Evans 1956: 121). Stonehenge was alternatively attributed to the Danes, Saxons, Romans, and either generically to the ancient Britons or specifically to the Druids.

As a result of their dependence on written records, throughout the eighteenth and into the early nineteenth centuries antiquarians generally despaired of ever learning much about the period before such records became available. In 1742 Richard Wise commented 'where history is silent and the monuments do not speak for themselves, demonstration cannot be expected; but the utmost is conjecture supported by probability' (Lynch and Lynch 1968: 57). Colt Hoare concluded 'we have evidence of the very high antiquity of our Wiltshire barrows, but none respecting the tribes to whom they appertained, that can rest on solid foundations'. Later in his *Tour in Ireland* he added: 'Alike will the histories of those stupendous temples at Avebury and Stonehenge . . . remain involved in obscurity and oblivion' (Daniel 1963a: 35–6). In 1802 the Danish antiquarian Rasmus Nyerup expressed a similar despair: 'everything which has come down to us from heathendom is wrapped in a thick fog; it belongs to a space of time we cannot measure. We know that it is older than Christendom but whether by a couple of years or a couple of centuries, or even by more than a millennium, we can do no more than guess' (ibid. 36). The English essayist and lexicographer Samuel Johnson, who had little patience with antiquarians, pressed the case against a future for their research even more trenchantly: 'All that is really known of the ancient state of Britain is contained in a few pages. We can know no more than what old writers have told us' (ibid. 35). Even J. Dobrovsky, 'the father of Czech prehistory', who in 1786 argued that archaeological finds were 'speaking documents' that by themselves might illuminate as yet unknown periods of national history (Sklenář 1983: 52), was not very successful in determining how this could be done.

Antiquarians continued to believe that the world had been created about 4000 B.C. They also thought that reliable written records were available as far back as the time of creation for the most crucial region of human history. If humanity had spread from the Near East to the rest of the world, in most regions there was likely to have been only a brief period between the earliest human occupation and the dawn of history. Antiquarians were uncertain whether the general course of human history had been one of development, degeneration, or cyclical change.

Yet the situation was not as stagnant as it is often represented. Between the fifteenth and eighteenth centuries European antiquaries had learned to describe and classify monuments and artifacts, to excavate and record finds, and to use various dating methods, including stratigraphy, to estimate the age of some finds. Some of them had concluded on the basis of archaeological evidence that there had probably been an age when only stone tools had been used in Europe prior to the use of metal and that the use of bronze might have preceded that of iron. These developments represented genuine progress and carried the study of prehistoric remains beyond what had been accomplished in China, Japan, and other parts of the world prior to Western influence. The most serious stumbling-block to the establishment of a relative chronology of prehistoric times and hence to acquiring a more systematic knowledge of early human development was the assumption that artifacts and monuments merely illustrated the historically recorded accomplishments of the past. This was based on the belief shared with classical archaeologists that historical knowledge can be acquired only from written documents or reliable oral traditions and that without these there can be no connected understanding of earlier times. The creation of prehistoric archaeology required that antiquarians find the means to liberate themselves from this restricting assumption.

CHAPTER 3

The beginnings of scientific archaeology

Within no very distant period the study of antiquities has passed, in popular esteem, from contempt to comparative honour.

E. OLDFIELD, Introductory Address, *Archaeological Journal* (1852), p. 1

The development of a self-contained and systematic study of prehistory, as distinguished from the antiquarianism of earlier times, involved two distinct movements that began in the early and middle parts of the nineteenth century respectively. The first originated in Scandinavia and was based on the invention of new techniques for dating archaeological finds that made possible the comprehensive study of the later periods of prehistory. This development marked the beginning of prehistoric archaeology, which was soon able to take its place alongside classical archaeology as a significant component in the study of human development. The second wave, which began in France and England, pioneered the study of the Palaeolithic period and added a vast, hitherto unimagined time depth to human history. Palaeolithic archaeology was concerned with questions of human origins that had become of major concern to the entire scientific community and to the general public as a result of the debates between evolutionists and creationists that followed the publication of *On the Origin of Species* in 1859.

Relative dating

The creation of a controlled chronology that did not rely on written records was the work of the Danish scholar Christian Jürgensen Thomsen (1788–1865). The principal motivation for Thomsen's work, like that of many earlier antiquaries, was patriotism. The antiquarian research of the eighteenth century and the evolutionary concepts of the Enlightenment were indispensable preconditions for his success. Yet these accomplishments would have been of little value if Thomsen had not developed a powerful new technique for dating archaeological finds without recourse to written records. Unfortunately, because Thomsen wrote little, the importance of what he accomplished has been underrated by historians and detractors. It is therefore necessary to clarify what he actually accomplished.

Thomsen was born in Copenhagen in 1788, the son of a wealthy merchant. As a young man he studied in Paris and, after he returned home, he undertook to arrange a local collection of Roman and Scandinavian coins. Collecting coins had become a popular gentleman's hobby during the eighteenth century (McKay 1976). From the inscriptions and dates they bore it was possible to arrange them in series according to the country and reign in which they had been minted. It was also often possible to assign coins on which dates and inscriptions were illegible to such series using stylistic criteria alone. Working with this coin collection may have made Thomsen aware of stylistic changes and their value for the relative dating of artifacts.

The beginning of the nineteenth century was a period of growing nationalism in Denmark, which was greatly strengthened when the British, who were fighting Napoleon and his reluctant continental allies, destroyed most of the Danish navy in Copenhagen harbour in 1801 and bombarded Copenhagen again in 1807. Worsaae later argued that these calamities encouraged Danes to study their past glories as a source of consolation and encouragement to face the future. Yet he also noted that the French Revolution, by encouraging greater respect for the political rights of a broader spectrum of the population everywhere, awakened in Denmark a new popular, as opposed to dynastic, interest in the past (Daniel 1950: 52). Many middle-class Western Europeans who lacked political rights saw in the Revolution, and later in Napoleon, hope for their own political and economic improvement; while those who enjoyed a measure of political power viewed them as a threat to their interests.

Denmark was at that time politically and economically less evolved than Western Europe. Hence the ideals of the French Revolution appealed to many middle-class Danes. These same Danes were also receptive to the teachings of the Enlightenment, which in popular thinking were closely associated with the Revolution (Hampson 1982: 251–83). Denmark had a strong antiquarian tradition, although it had not been as flourishing in recent decades as that in England. Most English antiquaries were conservatives who had rejected the ideals of the Enlightenment and taken refuge in romantic nationalism. By contrast, Scandinavian archaeologists were inspired to study the past for nationalistic reasons but these interests did not exclude an evolutionary approach. For them history and evolution were complementary rather than antithetical concepts.

In 1806 Rasmus Nyerup, the librarian at the University of Copenhagen, published a book protesting against the unchecked destruction of ancient monuments and advocating the founding of a National Museum of Antiquity modelled on the Museum of French Monuments established in Paris after the Revolution. In 1807 a Danish Royal Commission for the Preservation and Collection of Antiquities was established, with Nyerup as its secretary. It began to amass a collection of antiquities from all over Denmark. This collection soon became one of the largest and most representative in Europe. In 1816 the Commission invited Thomsen to catalogue and prepare it for exhibition. His chief qualifications for this post, which was not a salaried one, were his knowledge of numismatics and his independent means. For the rest of his life Thomsen was to divide his time between his family business and archaeological research.

The main problem that Thomsen faced was how the material in the collection could be exhibited most efficiently. Very early he decided to proceed chronologically by subdividing his prehistoric or heathen period into successive ages of stone, bronze, and iron. Presumably he knew of Lucretius' Three-Age scheme through the work of Vedel Simonsen, if not the writings of French antiquarians such as Montfaucon and Mahudel. He also appears to have been aware of archaeological evidence suggesting an era when stone but not metal tools had been used and of the classical and biblical texts which suggested that bronze had been used before iron. The notion of three successive ages of stone, bronze, and iron therefore was not mere speculation (as often has been maintained) but a hypothesis for which there was already some evidence.

In attempting to sort the prehistoric material in the collection into three successive periods, Thomsen faced a daunting task. He recognized that even for the stone and metal objects a mechanical sorting would not work. Bronze and stone artifacts had continued to be made in the Iron Age, just as stone tools had been used in the Bronze Age. The challenge was therefore to distinguish bronze tools made during the Iron Age from those made during the Bronze Age and to differentiate which stone tools had been made in each period. There was also the problem of assigning objects made of gold, silver, glass, and other substances to each period. Individual artifacts were no help in beginning this work. Yet in the collection there were sets of artifacts that had been found in the same grave, hoard, or other contexts and that one could safely assume had been buried at the same time. Thomsen called these 'closed finds' and believed that by carefully comparing the various items from each such discovery it would be possible to determine the sorts of artifacts that were characteristic of different periods (Gräslund 1974: 97–118, 1981).

Thomsen sorted and classified his artifacts into various use categories, such as knives, adzes, cooking vessels, safety pins, and necklaces. He further refined each category by distinguishing the artifacts according to the material from which they were made and their specific shapes. Once types had been defined, he began to examine closed finds in order to determine which types were and were not found together. He also examined the decorations on artifacts and found that these varied systematically from one closed find to another. On the basis of shape and decoration it became possible for Thomsen to distinguish bronze artifacts made in the Bronze Age from ones made in the Iron Age. He was also able to demonstrate that large flint knives and spearpoints that had similar shapes to bronze ones had been made in the Bronze Age. Eventually he could assign single artifacts to his sequence on the basis of stylistic similarities. In this fashion he worked out a rough chronological sequence for the whole of Danish prehistory.

Thomsen did not stop at that point but proceeded to examine the context in which artifacts were recorded as having been found. Ultimately this process yielded a developmental sequence of five stages. The first was the early Stone Age, when only stone tools were used. This was followed by a later Stone Age, which he described as the period when metal first came into use. At this time the dead were buried, uncremated, in megalithic tombs, accompanied by crude pottery vessels with incised decoration. In the full Bronze Age, weapons and cutting tools were made of copper or bronze, the dead were cremated and buried in urns under small tumuli, and artifacts

Bølgezirater:

Ringzirater:

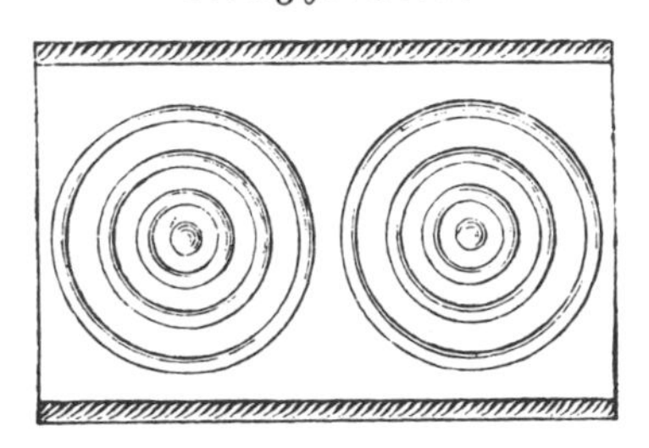

Spiralzirater:

Dobbeltspiralzirater:

Slangezirater:

Dragezirater:

10 Successive styles of ornamentation, from Thomsen's *Guidebook* (older forms at top)

were decorated with ring patterns. In the Iron Age, tools and weapons were made of tempered iron, while bronze continued to be used for ornaments and luxury goods. The Iron Age was divided into two stages, the earlier characterized by curvilinear serpent designs and the later by dragons and other fantastic animals. The latter forms of ornamentation continued into the historical period ([1837] Heizer 1962a: 21–6).

In the past a few archaeologists had attempted to subdivide prehistoric materials into various temporal segments. Possibly the most elaborate of these efforts was Pierre Legrand d'Aussy's (1737–1800) six-period classification of burial practices from earliest times to the Middle Ages (Laming-Emperaire 1964: 100–1). These schemes were based largely on intuition and failed to convince many people. Thomsen overcame this impasse by developing a crude but effective form of seriation, which provided scientific evidence to support the historical validity of his chronological series. For this scheme to work, it was insufficient that only one class of data formed a sequence. Instead, all the characteristics of individual artifacts and of those found together in closed finds had to be arranged in a sequence in which material, style, decoration, and the context of discovery formed a coherent pattern of variation. Discrepancies in any part of the pattern (such as the discovery of iron tools decorated with Bronze Age ring patterns) would have caused the entire scheme to fall apart. Thomsen's assumption that his sequence had evolved from stone to iron, rather than moved in the opposite direction, was confirmed by decorative continuities between his late Iron Age and the early historical period. Although some antiquarians mocked him for not adding ages of glass, wood, and gold to his sequence and others tried to ascribe his stone, bronze, and iron objects to different economies that had existed alongside one another, these critics failed to recognize that his phases were not the result of a mechanical sorting of artifacts but instead were based on the concurrent analysis of style, decoration, and context, which reinforced each other to produce a rough but effective chronology.

Thomsen's Museum of Northern Antiquities, with its collection arranged in accordance with his new system, was opened to the public in 1819, but the first written account of his research appeared only in 1836 in the *Ledetraad til Nordisk Oldkyndighed* (Guide Book to Scandinavian Antiquity), which was available in a German translation the next year but not in English until 1848. At least part of the appeal of Thomsen's work was that it offered independent support for an evolutionary view of early human development, which slowly became more popular, especially in England, as fear of the French Revolution and of Napoleon receded. It is true that neither Thomsen nor his successors regarded the Three Ages as constituting an evolutionary sequence within Scandinavia. Instead they argued

11 Thomsen showing visitors around the Museum of Northern Antiquities

that knowledge of bronze and iron working was brought into the region either by successive waves of immigrants from the south or as a result of 'intercourse with other nations' (Daniel 1967: 103). They did, however, assume that somewhere in Europe or the Near East an evolutionary development had taken place. Nineteenth-century archaeology did not view diffusion and migration as concepts that were antithetical to evolution but as factors that helped to promote evolutionary change (Harris 1968: 174).

The development and spread of Scandinavian archaeology

Even in his earliest work Thomsen was interested not merely in artifacts and their development over time but also in the contexts in which they had been found and what this might reveal about changing burial customs and other aspects of prehistoric life. During the first half of the nineteenth century archaeology continued to develop in Scandinavia as a discipline concerned with the evolution of ways of life throughout prehistoric times. This development was powerfully assisted by the work of Sven Nilsson (1787–1883), who had studied under the leading French palaeontologist Georges Cuvier and for many years was Professor of Zoology at the University of Lund. Nilsson strongly believed in cultural evolution but, unlike Thomsen, he was mainly interested in the development of subsistence economies rather than technology. Like some eighteenth-century philosophers, he believed that increasing population had been the principal factor compelling Scandinavian hunter–gatherers to become first pastoralists and then agriculturalists. His most important contribution to the study of prehistory was his systematic effort to determine the uses made of stone and bone artifacts by means of detailed comparisons with ethnographic specimens from around the world. Since many Scandinavian artifacts had been parts of compound tools now decayed, inferring the sort of implements to which they had belonged was often far from easy. As an exponent of unilinear evolution, he believed that ethnographic specimens from North America, the Arctic, and the Pacific Islands could shed light on prehistoric Scandinavian cultures that were at the same level of development. He also advocated that ethnographic parallels should be verified through the study of wear patterns on prehistoric artifacts, which could help to confirm what they had been used for (Nilsson 1868: 4). In these ways he sought to infer prehistoric patterns of hunting and fishing directly from archaeological data. His most important study of the Stone Age was published in four parts between 1836 and 1843 and was translated into English as *The Primitive Inhabitants of Scandinavia* in 1866.

An even more influential contributor to the development of Scandinavian archaeology was Jens J. A. Worsaae (1821–85). He became the first professional prehistoric archaeologist and was the first person to be trained in the discipline, albeit informally as a

12 Worsaae boring into one of the large tumuli at Jelling; he explains the procedure to King Frederik VII of Denmark

volunteer working with Thomsen. He was appointed Denmark's Inspector for the Conservation of Antiquarian Monuments in 1847 and the first Professor of Archaeology at the University of Copenhagen in 1855. Unlike Thomsen, who remained a museum researcher, Worsaae became a prolific field worker. His excavations helped to confirm Thomsen's chronology by providing more closed finds and also by means of stratigraphic excavations, which offered a more concrete demonstration of cultural change over time than did seriation. Major stratigraphic evidence in support of the Three-Age theory was provided by the excavations that the biologist Japetus Steenstrup carried out in the peat bogs of Denmark in his efforts to trace changes in the patterns of flora and fauna since the end of the last Ice Age. Many artifacts were found in the course of these excavations. These showed that the initial pine forests corresponded with the Stone Age occupation, while the Bronze Age was roughly coeval with the succeeding period of oak forests, and the Iron Age with beech forests. Steenstrup's findings were confirmed as archaeologists sought to relate their own discoveries to these environmental changes (Morlot 1861: 309–10).

Worsaae was a prolific writer and in his first book *Danmarks Oldtid* (The Primeval Antiquities of Denmark), published in 1843 (English translation 1849), he used Thomsen's findings as the basis for a prehistory of Denmark. In 1846–7, with financial support from King Christian VIII, he visited Britain and Ireland, mainly to study Viking remains there. His observations of prehistoric finds in these countries convinced him that Thomsen's Three-Age scheme was applicable to large parts, if not all, of Europe.

Worsaae also played an important role in developing interdisciplinary research related to archaeology. As early as 1837 on Sjaelland, mounds of oyster and cockle shells containing numerous prehistoric artifacts had been observed a short distance inland from the present coastline. As the result of a desire to learn more about geological changes, in 1848 the Royal Danish Academy of Sciences established a commission to study these shell middens. The commission was headed by Worsaae, the biologist Steenstrup and J. S. Forchhammer, the father of Danish geology. In the early 1850s these scholars published six volumes of reports on their studies of these 'kitchen middens'. Their interdisciplinary research demonstrated that the middens were of human origin and traced the patterns of their accumulation. They also determined that, when the middens had formed, the palaeo-environmental setting had consisted of fir and pine forests and some oak, that the only animals likely to have been domesticated were dogs, and that the middens had been occupied during the autumn, winter, and spring but not during the summer. The distributions of hearths and artifacts within the middens were also studied to learn more about human activities at these sites. Experiments, which involved feeding animal bones to dogs, were carried out in order to explain the numerical preponderance of the middle part of the long bones of birds over other parts of their skeleton (Morlot 1861: 300–1). The one issue Worsaae and Steenstrup did not agree about was the dating of the middens. Steenstrup maintained that they were Neolithic, and hence contemporary with the megalithic tombs, but, because they contained no ground or polished stone implements, Worsaae correctly believed them to be earlier (Klindt-Jensen 1975: 71–3).

The archaeology that was developing in Scandinavia provided a model for work elsewhere. Contacts with Worsaae inspired the Scottish antiquarian Daniel Wilson (1816–92) to use the Three-Age system to reorganize the large collection of artifacts belonging to the Society of Antiquaries of Scotland in Edinburgh. This work provided the basis for his book *The Archaeology and Prehistoric Annals of Scotland* published in 1851. In this first scientific synthesis of prehistoric times in the English language, Wilson assigned archaeological data to the Stone (Primeval), Bronze (Archaic), Iron, and Christian eras. Yet his study was not merely a slavish imitation of Scandinavian work. He demonstrated that, while Scotland and

Scandinavia had passed through the same stages of development in prehistoric times, Scottish artifacts differed stylistically from their Scandinavian counterparts, especially in the Iron Age. In this work Wilson also coined the term prehistory, which he defined as the study of the history of a region prior to the earliest appearance of written records relating to it. He stressed that the understanding of the past that could be derived from artifacts alone was very different from the kind of understanding that could be derived from written records. Yet he expressed the hope that in due course archaeologists would be able to learn about the social life and religious beliefs of prehistoric times. In his ready commitment to an evolutionary perspective Wilson showed himself to be a true product of the Scottish Enlightenment. Among English antiquarians there was much more resistance to accepting the Scandinavian approach (Daniel 1963a: 58–9) and Wilson's call to reorganize the collections of the British Museum in accordance with the new system long fell on deaf ears. Unfortunately for British archaeology, Wilson, although honoured for his accomplishments with a doctorate from the University of St Andrews, failed to find satisfactory employment in Scotland. In 1855 he left to teach English and history at University College in Toronto, Canada.

Scandinavian archaeology also provided a model for significant research in Switzerland. There, as the result of a drought in the winter of 1853, lake levels fell unprecedentedly low, revealing the remains of ancient settlements preserved in waterlogged environments. The first of these sites, a Bronze Age settlement at Obermeilen, was studied the following summer by Ferdinand Keller (1800–81), a Professor of English and President of the Zurich Antiquarian Society. His initial report led to the identification of several hundred such sites, including the Neolithic village at Robenhausen, which was excavated by Jakob Messikommer beginning in 1858 (Bibby 1956: 201–19). These so-called 'Lake Dwellings' were interpreted as settlements built on piles driven into lake bottoms on the basis of the traveller C. Dumont d'Urville's descriptions of villages of this sort in New Guinea (Gallay 1986: 167). They are now believed to have been constructed on what would have been swampy ground around the edge of lakes.

These excavations yielded the remains of wooden piles and house platforms, stone and bone tools still mounted in their wooden handles, matting, basketry, and a vast array of foodstuffs. Villages dating from both the Neolithic and Bronze Ages provided Swiss archaeologists with the opportunity to study changes in the natural environment, economies, and ways of life of these people. The Swiss finds not only revealed many sorts of perishable artifacts not usually found in Scandinavia and Scotland but also verified the reconstructions of stone and bone tools by Nilsson and others. Switzerland was already a major centre of tourism and the continuing study of these prehistoric remains attracted wide interest. It played a major role in convincing Western Europeans of the reality of cultural evolution and that ancient times could be studied using archaeological evidence alone (Morlot 1861: 321–36).

Prehistoric archaeology had thus developed as a well-defined discipline in Scandinavia, Scotland, and Switzerland prior to 1859. The basis for this new discipline was the ability to construct relative chronologies from archaeological data alone using seriation and stratigraphy. Thomsen had pioneered seriation using a large and representative museum collection, while Worsaae had employed stratigraphy to confirm his findings. For the first time relative chronologies were offered into which all known prehistoric data could be fitted. This demonstrated that artifacts from reasonably well-documented archaeological contexts could be used as a basis for understanding human history.

The development of prehistoric archaeology has long been ascribed to the influence of geological and biological evolution. It has been assumed that the stratigraphically derived chronologies of geological time constructed by geologists and palaeontologists provided a model for the development of archaeological chronologies of prehistory. Yet in Thomsen's pioneering work we see a seriational chronology of human prehistory inspired by social-evolutionary theories of the Enlightenment combining with the data collected by earlier antiquarians and with an implicit knowledge of stylistic change probably derived from the study of numismatics. Prehistoric archaeology did not begin as the result of borrowing a dating device from other disciplines. Instead it started with the development of a new technique for relative dating that was appropriate to archaeological material.

The kind of history produced by Scandinavian archaeology also made sense only in terms of the cultural-evolutionary perspective of the Enlightenment. History had traditionally been concerned with recounting the thoughts and deeds of famous individuals. Even classical archaeology and Egyptology, insofar as they were interested in material culture rather than epigraphy, were concerned with works of fine art understood in relation to recorded history. Yet Worsaae pointed out that in many cases prehistoric archaeologists could not even determine what people had made the implements they were studying. He and Wilson protested against the idea that the earliest people to be mentioned in recorded history were the original inhabitants of Europe (Daniel 1950: 50). A chronology offering independent confirmation of the development of European society from Stone Age beginnings was only of interest to people who were already predisposed to regard cultural evolution as a worthwhile topic. The groundwork for such an interest had been established by Enlightenment views of human nature. By the early nineteenth century, and despite periods of economic contraction such as the one that lasted from 1826 to 1847 (Wolf 1982: 291), many members of the expanding and now increasingly entrepreneurial middle class imagined themselves to be the spearhead of developments that were creating a new and better life for everyone. By identifying moral and social progress as concomitants of technological development and the latter as a fundamental characteristic of human history, Enlightenment theories reassured the middle classes of Western Europe of the cosmic significance and hence of the inevitable success of their role in history and portrayed their personal ambitions and those of their class as promoting the general good of society. Technological progress was also attributed to the initiative of individual human beings who used their innate intellectual capacities to control nature better. This was an optimistic view appropriate to the middle classes at the dawn of an era that was to see their power and prosperity increase throughout Western Europe. Thus, by providing what appeared to be material confirmation of the reality of progress throughout human history, Scandinavian-style archaeology appealed to those who were benefitting from the Industrial Revolution. While Danish archaeology continued to be strongly nationalistic and to enjoy the patronage of successive generations of the royal family, its innovators and increasingly its audience were members of a growing commercial middle class (Kristiansen 1981), for whom nationalism and evolutionism were both attractive concepts. By contrast, in the politically reactionary environment of post-Napoleonic Germany, archaeologists, while inspired by nationalism, tended to reject the Scandinavian approach partly because its evolutionism was too closely aligned with Enlightenment philosophy (Böhner 1981; Sklenář 1983: 87–91).

Scandinavian and Scandinavian-style archaeologists did not, however, limit their efforts to demonstrating the reality of cultural evolution. They also sought to understand the technologies and subsistence economies of prehistoric peoples and the environments in which they had lived, as well as something about their social life and religious beliefs. Their aim was to learn as much as the archaeological evidence would permit not only about the patterns of life at any one period but also about how those patterns had changed and developed over time. In order to understand the behavioural significance of archaeological finds they were prepared to make systematic comparisons of archaeological and ethnographic data, to carry out replicative experiments to determine how artifacts had been manufactured and used, and to perform experiments to explain the attrition patterns on bones found in archaeological sites. They also learned how to cooperate with geologists and biologists to reconstruct palaeoenvironments and determine prehistoric diets.

What archaeologists of this period did not do was to challenge the traditional biblical chronology which allowed a total of about 6,000 years for the whole of human history. For Thomsen, Worsaae, and others, several thousand years appeared long enough to encompass the past that was being revealed by the archaeological record. Worsaae dated the first arrival of human beings in Denmark around 3000 B.C. and the beginning of the Bronze Age between 1400 and 1000 B.C. By an ironic coincidence Scandinavia, Scotland, and Switzerland had all been covered by glaciers during the Würm glaciation and to this day have produced little evidence of human habitation prior to the Holocene era. Hence the absolute chronology imagined by the Scandinavians, Scots, and Swiss for their finds was not significantly out of line with reality as we currently understand it.

The antiquity of humanity

The prehistoric archaeology pioneered by the Scandinavians influenced archaeology in some of the smaller countries of Western and Northern Europe. Yet it was largely ignored by the antiquarians of France and England, who, although some of them were prepared to translate the writings of Thomsen and Worsaae into their languages, were unwilling to follow the example set by colleagues from a peripheral country such as Denmark. Their conservative attitude ensured that the scientific study of prehistory did not begin in these countries before the late 1850s and that it developed largely independently of Scandinavian-style archaeology. Unlike Scandinavia, early scientific archaeology in England and France was concerned primarily with the Palaeolithic period and ascertaining the antiquity of humanity. The presence in France and southern England of caves and glacial deposits containing traces of human activities going back into Lower Palaeolithic times provided archaeologists in these countries with an opportunity to study early phases of human existence that was wholly lacking in Scandinavia, Scotland, and Switzerland.

The development of Palaeolithic archaeology depended on the emergence of an evolutionary perspective in geology and also of some knowledge of palaeontology. Progress in these fields was necessary for a scientific study of human origins to replace reliance on the traditional biblical accounts. While the major archaeological breakthroughs in studying the antiquity of humanity slightly preceded the first major statement of Darwinian evolutionism, Palaeolithic archaeology was quickly drawn into the controversies that surrounded Darwin's work and was strongly influenced by concepts derived from biological evolution.

When a flint handaxe was found near the skeleton of what was probably a mammoth beneath a street in London towards the end of the seventeenth century, the antiquary John Bagford interpreted the find as that of a war elephant brought to Britain by the Roman emperor Claudius in A.D. 43 and slain by an ancient Briton armed with a stone-tipped spear (Grayson 1983: 7–8). This interpretation was clearly in the tradition of text-aided archaeology. On the other hand, in 1797 John Frere described a collection of Acheulean handaxes that were found together with the bones of unknown animals at

13 Acheulean handaxe found by Frere at Hoxne, published in *Archaeologia*, 1800

a depth of four metres in eastern England. He argued that the overlying strata, which included a presumed incursion of the sea and the formation of half a metre of vegetable earth, could only have been built up over a long period and concluded that 'the situation in which these weapons were found may tempt us to refer them to a very remote period indeed; even beyond that of the present world' ([1800] Heizer 1962a: 71). By this he meant that they were probably more than 6,000 years old. The Society of Antiquaries thought his paper worthy of publication but it aroused no contemporary discussion. While the intellectual climate was clearly opposed to assigning a great antiquity to humanity, Donald Grayson (1983: 58) has pointed out that Frere's failure to identify either the animal bones or the shells in his stratigraphy did not demand agreement with his claims.

In the course of the eighteenth century scientists such as Georges Buffon began to propose naturalistic origins for the world and to speculate that it might be tens of thousands or even millions of years old. This in turn suggested the need for a symbolic rather than a literal interpretation of the biblical account of the seven days of creation. The French zoologist Georges Cuvier (1769–1832), who established palaeontology as a scientific discipline, used his knowledge of comparative anatomy to reconstruct complete skeletons of hitherto unknown fossil quadrupeds. In this fashion he was able to assemble evidence that numerous species of animals had become extinct. He also observed that older geological strata contained animal remains that were increasingly dissimilar to those of modern times. Since he assumed a relatively short span since the creation of the world, he concluded that a series of natural catastrophes had destroyed entire species of animals and shaped the modern geological configuration of the planet. While he believed that devastated areas were repopulated by migrations of animals from areas that had been spared, other geologists, such as William Buckland (1784–1856), an Anglican priest and Professor of Mineralogy at Oxford University, viewed many catastrophes as universal ones that had wiped out most species. This required God to create new ones to replace them. The increasing complexity of plant and animal life observed in successive geological strata was therefore not viewed as a developmental sequence but rather as a series of ever more complex creations. He conceived of evolution as having occurred in God's mind rather than in the natural world.

In the first half of the nineteenth century naturalists and antiquarians encountered human physical remains and stone tools associated with the bones of extinct animals in stratified deposits in cave sites in many parts of Western Europe. The most important work was that of Paul Tournal (1805–72) near Narbonne and Jules de Christol (1802–61) northeast of Montpellier, both in France, Philippe-Charles Schmerling (1791–1836) near Liège in Belgium, and the Reverend John MacEnery (1796–1841) at Kent's Cavern in

England. Each of these men believed that his finds might constitute evidence of the contemporaneity of human beings and extinct animal species. Yet their techniques of excavation were not sufficiently developed to rule out the possibility that the human material was intrusive into older deposits. MacEnery's finds were sealed beneath a layer of hard travertine that must have taken a long time to form. Buckland maintained that ancient Britons had dug earth ovens through the travertine and that their stone tools had found their way through these pits into much older deposits containing the bones of fossil animals. While MacEnery denied this claim, he accepted that the human bones, while old, need not be contemporaneous with the extinct animals. It was argued that deposits elsewhere contained mixtures of animal bones and artifacts from diverse periods that had been washed into caves and mixed together in fairly recent times (Grayson 1983: 107). It became obvious that caves were not going to be conclusive. Their deposits were notoriously difficult to date and it was hard to rule out the possibility that human remains had become mixed with the bones of extinct animals as a result of human or geological activity in recent times.

A much-debated question was whether traces of human beings and their works should be found associated with extinct mammals. The bones of mammoth and woolly rhinoceros were encountered frequently in the glacial deposits that covered France and southern England. At the beginning of the nineteenth century these were generally believed to have resulted from Noah's flood, the last great catastrophe to convulse the earth's surface. Since the Bible recorded the existence of human beings prior to that time, it seemed possible that human remains might be found in these diluvial deposits. Yet fundamentalist Christians believed that the Bible implied that as a result of divine intervention all animal species had survived the flood; hence the presence of extinct species in these levels indicated that they dated before the creation of humanity rather than simply before the last flood. Even those palaeontologists who were inclined to interpret the Bible less literally believed that a beneficent God would have brought the earth to its modern state prior to creating the human species. By the 1830s it was generally accepted that all the diluvium had not been deposited at the same time. It was also believed to be older than the flood and therefore should not contain human remains (Grayson 1983: 69).

The intellectual problems of this period are clearly exemplified in the work of Jacques Boucher de Crèvecoeur de Perthes (1788–1868), who was the director of customs at Abbeville, in the Somme Valley of northwestern France. In the 1830s Casimir Picard, a local doctor, reported discoveries of stone and antler tools in the region. Boucher de Perthes began studying these finds in 1837. Soon after, in the canal and railway excavations of the period, he started to find Lower Palaeolithic handaxes associated with the bones of extinct mammoth and rhinoceros, deeply buried in the stratified gravel deposits of river terraces that predated the local peat formations.

Boucher de Perthes' sound stratigraphic observations convinced him that the stone tools and extinct animals were equally old. Yet, as a catastrophist, he decided that these tools belonged to an antediluvian human race that had been completely annihilated by a massive flood 'prior to the biblical deluge'. After a lengthy period of time God had created a new human race – that of Adam and Eve and their

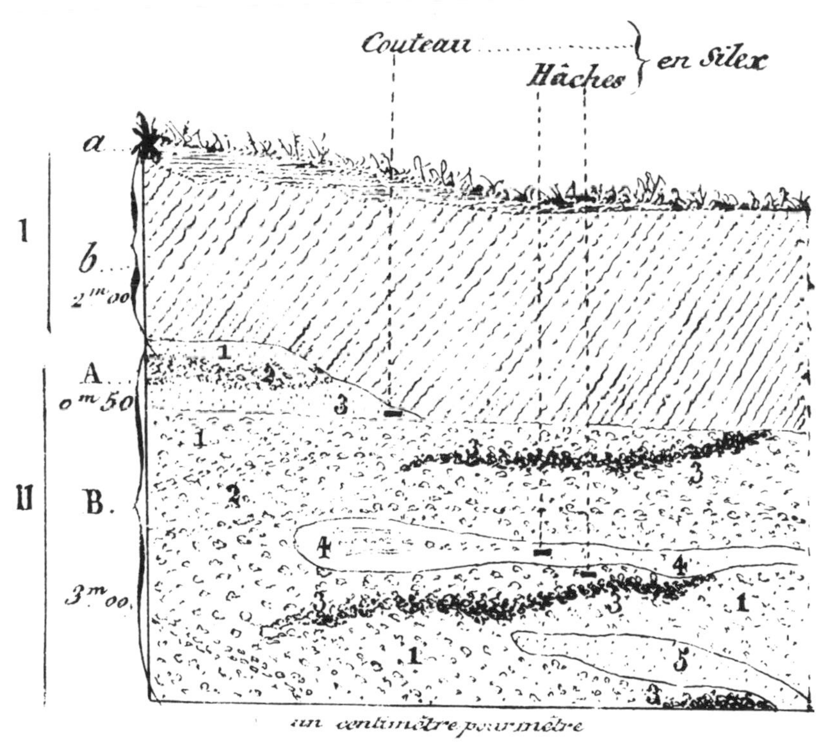

14 Profile showing location of Palaeolithic material from Boucher de Perthes' *Antiquités celtiques et antediluviennes*, 1847

descendants (Grayson 1983: 126–30). It is scarcely surprising that when these fanciful ideas were published in the first volume of his *Antiquités celtiques et antédiluviennes* in 1847, they were dismissed by French and English scholars alike. Yet even when his field observations were duplicated by the physician Marcel-Jérôme Rigollot (1786–1854) at St. Aucheul and another site near Amiens, 40 kilometres upstream from Abbeville, and these deposits were confirmed to be of 'diluvial age' by geologists, including Edmond Hébert from the Sorbonne, geologists and antiquarians continued to express concern that the artifacts might be intrusive. Grayson (1983: 207) has concluded that the rejection of Rigollot's sound evidence 'stemmed from the sheer belief that such things could not be' and Rigollot's status as an outsider with respect to the scientific elite of his day.

The resolution of such controversies concerning the antiquity of humanity required an improved understanding of the geological record. In 1785 the Edinburgh physician James Hutton (1726–97) proposed a uniformitarian view of geological history in which the slow erosion of rocks and soil was balanced by the uplifting of other land surfaces. He believed that all geological strata could be accounted for in terms of the forces currently at work operating over very long periods of time. In the years that followed William (Strata) Smith (1769–1839) in England and Georges Cuvier and Alexandre Brongniart in France, recognized that strata of different ages each possessed their own characteristic assemblage of organic fossils and concluded that such assemblages could be used to identify coeval formations over large areas. Smith, unlike Cuvier, accepted the principle of the orderly deposition of rock formations over long periods of time.

Between 1830 and 1833 the English geologist Charles Lyell (1797–1875) published his *Principles of Geology*, in which he assembled an overwhelming amount of data, much of it based on his observations around Mount Etna in Sicily, to support the uniformitarian assumption that geological changes had occurred in the past as a result of the same geological agencies acting over long periods and at approximately the same rate as they do at present. Lyell's book quickly won support for the principle of uniformitarianism in geology. Contrary to catastrophism, it indicated the past to have been a long and geologically uninterrupted period in which other events could have happened. This provided a setting for scholars to consider the possibility of biological evolution, a concept that Lyell rejected, although Jean-Baptiste Lamarck (1744–1829) had already argued in favour of it.

This new view of geological history also left the question of the antiquity of humanity as one that required an empirical answer. The favourable reception given to Lyell's geology reflected the increasing openness of British scholars and the public to evolutionary ideas. By the middle of the nineteenth century, Britain had become the 'workshop of the world' and the growth of industrialism had greatly strengthened the political power and self-confidence of the middle classes, who had come to view themselves as a major force in world history. This new attitude was reflected in the writings of Herbert Spencer (1820–1903), who in the 1850s began to champion a general evolutionary approach to scientific and philosophical problems. He argued that the development of the solar system, plant and animal life, and human society was from simple, uniform homogeneity to increasingly complex and differentiated entities. By emphasizing individualism and free enterprise as the driving forces behind cultural evolution, he rescued the latter from its former revolutionary associations and helped to make it the ideology of a substantial portion of the British middle class, whose faith in progress had already been expressed in the Great Exhibition held in London in 1851 (Harris 1968: 108 41). In so doing he inclined all but the religiously most conservative members of the middle classes to be sympathetic to arguments favouring biological evolution and the antiquity of humanity.

In 1858 William Pengelly (1812–94) excavated in Brixham Cave near Torquay in southwestern England. This was a newly discovered site known to contain fossilized bones. His work was sponsored by the Geological Society of London and was carefully supervised by a committee of prestigious scientists, including Charles Lyell. In the course of his excavations stone tools and fossil animal bones were found beneath an unbroken layer of stalagmitic deposit 7.5 cm thick, which suggested considerable antiquity (Gruber 1965). As a result of growing interest in the antiquity of humanity, in the spring and summer of 1859, first the geologist John Prestwich and the archaeologist John Evans and then a number of other British scientists, including Charles Lyell, visited the sites in the Somme Valley. All of these scientists were convinced of the validity of the finds Boucher de Perthes and Rigollot had made there and the geologists also recognized that the strata in which these finds occurred must have been deposited long before 4000 B.C. In their reports to leading British scientific associations, including the British Association for the Advancement of Science, the Royal Society of London, and the Geological Society of London, they agreed that there was now solid evidence that human beings had coexisted with extinct mammals at some time that was far removed from the present in terms of calendar years (Chorley *et al.* 1964: 447–9; Grayson 1983: 179–90). This new view of the antiquity of human beings won what amounted to official approval in Lyell's *The Geological Evidences of the Antiquity of Man* (1863).

Charles Darwin's *On the Origin of Species* was published in November 1859. This book, which summarized the results of almost 30 years of research that had been inspired by uniformitarian geology, accomplished for evolutionary biology what Lyell's *Principles* had done for geology. Darwin's concept of natural selection was accepted by many scientists and members of the general public as providing a mechanism that made it possible to believe that a process of biological evolution accounted for modern species and explained the changes observed in the palaeontological record. The obvious implication that humanity had evolved from some ape-like primate not only made the antiquity of the human species a burning issue that had to be empirically studied but also made this investigation a vital part of the broader controversy that was raging concerning Darwin's theory of biological evolution. Palaeolithic archaeology therefore quickly acquired a high-profile role alongside geology and palaeontology in the debates concerning a question of escalating public interest.

Palaeolithic archaeology

The subject-matter of Palaeolithic archaeology was first given its name in 1865 when, in his book *Pre-historic Times*, the English banker and naturalist John Lubbock divided the Stone Age into an earlier Palaeolithic or Archaeolithic (Old Stone) and a more recent Neolithic (New Stone) period. He was, however, merely formally labelling a distinction that was already obvious between an initial period, when all tools had been chipped from stone, and a later period, when some stone tools, such as axes and gouges, had been ground and polished (Daniel 1950: 85). After 1860 the main advances in Palaeolithic archaeology took place in France, where the river terraces of the north and the rock shelters of the south provided better evidence than was available in England. The principal goals of these studies were to determine how long human beings had been in the area and whether evolutionary trends could be detected within the Palaeolithic period. Evolutionary theory predicted that over time human beings would have become both morphologically and culturally more complex. The first goal of Palaeolithic archaeologists was therefore to arrange their sites in chronological order.

The leading figure in early Palaeolithic research was Edouard Lartet (1801–71), a magistrate who had turned to the study of palaeontology and had publicly acknowledged the importance of Boucher de Perthes' discoveries in 1860. Supported by the English banker Henry Christy, he began to explore cave sites in the Dordogne in 1863. He quickly realized that the Palaeolithic was not a single phase of human development but a series of phases that could be distinguished according to artifacts and associated prehistoric animals. He preferred a classification based on palaeontological criteria and distinguished four ages or periods, which from most recent to oldest were: (1) Aurochs or Bison, (2) Reindeer, of which the cave sites at Laugerie Basse and La Madeleine were typical, (3) Mammoth and Woolly Rhinoceros, and (4) Cave Bear, although he gradually recognized that the last two periods could not be temporally separated. The Le Moustier site was designated as typical of a new Cave Bear and Mammoth period. To Lartet's three periods Félix Garrigou added a still earlier Hippopotamus one when human beings had inhabited mainly open sites and which was not represented in the caves of southern France (Daniel 1950: 99–103).

Lartet's work was continued by Gabriel de Mortillet (1821–98), a geologist and palaeontologist who turned to the study of archaeology. He was assistant curator at the Museum of National Antiquities at Saint-Germain-en-Laye for seventeen years before becoming Professor of Prehistoric Anthropology at the School of Anthropology in Paris in 1876. Although he admired Lartet's work, he believed that an archaeological subdivision of the Palaeolithic had to be based on cultural rather than palaeontological criteria. In this respect he chose to follow the example of Lubbock and Worsaae.

In spite of this, his approach to archaeology was greatly influenced by his knowledge of geology and palaeontology. He sought to distinguish each period by specifying a limited number of artifact types that were characteristic of that period alone. These diagnostic artifacts were the archaeological equivalent of the index fossils that geologists and palaeontologists used to identify the strata belonging to a particular geological epoch. Mortillet also followed geological practice in naming each of his subdivisions of the Palaeolithic after the type site that had been used to define it. Like palaeontologists he relied on stratigraphy to establish a chronological sequence. In the Palaeolithic research of the nineteenth century, seriation played only a minor role as a means of establishing chronology. This was no doubt partly because technological and stylistic sequences were harder to recognize in Palaeolithic stone tools than in later artifacts and also because the issues being discussed were so controversial that only the clearest stratigraphic evidence was universally agreed to be able to provide conclusive temporal sequences. The reliance on stratigraphy also reflected Lartet's and Mortillet's training as natural scientists.

Lartet's Hippopotamus Age became the Chellean Epoch, named after a site near Paris, and most of Lartet's Cave Bear and Mammoth Age became the Mousterian, although Mortillet assigned finds from Aurignac that Lartet had placed late in his Cave Bear and Mammoth Age to a separate Aurignacian Epoch. Lartet's Reindeer Age was divided into an earlier Solutrean Epoch and a later Magdalenian one. Mortillet was uncertain about the date of the Aurignacian. He later placed it after the Solutrean and finally dropped it from his classification of 1872. He also added a Robenhausian Epoch to represent the Neolithic period and in later studies, such as *Formation de la nation française* (Development of the French Nation) (1897), he added still more epochs to incorporate the Bronze and Iron Ages into his system. It is doubtful, however, that he was ever serious about the universality of these highly distinctive Western European periods (Childe 1956a: 27).

Mortillet also invented a Thenaisian Epoch and later a Puycournian one to cover pre-Chellean finds. Between 1863 and 1940 archaeologists discovered eoliths, or presumed artifacts of exceptionally crude manufacture, in early Pleistocene as well as still earlier Pliocene and Miocene deposits in France, England, Portugal, and

TEMPS		AGES	PÉRIODES	ÉPOQUES
Quaternaires actuels.	Historiques.	du Fer.	Mérovingienne.	Wabenienne. (*Waben, Pas-de-Calais.*)
			Romaine.	Champdolienne. (*Champdolent, Seine-et-Oise.*)
				Lugdunienne. (*Lyon, Rhône.*)
	Protohistoriques.		Galatienne.	Beuvraysienne. (*Mont-Beuvray, Nièvre.*)
				Marnienne. (*Département de la Marne.*)
				Hallstattienne. (*Hallstatt, haute Autriche.*)
		du Bronze.	Tsiganienne.	Larnaudienne. (*Larnaud, Jura.*)
				Morgienne. (*Morges, canton de Vaud, Suisse.*)
	Préhistoriques.	de la Pierre.	Néolithique.	Robenhausienne. (*Robenhausen, Zurich.*)
				Campignyenne. (*Campigny, Seine-Inférieure.*)
				Tardenoisienne (*Fère-en-Tardenois, Aisne.*)
Quaternaires anciens.			Paléolithique.	Tourassienne. (*La Tourasse, Haute-Garonne.*) Ancien Hiatus.
				Magdalénienne. (*La Madeleine, Dordogne.*)
				Solutréenne. (*Solutré, Saône-et-Loire.*)
				Moustérienne. (*Le Moustier, Dordogne.*)
				Acheuléenne. (*Saint-Acheul, Somme.*)
				Chelléenne. (*Chelles, Seine-et-Marne.*)
Tertiaires.			Éolithique.	Puycournienne. (*Puy-Courny, Cantal.*)
				Thenaysienne. (*Thenay, Loir-et-Cher.*)

15 Mortillet's epochs of prehistory, from *Formation de la nation française*, 1897

Belgium. Evolutionary theory implied that the earliest tools would be so crude that they could not be distinguished from naturally broken rocks; hence in the absence of human bones or other convincing proofs of human presence the authenticity of these finds was challenged. In the late 1870s Mortillet and others who supported the artifactual status of eoliths began to develop a set of criteria that might be used to distinguish intentional stone working from natural breakage. Challenges to these criteria alternated with efforts to elaborate new and more convincing tests. Comparative studies were made of eoliths and rocks from formations hundreds of millions of years old and experimental work was carried out, including S. H. Warren's (1905) observations of striations on flints broken by mechanical pressure, Marcelin Boule's (1905) study of flints recovered from a cement mixer, and A. S. Barnes' (1939) quantitative analysis of edge angles fabricated by human hands and by natural processes. In the course of these studies much was learned about stone working and many sites were disqualified as evidence of human antiquity (Grayson 1986). Either as a result of direct influence or by coincidence, this research carried on the traditions of archaeological experimentation established by Scandinavian investigators in the 1840s.

Mortillet's training in the natural sciences was reflected in more than his classificatory approach. He and most other Palaeolithic archaeologists were primarily concerned with establishing the antiquity of humanity. Within their evolutionary framework, this meant trying to trace evidence of human presence back as far as possible in the archaeological record and demonstrating that older cultures were more primitive than later ones. The sequence that Lartet and Mortillet established stratigraphically and palaeontologically carried out this task admirably. Comparing later with earlier stages of the Palaeolithic, there was evidence of a greater variety of stone tools, more stages and greater precision in their preparation, and an increasing number of bone tools. This demonstrated that the technological progress that Thomsen and Worsaae had documented from the Stone to the Iron Ages could also be found within the Palaeolithic period.

While archaeologists discussed what Palaeolithic populations had eaten at different stages and it was debated whether certain art work might indicate that horses had been domesticated in the Magdalenian period (Bahn 1978), Palaeolithic archaeologists were far less interested in studying how people had lived in prehistoric times than Scandinavian archaeologists had been. In this respect Palaeolithic archaeologists resembled palaeontologists, who at that time were more concerned to demonstrate evolutionary sequences than they were to study ecological relations within rock formations from individual periods. The main units of archaeological excavation were strata, although even these were often recorded in surprisingly rudimentary fashion. Sites were frequently excavated with minimal supervision, which meant that detailed cultural stratigraphy and features within major levels went unrecorded. Particularly in rock shelters where living floors had been preserved, this resulted in a severe loss of information concerning how people had lived. The artifacts that were kept for study in museums were often only those recognized as being of diagnostic value for ascertaining the age and cultural affinities of sites. Debitage and artifacts that were not thought to have diagnostic significance were frequently discarded. This encouraged a non-cultural view of artifacts as dating devices and evidence of progress, which was very different from the Scandinavian approach to archaeological data. Even Boyd Dawkins, who criticized Mortillet for his preoccupation with evolutionary development and his failure to allow that some differences between Palaeolithic assemblages might reflect tribal or ethnic variation as well as varying access to different types of stone, did not produce any satisfactory alternative analyses (Daniel 1950: 108–9).

Mortillet, like the geologists and palaeontologists of the mid-nineteenth century, was caught up in the evolutionary enthusiasm that characterized scientific research at that time. He viewed his Palaeolithic sequence as a bridge between the geological and palaeontological evidence of biological evolution prior to the Pleistocene era and the already established documentation of cultural progress in Europe in post-Palaeolithic times. As Glyn Daniel (1950: 244) has noted, one of the keynotes of evolutionary archaeology was the idea that humanity's cultural development could be represented in a single sequence and read in a cave section, just as the geological sequence could be read in stratified rocks.

Mortillet was also influenced by a strong ethnological interest in cultural evolution during the second half of the nineteenth century. In 1851 the German ethnologist Adolf Bastian (1826–1905) began a series of voyages around the world in order to build up the collections of the Royal Museum of Ethnology in Berlin. Impressed by the cultural similarities that he encountered in widely separated regions, he emphasized the Enlightenment doctrine of psychic unity by arguing that as a result of universally shared 'elementary ideas' (*Elementargedanke*) peoples at the same level of development who are facing similar problems will, within the constraints imposed by their environments, tend to develop similar solutions to them.

After 1860 there was a great revival of theoretic history, as ethnologists sought, by comparing modern societies assumed to be at different levels of development, to work out the stages through which European societies had evolved in prehistoric times. These researches ranged from studies of specific issues, such as Johann Bachofen's (1861) theory that all societies had evolved from matrilineal beginnings and John McLennan's (1865) arguments that the oldest human societies had been polyandrous, to general delineations of development from savagery to civilization by E. B. Tylor (1865) and Lewis H. Morgan (1877). Unlike the 'theoretic' histories of the eighteenth century, these ethnological formulations were presented as scientific theories rather than as philosophical speculations. While reflecting the general vogue for evolutionary studies in the mid-nineteenth century and usually addressing questions that archaeological data were ill equipped to handle, these works derived much of their self-confidence from growing archaeological evidence that technological advances had been an important feature of human history. Reciprocally these ethnographic formulations encouraged archaeologists to interpret their data in a unilinear perspective.

In his guide to the archaeological displays at the Paris Exposition of 1867 Mortillet declared that prehistoric studies revealed human progress to be a law of nature, that all human groups passed through similar stages of development, and the great antiquity of humanity (Daniel 1967: 144). The first two concepts had their roots in the philosophy of the Enlightenment and the third had been recognized as a result of research carried out prior to the publication of *On the Origin of Species*. Yet, while Palaeolithic archaeology had vindicated an evolutionary origin for humanity, Mortillet's first two laws were far from validated. Not enough work had been done outside of Western Europe to determine whether or not human groups everywhere had developed – insofar as they had developed at all – through the same Palaeolithic sequence. While some scholars were prepared to accept the multiple invention of simple artifacts, such as spears or calabash containers, they suspected that more complex ones, such as boomerangs or bows and arrows, were more likely to be traced to a common origin (Huxley [1865] 1896: 213). Likewise, overly rigid applications of notions about what constituted progress led many archaeologists, although not Mortillet (Daniel 1950: 131), to reject the authenticity of cave paintings on the ground that they were too advanced to have been produced at an early stage of human development. This view was only overcome as fresh discoveries of bone carvings and cave paintings were made in contexts that clearly dated this art to the Upper Palaeolithic period (ibid. 131–2). Once validated, however, European cave art was largely interpreted in terms of the totemism associated with the Australian aborigines (Reinach 1903; Ucko and Rosenfeld 1967: 123–8).

Palaeolithic archaeology was scientifically important and aroused great public interest because it revealed the hitherto unexpected antiquity of humanity and the gradual evolution of European civilization from very primitive beginnings. It also set new standards for stratigraphic analysis in archaeology. Palaeolithic archaeology enjoyed great prestige because of its close ties with geology and palaeontology, which were both sciences in the forefront of creating a new vision of the history of the world. All three of these disciplines were valued because they were viewed as demonstrating the reality of progress in prehistoric times. Palaeolithic archaeology also was respected because it had evolved in France and England, which were the centres of political, economic, and cultural development in the world at that time. Because of its prestige Palaeolithic archaeology provided a model for studying post-Palaeolithic prehistory in Western Europe. Yet its view of artifacts mainly as dating devices and evidence of cultural evolution was a very narrow one by comparison with Scandinavian prehistoric archaeology, which was concerned with studying cultural evolution but also sought in a more rounded fashion to learn as much as possible about how human beings had lived in prehistoric environments. The interdisciplinary cooperation of Scandinavian archaeologists with geologists and biologists in their pursuit of these objectives contrasts with the wholesale modelling of archaeological research upon often inappropriate natural science methods by Palaeolithic archaeologists. As a result the prehistoric archaeology that developed in France and England was limited in the range of its interests just as it was enhanced in its time depth by comparison with Scandinavian archaeology.

Reaction against evolution

Those who objected to evolutionary accounts of human origins or the denial of biblical accounts of human history fought back in various ways. During the 1860s creationists who accepted current interpretations of the archaeological record could still hypothesize that human beings had been created much earlier than had previously been thought and hope that early hominid skeletons, when discovered, would resemble those of modern human beings rather than the 'pithecoid forms' predicted by the Darwinians (Grayson 1986: 211). Yet not everyone accepted an evolutionary interpretation of the archaeological record. As early as 1832 Richard Whately, Archbishop of Dublin (1787–1863), had breathed new life into the doctrine of degenerationism. He argued that there was no evidence that savages, unaided, had ever developed a less barbarous way of life. It followed that humanity originally must have existed in a state 'far superior' to that of modern savages, a view which he felt was in accord with the Book of Genesis (Grayson 1983: 217–20). This position became increasingly popular among conservatives in the 1860s, although not all degenerationists denied the great antiquity of humanity or attributed its earliest cultural achievements to divine revelation. One of the most eminent degenerationists was the Canadian geologist and amateur archaeologist John William Dawson, who was Principal of McGill University in Montreal from 1855 to 1893. Dawson accepted the association between human remains and extinct mammals but argued that these associations confirmed the recency of the Pleistocene gravels in which they were found. On a trip to Europe in 1865 he inspected the geological deposits of the Somme Valley and described his mentor Charles Lyell as taking 'very good-naturedly' his opinion that evidence was lacking 'of the excessive antiquity at that time attributed to [these formations] by some writers' (Dawson 1901: 145). He also maintained that North American ethnographic evidence revealed that the peoples who used the best-made stone implements also used the rudest and that the developmental sequence found in Europe might represent idiosyncratic local trends or the accidental interdigitation of neighbouring, contemporary groups with different cultures. From this he concluded that there was no evidence that cultures at different levels of complexity had not coexisted throughout human history (Dawson 1888: 166–7; 214; Trigger 1966). While in retrospect Dawson can be seen as defending a lost cause, in the nineteenth century it was easier for his opponents to ignore his objections than to refute them. Not enough was yet known about prehistoric sequences outside Europe to establish evolution as a general trend in human history.

Still more links existed between Near Eastern archaeologists and those who sought to prove the literal truth of the Bible. Interest in Mesopotamian archaeology was revived in the 1870s after George Smith published a clay tablet from Nineveh containing a Babylonian account of the deluge. The Daily Telegraph offered 1,000 pounds sterling to send an expedition to Iraq in search of the missing portions of this tablet, which were duly found (Daniel 1950: 132–3). Much of the early work of the Egypt Exploration Society was directed towards sites in the Delta, such as Tell el-Muskhuta, that were associated with biblical accounts. In 1896 W. M. F. Petrie was quick to identify the ethnic name *I. si. ri. ar?*, which appeared on a newly discovered stela of the Pharaoh Merneptah (reigned 1236–1223 B.C.), as the first known mention of Israel in Egyptian texts (Drower 1985: 221). As late as 1929 Leonard Woolley excited great interest by claiming that the thick silt deposits that he had found in his excavations of prehistoric levels at Ur attested a great flood in Mesopotamia that had given rise to the biblical account of the deluge (Woolley 1950: 20–3). While Egypt and Mesopotamia produced spectacular archaeological discoveries that excited the public in their own right, those that related to the Bible and appeared to confirm scriptural accounts ensured widespread support for archaeological research carried out in these countries as well as in Palestine. Individual archaeologists were on both sides in the struggle between the supporters of revealed religion and of evolutionism during the late nineteenth and early twentieth centuries (Casson 1939: 207–8).

Archaeology in North America

While European visitors and to a limited degree local scholars studied isolated facets of Latin American prehistory (Bernal 1980: 35–102), the United States was the only country outside Europe to develop an indigenous tradition of archaeological research prior to the late nineteenth century. By the time European settlement pressed westward beginning in the 1780s, racial myths had generally eclipsed religious ones as a justification for waging war on the Indians and violating their treaty rights. It was widely maintained that the Indians were brutal and warlike by nature and biologically incapable of significant cultural development. They were also pronounced, despite substantial evidence to the contrary, to be unable to adjust to a European style of life and therefore destined to die out as civilization spread westward (Vaughan 1982). Many white Americans saw these arrangements as a manifestation of divine providence, which indicates that the new biological explanations of alleged native inferiority did not exclude religious ones.

As Europeans began to settle west of the Appalachian Mountains they discovered mounds and earthworks throughout the Ohio and Mississippi watersheds. These are now known to have been built by the Adena and Hopewell cultures that had been centred in the Ohio Valley between 800 B.C. and A.D. 500 and the Mississippian culture distributed throughout the southeastern United States from A.D. 500 to 1500. These earthworks, which often contained elaborate artifacts made of pottery, shell, mica, and native copper, challenged the belief that native American cultures were invariably primitive. They also quickly became the focus of the most varied speculations. Some Americans, such as the naturalist William Bartram, the Reverend James Madison, and most importantly Dr. James McCulloh, concluded that they had been constructed by Indians but the traveller Benjamin Barton attributed them to Danes, who had gone on to become the Toltecs of Mexico, while Governor De Witt Clinton of Ohio said they were the work of Vikings, and Amos Stoddard identified them as being of Welsh origin. The sagacious ethnologist Albert Gallatin linked them with Mexico, although he was uncertain whether the Mexicans had moved north or the builders of these mounds had eventually moved south (Silverberg 1968; Willey and Sabloff 1980: 19–25; Blakeslee 1987).

The American public were anxious that their continent should have its own history to rival that of Europe and hence were intrigued by these finds, just as they were to be intrigued by John L. Stephens' discovery of lost Maya cities in the jungles of Central America in the 1840s. Yet, apart from those who interpreted them as evidence of degeneration (Bieder 1986: 33–4), most scholars and the general public were not prepared to ascribe the finds in the Mississippi and Ohio Valleys to the ancestors of the American Indians. They attributed them to a race of Moundbuilders who were imagined to have been destroyed or driven out of North America by savage hordes of Indians. The various Moundbuilder theories thus offered a chronicle of American prehistory but, by attributing the major accomplishments of the past to a vanished non-North American Indian people, they continued to emphasize the static and hence potentially uncivilizable nature of the Indians. The archaeological record was interpreted as further evidence of the menace posed by the Indians, who were revealed as destroyers of civilization when given the opportunity. Victims were thus portrayed as bloodthirsty monsters and new reasons were provided to justify white Americans waging war on them and seizing their lands. Books expounding the theory that the Moundbuilders were a lost race of civilized people, such as Josiah Priest's *American Antiquities and Discoveries in the West* (1833), quickly became best sellers. So great was the attraction of this theory that, even after the American physician and anatomist Samuel Morton (1799–1851) had failed to find any significant differences between the skulls of Moundbuilders and those of recently deceased Indians, he divided his American race into Toltec and Barbarous families on purely cultural grounds (Silverberg 1968).

More positively the discovery of mounds and earthworks west of the Appalachians created for the first time a widespread interest in describing prehistoric monuments and collecting artifacts from them. Between 1780 and 1860 archaeology in the central and eastern United States passed through an antiquarian phase which recapitulated the development of archaeology in England and Scandinavia between 1500 and 1800. In the late eighteenth century, army officers stationed in the Ohio Valley began to draw plans of the earthworks and the Reverend Manasseh Cutler counted the number of rings of trees that had grown on the top of the earthworks at Marietta as these were cleared for town building. In 1813 H. H. Brackenridge distinguished between burial and temple mounds and correctly suggested that the burial ones were earlier (Willey and Sabloff 1980: 23). Research and the publication of research gradually became more systematic. The American Philosophical Society took an active interest in the Moundbuilder debate. In 1799, as one of its numerous scientific projects, its President, Thomas Jefferson, distributed a circular soliciting information about prehistoric fortifications, tumuli, and Indian artifacts. In 1812 the publisher Isaiah Thomas founded the American Antiquarian Society, which provided a focal point for the diffuse but growing interest in archaeological questions. The first volume of the society's *Transactions*, which appeared in 1820, contained Caleb Atwater's 'Description of the antiquities discovered in the State of Ohio and other western states'. This study preserved valuable plans and descriptions of earthworks, many of which were later destroyed. He divided the remains into three classes: modern European, modern Indian, and Moundbuilder. He speculated, on the most meagre evidence, that the latter had been built by Hindus, who had come to North America from Asia and later moved south into Mexico.

The next major contribution to American archaeology was *Ancient Monuments of the Mississippi Valley* (1848) by Ephraim G. Squier (1821–88) and Edwin H. Davis (1811–88). Squier, a newspaper

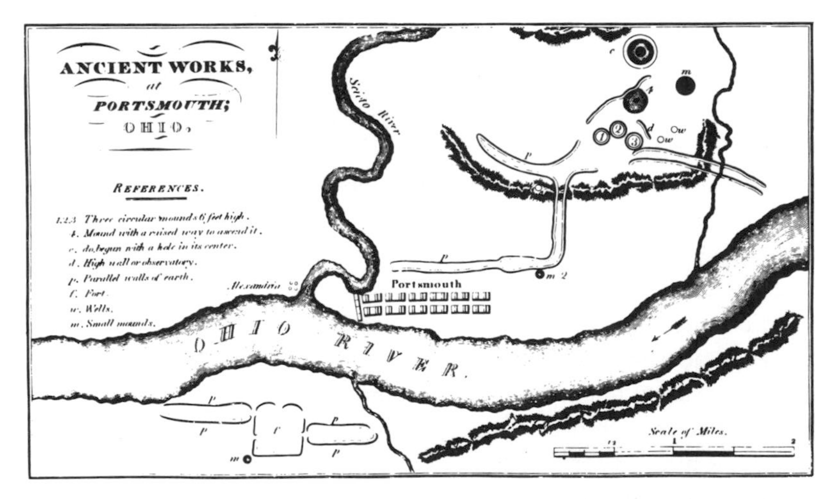

16 Plan of prehistoric earthworks at Portsmouth, Ohio, from Atwater's 'Description of the antiquities discovered in the State of Ohio', 1820

17 Grave Creek Mound, West Virginia, from Squier and Davis, *Ancient Monuments of the Mississippi Valley*, 1848

editor, and Davis, a physician, both lived in Ohio. They carefully surveyed a large number of mounds and earthworks, excavated some, and drew together the findings of other researchers. They assembled a vast amount of data about prehistoric earthworks over the eastern United States, many of which concern sites that have since been destroyed. Yet, while they were firm supporters of the Moundbuilder theory, their work was primarily descriptive in tone. Their classification, which was based on formal criteria, distinguished between the effigy mounds of the upper Mississippi Valley, the symmetrical enclosures of Ohio, and the truncated mounds to the south. Speculation was generally limited to posing some questions about the possible uses of such structures.

The general tone of the volume was set by Joseph Henry, a renowned physicist and the first secretary of the Smithsonian Institution, which had been founded in 1846. Their volume was the Smithsonian's first publication and began its *Contributions to Knowledge* series. Henry was determined to purge American archaeology of its speculative tendencies and to encourage scientific research in the inductive Baconian tradition. He insisted on excising all of

Squier and Davis' speculations about the Moundbuilders so that their 'positive addition to the sum of human knowledge should stand in bold relief' (Washburn 1967: 153; Tax 1975; Willey and Sabloff 1980: 36). Henry also commissioned Samuel Haven, the librarian of the American Antiquarian Society, to prepare a historical review of the *Archaeology of the United States*, which was published in 1856. In it numerous speculations about American prehistory were rigorously examined in the light of available information and shown to be untenable. The Moundbuilder theory was one of the principal objects of Haven's attacks. In order to encourage a more professional outlook Henry also published reports on developments in European archaeology in the *Annual Report of the Smithsonian Institution*, which was widely distributed in North America. The most successful of these was 'General Views on Archaeology', a translation of a paper originally published in French by the Swiss geologist and amateur archaeologist Adolf Morlot (1861). Morlot carefully summarized recent advances in European archaeology, especially in Denmark and Switzerland. In particular, his account of the excavation of Danish 'kitchen middens' stimulated the excavation of shell mounds along the east coast of North America from Nova Scotia to Florida beginning in the early 1860s (Trigger 1986a). Although Henry's conviction that the collection of data should precede theorizing did not significantly diminish the fanciful interpretations of the past that prevailed among amateur archaeologists and the general public, his official encouragement for archaeology and his promotion of more systematic research helped to prepare archaeologists for the more professional era that was to dawn after 1860.

Conclusion

In Europe prehistoric archaeology developed in the early and middle part of the nineteenth century, primarily as an evolutionary study of human history. It revealed not only that the most complex industrial technologies had developed from Stone Age beginnings but also that the Stone Age itself bore witness to the gradual elaboration of the ability of human beings to control their environment. Prehistoric archaeology originated in two complementary waves. The first, which began in Denmark in 1816, mainly studied cultural development in Neolithic, Bronze Age, and Iron Age times, while the second, which started 50 years later in England and France, developed around the study of the Palaeolithic period. While Palaeolithic archaeology did not begin completely independently of that practised in Scandinavia, they were distinctive in terms of goals and methods. Palaeolithic archaeology tended to model itself on the natural sciences, while Scandinavian archaeology was more interested in learning from archaeological data how specific peoples had lived in the past. It also pioneered seriation as a form of chronology appropriate to ordering cultural remains.

Both branches of prehistoric archaeology reveal themselves as intellectual products of the Enlightenment. They were committed to believing that the evolution of material culture betokens social and moral improvement as well. Large numbers of middle-class people, whose economic and political power was increasing as a result of the Industrial Revolution, were pleased to view themselves as a wave of progress that was inherent in human nature and perhaps in the very constitution of the universe. White Americans were happy to share this optimistic view but were not prepared to extend it to embrace the native peoples whose lands they were seizing. For them native people were an exception, who as a result of their biological inadequacies were unable to participate in the progress that destiny had made the prerogative of Europeans. Far from being discordant, these two views were soon to be combined in a powerful international synthesis.

CHAPTER 4

The imperial synthesis

Few of us can observe such indications of the habits and physical condition of the earliest inhabitants of this island [Britain] as are afforded by the remains of their rude dwellings, and by the rude implements occasionally found, without a sense of thankfulness that our lot has been mercifully cast in times of improved knowledge, of advanced civilization, and more refined habits.

EARL OF DEVON, 'Inaugural Address' at Exeter Congress, 1873, *Archaeological Journal* 30 (1873), 206

A shared commitment to an evolutionary approach promoted a close alignment between prehistoric archaeology and ethnology in Western Europe and the United States in the 1860s and 1870s. In Europe the basis of this alignment was the belief in unilinear cultural evolution evolved by Enlightenment philosophers. It was accepted that arranging modern cultures in a series from simplest to most complex illustrated the stages through which the most advanced cultures had developed in prehistoric times. Glyn Daniel (1950: 185–6) has argued that the meagreness of the archaeological record compelled archaeologists to employ the conclusions of physical anthropologists, linguists, and ethnologists in their efforts to reconstruct the past. Yet it appears that French and British archaeologists did not try harder to elucidate the past using archaeological data because, as a result of their commitment to unilinear evolutionism, they believed that ethnology revealed almost everything that they wished to know about prehistoric times. From this stricture we must exempt the Scandinavian archaeologists, especially Nilsson, who used ethnographic parallels to infer specific forms of behaviour, such as the use that had been made of particular types of artifacts, rather than the nature of whole cultures.

In the United States, where it was assumed that relatively little cultural evolution had occurred in prehistoric times, archaeology, ethnology, physical anthropology, and linguistics had begun by the

1840s to be regarded as different branches of anthropology, which was identified as the study of native peoples. The principal goal of American anthropology was romantically defined by the ethnologist Henry Schoolcraft as being to preserve some records of a dying race for future ages (Hinsley 1981: 20).

One of the main problems that had confronted cultural evolutionism from the beginning was to explain why some societies had developed rapidly while others apparently had remained static over thousands of years. In the eighteenth century such disparities commonly had been attributed to environmental factors. Yet specific environmental explanations often were far from convincing. A growing interest in cultural evolution could not fail to draw attention to this deficiency.

The rise of racism

At the same time that this close relationship between prehistoric archaeology and ethnology was developing in Western Europe and America, some of the principal ideas of the Enlightenment on which it was based were undergoing significant changes and even being abandoned. In particular the nineteenth century witnessed the slow decline in Western Europe of the belief in psychic unity. The Napoleonic conquests had stimulated a nationalistic reaction, which was encouraged by the conservative regimes that were restored to power in France, Germany, and Italy after his defeat. In place of the rationalism of the Enlightenment, this new conservatism favoured a romantic idealization of national and ethnic differences. This encouraged intellectuals to view alleged national characteristics as being rooted in biological disparities between human groups. In place of the eighteenth-century belief in the intellectual and emotional similarity of different ethnic groups and in relatively quickly acting environmental influences as the main causes of physical and behavioural differences (Grayson 1983: 142–9), some scholars began to view these differences as rooted in biological factors that were impervious to change. These ideas found expression in the writings of Joseph-Arthur, comte de Gobineau (1816–82), especially his four volume *Essai sur l'inégalité des races humains* (Essay on the Inequality of the Human Races) (1853–5). A member of an aristocratic and royalist French family, Gobineau believed that the fate of civilizations was determined by their racial composition and that the more a successful civilization's racial character was 'diluted', the more likely it was to sink into stagnation and corruption. In particular he proclaimed that European societies would flourish only so long as their members avoided 'miscegenation' with non-European strains. Gobineau's teachings were to influence European racists from Richard Wagner to Adolf Hitler and in America they were popularized by works such as Madison Grant's *The Passing of the Great Race* (1916). It was not long before novelists as well as scholars were invoking alleged racial factors instead of environmental ones to explain variations in the degree to which different groups had evolved in the course of human history.

Some of these theories were related to the doctrine of polygenesis, which can be traced back to the twelfth century (Slotkin 1965: 5–6), but was first raised as a major issue in modern times by the French Calvinist librarian Isaac de La Peyrère (1594–1676) in 1655. He argued that the biblical Adam was the ancestor of the Jews alone, while the ancestors of other human groups had been created separately and earlier. While church authorities compelled La Peyrère to retract his thesis, his ideas continued to be debated. In 1774 Edward Long (1734–1813), who had worked in the West Indies, argued that Europeans and negroes were separate species, while in 1799 Charles White (1728–1813) proclaimed that Europeans, Asians, Americans, black Africans, and Hottentots constituted a graded sequence of increasingly primitive species.

Samuel Morton suggested in his *Crania Americana* (1839) that the American Indian constituted a homogeneous type that providence had adapted from the beginning for life in the New World. In his *Crania Aegyptiaca*, published five years later, he argued that Egyptian skulls and depictions on their monuments revealed that human types had not changed in that part of the world for 4,500 years; almost as far back as the biblically recorded creation of the earth. While Morton initially believed that God had differentiated the races after he had created a common humanity, by 1849 he was advocating divine polygenesis, a position that was endorsed by the influential Swiss-American naturalist Louis Agassiz (1807–73) and popularized by the Alabama physician Josiah C. Nott (1804–73) and the amateur Egyptologist George R. Gliddon (1809–57) in their book *Types of Mankind* (1854). Yet polygenism remained a scientific fad which was generally repudiated by devout Christians, who were offended by its rejection of biblical authority. Despite their alleged proof that negroes were inferior to whites, Nott and Gliddon's ideas were not popular in the slave-owning southeastern United States because their attacks on biblical authority offended the conservative religious sensibilities of that region (Stanton 1960: 161–73). Even the leading British monogenist James Cowles Prichard (1786–1848), who argued that human beings had differentiated as the result of a process of self-domestication, maintained that the more civilized peoples became the more they grew to resemble Europeans. Hence while the most primitive groups had black skins, more civilized ones became progressively lighter (Prichard 1813: 174–242).

Belief in the inequality of races gained scientific credibility as a result of Darwinian evolutionism. In their desire to make credible the evolutionary origins of the human species, Darwin and many of his supporters argued that human societies varied in their biological evolutionary status from highly evolved groups to ones that differed only slightly from the most evolved apes. Darwin believed that less civilized peoples were also less developed intellectually and emotionally than were Europeans; hence his estimation of biological development corresponded with the conventional scale of cultural evolution. In 1863 Thomas Huxley noted the similarities between two Neanderthal skulls and those of modern Australian aborigines and argued that they were also culturally alike (Huxley [1863] 1896). Culturally advanced societies were viewed as ones in which the operation of natural selection had produced individuals who possessed superior intelligence and greater self-control. Alfred Wallace (1823–1913), the co-discoverer of natural selection, had as a naturalist lived for long periods of time among tribal groups in South America and Southeast Asia. On the basis of his personal knowledge of such groups he denied that these peoples differed significantly from Europeans in intelligence or other innate abilities and maintained that humanity's higher mental capacities could not have been produced by natural selection. Darwin deplored these observations as lack of support for their joint theory (Eiseley 1958). To those who were predisposed to believe it, Darwin's view of natural selection offered a far more convincing explanation of how biological inequalities had developed among human groups than polygenism had done. Darwinism also reinforced an evolutionary perspective on cultural evolution by making it appear to be an extension of biological evolution and implying that they were inseparable. While Darwin vehemently opposed the mistreatment and exploitation of non-Western peoples, his theorizing about human evolution gave an unprecedented measure of scientific respectability to racial interpretations of human behaviour. These interpretations provided a biological counterpart to romantic nationalism in challenging and ultimately superseding a belief in psychic unity.

Lubbock's synthesis

A Darwinian view of human nature was incorporated into prehistoric archaeology by the versatile John Lubbock (1834–1913), who later became Lord Avebury, with his book *Pre-historic Times, as Illustrated by Ancient Remains, and the Manners and Customs of Modern Savages*. Between 1865 and 1913 this book went through seven editions both in England and the United States and it long served as a textbook of archaeology. It was almost certainly the most influential work dealing with archaeology published during the nineteenth century. A second book *The Origin of Civilisation and the Primitive*

18 John Lubbock (Lord Avebury) (1834–1913)

Condition of Man (1870) also went through several editions. It expounded Lubbock's ideas in a more extreme fashion and with less emphasis on archaeological data. Lubbock grew up as a neighbour of Charles Darwin, whose house bordered on the Lubbock family's estate in Kent. At the age of 22 he became a partner in his father's bank and later as a member of parliament he secured passage of the Bank Holidays Act (1871) and of an act to provide protection for ancient monuments (1882). His research as a naturalist established him as a leading authority on animal behaviour. It was as an early supporter of Darwin's theory of evolution that he began to study prehistoric archaeology.

At first glance, *Prehistoric Times* (to adopt the spelling of later editions) appears to be a curious collection of disparate material. A first section, comprising more than half the book, presents a series of chapters dealing in roughly chronological order with archaeological topics: the use of bronze in ancient times, the Bronze Age, the use of stone, megaliths and tumuli, lake-dwellings, kitchen middens, North American archaeology, Quaternary mammals, 'primeval man', Pleistocene deposits, and the antiquity of human beings. Lubbock then argued that just as modern elephants provide information about the nature of extinct mammoths, so modern primitive societies shed light on the behaviour of prehistoric human beings. This is followed by a series of sketches of the ways of life of modern tribal societies: Hottentots, Veddahs, Andaman Islanders, Australian Aborigines, Tasmanians, Fijians, Maoris, Tahitians, Tongans, Eskimos, North American Indians, Paraguayans, Patagonians, and Fuegans. The ordering of these chapters is clearly geographical rather that evolutionary and no attempt was made to indicate what particular modern groups provide evidence about specific stages of prehistoric development. Among the few specific parallels that he suggested was the long-standing Scandinavian claim that Eskimo stone tools were very similar to those of the European Upper Palaeolithic. He also drew a parallel between the Fuegans and the nameless people who had produced the Danish kitchen middens, although he noted that the latter had excelled the Fuegans because they manufactured crude pottery.

Lubbock was deeply committed to the idea of unilinear cultural evolution. The parallel that he drew between palaeontological analogies and those involving modern 'primitive' peoples and prehistoric ones seems to have been an attempt to enhance the scientific respectability of the cultural comparisons rather than methodologically innovative. He noted, however, that there was no clear evidence that humanity had invented specific types of tools in any one particular sequence. Environmental factors had produced variations in 'kind' as well as 'degree' among human groups. None of these arguments limiting the usefulness of a unilinear approach was new.

What was new was his Darwinian insistence that as a result of natural selection human groups had become different from each other not only culturally but also in their biological capacities to utilize culture. Lubbock viewed modern Europeans as the product of intensive cultural and biological evolution. He believed that technologically less advanced peoples were not only culturally but also intellectually and emotionally more primitive than civilized ones. He also maintained that as a result of the differential operation of natural selection among Europeans, the criminally inclined and lower classes were biologically inferior to the more successful middle and upper classes. Thus a single explanation accounted for social inequality in Western societies and for the alleged superiority of European societies over other human groups.

Like other evolutionists, Lubbock argued forcefully against the idea that cultural degeneration had played a significant role in human history. He consistently portrayed degenerationism as an old-fashioned and discredited doctrine. He also sought to counter romantic followers of Jean-Jacques Rousseau, who questioned that the development of civilization had led to an increase in human happiness. In order to reinforce an evolutionary perspective, he went out of his way to portray primitive peoples as inevitably few in number, wretched, and depraved. He described modern tribal groups as being unable to control nature and having intellects resembling those of children. Their languages were alleged to lack abstract words and they were claimed to be incapable of understanding abstract concepts. They were also said to be slaves to their passions, being unable to control anger or to follow any specific course of action for more than a short time. He maintained that they were more deficient in moral sense than was generally believed and took pains to document how specific groups regularly mistreated children, murdered aged parents, ate human flesh, and practised human sacrifice. To demonstrate their lack of routine Victorian values, he also emphasized their dirtiness. He argued that cultural development resulted in an increasing population; while left to their own devices primitive peoples remained static or declined in numbers. Cultural development also expanded human consciousness and led to growing material prosperity and spiritual progress. He viewed cultural evolution as continuing indefinitely in a future marked by ever greater technological and moral improvement and by increasing human happiness and comfort. *Pre-historic Times* ended with a rousing expression of this evolutionary credo:

> Even in our own time, we may hope to see some improvement; but the unselfish mind will find its highest gratification in the belief that, whatever may be the case with ourselves, our descendants will understand many things which are hidden from us now, will better appreciate the beautiful world in which we live, avoid much of that suffering to which we are subject, enjoy many blessings of which we are not yet worthy, and escape many of those temptations which we deplore, but cannot wholly resist. (Lubbock 1869: 591)

The growth of a capitalist industrial economy, in conjunction with the operation of natural selection on human beings, was clearly leading to an earthly paradise. By offering evidence that such progress was the continuation of what had been occurring ever more rapidly throughout human history, prehistoric archaeology bolstered the confidence of the British middle classes and strengthened their pride in the leading role that they were playing in that process.

Yet not all human groups were to share in this happiness. The most primitive were doomed to vanish as a result of the spread of civilization, since no amount of education could compensate for the thousands of years during which natural selection had failed to adapt them biologically to a more complex and orderly way of life. Nor was their replacement by more evolved peoples to be seriously regretted, since this resulted in an overall improvement of the human race. Thus, by applying Darwinian principles, Lubbock came to much the same conclusion about the unbridgeable biological differences between Europeans and native peoples that American anthropologists and historians had evolved in the late eighteenth and early nineteenth centuries. His views of native peoples justified British colonization and the establishment of political and economic control abroad on the grounds that they promoted the general progress of the human species. He also absolved British and American settlers of much of the moral responsibility for the rapid decline of native peoples in North America, Australia, and the Pacific. These populations were vanishing not because of what colonists were doing to them but rather because, over thousands of years, natural selection had not equipped them to survive as civilization spread. The imposition of inferior roles on native groups was made to appear less a political act than a consequence of their limited natural abilities. Whether dealing with the working classes in Britain or with native peoples abroad, social Darwinism transferred human inequality from the political to the natural realm by explaining it as a consequence of biological differences that could be altered only very slowly, if at all.

This view marked a major break with the ideals of the Enlightenment. The aspiring bourgeoisie of eighteenth-century France had expressed their hopes for the future in terms of a belief in progress in which all human beings could participate. In contrast the middle classes that dominated Britain in the mid-nineteenth century were increasingly concerned to defend their gains and did so by trying to define natural limits to those who could reasonably hope to share in them. Beginning in the 1860s, Darwinian evolutionism performed this function admirably. Through Lubbock's version of cultural evolution, prehistory was linked to a doctrine of European preeminence.

While Lubbock's synthesis was clearly a product of Victorian England, there was nothing narrowly chauvinistic about it. Arguments about superiority were formulated in terms of a contrast between European civilization and technologically less developed societies. They sought to explain the expanding world system that was dominated by Western Europe. England's political and economic hegemony was so great compared to that of any other nation that it did not require any specific defence. In framing arguments in terms of European civilization, Lubbock took his own country's leadership for granted. Because of that his works had appeal far beyond Britian and influenced the interpretation of archaeological data in many parts of the world.

Colonial archaeology in America

Lubbock's writings played a significant role in reinforcing and shaping the development of American evolutionary archaeology in the late nineteenth century, even if some leading American archaeologists did not whole-heartedly accept the relevance of Darwinism for understanding human affairs (Meltzer 1983: 13). Euroamerican anthropologists had no difficulty applying an evolutionary perspective to their own society. The Enlightenment concepts of reason and progress that had played an important role in the American Revolution, and the economic and territorial expansion of the United States throughout the nineteenth century, sustained a belief that progress was inherent in the human condition. In works such as Lewis Henry Morgan's (1818–81) *Ancient Society* (1877) and Otis Mason's (1838–1908) *The Origins of Invention* (1895) anthropologists traced the development of culture in a perspective that placed Euroamerican society in the forefront of human advancement. Lubbock provided Americans with a Darwinian explanation for the biological inferiority that they had attributed to American Indians since the late eighteenth century. Many found his explanation more persuasive than any previous one, no doubt partly as a result of the great prestige that leading biologists and the general public accorded to Darwin's work. The declining numbers of native people and their lessening ability to withstand Euroamerican expansion also encouraged a growing belief that they were doomed to extinction, which accorded with Lubbock's views. As a result most North American archaeologists continued to stress the changeless quality of the archaeological record and tried hard to attribute changes to processes other than alterations in native cultures.

The archaeology of Mexico, Central America, and Peru constituted a challenge to this view. Some writers, including those who identified the native peoples of Mexico with the Moundbuilders, regarded them as racially superior to the North American Indians. J. L. Stephens' discovery of the ruins of Maya cities in Mexico and Central America was welcomed as proof that the New World had developed its own civilizations by American scholars who were anxious to refute the claims advanced by eighteenth-century European naturalists and historians, such as Georges-Louis Leclerc, comte de Buffon, Guillaume-Thomas Raynal, and William Robertson, that the climate of North America was conducive to the degeneration of animal and human life (Haven 1856: 94). William H. Prescott's celebrated *History of the Conquest of Mexico* (1843) and his later *History of the Conquest of Peru* (1847) portrayed the Aztecs and Incas as civilized peoples, although he maintained that, as a result of their superstitions and aggressiveness, the Aztecs were destroying the accomplishments of their more civilized predecessors. The ethnologist Albert Gallatin (1761–1849) defended Enlightenment views of cultural evolutionism and strongly opposed polygenesis, but by the 1840s his arguments appeared old-fashioned and unconvincing (Bieder 1975). Nevertheless E. G. Squier continued to defend both unilinear evolutionism and psychic unity (Bieder 1986: 104–45). Finally in 1862 Daniel Wilson, who was now teaching at University College in Toronto, published the first edition of *Prehistoric Man: Researches into the Origin of Civilization in the Old and the New World*. This book was a remarkable synthesis of all that was known about the anthropology of the New World. Wilson, as a product of the Edinburgh Enlightenment, continued, like Gallatin, to resist racial interpretations of human behaviour. A significant portion of his book was concerned with the impact that European colonists and African slaves were having upon the native peoples of the western hemisphere and the effects that a new environment was having on them. In the section of his book dealing with prehistory, Wilson, while accepting the Moundbuilder myth, sketched an evolutionary sequence which, independently of outside influence, had produced in Mexico and Peru civilizations that were comparable to those of ancient Egypt and Mesopotamia.

These views encountered great opposition. The war between the United States and Mexico that ended in 1848 unleashed a flood of anti-Mexican feeling in the United States. The Mexicans were widely agreed to be racially inferior to Euroamericans because Spanish settlers had interbred with the native population (Horsman 1975). The ethnologist Lewis Henry Morgan, doggedly ignoring archaeological evidence, maintained that the sixteenth-century Spanish had exaggerated the sophistication of the Aztecs and Incas in order to glorify their own achievements in conquering them. He argued that the traditional ways of life of these peoples had differed little from that of the Iroquois of New York State and that no native group in the New World had ever evolved beyond the level of a tribal society (Morgan 1876). He did not rule out the possibility that native Americans on their own might have evolved more complex ways of life, but he believed that any cultural advancement depended on an increase in brain size which could occur only very slowly (Bieder 1986: 194–246). This position was long maintained by many Euro-americans who saw little to admire in the native peoples of the United States. There was strong support by the 1860s for the view that the native cultures not only of North America but of the entire New World were inherently primitive and had been static throughout prehistoric times.

It has been suggested that the lack of concern with chronology in North American archaeology prior to the twentieth century resulted from the failure of any native group to advance beyond the Stone Age, a dearth of stratified sites, and lack of familiarity with techniques for deriving chronology in the absence of major technological changes (Willey and Sabloff 1980: 80–1). These factors do not explain, however, what happened. A low frequency of stratified post-Palaeolithic sites among those that were known in northern and western Europe in the nineteenth century did not inhibit the construction of detailed chronologies in those regions, mainly by employing Thomsen's principles of seriation (Childe 1932: 207). Moreover, all of the chronological methods used in Europe were known in America and had been successfully applied by archaeologists in situations where they sought to emulate European research. After 1860 shell mounds were studied both seriationally and stratigraphically and on the basis of such evidence local cultural chronologies were constructed that were characterized by changing pottery styles or adaptive patterns. Such observations were made by Jeffries Wyman (1875), S. T. Walker (1883), and Clarence B. Moore (1892) in the southeastern United States; William Dall (1877) in Alaska; and the visiting German archaeologist Max Uhle (1907) in California. Stratigraphic methods were also employed in mound studies by Squier and Davis in the 1840s and by Cyrus Thomas in the 1880s, as well as by W. H. Holmes and F. W. Putnam in their 'Palaeolithic' research in the 1880s (Meltzer 1983: 39). The evidence of local cultural change that these archaeologists adduced was rejected or dismissed as being of trivial significance by most contemporary archaeologists, including sometimes those who employed these methods (Thomas 1898: 29–34). Discussing Uhle's evidence for 'the gradual elaboration and refinement of technical processes' within the Emeryville shellmound in California, A. L. Kroeber (1909: 16) proposed that the native cultures found in that region in historical times had been so primitive as to rule out any possibility that there could have been significant cultural change in the past. It is also significant that not even local studies of shell mounds displayed cumulative development at this period. The most insightful and productive research in any one region was not necessarily the most recent (Trigger 1986a).

In accordance with the belief that change had been minimal in prehistoric times, the systematic study of cultural variation in the archaeological record was oriented primarily towards defining geographical rather than chronological patterns. This paralleled the tendency of American ethnologists late in the nineteenth century to organize the study of cultural similarities and differences in terms of cultural areas. In 1887 the ethnologist Franz Boas had argued that the ethnological material from across the United States that was accumulating in major museums should be exhibited according to geographical areas and tribes rather than in terms of hypothetical evolutionary sequences or typological categories applicable to the entire continent. Otis Mason published the first detailed ethnographical treatment of the cultural areas of North America in 1896 and was followed in this approach by Clark Wissler (1914).

Archaeologists had long been aware of geographical variations in the distributions of certain classes of archaeological data, such as different types of mounds. Cyrus Thomas (1825–1910), an entomologist who worked as an archaeologist for the Bureau of American Ethnology, subdivided these mounds into eight geographical units which he suggested represented more than one nation or group of tribes, some of which had survived into historical times (1894). Later, in his *Introduction to the Study of North American Archaeology* (1898), he divided all of North America into three major cultural zones: Arctic, Atlantic, and Pacific, with the latter subdivided into several districts. J. D. McGuire (1842–1916) examined the distribution of different types of Indian pipes in terms of fifteen geographical divisions (1899) and W. H. Holmes (1846–1933), who had been trained as an artist, used stylistic analyses as well as technological criteria to define a series of pottery regions for the eastern United States (1903). In 1914 he divided the whole of North America into

19 'Cultural characterization areas' of North America based on archaeological criteria, by Holmes, 1914

26 'cultural characterization areas' on the basis of archaeological data, in a manner that paralleled the procedures being followed by ethnologists. In all of this work little effort was made to assign relative chronological significance to different units or to trace chronological changes within them.

It was generally assumed that the way of life of each prehistoric tribe had not changed significantly over time. Evidence of change in the archaeological record was interpreted as resulting from movements of people rather than from alterations within individual cultures. For example, the change from what would now be called Archaic to Middle Woodland cultures in upper New York State was attributed to the replacement of an Inuit-like population by Algonkian-speakers, who in turn were displaced by Iroquoian-speaking peoples carrying yet another distinctive cultural pattern northward from the Mississippi Valley. That pattern included an agricultural subsistence economy and incised pottery and in general was thought to resemble more closely the ways of life found in the southeastern United States than it did earlier cultures that had existed in its historical homeland (Beauchamp 1900; Parker 1916, 1920). The ethnologist R. B. Dixon (1913) interpreted the complexity of the archaeological record, which by that time was becoming evident in eastern North America, as a 'palimpsest' resulting from repeated shifts of population in prehistoric times. These shifts were viewed as largely random movements that characterized aboriginal life on a large and thinly populated continent.

It was also agreed that, where there had been no major shifts in population, ethnographic data concerning tribes that had lived in a region in historical times could be used relatively straightforwardly to explain prehistoric archaeological data. Cyrus Thomas (1898: 23) argued that once America had been settled by native peoples they tended to remain in the same place; hence the archaeological record had been mostly produced by the same people who had lived in particular regions in historical times. He suggested that such stability could be assumed unless there was clear evidence to the contrary. Archaeologists such as Frank Cushing (1857–1900) and J. W. Fewkes (1850–1930), in their studies of the Pueblo Indians of the southwestern United States, paid much attention to determining by means of careful ethnographic parallels what prehistoric artifacts had been used for and how they had been made (Cushing 1886; Fewkes 1896). It was generally assumed that there were no significant differences between life in prehistoric pueblos and in modern ones. Hence efforts to learn about the past brought archaeologists into close contact with ethnologists and often with native people. Studies of this sort constitute early examples of the direct historical approach to the interpretation of archaeological data. Only Edgar Lee Hewett (1865–1946) expressed significant reservations about the relevance of this method (1906: 12).

For the anthropologists employed by the Bureau of Ethnology (renamed the Bureau of American Ethnology in 1894) this 'flat' view of native history unified the study of ethnology and prehistoric archaeology as closely related branches of anthropology. Founded as an arm of the Smithsonian Institution in 1879, the Bureau grew under the leadership of its director, the renowned geologist and explorer John Wesley Powell (1834–1902), into the leading centre of anthropological research in North America. Although originally intended to study ethnographic and linguistic problems in order to promote the more effective administration of Indian affairs, it also laid 'the empirical foundations of archeology in the United States . . . on a broad geographical scale' (Hallowell 1960: 84). While the 'flat' past was advocated as a self-evident means for understanding archaeological data, it depended on the assumption that prehistoric times were not qualitatively distinct from the ethnographic present. Samuel Haven (1864: 37) had observed that 'The flint utensils of the Age of Stone lie upon the surface of the ground . . . The peoples that made and used them have not yet entirely disappeared'. Yet this denial of cultural change, to no less a degree than the extreme unilinear evolutionism of European archaeologists, subordinated archaeological to ethnological research by suggesting that nothing could be learned from archaeological data that could not be ascertained more easily by means of ethnographic research. While unifying anthropology, the 'flat' view also reinforced negative stereotypes of native peoples. As Meltzer (1983: 40) has noted, this view was 'a predictable consequence of the government approach to archaeological research [which was] grounded in a subliminal and denigrating stereotype of the Native American'.

In order to pursue their programme, the anthropologists at the Bureau of American Ethnology sought to eliminate those aspects of prehistory that could not be studied by means of the direct historical approach (Meltzer 1983). The first of these anomalies was the lost Moundbuilder race. Because of great public interest, the United States Congress had insisted that the Bureau should spend $5,000 each year on mound studies. In 1882 Powell selected Cyrus Thomas to head this research. Thomas began an extensive programme of survey and excavation which led him to conclude that many mounds had been constructed after earliest European contact and that all of them had been built by the ancestors of modern native Americans

(Thomas 1894). He also sought to demonstrate that the cultures of the Indians who had built the mounds in no way excelled those of the Indian groups who had lived in the eastern United States in the seventeenth and eighteenth centuries. Thus the refutation of the Moundbuilder myth involved not only the wholesale rejection of inflated claims that had been made about them (such as that they were able to produce iron) but also undervaluing many of the genuine accomplishments of the various groups that had built the mounds. It appears that at this time archaeologists had either to credit the Moundbuilders with possessing an advanced culture and deny that they were Indians or to accept them as Indians and deny that their culture was more advanced than those of any Indian groups living north of Mexico in historical times. No archaeologist was prepared to believe that in prehistoric times native North Americans might have evolved cultures that were more complex than those observed in the historical period, although by then most Indian groups had been severely reduced by epidemics of European diseases and many had also been shattered and dislocated by European aggression and by warfare arising as a result of European settlement. Under these circumstances, it is scarcely surprising that the demolition of the Moundbuilder myth 'did nothing to change the prevailing popular attitudes against the American Indian' (Willey and Sabloff 1980: 42).

The archaeologists at the Bureau of American Ethnology also adopted a very sceptical attitude towards claims that there existed in North America evidence of human antiquity to rival the Palaeolithic assemblages of Europe. The most significant of these assertions was based on excavations that Charles C. Abbott (1843–1919), a physician by training, carried out in gravel deposits on his ancestral farm near Trenton, New Jersey. By 1877 he was convinced that these finds had been produced not by the recently arrived ancestors of modern Native Americans but by inhabitants of the region during the glacial period who were probably not related to the American Indians. He later suggested that this earlier race might have been the ancestors of the Inuit (Abbott 1881). For a time his research enjoyed the limited support and patronage of Frederic W. Putnam (1839–1915), who had been trained as an ichthyologist but since 1874 had been the curator of the Peabody Museum of American Archaeology and Ethnology at Harvard University. Meanwhile, scientists in other parts of the

United States began to find similar 'Palaeolithic' tools, sometimes in geological contexts suggesting great antiquity. Holmes and Thomas led the attack on these claims. They argued that the so-called Palaeolithic tools were quarry refuse marking the early stages in the manufacture of implements by American Indians. Doubt was also cast on the geological contexts in which these finds were being made. Later Aleš Hrdlička (1869–1943), a Czech physical anthropologist who was brought to the United States National Museum in 1903, studied all of the skeletal material that had been claimed as evidence of 'Early Man' and demonstrated that there was no clear evidence that any of it dated prior to the post-glacial period. While these onslaughts led archaeologists and geologists to abandon the idea of a strictly Palaeolithic age in North America, they did not exclude the possibility that human beings had lived in the New World for many thousands of years. They did, however, demonstrate the need for more rigorous evidence. It is clear that in this case scientists in the employ of the federal government were using their power and prestige not only to put archaeology on 'a really scientific basis' but also to promote a view of the past that accorded with their commitment to their own conception of how archaeology and ethnology fitted together as branches of anthropology (Meltzer 1983).

Archaeologists were prepared to acknowledge that a limited amount of innovation had occurred in prehistoric times. Warren K. Moorehead (1866–1939) even believed that some progress was likely because 'the Indian brain is finer than the Australian or African brain' (1910, 1: 331). There was, however, a tendency, where clear chronological indications to the contrary were lacking, to interpret high-quality artifacts, such as stone effigy pipes or elaborately decorated stone and metal ornaments, as reflecting European influence, which took the form of iron tools and artistic inspiration. The implication of such interpretations was that native cultures had been even simpler in prehistoric times than the archaeological remains of the past viewed as a whole would suggest.

The period between 1860 and 1910 witnessed the growing professionalization of archaeology in the United States. Full-time positions became available for prehistoric archaeologists in major museums in the larger cities and later teaching positions were established in universities, beginning with Putnam's appointment as Peabody Professor of American Archaeology and Ethnology at

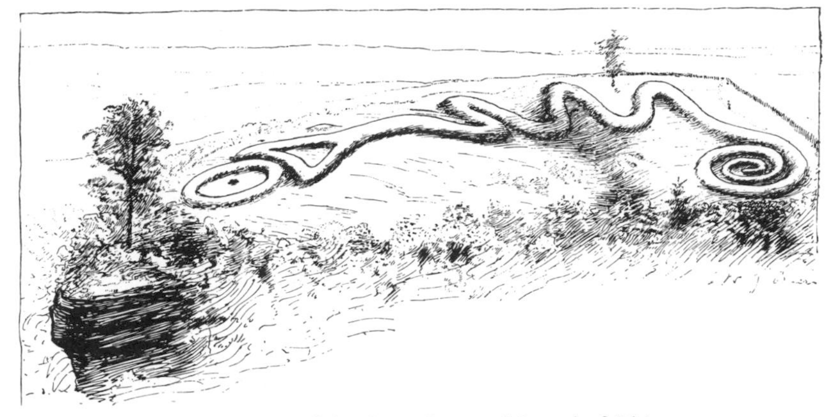

20 Drawing of the Great Serpent Mound of Ohio,
from a popular article by Putnam, 1890

Harvard in 1887. The first doctorate in prehistoric archaeology in the United States was granted at Harvard in 1894 (Hinsley 1985: 72). Euroamericans expressed their convictions about their own ethnic superiority by locating collections of native American archaeology and ethnology in museums of natural history rather than together with European and Near Eastern antiquities in museums of fine art and by teaching prehistory in departments of anthropology rather than of history. Despite the pleas of anthropologists such as John W. Powell and Lewis H. Morgan that 'humble Indian antiquities' should not be allowed to perish, it was generally more difficult to secure the support of wealthy patrons for research on North American Indian prehistory than for collecting the classical antiquities of Europe, which it was argued would 'increase the standard of our civilization and culture' (Hinsley 1985: 55). Despite these problems, much new information was collected, new standards of research were established, and the first steps were taken to preserve major prehistoric monuments, such as the Great Serpent Mound in Ohio and Casa Grande in Arizona. The Smithsonian Institution and the Bureau of American Ethnology played a major role in providing leadership to archaeology. This sometimes involved directing their prestige and resources against amateurs, who bitterly resented interference in their activities by professional scientists employed by the federal government (McKusick 1970). Yet, despite these developments, there was no change in the view of Indians that had prevailed in archaeology and American society generally since the late eighteenth century. Instead, the belief that Indian societies were fossilized entities, incapable of progress, and therefore doomed to extinction was reinforced as a result of being rationalized in terms of Darwinian evolution and seen to accord with the universal perspective on human evolution that had been popularized by John Lubbock. The view of native Americans as inherently primitive and static was now shared not only by vast numbers of white Americans at all social levels but also by an international scientific community that was increasingly receptive to racist explanations of human behaviour. Without significant changes, the traditional view that Euroamerican archaeologists had held of American prehistory could be identified as congruent with that part of Lubbock's imperialist archaeology that applied to colonial situations.

Racist archaeology in Africa

These developments in American archaeology foreshadowed ones that were to occur later in other colonial settings. Archaeological research was carried out sporadically in sub-Saharan Africa by European visitors beginning in the eighteenth century. According to Brian Fagan the earliest recorded excavation was by the Swedish naturalist Andrew Sparrman in 1776. He dug into one of a number of stone mounds near the Great Fish River in southern Africa. Although he discovered nothing, he concluded that these mounds offered irrefutable proof that a more powerful and numerous population had lived in the area before being 'degraded to the present race of Cafres, Hottentots, Boshiesmen, and savages' (Fagan 1981: 42).

Systematic archaeological research did not begin in Africa before the 1890s, by which time the continent had been divided among the various European colonial powers. Archaeologists and colonizers both regarded the indigenous cultures of sub-Saharan Africa as a living museum of the human past. There was much more diversity among these cultures than among those of North America, which could all be formally assigned to the Stone Age. In Africa technologies were based on iron as well as stone tools, while societies ranged in complexity from tiny hunting bands to large kingdoms. Yet most Europeans agreed that the technological, cultural, and political achievements of African people were less significant than they appeared to be. This position was sustained by attributing such accomplishments as were recognized to diffusion from the north. Explorers and missionaries who first encountered black Africa's many complex societies concluded that agriculture, metallurgy, urban life, and various art forms had been introduced by the ancient Egyptians or from other Mediterranean or Near Eastern civilizations (Fagan 1981: 43; Schrire *et al.* 1986). In his study of the archaeology of southern Africa, Miles Burkitt (1890–1971), a lecturer in Prehistory at Cambridge University, saw northern, and frequently specifically European Lower Palaeolithic, Mousterian, and Upper Palaeolithic, influences in stone-tool assemblages and rock art (1928). His view of the region as a cul-de-sac was shared in a less extreme form by his pupil A. J. H. Goodwin (Goodwin and Van Riet Lowe 1929).

In 1880 the German Egyptologist Karl Lepsius suggested that the indigenous peoples of Africa were composed of two major stocks: a lighter-skinned Hamitic population in the north and a Negro population to the south. A large number of ethnologists, including Charles Seligman (1930), identified the Hamites as the 'great civilizing force' of black Africa. They sought to account for the more advanced aspects of sub-Saharan cultures by claiming that culturally more creative Hamitic pastoralists had conquered and imposed the rudiments of a more advanced technology and culture, that was ultimately of Near Eastern origin, upon the culturally inert Negro populations of Africa until their own creativity was undermined as a result of 'miscegenation'. This dichotomy between Negroids and Caucasoids, and the accompanying disparagement of African creativity, lingered on in studies of prehistory and ethnology into the 1960s. The role that was assigned to the prehistoric Hamitic conquerors bore a striking resemblance to the civilizing missions that European colonists had been claiming for themselves since the late nineteenth century (MacGaffey 1966).

Soon archaeological discoveries were made that seemed to be too extensive or sophisticated to be the work of people who were as primitive or indolent as the Africans were supposed to be. The most spectacular example of the colonialist mentality at work in African archaeology is provided by the controversies surrounding the stone ruins found in what is now Zimbabwe. Fagan (1981: 43–4) has observed that these controversies constitute an African counterpart to the Moundbuilder debate in North America. Early European investigators of these monuments saw them as proof of prehistoric white colonization in southern Africa.

In the sixteenth century Portuguese colonists in Mozambique recorded Swahili reports of stone cities in the interior. These accounts encouraged European speculation that these cities had been built by King Solomon or the Queen of Sheba in the course of gold-mining activities. The identification of the stone constructions of Zimbabwe with the biblical land of Ophir continued to excite the imagination of those who studied the geography of Africa in succeeding centuries. In the late nineteenth century these speculations had particular appeal to the Afrikaaners, who were newly settled in the Transvaal and whose Calvinist faith led them to hope that their new homeland bordered on a region that had biblical associations. Information collected in the Transvaal about ruins to the north inspired H. M. Walmsley's *The Ruined Cities of Zululand*, a novel published in 1869. Already in 1868 the German missionary A. Merensky had persuaded the young German geologist Carl Mauch to look for these ruins. In 1871 Mauch became the first European known to have visited the ruins of Great Zimbabwe, which, on the basis of what Merensky had told him, he concluded was the lost palace of the Queen of Sheba.

Speculations of this sort were actively promoted by Cecil Rhodes after his British South Africa Company forcibly occupied Mashonaland in 1890, and neighbouring Matabeleland three years later, in order to exploit the region's gold resources. Great Zimbabwe soon became a symbol of the justice of European colonization, which was portrayed as the white race returning to a land that it had formerly ruled. The first serious study of Great Zimbabwe was sponsored by the British South Africa Company with the help of the Royal Geographical Society and the British Association for the Advancement of Science. The man chosen for this task was J. Theodore Bent (1852–97), a Near Eastern explorer with antiquarian interests. Although his excavations revealed evidence of Bantu occupation containing foreign trade goods no more than a few centuries old, he concluded on the basis of an unscientific selection of architectural and stylistic features that the ruins had been built by 'a northern race' that had come to southern Africa from Arabia in biblical times. On the basis of alleged astronomical orientations the stone ruins were dated between 1000 and 2000 B.C. (Bent 1892).

21 'Approach to the acropolis', from Bent's *The Ruined Cities of Mashonaland*, 1892

In 1895 a company called Rhodesia Ancient Ruins Limited was licensed to hunt for gold in all the architectural sites in Matabeleland except Great Zimbabwe. This operation, which mainly involved grave robbing, was stopped in 1901; after which, in an effort to give his plundering some respectability, one of the prospectors, W. G. Neil, collaborated with Richard Hall (1853–1914), a local journalist, to produce *The Ancient Ruins of Rhodesia* (Hall and Neal 1902). This book presented the first general survey of the ruins of the region. On the strength of it, the British South Africa Company appointed Hall as Curator of Great Zimbabwe, where he proceeded to remove stratified archaeological deposits on the grounds that by doing so he was clearing the site of 'the filth and decadence of the Kaffir occupation'. In his second book he defined three architectural styles, which he claimed revealed progressive degeneration from the finely dressed walls of the elliptical enclosure, and interpreted Great Zimbabwe as the lost metropolis of a Phoenician colony. In recent years careful architectural studies have revealed that the regularly coursed and dressed walls at Zimbabwe are later than short, wavy ones but were followed by walls with uncoursed stones (Garlake 1973: 21–3).

Archaeological criticism of Hall's work led to his dismissal in 1904, following which the British Association for the Advancement of Science, using funds provided by the Rhodes Trustees, invited David Randall-MacIver (1873–1945), a professional archaeologist who had worked with the Egyptologist Petrie, to investigate Great Zimbabwe and other ruins in Rhodesia (1906). More extensive and stratigraphically sophisticated work was carried out under the same auspices by the celebrated British archaeologist Gertrude Caton Thompson (1893–1985) in 1929 (Caton Thompson 1931). These two archaeologists demonstrated conclusively that these ruins were entirely of Bantu origin and dated from the Christian era. While their conclusions were accepted by the world archaeological community, they were unwelcome among the white settlers in Rhodesia and South Africa, where amateur archaeologists kept alive the notion that the ruins of Zimbabwe were the work of invaders, merchants, or metalworkers coming from such varied places as the Near East, India, and Indonesia (Posnansky 1982: 347). In 1909 Hall, supported by subscriptions from a broad cross-section of leading white South Africans, published *Prehistoric Rhodesia*, a massive and emotional work in which he attempted to refute Randall-MacIver's findings. He maintained that the 'decadence' of the Bantu is a 'process which has been in operation for very many centuries [and] is admitted by all authorities', attributing this process to a 'sudden arrest of intelligence' that 'befalls every member of the Bantu at the age of puberty'(p. 13). Thus, as Peter Garlake (1973: 79) has noted, Hall made explicit for the first time the racial theories that were implicit in excluding Africans from the consideration of Zimbabwe's past. Notions of exotic origin have been kept alive since that time by A. J. Bruwer (1965), R. Gayre (1972), Wilfrid Mallows (1985), and Thomas Huffman in an official guidebook to Great Zimbabwe written under the Ian Smith regime. For the white settlers, who constituted less than ten per cent of the population of Southern Rhodesia, such claims served to depreciate African talents and past accomplishments and to justify their own domination of the country. These claims became particularly insistent after they illegally proclaimed the colony to be independent in 1965. In 1971 Peter Garlake, who had been Inspector of Monuments since 1964, resigned in protest over a secret order issued by the Smith government that no official publication should indicate that Great Zimbabwe had been built by blacks. By this time the government was particularly concerned that the ruins had become a symbol of their cultural heritage to local Africans struggling for majority rule. Since the independence of Zimbabwe in 1980, some nationalists have claimed that only Africans have the moral right or understanding necessary to interpret the ancient ruins of Zimbabwe and attempts have been made to promote new, and in this case black African, mythologies (Mufuka 1983; Garlake 1984).

A comparison of the controversies surrounding the Moundbuilders in North America in the nineteenth century and Zimbabwe beginning in the 1890s reveals striking similarities but also significant differences. In both cases amateur archaeologists and public opinion rejected an association of these remains with indigenous native peoples in an effort to disparage the latter's accomplishments. Similarly, the scientific establishment of the day expressed some reservations about the more fanciful interpretations that were being offered of these monuments. What is significant, however, is that after 1905 the international archaeological community unanimously rejected the claims that Zimbabwe had not been constructed by the Bantus, leaving the maintenance of the Zimbabwe myth to local amateur archaeologists and the general public. This suggests that, while the same social pressures to distort the past existed in both situations, by 1905 advances in archaeological techniques for resolving historical questions had reached the point where these pressures no longer distorted the interpretations of most professional archaeologists. Work done in Zimbabwe since the 1950s by locally based professional archaeologists such as Keith Robinson, R. Summers, and Peter Garlake has made a distinguished contribution to understanding the history of Zimbabwe during the late Iron Age. During the Smith regime only one professional archaeologist yielded, against his own better judgement according to later statements attributed to him (S. Taylor 1982), to pressures to satisfy the political requirements of white settlers.

Another feature of African colonial archaeology was the great attention paid to Palaeolithic studies. In the 1890s the geologist J. P. Johnson studied the geological contexts of Palaeolithic tools in the Orange Free State and Transvaal. In 1911 Louis Péringuey, the Director of the South African Museum in Cape Town, divided South African prehistory into a Palaeolithic phase, characterized by implements from river gravels, and a later Bushman phase, represented in shell middens and rock shelters (Fagan 1981: 42–3). Between 1913 and 1924 remains of fossil humans were discovered in South Africa covering the range of human development from Upper Palaeolithic *Homo sapiens* to the first identified skull of an Australopithecine.

Stone tools were identified in Kenya as early as 1893 but systematic work did not begin there until 1926, when the Kenyan-born Louis Leakey (1903–72) organized the first East African Archaeological Expedition from Cambridge University. In *The Stone Age Cultures of Kenya Colony* (1931) Leakey outlined a culture-historical framework for East Africa that continued to be used into the 1950s. Stone tool assemblages were labelled, as before, with terms used in European Palaeolithic studies, such as Chellean, Acheulean, Mousterian, and Aurignacian, and he worked out a succession of pluvial and interpluvial periods that were generally believed to correlate with glacial and interglacial periods in Europe. In due course it was realized that many finds did not conform to European categories and in the late 1920s a set of designations for cultural assemblages that were recognized to be specific to Africa was proposed (Goodwin and Van Riet

Lowe 1929). The two systems continued to be used alongside one another until the European terms were discarded, except to designate tool-manufacturing techniques (Posnansky 1982: 348).

Between 1936 and 1962 a large number of Australopithecine discoveries were made at Sterkfontein, Kromdraai, Makapansgat, and Swartkrans in South Africa. These finds encouraged growing interest in an earlier phase of the archaeological record than had hitherto been studied anywhere else in the world. In the late 1950s new geological chronologies were established for the Pleistocene and Pliocene epochs in Africa, potassium–argon dating stretched the period that was covered by evidence of cultural remains from an assumed 600,000 to 2,000,000 years, Palaeolithic artifacts found in river gravels were shown to be of limited interpretative value, and interest shifted to the excavation of presumed 'living floors', which favoured the preservation of fossil pollens and other palaeoenvironmental data. In 1959 Louis and Mary Leakey, who had pioneered Palaeolithic living-floor archaeology at Olorgesaillie in the 1940s, made the first of many spectacular early hominid finds in the primitive Oldowan tool levels at Oldovai Gorge (M. Leakey 1984). These finds aroused world-wide interest in Lower Palaeolithic archaeology. International funding for such research vastly increased and large numbers of archaeologists from America and Europe began to work in East Africa. Their discoveries were seen as confirming Darwin's conclusion that Africa was likely to have been the cradle of humanity. While these finds were proclaimed to be of great scientific importance, much of the interest resulted from their being perceived as marking the origins not only of humanity as a whole but more specifically of Europeans and Euroamericans. Although the earliest segments of European and Euroamerican prehistory were clearly not going to be found in Europe, it now appeared that they could be traced in Africa.

By contrast, prior to the late 1950s Europeans generally regarded more recent phases of African prehistory as a time of cultural stagnation. To archaeologists in other parts of the world these periods were of little interest compared to early Palaeolithic ones and many resident archaeologists tended to be preoccupied with Palaeolithic archaeology. Fagan (1981: 49) has observed that almost no historians were concerned with pre-European Africa. In their view, the history of Africa began with the earliest records of European activities. This reinforced the belief that there was little for archaeologists to discover about recent millennia. There were, however, significant exceptions. Kenneth Murray, an art teacher who had long sought to conserve Nigeria's indigenous traditions and to convince scholars that these traditions were worth studying, was appointed first Director of the Nigerian Antiquities Service in 1943. He persuaded Bernard Fagg, a Cambridge-trained archaeologist, to join his staff and founded a number of regional museums throughout the colony. This work brought traditional art and culture closer to the currents of emerging African nationalism. John Schofield's *Primitive Pottery* (1948) presented the first typology of Iron Age ceramics from sites in Rhodesia and the Transvaal but major uncertainties about the chronology of the Iron Age were not resolved until the 1950s (Fagan 1981: 48–9).

Especially after 1945 there was a marked expansion of museums, antiquities services, and university departments employing archaeologists, especially in the British and French colonies. Newly trained expatriate scholars combined the latest technical and conceptual advances of Western European archaeology with the pioneer efforts of local (usually white) amateurs. As the prospects for independence brightened there was in some colonies a growing interest in learning more 'about the actual peoples who were now to govern Africa rather than about their remote Stone Age ancestors' (Posnansky 1982: 349). There was also an increasing demand to teach African and not solely European and colonial history in African schools, as had been done in the past. Archaeologists began to study the development of early African states and to investigate important late precolonial sites such as Benin, Gedi, and Kilwa. At the same time African historians insisted that more attention be paid to the Iron Age. In the 1960s they encouraged the introduction of the first regular courses in archaeology in Uganda and Ghana (Posnansky 1976). Iron Age archaeology learned to draw upon historical and ethnographic sources. At the same time archaeologists ceased to attribute changes in prehistoric times almost exclusively to external stimuli and began to try to understand the internal dynamics of the later phases of prehistoric African development. This reorientation was supported by a rapid accumulation of evidence that in precolonial times Africa had played a major role in the development of agriculture and metallurgy and that without major external stimuli its peoples had created numerous civilizations.

The history of African archaeology reveals that changing social conditions have influenced the periods of prehistory that were studied at different times, the questions that have been posed, and the degree to which internal or external factors have been invoked to explain change. It is also clear that a growing corpus of archaeological data, produced by an increasing number of professional archaeologists, and new internationally accepted techniques for studying the past have restricted the freedom of archaeologists to support the views of prehistory that were congenial to colonial ideologies. At the same time changing fashions in archaeological interpretations in the European countries where most archaeologists who have worked in Africa were trained have also influenced the interpretation of African prehistory. These fashions were not directly related to the changing colonial milieu. This suggests a significant but complex relationship between archaeology and the colonial setting in which it was practised in Africa.

Archaeology in New Zealand

In New Zealand the small and dispersed British settlements that began to be established in the 1840s, in the wake of earlier activities by European missionaries and whalers, were for a long time unable to subdue the indigenous Maori, who, especially on the North Island, were numerous and warlike. Armed conflict between the natives and settlers lasted until 1847 and broke out again in the 1860s. Although the Maori were weakened by European diseases, their continuing resistance won them a measure of grudging respect from the European settlers.

No full-time archaeologist was appointed to a university position in New Zealand prior to 1954. Yet as early as 1843 European settlers had noted stone tools associated with the bones of the giant moa and other extinct species of birds. In the 1870s Julius von Haast (1822–87), who was influenced by the writings of Lyell and Lubbock concerning the antiquity of human beings in Europe, argued that the Moa-hunters were a vanished Palaeolithic people, who had subsisted mainly on fish and shellfish and were distinct from the much later Neolithic Maori. He was soon compelled, however, to admit that the Moa-hunters were culturally not very different from the Maori (1871, 1874).

Hereafter the main historical research concerned the origins of the Maori. In the course of the nineteenth century a strong interest developed in their customs, mythology, folklore, and physical anthropology. Much of this research was stimulated by a decline in Maori population and by rapid cultural change, which suggested that soon little of their traditional culture might be available for study. Between 1898 and 1915 Percy Smith (1913, 1915) sought to synthesize various tribal accounts of Maori migrations that had been collected in the 1850s, in order to create a uniform history of their settlement in New Zealand. He concluded that they were Polynesian seafarers who had ultimately originated in India. New Zealand had first been settled by the Maruiwi, an allegedly inferior Melanesian people who were later conquered by the Maori. In 1916 Elsdon Best (1856–1931) identified the Maruiwi with the South Island Moa-hunters. Some Maori tribes were claimed on the basis of oral traditions to have reached New Zealand around A.D. 950 and 1150 and these were followed in A.D. 1350 by a Great Fleet, which carried the groups from whom the major tribes are descended. It was generally concluded that the basic pattern of Maori culture had not changed since that time (Sorrenson 1977).

This scheme of origins was widely accepted by white and Maori New Zealanders, including the Maori anthropologist Peter Buck (Te Rangihiroa, 1877–1951). Peter Gathercole (1981: 163) has drawn attention to the parallels that this account, based on Maori traditional scholarship, drew between the coming of the Maori and the arrival of the Europeans in New Zealand. The Maoris were established in European opinion as being recent colonists in New Zealand, who had seized it from an earlier, culturally less developed people. Therefore they had little more historical claim to the land than the European settlers had. It was also assumed that ethnology and oral traditions revealed all that needed to be known about Maori prehistory.

In the 1920s, Henry D. Skinner, who had studied anthropology at Cambridge University, began to examine Moa-hunter sites on the South Island. Combining archaeological, ethnographic, physical anthropological, and linguistic data with oral traditions, he sought to demonstrate that the Moa-hunters were Maori, and hence Polynesian, in origin. By debunking the Maruiwi myth, he established the role of the Maori as the 'first people of the land' and put archaeology in the forefront of the movement for re-enfranchising them (Sutton 1985). Skinner was also sensitive to regional variations in Maori culture, which he interpreted as partly adaptive in nature, and he argued that indigenous cultural changes had taken place (Sutton, personal communication). Yet his archaeological work lacked any systematic treatment of sequence or cultural change apart from the economic impact of the extinction of the moa (Skinner 1921). Like colonialist archaeologists elsewhere, he continued to view archaeology mainly as a way to recover material culture that would augment and complement ethnological collections rather than as an independent source of historical information. He did, however, support the expansion of archaeological research, including the appointment of David Teviotdale (1932) at the Otago Museum. Teviotdale thus became the first professional archaeologist in New Zealand. Into the 1950s archaeological research continued to concentrate on the study of the Moa-hunters (Duff 1950), while later periods remained understudied (Gathercole 1981). Although oral traditions had involved an awareness of historical events, New Zealand archaeologists had not yet developed an interest in accompanying changes in material culture and styles of life that would have stimulated a comprehensive study of changes in the archaeological record.

In recent years New Zealand archaeology has become increasingly professionalized and redefined its traditional association with Maori ethnology, which had discouraged the study of later prehistory. Much recent work has been done on the North Island, which archaeologists had hitherto ignored, but where most of the Maori population lived and the greatest elaboration of their prehistoric culture had occurred. This work, which is increasingly involving the Maori themselves, has not only already pushed the original settlement of New Zealand back several centuries but also revealed dramatic changes in the material culture and the economic and social organization of the Maori, as well as the effects of climatic change and considerable regional diversification as they adjusted to life in New Zealand. The Moa-hunters are now interpreted as an episode in the Polynesian settlement of the South Island (Davidson 1979). There is also increasing interest in the archaeological investigation of contact between New Zealand and neighbouring regions of the Pacific (D. G. Sutton, personal communication). New Zealand provides an example of a colonial situation in which there was a measure of respect for the native inhabitants. Yet amateur archaeologists there, as elsewhere, viewed native cultures as static and attributed alterations in the archaeological record to ethnic changes rather than to internal developments. It is also true, however, that in the course of the twentieth century a more professionalized archaeology has played a significant role in dispelling such beliefs.

Australian prehistory

In Australia studies of Aboriginal customs began with the first European explorers and settlers. By 1850 most of southern Australia was occupied by Europeans and the Aborigines had been driven from their lands or were dead as a result of disease, neglect, and outright murder. As in North America racial prejudice helped to reduce any feelings of guilt that European settlers may have had about the way they were treating native people.

Beginning in the second half of the nineteenth century, ethnologists in Europe and America encouraged the study of Aborigines as examples of the 'most primitive tribes' known to anthropological science. By 1900 major studies, such as Baldwin Spencer and F. J. Gillen's *The Native Tribes of Central Australia* (1899), had placed Aboriginal ethnography on an internationally respected basis. Spencer, like his English mentors, was to describe the Aborigines as 'a relic of the early childhood of mankind left stranded . . . in a low condition of savagery' (Spencer 1901: 12).

Early investigations of Aboriginal prehistory failed to uncover any clear evidence of the association between human beings and prehistoric animals, such as had been found in Europe. Nor did the artifacts discovered in archaeological sites appear to differ significantly from those in recent use. By 1910 naturalists abandoned the search for early evidence of native people in Australia. The assumptions that they had arrived recently and that their cultures had not changed significantly accorded with the ethnologists' belief that these cultures were primitive and essentially static. From 1910 until the 1950s amateur archaeologists collected artifacts 'secure in the knowledge that Aborigines were an unchanging people, with an unchanging technology' (Murray and White 1981: 256). Spencer, alleging technological opportunism and lack of concern with formal

22 'Native police dispersing the blacks', Western Queensland, c. 1882

tool types in Aboriginal culture, attributed variations in the form and function of artifacts to differences in raw material, thus ignoring the alternative possibilities of change over time, idiosyncratic cultural preferences, and functional adaptation (Mulvaney 1981: 63). John Mulvaney (1981: 63–4) has argued that this concept of the 'unchanging savage', which was in accord with the popular denigration of Aboriginal culture, inhibited the development of prehistoric archaeology in Australia throughout this period. It is also noteworthy that the first archaeology department that was established in Australia, at the University of Sydney in 1948, initially studied only the archaeology of Europe and the Near East.

The excavation in southern Australia, beginning in 1929, of a stratified series of different tool types suggested a longer human occupation and called into question the image of a static prehistory. Cultural change was attributed initially, however, to various groups replacing one another, some of them recent invaders. In 1938 Norman Tindale linked his sequence to the American physical anthropologist, J. B. Birdsell's, tri-racial hybrid theory of Australian racial origins. Tindale also suggested that environmental changes might have occurred during the period of Aboriginal occupation. Concern with cultural change and regional variation did not characterize Australian archaeology until a number of young professional archaeologists began to study Australian prehistory following John Mulvaney's appointment at the University of Melbourne in 1953. Most of these archaeologists had been trained at Cambridge University, where Grahame Clark had encouraged them to work in Australia. As a result of their research, it has become clear that human beings have lived in Australia for at least 40,000 years. Archaeologists have documented numerous changes in technology, environment, adaptation, and non-technological aspects of native culture. Their cultural chronologies have also dispelled the belief that all cultural changes in prehistoric times came about as a result of external stimuli.

Since the 1970s the interpretation of archaeological data has also reflected a growing concern for a distinctive national identity among white Australians. White artists draw inspiration from native art forms and Aboriginal art is viewed as part of Australia's national heritage to a far greater degree than is the case with native arts in North America. Within the context of this growing nationalism,

Australian archaeologists are no longer content to treat their country's prehistory as a mirror of the Palaeolithic stage of human development. Instead they have begun to emphasize the singularity of Australian prehistory, including the considerable degree to which Australian Aborigines managed and altered significant aspects of their environment. The current image of prehistoric Aborigines as 'firestick farmers' is far removed from the traditional one of them as Upper Palaeolithic hunter–gatherers.

It is taking longer for Australian archaeologists to consider the possibility that their country's prehistory may be more than nineteenth-century ethnology retrodicted for 50 millennia (Murray and White 1981: 258; Mulvaney and White 1987). There is now, however, lively discussion about whether it is scientifically legitimate to regard the whole of Australian prehistory as that of the ancestors of the modern Aborigines (cf. White and O'Connell 1982: 6; Flood 1983).

Archaeologists have also been compelled to reassess their goals as a result of the increasing political activities of Aborigines. The federal Labour Party that was elected in 1972 passed legislation granting Aborigines significant membership on decision-making bodies considering matters of concern to them, including the protection of archaeological sites. As a result archaeologists have come under growing pressure to consider the relevance of their research for native people (Ucko 1983; McBryde 1986). The situation has been a complex and rapidly changing one. Some Aborigines' traditional world view leads them to regard all archaeological activity as useless or profaning; others appreciate the value of archaeological work for land-claim disputes and for enhancing their general image. The desire of the latter to use archaeological findings for political ends sometimes brings them into conflict with white archaeologists wishing to pursue 'scientific' goals. Difficult cultural issues include whether or not female archaeologists may visit sacred sites, which only male Aborigines may approach.

Among white Australian academics there are significant differences of opinion concerning the degree to which Australian prehistory should be regarded as a national heritage or as the exclusive possession of the Aborigines. At least some Aborigine activists view a white Australian interest in their heritage as yet another attempt to appropriate what belongs to native people. They remind Australian archaeologists of their past complicity in denigrating Aborigines as a primitive people who were doomed to extinction (Langford 1983). The resolution of such conflicts between Aborigines and archaeologists cannot occur independently of a resolution of the major grievances that Aborigines have against modern Australian society. Nevertheless Australian archaeologists have been making significant efforts to involve Aboriginal people in their work. The general orientation of modern Australian archaeologists towards a historical rather than an evolutionary view of prehistory, which results from their British training, makes the resolution of these problems in some respects easier than it is for anthropologically trained North American archaeologists.

Lubbock's legacy

In the 1860s and 1870s archaeologists continued to believe in the evolutionary origins of European society. Yet by that period they were inclined to offer racial explanations for the failure of other societies to evolve to the same extent as they had done. The Darwinian explanation of these racial differences that was popularized by Lubbock reinforced the racist views inherent in colonial situations and which had already influenced the interpretations of archaeological evidence in the United States. The archaeology that developed wherever European colonists were seeking to establish themselves in the midst of native populations had much in common. Native societies were assumed to be static and evidence of change in the archaeological record, when noted, was attributed to migrations rather than to internal dynamism. The racist views underlying specific interpretations were more often implicit than explicit. Either way, colonialist archaeology served to denigrate the native societies that European colonists were seeking to dominate or replace by offering evidence that in prehistoric times they had lacked the initiative to develop on their own. Such archaeology was closely aligned with ethnology, which documented the primitive condition of traditional native cultures and their general inability to change. This primitiveness was widely believed to justify Europeans seizing control of the territories of such peoples. While these archaeological views did not survive the collection of archaeological evidence which indicated that internal changes had taken place in native cultures, they impeded the search for such evidence and significantly delayed the development of prehistoric archaeology in countries such as Australia, where it was assumed that archaeology had little to reveal about the past. Moreover, this development did not occur until evolutionary archaeology had been replaced in Europe by a historical view of prehistory.

This was because unilinear evolutionism, whether of Lubbock's racist variety or the older, universalistic sort championed by Mortillet, shared certain major weaknesses as a model for collecting and interpreting archaeological data. These weaknesses were especially evident in the evolutionary archaeology that had evolved in England and France around the study of the Palaeolithic period. By arguing that modern cultures arranged from simplest to most complex recapitulated the sequence through which European societies had evolved, unilinear evolution denied that there was anything novel to be learned from the archaeological record. The main value of archaeology was its proof that evolution had in fact occurred, to varying degrees and hence at varying rates in different parts of the world. Lubbock and other archaeologists argued that ethnographic evidence provided an easy way to achieve a rounded understanding of how people had lived in prehistoric times. As long as archaeological data, in the form of diagnostic artifacts, could reveal the level of development that a particular culture had reached, ethnographic data concerning modern societies at the same stage were capable of supplying all that needed to be known about the nature of life associated with that culture. Only the earliest archaeological finds were believed to lack corresponding ethnographic evidence. As late as 1911 Lower and Middle Palaeolithic cultures were being equated with the Tasmanians and Australian Aborigines (Sollas 1911). These holistic analogies invited a revival of antiquarianism, to the extent that they returned archaeology to a situation where artifacts once again merely illustrated the past, rather than constituted a basis for studying prehistoric human behaviour. Within the context of unilinear evolutionism the matrix for understanding archaeological data was no longer historical documentation, as it had been prior to Thomsen's work or remained in classical studies, but rather had become ethnography.

Another major problem was that none of the unilinear evolutionary archaeologists succeeded in devising a methodology for implementing holistic comparisons. No systematic effort was made to correlate specific tool types with ethnographic cultures so that these tool types could in turn be used to draw detailed and controlled comparisons between ethnographic and archaeological assemblages. Efforts to do this might have revealed in greater detail some of the problems of unilinear evolutionism. Archaeologists were aware of the difficulties posed by geographical and environmental variations, but they never confronted this issue systematically. As a result, comparisons between archaeological assemblages and ethnographic cultures remained impressionistic.

The failure to deal adequately with these problems produced a growing sense of impasse and sterility in evolutionary archaeology after the European Palaeolithic sequence had been delineated. The problem with unilinear evolutionary archaeology was that it had become too integral a part of anthropology and too dependent on ethnology. Far more creativity had survived in Scandinavian-style post-Palaeolithic archaeology, although it had been temporarily eclipsed by the momentous discoveries concerning still earlier phases of human development. While Scandinavian archaeology had been inspired by an evolutionary perspective, it shunned holistic analogies and sought to use parallels to interpret individual facets of the archaeological record. Because of their growing realization of the inadequacies of the unilinear evolutionary approach, a new generation of professional archaeologists was to view its decline as a liberation rather than a loss.

CHAPTER 5

Culture-historical archaeology

Generally speaking, nationalist ideology suffers from pervasive false consciousness. Its myths invert reality: it . . . claims to protect an old folk society while in fact helping to build up an anonymous mass society.

E. GELLNER, *Nations and Nationalism* (1983), p. 124

The true patriot becomes of necessity the antiquarian.

O. F. OWEN, *Surrey Archaeological Collections* 1 (1858), pp. 2–3

In the late nineteenth century, cultural evolutionism was simultaneously challenged across Europe by growing nationalism and declining faith in the benefits of technological progress. These two developments were closely linked, since a reduced commitment to evolutionism made ethnicity appear to be the most important factor in human history. In Western Europe nationalism increased as spreading industrialization heightened competition for markets and resources. Towards the end of the century it was encouraged by intellectuals who sought to promote solidarity within their own countries in the face of growing social unrest by blaming economic and social problems on neighbouring states.

In England and France nationalism expressed itself strongly in historical writing, which emphasized the solidarity of these national groups. Yet its impact on archaeology was quite muted, in part as a result of the continuing influence of Lubbock and Mortillet. The French Emperor Napoleon III ordered large-scale excavations to be carried out between 1861 and 1865 at the Celtic oppida, or fortified towns, at Mont Auxois and Mont Réa in Burgundy. These sites, which had been besieged by Julius Caesar when he invaded Gaul, revealed the material culture of the Celtic inhabitants of France in the first century B.C. Napoleon sought, by encouraging nationalism, to enhance the power of his regime (Daniel 1950: 110–11). By contrast, in a self-confident Britain, fantasizing about possible

Druidical associations of Neolithic and Bronze Age sites, which had been the main form of patriotism indulged in by antiquarians in the eighteenth century, was banished to the realms of popular history and folklore (A. Owen 1962: 239).

In Central and Northern Europe, archaeology was associated with nationalism throughout the whole of the nineteenth century. By promoting a sense of ethnic identity, it played a significant role in the unification of Germany in 1871 and afterwards by expressing the pride of the Germans in their accomplishments as a people. The revival of German literature in the eighteenth century had been characterized by a revolt against the classical heritage of Western Europe and a glorification of Germany's medieval and ancient past. At the same time the philosopher Johann Herder had defined history as the account of the development of a people as exemplified by their language, traditions, and institutions (Hampson 1982: 241, 248–9). The study of prehistory continued to be part of the Danish reaction to territorial losses to more powerful neighbours. In Eastern Europe archaeology, by encouraging a sense of ethnic identity among Poles, Czechs, Hungarians, and other groups living under Austrian, Russian, and Prussian domination, played an important role in the destruction of these empires and the eventual emergence of a series of national states.

Throughout the nineteenth century, growing amounts of archaeological material were recovered throughout Central Europe as a result of the construction of roads, railways, canals, and factories; the founding of museums and research institutes; and the establishment of teaching positions for archaeologists in universities. As more evidence was collected, the attention of archaeologists turned from a preoccupation with megaliths, hillforts, and tumuli to the study of artifacts. Their main objective was to determine, often using fanciful criteria, to which ethnic groups various finds belonged, so that emerging nations might learn more about their early history and how their ancestors had lived (Sklenář 1983: 91). In the 1870s and 1880s archaeological research in this region was influenced by the evolutionary archaeology of France and England. This encouraged the more careful classification and comparison of archaeological finds. The development of local chronologies was retarded, however, by a reluctance to adopt the Scandinavian Three-Age system, which was opposed, largely for nationalistic reasons, by a number of prominent German archaeologists (Böhner 1981; Sklenář 1983: 87–91). Yet this flirtation with evolutionary anthropology was short-lived and in the late nineteenth century archaeology once again reaffirmed its ties to the study of national histories. A concern with historical and ethnic problems led archaeologists to pay increasing attention to the geographical distribution of distinctive types of artifacts and artifact assemblages in an effort to relate them to historical groups. A nationalistic orientation encouraged the archaeology of Central Europe to concentrate on the study of the Neolithic and more recent periods rather than on Palaeolithic times. Because of the role that archaeologists played in promoting a sense of ethnic identity, imperial governments sometimes sought to hinder or prevent archaeological research. For the same reason, it enjoyed the support of nationalist elements, such as the Czech middle class and the Polish landed aristocracy.

Diffusionism

By the 1880s growing social and economic problems in Western Europe were encouraging a new emphasis on conservatism and the rigidity of human nature, and hence on ethnicity, in the heartland of evolutionary anthropology. The problems of the Industrial Revolution were becoming increasingly evident, especially in Britain where it had been going on the longest, in the form of slums, economic crises, and growing foreign competition. At the same time the political supremacy of the middle classes was being challenged by the first labour movements. As a result of these developments, the younger generation of intellectuals turned against the idea of progress. Industrialism, which had formerly been a source of pride, was now seen as a cause of social chaos and ugliness (Trevelyan 1952: 119). The efforts that were made to externalize conflicts encouraged a growing emphasis on racial doctrines. It was argued that French, Germans, and English were biologically different from one another and that their behaviour was determined, not by economic and political factors, but by essentially immutable racial differences. National unity was encouraged by arguing that within each nation everyone, regardless of social class, was united by a common biological heritage, which constituted the strongest of all human bonds.

Disillusionment with progress, together with the belief that human behaviour was biologically determined, promoted growing scepticism about human creativity. Writers and social analysts maintained that people were not inherently inventive and that change was contrary to human nature and potentially harmful to people. It was argued that a static condition was most congenial to human beings, who were naturally predisposed to resist alterations in their styles of life. This led to declining credence in independent development, a belief that particular inventions were unlikely to be made more than once in human history, and hence a growing reliance on diffusion and migration to explain cultural change. It also encouraged an increasing interest in the idiosyncratic features associated with particular ethnic groups rather than with the general characteristics of successive stages of cultural development. If the insecurity of the middle classes of Western Europe in the 1860s had led Lubbock and other Darwinians to abandon the doctrine of psychic unity and view native peoples as biologically inferior to Europeans, the still greater insecurity of the 1880s led intellectuals to jettison the doctrine of progress and regard human beings as far more resistant to change than they had been viewed since before the Enlightenment.

Increasing reliance on diffusion and migration, as well as the concept of cultures as ways of life related to specific ethnic groups, were soon evident in the work of German ethnologists such as Friedrich Ratzel (1844–1901) and Franz Boas (1858–1942). Ratzel, a geographer and ethnologist, rejected Bastian's concept of psychic unity. In works such as *Anthropogeographie* (1882–91) and *The History of Mankind* ([1885–8] 1896–8) he argued that, because the world was small, ethnologists must beware of thinking that even the simplest inventions were likely to have been made more than once, let alone repeatedly. Both invention and diffusion were described as capricious processes; hence it became impossible to predict whether a particular group will borrow even a useful invention from its neighbours. Ratzel argued that because of this it was necessary to rule out the possibility of diffusion in order to prove that the same type of artifact had been invented more than once. He tried to demonstrate that items such as the blowpipe and the bow and arrow, wherever they occurred in the world, could be traced back to a common source. He also sought to show that, despite its capriciousness, diffusion created culture areas, or blocks of similar cultures adjacent to each other.

Ratzel's ideas influenced the younger Boas, who introduced them into North America. Boas opposed the doctrine of cultural evolutionism and argued that each culture was a unique entity that had to be understood on its own terms. This involved accepting two doctrines: cultural relativism, which denied the existence of any universal standard that could be used to compare the degree of development or worth of different cultures, and historical particularism, which viewed each culture as the product of a unique sequence of development in which the largely chance operation of diffusion played the major role in bringing about change. Boas believed that if the development of cultures displayed any regularities, these were so complex as to defy understanding. The only way to explain the past was to determine the successive idiosyncratic diffusionary episodes that had shaped the development of each culture (Harris 1968: 250–89). About the same time the Viennese school of anthropology, developed by the Roman Catholic priests Fritz Graebner and Wilhelm Schmidt, argued that a single series of cultures had developed in Central Asia, from where cultures of different types had been carried to various parts of the world. The complex cultural variations observed on every continent resulted from the mingling of cultures at different levels of development (ibid. 382–92; Andriolo 1979).

Diffusion displaced an evolutionary approach in English ethnology as a result of the work of the Cambridge scholar W. H. R. Rivers (1914). Unable to detect an evolutionary pattern in his detailed study of the distribution of cultural traits in Oceanic societies, he rejected an evolutionary approach and adopted a diffusionist one (Slobodin 1978). Diffusionism was carried further in British anthropology by Grafton Elliot Smith (1871–1937). Born in Australia, Smith studied medicine and became interested in mummification while he taught anatomy at the University of Cairo, prior to moving to the University of London. Noting that embalming was practised in various forms elsewhere, he decided that it had been invented in Egypt, where it had reached its most highly developed form, and that it had degenerated as it spread to other parts of the world. He then theorized that all early cultural development had occurred in Egypt. Prior to 4000 B.C. there had been no agriculture, architecture, religion, or government anywhere in the world. Then the accidental harvesting of wild barley and millet led to the development of agriculture, which was followed by the invention of pottery, clothing, monumental architecture, and divine kingship. Smith believed that these events had occurred in a unique environment and were unlikely ever to have happened elsewhere. Egyptian innovations had been carried to all parts of the world by Egyptian merchants who were searching for raw materials that had the power to prolong human life. While these influences acted as an 'exotic leaven' encouraging the development of agriculture and civilization in other parts of the world, civilizations such as that of the Maya declined when cut off from direct contact with Egypt (Smith 1923, 1933).

Smith's hyper-diffusionist ideas were elaborated using ethnographic data by W. J. Perry, who taught cultural anthropology at the University of London. His two major works, *The Children of the Sun* (1923) and *The Growth of Civilization* (1924) still make fascinating reading, although the explanation of his world-wide parallels in political organization and religious beliefs remains illusive. Lord Raglan (1939) also advocated hyper-diffusionism but believed Mesopotamia rather than Egypt to have been its source. The ideas on which these three men agreed were that most human beings are naturally primitive and will always revert to a stage of savagery if not stopped from doing so by the ruling classes; that savages never invent anything; that the development of civilization, and by extrapolation the Industrial Revolution, were accidents that produced results contrary to human nature; and that religion was a prime factor promoting the development and spread of civilization. Yet, in denying that progress was natural or that there was any plan to human history, the hyper-diffusionists were only carrying to an extreme ideas that had been shared by a growing number of anthropologists since the 1880s. Marvin Harris (1968: 174) has observed that diffusionists generally were far more dogmatic in dismissing the possibility that the same invention had been made twice than evolutionists ever had been in denying the importance of diffusion.

Some European archaeologists were influenced by Elliot Smith to the extent that they argued that megalithic tombs might be a degenerate form of pyramid, the idea of which had been carried to Western Europe by Egyptians seeking for life-giving natural substances (Childe 1939: 301–2, 1954: 69). Yet, by the 1920s the archaeological record was sufficiently well known that hyper-diffusionism had little appeal to archaeologists as an explanation of world prehistory. Insofar as archaeologists thought about the problem, cultures in the Old and New Worlds were recognized to be stylistically distinct and were believed to have developed independently from hunting and gathering to civilization. Yet, within the diffusionist milieu that had begun to evolve in the 1880s, the human capacity for innovation was considered to be sufficiently limited and quixotic that basic discoveries, such as pottery and bronze working, seemed unlikely to have been invented twice and hence were believed to have spread from one part of the world to another. The chronologies that had been elaborated prior to radiocarbon dating, especially on an intercontinental scale, were not sufficiently calibrated to rule out such interpretations. Almost all cultural change in the archaeological record was attributed to the diffusion of ideas from one group to another or to migrations that had led to the replacement of one people and their culture by another. Because they accepted the capacity of one group to learn from another, archaeologists who stressed diffusion were generally more optimistic about the capacity of human societies to change than were those who attributed almost all change to migration. The latter fashion is exemplified in the work of W. M. F. Petrie (1939), who, in discussing the prehistoric development of Egypt, explained all cultural changes in terms of mass migrations or the arrival of smaller groups who brought about cultural change by mingling culturally and biologically with the existing population. Petrie saw no possibility of significant cultural change without accompanying biological change.

The transition between evolutionary and diffusionist modes of thought was gradual and diffusionist explanations often shared many of the features of evolutionary ones. W. J. Sollas, in his *Ancient Hunters and their Modern Representatives* (1911), based on a series of lectures delivered in 1906, appears to be following an evolutionary model when he compares successive ages of Palaeolithic development with different modern hunter–gatherer groups. Thus the Mousterians are 'represented' by the Tasmanians, the Aurignacians in part by the Bushmen, and the Magdalenians by the Inuit and the American Indians. Yet he maintains that most of these modern counterparts are appropriate analogues because they are the literal descendants of these Palaeolithic groups, who, as more 'intelligent' races emerged, were 'expelled and driven to the uttermost parts of the earth' where they remained in an arrested state of development (1924: 599). Under the impact of diffusionism, holistic analogies based on the assumption that historically unrelated groups at the same level of development are culturally similar gradually were replaced by the assumption that because cultures are inherently static only the comparison of historically related ones could facilitate the interpretation of archaeological data (Wylie 1985a: 66–7).

The Montelian synthesis of European prehistory

The growing interest in cultural variation and diffusion in the social sciences provided a framework that allowed archaeologists to account for the evidence of spatial as well as temporal variation that was becoming obvious as archaeological data accumulated across Europe. As early as 1851 Daniel Wilson had noted major stylistic differences between Iron Age artifacts in Scandinavia and Scotland. In the course of the nineteenth century archaeologists in Britain, France, Switzerland, Germany, and Central Europe traced the geographical distributions of coins (J. Evans 1850), megaliths, and other Stone, Bronze, and Iron Age remains (Daniel 1950: 303–5; Sklenář 1983: 111–12). As La Tène finds were more firmly identified with late prehistoric Celtic groups, its status as a culture rather than a stage of development or a period became clearer; a process that was accelerated in 1870 when Mortillet interpreted La Tène artifacts found in northern Italy as archaeological evidence of a historically recorded Celtic invasion of that country (Daniel 1950: 111). In 1890 Arthur Evans identified a late Celtic urnfield in southeastern England with the Belgae, who the Romans reported had invaded England in the first century B.C. John Abercromby (1902) associated Early Bronze Age beaker pottery, probably wrongly (Harrison 1980), with a putative 'Beaker folk' whom he had migrating over much of Western Europe. In 1898 the Danish archaeologist Sophus Müller (1846–1934) argued that, although the Single Graves and Megalithic Burials of the Danish Neolithic were at least partly contemporary, the weapons, pottery, and ornaments associated with them were different and hence they must represent two distinct peoples (Childe 1953: 9). By 1909 the Mesolithic period in Western Europe had been divided into contemporary Azilian and Tardenoisian assemblages. As early as 1874 Boyd Dawkins (p. 353) suggested the possibility of

23 Oscar Montelius (1843–1921)

regional variations in the Palaeolithic and by 1916 Henri Obermaier had divided the Lower Palaeolithic into contemporary flake and core traditions.

This growing emphasis on the geographical distribution as well as the chronology of archaeological finds led to important creative work being done by archaeologists who were interested primarily in the European Neolithic, Bronze, and Iron Ages rather than the Palaeolithic period. Their work was to replace the evolutionary preoccupation of Western European prehistoric archaeology with a historical orientation, but this change came about slowly. The first major figure in this transition was the Swedish archaeologist Gustav Oscar Montelius (1843–1921). He was trained in the natural sciences but soon became interested in archaeology and began to work at the State Historical Museum in Stockholm in 1863. He shared Thomsen's and Worsaae's interest in elaborating a prehistoric chronology, to the extent that he was less concerned than were many of his Scandinavian contemporaries with understanding the ecological background of prehistoric cultures. He spent part of each year travelling throughout Europe in order to study collections and thus became the first archaeologist to investigate prehistory on a continental scale. The enlarged scope of his research was made possible by the increasing tempo of archaeological activity throughout Europe and by the development of a network of railways, which made travel easier.

The typological method, as Montelius developed it, was a refinement of Thomsen's seriational approach. He noted variations in form and decoration for various classes of artifacts throughout Europe and on this basis sought to work out and correlate a series of regional chronologies. He did this by examining material from closed finds, such as graves, hoards, and individual rooms, to determine what types of artifacts occurred and never occurred together. Experience taught him that, after comparing 200 to 300 finds of this sort, clusters of association would form that represented, not large units of time such as the Bronze Age, but subdivisions of these ages that he believed could each have lasted only a few hundred years. By arranging these clusters so that elements that were most alike were placed adjacent to each other, he created a chronological sequence. For such a sequence to be convincing, however, materials, techniques of manufacture, shape, and decoration had to form an internally coherent series, just as they had done with Thomsen's cruder seriation (Bibby 1956: 176–81; Klindt-Jensen 1975: 87–96).

Montelius noted evolutionary trends over the course of his periods. Bronze celts, for example, began as flat axes that were later flanged to strengthen them. Next they were provided with a crossbar and cylindrical shaft and finally with a heavy cast socket to facilitate mounting. He viewed such a sequence as a natural and logical one and drew parallels between the evolution of material culture and of biological organisms. Yet, as Gräslund (1974) has shown, despite his training in the natural sciences, Montelius' thinking about human behaviour owed little to Darwinism. On the contrary it continued the traditions of Scandinavian archaeology. Montelius believed, as had the philosophers of the Enlightenment, that technology developed because human beings used their powers of reason to devise more effective ways of coping with nature and thereby make their lives easier and more secure. His references to biological evolution seem to have been intended mainly as analogies that would enhance the status of archaeology in an era dominated by Darwinian evolution. It is significant that not all of Montelius' evolutionary patterns were unilinear. He demonstrated, for example, that during the Bronze Age fibulae (safety pins), which were used to fasten clothing, had been manufactured in Italy as one piece with a coiled spring and in Scandinavia as two pieces with a hinge (Bibby 1956: 180–1). In due course the best features of both types were merged to form a new pan-European variety. Hence he took account of how historical factors as well as logical ones influenced the evolution of material culture.

In the 1880s Montelius developed his typological method and divided the European Bronze Age into six periods. In the following decade he divided the Neolithic into four periods and the Iron Age into ten. While he regarded these periods as applicable to the whole of Europe, he noted considerable regional variation within each one and rejected the idea that all parts of Europe had reached the same stage of development at the same time. Instead he sought to use artifacts which he assumed had been exchanged from one region to another, or copied from more advanced areas, to correlate various periods in different parts of Europe. As a result of the discovery of Mycenaean Greek pottery in historically dated Egyptian sites and Egyptian goods in Greece, it was possible for archaeologists to date the Mycenaean period in Greece to the fifteenth century B.C. Faience beads found across Europe that were presumed to have come from Egypt through the Mycenaean civilization provided a bench-mark calendrical dating for Bronze Age cultures. This correlation also gave rise to what was later called the 'short chronology' of European prehistory (Bibby 1956: 181–2).

Montelius believed that his cultural chronology of European prehistory was derived objectively from the archaeological evidence. Today we are not so certain that presuppositions did not play a significant role in determining his selection of the cross-ties that he used to correlate the chronologies of different parts of Europe. He thought that his chronology indicated that in prehistoric times cultural development had occurred in the Near East and that achievements had been carried from there to Europe by waves of diffusion and migration making their way through the Balkans and Italy. Because of that the level of cultural development in southeastern Europe in prehistoric times was always ahead of that to the north and west and Europe as a whole 'was for long but the pale reflection

24 Bronze Age artifacts arranged according to Montelius' system, 1881

of Eastern civilization'. Montelius became the most distinguished exponent of a diffusionist explanation of European cultural development, the so-called *ex oriente lux* ('light from the east') school (Renfrew 1973a: 36–7).

Montelius' (1899, 1903) interpretation of the development of European civilization required a belief not only in diffusion but also that over long periods innovation tended to occur in particular areas and to diffuse outwards from these areas to peripheries. A similar belief in cultural cores and peripheries played a significant role in Boasian anthropology, together with the age/area assumption, which maintained that more widely distributed traits tended to be older than ones spread over a smaller territory. In general broad natural zones, such as the Great Plains or boreal forests of North America, were seen as constituting the most active spheres of diffusion by American anthropologists. The concepts of cultural cores and age/area were subjected to a withering critique by the anthropologist R. B. Dixon in 1928. In Europe, however, these theoretical assumptions were neither articulated nor criticized so clearly.

Many archaeologists supported Montelius' interpretation of European prehistory. Moreover, the most vocal objections were directed not against his idea of diffusion from a centre of innovation but rather against his claim that this centre was located in the Near East. Many scholars objected to an interpretation that ran counter to European convictions of their own superior creativity and which derived civilization from outside Europe. Carl Schuchardt, Adolf Furtwängler, and other German archaeologists maintained that Mycenaean civilization was the creation of 'Aryan' invaders from the north; while Montelius' thesis was opposed in a more general fashion by scholars such as Matthäus Much (1907) and the French prehistorian Salomon Reinach in his book *Le Mirage oriental* (The Eastern Mirage) (1893) (Sklenář 1983: 145). Overthrowing Montelius' scheme required, however, either ignoring or refuting his chronology, which most impartial prehistorians were convinced was based on sound evidence.

There were, however, non-scientific reasons as well as scientific ones for the support given to Montelius. His diffusionist views clearly accorded with the conservative opinions about human creativeness that were fashionable at the end of the nineteenth century. Tracing the origins of European civilization to the Near

East also appealed to many Christians as a reaffirmation of the biblical view of world history. It further accorded with a biblically based interpretation of history dating from the medieval period that saw successive empires – Babylonian, Persian, Hellenistic Greek, and Roman – transferring the centre of power and creativity westward from the Near East to Europe. Finally, throughout the nineteenth century European powers, especially England and France, had been intervening to an ever greater degree in the political and economic affairs of the Near East (Silberman 1982). A view of prehistory which saw the Western European nations rather than the Arab peoples as the true heirs of the ancient civilizations of the Near East helped to justify Europe's colonial interventions in that region, just as such folk lore justified the European colonization of Africa. This interpretation of early cultural development in the Near East as constituting the origins of European civilization may help to explain why Montelius' arguments were more popular in France and England than in Germany, where interventions in the Near East began only towards the end of the nineteenth century.

Montelius did not subscribe to racial interpretations of human history. Moreover, while he believed that diffusionary processes accounted for the spread of civilization to Europe in prehistoric times, he saw evolutionary ones explaining its origins in the Near East. As the citizen of a geographically peripheral nation whose cultural and academic life was being transformed in the nineteenth century by influences coming principally from Germany, he must have regarded diffusion as a powerful stimulus for change. While he was the first great archaeological innovator to be strongly influenced by a specifically diffusionist view of culture, his position in the debate about human inventiveness was a moderate one and much of his thinking continued in an evolutionist mode.

The concept of culture

In the late nineteenth century a growing preoccupation with ethnicity encouraged the development of the concept of the archaeological culture and of the culture-historical approach to the study of prehistory. Archaeologists in Scandinavia and Central Europe began to draw an explicit analogy between the numerous geographically restricted remains of a distinctive character that they were finding and ethnographic cultures. Kroeber and Kluckhohn (1952) have documented how in the course of the eighteenth century French and German philosophers began to use the French word 'culture', which originally had been applied to agricultural pursuits, to designate human progress and enlightenment (self-cultivation). In Germany the word came to designate the customs of individual societies, especially the cohesive, slowly changing ways of life ascribed to peasant and tribal groups as opposed to the cosmopolitan, rapidly changing 'civilization' of modern urban centres. After 1780 works on *Kulturgeschichte* (culture history) began to proliferate and, beginning in 1843, the German ethnologist Gustav Klemm (1802–67) published ethnographic data in books titled *Allgemeine Cultur-Geschichte der Menschheit* (General Culture History of Humanity) (1843–52). The English ethnologist E. B. Tylor was aware of Klemm's usage as early as 1865 but it was only in *Primitive Culture* (1871) that he adopted the word culture and provided it with its classic definition as 'that complex whole which includes knowledge, belief, art, morals, law, custom, and other capabilities and habits acquired by man as a member of society' (p. 1). From this holistic or processual view of culture it was an easy step to a partitive one of individual cultures as ways of life transmitted by specific peoples from generation to generation, a concept popularized by Ratzel along with diffusionism. In his *Geschichte des Alterthums* (History of Ancient Times), which began to appear in 1884, the historian Eduard Meyer (1855–1930) wrote of Egyptian, Greek, Trojan, and Mycenaean cultures (Meinander 1981: 101). In the works of Heinrich Schliemann and others the terms Aegean, Mycenaean, Minoan, Helladic, and Cycladic distinguished specific Bronze Age civilizations of the eastern Mediterranean (Daniel 1950: 243).

The labelling of geographically and temporally restricted assemblages of prehistoric archaeological material as cultures or civilizations and their identification as the remains of ethnic groups seems to have occurred independently to a number of archaeologists. In Childe's (1935b: 3) view, the concept of the archaeological culture was 'forced' upon Scandinavian, Central European, and Italian archaeologists by the wealth of material that their excavations were revealing for Neolithic and later periods. Yet it is also clear that this generally occurred first in Central Europe and adjacent regions where there had been a longstanding interest in tracing ethnic identities in the archaeological record. As early as 1866 the Norwegian archaeologist Olof Rygh interpreted distinctive spear points and arrowheads found in his country as the products of a particular Stone Age 'culture and people' and by 1871 he had noted the existence of 'two Stone Age cultures and two Stone Age peoples' in Norway (Meinander 1981: 106). A. Götze was referring to the Bandkeramik and other Neolithic cultures in 1891; V. V. Hvojko to the Tripolye culture in 1901; and A. A. Spitsyn to the Fatyanovo culture in 1905 (ibid. 103, 107). In 1908 Raphael Pumpelly, an American geologist turned archaeologist, who was excavating at the stratified site of Anau in Central Asia, used the term culture to distinguish successive levels of occupation at that site, explaining that 'culture' was employed as a synonym for civilization (p. xxxv). In some cases it is possible to trace the process by which specific cultures were recognized. Following the excavations at a Bronze Age cemetery at Únětice in Czechoslovakia, archaeologists began to identify Únětice-like finds in nearby regions and finally organized these to establish a Únětice culture. In a similar manner the proto-Slavic Burgwall-type pottery that the German prehistorian Rudolf Virchow (1821–1902) had defined in Central Europe in 1870 was broadened into the concept of a Burgwall culture (Sklenář 1983: 110).

Kossinna and the culture-historical approach

Despite these diverse beginnings, the concept of the archaeological culture was not defined and systematically applied to the interpretation of archaeological data until Gustaf Kossinna (1858–1931) published *Die Herkunft der Germanen* (The Origin of the Germans) in 1911. Inspired by a fanatical patriotism, Kossinna declared archaeology to be the most national of sciences and the ancient Germans to be the most noble subject for archaeological research. Although he had been trained in philosophy, he turned to archaeology in an effort to ascertain the original homeland of the Indo-European-speaking peoples and hence of the Germans. He was appointed Professor of Archaeology at the University of Berlin and in 1909 founded the German Society for Prehistory, which was soon renamed the Society for German Prehistory to emphasize its nationalistic goals. He attacked fellow-German archaeologists for their interests in classical archaeology and Egyptology, which he implied were evidence of a lack of patriotism, if not a betrayal of the German nation (Sklenář 1983: 148–9). *Die Herkunft der Germanen* was the first systematic exposition of his approach to archaeology, which was a mixture of important theoretical innovations and a fanciful glorification of German prehistory as that of a biologically pure master race. His work helped to reinforce German nationalism and won the favour of conservatives, such as Field Marshal Paul von Hindenburg, and later of the National Socialist movement. Although Kossinna died in 1931, his interpretation of German prehistory became the main component in the curriculum that the Nazi government adopted for teaching prehistory in German schools (Frick 1934). Under the Nazi regime his Society for German Prehistory was renamed the Imperial Union for German Prehistory and a large number of new teaching positions was established for his followers in German universities; while many archaeologists who were politically or racially anathema to the government or who opposed Kossinna's views were dismissed from their positions and had to leave Germany (Sklenář 1983: 159; Fowler 1987).

Despite Germany's imperialistic ambitions dating from before World War I and the Nazis' desire to establish a new world order, German archaeologists produced only an extremely strident version of the nationalist archaeology that more often sought to defend the interests of smaller or weaker ethnic groups. They did not succeed, as Lubbock had done, in creating a truly imperialistic archaeology, based on a vision of what had happened in the past that would serve the interests of their country by winning widespread support abroad. Because of Kossinna's political orientation, it is necessary to maintain an unusual level of objectivity if his positive contributions are to be separated from the pernicious aspects of his work. It should also be remembered that in interpreting archaeological evidence in a way that encouraged Germans to regard Slavs and all other peoples as inferior to themselves and excused aggression against these peoples, Kossinna was not acting differently from the amateur and semi-professional archaeologists who in North America, Africa, and Australia were portraying native peoples as inferior to Europeans. In different ways archaeology in each region reflected racist attitudes that had become widespread in Western civilization in the course of the twentieth century.

Kossinna proposed that from Upper Palaeolithic times onward

the archaeological record of Central Europe could be organized as a mosaic of cultures (*Kulturen* or *Kultur-Gruppe*), the location and contents of which altered over time. On the basis of his belief that cultures are inevitably a reflection of ethnicity, he argued that similarities and differences in material culture correlate with similarities and differences in ethnicity. Hence clearly defined cultural provinces always correlate with major ethnic groups or peoples, such as the Germans, Celts, and Slavs, while individual cultures correspond with tribes, such as the Germanic-speaking Saxons, Vandals, Lombards, and Burgundians. Like many other archaeologists, including Montelius, Kossinna believed that cultural continuity indicated ethnic continuity. Hence he argued that, by mapping the distributions of types of artifacts that were characteristic of specific tribal groups, it would be possible to determine where these groups had lived at different periods in prehistory, a procedure that he called settlement archaeology (*Siedlungsarchäologie*). By this he did not mean the study of habitation sites but rather the delineation of where particular ethnic groups had lived. He believed that by identifying historically known tribal groups with particular archaeological cultures for the early historical period, it would become possible to trace them backwards in time archaeologically. At some point it would no longer be possible to distinguish individual German tribes, since they would not yet have differentiated from each other, but archaeologists could still distinguish between Germans, Slavs, Celts, and other major groups of Indo-Europeans. For still more remote periods it might only be possible to differentiate Indo-Europeans from non-Indo-Europeans. Kossinna was not only the first archaeologist to use the concept of the archaeological culture systematically but also the first to apply the direct historical approach to the study of a large region.

In all of his later writings Kossinna specifically identified cultural and ethnic variations with racial differences. In particular he accepted the commonly held belief that the original Indo-European-speaking peoples and hence the direct ancestors of the Germans were members of the blond, longheaded Nordic (or Aryan) racial group and that racial characteristics were the fundamental determinants of human behaviour. Kossinna also accepted Klemm's distinction between *Kulturvolker*, or culturally creative peoples, and *Naturvolker*, or culturally passive peoples. For him this was a distinction between Indo-Europeans, and above all Germans, and all other peoples. He believed that the Indo-Europeans could be traced back to the early Mesolithic Maglemosian culture found in northern Germany. In particular he traced their origins to the vicinity of Schleswig and Holstein, which Germany had recently annexed from Denmark. By claiming maximum antiquity for the cultural chronology of Germany, he sought to demonstrate that this region had been the centre of cultural development for Europe and the Near East. Late Neolithic flint daggers were interpreted as evidence of a noble German pride in weapons and as prototypes for later bronze ones, while Bronze Age trumpets were construed as evidence of the superior musical ability of the Germans in prehistoric times. In a flight of fantasy he proposed that even the alphabet had a Stone Age European origin rather than a Phoenician one.

Because more advanced cultures were an expression of biological superiority, they could be spread from one region to another only by migrations of people, not by diffusion. Waves of Indo-Europeans were imagined to have migrated south and east, conquering native populations and using them to build civilizations in the Near East, Greece, and Italy. Each of these waves in turn, however, had interbred with local populations and as a result had impaired their creative abilities. Hence even the Indo-European-speaking peoples of ancient Greece and Italy eventually became incapable of sustained cultural creativity. Kossinna argued that because the Germans had stayed in their original homeland they remained the racially purest and therefore the most talented and creative of all the Indo-European peoples. They alone remained capable of carrying out the historical responsibility of creating civilization and imposing it upon inferior peoples. Hence the Germans became the first-born (*Erstgeborenen*) of the Indo-Europeans. Kossinna also viewed archaeology as establishing a historical right to territory. Wherever allegedly German artifacts were found was declared ancient German territory, which modern Germany either held by right or was entitled to win back. The same argument did not, of course, apply to non-German groups, such as the Slavs, who in medieval times had settled as far west as the modern border between East and West Germany (Klejn 1974).

Finally and more positively Kossinna stressed the need to learn as much as possible about how human groups, or at least Germans, had lived in prehistoric times. Cultures were not to be defined simply as artifact assemblages but archaeologists were urged to try to determine the nature of prehistoric life-styles. In his own work, Kossinna paid little attention to archaeological evidence of house types, burial customs, and rituals but based his interpretations on artifacts in museum collections. His speculations about prehistoric German life often were fanciful in the tradition of Stukeley and his latter-day followers. Yet, in its intention, his holistic view of individual archaeological cultures had more in common with the Scandinavian approach to archaeology than it had with 'scientific' archaeology modelled on French and English Palaeolithic studies.

Kossinna's work, for all of its chauvinistic nonsense and its often amateurish quality, marked the final replacement of an evolutionary approach to prehistory by a historical one. By organizing archaeological data for each period of prehistory into a mosaic of archaeological cultures, he sought not simply to document how Europeans had lived at different stages of prehistoric development but also to learn how particular peoples, many of whom could be identified as the ancestors of modern groups, had lived in the past and what had happened to them over time. His approach offered a means to account for the growing evidence of geographical as well as chronological variations in the archaeological record. He must therefore be recognized as an innovator whose work was of major importance for the development of archaeology.

Childe and The Dawn of European Civilization

Yet Kossinna had little direct influence outside the German-speaking countries, no doubt because his chauvinistic interpretations of prehistory were so repellent to other nationalities. The British of the Edwardian period were as proud of their supposed Nordic or Aryan racial affinities as were the Germans. Yet, unlike the Germans, who could trace their ethnic group back into prehistoric times as the sole occupants of most of their modern homeland, the British were keenly aware that England had been conquered and settled in turn by Romans, Saxons, Danes, and Normans. British archaeologists postulated that similar invasions had occurred in prehistoric times. While some English claimed that the prehistoric Celtic peoples were only their predecessors and not their ancestors, most historians argued that what was biologically and culturally most desirable in successive indigenous populations had combined with what was most advanced in invading groups to produce a people whose hybrid vigour, composed of various European stocks, made them the best in the world (Rouse 1972: 71–2). This historical chain of increasing superiority corresponded with a modern regional and ethnic hierarchy within Britain. The dominant upper and upper-middle classes viewed themselves as the spiritual if not the biological heirs of the Normans, while the English as a whole were identified with the earlier Saxons, and the more remote Celtic fringe with the still earlier and more primitive British.

Because of their positive attitude towards foreign influence, British archaeologists were receptive to Montelius' arguments that prehistoric Europe owed much of its cultural development to the Near East. Yet they did not hold his views and those of more Eurocentric archaeologists to be mutually exclusive. One of the two main themes of John Myres' *The Dawn of History* (1911) was the spread of technology from Egypt and Mesopotamia to Europe. The second was his belief that all hierarchical societies developed when politically dynamic, pastoral peoples, such as the Semites and the Indo-Europeans, were forced by drought to leave their homelands and to conquer and rule politically less innovative peasant societies. According to Myres the Indo-Europeans, whom he believed to be nomads from the steppes of Central Asia, were particularly adept at imposing their language, beliefs, and social customs on conquered peoples, while adopting the latter's material culture. Out of the encounter between cultural influences that had been transmitted to Europe from the Near East and Indo-European political skills a vital and distinctive European way of life was created. Similar views were held by Arthur Evans (1896), who was Myres' colleague at Oxford University. Yet, while Myres wrote of peoples in *The Dawn of History*, he did not yet refer to archaeological cultures. Later individual cultures were mentioned by archaeologists such as Myres (1923a, b), Harold Peake (1922), and Cyril Fox (1923) and in *Man and his Past* O. G. S. Crawford (1921: 78–9) discussed geographical methods for delineating their origins, extent, and frontiers. Yet no effort was made to apply the concept of the archaeological culture in a systematic fashion prior to the publication of V. Gordon Childe's (1893–1957) *The Dawn of European Civilization* (1925a). Through this

25 Childe with a party of workmen at Skara Brae, Orkney, 1928–30

book, which Glyn Daniel (1950: 247) has called 'a new starting-point for prehistoric archaeology', the archaeological culture became the working tool of all European archaeologists.

Childe was born in Sydney, Australia in 1893, the son of a conservative Church of England minister. He studied Classics at the University of Sydney, where he became committed to socialist politics. At an early stage he also grew interested, like Kossinna, in locating the homeland of the Indo-European-speaking peoples. He went on to Oxford University where he studied with Myres and Evans. In 1916 he returned to Australia. There he engaged in various left-wing political activities until 1921. Then, disillusioned with politics, he returned to the study of archaeology. His already extensive command of European languages and an acute visual memory enabled him to visit and assemble data from museums and excavations across the whole of Europe. He presented the results of this research in two books: *The Dawn of European Civilization*, which was a synthesis of European prehistory to the end of the Bronze Age, and *The Danube in Prehistory* (1929), a more detailed study of a hitherto little-known region. The theoretical basis of his approach was outlined at the beginning of the latter book.

In *The Dawn of European Civilization* Childe adopted Kossinna's basic concept of the archaeological culture and his identification of such cultures as the remains of prehistoric peoples, while rejecting all of the racist connotations that Kossinna had attributed to them. He combined this concept with Montelius' chronology and the belief that in prehistoric times technological skills had diffused to Europe from their place of origin in the Near East. His interpretations of European prehistory were also influenced by those of Myres and Evans, inasmuch as he stressed the creativity of prehistoric Europeans to a much greater extent than Montelius had done. He defined an archaeological culture, unfortunately with misleading brevity, as 'certain types of remains – pots, implements, ornaments, burial rites, house forms – constantly recurring together' (1929: v–vi). He stressed that each culture had to be delineated individually in terms of constituent artifacts and that cultures could not be defined simply by subdividing the ages or epochs of the evolutionary archaeologists either spatially or temporally. Instead the duration and geographical limits of each culture had to be established empirically and individual cultures aligned chronologically by means of stratigraphy, seriations, and synchronisms. In this way he interpreted the prehistory of the whole of Europe in terms of a complex mosaic of cultures. While this mosaic was approximated using maps and tables in *The Dawn of European Civilization*, a detailed chart showing the chronological and geographical distributions of all the archaeological cultures known in the Danube Valley was published in *The Danube in Prehistory* and a chart by Childe and M. C. Burkitt covering all of Europe appeared in *Antiquity* in 1932. These charts were prototypes for ones that other archaeologists would use to represent regional cultural chronologies around the world.

Most of Childe's cultures were defined on the basis of a small number of diagnostic artifacts. Yet his selection of these artifacts involved a functionalist view of material culture. He argued that the historical significance of different types of artifacts could only be ascertained by considering what role they had played in prehistoric

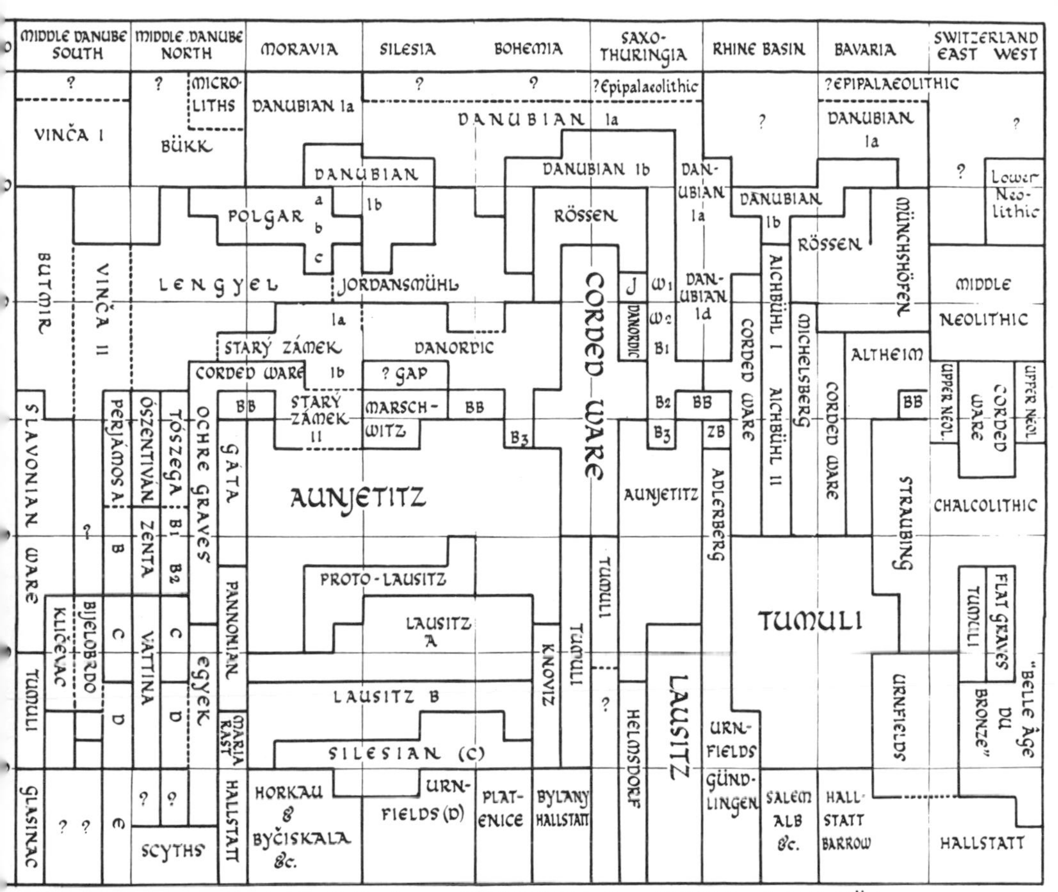

26 Childe's first chart correlating the archaeological cultures of Central Europe, from *The Danube in Prehistory*, 1929

cultures. He decided that home-made pottery, ornaments, and burial rites tended to reflect local tastes and were relatively resistant to change; hence they were useful for identifying specific ethnic groups. On the other hand the marked utilitarian value of tools, weapons, and many other items of technology caused them to diffuse rapidly from one group to another, either as a result of trade or copying. Hence these types of artifacts were especially valuable for assigning neighbouring cultures to the same period and establishing cultural chronologies prior to the invention of radiocarbon dating (Childe 1929: viii, 248; cf. Binford 1983a: 399–400). Childe concluded that this operation supported the same picture of the diffusion of material culture westward across Europe as had emerged from Montelius' work.

While diagnostic artifacts might serve to define an archaeological culture, they did not suffice to describe it. For that purpose every artifact was relevant. Childe was interested in viewing archaeological cultures not simply as collections of traits but also as the means of providing an ethnographic interpretation of how specific groups had lived in prehistoric times. In the first edition of *The Dawn of European Civilization* he attempted to summarize what could be inferred about the way of life associated with each major culture. In later editions, he surveyed each culture more systematically, covering – insofar as this was possible – economy, social and political organization, and religious beliefs (Childe 1939; 1956a: 129–31). How people had lived in the past was a concern that both he and Kossinna shared. When it came to interpreting cultural change Childe had recourse, as Montelius had done, to diffusion and migration, which were both external factors. Cultural continuity was ascribed to the absence of these factors. His approach thus bore a close resemblance to the diffusionist ethnology found in Europe and North America in the 1920s.

The Dawn of European Civilization provided a model that was to be applied to the study of archaeology throughout Europe into the 1950s. It was an approach that Childe, despite his own changing interests, followed closely in his later regional syntheses, such as *The Prehistory of Scotland* (1935a) and *Prehistoric Communities of the British Isles* (1940a). The primary aim of archaeologists who adopted this approach was no longer to interpret the archaeological record as evidence of stages of cultural development. Instead they sought to identify often nameless prehistoric peoples by means of archaeological cultures and to trace their origin, movements, and interaction. The Neolithic period was no longer seen primarily as a stage of cultural development but rather as a mosaic of sharply delineated cultural groups. The questions being addressed were of a particularist, historical variety. There was also a general interest in learning how specific peoples had lived in prehistoric times.

Childe was fully aware of the revolution that he had brought about in archaeology. In 1925 he noted with satisfaction that the clarity with which the migrations of nameless prehistoric peoples stood out in the archaeological record when it was studied as a mosaic of cultures was a revelation to fellow archaeologists (Childe 1925b). He thus distinguished between an older evolutionary archaeology and a new culture-historical approach. He also observed, with reference to the British and French rather than the Scandinavian school, that in the nineteenth century evolutionary archaeologists had become more interested in artifacts than in their makers. He claimed that in constructing evolutionary sequences they had treated artifacts as dead fossils rather than as expressions of living societies (1940a: 3). In his opinion scientific progress had left archaeologists with no alternative but to adopt the concrete methods of history. He was correct in portraying the development of a historical approach to archaeology as a natural and logical progression, to the extent that culture-historical archaeology was equipped, as evolutionary archaeology had not been, to study and try to explain geographical as well as temporal variation in the archaeological record. He was wrong, however, in implying that his method for interpreting the archaeological record was necessarily more objective than evolutionary archaeology. The concept of the archaeological culture, which he had borrowed from Kossinna, and the diffusionist views of Montelius were both closely related to the widely held interpretations of human behaviour that had developed as a reaction against cultural evolutionism in Western Europe beginning in the late nineteenth century. The new culture-historical view of prehistory was as deeply rooted in a pessimistic assessment of cultural change and human creativity as the previous evolutionary view had been rooted in an optimistic one.

Childe, despite his left-wing political radicalism, did not wholly escape the racism that was part of this new outlook. In *The Aryans* (1926) he argued that the Indo-Europeans did not succeed because they possessed a material culture or natural intelligence that was superior to those of other people. Instead they were successful because they spoke a superior language and benefitted from the more competent mentality it made possible. He pointed out that the Greeks and Romans had only a diluted Nordic physical type but that each had realized the high cultural potential that was inherent in their language. This interpretation contrasted with Kossinna's belief that ethnic and racial mixture in these countries had resulted in cultural decline. Yet at the end of *The Aryans* Childe bowed to prevailing racist sentiments by suggesting that the 'superiority in physique' of the Nordic peoples made them the appropriate initial bearers of a superior language (Childe 1926: 211). In later years, as he adopted other explanations for cultural variation, he repudiated these early speculations.

National archaeology

The culture-historical approach, with its emphasis on the prehistory of specific peoples, provided a model for national archaeologies not only in Europe but around the world. It remains the dominant approach to archaeology in many countries. Like nationalist history, to which it is usually closely linked, the culture-historical approach can be used to bolster the pride and morale of nations or ethnic groups. It is most often used for this purpose among peoples who feel thwarted, threatened, or deprived of their collective rights by more powerful nations or in countries where appeals for national unity are being made to counteract serious internal divisions. Nationalist archaeology tends to emphasize the more recent past rather than the Palaeolithic period and draws attention to the political and cultural achievements of indigenous ancient civilizations. There is also, as Daniel Wilson (1876, 1: 247) noted long ago, a tendency to glorify the 'primitive vigour' and creativity of people assumed to be national ancestors rather than to draw attention to their low cultural status.

The political problems and revolutionary changes that overtook China beginning in the nineteenth century produced a renewed interest in historiography. In particular it led to the development of a more critical attitude towards ancient texts (Wang 1985: 184–8). The study of art objects and calligraphy was a long-established part of the Chinese tradition of historiography. Field archaeology developed, however, within the context of the reformist May 4th Movement, which, beginning in 1919, sought to replace traditional literary scholarship with scientific knowledge from the West. There was a receptive audience for geology, palaeontology, and other sciences capable of collecting empirical data from the earth.

The first major archaeological fieldwork was carried out by Western scientists attached to the Geological Survey of China, which had been established in Peking in 1916. The Swedish geologist J. G. Andersson (1934: 163–87) identified the Neolithic Yangshao culture in 1921, while major work at the Palaeolithic site of Zhoukoudian began under the direction of the Canadian anatomist Davidson

Black in 1926 (Hood 1964). The first native Chinese scholar to direct the excavation of an archaeological site was Li Ji (Li Chi) (1896–1979), who had earned a doctorate at Harvard University in 1923. From 1928 to 1937, as first head of the Department of Archaeology in the National Research Institute of History and Philology of Academia Sinica, he dug at the important late Shang site of Yinxu, near Anyang. These excavations, carried out at an early historical site that yielded many inscriptions and works of art, played a major role in training a generation of Chinese archaeologists and also in turning the new science of archaeology into an instrument for studying Chinese history. They also fuelled a resurgence of pride in China's ancient past. This turning towards history is all the more significant in view of Li's training as an anthropologist.

Foreign scholars, such as Andersson, sought to trace the origins of Chinese culture, or at least of major aspects of it, such as the Neolithic painted pottery, back to the Near East, thereby implying that Chinese civilization was derivative from the West. Chinese archaeologists sought the origin of Chinese civilization in the Neolithic Longshan culture, where Western influence seemed less evident. Later they argued that Yangshao and Longshan represented a continuum of development that culminated in Shang civilization (W. Watson 1981: 65–6). Archaeological research was curtailed by the Japanese invasion in 1937 and, following the Communist victory in 1949, many archaeologists, including Li, retreated to Taiwan taking valuable collections with them.

Marxism had begun to influence the study of ancient China as early as 1930 in the writings of Guo Moruo (1892–1978). A writer and revolutionary, Guo was forced to flee to a still relatively liberal Japan in 1927 to escape Chiang Kai-Shek's death squads. During the ten years he lived there he produced a series of studies on ancient inscriptions and the stylistic evolution of bronze artifacts. Unlike Li and his associates, who were primarily interested in art, religion, and ideology, Guo stressed production as the basis of society and interpreted the Shang and Zhou Dynasties as examples of a slave society. More than any other Chinese scholar, Guo sought to place his country in a comparative framework of world history (Wang 1985: 188). After the Communist revolution he became a major figure in Chinese intellectual life. From 1950 until his death in 1978 he was President of the Chinese Academy of Sciences.

After 1949 archaeology became a state-directed activity. Except when the value of any study of the past was challenged by extremists during the Cultural Revolution, archaeology has been supported, as it always has been in the Soviet Union, as an important instrument of political education. This is done in accordance with Mao Zedong's dictum that 'the past should serve the present'. A National Bureau of Cultural Relics administers thousands of provincial and local museums either directly or through provincial and district Bureaus of Culture. Vast amounts of archaeological data have been unearthed throughout China in the course of unprecedented industrial and agricultural development and, because accidental finds now quickly come to the attention of professional archaeologists, information about the past has increased very rapidly (Chang 1981: 168). Within the research divisions of Academia Sinica, Palaeolithic archaeology is separated from the study of the Neolithic and historical periods and attached to the Institute of Vertebrate Palaeontology and Palaeoanthropology. This arrangement may reflect a lack of close identification of the earliest periods of human development with a specifically national history, although there is much pride in the antiquity of China's Palaeolithic record. On a practical level this division reflects the close working relationship among Palaeolithic archaeologists, geologists, and palaeontologists.

In keeping with nationally accepted Marxist tenets, the Chinese past is conceptualized in terms of a unilinear sequence of stages: primitive society, slave society, and feudal society. There is no questioning of this model. So far very little archaeological research has been directed towards examining Marxist theories of social evolution, which would involve the investigation of subsistence systems, settlement patterns, trade, and social and political organization. This may partly reflect the scarcity of well-trained personnel, but it has also been attributed to unpredictable shifts in Chinese government policy, which have discouraged the expression of opinions on topics that are potentially politically sensitive. Instead, archaeological finds are interpreted pragmatically to promote a variety of political goals. They dramatize the cruelty and oppression that characterized life for the Chinese masses under successive royal dynasties, and which contrast with the beneficial social and economic changes that have been the goal of government policy in China since 1949. The great tombs, temples, and other monuments of the past are also interpreted as testimonials to the skill and energy of the workers and artisans who created them. Last, but not least, archaeological finds are used to cultivate national dignity and pride by documenting China's accomplishments over the ages.

Despite a Marxist veneer, Chinese archaeology has continued to display strongly traditional features. It plays a significant role in promoting national unity, as historiography in general did prior to 1949. Until recently the interpretation of the archaeological record accorded with longstanding northern-centred Chinese traditions. Chinese material culture and institutions have been interpreted as first evolving in the Huang-he Valley and gradually spreading from there southward to produce the pan-Chinese culture of the Iron Age. The cultural creativity of other parts of China was thereby minimized. In the past at least one Western archaeologist has been attacked for drawing attention to the sophistication and independent character of the 'provincial' Neolithic and Bronze Age cultures of southern China (W. Watson 1981: 68–9). This Chinese view has been vigorously rejected by Vietnamese archaeologists who see in the Bronze Age Dong-s'on culture of Southeast Asia evidence of a 'deep and solid basis' for a distinctive cultural tradition, which in their own country 'absolutely refused to be submerged by Chinese culture while many other cultures at that time were subjugated and annihilated' (Van Trong 1979: 6). It has remained for scholars working outside China to identify the distinctive cultural characteristics and early development of central and southern China (Meacham 1977).

Western-style field archaeology was introduced into Japan even earlier than into China by American and European natural scientists and physicians who were hired to teach there, especially after the Meiji revolution of 1868, when the new government determined to catch up with advances in Western science, technology, and medicine. The most important of these visitors was the American zoologist Edward Morse (1838–1925), who had participated in shell-mound research in the eastern United States. He identified and excavated the shell mound at Omori in 1877. While none of his students became professional archaeologists, he interested some of them in doing archaeological research. Ikawa-Smith (1982: 299) points out that the leading Japanese archaeologists of the late nineteenth and early twentieth centuries were trained in geology, zoology, or medicine and that many of them had studied in Europe or America. Hence their backgrounds were similar to those of the self-trained or informally trained professional archaeologists in the West during the nineteenth century.

Although Morse was an evolutionist, the Japanese archaeologists who followed him had more in common with the European culture-historical archaeologists of the late nineteenth century. The first generation of Japanese professional archaeologists was led by Tsuboi Shogoro (1863–1913). In 1884 he and several other science students established the Anthropological Society of Tokyo and nine years later he was appointed Professor of Anthropology at the University of Tokyo. He conceived of anthropology, in the continental European fashion, as a branch of zoology interested in human physical remains and regarded archaeological evidence as clues for identifying racial groups. He specialized in the study of the Mesolithic Jomon period and by the 1930s had established a general chronology for it.

In 1895 historians working at the Imperial Museum (today the Tokyo National Museum) founded the Archaeological Society. It had closer links with pre-Meiji antiquarian scholarship than did the Anthropological Society of Tokyo. Its aims were to study the 'archaeology of our country, with the view to throwing light on customs, institutions, culture and technologies in the successive periods of our national history' (Ikawa-Smith 1982: 301). These scholars concentrated on the late prehistoric Yayoi and the protohistoric Kofun periods and had a special interest in fine art, as exemplified by bronze mirrors and weapons.

Japanese archaeologists of all schools continued to pursue a culture-historically oriented archaeology, which did not preclude an interest in understanding 'the outline of human development and regularities of social transformations' (Ikawa-Smith 1982: 302). Political pressures, particularly those associated with efforts to promote national unity by stressing the veneration of the emperor as the descendant of the gods and the divinely appointed head of the Japanese national family, impeded archaeological development at certain periods. Government regulations issued in 1874 and 1880 made it difficult to excavate large burial mounds, especially ones identified as possible tombs of the royal family. Such excavations were carried out in the politically relaxed atmosphere of the 1920s.

At this time some historians also published Marxist interpretations of Japanese history in which archaeological data were used. From the nineteenth century onwards, however, most archaeologists were careful not to contradict officially sponsored accounts of ancient Japanese history based on the *Kojiki*, *Nihon Shoki*, and other chronicles recorded in the eighth century A.D. The primitive Jomon culture, which was dated prior to 1500 B.C. and therefore antedated the events described in these accounts, was ascribed to the Ainu by the anatomist Kogenei Yoshikiyo and to a pre-Ainu people by Morse and Tsuboi, but was not considered to be ancestral to the modern Japanese. Either interpretation justified the late-nineteenth-century colonization of the island of Hokkaido, where the Ainu lived, by representing it as the continuation of a historical expansion of the Japanese people northward through the Japanese archipelago (Fawcett 1986). In the ultra-nationalist atmosphere of the 1930s it became extremely dangerous to engage in any research that even inadvertently might cast doubt on Shinto myths concerning the divine origin of the royal family. Those involved in such activities risked removal from their posts and even imprisonment. As a result of these pressures physical anthropologists and linguists avoided discussions of ethnicity, while archaeologists concentrated on elaborating artifact typologies and did not engage in discussions of cultural change that could have any bearing on the official version of history.

Since World War II archaeological activities have increased enormously in Japan. Japanese archaeologists are proud of the technical excellence of their work and strive to advance their understanding of culture-history and chronology. The vast majority of them are interested in studying material remains within Japan from the perspective of national history. Public interest in archaeology is high, surveys and rescue work mandatory, and archaeological finds are widely exhibited to the public (Tanaka 1984). Archaeology has provided a view of the development of the Japanese nation, people, and culture that has helped to fill the ideological vacuum left after the militarist defeat in World War II. For many Japanese, archaeological finds provide tangible contact with the past and help to reinforce a sense of stability in a period of great social and cultural change and uncertainty. In particular, archaeological research and popular accounts of archaeology are characterized by a fascination with the origin of the Japanese people and culture. There is a growing tendency to trace the Japanese as an ethnic group as far back as the Jomon or even the Palaeolithic periods (Fawcett 1986). The theory that the Japanese ruling class came as conquerors from the Asian mainland during the Yayoi period, which was advanced in the wake of Japanese militarism in the 1940s, has also been abandoned. Nevertheless a traditional pattern continues of portraying the Japanese ruling elite as the patrons of new influences, such as writing, bureaucracy, and Buddhism, which entered the country from Korea and China. This view relates class to history in a way that resembles interpretations offered by nationalistic historians and prehistorians in England in the late nineteenth and early twentieth centuries.

In Mexico the past was an object of political manipulation even before the Spanish conquest in 1519 (Carrasco 1982). Following the conquest the Spanish attempted as far as possible to eliminate non-Christian religious beliefs and traditional political loyalties by discouraging an interest in Mesoamerican history and culture (Diehl 1983: 169). During the struggles preceding Mexican independence in 1821, Spanish officials continued to discourage the study of the pre-hispanic period, but creoles turned to it as a source of inspiration and national identity. In the nineteenth century the conservatives among the ruling elite regarded the study of this period as a worthless preoccupation with barbarism, while liberals supported it as the investigation of a significant period of Mexico's national history (Lorenzo 1981). The national revolution of 1910 was successful largely as a result of armed support by peasants, who were mainly Indians and who constituted a majority of the population. The revolution resulted in major changes in government policy towards these people. The injustices of the colonial period were acknowledged and far-reaching economic and social reforms were promised. The government also undertook to integrate Indians into national life and to heighten their sense of self-respect by encouraging the study of Mexico's rich pre-hispanic heritage and making its findings an integral part of Mexican history. In this way the government also sought to assert Mexico's cultural distinctiveness to the rest of the world (Gamio 1916). Large sums of money were allocated for archaeological instruction and research. A Department of Anthropology was established in 1937 at the National Polytechnical School, which had as one of its duties to train archaeologists. It later became part of the National Institute of Anthropology and History, which was granted an absolute monopoly to license archaeological excavations throughout Mexico.

While this Institute and Mexican archaeology as a whole have been influenced by trends in United States archaeology, they have maintained a strongly historicist orientation. Archaeologists see it as their duty to provide Mexicans with a past of their own, which promotes national integration through the formation of a historical perspective that can be shared by all elements in the population. This requires the humanization and popularization of prehistory. An important aspect of this policy has been the creation of large public museums and the development of major archaeological sites as open-air museums for the entertainment and instruction of Mexicans and foreign visitors alike (Lorenzo 1981, 1984). Within this common framework there are striking divergences in the interpretation of archaeological data, some of which have clearly political connotations. These run the gamut from various types of Marxism on the one hand to varying degrees of commitment to North American positivism on the other. The political uses of archaeology have been accompanied by an underfunding of scientifically oriented research. As a result many of the most important long-term research projects have been carried out by foreign archaeologists.

Archaeological research in India began in a colonial setting and for a long time remained remote from traditional Indian scholarship. European travellers began to note ancient monuments as early as the sixteenth century and systematic scholarly interest in these monuments dates from about 1750. This interest was stimulated by the realization that Sanskrit and the modern languages of northern India that are descended from it were related to the major languages of Europe; hence studying India might be relevant for understanding ancient Indo-European culture. Amateur British archaeologists began to examine megaliths, Buddhist stupas, and other archaeological sites with some regularity, while the Archaeological Survey of India, first established in 1861, published an immense amount of research under directors such as Alexander Cunningham (1861–5), John Marshall (1902–31), who discovered the Indus Valley civilization, and Mortimer Wheeler (1944–8). Wheeler trained many Indian students in modern field methods and encouraged several

Indian universities to begin offering instruction in archaeology. Yet, while India owes the introduction of archaeology to British rule, Lallanji Gopal (1985: i) has observed that the 'glorious cultural heritage, which was unearthed by archaeologists . . . aroused the self-confidence of the Indian people [and] was one of the major factors contributing to the Indian renaissance, which ultimately ushered in independence'. Chakrabarti (1982: 335) notes that, by the time John Marshall began to excavate, the outlines of ancient Indian history and culture had been established from textual and art-historical sources. Yet the historical image of ancient India remained shadowy. His excavations of sites of the Buddhist period in the Ganges Valley and the northwest enlivened this crucial phase in the development of India in the Indian cultural consciousness and hence contributed to the growth of nationalism.

The ties between archaeology and history were made easier by close similarities between the culture-historical approach in archaeology and the newly emerging Indian historiography. Historians tended to think in terms of different racial groups and viewed the past as a series of migrations of peoples who brought innovations into India but eventually were absorbed into the Indian way of life. By labelling the Indus civilization as pre-Vedic and attributing its destruction to Aryan invaders, archaeologists made prehistory conform to the established pattern of Indian historical interpretation (Chakrabarti 1982: 339).

Archaeology has made significant progress in India since Independence in 1947. It is well-established in universities and much research is carried out each year (Thapar 1984). Yet, while Indian archaeologists keep abreast of world-wide trends in their discipline and are more attracted by American anthropological archaeology than are Japanese or Chinese researchers (Jacobson 1979; Paddayya 1983; Lal 1984), archaeology remains closely linked to the study of ancient history. Many Indian archaeologists are content to attach ethnic and linguistic labels to newly discovered cultures and to interpret them in a general, descriptive fashion. It remains to be seen how, as research of a processual nature becomes more familiar to Indian archaeologists, they will relate it to this orthodox historical framework.

Archaeology was also introduced to the Near East by Europeans, who developed local institutions for research and teaching under *de facto*, if not official, colonial regimes. In particular, Western scholars were attracted to Egypt, Iraq, and Palestine by the remains of ancient civilizations that were of special interest to Europeans because they were mentioned in the Bible. On the other hand, local attitudes toward archaeology have been coloured by a traditionally negative view of pre-Islamic times as an age of religious ignorance. In Egypt the indigenous middle class displayed considerable interest in Pharaonic civilization within the context of secular nationalism that prevailed in the early part of the twentieth century. This interest expressed itself in strenuous efforts to ensure that Egyptians controlled the archaeological work being done in their country and that Egyptian scholars were involved in it (J. Wilson 1964: 159–77). The late Shah of Iran sought to emphasize the pre-Islamic glories of his country and in particular to identify his regime with the ancient Persian monarchy. This included a magnificent celebration of the supposed 2,500th anniversary of the ancient Persian kings at the ruins of their palace in Persepolis in 1971. In the face of growing difficulties with neighbouring Islamic, and in some cases also Arab, states the Iraqi government has likewise paid increasing attention to their country's distinctive Babylonian heritage. On the other hand, interest in pre-Islamic times declined rapidly in Egypt following the overthrow of the monarchy and the coming to power of the Gamal Abdul Nasser regime, which promoted a pan-Arab rather than a specifically Egyptian sense of identity. Likewise in Iran the overthrow of the Shah brought to power a strongly Islamic government that discouraged identification with pre-Islamic times both on religious grounds and because of the symbolic associations between ancient Persia and the recent monarchy. Throughout the Near East there is increasing emphasis on Islamic archaeology as research comes to be controlled by and carried out by local scholars (Masry 1981).

In modern Israel archaeology plays the very different role of affirming the links between a recently arrived population and its own ancient past. By providing a sense of concrete reality to biblical traditions, it heightens national consciousness and strengthens the claims of Israeli settlers to the land they are occupying. In particular, Masada, the site of the last Zealot resistance to the Romans in A.D. 73, has become a monument possessing great emotional and ceremonial value as a symbol of the will to survive of the new Israeli state. Its excavation was one of the most massive archaeological projects undertaken by Israeli archaeologists and received a vast amount of publicity.

A strong biblical emphasis in Israeli and still earlier Palestinian archaeology has 'helped to create an individual discipline measurably unaffected by methodological and intellectual developments elsewhere' (Hanbury-Tenison 1986: 108). Most Israeli archaeologists are trained in historical and biblical research and devote much time to studying history, philology, and art history. Palaeolithic archaeology is much less important and the influence of anthropological-style archaeology has generally been limited to encouraging the use of technical aids in the analysis of data. Relatively little attention is paid to the archaeology of the Christian and Islamic periods (Bar-Yosef and Mazar 1982). While most Israelis view archaeological research as playing a positive role in their society, some ultra-conservative religious groups oppose it on the grounds that it disturbs ancient Hebrew burials (Paine 1983).

The decolonization of sub-Saharan Africa has accelerated the changes in the archaeology of that region that had begun in the late colonial period. Posnansky (1982: 355) has pointed out that African archaeologists and historians are not necessarily interested in the same problems as foreign scholars. They are more concerned with recent prehistory and with problems of national history than with Palaeolithic archaeology. Topics of interest include the origin of specific states, the development of trade, the evolution of historically attested social and economic institutions, and relations among ethnic groups that live within the boundaries of modern African states (Tardits 1981; Andah 1985). There is also an interest in the study and preservation of major sites that relate to pre-colonial African history. While archaeology is seen as a means of increasing awareness of, and pride in, Africa's past, there is political concern about how the presentation of archaeological findings may enhance national unity or promote regional and local self-awareness (Nzewunwa 1984). While African archaeologists, who are often tied to administrative positions, generally welcome research by anthropologically trained colleagues from abroad, anthropology as a discipline is not well regarded. Across Africa archaeology is becoming increasingly aligned with history, just as ethnological studies are being redefined as sociology (Ki-Zerbo 1981). As a result of this realignment, as well as a growing involvement with the study of oral traditions and historical linguistics, history is now equipped to investigate periods for which few or no written records are available. It thus becomes African rather than colonial in its orientation (D. McCall 1964; Ehret and Posnansky 1982). By actively participating in this process, African archaeology is transformed from being colonial to national in character.

In Europe the cruder and more obvious relationships between archaeological interpretation and nationalism tended to disappear after World War II, as growing political and economic cooperation and a generally improving standard of living led to a decline in nationalism. In recent years this has promoted a growing awareness of how fundamentally different prehistoric European cultures were from modern ones and has encouraged archaeologists once again to rely on ethnographic studies of non-European cultures to interpret their data. The result has been a growing *rapprochement* between Western European (especially British) and American archaeology. Yet archaeological interpretation continues to be influenced in various ways by political issues (Gjessing 1968). In countries such as Greece, Poland, and to a lesser degree Italy, where various grievances still nurture nationalism, archaeology continues to be valued as a chronicle of past glories and a source of hope for the future. In Scandinavia a dedication to peace and social welfare is accompanied by a whimsical fascination with the Viking period, which is conceptualized as violent, wanton, and romantic in contrast to the present. In the 1970s, 20 to 25 per cent of all archaeological publications were devoted to these 300 years (Moberg 1981: 215). In England, however, the discovery that during the Dark Ages the Viking settlement at York was a centre of manufacturing and trade has confirmed to northerners that their region was culturally as advanced as southern England, contrary to establishment history which portrays Saxon Wessex as an outpost of civilization valiantly resisting the incursions of barbarous Scandinavians who eventually settled in the north (Graham-Campbell and Kidd 1980). The revelation, as a result of the excavations at Wood Quay, that in the Dark Ages Dublin was a major Viking centre, while exciting great public interest, accords less well with a Celtocentric nationalist view of Irish history (Sheehy 1980).

As the role of Europe, and in particular that of Britain, as a centre of world power has declined, new views of European prehistory have replaced those formulated by Childe in the 1920s. Colin Renfrew (1973a), in particular, has played a major role in discrediting the Montelius–Childe diffusionary model of European prehistory, once again emphasizing the technological superiority of Europe in prehistoric times. He has used calibrated radiocarbon dates to argue that metallurgy developed in Europe independently and as early as it did in the Near East and that megalithic structures were being erected in Malta and Western Europe prior to any monumental constructions in the Near East. Renfrew views European prehistory in much the same way that Montelius' Eurocentric opponents did in the late nineteenth century. Although his interpretations are conceived in terms of a neo-evolutionary perspective that affirms the creativity of all human groups, no specific explanation is offered for the precociousness of European culture, which thus appears to be taken for granted.

There has also been a resurgence of popular interest in Britain's rich assemblage of megalithic circles and alignments as evidence that highly skilled engineers and 'astronomer priests' lived there in prehistoric times. As a result of Renfrew's new 'long chronology', the scientific knowledge encoded in these monuments is interpreted as being of indigenous rather than exotic origin. On these grounds some scholars assert that Britain has been a centre of scientific achievement since the Neolithic period (Ellegård 1981; Fowler 1987). It thus appears that the decline of Britain as a world power has produced at least a minor nationalist reaction. This has been accompanied by a more widespread resurgent emphasis on economic dynamism, equality before the law, and the sharing of political power as exclusive features of Western civilization (Wells 1984; Gosden 1985; Lamberg-Karlovsky 1985b; Willey 1985).

Culture-historical archaeology in North America

In the United States a culture-historical approach was adopted soon after 1910 as a response to growing familiarity with the archaeological record. Continuing research revealed temporal changes that could not be explained by the simple replacement of one group of people by another. As a result of the first confirmed Palaeo-Indian finds, which date from the 1920s, it also became evident that native people had lived in North America far longer than most archaeologists had hitherto believed (Willey and Sabloff 1980: 121–3). These observations were interpreted in the context of general developments in American anthropology. Boasian anthropology had popularized the concept of the ethnographic culture as a basic unit of study and of diffusion as a major cause of cultural change. In addition Boas' persuasive advocacy of cultural relativism and his strong opposition to racism encouraged the view that Indians were capable of change. Yet, while he had some interest in archaeology, which he actively promoted in Mexico (ibid. 84–5), there is no evidence that he introduced the European concept of the archaeological culture to the United States. On the contrary, the way in which this concept developed in North America and the fact that it was used prior to any formal definition in Europe suggest an independent origin. Both the European and the American version had their roots in the ethnology of Friedrich Ratzel.

We have already noted that during the nineteenth century American archaeologists became increasingly aware of geographically circumscribed cultural manifestations in the archaeological record, especially in the central United States, where a concern with the Moundbuilders had led to much archaeological activity. In 1890 G. P. Thruston defined a prehistoric Stone Grave 'race' in Tennessee, which he believed was the remains of a single tribe or a group of related tribes (pp. 5, 28). The term culture was first applied to groups of sites containing distinctive artifact assemblages in the Ohio Valley. By 1902 William C. Mills had distinguished the Fort Ancient and Hopewell cultures. In 1909 W. K. Moorehead identified the Glacial Kame culture and soon after H. C. Shetrone (1920) was noting more such units in that area. These archaeological cultures differed from European or later American ones inasmuch as they remained primarily geographical entities. It was, for example, not until 1936 that the Hopewell culture was securely dated earlier than the Fort Ancient one.

In 1913 the American ethnologist Berthold Laufer (1913: 577) correctly diagnosed the most serious shortcoming of American archaeology as being its lack of chronological control. This was a problem that American archaeologists had already recognized and begun to remedy. Stratigraphic excavations had been undertaken with increasing frequency since the 1860s but for a long time this technique was not used regularly even though it was recognized that important conclusions flowed from it, such as Richard Wetherill's demonstration that the Basketmaker culture had preceded the more sedentary Pueblo one in the American Southwest (Kidder 1924: 161). On somewhat speculative typological grounds Adolf Bandelier in the 1880s and Edgar Lee Hewett in 1904 attempted to work out a rough chronology of prehistoric Pueblo sites (Schwartz 1981). Work of this sort was, however, only a beginning. Willey and Sabloff (1980: 83) state that American archaeologists were mainly concerned with chronology only between 1914 and 1940.

In 1913 archaeologists began to study the cultural chronology of the Southwest in a systematic fashion. Nels C. Nelson (1875–1964) (1916) and Alfred V. Kidder (1885–1963) carried out extensive stratigraphic excavations. Nelson had observed and participated in excavations at Palaeolithic sites in France and Spain, and still earlier, as a student in California, he had dug stratified shell mounds under the direction of Max Uhle. Kidder had taken a course in field methods at Harvard University with the Egyptologist George Reisner (1867–1942), who was one of the best excavators of the early twentieth century. In 1916 and 1917 A. L. Kroeber and Leslie Spier used seriation techniques to determine the chronological ordering of sites in the Zuñi region from which they had surface-collected potsherds. Spier went on to excavate Zuñi sites stratigraphically and to compare the results of both techniques.

In his *An Introduction to the Study of Southwestern Archaeology* Kidder (1924) attempted the first culture-historical synthesis of the archaeology of any part of the United States. This study was published one year before Childe's *The Dawn of European Civilization*. In it Kidder discussed the archaeological material from nine river drainages in terms of four successive periods, or stages, of cultural development: Basket Maker, Post-Basket Maker, Pre-Pueblo, and Pueblo. Each period was sometimes called a culture, while the regional variants associated with individual river drainages were also designated as Chihuahua Basin culture, Mimbres culture, and Lower Gila culture. Although the term culture had not yet acquired a standard meaning in the Southwest, as a result of chronological studies supplementing a knowledge of geographical variation, something approaching the concept of an archaeological culture was now evolving.

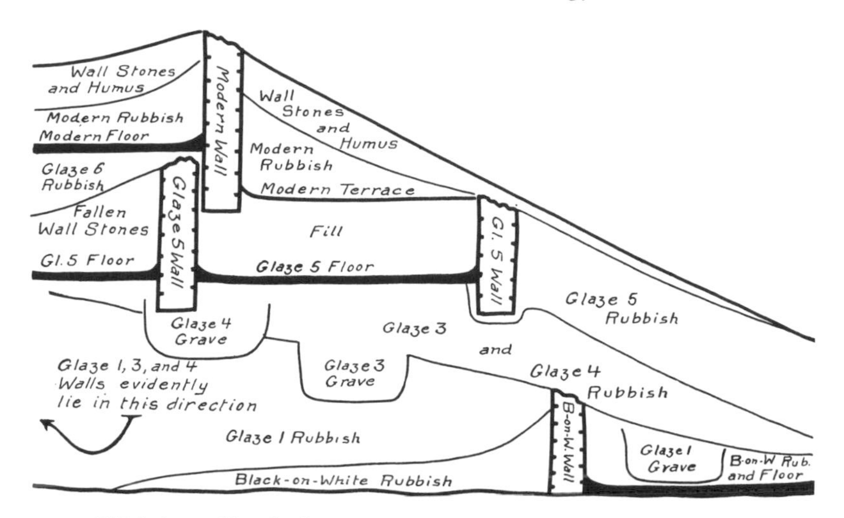

27 Kidder's profile of refuse stratigraphy and construction levels at Pecos Ruin, New Mexico, from *An Introduction to the Study of Southwestern Archaeology*, 1924

Yet what interested other archaeologists most about Kidder's work was his chronology. At the first Pecos Conference, held in 1927, the archaeologists who were working in the area adopted a general classificatory scheme made up of three Basketmaker periods followed by five Pueblo ones. H. S. Gladwin complained, however, that among its other shortcomings the Pecos classification was better suited to the northern Pueblo area of the Southwest than to more southerly regions, where quite different cultures were found. In a paper entitled 'A method for designation of cultures and their variations' (1934), he and his wife Winifred proposed a hierarchical classification of cultural units for the region, the most general of which were three roots called Basketmaker (later Anasazi), Hohokam, and Caddoan (later Mogollon). Each of these roots, which were found in the northern, southern, and intervening mountainous areas of the Southwest, was subdivided into stems, that were named after regions, and these in turn into branches and phases that were given more specific geographical names. Some phases could follow one another in the same locality and each one was defined as a set of sites with a high degree of similarity in artifact types. While the Gladwin classificatory hierarchy was based on relative degrees of trait similarities, its dendritic pattern involved geographical considerations and it was implicitly chronological; roots formed before stems and stems before branches. Willey and Sabloff (1980: 105) observe that the system implies that the prehistoric cultures of the southwestern United States had become increasingly differentiated through time, which 'while a possibility, was by no means demonstrated'.

A similar but even more influential scheme was proposed in 1932, under the leadership of W. C. McKern (1939), by a group of archaeologists working in the midwestern United States. The Midwestern Taxonomic Method was soon applied throughout the central and eastern United States. It was used to classify large amounts of material that had been collected by amateur archaeologists in a region where few stratified sites representing occupations over long periods of time were known. The Midwestern Taxonomic Method proposed to classify these finds on the basis of formal criteria alone. Yet, while its authors denied that the system had historical implictions (Rouse 1953: 64), they generally acted on the assumption that cultural differences in a single locality indicated temporal differences, while similar cultures distributed over large areas dated from the same period (Snow 1980: 11). Artifact assemblages representing a single period of occupation at a site were called a component; components sharing an almost identical set of artifact types were assigned to the same focus; foci with 'a preponderating majority of traits' to the same aspect; aspects sharing only more general characteristics to the same phase; and phases sharing a few broad traits to the same pattern. The traits used to define a pattern were said to be 'a cultural reflection of the primary adjustments of peoples to environment, as defined by tradition'. The patterns that were identified were Woodland, characterized by semi-sedentary sites, cordmarked pottery, and stemmed or sidenotched projectile points; Mississippian, with sedentary sites, incised pottery, and small triangular points; and Archaic, which lacked pottery but contained ground slate artifacts.

Foci and aspects were defined by drawing up lists of artifact types for each component and seeing how many types different components had in common. This approach corresponded with the historical particularist conception, championed by Boas, which viewed cultures not as integrated systems but as collections of individual traits that had come together as the result of historical accidents. No inferences about human behaviour were included in these definitions nor was any attention paid, as Childe had done, to the functional significance of different classes of artifacts or to the ecological significance of what was being found. Quantitative comparison of different classes of artifacts was neglected in favour of simply noting the presence or absence of artifact types. Changing frequencies of types were not seen as having chronological or functional significance. Neither was attention paid to the fact that artifacts that were stylistically highly variable, such as pottery, often were divided into more types than were stone or bone ones. It was recognized, however, that cemeteries and habitation sites belonging to the same culture might contain a different selection of artifact types. Because of this, some archaeologists proposed to base foci on a range of sites representing the complete cultural manifestations of a people, rather than on components (McKern 1939: 310–11). It was argued that these considerations, as well as the incompleteness of archaeological data, precluded specific percentages from being used to establish degrees of relationship among components. Yet it was maintained that 'quantitative similarity', as measured by the percentage of shared artifact types, was important for determining the classificatory status of archaeological manifestations.

Both the Gladwin system and the Midwestern Taxonomic Method eschewed the term culture, which McKern (1939: 303) believed was used by archaeologists to designate too broad a range of phenomena. Nevertheless these two systems initiated systematic use of cultural units for classifying archaeological data in the United States, in the guise of the Gladwins' phases and McKern's foci and aspects. These units were seen as the archaeological equivalent of a tribe or group of closely related tribes. Their dendritic schemes implied that cultures, like biological species, differentiated along irreversible paths, thereby ignoring the convergence brought about by diffusion. In both cases shared traits were assumed to signify common origins, history, and ethnicity. It was also believed that more generally shared traits were older than more culturally specific ones, a fallacy that even in the 1930s would have made the Coca-Cola bottle older than the Acheulean handaxe. This viewpoint had some bad effects on the interpretation of archaeological data. For example, in New York State McKern's Woodland pattern embraced prehistoric cultures that archaeologists traditionally had associated with Algonkian-speakers, while his Mississippian pattern embraced the historical cultures of the linguistically unrelated Iroquoians. The assumption that cultures could not evolve from one pattern to another, any more than an Algonkian language could change into an Iroquoian one, severely hindered the realization that the historical Iroquoian cultures had developed from local Middle Woodland antecedents (MacNeish 1952). In this respect, the Midwestern Taxonomic Method, while struggling for classificatory objectivity and quantitative precision, perpetuated the pessimistic views about the Indians' capacity to change that had characterized American archaeology during the nineteenth century.

Yet in practice this weakness was of short duration. Phases and foci were soon being arranged to form local chronologies by means of stratigraphy and seriation, as was being done with cultures in Europe. As this happened, the higher levels of the American classificatory schemes were abandoned and archaeological cultures were viewed as forming mosaics, in which each unit had its own empirically defined spatial and temporal limits. Cultures, as well as artifact types, were viewed as persisting, possibly with slow modifications, to form traditions, or spreading geographically to create cultural horizons, which were one of the devices used to align traditions chronologically. These concepts were systematized by G. R. Willey and Philip Phillips in *Method and Theory in American Archaeology* (1958). As regional cultural chronologies were constructed, the dendritic view of cultural development became untenable and archaeologists began to credit diffusion with playing a significant role in bringing about cultural change. Yet diffusion was employed mechanically. Most archaeologists paid little attention to understanding the internal dynamics of change or trying to determine why a particular innovation did or did not diffuse from one group to another. By 1941 enough data had been collected for James A. Ford and G. R. Willey to present a synthesis of the culture history of eastern North America in which the known cultures were grouped to form five stages of development: Archaic, Burial Mound I (Early Woodland), Burial Mound II (Middle Woodland), Temple Mound I (Early Mississippian), and Temple Mound II (Late Mississippian). Each stage was viewed as coming from the south, and ultimately in some general form from Mesoamerica, and then spreading north through the Mississippi Valley. Thus an interpretation of eastern North American prehistory was created that resembled that presented for prehistoric Europe in *The Dawn of European Civilization*.

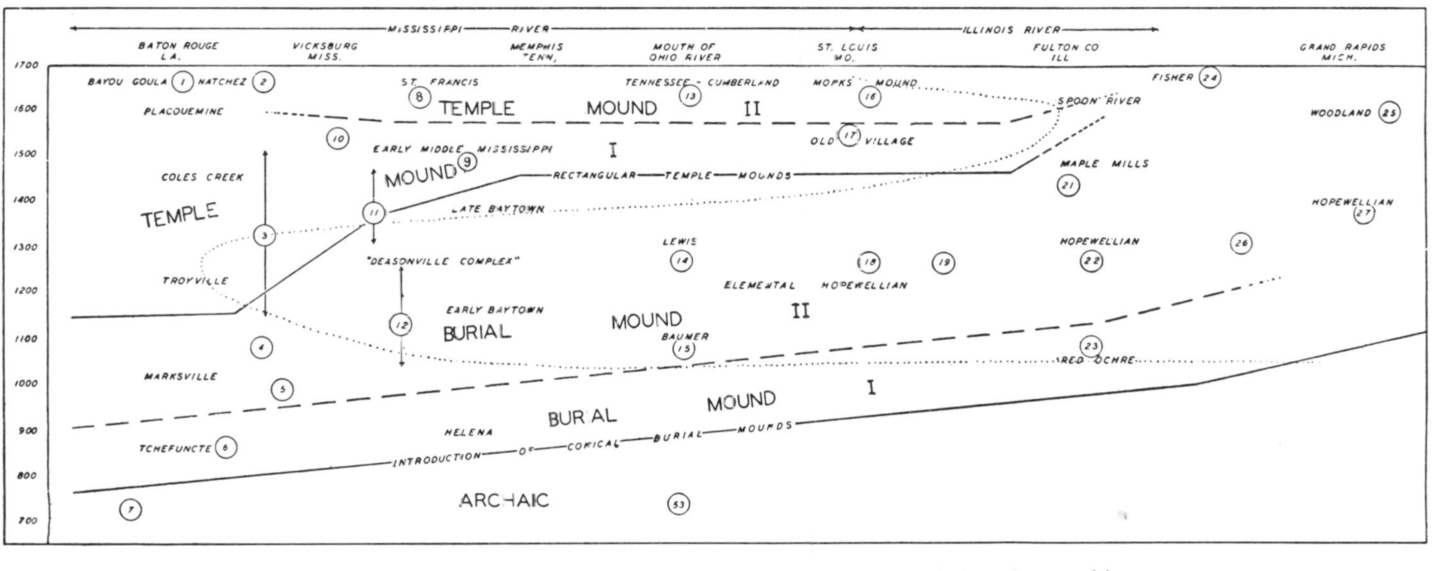

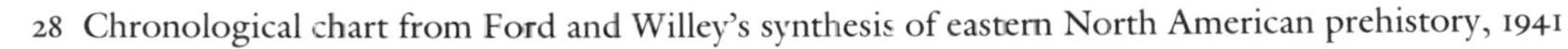

28 Chronological chart from Ford and Willey's synthesis of eastern North American prehistory, 1941

While diffusion implied a greater capacity for native cultures to change than had hitherto been recognized, diffusionist explanations were employed in a very conservative fashion. New ideas, such as pottery, burial mounds, metal working, and agriculture were almost always assigned an East Asian or Mesoamerican origin (Spinden 1928; McKern 1937; Spaulding 1946), thus implying that native North Americans were imitative rather than creative. Moreover, archaeologists still tended to attribute major changes in the archaeological record to migrations. For example, into the 1950s the transitions from the Archaic to the Woodland pattern and from Woodland to Mississippian in the northeastern United States were interpreted as resulting from the entry of new populations into that region. As had happened in Europe, theories of cultural change and chronologies became linked to form a closed system of interpretation. A very short chronology was adopted in which late Archaic cultures, that are now radiocarbon dated around 2500 B.C., were placed no earlier than A.D. 300 (Ritchie 1944). This short chronology reflected the belief that major changes had occurred as a result of migrations. Yet, so long as it was accepted, it discouraged archaeologists from considering internal developments as an alternative explanation of cultural change in this area.

With the notable exception of Ford and Willey (1941), interpretations of archaeological data were characterized by a lack of will to discover, or even to search for, any overall pattern or meaning to North American prehistory. Only a tiny portion of the most ambitious synthesis produced during the culture-historical period, P. S. Martin, G. I. Quimby, and Donald Collier's *Indians Before Columbus* (1947), was devoted to interpreting rather than describing the archaeological record. The authors concluded that from the arrival of the first Asian immigrants 'there existed a continuous process of adaptation to local environments, of specialization, and of independent invention' that 'led to the development of a series of regional Indian cultures' (p. 520). Yet they believed that the two innovations they selected as representing basic trends of cultural development, pottery making and agriculture, were of external origin. While the book documented change as a basic feature of North American prehistory, it made little effort to explain that change. Kidder was a rare exception to a diffusionist perspective when he maintained in 1924 that the prehistoric southwestern United States owed little more than the 'germ' of its culture to the outside and that its development had been a local and almost wholly independent one that was cut short by the 'devastating blight of the white man's arrival' (1962: 344). In this, as in much else, Kidder was an innovator.

American archaeology did not remain a passive victim of the stereotypes of Indians as being incapable of change that had dominated it throughout the nineteenth century. Yet, while cultural change and development were perceived for the first time as being a conspicuous feature of the archaeological record for North America in the decades after 1914, the main product of this period was a series of regional chronologies. While overtly racist views about native people were abandoned, the stereotypes of the American Indian that had been formulated before 1914 remained largely unchallenged. Major changes documented in the archaeological record continued to be attributed to migration and diffusion was only grudgingly admitted to indicate creativity on the part of North American Indians. Because there was less concern than previously with reconstructing prehistoric patterns of life, the links between archaeology and ethnology, as well as between archaeologists and native people, were weakened. No alternative links were formed and to a large degree American archaeology came to be preoccupied with typologies of artifacts and cultures and working out cultural chronologies.

American archaeologists did not simply adopt a culture-historical approach from European ones but reinvented much of it, as increasing knowledge of chronological variations in the archaeological record supplemented an older awareness of geographical variations. The culture-chronological approach developed differently in Europe, where a growing sense of geographical variation in the archaeological record complemented a longstanding evolutionary preoccupation with chronological variation (Trigger 1978a: 75–95). Yet American archaeology did not, as a result of this enhanced perception of change in prehistory, overcome the views about native people that had characterized the 'colonial' phase of its development. The minimal acceptance of change in prehistoric times was primarily an adjustment of cherished beliefs to fit new archaeological facts. American archaeology remained colonial in spirit at the same time that it adopted a culture-historical methodology. The price that American archaeologists paid for their conservatism was a growing disillusionment with their discipline, which was perceived to be without theoretical or historical interest.

Technical developments

The development of the culture-historical approach resulted in a significant elaboration of archaeological methods. This is especially evident in terms of stratigraphy, seriation, classification, and learning more about how people had lived in the past. As archaeologists became increasingly interested in historical rather than evolutionary problems, they perceived the need for increasingly tight controls over chronological as well as cultural variation. Temporal changes within sites over relatively short periods of time became crucial for answering questions of a historical rather than an evolutionary nature. This need was first perceived in classical archaeology, which always had a historical orientation. In the late nineteenth century classical archaeologists began to search for ways to recover information from historical sites that would corroborate and expand what was known about their history from written records. One of the pioneers of this sort of stratigraphic analysis was Giuseppe Fiorelli (1823–96), who took charge of the excavations at Pompeii in 1860. He proclaimed the recovery of works of art, which hitherto had dominated work at the site, to be secondary to the detailed excavation of all kinds of buildings and learning how they had been constructed and for what purposes each part of them had been used. This involved careful stratigraphic excavations so that the ruined upper storeys of houses could be reconstructed. He also recovered the outlines of decayed organic remains, including human bodies, by filling the holes they left in the ash with liquid plaster of Paris. Fiorelli established an archaeological school at Pompeii where students could learn his techniques (Daniel 1950: 165).

His work was carried forward by the Austrian archaeologist Alexander Conze (1831–1914), who began to excavate on the island of Samothrace in 1873, and the German archaeologist Ernst Curtius (1814–96), who started to dig at Olympia two years later. These excavations initiated 30 years of major excavations at classical sites in the eastern Mediterranean. Both archaeologists aimed to record the plans and stratigraphy of their excavations of major ancient buildings in sufficient detail that their reports would be a substitute for what their digging had destroyed. The report on Samothrace was the first to contain plans recorded by professional architects, as well as photographic documentation of the work. Wilhelm Dörpfeld

(1853–1940), who had excavated at Olympia, worked for Heinrich Schliemann (1822–90) at Hisarlik, in Turkey, from 1882 to 1890. Schliemann, who had begun there in 1871, had pioneered the stratigraphic excavation of multi-layered 'tell' sites in an effort to discover the remains of Homer's Troy. He had identified seven superimposed settlements at the site. Using more refined excavation methods, Dörpfeld identified nine levels and revised Schliemann's chronology (Daniel 1950: 166–9).

These new techniques of excavating and recording data gradually spread throughout the Near East. W. M. F. Petrie (1853–1942), who began to work in Egypt in 1880, recorded the plans of his excavations and noted where major finds were made but generally did not record stratigraphic sections. He regarded the latter as being of relatively minor importance, since most of the sites he dug had been occupied for relatively short periods. He did record stratigraphic profiles at Tell el Hesy, a stratified site in southern Palestine where he began excavating in 1890 (Drower 1985). George Reisner, who excavated in Egypt and the Sudan beginning in 1899, introduced the recording of sections as well as plans and brought Egyptian archaeology to its modern standard (J. Wilson 1964: 145–9).

Although prehistoric monuments occasionally were excavated with considerable attention to detail beginning in the seventeenth century (Klindt-Jensen 1975: 30), detailed recording techniques developed more slowly in this field than in classical archaeology. Until the 1870s, as a result of evolutionary preoccupations, interest was focused on the recording, frequently in an idealized fashion, of cross-sections of excavations, the main exception being richly furnished graves, such as those found in the early Iron Age cemetery at Hallstatt in Austria in the 1850s (Sklenář 1983: 71–2, 77). General Augustus Lane-Fox Pitt-Rivers (1827–1900) altered this situation with his slow and detailed excavations of sites on his extensive estate in southern England beginning in the 1870s. In the 1850s he had become interested in anthropology as the result of a detailed study he made of the history of firearms in order to improve the rifles used by the British Army. Throughout the 1860s he built up a large ethnographic collection and wrote on primitive warfare, navigation, and the principles of classification (Pitt-Rivers 1906). His daughter was married to John Lubbock. Although an evolutionist (Pitt-Rivers 1906), Pitt-Rivers' principal aim as an archaeologist was to

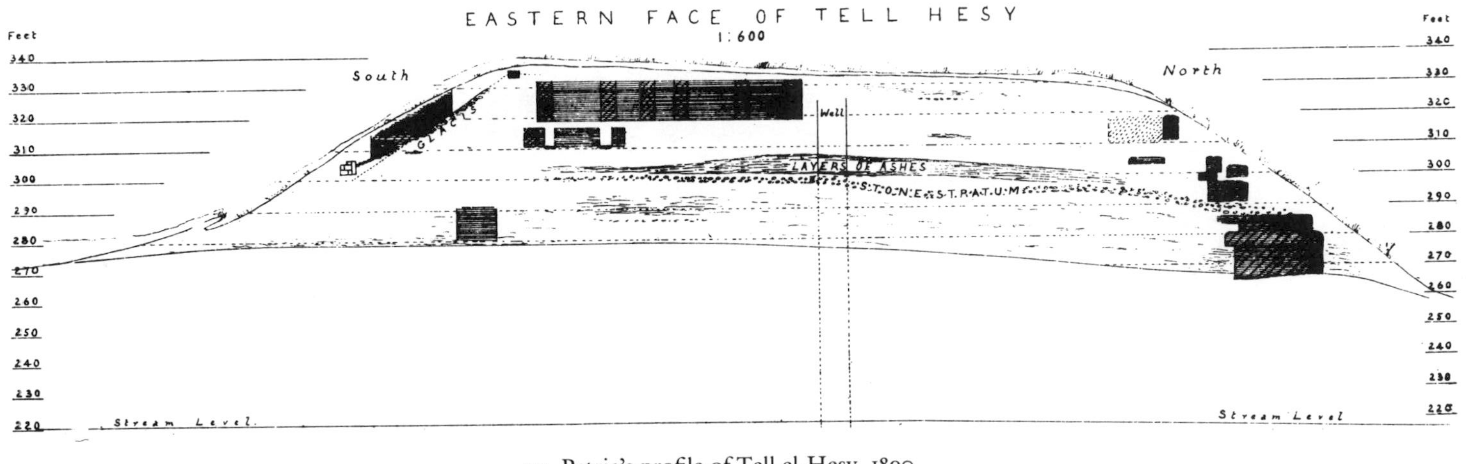

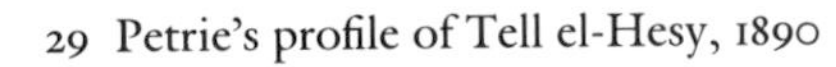
29 Petrie's profile of Tell el-Hesy, 1890

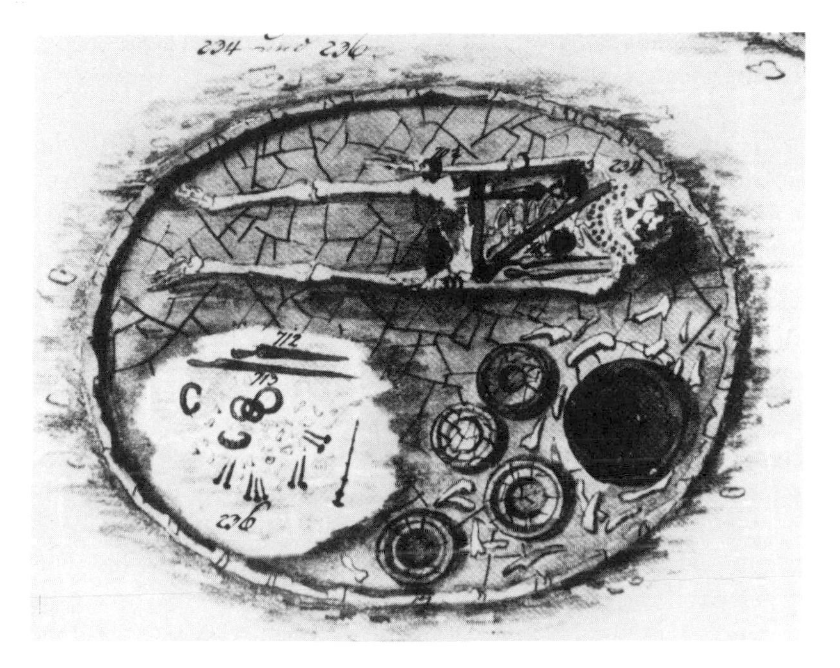

30 Grave from Hallstatt cemetery, Austria, recorded by the painter Isidor Engel in the mid-nineteenth century

understand the history of particular sites. He did this by trenching ditches at right angles, leaving baulks to record stratigraphy, and carefully relating finds to their stratigraphic contexts. In his lavish excavation reports he stressed the need for archaeologists to publish a complete record of their works, rather than only what was of interest to them (M. Thompson 1977). While Pitt-Rivers is often treated as an isolated figure, his work signalled a general improvement in the standard of recording prehistoric sites. A. H. Bulleid and H. S. Gray (1911, 1917) recorded their work at the late Iron Age settlement at Glastonbury between 1892 and 1911 in sufficient detail that their data concerning houses and building levels could be re-analysed in the 1970s (Clarke 1972b). Through the advocacy of Mortimer Wheeler (1890–1976), one of the few young archaeologists to survive World War I, modern forms of three-dimensional excavation and recording became standard throughout Europe and much of the Old World beginning in the 1930s (1954). Wheeler established the primacy of archaeological evidence and its reliability and availability foremost in the minds of British and Indian archaeologists and made it clear that bad data could vitiate a good theory. By the 1930s similar techniques were being followed routinely in North America (Willey and Sabloff 1980: 123–6).

Techniques of seriation were also refined in response to growing historical interests. In the 1880s Petrie, who normally dated Egyptian sites by means of inscriptions, excavated a number of large cemeteries in southern Egypt that contained material that was unfamiliar to him and no inscriptions. Eventually it was realized that these cemeteries dated from the late prehistoric period. There was considerable stylistic variation in the artifacts found in different graves, suggesting that the cemeteries had been used for a long time, but no stratigraphy or obvious general patterns of expansion that could be used to arrange the graves even roughly in a chronological sequence. In order to devise a chronology, Petrie (1901) divided the pottery from the cemeteries at Diospolis Parva into nine major groups or classes and over 700 types. He then recorded what types occurred in each of 500 graves and tried to seriate the graves to produce a maximum concentration of each type (Heizer 1959: 376–83). This formidable task, even using modern computers (Kendall 1969, 1971), was facilitated by Petrie's having inferred certain trends in major wares, in particular the tendency of Wavy-handled vessels to become smaller, cylindrical rather than globular, and their handles more vestigial as the historical period was approached. He was finally able to divide his 500 graves into 50 divisions of ten graves each, which were arranged to form a series of 'sequence dates'. The resulting chronological sequence was then tested against trends in non-ceramic artifacts from the graves and overlaps resulting from later graves being cut into earlier ones. Petrie's chronology for Predynastic Egypt, which in general terms has stood the test of time (Kaiser 1957), differed from Montelius' seriation by defining intervals that in some cases may have been less than a decade rather than periods lasting several hundred years.

In 1916 A. L. Kroeber, who was doing ethnographic fieldwork among the Zuñi, noted a number of archaeological sites nearby and that the pottery differed from one site to another. He collected potsherds from eighteen of these sites, divided them into three general types, and by comparing changes in the frequencies of each type worked out a historical sequence of these sites (Heizer 1959: 383–93). This approach to seriation was adopted by Leslie Spier

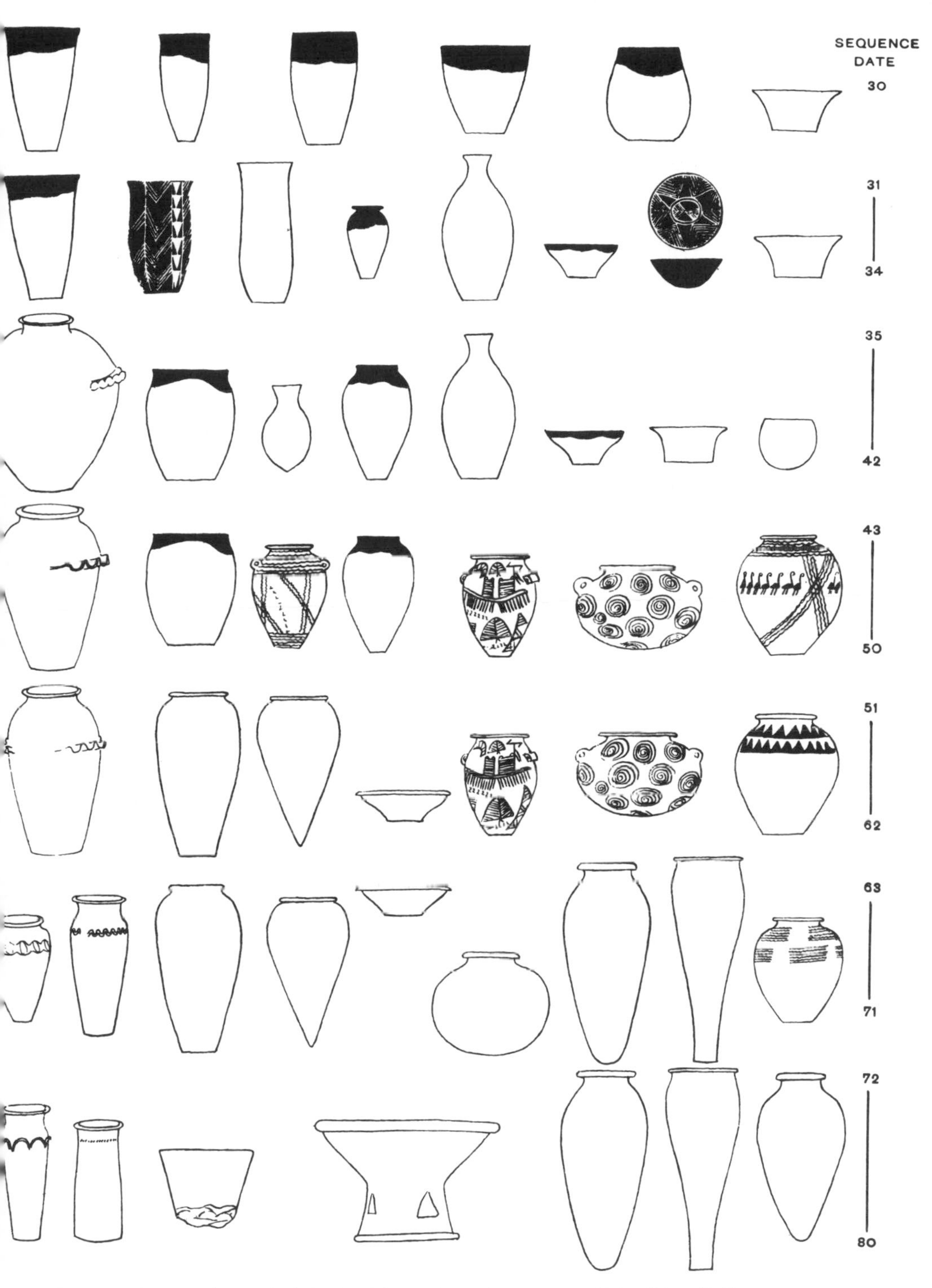

31 Pottery of successive periods in Petrie's predynastic sequence, from *Diospolis Parva*, 1901

(1917), who applied it to a larger number of Zuñi sites, while James Ford (1936) made it the basis for working out much of the culture-chronology of the Mississippi Valley beginning in the 1930s. Although Kroeber may have learned the basic principles of typology and seriation from Boas and known of Petrie's work (Willey and Sabloff 1980: 94–5), his technique of seriation was not based on the same principles as Petrie's. Petrie's 'occurrence seriation' depended on the individual occurrence or non-occurrence in specific closed finds of a large number of different types, while Kroeber's 'frequency seriation' depended on the changing frequencies of a much smaller number of types (Dunnell 1970). This suggests the separate development of the two approaches. In both cases seriation was being used to establish a detailed historical sequence of villages or graves rather than a succession of periods, as evolutionary archaeologists from Thomsen to Montelius had done. Petrie and Kroeber both chose to work with pottery because its stylistic attributes provided more sensitive indices of change than did the stone and metal tools that had been studied by the Scandinavian archaeologists.

This growing interest in defining cultures and working out more detailed seriations resulted in more elaborate classifications of artifacts in both Europe and North America. In Europe these classifications tended to build on ones established by evolutionary archaeologists, usually by splitting or otherwise refining existing types. Types tended to be viewed pragmatically as a means for achieving chronological objectives or for understanding prehistoric life. Perhaps for these reasons, the discussion of the nature and significance of types has generally remained low-keyed in Europe, although complex typologies have been devised there (Bordes 1953; Childe 1956a). The major exception to this is the work of David Clarke, who has provided a systematic treatment of archaeological typology at all levels (1968). In the United States the theoretical significance of artifact classification has been discussed in great detail over the years. While Winifred and Harry Gladwin (1930) saw pottery styles as sensitive indicators of spatial and temporal variations in culture, they believed that it was necessary to define pottery types in terms that were free from temporal implications if subjectivity was to be avoided. They therefore proposed a binomial designation, in which the first term indicated a geographical location where the type was found and the second its colour or surface treatment, such as Tularosa black-on-white. Type descriptions were published in a set format involving name, vessel shape, design, type site, geographical distribution, cultural affiliations, and inferred chronological range (Colton and Hargrave 1937). James Ford (1938), on the other hand, stressed that types should be recognized only if they could be demonstrated to be useful tools for interpreting culture-history and that there should be no formal splitting of them unless the results clearly correlated with spatial or temporal differences. He regarded types merely as tools for historical analysis. Later discussions centred on the reality of types to those who had made and used artifacts, on the relationship between types and the attributes or modes that are used to define them, and on the nature of attributes and their usefulness for artifact seriation (Rouse 1939). In the 1950s it was maintained that types could be discovered as regular clusterings of attributes and that these 'natural' types would reveal much more about human behaviour and cultural change than would Ford's arbitrary creations (Spaulding 1953). This prolonged discussion of artifact classification was the first substantial manifestation of the concern of American archaeologists to articulate and make explicit the analytical basis of their discipline.

A growing interest in how particular groups of Europeans had lived in prehistoric times, which was encouraged by nationalism but had its roots in the Scandinavian archaeology of the early nineteenth century, led archaeologists to pay attention to classes of archaeological data that previously had been ignored. A long-standing interest in cemeteries was supplemented by the increasing study of the remains of settlements. This required large-scale horizontal excavations rather than vertical stratigraphic ones, as well as the recording of many new types of observations. The first post moulds are believed to have been noted by Pitt-Rivers in 1878, after which their value for reconstructing the plans of decayed wooden structures was quickly recognized. In the 1890s the Roman–German Boundary Commission, which was studying sites along the northern frontier of the Roman empire in Central Europe, developed techniques for recognizing post moulds in all kinds of soils (Childe 1953: 13). Archaeologists also began to record more systematically the locations where artifacts were found, so that these could be plotted in relation to features such as hearths and house walls. Gradually lithic debitage and minor floral and faunal remains that hitherto had generally been dismissed as unimportant were saved and studied.

All of this encouraged a new concern for precision in archaeological methods. The principal aim of such research was to reconstruct a visual impression of life in the past. That involved determining what houses looked like, what kind of clothing people wore, what utensils they used, and in what activities they engaged. These impressions could be reconstructed in drawings or three-dimensionally in the form of open-air museums. One site that did not require much reconstruction was Skara Brae, a Neolithic settlement in the Orkneys that was excavated by Gordon Childe (1931). In this site not only houses but also furniture, such as beds and cupboards, were preserved as a result of being constructed from stone slabs. The most impressive developments in this sort of field archaeology occurred in Europe between 1920 and 1940. Houses and their surroundings were completely excavated and post moulds, hearths, pits, and artifact distributions interpreted as evidence of patterns of daily life (De Laet 1957: 101–3; Sieveking 1976: xvi). In Poland a unique timber-built fortress of the Urnfield culture was excavated at Biskupin beginning in 1934 and soon became the best-known archaeological site in the country (Bibby 1956: 384–94).

In the United States the development of a culture-historical approach initially encouraged archaeologists to excavate sites mainly to recover artifact samples that could be used to elaborate trait lists and define cultures. It was assumed that any part of a site was typical of the whole and therefore excavations were frequently directed towards middens, where artifacts were most abundant and could be recovered most cheaply. In addition to artifacts, archaeologists sought to recover floral and faunal data as evidence of subsistence patterns and skeletal remains that could identify the physical types of the people that had occupied sites. During the economic depression of the 1930s, United States federal government relief agencies, working through park services, museums, and universities, made large sums of money available for archaeological research. As a result entire sites were excavated, especially in areas that were to be flooded by the construction of hydro-electric dams (Willey and Sabloff 1980: 115, 127). These massive horizontal excavations resulted in more attention being paid to settlement patterns.

This convergence in research programmes does not indicate a growing similarity in attitudes towards the past. While Europeans were emotionally involved in what they regarded as the study of their own prehistory, Euroamericans continued to view the archaeological record as the product of an alien people. Yet, on both sides of the Atlantic Ocean, the development of a culture-historical approach to archaeology led to an elaboration, which in terms of classification, chronology, and cultural reconstruction, carried methodology far beyond the point it had reached in the context of evolutionary archaeology. The switch from 'scientific' to 'historical' objectives stimulated rather than inhibited the development of archaeological methodology.

Conclusions

An approach centred upon defining archaeological cultures and trying to account for their origins in terms of diffusion and migration developed as Western Europeans ceased to view cultural evolution as a natural or necessarily desirable process. European archaeology became closely aligned with history and was seen as offering insights into the development of particular peoples in prehistoric times. Its findings thus became a part of struggles for national self-determination, the assertion and defence of national identity, and promoting national unity in opposition to class conflict. Archaeology of this sort obviously had a widespread appeal in other parts of the world. Ethnic and national groups continue to desire to learn more about their prehistory and such knowledge can play a significant role in the development of group pride and solidarity and help to promote economic and social development. This is particularly important for peoples whose past has been neglected or denigrated by a colonial approach to archaeology and history. While the findings of culture-historical archaeology can be enriched by techniques for reconstructing prehistoric cultures and explaining cultural change that have been developed outside the framework of this kind of archaeology, only an approach that is focused on understanding the prehistory of specific peoples can fulfil the needs of nations in a post-colonial phase. For this reason culture-historical archaeology remains socially attractive in many parts of the world.

In the United States a culture-historical approach evolved as a response to a growing awareness of complexity in the archaeological record. In this case, however, archaeologists did not feel any heightened sense of identity with the people they studied. In Europe archaeologists continued to take pride in the accomplishments of their forefathers. Yet after 1880 there was declining faith in human creativity and diffusion and migration were relied on to a much greater degree than they had been previously to explain changes in the archaeological record. By contrast, in the United States growing awareness of prehistoric change that could not be explained by migration led to an increasing reliance on diffusion. In this case diffusionism represented not growing pessimism about human creativity but a grudging and limited acceptance of the capacity of native Americans to change.

The culture-historical paradigm was focused on the archaeological culture rather than on general stages of development. It thus tried to explain the archaeological record in more specific detail than had been done in the past. In the nationalistic contexts where it first developed, there was a strong desire to learn as much as possible about how specific groups had lived at various times in the past, which meant that archaeologists tried to reconstruct synchronic descriptions of these cultures. In America this tendency developed more slowly because of a commitment to 'scientifically objective' trait lists which reflected the continuing alienation between archaeologists and the peoples whose history they studied. Yet in both cases change in archaeological cultures was routinely attributed to external factors, that were subsumed under the general headings of migration and diffusion. In cases where the internal origin of innovations appeared evident, the process either was not explained or was attributed to special racial characteristics. The most striking failure of culture-historical archaeologists was their refusal, following their repudiation of cultural evolutionism, to extend their concern with change to properties of cultural systems that either make innovation possible or lead to the acceptance of innovations coming from the outside. Without such understanding, diffusion was doomed to remain a non-explanation.

CHAPTER 6

Soviet archaeology

It is not only a new economic system which has been born. A new culture . . . a new science . . . a new style of life has been born.

N. I. BUKHARIN, 'Theory and practice from the standpoint of dialectical materialism' (1931), p. 33

Since the Communist Party came to power in 1917, archaeology has been generously funded in the Soviet Union, which now possesses the world's largest centralized network for archaeological research. Every year more than 500 expeditions carry out archaeological reconnaissance and excavations, and more than 5,000 scholarly reports are published. Archaeology is sponsored as an instrument for cultural enhancement and public education. Its findings are actively disseminated through popular writings and museum displays. Part of archaeology's task is to enrich an understanding of the origins and history of the many ethnic groups that make up the Soviet Union. A still more fundamental mission is to promote a materialist understanding of human history that accords with the guiding philosophy of the Communist Party. Soviet archaeology also adds time depth and verisimilitude to a cultural-evolutionary scheme which, while careful not to deny the creative potential of any human group, emphasizes the world-wide historical significance of the Soviet Union as the first association of states to evolve socialist societies, and thus to achieve a goal that other nations have yet to attain.

The Soviet Union was the first country where archaeological data were interpreted within the framework of Marxist historical materialism. Since the late 1920s this paradigm has guided all archaeological research done there. The resulting unity of theoretical outlook, which is shared by all of the humanistic sciences in the Soviet Union, has given Soviet archaeology a distinctive character which has been enhanced by a major linguistic barrier and by long periods of political and ideological estrangement from Western

Europe and the United States. Soviet archaeology has not remained static and enmired in 'nineteenth century dogmas', nor has it simply changed course as required to serve the shifting exigencies of government policies, as some of its Western critics have maintained (M. Miller 1956; M. Thompson 1965). Instead it has developed in the past, and continues to develop, within the framework of Marxist philosophy. In the less regimented intellectual atmosphere of the post-Stalin era, Soviet archaeology has also become less monolithic and been characterized by a growing diversity of approaches within a Marxist framework. Moreover, although Soviet archaeology is largely unknown to most Western archaeologists, it has influenced, both directly and indirectly, archaeological research far beyond the sphere of Soviet political control. For all these reasons Soviet archaeology is of world-wide significance. It also seems possible, by comparing the similarities and differences between archaeology as it has developed under very different conceptual schemes and political orientations in the Soviet Union and the West, to understand better the general factors that influence archaeological interpretation.

Archaeology in tsarist Russia

Archaeology was already a well-established discipline in tsarist Russia. The first substantial interest in the remains of prehistoric times was directed to the kurgans, or tumuli, many thousands of which had been constructed over a period of 5,000 years in the steppe lands that stretch from the Ukraine eastward into Siberia. For centuries, if not millennia, these tombs had been plundered for treasure. As Russian colonization spread eastward into Siberia in the seventeenth century, the plundering of kurgans in that region was carried out on a massive scale, sometimes under government licence. By the 1760s not enough Siberian tumuli remained unplundered for these large-scale operations to remain profitable (Miller 1956: 15).

As early as the 1680s Tsar Fyodor Alekseyevitch ordered that the bones of a 'giant' (probably a mammoth) found in the Kharkov region should be excavated, measured, and described (Miller 1956: 12). In 1718 Peter the Great issued a more general order that district governors and commanders of cities should collect and forward to St Petersburg (now Leningrad) old and rare objects as these were discovered. His interests embraced geological and palaeontological as well as archaeological specimens and his scientific interests were evident in his request that sketches should be made of the circumstances in which interesting objects were found. In 1721 a Dr Messerschmidt was sent to Siberia to make collections of various kinds, including archaeological ones, and five years later a government office turned over more than 250 objects of gold and silver weighing more than 33 kilograms to the Imperial Art Collection. In 1739 Gerhard Müller (Gerard F. Miller, 1705–83), a professor of German attached to the Russian Academy of Sciences, who had been sent to study the peoples and resources of Siberia, supervised the excavations of kurgans in the vicinity of Krasnoiarsk. He recovered a large number of bronze weapons and ornaments that he prepared for publication (Black 1986: 71).

After the Russians annexed and began to settle the steppes along the north coast of the Black Sea in the second half of the eighteenth century, the archaeological interests of the government and the general public shifted to that region. Landowners and peasants began to dig into kurgans in hopes of recovering precious metals and antiquities. As early as 1763 the governor of the region, General Aleksey Mel'gunov, excavated the Scythian royal kurgan of Mel'gunovsky, recovering valuable finds that are now in the Hermitage Museum. Classical Greek settlements along the north shore of the Black Sea also attracted attention. Some of the best archaeological research in Russia in the early nineteenth century was done by French *émigré* archaeologists working in the Crimea (Miller 1956: 22; Sklenář 1983: 94). The study of classical antiquities was vigorously pursued by the Imperial Odessa Society of History and Antiquity, founded in 1839 (Miller 1956: 27). By 1826 so many finds had been assembled in the Crimean city of Kerch that an archaeological museum was opened there.

Prior to 1850 the Russian aristocrats who patronized antiquarian research were far more interested in the valuable and exotic works of art recovered from kurgans and Greek cities than in humbler finds relating to Slavic prehistory. In Russia, unlike Central Europe, class interests overtly continued to outweigh a sense of ethnic identity. Among themselves, the upper classes often spoke French and German rather than Russian. Moreover, although the Russians, like the Americans, were expanding into regions occupied by tribal peoples, they did not invoke archaeological evidence to provide racial justifications for their actions. Having been conquered and ruled for centuries by the Mongols, the Russians were less inclined to despise their technologically less developed neighbours than were the Americans.

In the second half of the nineteenth century, Russia experienced rapid development in industry, transport, trade, and educational opportunities. The middle classes expanded rapidly and among the educated segment of the population there was a growing interest in natural science, philosophy, history, and political economy. There was a rapid proliferation of archaeological research, publications, museums, associations, and congresses. All of the archaeologists at this period were teachers, landowners, civil servants, and military officers who were self-instructed in the discipline. Yet they carried out research comparable to that being done elsewhere in Europe (Miller 1956: 28). The rapid development of archaeology in Russia, and a growing number of remarkable finds, led the government to establish the Imperial Archaeological Commission in St Petersburg. In 1859 this commission was empowered to grant licences for excavations on government and public lands and assigned general responsibility for safeguarding all archaeological remains in Russia. In 1851 an Imperial Archaeology Society was founded in St Petersburg and in 1864 Count Aleksey Uvarov organized the Imperial Russian Archaeological Society in Moscow, which he, and later his widow, directed until 1917. Each of these bodies established major publication series which continued until the revolution. In the 1870s and 1880s regional archaeological societies were established in Tiblisi, Kazan, Pskov, and other provincial cities.

Beginning in the 1870s and continuing into the early twentieth century, archaeological interests diversified. Kurgans and classical sites continued to be excavated, but there was a growing emphasis on settlements and cemeteries from all periods of Russian history. The Palaeolithic sites at Kostenki, in the Ukraine, began to be studied, while Neolithic sites, including those of the Tripolye culture, as well as Bronze and Iron Age ones were excavated in western Russia. There was also considerable interest in Slavic and medieval Russian archaeology, especially among the members of the Imperial Archaeology Society, where a special section was established for such research. This particular interest reflected the pan-Slavism that played a significant role in Russian foreign policy in the late nineteenth century and which supported the government's efforts to extend Russian influence throughout Eastern Europe. By this time archaeology was being taught at the universities in St Petersburg and Moscow.

This same period witnessed a considerable, if uneven, improvement in archaeological methodology and interpretation. Treasure hunting continued and was popular among landowners, who legally owned all the wealth on their estates, including archaeological finds. This approach was provided with some degree of scientific respectability by old-fashioned archaeologists and art historians who believed that kurgans and classical sites were the only archaeological remains worth studying and by an aestheticizing trend that viewed only works of art as deserving of attention. The latter approach was cultivated particularly at the Hermitage Museum in St Petersburg where a remarkable collection of prehistoric and medieval art had been assembled (Miller 1956: 53).

Other archaeologists working in Moscow and St Petersburg were influenced by recent developments in prehistoric archaeology in the rest of Europe. The most prominent of these was Vasily Gorodtsov (1860–1945), a retired infantry officer who began to excavate in the 1890s with financial support from the Countess Uvarova. In the early 1900s he became director of the Moscow Historical Museum and one of the founders of the Moscow Archaeological Institute. He also trained a large number of professional archaeologists. Gorodtsov was the outstanding exponent of what later was called the formalist school of Russian archaeology, which was inspired by the work of Oscar Montelius, Joseph Déchelette, and other typologists. Formalists studied the morphology of artifacts and sought to arrange them in chronological sequences. As a result of his excavations along the Don River, Gorodtsov was able to demonstrate the existence of a Bronze Age in Russia and to divide it into successive periods. He systematically periodized Russian antiquities and proposed his own terminology, although it was not widely accepted. He also stressed the importance of studying settlements and ordinary cemeteries as well as kurgans (Miller 1956: 37).

Aleksandr Spitsyn (1858–1931), who was a member of the Imperial Archaeological Commission, was a founder of the empirical school. The school maintained that the basic task of archaeologists was to provide the most detailed and accurate descriptions of artifacts, while eschewing premature conclusions of a historical or sociological nature (Miller 1956: 32–3). Such an approach had much in common with that of Joseph Henry in the United States. The eventual leader of the empirical school was Aleksandr Miller (1875–1935), a student of Mortillet who began to excavate in Russia in 1902. He greatly improved the standards of excavation techniques, as well as of the study and conservation of artifacts. As Professor of Archaeology at the University of St Petersburg, he trained many Russian archaeologists. Yet, despite the good work that was being done, no Russian archaeologist established an international reputation equivalent to that of Lobachevsky in mathematics, Mendeleyev in the physical sciences, or Pavlov in biology.

Archaeology during the New Economic Policy

It has been claimed that 'no previous government in history was so openly and energetically in favor of science' as was the Soviet regime that came to power in the autumn of 1917 (Graham 1967: 32–3). The revolutionary leaders of the new state looked to scientific knowledge to modernize the Russian economy and to eliminate Russia's age-old mysticism, which was viewed as a hindrance to social and economic progress. The social sciences, including archaeology, had a crucial role to play in the ensuing ideological struggle. In a decree of the Council of People's Commissars dated 18 April 1919 and signed by V.I. Lenin, the Imperial Archaeological Commission in Petrograd (formerly St Petersburg) was reorganized as the Russian Academy for the History of Material Culture (RAIMK). The organization was entrusted to its first director Nikolay Marr (1865–1934). Like Kossinna, a linguist with archaeological interests, Marr rejected the universally held belief that new languages evolve as the result of a gradual process of phonological, lexical, and grammatical differentiation from ancestral forms. Instead he believed that linguistic changes occur as a response to alterations in the socio-economic organization of the societies in which their speakers live; hence similarities among languages indicate the stage of evolution that societies have reached rather than historical affinities. On the basis of a superficial resemblance between this theory and Marxist explanations of sociocultural change, Marr's teachings enjoyed official esteem within the Soviet Union until 1950.

Following the creation of the Soviet Union the RAIMK became the State Academy for the History of Material Culture (GAIMK) and was given ultimate jurisdiction over archaeological activities and institutions not only in the Russian Republic but throughout the Union (Miller 1956: 47). From the start this was a larger and more powerful institute than the Imperial Archaeological Commission had been (Bulkin *et al.* 1982: 274). In 1922 the chairs of archaeology at the universities of Leningrad and Moscow were transformed into archaeology departments. Talented students who completed their undergraduate studies in these and other departments were admitted to the Institute of Postgraduate Studies of the GAIMK. The best of these students could hope to remain in the GAIMK as junior and then senior research associates. Thus a pattern of largely separating research and undergraduate teaching was established that has persisted to the present in the Soviet Union (Davis 1983: 409). In addition to allowing a large number of archaeologists to engage in full-time research, the institute structure gave these archaeologists access to technical experts who could scientifically analyse artifacts, floral and faunal remains, and geological and climatological data relating to archaeological problems.

In Moscow in the mid-1920s a rival archaeological centre was established in the form of an Archaeological Section of the Russian Association of Scientific Institutes of the Social Sciences (RANION). The latter was an amalgamation of 15 separate institutes in Moscow and Leningrad that sought to produce good researchers and teachers by employing Communist Party and selected non-party personnel working under close communist supervision (Shapiro 1982: 89). The encouragement by the Communist Party of the popularization and democratization of scientific knowledge and research also led to the formation of many regional studies organizations in the early 1920s. Archaeology was a popular subject in these societies, in which professional archaeologists, students, and interested amateurs united to carry out and publish research (Miller 1956: 44–5).

Almost no archaeological fieldwork was done during World War I or the civil war that followed it. In 1921, in an effort to promote economic recovery and broaden the basis of support for the revolution, especially among the peasantry, Lenin inaugurated the New Economic Policy, which restored a limited market economy in the

Soviet Union. As part of this move, the Soviet government adopted an accommodative policy toward the intelligentsia, although most of the latter had not supported the Bolshevik revolution. Lenin was convinced that, because of the lack of education among working-class people, the party could not manage the economy, conduct scientific research, or run the government without the services of the educated classes. He also rejected the radical proposal that cultural power could be seized by revolutionary action. Instead he believed that a socialist society had to be built on the foundations of bourgeois cultural achievements and that peasants and industrial workers had to learn about that culture gradually from the intelligentsia. Some other Communists, including Anatoly Lunacharsky, the Commissar of Enlightenment, went further and hoped that, by being assigned a positive role in the building of socialism, the intelligentsia could be brought into the mainstream of Soviet life and turned into Communists (O'Connor 1983: 36–7). During the period of the New Economic Policy (1921–8) established intellectuals, to the disgust of hardline revolutionaries, were trusted with positions of influence and power, given well-paid jobs, and allowed a reasonable measure of scholarly independence, so long as they did not openly criticize the regime.

As a result of the revolution, a few well-known Russian archaeologists left the Soviet Union, most notably M.I. Rostovtsev (1870–1952), who was to become one of the world's leading experts on the economy and society of ancient Greece and Rome. Those who remained continued to occupy prominent positions. Gorodtsov was still a leading archaeologist in the Moscow area, where his principal collaborators were his former students. Spitsyn, Miller, and other archaeologists with pre-revolutionary views all remained active members of the GAIMK. Because of their influence its scientific character and direction were little different from those of the former Imperial Archaeological Commission. Although Marr continued to elaborate his bizarre linguistic theories, his leadership of the GAIMK did not result in significant changes in its approach to archaeology (Miller 1956: 46).

During the period of the New Economic Policy a large amount of archaeological research was accomplished and many new archaeologists were trained. The more spectacular manifestations of amateurish archaeology that had flourished in the nineteenth century disappeared as the confiscation of the wealth of the aristocracy brought the financing of research under government control. Professional archaeologists also wrote the first generalizing works in Russian dealing with archaeology and prehistory. Although these studies were of varying quality, they set new standards for students and provincial researchers (Miller 1956: 60). On the other hand, the main interpretive schools that had been founded before the revolution still dominated archaeology. The formalists continued to elaborate a typological approach and followed Montelius in viewing the development of technology as the cumulative result of the use of human intellect to gain increasing control over nature. Diffusion and migration were relied on to explain changes in the archaeological record. The empirical school remained content to describe archaeological finds as precisely as possible, without making generalizations or trying to relate these finds to the societies that had produced them (Miller 1956: 49–55). Contacts with foreign archaeologists were unimpeded and Soviet archaeologists continued to publish their works abroad. The journal *Eurasia Septentrionalis Antiqua*, edited by the Finnish archaeologist A.M. Tallgren (1885–1945), was devoted largely to Russian archaeology and published papers by Russian archaeologists in French, English, and German translations. Through these contacts European archaeology continued to exert significant influence on work done throughout the Soviet Union. Mikhail Miller (1956: 53–5) notes the impact of contemporary European thought, such as the diffusionist Viennese school of anthropology, Oswald Spengler's cyclical views of history, and even racist theories, on the interpretation of Soviet archaeological data.

On the other hand, most archaeologists avoided applying the concepts of historical materialism to archaeology. They appear to have assumed that, because they were studying the history of material culture, their work accorded sufficiently with the materialist perspective of the new social and political order. Yet even formalists, who believed technological innovation to be a major cause of social change, did not interpret their data as if it were a basis for understanding historical and cultural processes. Instead they treated them as objects unrelated to a social context. The history of the socio-economic relations that had produced the archaeological record was viewed as something to be studied by historians using written records (Miller 1956: 55). The New Economic Policy has been described as a 'golden era of Marxist thought in the USSR' (S. Cohen 1973: 272). There is no evidence that any archaeologists participated in this intellectual ferment. Even within the framework of traditional interpretations, Russian archaeologists appear to have been cautious and reactionary rather than innovative.

The birth of Soviet archaeology

During the 1920s revolutionary veterans, cultural radicals, industrial workers, members of the Union of Communist Youth (Komsomol), and Communist students became increasingly critical of the New Economic Policy as it was applied to cultural affairs. They resented the skills of the old cultural and educational elites and saw the entrenched privileges and opposition to educational reforms of this group as impediments to their own advancement. They therefore denounced the accommodation with the old intelligentsia as a betrayal of the October revolution and demanded that the political revolution be extended into the cultural realm. Political struggles within the leadership of the Communist Party following the death of Lenin played a role in deciding cultural policy at this juncture. Joseph Stalin's programme of intensive industrialization and the collectivization of agriculture, which began with the first Five-Year Plan in 1928–9, reversed the basic economic principles of the New Economic Policy. As part of his campaign to consolidate power, he allied himself with the cultural radicals who demanded that intellectuals should be subjected to strict party discipline (Fitzpatrick 1974; O'Conner 1983: 54, 89). The cultural revolution, which was initiated by the arrest of engineers and technicians on charges of sabotage and treason, lasted from 1928 to 1932. It involved a massive campaign to bring Soviet intellectual life into line with the tenets of Marxist philosophy as they were understood by the Soviet Communist Party. Many non-Marxist intellectuals and institutions were purged as the Stalinist bureaucracy sought to suppress all opposition. Among the early victims of this campaign were the regional studies societies. They were disbanded and later replaced by government-controlled regional studies bureaux, which did not command popular support. From 1930 on contacts between Soviet and foreign scholars were forbidden and for a time current issues of foreign archaeological publications could be found only in the GAIMK library (Miller 1956: 73, 93–4).

In the late 1920s a Communist cell had been established in the GAIMK. It was composed mainly of postgraduate students and research associates. At the beginning of the cultural revolution this group started to criticize archaeologists of the old schools, challenging them to reveal their attitude towards Marxism. In 1929 Professor Vladislav I. Ravdonikas (1894–1976), a middle-aged archaeologist who had joined the Communist Party a number of years before, on orders from the GAIMK party organization read a report in the academy entitled 'For a Soviet history of material culture'. This paper was published the following year and widely read by archaeologists throughout the Soviet Union. It criticized the theoretical positions of prominent archaeologists and called for a 'Marxist history of material culture' to replace the old archaeology. The very concept of archaeology was rejected as that of a bourgeois science

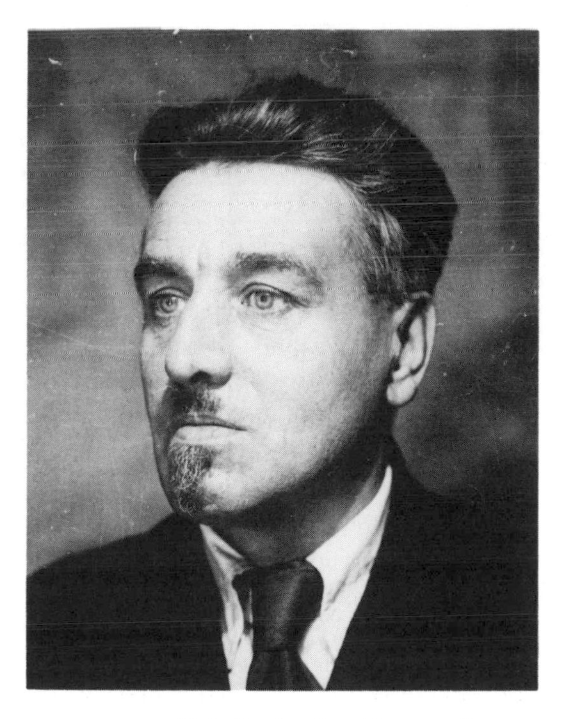

32 V. I. Ravdonikas (1894–1976)

hostile to Marxism. At the Pan-Russian Conference for Archaeology and Ethnography held at the GAIMK the following May, the party organization of the academy mounted an exhibition of Soviet archaeological literature in which books and papers written since 1917 were denounced for their adherence to formalism, bourgeois nationalism, and other anti-communist tendencies. The Montelian typological method was criticized for its idealism, for making fetishes of artifacts (artifactology), and for improperly interpreting human history in biological terms (Miller 1956: 71–8). The counter-suggestion that archaeology might cut its links with history and seek within a Marxist framework to develop its own methods to study past human behaviour was also firmly rejected (Dolitsky 1985: 361).

This criticism was followed by the dismissal, and in some cases the arrest and exiling, of archaeologists who were unable or unwilling to alter their views. At least 20 archaeologists in Leningrad, including Aleksandr Miller, were exiled. In Moscow Gorodtsov was dismissed from all his duties, although the Soviet government later awarded him the Order of the Red Banner for his contributions to Russian archaeology. This suppression was documented and condemned by Tallgren (1936) after he visited Leningrad in 1935. In retaliation he was deprived of his honorary membership in the GAIMK and denied further entry to the Soviet Union. The events of this period have since been chronicled in greater detail by the *émigré* Russian archaeologist Mikhail Miller (1956: 96–105). At the same time that this was happening, the power of the GAIMK and its centralized control of Soviet archaeology was enhanced when RANION, together with its Archaeological Section in Moscow, was completely abolished. In its place a Moscow Branch of the GAIMK (MOGAIMK) was organized in 1932 with the historian A. Udal'tsov as its director.

The younger generation of Marxist archaeologists, who under Ravdonikas' leadership came to occupy leading positions, had to elaborate a Marxist approach to archaeology. These scholars included Yevgeni Krichevsky (1910–42), who studied Neolithic cultures, A. P. Kruglov (1904–42) and G. P. Podgayetsky (1908–41), who studied the Bronze Age in southern Russia, and P. N. Tret'yakov, who studied the Old Russian and Slavic cultures. Most of them were enthusiastic, but not very experienced in Marxism or in archaeology (Bulkin *et al.* 1982: 274). The leading theoretician in these formative years was Ravdonikas, whom even his enemies credited with exceptional ability. The Communist Party, while supporting the creation of a Marxist approach to archaeology and reserving the right to pass judgement on its theory and practice, does not appear to have provided archaeologists with explicit guidelines. Nor could these guidelines be found in the writings of Marx and Engels. The most relevant statement that Marx had made about archaeology was that

> Relics of by-gone instruments of labour possess the same importance for the investigation of extinct economical forms of society, as do fossil bones for the determination of extinct species of animals. It is not the articles made, but how they are made, and by what instruments, that enables us to distinguish different economical epochs. Instruments of labour not only supply a standard of the degree of development to which human labour has attained, but they are also indicators of the social conditions under which labour is carried on.
>
> (Marx 1906: 200)

Moreover, Marx had devoted most of his career to studying capitalist societies and how they had developed from feudal ones. He had begun to investigate pre-class and early class societies late in life and had to depend on the highly defective and polemical anthropological literature that was available in the late nineteenth century (Bloch 1985: 21–94). Thus he and Engels left many questions about the sorts of societies that archaeologists study unanswered, including how these societies had evolved. This meant that archaeologists had to rely, not on the well-developed concepts that were available to most other social scientists, but on the basic principles of Marxism, as these were formulated in Marx's and Engels' own writings and in later exegeses.

Marx summarized the basic principles on which he based his analyses of society in the preface to his *Contribution to the Critique of Political Economy* (1859):

> In the social production that human beings carry on, they enter into definite relations that are indispensable and independent of their will, relations of production which correspond to a definite stage of development of their material forces of production . . . The mode of production in material life determines the general character of the social, political, and intellectual processes of life. It is not the consciousness of humans that determines their existence; it is

> on the contrary their social existence that determines their consciousness. (Marx and Engels 1962, 1: 362–3)

Traditionally Marxism is characterized by an unswerving devotion to a materialist analysis of the human condition. It is frequently asserted that at the same time it rejects the positivist doctrine that science can be based only on the direct data of sensory experience, in favour of philosophical realism, which emphasizes the discovery of unobservable underlying structures which generate observable phenomena, in this case the inner essence of socioeconomic formations (Davis 1983: 408). Yet this distinction may be exaggerated. Lenin argued that 'Marxism does not base itself on anything other than the facts of history and reality' (Petrova-Averkieva 1980: 24). Marx and Engels emphasized the systemic interdependence of all aspects of social life and more particularly viewed human societies as systems that organized production and reproduction. They also stressed internal contradictions and conflicts as prominent features of complex (historical) human societies and the most important source of social change.

Marx, like many other nineteenth-century social theorists, viewed human beings as having evolved the ability to cooperate as members of social groups to the extraordinary extent that societies were able routinely to transform their relations to the natural world and to modify human nature. Yet he differed from most analysts in identifying the organization of labour as the most important means by which human beings were able to confront nature as one of her own forces. The crucial factor shaping social systems was the economic base, which consists of the forces and relations of production. While there have been serious differences of opinion among Marxists concerning the definitions of these terms, the forces of production are widely interpreted as embracing not only all forms of technology but also all utilized resources, human and non-human, and all scientific knowledge (Graham 1967: 34–5). The relations of production signify the ways in which individual human beings relate with one another to utilize the forces of production to produce and distribute goods. They therefore embrace not only what Western anthropologists would identify as economic behaviour, but also various facets of social behaviour. The economic base is seen as playing a powerful role in shaping other aspects of society, such as concepts of property, family life, political organization, law, religious beliefs, aesthetics, and philosophical and organizational aspects of scientific activities. All of these are collectively referred to as society's superstructure. Marx did not believe that technological change came about as a result of human beings using their intellect to develop more effective ways to control their environment, as Victorian evolutionists and Enlightenment philosophers had assumed. Instead he argued that technological change itself must be understood in a social context. While new technologies bring about social and political changes, they themselves are the products of specific social contexts that influence what innovations are likely or unlikely to occur. This is what Engels meant when he wrote that 'the determining element in the historical process in the final analysis is production, and the reproduction of human life . . . If somebody distorts this principle into the belief that the economic element is the only determining element, then [that person] has transformed [the materialist understanding of history] into an empty, abstract phrase' (Marx and Engels 1962, 2: 488).

Marxism analyses every society as containing within itself tendencies that promote and oppose change. Thus each society contains the seeds of the destruction of its present state and at the same time the embryo of a future condition. The antagonism between these two tendencies produces the energy that brings about change. Marx did not deny that superstructural factors, such as entrenched political hierarchies or powerful religious beliefs, can be of great historical importance but he maintained that this is so only insofar as they are capable of preventing change. Wholesome changes can occur only when economic transformations are not overwhelmed by such forces. A progressive society is therefore one that provides a large number of possibilities for the unfettered development of human productive forces (Petrova-Averkieva 1980: 20; Tringham 1983: 95–6).

In his own research Marx endeavoured both to explain concrete historical events and to generalize about evolutionary trends in human history. In *The XVIIIth Brumaire of Louis Bonaparte* and *The Class Struggle in France, 1848–50* he sought to account for historical events not as collective responses to environmental and economic conditions but in terms of the conflicting interests of social and economic groups that were seeking to preserve or enhance their power. These studies stress intentionality and the social reproduction of reality rather than treating human behaviour as the passive consequence of social forces. He also observed that every society was the product of its own separate history and therefore responded to economic changes in a distinctive fashion. Because of this it was impossible to formulate general laws that would explain all of the concrete reality of cultural change in a predictive fashion. In some of his writings there is a suggestion that he believed in multilinear evolution, at least in the short and middle range (Hobsbawm 1964). Yet he also believed in an ideal course for human development that would run from primitive egalitarian societies, through class societies, to the technologically advanced, egalitarian societies of the future. Over the years Marxists have varied in the degree to which they have emphasized the historical complexity or evolutionary regularity of human history. Soviet scholarship, rooted in the writings of G. V. Plekhanov (1856–1918) and reinforced by Stalin's own views, tended to stress a strongly evolutionary and deterministic view of social change (Bloch 1985: 95–123).

Finally Marx denied that human behaviour is biologically determined to a significant degree or that a large number of generalizations are applicable to all human societies (Childe 1947a). Instead he believed that most of the rules governing societies change as the mode of production changes. Social evolution thus produces genuine novelties in the rules governing human behaviour rather than merely varied permutations and combinations of a fixed set of regularities. He also denied that it was possible to create a socially and politically neutral social science in a class society, since such studies inevitably are influenced by the class prejudices of the scholars who undertake them. Yet Marx would not have viewed the ancient Sumerian and modern capitalist world views relativistically. Instead he would have interpreted them as positions that are qualitatively distinct in terms of their potential for human action. He would also have claimed for Marxism a privileged position compared to all other philosophical or scientific approaches to understanding human behaviour.

Ravdonikas and his colleagues attempted to render archaeological data of value to society by making them useful for the Marxist study of history. Archaeologists were to use their data to illustrate the laws and regularities of historical processes and by doing so demonstrate the accuracy and utility of Marxist concepts. The specific task they set themselves was to explain in Marxist terms the changes that had occurred in prehistoric times. The primary context in which such changes were held to be comprehensible was no longer technology but social organization. The concept of successive ages of stone, bronze, and iron was abandoned on the ground that it had its source in an understanding not of society but too narrowly of the raw materials prevailing in the development of technology. Archaeologists were called upon not only to describe their finds but also to reconstruct the societies that had produced them. This involved defining their modes of production and determining as much as possible about their technology, social organization, and ideological concepts (Miller 1956: 79).

This approach had many valuable consequences. By directing the attention of archaeologists to how ordinary people had lived, it encouraged them to undertake large-scale horizontal excavations of settlements, camp sites and workshops (Davis 1983: 410). Greater attention also was paid to the evidence of dwellings and the relationship of different types of artifacts to these structures. This resulted in the first identification of Palaeolithic dwellings anywhere in the world (Childe 1950) and some of the first total excavations of Neolithic villages. When cemeteries were excavated it was mainly to investigate religious beliefs and to ascertain the social structures of the societies that had produced them.

Some of the interpretations of this period were unsound, such as P. I. Boriskovsky's suggestion that female statuettes were evidence of matriarchal clan societies in Upper Palaeolithic times (Davis 1983: 413–4). On the other hand, in 1934 P. N. Tret'yakov determined from fingerprints on the interiors of vessels that the pottery associated with prehistoric hunter–fisher cultures of northern and central Russia was manufactured by women. He went on to argue that the uniformity of pottery styles within individual sites and the considerable variation between sites indicated a matrilocal marriage pattern, which resulted in the potters of each small community handing on their traditions from one generation to the next undisturbed by external influences (Childe 1943: 6). Similar interpretations were not attempted by American archaeologists prior to the 1960s and these studies were less archaeological in that the identification of the sex of the potters depended entirely on the direct historical approach (Binford 1972: 61).

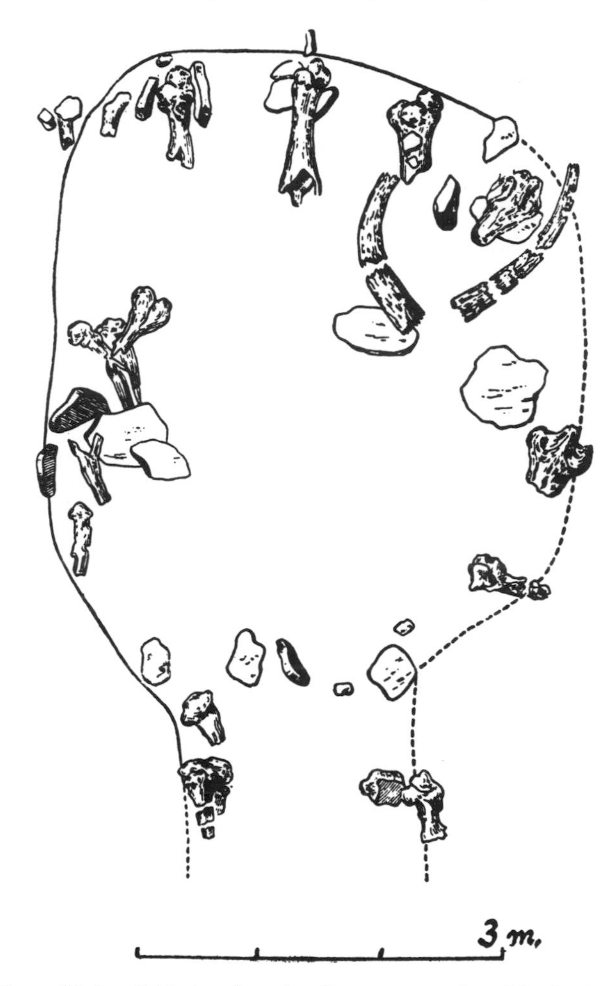

33 Plan of Palaeolithic hut found at Buryet, reproduced in *Antiquity* by Childe, 1950

Archaeologists were also encouraged to explain changes in the archaeological record not in terms of migration and diffusion but as the result of internal social developments. For example, in their *Clan Societies of the Steppes of Eastern Europe* Kruglov and Podgayetsky (1935) related changes in Copper Age burial customs in southern Russia to developing concepts of property. They suggested that collective tombs correlated with the communal ownership of the means of production and individual barrows with patriarchal pastoral societies. They also suggested that as property became more important in evolving societies, the greed of heirs gradually curtailed the burial of large amounts of valuable possessions with the dead (Childe 1942d: 133). The latter argument was to inspire Childe's (1945a) cross-cultural generalizations about the development of funerary customs, which after decades of neglect have once again become of interest to archaeologists (M. Pearson 1982). Because of their concern with social change Soviet archaeologists also revived an interest in cultural evolution as well as in associated concepts of development and progress, at a time when diffusionism was still in the ascendant in North America and the rest of Europe.

Yet Marxist studies of archaeological data laboured under severe conceptual restrictions at this time. Social evolution was conceptualized in terms of a unilinear scheme of socioeconomic formations loosely derived from Engels' *The Origin of the Family, Private Property, and the State*, which in turn had been based largely on Marx's study of Morgan's *Ancient Society*. Pre-class societies were divided into successive pre-clan, matriarchal clan, patriarchal clan, and terminal clan stages followed by three forms of class society: slave, feudal, and capitalist; and two more forms of classless society: socialist and communist. The latter was regarded as the final stage of human development and not subject to further change (Miller 1956: 78–9; Yu. Semenov 1980). This formulation was accorded canonical status during the Stalin period and scientific criticism of it was not allowed. Archaeologists had to interpret their findings in accordance with this scheme and also in agreement with the classics of Marxism–Leninism. The only leeway allowed reflected the recognition that many cultures were in a transitional rather than a pure state with respect to their stage of development. There was also debate concerning the archaeological criteria that might reveal to which stage of development an archaeological culture belonged. The dogmatism with which social scientists adhered to this scheme contrasts sharply with the views expressed by Marx and Engels, who were prepared to consider multilinear models of social evolution, especially with regard to earlier and less well understood periods of human development.

Still worse, within the GAIMK, Soviet archaeological research was now subjected to the intellectual influence as well as the administrative direction of Marr. By denying commonly accepted evidence of linguistic continuity, his theory of linguistic change encouraged archaeologists to ignore even the most blatant evidence of ethnic movements in the archaeological record and to interpret the archaeological sequence for each region from earliest times to the present as stages in the history of a single people. Ravdonikas argued that in the Crimea an autochthonous population had in turn been Iranian-speaking Scythians, German-speaking Goths (whose language was nevertheless proclaimed to be historically unrelated to German languages farther west), and finally Slavs. Mikhail Artamonov maintained that the Khazars had not come from farther east to the Don Valley and the northern Caucasus but had evolved locally and hence were not Turks; while M. Khudyakov asserted that the Volga Tatars were likewise not Turks but had developed as a result of the amalgamation of local tribes (Miller 1956: 81–2). This view also tended to inhibit an interest in physical anthropology, insofar as the latter was directed towards distinguishing ethnic groups in the archaeological record (letter of V.G. Childe cited in Trigger 1980a: 104). While Soviet archaeologists professed to be interested in the prehistory of various ethnic groups, their unilinear evolutionary approach discouraged the investigation of the sorts of cultural variation that might have had ethnic significance. Diffusion was also rejected as a denigration of human creativity. Marr's concept of the autochthonous development of peoples was seen as a rejection of the anti-evolutionary and often racist theories of cultural development prevailing in Western Europe. Interpretations that invoked processes of diffusion and migration were condemned for embodying concepts of bourgeois nationalism and trying to provide a spurious scientific basis for chauvinist, imperialist, and racist doctrines. Hence to advocate such views became evidence of counter-revolutionary sympathies (Miller 1956: 80–4). After Marr died in 1934 his doctrines continued to enjoy official esteem and patronage and dominated archaeological interpretations until 1950. At that time Stalin, in his essay 'Concerning Marxism in linguistics' denounced Marr's teachings as absurd; pointing out that the same Russian language continued to be spoken in the Soviet Union as had been spoken in tsarist Russia.

The heavy emphasis that was placed on the sociological interpretation of archaeological data and the rejection of the Montelian approach inhibited an interest in the systematic classification of artifacts, which was labelled *goloye veshchevedeniye* (naked artifactology). The attention paid to classification in the past was condemned as part of a bourgeois tendency to ignore the social and political significance of archaeological data. Hence it, like diffusion and migration, acquired negative political connotations. The neglect of classification has had long-term adverse effects on Soviet archaeology, which to the present day has continued, in terms of typology, cultural chronology, and the defining of cultural units to lag behind research being done in Central and Western Europe (Bulkin *et al.* 1982: 288–90).

Although the Soviet cultural revolution is generally described as a period when creativity was swamped by aggressive and intolerant sectarianism (Fitzpatrick 1974: 52), the approach to archaeological interpretation that was pioneered at that time was one of great originality and importance. The conceptualizations of this initial phase in the development of Soviet archaeology were not without flaws and excesses. Chief among these was a superficial and politically constrained understanding of Marxism, which was accompanied by an overenthusiasm for interpreting archaeological data in terms of human behaviour, often without necessary formal studies. Such shortcomings were to be expected in the early stages of a new approach to archaeological interpretation. These flaws were identified and have been increasingly overcome as Soviet archaeology has matured.

Soviet archaeologists shared an interest in cultural evolution and learning how people had lived in prehistoric times with the Scandinavian archaeologists of the early nineteenth century. What was completely new was their determination to understand how social and cultural systems changed in terms of their own internal dynamics. This marked a sharp break with earlier efforts by archaeologists to explain cultural change in terms of external influences or human inventiveness considered without reference to social and economic conditions. The new approach was also characterized by an explicit rejection of the racism and pessimism about human creativity that characterized archaeology in Central and Western Europe in the 1920s. Instead it adopted a dynamic view of society that accorded with the new social outlook within the Soviet Union. In particular, it reflected the beliefs of a new generation of archaeologists, trained since the revolution, that society could be altered and improved through collective social efforts.

Consolidation

The cultural revolution was followed by a period of consolidation. Beginning in 1934 there was a call, in all branches of Soviet historical scholarship, for greater professionalization, better techniques, and higher-quality work. The polemical and programmatic literature that had dominated the previous period was abandoned in favour of more conventional empirical studies. The latter became more popular as growing insistence on political orthodoxy made any innovation within the Marxist tradition, or even the serious academic discussion of theoretical problems, increasingly dangerous. Postgraduate degrees and the defence of dissertations, which had been abolished after the revolution (Graham 1967: 141), were reintroduced. As part of this consolidation the term archaeology was revived, early in 1931, as the name of a discipline, although to distinguish it from 'bourgeois archaeology' the form practised in the Soviet Union was henceforth to be called Soviet archaeology (Miller 1956: 108–9). Archaeology continued to be regarded as a branch of history, but was seen as embracing a set of problems that were studied by means of material culture. It was also possible once again to refer to the traditional technological stages of development, although technology alone was no longer accorded explanatory significance.

While Soviet archaeology was accepted as being adequately developed in a political sense, greater technical expertise was now said to be required to improve the general standard of the discipline. The GAIMK was expanded and given the right to award postgraduate degrees. In 1934 it was divided into four branches, one each to study the history of pre-class, slave-holding, and feudal societies and a fourth to deal with technical aspects of research common to archaeology. A separate chair (professorship) was established for each socioeconomic period. In 1937 the GAIMK was renamed the Institute for the History of Material Culture and attached to the prestigious Soviet Academy of Sciences, which by the 1930s had regained the role that the Imperial Russian Academy had played under the tsars as the 'directorate of the cultural and scientific life of the nation' (Graham 1967: 23). The main centre of the Institute for the History of Material Culture was now located in Moscow, although a branch remained in Leningrad. In the mid-1950s the Institute was renamed the Institute of Archaeology. It has continued to exert a controlling influence on setting the objectives of archaeological research for five-year plans, organizing major conferences, allocating space for publications in major journals and monograph series, and regulating foreign contacts. It also continues to grant a large number of the higher degrees in archaeology (Davis 1983: 408).

During the 1930s chairs and departments of archaeology were established in a large number of universities, new monographs and monograph series were published, and *Sovetskaya Arkheologiya*, which was to become the leading Soviet archaeological journal, was begun. Archaeological salvage work expanded rapidly in conjunction with the massive industrial projects that started in 1928. Special archaeological expeditions were attached to each major construction project. These investigated the affected terrain before and during construction, carried out excavations, and studied the findings. In the 1930s nearly 300 expeditions were at work annually (Bulkin *et al.* 1982: 276). Tours of excavations, exhibitions, and popular publications served as means of public instruction. Archaeologists also applied themselves to practical work, such as studying ancient irrigation systems as guides to modern development and locating ancient mining sites which might still be of commercial value. This practice was especially common between 1935 and 1941 (Miller 1956: 112).

During the 1930s there was a dramatic increase in knowledge of the prehistoric archaeology of the Caucasus, Central Asia, and Siberia. These regions were studied in order to enhance the cultures of national groups that had been exploited and kept underdeveloped in tsarist Russia (Frumkin 1962). Various rich finds were made in these areas, such as remains of the ancient states of Urartu and Parthia and the tumuli at Trialeti and Pazyryk. The cultural diversity of the archaeological record became increasingly evident and this in turn raised questions about how such data were to be analysed and related to the prevailing unilinear evolutionary scheme. These questions acquired greater urgency in the late 1930s and during World War II, when the sovereignty and very survival of the peoples of the Soviet Union were threatened by German military expansion. Soviet scholars responded with an assertion of patriotism and by fostering national self-consciousness, which continued during the period of the Cold War.

In archaeology this new interest expressed itself in a growing concern with ethnogenesis, which involved searching for ways to distinguish ethnic differences from other forms of cultural variation in order to trace the origins of specific national groups. Archaeologists began to specialize in the study of specific periods and cultures and thus to move in the direction of a culture-historical approach. Previously Soviet archaeologists had ridiculed the debates carried on between Polish and German archaeologists as to whether the late Neolithic and early Bronze Age Lusatian culture was Slavic or German. They rightly observed that these two linguistic groups had probably not yet differentiated at that time (Miller 1956: 83–4). They also noted that Marx had rejected the notion that historical claims gave national groups rights to territories they did not currently occupy. Nevertheless, in the late 1930s, Russian archaeologists became anxious to demonstrate that from ancient times their ancestors, the East Slavs, had occupied the European territory of the Soviet Union, as well as to refute German claims that throughout history the Slavs had been culturally backward peoples. Both before and after World War II research was carried out that sought to trace the origins of the Russian people and the development of their ancient culture and handicrafts (Miller 1956: 135–44). The study of medieval Russian towns, especially the excavations at Novgorod, set new standards for urban archaeology for that period. The recovery there of numerous letters written on birch bark revealed an unexpected degree of literacy outside of the clergy. These studies demonstrated that the development of towns in ancient Russia started at the same time as, and went on simultaneously with, the development of towns in Western and Central Europe. They also showed that the Russians were abreast of other European groups in the development of crafts, trade, and culture (M. Thompson 1967). The long-held view that Russian towns had begun as Scandinavian colonies was vehemently rejected. Yet, in the course of these studies of ethnogenesis, the concept of autochthonous development was frequently ignored and cautious use was made of diffusion and migration to explain changes in the archaeological record.

These tendencies were strengthened when Marr's linguistic theories were repudiated in 1950 and with them the main ideological underpinning for the concept of autochthonous development. Faith diminished in formerly respectable stationary schemes of ethnogenesis and by the 1960s some migrations were seen as coming from

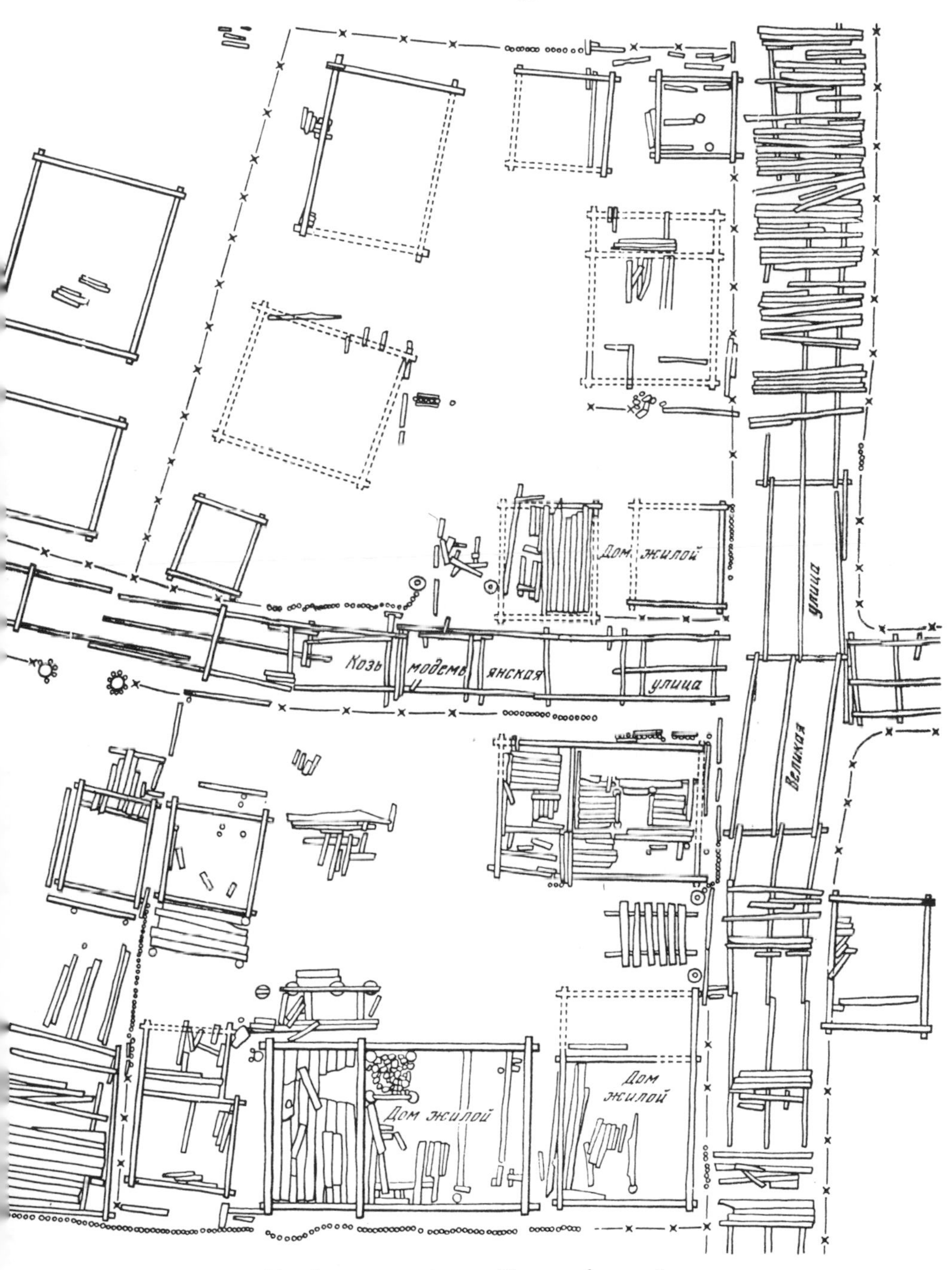

34 Plan from excavations at Novgorod, 1977–83

35 Excavations at Novgorod, 1977–82

distant homelands. Researchers were now taking account of characteristics of the archaeological record and of prehistoric human behaviour which they had previously ignored. The archaeological record was becoming more diverse and colourful as it was seen to be filled with ethnic groups whose cultural differences were of considerable interest (Bulkin *et al.* 1982: 276–8). While these developments were less innovative than those of the early 1930s and had their roots in nineteenth-century European culture-historical archaeology, their incorporation into Soviet archaeology represented a definite enrichment of that approach.

At the same time Soviet archaeology made significant advances along its own lines. S. A. Semenov had considerable success in determining the uses that had been made of prehistoric stone and

36 Excavations at Novgorod

bone tools by experimentally identifying the processes that had caused the patterns of use-wear found on them. While this approach, which is closely aligned to a Marxist interest in production, had been pioneered by Nilsson in the first half of the nineteenth century, it was almost completely ignored by Western archaeologists until a translation of Semenov's *Prehistoric Technology* (1964) was published. Thus, without in any way abandoning the Marxist goal of explaining cultural transformations in relationship to changing modes of production, archaeologists became aware that there was more evidence that required explanation. While staying within the Marxist tradition, they adopted a more historical, as opposed to an evolutionary, view of the past.

Recent developments

The post-Stalin era saw significant liberalization of Soviet scholarship and in Soviet life generally. While this period has been described as one of problems (Gening 1982) or even crisis (Soffer 1985: 8–15) in Soviet archaeology, it has also been a time of growing complexity and diversity in the interpretation of archaeological data. The centralized control of archaeology lessened somewhat as new degree-granting centres of the Institute of Archaeology were established in Novosibirsk, Irkutsk, Chita, Kemerovo, Magadan, Dushanbe, and Samarkand and the amount of research originating in Moscow and Leningrad dropped to 25 percent by 1970 (Davis 1983: 409). Western books became more widely available and more contacts were established with Western archaeologists. These contacts have been justified on the basis of Lenin's observation that every important trend in bourgeois science reflects as well as distorts reality and that by applying a dialectical materialist critique to such work it is possible for Marxists to discover what is of value in these approaches (Bulkin *et al.* 1982: 278). Soviet archaeologists now recognize that valuable insights can be derived from Western archaeology, whereas in the past such behaviour would have been denounced as a 'manifestation of fawning and subservience to the West and its capitalist culture' (Miller 1956: 146). According to Soviet archaeologists this new confidence does not mean 'the end of ideological struggle' but signifies that it has become 'less sharp in form but more profound in substance' (Bulkin *et al.* 1982: 278).

Greater self-consciousness and creativity are also manifested in theoretical discussions of Marxism, which is no longer obligatorily identified with the traditional Soviet scheme of unilinear evolution. In recent years the status of the Asiatic mode of production has been hotly debated (Dunn 1982), as have the relationship between socio-economic formations and specific cultures, the impact that interacting societies at different levels of development have on one another, and the nature of sociocultural change in precapitalist societies (Danilova 1971). Western observers have noted a rejection of dogmatism and a trend towards theoretical diversification, although always within the framework of Marxist philosophy (Fortes 1980: xix). What is happening is perhaps more accurately described as a continuing shift from the evolutionary to the historical poles that have been complementary approaches in Marxism from the beginning.

All Soviet archaeologists work within the framework of Marxist historical or dialectical materialism, which constitutes the ideological basis of Soviet society. This requires all studies of human behaviour to be conceptualized developmentally, with special attention being paid to the causes and conditions that bring about change. Marxism also encourages the analysis of behavioural phenomena in as holistic a context as possible. The marked divisions between social science disciplines in the West are viewed as an arbitrary impediment to a scientific understanding of human behaviour. Such divisions are interpreted as symptomatic of a declining society in which an objective understanding of human behaviour is no longer desired by the dominant class. Soviet archaeology is also not separated into self-contained branches, such as prehistoric, classical, and Near Eastern archaeology. These different types of archaeology are all studied in history departments and higher degrees in archaeology are always in history. It is argued that this unity of history and archaeology and their shared commitment to a historical approach helps archaeologists to understand their material from a holistic perspective that combines an interest in specific culture-historical processes with a more general concern with the evolution of society and culture. Soviet archaeology thus lacks much of the theoretical tension that – rightly or wrongly – has pitted culture-historical and evolutionary approaches against one another in Western Europe and America since the nineteenth century and which also has encouraged much methodological innovation in the West in recent decades.

Yet there is growing discussion about how archaeological data can contribute most effectively to a Marxist analysis of human behaviour. Many of the more traditional Soviet archaeologists believe that historical information can be extracted from archaeological data using only common sense and the theoretical apparatus of conventional historical analysis. These data can then be combined with written historical sources, ethnography, historical linguistics, art history, folk lore, and any other information that is relevant for the study of the past. While not denying that they employ distinctive methods to recover and analyse their data, these archaeologists do not believe that it is necessary to elaborate any specifically archaeological concepts that would distinguish archaeological interpretation from the general stream of historical analysis.

This approach characterizes the work of archaeologists who are interested in studying not only specific cultures but also the evolution of society. The evolutionary approach, which V. M. Masson calls 'sociological archaeology', especially embraces research being done in the Caucasus and Central Asia, where the earliest agricultural economies and the first urban civilizations evolved within the territory of the Soviet Union. Sociological archaeology seeks to reconstruct the economic, social, and ideological structures of ancient societies in order to establish the laws as well as the particular phenomena and processes that bring about change (Bulkin *et al.* 1982: 281). Systematic studies begun in 1937 by S. P. Tolstoy in Turkmenia documented the development of ancient irrigation systems. Since then research in southern Turkmenia has demonstrated the development of a food-producing economy and later of Bronze-Age class societies in that region (Kohl 1981a).

Although major efforts have been made to reconstruct tool use, the operation of irrigation systems, and the economy and social composition of urban centres, at least one American commentator has noted the absence of detailed discussions of the relative importance of population pressure, irrigation agriculture, settlement patterns, warfare, economic exchanges, and religious integration as factors bringing about change (Lamberg-Karlovsky 1981: 388). He attributes this to the 'historical–descriptive' rather than 'analytical–explanatory' models that characterize Soviet archaeological research. On the other hand, some Soviet archaeologists have suggested that the chief shortcoming of their evolutionary interpretations is that evolutionary patterns, often derived in part from the writings of Western archaeologists such as V. G. Childe, R. J. Braidwood, and R. McC. Adams, are imposed on the data, rather than derived from a detailed study of the objective characteristics of the archaeological record (Bulkin *et al.* 1982: 281). To at least some degree this approach reflects a continuing belief that Marxist stadial theory already provides a detailed explanation of cultural change rather than a desire to use archaeological data to refine and elaborate an understanding that would take account of the distinctive features of the archaeological record, such as the weak dichotomy between urban and rural society found in Central Asia during the Bronze Age (Kohl 1984: 131–2).

A more critical attitude towards traditional stadial theory has developed in Palaeolithic archaeology, where archaeologists have attempted to determine in a rigorous fashion the archaeological indices by which the various stages of social evolution can be recognized. In 1935 Boriskovsky maintained that matriarchal clan society had replaced the primeval horde at the beginning of the Upper Palaeolithic period. He cited Venus figurines and what appeared to be the remains of large longhouses as evidence of this. Since the late 1950s, however, the social contrasts between the Mousterian and Upper Palaeolithic periods have become less apparent. More recently G. P. Grigor'ev has maintained that no major differences can be detected in communal organization from late Acheulean through Upper Palaeolithic times. He concludes that the nuclear family probably existed already in the Lower Palaeolithic and that there is no compelling evidence to demonstrate the existence of clan organization in Upper Palaeolithic times. It is now widely recognized by Soviet archaeologists that existing stadial theory provides no visible transition markers for the Palaeolithic sequence and that archaeological finds cannot be interpreted in socioevolutionary terms (Davis 1983: 411–15). This critique has developed as part of a general reappraisal of periodization schemes by Soviet ethnologists and historians (Gellner 1980).

Since the 1930s archaeologists interested in ethnogenesis have sought to discover 'ethnic indicators' and to use these to identify prehistoric ethnic groups. Yet ethnographic research has weakened this position by demonstrating the complexity of the relationship between material culture, language, and group identity as revealed by a self-appointed name (Dragadze 1980). This has led to the realization of the polyethnicity of certain archaeological cultures, including ones that have played a decisive role in interpreting the origins of modern ethnic groups (Bulkin *et al.* 1982: 280). V. P. Liubin's contention that systematic variations in Mousterian assemblages in the Caucasus reflect ethnic divisions has been challenged by I. I. Korobkov and M. M. Mansurov's arguments that these differences reflect functional variations in site behaviour, giving rise to a debate that has much in common with that between Bordes and Binford concerning the Mousterian of Western Europe. G. P. Grigor'ev maintains that, because the 'pre-tribes' that existed prior to the Upper Palaeolithic were closed systems, stone tools provide adequate indices of tribal or ethnic affiliations that extend as far back as late Acheulean times. A number of Soviet Palaeolithic archaeologists do not agree with Grigor'ev or Liubin that formally defined stone tool assemblages are adequate indicators of ethnicity (Davis 1983: 419).

A growing number of Soviet archaeologists appear to believe that the progress of their discipline has been hampered by failure to pay adequate attention to the particular characteristics of archaeological data. No one publicly questions the status of archaeology as a historical discipline or the appropriateness of interpreting human behaviour in terms of Marxist theory. The question is how human behaviour is to be inferred from the material remains of the past, which by their very nature do 'not contain evidence fixed by means of language' (Kamenetsky, Marshak and Sher 1975, cited by Bulkin *et al.* 1982: 282). These archaeologists believe that treating archaeological findings humanistically, as merely another form of historical or sociological data, fails to deal with this problem. A variety of trends in current Soviet archaeology represent implicit or explicit attempts to overcome this shortcoming.

The most conventional of these trends, within the context of Soviet archaeology, is the increasing attention being paid to the study of prehistoric technology. The findings of petrography, metallurgy, and other natural science disciplines, as well as the use-wear analysis pioneered by Semenov, are used to identify sources of raw materials and to determine how artifacts were made and what they were used for. The advocates of these approaches, like their counterparts in the West, are fond of contrasting the scientific rigour of their work with the guesswork of traditional archaeologists (Bulkin *et al.* 1982: 282–3).

There is also growing interest in the Soviet Union, as in the West, in ecological analyses of the relations between prehistoric societies and their natural environments. For Soviet archaeologists the guiding principle of this approach, which structured earlier interests in prehistoric environments and subsistence patterns, is Marx and Engels' observation that 'the history of humanity and the history of nature . . . are inseparable . . . While the human race exists, the history of humans and the history of nature mutually influence one another' (cited by Dolukhanov 1979: 200). Soviet archaeologists carefully locate the source of sociocultural development in the forces and relations of production rather than in the natural realm or the general adjustment of changing subsystems to one another. The sphere of 'social production' is viewed as central to understanding human responses even to the most dramatic changes in the natural environment. Thus, even in the sphere of ecology, Marxists adopt a human-centred rather than an ecosystemic approach (Dolukhanov 1979). It has been observed, however, that the analysis of empirical data is still the weakest point in the study of prehistoric ecology as well as in archaeology generally. Paul Dolukhanov (1979: 200) has pointed to ambiguities in such elementary concepts as attribute, type, assemblage, and culture.

This concern has given rise to a growing interest in the formal analysis of archaeological data. Rather than dismissing such concerns as evidence of bourgeois obscurantism, as was done in the 1930s, many Soviet archaeologists now regard these studies as essential for achieving a detailed historical and social understanding of archaeological data. Proponents of the descriptive approach have urged the necessity for strict operational definitions and standardized procedures for the analysis of archaeological data. The importance of standardized analysis is particularly evident in situations where vast amounts of data have to be processed. As a result of years of neglect, much research of this sort remains to be done. While Central European archaeologists can refer to specific types of fibulae, such as Almgren 67 or 236, which have carefully defined formal characteristics and temporal associations, Soviet archaeologists use descriptive terms, such as 'fibula with a high catch-guard' (Bulkin *et al.* 1982: 288; Klejn 1982). In the Soviet Union there is still no widely accepted typology for Palaeolithic artifacts, although attempts are being made to develop such systems (Davis 1983: 419–21). Some work is being done using attribute analyses and complex mathematical–statistical procedures (Bulkin *et al.* 1982: 282). These procedures are making it possible to recognize artifacts as multivariate phenomena rather than simply as products of cultural norms. Some typological studies raise issues of technological and historical importance, such as the debate between Liubin and Grigor'ev about whether the Levallois technique for manufacturing stone flakes represents a necessary intermediate step between discoidal and prismatic blade cores (Davis 1983: 421). Opponents of this trend in archaeology accuse it of exaggerating the correlation between formal traits and their historical significance and more generally of overestimating the potential of a typological approach to reveal historical information (Bulkin *et al.* 1982: 282).

In the Soviet Union archaeological cultures are generally large-scale taxonomic units, whereas in Central and Western Europe smaller divisions, corresponding to individual, socially significant site clusters, are being identified. This discrepancy is partly accounted for by the large areas that have to be studied in the Soviet Union even in relation to the extensive archaeological resources. It is also seen, however, like the rudimentary development of typology, as reflecting a poorly developed concern for the formal properties of the archaeological record, that stems from the approach towards archaeology that was adopted in the early 1930s. Today there is a growing interest in defining archaeological cultures (Bulkin *et al.* 1982: 289–90). Soviet archaeologists follow ethnologists in distinguishing between 'historical–ethnographic communities', which denote specific social groups, and 'economic–culture types', which may embrace a number of ethnic groups at a similar level of development and occupying similar environmental zones. Most Palaeolithic archaeologists define their archaeological cultures as being economic–culture types, while more recent cultures tend to be regarded as historical–ethnographic entities (Davis 1983: 415–16). Since the early 1970s efforts have been made to formulate a uniform definition of the archaeological culture for use throughout the Soviet Union. In 1972 V. M. Masson suggested a hierarchy of units – local variant, archaeological culture, and culture group – which was explicitly modelled on the scheme that D. L. Clarke had presented in his *Analytical Archaeology* (1968). Masson also proposed that the levels of this hierarchy could be defined in terms of coincidence of artifact types. An even more elaborate system has been proposed by Leo Klejn (1982). As yet, however, there is no general agreement about how archaeological cultures are to be defined, what is their precise sociological meaning, and how they fit into a Marxist analysis of social change.

It is also objected that in the past, in order to escape the sin of 'artifactology', Soviet archaeologists shunned not only artifact typology and defining archaeological cultures but also the construction of relative chronologies by means of seriation. Since the 1950s this tendency has been reinforced by a growing reliance on radiocarbon dates. Leo Klejn and other adherents of 'theoretical archaeology' argue that, because of their failure to evolve a more detailed chronology, Soviet archaeologists are unable to correlate changes observed in material culture in adjacent regions with sufficient precision and to relate these changes to known historical events. They urge that, as a first step in their research, archaeologists should arrange historically related cultures as co-traditions and determine the influences that contemporary cultures exerted upon one another. This approach was alien to Soviet archaeology in its early stages as a result of its preoccupation with unilinear evolution and autochthonous development. Once these external comparisons have been made, it becomes possible to assess the historical role that migrations and diffusion have played in shaping the archaeological record. Only then can archaeologists proceed to interpret the archaeological record in terms of the economies, social structures, and belief systems of ancient societies and to explain the development of these societies in terms of laws, causal mechanisms, and specific processes (Bulkin *et al.* 1982).

No Soviet archaeologist questions the validity of historical materialism as an explanation of human behaviour. His or her aim is to provide information about human behaviour that will contribute to the development of Marxist palaeohistory (prehistory, protohistory, and ancient history), historical sociology, and the study of cultural evolution. Klejn and some other Soviet archaeologists emphasize that material culture constitutes a very different source of information about human behaviour than do written records. They also argue that Marxism, as a study of human behaviour, does not provide a detailed guide for transforming archaeological data into information about human behaviour. It is therefore the duty of archaeologists to elaborate such methods. They also imply that many of the basic techniques used to analyse archaeological data are relatively immune to social and political bias. This explains why Soviet archaeologists, including many who reject 'theoretical archaeology', have been able successfully to borrow numerous techniques from Western archaeology in recent years. Thoroughly delineating spatial, temporal, and formal variations in the archaeological record and documenting the external factors, such as environmental changes, intersocietal competition, diffusion, and migration, that account for some of these variations, are necessary prerequisites for understanding how the forces and relations of production bring about change within the context of specific societies.

Conclusions

Soviet and Western archaeology have developed in ways that contrast with each other. Yet over time both appear to have come to address the same range of problems. In the 1930s Soviet archaeologists pioneered the development of settlement archaeology and the societal explanation of archaeological data. Later they spearheaded the modern revival of use-wear analysis. A Marxist orientation led them to become the first archaeologists to attempt to explain changes in the archaeological record in terms of internal social factors. Only in the 1950s did these start to become frontier areas of research in Western archaeology. Conversely, an increasing number of Soviet archaeologists are currently advocating that more systematic attention should be paid to the construction of cultural chronologies and the study of diffusion and migration at a time when these topics have come to seem routine, and even old-fashioned, to many Western archaeologists. At the same time both Soviet and Western archaeologists share a growing interest in studying their data from an ecological viewpoint.

Soviet archaeologists began to take account of external factors bringing about change in social systems at the same time that Western ones were becoming more interested in internal factors. The political and economic influences that adjacent societies exert upon one another can be analysed easily in terms of a traditional Marxist framework by enlarging the scale of the unit being studied and thereby treating a number of interacting cultures as parts of a world system. Yet ecological analyses and the study of cultural diffusion require the consideration of external factors that Marxist archaeologists have hitherto avoided. This does not constitute, however, a break with Marxist theory but rather an attempt to elaborate it to take account of the complexity of the archaeological record. By avoiding external determinism and stressing the socially conditioned evolution of the relations of production as the principal factor bringing about cultural evolution, Soviet archaeology remains unique in terms of the primary role that it assigns to human action in explaining history.

Soviet archaeologists initially rejected a formalist, or Montelian, methodology because they saw it as standing in the way of developing a Marxist approach to interpreting archaeological data. It continued to be rejected during the ideologically regimented Stalinist period because of its Western and bourgeois connotations. Today Soviet archaeologists are once again employing 'formalist' approaches to examine the archaeological record and discover the full range of regularities that require explanation. The growing debates in Soviet archaeology and the widening range of analytical techniques being employed by Soviet archaeologists are indications, not of their rejection of Marxism, but on the contrary of their growing self-confidence as Marxist historians. There is no basis for Western archaeologists, including self-styled Marxists, who know little or nothing about what is going on in Soviet archaeology, to dismiss it as a fossilized relic of the past from which there is little to be learned.

CHAPTER 7

Functionalism in Western archaeology

Forms and types, that is, products, have been regarded as more real and alive than the society which created them and whose needs determined these manifestations of life.

A. M. TALLGREN, 'The method of prehistoric archaeology' (1937), p. 155

Although the culture-historical approach has continued to serve significant needs until the present, especially in countries where interests in ethnic origins remain strong or where detailed cultural chronologies have not yet been worked out (Schrire *et al.* 1986), its inadequacies for understanding how prehistoric cultures functioned and how they changed soon became evident to an increasing number of Western archaeologists, just as they had become evident to archaeologists in the Soviet Union. While Childe (1935a, 1940a) continued to produce detailed regional culture-historical syntheses, long before these works were published he began to doubt that much could be learned about ethnicity from archaeological data alone or that ethnicity was a concept that could be central to the study of prehistory (Childe 1930: 240–7). He dismissed the culture-historical approach as an archaeological substitute for old-fashioned political history in which cultures replaced statesmen and migrations replaced battles (Childe 1958b: 70; see also MacWhite 1956). In due course other Western European and American archaeologists came to share this view and adopted a new approach to the study of prehistory which was based upon a systemic understanding of human behaviour. This approach was stimulated by the ecological tradition of Scandinavian archaeology, the example of Soviet archaeology, and the rejection of diffusionism by Western European ethnologists.

The development of social anthropology

In the United Kingdom ethnologists reacted against the sterile diffusionism of Elliot Smith and his followers by adopting the structural–functionalist approach of Bronislaw Malinowski (1884–1942) and E. R. Radcliffe-Brown (1881–1955). Their first major works, Malinowski's *Argonauts of the Western Pacific* and Radcliffe-Brown's *The Andaman Islanders*, were both published in 1922, although Malinowski had done his unprecedentedly detailed fieldwork in the Trobriand Islands between 1915 and 1918 and Radcliffe-Brown had worked in the Andaman Islands between 1906 and 1908. Both men argued that human behaviour can be understood best in relation to social systems that are conceived as made up of functionally interdependent elements. Malinowski stressed that the institutions that composed social systems were grounded in biological needs, a view not shared by Radcliffe-Brown, who sought only to define the social role played by institutions. Their common approach came to be called social anthropology to distinguish it from ethnology, which was associated with unilinear evolutionism and diffusionism.

British social anthropology was grounded on the earlier work of the French sociologist Emile Durkheim (1858–1917). Like Karl Marx, Durkheim viewed societies as systems made up of interdependent parts. Coming from a family of modest means whose status was threatened by the rapid social and economic changes taking place in late nineteenth-century France, he regarded these changes as encouraging rapacity and an excess of individualism which threatened the equilibrium of society. As a Jew, and hence a member of a threatened minority group, he did not seek to promote social cohesion by emphasizing racial or ethnic unity. Instead he assumed that only stable societies were healthy and vigorous ones. Like Henri de Saint-Simon (1760–1825) and Auguste Comte (1798–1857), he advocated sociology as a practical means to counteract what he saw as social disintegration in a capitalist society. At the same time he avoided a critique of the economic basis of such societies by viewing social relations as causal in their own right and therefore capable of being regulated without significant reference to the economy (Wolf 1982: 9). While Marx had elaborated theories of internal conflict to explain social change, Durkheim directed his attention towards factors that promoted social stability. His interpretations were elaborated in a series of major publications: *De la division du travail social* (1893), *Les Règles de la méthode sociologique* (1895), *Le Suicide* (1897), and *Les Formes élémentaires de la vie religieuse* (1912).

Durkheim argued that the objective of social science studies was to understand social relations and that the origin of all social processes should be sought in the internal constitution of human groups. Individual aspects of culture, whether they were invented internally or externally, were said to acquire their significance in terms of their functional relationship to specific social systems. He rejected the culture-historical view that social systems and the cultural norms that were associated with them could be understood as a mechanical collection of traits that diffusion had brought together largely as a result of the operation of chance. Instead he argued that societies constituted integrated systems, whose institutions were interrelated like the parts of a living organism. The science of society was thus conceptualized as a comparative study of social morphologies, similar in its objectives to comparative anatomy.

Durkheim also maintained that no change could occur in one part of a social system without bringing about varying degrees of change in other parts. Yet he believed that the normal state of society was one of social solidarity and that rapid changes led to a feeling of anomie or alienation. Thus he agreed with the diffusionists that change was contrary to human nature. This suggests that in his interpretations of change he aligned himself with the anti-evolutionists of the late nineteenth century. Nevertheless he was interested to some degree in problems of social evolution, which he studied using ethnographic data. He argued that as societies became more complex they ceased to be held together by mechanical solidarity, or shared beliefs, and were increasingly united by organic solidarity, resulting from economic interdependence. This new form of cohesion freed individuals from the tyranny of custom and tradition. Malinowski and to a still greater extent Radcliffe-Brown rejected all evolutionary and historical interpretations of ethnographic data as speculative and argued that the comparative study of the structure and functioning of societies currently available for detailed examination was sufficient to produce generalizations that would explain the morphological variation among all societies. For Radcliffe-Brown in particular, the study of change had no significance apart from the investigation of this morphological variation.

While this rejection of an interest in historical processes might seem to have been an unpromising basis for a relationship between social anthropology and archaeology, social anthropology and Durkheimian sociology encouraged an interest among archaeologists in how prehistoric cultures had functioned as systems. This interest increased as archaeologists became disillusioned with the limitations of a diffusionist or culture-historical approach. With its conservative views of human behaviour, social anthropology provided a respectable alternative to Marxism for archaeologists who were primarily interested in how societies worked rather than in how change came about. Yet it is clear that a functional view of archaeological data had begun in archaeology prior to the development of social anthropology. In its early stages this interest had taken the form of a concern with relations between prehistoric cultures and their environments.

Environmental functionalism

As early as the 1840s Worsaae had argued that archaeological finds had to be studied in relationship to their palaeoenvironmental settings and had cooperated with biologists and geologists to do this. Thus began a tradition that has continued to the present in Scandinavian archaeology. Archaeologists studied the retreat of glaciers and the combined results of changing sea levels and isostatic rebound in altering the distributions of land surfaces, lakes, and oceans as a background for determining the impact that these changes had on the prehistoric populations of Scandinavia. They also investigated changes in climate and in the reciprocal relations between flora, fauna, and human land use. Beginning in 1905 the geologist Gerard de Geer (1858–1943) used successions of overlapping annually deposited varves to date the retreating ice front in Sweden beginning 12,000 years ago. This varve sequence was tied in with 30 metres of annual silt deposits on the bed of former Lake Raganda, which had been drained in 1796. Another Swede, E.J. Lennart von Post (1884–1951), utilized Gustav Lagerheim's observation that pollen grains could be preserved for thousands of years to elaborate Steenstrup's pioneering studies of post-glacial floral changes. By 1916 he had produced graphs that purported to show the percentages of various trees at successive periods of Scandinavian prehistory. The old sequence of birch, pine, oak, and beech forest was vindicated but, because pollen floats through the air and is preserved elsewhere than in bogs, it was now possible to examine plant communities over larger areas and to provide evidence of tree cutting and the introduction of domestic plants. It also became possible to trace fluctuations in different plant species over much smaller intervals of time than had been done previously. Forest contour lines were worked out showing the northern limits of various trees at different periods and these were correlated with De Geer's geochronology of glacial margins to achieve a high degree of calendrical precision (Bibby 1956: 183–94). Pollen analysis was introduced into England and applied to archaeological problems by the biologist Harry Godwin (1933).

In 1898 the geologist Robert Gradmann noted a close correlation between wind-deposited loess soils and early Neolithic settlement in Central Europe and concluded that, because early farmers were incapable of clearing forests, the first agricultural settlements had been in areas that were naturally either devoid of trees or lightly forested (Gradmann 1906). The relationship between loess soils and Neolithic settlement continued to be examined by Alfred Schliz (1906), Ernst Wahle (1915), and Max Hellmich (1923) and inspired similar studies of the correlations between soil types and archaeological cultures in England (Daniel 1950: 304–5). It was not until the 1940s that pollen analysis made it clear that loess and other light soils had been forested when they were first settled by Neolithic farmers and that their original attraction had not been lack of trees but rather the presence of soil that was easy to till (G. Clark 1974: 43).

In the account of his excavations at the stratified site of Anau in Russian Turkestan in 1904, the American geologist and archaeologist Raphael Pumpelly (1837–1923) proposed the desiccation or oasis theory of the origins of food-production (1908, 1:65–6). He argued that, as the Near East became much drier following the last Ice Age, hunter–gatherers were compelled to gather around surviving sources of water and to 'conquer new means of support' by domesticating wild animals and grasses. This theory was to become extremely popular among Old-World archaeologists in succeeding decades.

In *Origines Celticae* the Oxford University historian Edwin Guest (1800–80) urged that the history of England had to be understood against the background of British geography (1883). Shortly after, the Oxford geographer H. J. Mackinder (1861–1947) argued that the geographical location of nations in relation to each other played a major role in shaping their political and economic history. In 1912 F.J. Haverfield (1860–1919) demonstrated a correlation between the extent of Roman settlement in Britain and particular types of geographical terrain, while John Myres was inspired by Guest and Mackinder to expound the value of a geographical approach to archaeology. Beginning in 1912, O.G.S. Crawford (1886–1957), who had studied at Oxford and was to work for many years for the Ordnance Survey, concentrated on studying prehistory in relation to the geographical environment. Among his many contributions, he encouraged the use of aerial photography to detect ancient ditches, banks, and crop marks that were not visible from the ground. The importance of aerial reconnaissance for archaeological research had first been recognized during military operations in the course of World War I (Crawford 1923; Crawford and Keiller 1928). The mapping of artifact distributions led to detailed studies of specific periods, with a special emphasis on reconstructing original patterns of vegetation. W. G. Clark, J. P. Williams-Freeman, Herbert Fleure, W. E. Whitehouse, and Cyril Fox undertook studies of the relationship between prehistoric settlement and ecology in various parts of Britain (Daniel 1950: 303–6). This work, which culminated in Fox's (1882–1967) *The Archaeology of the Cambridge Region* (1923), showed that early agricultural settlement had been on light, permeable soils, whereas in the Iron Age and even more in Anglo-Saxon times it had shifted to heavier soils, that were harder to work but more drought resistant and productive. In *The Personality of Britain* Fox (1932) combined the ecological–distributional approach of Gradmann and Crawford with the positional geography of Mackinder to produce some major generalizations about the relationship between landscapes and culture-history. His principal contribution was a distinction between the lowlands of southeastern England, which he saw as exposed to migrations and diffusion of culture from continental Europe, and the highland areas of western and northern Britain, which were more sheltered from such disruptions and hence more selective in adopting new items of culture. This approach has since been applied to other areas (Daniel 1963b; Trigger 1969).

As early as 1915 Elliot Smith had championed the idea that the invention of agriculture, which he believed had occurred as a result of fortuitous circumstances in Egypt, was the primary criterion of the Neolithic and marked one of the crucial turning-points in human history. Both this idea and Pumpelly's oasis hypothesis were popularized by Harold Peake (1867–1946) and H. J. Fleure (1877–1969) in the third volume of their *The Corridors of Time* (1927), a widely read multi-volume series dealing with prehistory. About the same time W. J. Perry (1924: 29–32) popularized the claim of the agronomist T. Cherry that agriculture had been invented in Egypt when people began to increase the amount of millet and barley that grew spontaneously on the flood plain by irrigating dry land adjacent to wild stands and scattering barley seeds in the wet mud left behind at the end of the annual flood. These contributions raised the discussion of the origins of agriculture to a new level of theoretical importance.

While not constituting analyses of whole cultures, growing interest in the relationship between human societies and their environmental settings encouraged a functional view of one major aspect of human behaviour. This stimulated the analysis of palaeoenvironments and of the ecological adaptation of cultures to these environments. It was generally assumed that the natural environment set limits to the sorts of adaptations that were possible rather than determined the specific nature of the response, which was also influenced by historical traditions and unpredictable human choices. This view accorded with the human geography of the period which was dominated by the environmental possibilist approach of the French geographer Paul Vidal de La Blache (1845–1918). Possibilism and diffusionism both stressed indeterminacy as the dominant feature of cultural change.

Economic approaches

As Childe turned away from the culture-historical approach, which he came to regard as an intellectual dead end, he did not deny the importance of diffusion as a force bringing about cultural change. He did, however, realize that diffusion was of no more value for explaining such changes than unilinear evolutionary concepts had been unless archaeologists could determine what factors within prehistoric cultures favoured the adoption of new ideas and influenced the roles that these ideas would play. Childe sought to emulate the work of economic historians by searching for broad economic trends in prehistory, in terms of which specific instances of diffusion might be explained. He presented the results of this research in three books: *The Most Ancient East* (1928), *The Bronze Age* (1930), and *New Light on the Most Ancient East* (1934). Economic interpretations of prehistoric data also played a significant role in *The Danube in Prehistory* (1929), which was written prior to *The Most Ancient East*.

While Childe's concern with economic factors has been interpreted as an early reflection of his commitment to Marxism, he did not claim to be a Marxist at this time and nothing that is specifically Marxist is evident in his work of this period. British archaeologists such as Peake and Fleure had already been offering economic interpretations of the archaeological record and Childe used many of their ideas to construct a more comprehensive model of economic development. It is also evident that his thinking evolved only slowly from a primary interest in subsistence patterns to a view that emphasized aspects of the economy that were not primarily related to subsistence patterns. The importance that he ascribed to viewing prehistoric cultures as patterns of social relations reflects a knowledge of Durkheimian sociology that he acquired primarily as a result of translating into English *From Tribe to Empire* by Alexandre Moret and Georges Davy (1926). Davy was a student of Durkheim who had collaborated with Moret, an Egyptologist, to produce a Durkheimian interpretation of the development of ancient Egyptian civilization.

The Most Ancient East was written as a textbook and a companion volume to *The Dawn of European Civilization*. It sought to trace the origins of the technological innovations that had later spread to Europe. Childe followed Smith and Fleure in stressing the development of agriculture as a crucial turning-point in human history. He also agreed with Pumpelly that desiccation in the Near East at the end of the last Ice Age had caused people to domesticate plants and animals in order to feed the higher densities of population that gathered around surviving sources of water. In keeping with the environmental possibilism that currently was fashionable in non-

Marxist geography, he stressed that individual hunter–gatherer bands could have perished or moved north or south into areas where big game survived rather than developing agriculture. Only three regions in the Near East had enough fertile soil to support the development of a major early civilization: the Nile, Tigris–Euphrates, and Indus Valleys. In each of these areas surplus wealth increased even faster than population, resulting in the concentration of political power, the rise of city life, and the progress of the industrial arts. Yet, while these civilizations evolved from a common Neolithic base and maintained contact with each other, Mesopotamia developed as a series of city states while Egypt quickly was united as a divine monarchy. Technological knowledge spread from these early civilizations to outlying regions, such as Europe, as a result of the trading of surplus food and manufactured goods for raw materials, especially copper and tin. While Childe based this model on relations between modern industrial and Third-World countries, he argued that it was necessary to give 'trade' a precise definition whenever the term was used by specifying the particular sociological, economic, and environmental conditions that shaped such activities in a specific area and at a given point in time (Childe 1928: 221).

In *The Bronze Age* Childe studied the origins and spread of metallurgy, as documented in the archaeological record. He considered the possibility that metallurgy might have been invented independently in Egypt, the Near East, Hungary, and Spain, but, like most diffusionists, concluded that it was such a complex process that it likely was invented only once in human history. He also interpreted specific similarities in the processes used to work bronze and in the shapes of the earliest metal artifacts in Europe and the Near East as proofs of a single origin. Childe was convinced, almost certainly wrongly, on the basis of Homeric texts that metal casting required full time, although initially itinerant, specialists, who, along with prospectors and miners, became the first human beings to function independently of tribal affiliations. The adoption of a metal tool technology therefore was thought to have produced a double loss of Neolithic self-sufficiency, since it required communities to become dependent on craftsmen who were often unrelated to them as well as on the development of extensive trade routes that were not interrupted by periodic outbreaks of tribal warfare in order to ensure the regular delivery of supplies of copper and tin. While he viewed bronze working as an important prerequisite for the development of civilization in the Near East, he argued that in Europe it was mainly used to supply weapons to tribal societies, as an increasing population and spreading forests (resulting from climatic changes) led to greater competition for agricultural land.

In *New Light on the Most Ancient East*, which was written after a visit to major archaeological excavations in Iraq and the Indus Valley, Childe synthesized and elaborated the arguments advanced in his two previous books. He maintained that two revolutions had occurred in prehistoric times in the Near East that were equivalent in their importance to the Industrial Revolution. These were the transition from food-collecting to food-producing and from self-sufficient food-producing villages to urban societies. He believed that each of these revolutions had resulted in a more productive technology and a massive increase in population. The population increase was, however, assumed rather than demonstrated. He also overestimated the extent to which the inhabitants of ancient Near Eastern cities engaged in industry, trade, and commerce rather than agricultural activities. Migrations of surplus population, the exchange of manufactured goods for raw materials, and surplus craftsmen seeking employment spread the technologies produced by these revolutions to Europe. The result was the development in Europe of Neolithic and Bronze Age societies that were structurally different from those that had evolved in the Near East. In due course conspicuous consumption by the upper classes and the military conflicts of the Near Eastern civilizations began to waste more goods than they produced, while the growth of secondary civilizations reduced the amount of raw materials that was reaching them. As a result of both processes, economic progress eventually ground to a halt in the Near East. At the same time European societies continued to progress until they were able to outstrip and dominate those of the Near East. With this economic explanation Childe was able to exorcize the ethnic stereotypes and semi-racist theories that he had invoked to explain the ultimate dominance of European cultures in *The Aryans*.

Childe's interest in economic development in prehistoric times drew its inspiration from trends that were active in the European, and more specifically the British, archaeology of that period. Yet he advanced beyond the interpretations of Elliot Smith, Peake, and Fleure in the consistency with which he applied an economic approach to the study of prehistory and in the scope of his formulations. Also, instead of interpreting cultural change as the result of technological innovation, he saw broader economic and political contexts influencing the uses that were made of innovations. This allowed him to explain how the same technological innovations could produce very different types of societies in Europe and the Near East.

A multilinear evolutionary perspective was inherent in such an economic approach. Yet Childe was not primarily concerned with cultural evolution at this time. He stated categorically that 'archaeology's revelations . . . disclose not abstract evolution but the interaction of multiple concrete groups and the blending of contributions from far-sundered regions' (Childe 1928: 11). Like other European archaeologists he accepted that increasingly complex technologies had developed in the Near East and later in Europe. Yet he regarded human beings as inherently uninventive and relied heavily on diffusion and migration to explain cultural change. Readers were told at the end of *New Light on the Most Ancient East* that the principal aim of the book was to justify 'the general doctrine of cultural diffusion' (Childe 1934: 301). Nor was his materialist perspective complete at this time. While he interpreted some economic change as a response to environmental challenges, much innovation was attributed in a Montelian fashion to the spontaneous exercise of human intelligence to achieve greater control over nature and make human life easier and more secure. Nevertheless, by examining the way in which economic activities brought about changes within cultures, he had helped to narrow the gap between static reconstructions of prehistoric cultures and the appeal to external factors to explain change that had characterized his earlier culture-historical studies.

Childe and Soviet archaeology

In 1935 Childe visited the Soviet Union for the first time. While he was there he met Russian archaeologists, toured museums, and gathered information about recent archaeological discoveries relating to the prehistory of Eastern Europe (S. Green 1981: 76–7). He was impressed by the lavish government support for archaeology, the vast scale on which archaeological research was being conducted, and the use being made of archaeological finds for public education. Above all he was fascinated by the efforts of Soviet archaeologists to explain prehistory in terms of processes internal to societies and on explicitly materialist principles. Their work revealed the narrowness of his own economic interpretations, which he henceforth contrasted unfavourably with the Marxist view that the forces and relations of production play a major role in determining the general character of societies.

On the basis of his own experience, Childe did not accept the entire programme of Soviet archaeology. He refused to adopt its detailed scheme of socioeconomic formations or any other unilinear formulation of social evolution. Later he was to criticize the Soviet approach for compelling archaeologists to assume in advance to be true what it was their duty to prove was so (Childe 1951: 28–9). Moreover, he did not see how archaeologists might hope to infer many of the specific details of social organization that could relate this formulation to their work.

He also refused to stop viewing diffusion as a major factor promoting cultural development. For Childe diffusion was a concept that had moral relevance. Hitler's seizure of power in Germany in 1933 had made him more keenly aware of how disastrously archaeology and racist political movements had become intertwined in that country. Long before, he had invoked diffusion as an antidote to the nationalist theories of Kossinna and other German archaeologists. Now, like Boasian anthropologists in the United States, he argued that increasingly rapid cultural progress had resulted from the breakdown of isolation among neighbouring groups and the pooling on an ever increasing scale of the innovations of all branches of the human family (Childe 1933a,b). Because of this he was distressed to discover that Soviet archaeologists, under the influence of Nikolay Marr, had rejected this concept. While agreeing that as far as possible archaeologists should attempt to explain changes in terms of developments within cultures and alterations in the natural environment, he asserted that it 'cannot be unMarxian' to invoke diffusion to account for the spread of domestic plants and animals and by extension many other classes of ideas (Childe 1946a: 24).

He also refused to abandon the major emphasis he had placed on typology, which he saw as essential for constructing regional chronologies and tracing cultural influences between one region and another. He had little respect for the sloppy manner in which Soviet archaeologists handled these matters. In 1957 he described their prehistoric chronologies as a series of hopelessly vague guesses that did 'not even attract, still less convince' him (Daniel 1958: 66). His experience as a prehistoric archaeologist led him to incorporate what he believed were the important innovations of Soviet archaeology into his own work and to reject what he saw as its shortcomings. In the post-Stalin era Soviet archaeologists have confirmed the wisdom of his choices by working to modify precisely those features of early Soviet archaeology that Childe found objectionable.

Following his visit to the Soviet Union Childe sought to replace his earlier emphasis on economic factors as the principal cause of social change with analyses that were more in accord with Marxist principles. He also paid attention for the first time to cultural evolution, which was a topic of theoretical interest that had remained important in Marxist scholarship but which had not been significant in his own writings or in creative Western European archaeology since the 1880s. In the course of a decade he published three books dealing with cultural evolution: *Man Makes Himself* (1936), *What Happened in History* (1942a), and *Progress in Archaeology* (1944a), as well as a case study *Scotland Before the Scots* (1946a). The first two were written for the general public as well as for professional archaeologists and continue to be read widely.

In *Man Makes Himself* Childe interpreted the archaeological record as evidence of a directional process whereby the scientific knowledge accumulated by human beings gave progressive societies ever greater control over nature and led to the formation of new and more complex sociopolitical systems. He later regarded these views as not being significantly different from the idealist Montelian conception of cultural change (Childe 1958b: 72). In *What Happened in History* he attempted in a more explicitly Marxist fashion to formulate explanations of cultural change that were focused not on technological knowledge as a prime mover but on social, political, and economic institutions and the role they played in bringing it about. In accordance with the principles of dialectical materialism, he viewed every society as containing within itself both progressive and conservative tendencies. The contradictions between these tendencies provided the energy that brought about irreversible social change.

He did not embrace unilinear evolutionism in these studies any more than he had done previously or was to do later. Yet he was erroneously accused of doing so by Julian Steward (1953; 1955: 12), who influenced many American anthropologists to regard Childe as a typical nineteenth-century evolutionist. In *Man Makes Himself* and *What Happened in History*, by concentrating on the development of cultures in the Near East, Childe presents a more unilinear view of cultural change than in his works where developments in Europe and the Near East are examined alongside one another. Nevertheless even in these studies he attributed the differences between the city states that developed in Mesopotamia and the divine monarchy that united Old Kingdom Egypt to divergent social and political techniques for controlling agricultural surpluses that had been created in the course of the transformation of tribal societies into class societies. Writing under the shadow of expanding Nazi power and World War II, he also rejected the naive faith in the inevitability of progress that characterized many vulgarized versions of Marxism as well as the unilinear cultural evolutionism of the nineteenth century. Yet his pessimism led him to make a significant contribution to Marxist studies of change by providing a detailed analysis of the social conditions that impede progress.

Childe argued that at any level of social development, but especially in the early civilizations, entrenched political hierarchies and inflexible systems of religious beliefs can slow or even halt social and economic change. He distinguished between progressive societies, where relations of production favour an expansion of productive forces and there is a harmonious relationship among the means of production, social institutions, and the dominant system of beliefs, and conservative ones, in which social and political factors block change. The ruling classes, according to Childe, sought to prevent technological changes that might threaten their control of society. They did this by monopolizing surplus wealth, exercising bureaucratic control over craftsmen, inhibiting the pursuit of technical knowledge, and patronizing magic and superstition on a lavish scale, as well as by the exercise of force. They only succeeded, however, at the cost of making it more difficult for their own societies to compete with more progressive neighbouring ones. This explanation of the eventual backwardness of Near Eastern civilizations by comparison with those of Europe replaced his own more narrowly economic explanation in *New Light on the Most Ancient East*. Childe now ascribed important roles in shaping history to both the economic base and the superstructure of societies. Yet he was careful to specify that where the superstructure is dominant, its influence can only be negative. Soviet anthropologists have since maintained that this view accords with orthodox Marxism (Petrova-Averkieva 1980: 24).

This position provides a definitive answer to those British Marxists, such as George Thomson (1949), who accused him of ignoring class conflict in the early civilizations. Childe argued that social evolution occurred slowly, if at all, in those early civilizations precisely because such struggles were blunted by highly effective political and religious techniques of social control. He did not ignore the concept of class struggle in the early civilizations or reject it because he thought it inapplicable for studies based on archaeological data. On the contrary, he did not find it useful for explaining ancient Near Eastern civilizations, which he believed remained static for long periods. In his analyses of classical civilizations and in particular of the Roman Empire, he placed greater emphasis on struggles among groups within societies to control wealth and power and on the shifting patterns of political control. His differing treatment of ancient Near Eastern and classical civilizations may have been based on Marx's own distinction between Oriental and Slave societies. Yet it seems more likely that he was unaware of this distinction, since orthodox Marxists did not discuss or write about the concept of Oriental Society during the Stalin period (Bailey and Llobera 1981; Dunn 1982). In either case, his analysis was filling a major gap in current Marxist theory.

Despite his growing interest in evolutionary processes he remained as sceptical as were most culture-historical archaeologists about the value of ethnographic analogies, except where historical continuities were apparent. He regarded modern hunter–gatherer societies as ones that had failed to develop technologically. He suspected that instead they had elaborated complex forms of social organization and 'painful' and 'incoherent' rituals that had blocked further technological development. Hence in crucial respects modern hunter–gatherer societies were probably unlike the Palaeolithic ones from which more complex societies had evolved. The same dichotomy held at the level of tribal cultivators. Childe thus proposed two general lines of cultural evolution: a progressive one, characterized by continuous technological development combined with a flexible social organization and ideology, and a conservative one, characterized by static technology and the elaboration of convoluted social structures and ideologies (1936: 46). While based on Marxist ideas, this model bore little relationship to generally held Marxist evolutionary concepts. His interpretation of cultural development, like his changing efforts to explain the eventual superiority of European culture, looks curiously like an attempt to reformulate Lubbock's view of human evolution in non-racist terms.

In *Scotland Before the Scots* Childe attempted to apply a Soviet-style approach to the interpretation of a specific corpus of Western archaeological data. He sought to use information concerning subsistence patterns, houses, handicrafts, trade, and burial customs to infer changing modes of production and the accompanying development of larger and more unequal groups and new ideologies. Inspired by Kruglov and Podgayetsky's explanation of the evolution of Bronze Age society in southern Russia, he saw Scotland developing from a network of egalitarian tribal societies based on communal property into a hierarchical state society. The key factor bringing about change was the emergence of private property, which he believed was mirrored in the replacement of communal tombs by individual ones expressing status differences. Childe concluded that this approach produced 'a picture of Scotland's development which was far more realistic and far more historical' than he had achieved by means of migrationist hypotheses in his early studies of Scottish prehistory (1958b: 73). Yet he refused categorically to subscribe to the dogmatic scheme of social evolution used by Soviet archaeologists or to rule out diffusion and migration as significant factors bringing about social and cultural change.

Childe as a Marxist archaeologist

After World War II Childe continued to refine and develop a Marxist understanding of social change. As a result of growing disillusionment with the quality of archaeological research then being done in the Soviet Union, he turned away from Soviet archaeology as a major source of creative inspiration and began to investigate the philosophical basis of Marxism itself. In the last decade of his life he worked hard to acquire a more profound and less dogmatic understanding of Marxism as an analytical tool and to apply it to the study of archaeological data. As part of this effort he read widely in the field of philosophy in order to gain a better understanding of Marxism.

Like all Marxists he regarded a historical approach as uniting all of the social sciences. He believed that no general formulae can disclose the total order of history – 'that can only be reproduced in the concrete whole of history itself, which no book and no library of books . . . could contain' (Childe 1947a: 69). Laws are merely general descriptions of what is observed and, as such, statements of probabilities with varying degrees of applicability. He argued that there were a certain number of general laws of history, such as the primacy of the social relations of production with respect to the superstructure, the periodic development of conflicts between the forces and relations of production, and the revolutionary resolution of these contradictions. Yet he believed that a far larger number of cross-cultural generalizations were valid only for societies that shared a particular mode of production and hence were at the same general stage of development (Childe 1947a).

He further argued that the significance of any generalization can only be established in relation to specific historical contexts because the rules that account for human behaviour, and human behaviour itself, change as new forms of societies develop. Because of this, human evolution is genuinely creative. It is capable of bringing into existence novel and often unforeseen social orders and new forms of human self-awareness. Yet he continued to be convinced that such progress was not inevitable. Some societies remain static, while others regress or even destroy themselves (Childe 1947a).

In Childe's view a Marxist analysis, while assigning a privileged role to the relations of production, ruled out any form of narrow determinism. Functional constraints account for many similar features of social organization and ideology possessed by historically unrelated cultures that share a common mode of production. Nevertheless the specific content of cultures and of individual sequences of change is determined to so great a degree by pre-existing cultural patterns, fortuitous contacts with other cultures, and interaction between neighbouring societies that it cannot be predicted in detail. Childe already had observed that the precise form of the British constitution in the nineteenth century could never be deduced from the capitalist mode of production alone (Childe 1936: 98). This analysis implied that there was no easy way to predict the precise nature of one aspect of a society on the basis of knowledge of some other aspect. Insofar as each feature of a prehistoric culture was to be reconstructed, this would have to be done inductively, using archaeological data. Childe's rejection of determinism is now widely recognized as being in accord with orthodox Marxism, which denies that general laws can explain all of the diverse features of concrete human development (Petrova-Averkieva 1980: 24).

In *Social Evolution* (1951) Childe reaffirmed his belief in multilinear evolution, but argued in accordance with Marxist principles that over time cultures sharing the same mode of production tend to evolve increasingly similar social, political, and cultural institutions, which would be in ever greater harmony with the economic base. Yet these institutions develop in varied ways and in different sequences even in adjacent cultures because of environmental differences, historical accidents, and the societies involved being initially dissimilar. Thus there are many more ways to move from one level of social organization to another than there are forms in which the superstructure is in close accord with the base. Because of this, social reality rarely corresponds with an ideal type. This view of cultures as less than perfectly integrated systems was shared by a number of non-Marxist American anthropologists, most notably G. P. Murdock (1949).

Childe gradually extended his materialist analysis of society to embrace cognitive aspects of behaviour. He defined knowledge as shared mental approximations of the real world that permitted human beings to act upon it and insisted that archaeologists must treat artifacts as concrete expressions of human thoughts and ideas. He also argued that human beings adapt not to real environments but to their ideas about them, even if an effective adaptation requires a reasonably close correspondence between reality and how it is perceived. Innovations and their applications to social needs also require new forms of thought that have ramifications extending through entire societies. Advances in technology thus reflect not simply an increase in scientific information but also the evolution of the total knowledge at the disposal of a society, including how human beings perceive themselves and their relations to nature. He maintained that notions of causality had remained anthropomorphic until the growing use of inanimate power to work machines had engendered the idea of mechanical causality embodied in the thinking of Isaac Newton. He had no qualms about pronouncing modern civilization to be superior to all preceding ones insofar as it was able to provide a reliable guide to a far greater number of actions (Childe 1949).

In *Society and Knowledge* (1956b) he elaborated his concept of knowledge in terms of the Marxist dichotomy between true and false consciousness. True consciousness is characterized by the operational correspondence between views of reality and external reality itself. In the form of technological knowledge, it exists to varying degrees in all societies. By contrast, an objective understanding of social relations and of the social significance of beliefs and values is rare in any ancient or modern society, although Marxists maintain that such understanding will characterize the technologically advanced, classless societies of the future. False consciousness occurs in situations where there is no operational correspondence between what is believed and external reality. It embraces the myths that all societies create to mask and compensate for their technological incompetence and that class societies use to disguise exploitation as altruism. Childe observed that false consciousness, in the form of religious beliefs, magic, and superstition, leaves its mark on the archaeological record no less conspicuously than does technological knowledge. Yet, because the possible variations in the details of magical and religious beliefs are infinite, the archaeologist has no hope of being able to infer the specific content of these beliefs in the absence of written records or oral traditions. By contrast, the number of practical solutions to any technological problem is limited by material constraints that can be inferred with a high degree of accuracy, using the laws of physics and chemistry. Childe therefore concluded that the archaeological study of knowledge must be restricted largely to technological matters and framed in terms of practical results rather than the subjective goals of those who possessed it. Because of this the investigation of prehistoric technology becomes a chronicle of the triumph of true over false consciousness.

Yet Childe also believed that the evolution and functioning of technology could only be understood if archaeologists were able to reconstruct the social context in which it had operated. This was the problem that he turned to in his last book, *The Prehistory of European Society* (1958a). He identified social relations, which in a Marxist fashion he viewed as including the relations of production, as the principal aspect of human behaviour that was capable of orderly cross-cultural explanation. He observed that variation in the essential features of economic, social, and political organization was far more limited than variation in most cultural traits and argued that the latter acquired their functional significance in terms of their relation to the social system. The main practical problem that he confronted was how archaeological evidence could be used more effectively to infer prehistoric sociopolitical systems. This problem troubled him more than it did Soviet archaeologists in the 1950s, since he believed that archaeological evidence must be used objectively to test Marxist theories (Childe 1951: 29). Hence independent and verifiable means had to be found for inferring social organization from archaeological data.

He was not optimistic about how much could be accomplished along these lines (Childe 1958a: 12–14). At this time he seemed more constrained than ever by the typological method that had been the basis of his early work and less able to make effective use of settlement-pattern or funerary data. While he had done much archaeological field work in Scotland, his most innovative results came from his early use of ethnographic comparisons with rustic highland Scottish houses to interpret the use of house-space in the Neolithic village of Skara Brae (Childe 1931) and his survey of megalithic tombs to estimate the size and distribution of the population on the island of Rousay in the Neolithic period (Childe 1942f). Although he had evolved some very sophisticated models of social change, he now seemed unable to apply these results to the synthesis of archaeological data. It is perhaps indicative of failing creativity in the last years of his life that his earlier involvement in settlement-pattern research did not suggest to him effective techniques for studying prehistoric social and political organization.

Grahame Clark

An alternative and in many ways complementary functionalist approach was pioneered by Grahame (J. G. D.) Clark. Through his training of numerous graduate students at Cambridge University this approach has exerted a strong influence on the development of archaeology in many parts of the world (Murray and White 1981; Clark 1988a). Although he was committed to a materialist perspective for most of his career, he consistently criticized Childe's attempts to apply Marxist concepts to archaeology. He also attempted to develop new methods of fieldwork to complement his theoretical innovations.

Clark studied at Cambridge University, where he became a lecturer in 1935. His doctoral thesis was a conventional typological study of Mesolithic material from Britain and a comparison of this material with Mesolithic finds from continental Europe (Clark 1932). Yet during his early years at Cambridge three different influences oriented him towards a functionalist view of prehistoric cultures. The first was his growing awareness of the manner in which Scandinavian archaeologists studied prehistoric cultures in their environmental setting. This awareness was encouraged by the close similarities between Mesolithic finds in England and the Maglemosian culture of Denmark and the eventual realization that the latter culture had exploited marshlands extending across the present bed of the North Sea prior to their flooding by rising sea levels. He also worked closely with Harry Godwin, the biologist who had introduced pollen analysis into Britain. Secondly he was exposed to the functionalist views of social anthropologists such as Malinowski and Radcliffe-Brown. Finally he 'responded eagerly' to the call by the Finnish archaeologist A. M. Tallgren (1885–1945) that archaeologists should stop regarding artifacts as more real and alive than the societies that had created them and the people whose needs had brought them into being (Tallgren 1937; Clark 1974). Ironically Tallgren's views had been shaped in large part through his close contacts with Soviet archaeologists.

In 1939 Clark published the first edition of *Archaeology and Society*, a theoretical study of archaeology which remains a milestone in the history of the discipline. He maintained that archaeology should be 'the study of how [human beings] lived in the past' (p. 1) and that to achieve that goal archaeological finds had to be examined from a functionalist point of view. He further argued that the primary function of a culture, or way of life, was to ensure the survival of a society; which implied that all aspects of cultures were influenced at least to some degree by ecological constraints. The aim of archaeologists should be to determine how human beings had lived in prehistoric times by reconstructing as far as possible their economies, social and political organizations, and systems of beliefs and values and trying to understand how these different aspects of culture related to each other as parts of functioning systems. Like many social anthropologists, Clark stressed the role of culture as an adaptive system at the same time that he stated that his aim was to document social life. This formulation reflected the conviction that, by influencing individual human behaviour, culturally transmitted patterns facilitated the social interaction upon which the survival of individuals and groups depended.

Clark systematically assessed the strengths and limitations of archaeological data for studying prehistoric social life. He noted that some aspects of material culture are better preserved in the archaeological record than are others: bronze survives better than iron or silver and bone better than soft plant parts. On the other hand, because of its value, gold is less likely to make its way into the archaeological record or to escape plundering than is a less valuable metal. He also observed that material culture generally survives better in desert or arctic environments than in tropical forests. Because people living in tropical forests tend to use perishable materials and because of the difficulties of preservation and recovery, it is likely that archaeologists will always know less about prehistoric cultural development in these regions than in deserts or the high arctic. Finally, he concluded that, when working only with archaeological data, archaeologists are likely to learn more about the economies of prehistoric societies than about their social organization and religious beliefs. This is because the technologies and economies of societies are largely shaped by material constraints that can be understood through the natural sciences. On the other hand, economic factors merely constrain rather than determine the nature of social organization and religious beliefs; hence much of the specific content of these higher levels of human behaviour is not subject to the same kind of scientific analysis as are technology, subsistence economies, and trading patterns. Although Clark's general view of culture was formulated in ecological terms rather than on the priority of the mode of production, his conclusions about the potential of the archaeological record for reconstructing different aspects of cultures closely resembled those reached by Childe. The notion of a scale of ascending difficulty in reconstructing prehistoric technology, economies, sociopolitical organization, and religious beliefs has continued to play a major role in British discussions of prehistory from the 1930s to the present (Piggott 1959: 9–12; Friedman and Rowlands 1978b: 203–4). This concept was given its most elaborate treatment by Christopher Hawkes (1954), who concluded that archaeology, unaided by written texts or oral traditions, is able to reveal more about what is generically animal in human behaviour than about what is specifically human. This scale of ascending difficulty is frequently called 'Hawkes' hierarchy' or 'ladder' after his study.

In *Archaeology and Society* Clark asserted that the ultimate aim of archaeologists should be to interpret their data in terms of social history. They could do that, however, only after they had defined a succession of cultures in the archaeological record and had a clear idea of how the prehistoric communities associated with these cultures had functioned. He regarded an archaeologist studying a prehistoric habitation site as the equivalent of an ethnologist studying a living community. Very little attention was paid to the appropriateness of this analogy or to the social anthropologists' assumption that a single community was representative of some larger cultural unit, a conclusion now generally repudiated. He also accepted that ethnographic analogies had to be used to interpret archaeological data. He repeated the Victorian argument that just as palaeontologists use living animals to reconstruct the anatomy of fossil finds, so archaeologists must use ethnographic data to interpret their discoveries. Yet his belief in the relatively loose articulation between the different parts of a cultural system led him to reject the unilinear evolutionary view that cultures at the same stage of development would be similar to one another in any detailed fashion. He specified that ethnographic analogies had to be drawn between individual artifacts, as Nilsson had done, rather than between whole cultures, in the unilinear evolutionary fashion, and that they had to be treated as suggestive rather than definitive. In general he preferred to use analogies derived from folk lore rather than from comparative ethnology for the interpretation of European prehistory, because he believed that historical continuity guaranteed the greater relevance of the former. He argued that when archaeologists were seeking to interpret data about prehistoric times 'it was helpful to know how people occupying the same territory managed to provide for themselves before the rise of modern economies' (Clark 1974: 41). In this respect as well, his position was similar to that of Childe and in line with earlier diffusionist doctrines.

During the next decade Clark sought to develop techniques for using archaeological evidence to document social life and particularly the ways in which natural resources had been utilized. In *Prehistoric England* (1940) his chapters were organized not chronologically but functionally to provide a review of what was known about subsistence patterns, dwellings, handicrafts, mining, trade, communications, defence, burial, and sacred sites from Palaeolithic times to the end of the Iron Age. This was followed by a series of papers on the utilization of various resources in prehistory and on basic subsistence activities such as seal hunting, whaling, fowling, fishing, forest clearance, farming, and stock raising. In a paper on 'Bees in antiquity' he outlined an ecological perspective that linked an increase in the number of wild bees in Europe to the introduction of farming and demonstrated how the resulting increase in the supply of beeswax facilitated bronze casting (Clark 1942). While these papers all addressed biological problems, Clark sought, by identifying the functions of artifacts and the seasons when specific subsistence activities took place, to use the archaeological record to document economic and social life. The need to do this was stressed by Donald Thomson (1939), who demonstrated ethnographically that the same group of Australian aborigines used totally different material culture assemblages at different times of the year, when they exploited the resources of different areas. These remains could easily be mistaken for different cultures within a traditional cultural–historical framework.

Between 1949 and 1951 Clark excavated a waterlogged Mesolithic site at Star Carr in East Yorkshire. The primary objectives of this excavation were to recover organic materials as well as stone tools, to date the site in relation to post-glacial vegetation patterns, to recover food remains that would reveal the subsistence pattern, and to

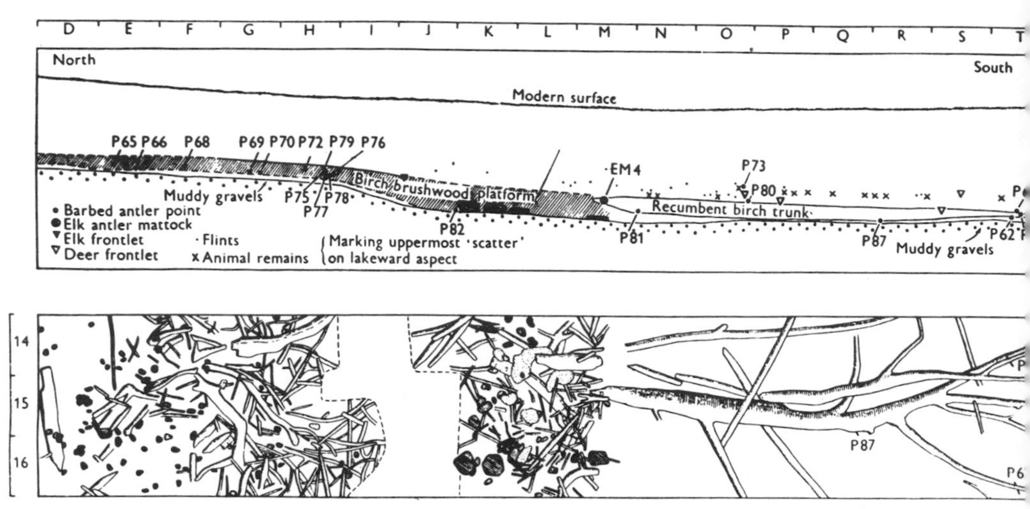

37 Plan and section of Cutting II, Star Carr

determine what sort of social group had used the site. With the help of palaeobotanists and zoologists he was able to conclude that a small group of hunters had visited it over a number of winters in order to hunt deer. This study set a new standard for the archaeological investigation of hunter–gatherer sites and called into question the value of all previously excavated sites for economic studies of prehistory (Clark 1954, 1972; cf. Andresen *et al.* 1981).

At the same time Clark was excavating at Star Carr, he was writing *Prehistoric Europe: The Economic Basis* (1952). In this book he sought to 'mine and quarry' existing archaeological literature and museum collections to see what could be learned from them about the economic development of Europe from late glacial times to the historical period. The main topics that he addressed were subsistence patterns, shelter, technology, trade, travel, and transportation. He did not examine data in relation to specific societies or archaeological cultures but sought to trace economic changes as they related to three major climatic and vegetation zones: Circumpolar, Temperate, and Mediterranean. The relationship between culture and environment was viewed as reciprocal and the economy defined as 'an adjustment to specific physical and biological conditions of certain needs, capacities, aspirations and values' (p. 7). *Prehistoric*

Europe was the first application to archaeology of the botanist A. G. Tansley's (1871–1955) concept of the ecosystem, with its notion of a self-correcting mechanism, or homeostat, which keeps the whole system in balance (Tansley 1935; Odum 1953). Similar ecological concepts had been applied by the social anthropologist E. E. Evans-Pritchard (1940) in his study of the ecology of the Nuer people of the southern Sudan and they were in accord with a Durkheimian emphasis on social integration and equilibrium. Clark viewed cultural change as a response to 'temporary disequilibrium' brought about by environmental changes, fluctuations in population, labour-saving innovations, and cultural contact. He thus ascribed change to all the major factors that evolutionary and diffusionist archaeologists had invoked over the previous century, without reviewing the status of these concepts. Nor did he attempt to interrelate them, apart from the commonplace observation that the natural environment imposed certain restrictions on economic exploitation at particular stages of technology.

In *Prehistoric Europe* Clark was concerned primarily with economic processes. In later studies he paid increasing attention to how the integrity and cohesion of social groups are reinforced by distinctive patterns of behaviour in the same way that individuals signal their identity by conforming to or ignoring social norms. His interests turned to the social and symbolic significance of artifacts. More recently he has argued that so long as form and style are studied in order to define the territories of social groups rather than as ends in themselves, they have a significant role to play in scientific archaeology (Clark 1974: 53–4; 1975).

At the same time his ideas about the forces that bring about social change appear to have moved away from a materialist perspective. He maintains that human beings are free to the extent that they can reason but emphasizes cultural traditions as a major constraint on change. Innovation occurs only when the cost of maintaining the status quo exceeds that of change. The Industrial Revolution is attributed to major alterations in patterns of thinking rather than to economic developments, while the preindustrial civilizations are seen as contributing to cultural elaboration and diversification because resources, power, and patronage were concentrated in the hands of a wealthy and sophisticated ruling class (Clark 1983, 1986). Clark played a major role in moving British archaeology away from a preoccupation with typology and encouraging efforts to understand prehistoric economies and related forms of social organization. Yet, if he excelled Childe in the detailed reconstruction of prehistoric subsistence activities from archaeological data, his work falls short of Childe's as an attempt to explain cultural change. This in turn reflects his failure to develop an explicit model of cultural change to complement his behavioural interpretations of archaeological data.

Clark spurred major developments in British archaeology. The laboratory study of biological remains, such as animal bones and plant seeds, recovered from archaeological sites, and their interpretation in ecological and economic terms, has become a major interdisciplinary specialization, partly covered by terms such as zooarchaeology, palaeoethnobotany, and bioarchaeology. Under the leadership of his student Eric Higgs (1908–1976) and the British Academy Major Research Project in the Early History of Agriculture, a school of palaeoeconomy has developed that attempts to interpret these findings in relation to the total resources available in the vicinity of the settlement where they were discarded and a presumed seasonal pattern of exploitation (Sieveking 1976: xxii). This involves site catchment analysis, which strives to determine the resources that would have been available prehistorically within an exploitable radius around an archaeological site (Vita-Finzi and Higgs 1970; Higgs 1972, 1975; Jarman *et al.* 1982). Both Higgs and Jarman claimed that artifactual analysis has not been very informative about the nature of prehistoric subsistence adaptations and denied it a 'prior place' in archaeological investigations, although they did not rule out the importance of technological development. They also viewed economic factors as being the only ones that are of long-term explanatory importance or significantly detectable in the archaeological record. Much of the work of David Clarke (1968) was a reaction against the narrowness and determinism of the Higgsian approach (Sherratt 1979: 199–200).

Early functionalism in the United States

In the United States a functionalist approach to archaeological analysis began in the nineteenth century. It took the form of an interest in how artifacts were manufactured and what use had been made of them. This approach was developed and systematized in

Harlan Smith's (1872–1940) *The Prehistoric Ethnology of a Kentucky Site* (1910), which was based on the analysis of artifacts that he had recovered from the Fox Farm site in 1895. He sought to reconstruct the lifeways of the inhabitants of that site, which was later assigned to the late prehistoric Fort Ancient aspect. Artifacts were described and analysed in terms of a series of functional categories: Resources in Animal and Plant Materials; Securing Food; Preparation of Food; Habitations; Tools used by Men; Tools used by Women; Processes of Manufacture; History of Manufactured Objects (stages in the manufacture of tools as illustrated by unfinished artifacts); Games; Religious Objects; Pipes and Amusements; Warfare; Dress and Ornament; Art; Injuries and Diseases; and Methods of Burial. Individual artifacts were discussed from different points of view under multiple headings. Although ethnographic analogies were employed to determine the functions of specific artifacts, guesswork played a major role in assigning artifacts to specific classes.

There was widespread interest in this sort of functional interpretation in the early twentieth century. William Wintemberg (1876–1941), whose professional career developed under the supervision of Smith, followed this approach in his analysis of material from the Iroquoian sites that he excavated in southern Ontario (Trigger 1978c). A former craftsman, he conducted many experiments to determine how artifacts were made and used. He also acquired an extensive knowledge of traditional Indian material culture and ways of life (Swayze 1960: 178). A. C. Parker's (1881–1955) report on the Iroquoian Ripley site, in northwestern New York State (1907), has been described as 'an early attempt to delineate the entire culture of a group from archaeological remains interpreted in the light of ethnography' (Brose 1973: 92). M. R. Harrington, who worked for the American Museum of Natural History when Smith was employed there, consulted local Indians in order to extend his knowledge of the material he excavated at the Shinnecock site on Long Island in 1902 (Harrington 1924). Beginning with *Ancient Life in Kentucky* (Webb and Funkhouser 1928), William S. Webb (1882–1964) studied how prehistoric Indians had made and used artifacts and how these artifacts reflected less tangible ancient customs. He was trained as a physicist and is said to have approached archaeology with an amateur's 'interest in local antiquities and the ancient life of the local Indians' (Taylor 1948: 75). Working in Kentucky he had special reason to be influenced by Smith's report on the Fox Farm site. Similarly William Ritchie's early publications on the 'pre-Iroquoian' sites of New York State had been manifesting a widely ranging, if unsystematic, interest in using artifacts to reconstruct prehistoric human behaviour. After they were influenced by the Midwestern Taxonomic Method, both Webb and Ritchie concentrated on the elaboration of trait lists and ceased (in Ritchie's case only until the 1950s) to study the behaviour of prehistoric peoples (Taylor 1948: 70–80).

The large horizontal excavations carried out during the depression years helped to revive the interest of American archaeologists in the functional analysis of archaeological data. Now, however, instead of this concern being mainly with artifacts, it was focused increasingly on features, house patterns, and village plans, in relation to which the distribution of artifacts took on additional significance. These excavations expanded knowledge about the construction of houses and sacred structures, while plans of entire villages added a new dimension to the understanding of the prehistoric social organization of eastern North America (Willey and Sabloff 1980: 123–7).

Yet this work was initially justified as a means of expanding trait lists and only slowly stimulated an interest in how people had lived in prehistoric times. In *Rediscovering Illinois* (1937), a report on archaeological excavations carried out in and around Fulton County, Illinois, Fay-Cooper Cole (1881–1961) and Thorne Deuel listed all the artifact types from a single occupation level within a site under a number of broad functional headings, which they labelled complexes. These included Architecture and House Life, Costume and Dress, Ceremonial, Military and Hunting, Economic and Artistic, Agricultural and Food-Getting, and Pottery. Yet they made no attempt to infer specific activities from these artifacts. The same is true of Charles Fairbanks' (1942) effort to arrange a list of artifact types from the Stallings Island midden in Georgia in a functional order according to whether they appeared to relate to subsistence, community plan, burial, or technological and artistic activities. In Martin, Quimby, and Collier's *Indians Before Columbus* (1947) all of the major archaeological cultures so far defined for North America were summarized by regions and successive periods under the headings: location, people (physical type), village, livelihood, pottery,

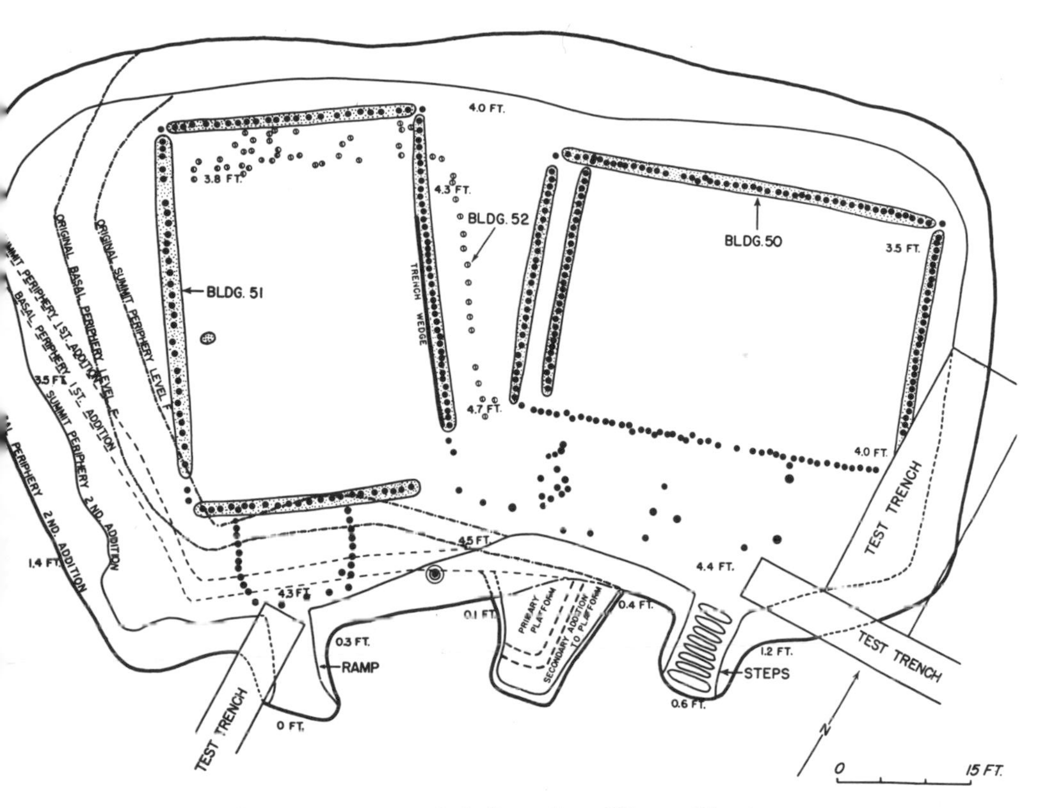

38 Structures on mound platform, from *Hiwassee Island*, by T. Lewis and M. Kneberg, 1946

tools, utensils, weapons, pipes, costumes, ornaments, and burials. In each of these cases, despite a growing variety of data, the emphasis was largely on listing traits in an ethnographic or pseudo-ethnographic format rather than on trying to interpret material culture as evidence of human behaviour. Although interpretations prior to the 1930s have been castigated for remaining 'on a relatively superficial level' consisting 'mainly of the obvious inferences to be drawn from artifacts . . . by visualizing how they might have been used' (Rouse 1972: 147), they constituted a more serious effort to infer human behaviour from archaeological remains than did the ethnographic trait lists of the 1930s and 1940s. This indicates that the classificatory orientation of the Midwestern Taxonomic Method, and of chronological studies generally, suppressed a professional interest in the behavioural interpretation of archaeological data in North America for a longer period than Taylor (1948: 91) or Willey and Sabloff (1980: 134) have believed.

Nevertheless a growing minority of American archaeologists began to call for the functional interpretation of archaeological data within the framework of more holistic views of culture than had been adopted hitherto in American archaeology. They may have been responding to the more functionalist views of human behaviour that were being popularized in American anthropology by Radcliffe-Brown, who taught at the University of Chicago from 1931 to 1937, and by Malinowski, who taught at Yale University from 1938 until his death in 1942. Archaeologists were also increasingly aware of the interpretations of archaeological data offered by Childe, Clark, and other European archaeologists. This provided theoretical as well as practical evidence that leading American ethnologists, such as Robert Lowie and Frank Speck, erred when they claimed that, because archaeologists could study only material culture, they were unable to say anything significant about non-material aspects of human behaviour. To do this, however, archaeologists had to interpret artifacts as parts of total cultural systems and as integrated within social, political, and economic organizations, rather than as material objects that had only typological significance.

This desire to understand archaeological remains from a functional point of view led archaeologists to renew their ties with ethnologists, which had become attenuated during the period when their primary interest had been to construct cultural chronologies. In 1936 William D. Strong (1899–1962) stressed the interdependence of archaeology and ethnology and argued that archaeologists should look to ethnologists for theoretical leads as well as factual information. He applied this principle in his direct-historical approach to Nebraskan prehistory, as did Paul Martin (1899–1974) when he used Robert Redfield's concept of 'folk culture' to explain variations in the size and contents of Pueblo ruins (Martin *et al.* 1938; Martin and Rinaldo 1939). In his study of native subsistence economies on the Great Plains, Waldo R. Wedel (1941) stressed the importance of the relation between culture and environment and argued that factors other than historical accidents shaped archaeological cultures. A. J. Waring, Jr and Preston Holder (1945) interpreted elaborately decorated copper and shell artifacts in widely dispersed Mississippian sites as evidence of a widespread religious cult.

Similar functional explanations were used to account for stylistic distributions in Mexico and Peru, such as the Chavin and Tiahuanaco horizons, which had hitherto been interpreted purely in diffusionist terms. In each of these studies efforts were made to identify sociopolitical or religious characteristics of the material by considering their intrasite provenience or other features that typological studies had ignored (W. Bennett 1945; Willey 1948). In a study of the contentious issue of Mesoamerican influences on the cultures of the southeastern United States, John W. Bennett (1944) stressed the need to consider the functional implications of traits, the social context from which they were derived, and, above all, the context into which they would have been introduced. He hypothesized that some Mesoamerican traits would have been readily accepted by the less complex cultures of the United States, while others would have been rejected, however many times they were transmitted. Hence he maintained that diffusionist explanations require a detailed functional understanding of the recipient cultures. Still other archaeologists sought to interpret the interaction between neighbouring cultures in terms of the concept of acculturation, which was becoming popular at that time among ethnologists (Keur 1941; Lewis and Kneberg 1941). While these and other studies were highly disparate and provisional, enough of them had appeared by 1943 to be recognized as constituting a trend in American archaeology, which J. W. Bennett (1943) labelled as a 'functional' or 'sociological' approach to archaeological interpretation. These studies and Kluckhohn's (1940) advocacy of a 'scientific' approach prepared the way for Walter Taylor's *A Study of Archeology* (1948), a polemical work that examined the differences between traditional culture-historical archaeology and the new functionalist interests.

The conjunctive approach

Taylor observed that the majority of American archaeologists said that their goal was to reconstruct prehistory, while some of them, like Kidder, went further and expressed the hope that eventually archaeological data would provide a basis for generalizing about human behaviour and cultural change. Yet few culture-historical archaeologists displayed any interest in systematically reconstructing prehistoric ways of life or explaining events that had taken place in prehistoric times. Instead they occupied themselves with 'mere chronicle', working out the geographical and temporal distributions of archaeological material and explaining changes by attributing them to external factors grouped under the headings of diffusion and migration.

Taylor proceeded to demonstrate that the limited goals of archaeologists encouraged slackness in archaeological fieldwork and analysis. Many classes of artifacts, especially those that were not regarded as important for defining cultures, were not examined and described in detail. Pottery and lithic material were studied much more carefully than was surviving evidence of basketry. Floral and faunal remains often were inadequately recovered and identified; hence archaeologists did not know what foods were eaten and why particular sites were used or at what season. Archaeologists also failed to record, and more often to report, the intrasite provenience of artifacts in sufficient detail. Because of this it was difficult for them to define activity areas within sites and to determine how artifacts might vary from one part of a site to another. Finally, although archaeologists sought to elaborate lists of all the types of artifacts associated with particular sites and made statistical comparisons of these lists in an effort to determine their degrees of cultural affinity, they were normally content to compare merely the presence or absence of types. As a result, quantified data, that might be very important for understanding the role played by particular kinds of artifacts, were lacking. Taylor devoted much of his study to providing a detailed critique of the shortcomings of the work of leading American archaeologists in order to demonstrate how their cultural–chronological objectives had limited their investigations of the archaeological record.

To remedy these defects Taylor offered the conjunctive approach. To the traditional investigation of chronological problems and intersite relations he proposed to add detailed intrasite studies in which careful attention would be paid to all artifacts and features and how they were interrelated. Special note would be taken of the quantitative aspects and spatial distributions of archaeological finds, as well as of their formal properties and evidence of how they were made and used. In this way archaeologists might hope to learn as much as possible about the nature of life in prehistoric times and about the functional relations within a prehistoric culture. A distinctive aspect of the conjunctive approach was the importance that Taylor, like Clark, attached to sites as primary units of analysis.

He sought to avoid the problems inherent for archaeologists in the concept of material culture by following Kroeber and other Boasian anthropologists in defining culture as mental constructs and viewing material remains as products of culture rather than culture itself (Osgood 1951). Mental constructs, which are partly a heritage of the past and either idiosyncratic or shared by varying numbers of people, constitute beliefs and values and provide guides for social activities as well as the technical knowledge required to produce material culture. He concluded that, while culture was ideational and hence did not survive in the archaeological record, many aspects of culture other than the knowledge that went into manufacturing artifacts were reflected archaeologically. He also distinguished between culture as a holistic concept, or process, and culture as a partitive one (the individual archaeological culture).

Taylor maintained that archaeologists must strive to recover as much information as possible concerning archaeological sites, including seemingly trivial evidence. They must also collect information concerning the palaeoenvironmental context of the site and any related historical or ethnographic data. This material had to be studied and classified as well as reported in sufficient detail that it could be reanalysed by other archaeologists. The first analytical task relating to the site as a whole was to work out its internal chronology and thus to determine what evidence was synchronous or successive. Archaeologists should next turn to the major task of synthesizing the material from the site, or from each period that it was occupied. Two sorts of synthesis had to be done. The ethnographic synthesis consisted of determining everything possible about how people lived at the site. The archaeologist, like an ethnographer, should try to fill out the *Outline of Cultural Materials* (Murdock *et al.* 1938), a checklist documenting all conceivable patterns of cultural behaviour. The conjunctive approach also required that archaeologists should try to understand how life was lived at a site as a functionally integrated pattern. The ethnographic synthesis was to be followed by a historiographic one that traced how ways of life at a site changed in the course of its occupation and tried to account for how these changes came about.

Having synthesized the cultural significance of individual sites, archaeologists could undertake comparative studies. Taylor believed that these should involve the comparison of whole cultural contexts as manifested at individual sites rather than of individual items of culture, and that their immediate aim should be to understand how a site related to the broader pattern of life in a surrounding territory. In this way, seasonally occupied hunter–gatherer sites could be linked to form year-round patterns or peasant hamlets associated with elite centres to provide information about the hierarchical structures of ancient civilizations. Thus a functional understanding could be gained that was equivalent to the ethnologists' insight into the nature of living cultures. Archaeologists could then proceed to work alongside ethnologists to achieve the principal goal of anthropology: a general understanding of the nature and working of culture.

There has been considerable discussion concerning to what extent Taylor's approach represented a break with the past and marked the beginning of the New Archaeology of the 1960s (Taylor 1972; Binford 1972: 8–9; 1983a: 229–33). At the same time lateral connections have received little attention. Taylor's emphasis upon the first task of archaeologists as that of using archaeological evidence to reconstruct how people lived at individual prehistoric sites closely paralleled the approach Clark had advocated in 1939. So too did his insistence upon palaeoethnography as a vital goal of archaeology and his view of cultures as functioning entities embracing social, political, and ideological as well as economic components that the archaeologist must try to study holistically from the inside. Yet he did not follow Clark or anticipate the New Archaeology in viewing cultures as ecologically adaptive systems. Instead he adopted an idealist view of culture as a collection of shared concepts, a view which closely resembles the traditional Boasian position. Like the Boasians he did not presuppose that any one part of a culture plays a more important role than any other in bringing about cultural change. Instead he regarded defining the relations between parts and explaining change as problems that must be approached inductively. He was amenable to the idea that different aspects of culture might play a leading role in bringing about change in different societies and continued to believe that much change occurs as a result of fortuitous contacts between human groups.

Taylor's concept of the integration of individual cultures also tended to be weaker than that adopted by Clark. It relates more closely to the notion of configuration or psychological consistency advocated by Boasian anthropologists such as Ruth Benedict (1934) than to the ideas of structural and functional integration championed by social anthropologists. He contrasted the lack of symmetry in Coahuila Cave basketry designs in the southwestern United States with the regularized patterns that dominate San Juan baskets several hundred miles to the south. These variations, which cannot be attributed to differences in materials or weaving techniques, constituted a discontinuity in cultural pattern that Taylor believed deserved a functional explanation. Finally, because of his idealistic and inductive approach, he was compelled to remain at the level of discussing how prehistoric patterns might be reconstructed. He contributed almost nothing towards explaining how or why changes occurred. Like Clark he failed to use a functional view of prehistoric cultures to promote a new understanding of cultural change. His work was mainly important as a critique of current standards of archaeological research and as a call for archaeologists to recover and analyse archaeological data in far greater detail than they had done hitherto. The result was to reinforce the trend toward functional interpretation already under way in American archaeology rather than to challenge the basic tenets of Boasian historical particularism or introduce any major innovations into archaeological interpretation.

Ecological and settlement archaeology

Julian Steward (1902–72), who was one of the first American ethnologists to adopt an explicitly materialist view of human behaviour, greatly enhanced an awareness of the role played by ecological factors in shaping prehistoric sociocultural systems. In 1938 he and F. M. Setzler published a paper in which they argued that archaeologists as well as ethnologists should seek to understand the nature of cultural change and that both disciplines could contribute to an ecological analysis of human behaviour. To play a significant role, however, archaeologists would have to stop concentrating on the stylistic analysis of artifacts and begin to use their data to study changes in subsistence economies, population size, and settlement patterns. Steward himself had carried out and published archaeological research on the *Ancient Caves of the Great Salt Lake Region* (1937a) and written a paper in which he had drawn together archaeological and ethnographic settlement-pattern data in a study of interaction between culture and environment in the southwestern United States (1937b). Of all the American ethnologists of this period, he had the greatest respect for archaeological data and awareness of their potential value for studying problems of human behaviour over long periods.

After World War II increasing awareness of the importance of an ecological approach, resulting from the writings of Steward and Clark, stimulated major American research programmes involving interdisciplinary teams. One of the most important of these was the Iraq Jarmo Project, directed by Robert Braidwood, which between 1948 and 1955 examined a series of late Palaeolithic to early Neolithic sites in the Kirkuk region of the Near East (Braidwood 1974). Another was the Tehuacan Archaeological–Botanical Project, led by Richard S. MacNeish, which between 1960 and 1968 revealed an unbroken 12,000-year cultural sequence from PalaeoIndian times to the Spanish conquest in highland Mexico (MacNeish 1974, 1978). Both of these projects, which were funded at least in part by the United States National Science Foundation, brought together archaeologists, botanists, zoologists, geologists, and other specialists to carry out research relating to the origin of food-production in the Near East and Mesoamerica. They succeeded in delineating changes in the subsistence economies of their respective regions, while MacNeish, with a sample of 456 sites, was also able to infer changes in group composition and land utilization. With the help of radiocarbon dates they demonstrated that in both the Old and the New Worlds food-production had begun earlier and increased in economic importance far more slowly than archaeologists, including Childe, had previously believed. In the Cold War atmosphere prevailing in the United States, these findings were welcomed as proof of the normalcy of gradual evolutionary changes and a major set-back for Childe's apparently Marxist-inspired theory of a Neolithic 'revolution'. Braidwood's work also ruled out the likelihood that desiccation had played a significant role in initiating the development of food-producing economies in the Near East. Both of these studies were landmarks in the use of archaeological data to study one of the major economic and social transformations of human history. They also demonstrated the importance of a multidisciplinary approach in which archaeologists and natural science specialists worked together to analyse archaeological data.

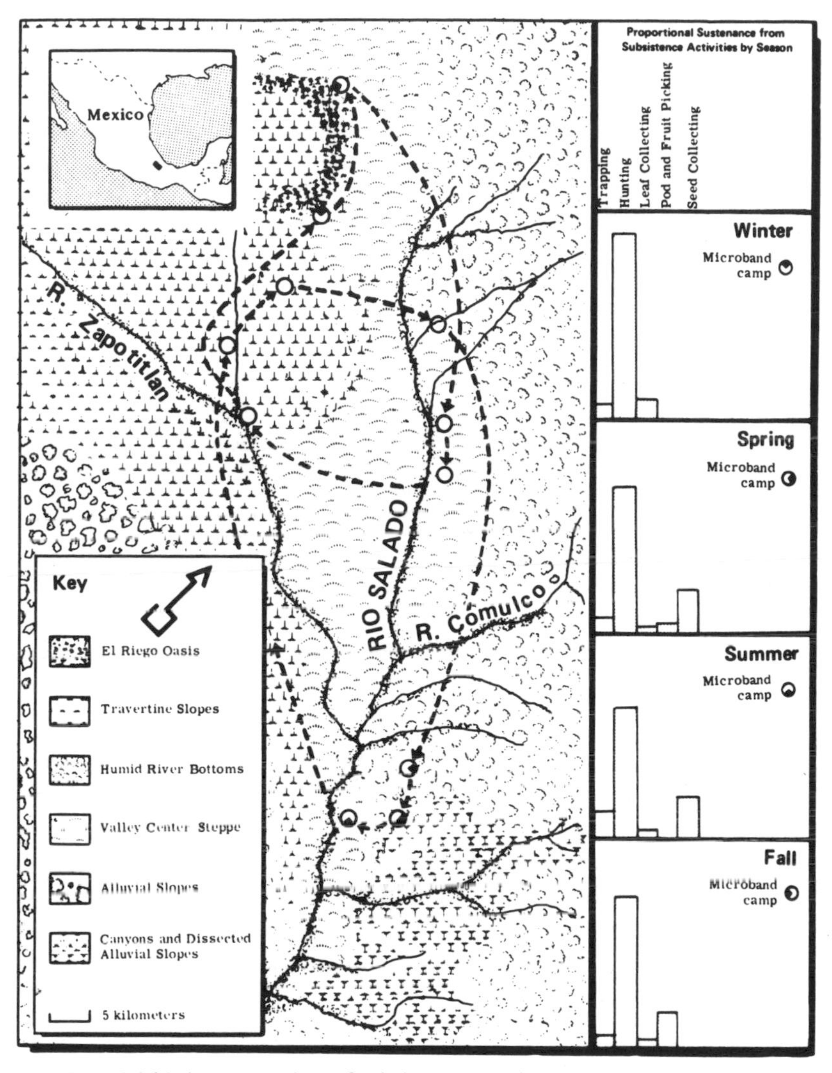

39 MacNeish's interpretation of subsistence–settlement pattern of Ajuereado Phase (11,000–7,000 B.C.) in Tehuacan Valley

In *Trend and Tradition in the Prehistory of the Eastern United States*, Joseph Caldwell (1916–73) adopted an ecological approach to understanding cultural change (1958). He argued that ecological adjustments to the disappearance of big game at the end of the last Ice Age had resulted in more complex and intensive patterns of food collection that had increased the carrying capacity of most areas and promoted sedentarization and denser populations throughout the region. These developments encouraged the acquisition of heavier and more varied types of equipment than had been useful previously, including soapstone, and later ceramic, cooking vessels. He stressed not only the capacity for internally initiated change among the native cultures of the Eastern Woodlands but also the need for archaeologists to understand artifacts such as pottery vessels with reference to the roles they had played within adaptive systems. Such interpretations had been foreshadowed in Ralph Linton's (1944) study of developmental trends in the shape of eastern North American ceramic vessels.

Steward also inspired the development of settlement archaeology, which was initiated by Gordon Willey's *Prehistoric Settlement Patterns in the Virú Valley, Peru* (1953), a study that was carried out in connection with a combined archaeological and anthropological investigation of a small coastal valley in Peru by American and Peruvian anthropologists in 1946. It was Steward who persuaded Willey to conduct a settlement-pattern survey as part of the project (Willey 1974b: 153). Yet Willey's interpretation of the data collected by this survey marked a significant departure from Steward's ecological approach. In previous studies archaeological settlement patterns had been viewed as evidence of relations between human groups and the natural environment. Willey chose instead to view settlement patterns as a 'strategic starting point for the functional interpretation of archaeological cultures'. He went on to assert that settlement patterns 'reflect the natural environment, the level of technology on which the builders operated, and various institutions of social interaction and control which the culture maintained' (p. 1). He did not deny that ecological factors played a significant role in shaping settlement patterns but observed that many other factors of a social or cultural nature were also reflected in the archaeological record and was unprepared to view these factors as merely a reflection of the general patterns of ecological adaptation. Instead he treated settlement patterns as a source of information about many aspects of human behaviour. The great advantage of settlement patterns over artifacts was that, while artifacts frequently were found in contexts where they had been disposed, settlement patterns provided direct evidence about the settings in which human activities were carried out. Willey recognized the potential of

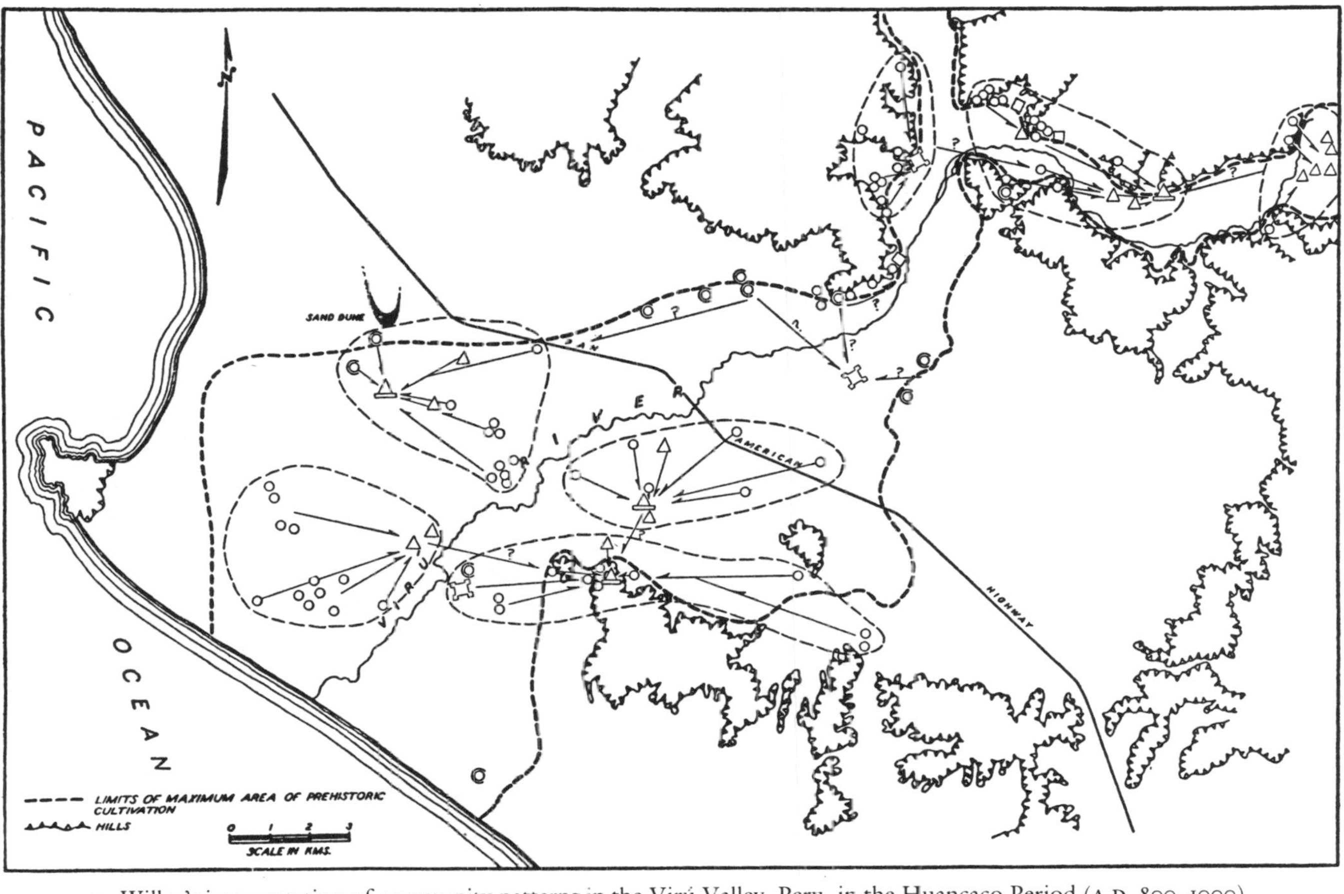

40 Willey's interpretation of community patterns in the Virú Valley, Peru, in the Huancaco Period (A.D. 800–1000)

settlement-pattern data for the systematic study of the economic, social, and political organization of ancient societies.

Although he viewed settlement patterns as a strategic starting-point for the functional interpretation of archaeological cultures, he mainly used the concept of culture to distinguish successive phases in the development of the Virú Valley and hence to group together sites that had been in use at approximately the same time. Cemeteries, habitation sites, palaces, temples, forts, and irrigation networks that appeared to be contemporary were used to try to reconstruct the changing patterns of social and political organization of the valley over several millennia. Instead of viewing social and political phenomena as attributes of culture, he interpreted them as an evolving system of social relations that provided a behavioural context integrating other aspects of culture. Thus, in addition to recognizing social organization as a legitimate object of archaeological study, as Childe was to do in *The Prehistory of European Society* (1958a), Willey provided an analytical device for studying prehistoric social organization, which Childe failed to do. Recognizing long-term continuities in the population inhabiting the Virú Valley also led Willey to emphasize understanding changes in the archaeological record in terms of internal transformations rather than attributing them to diffusion and migration as had commonly been done in the past. His study was therefore an important pioneering effort in using archaeological data to interpret long-term social change.

Within the context of settlement archaeology, individual sites ceased to be studied as ends in themselves or to be regarded as representative of a particular culture or region. Instead they were seen as forming networks in which single sites played very different and complementary roles. Site surveys no longer sought to locate the largest or most representative sites for excavation but instead sought to recover information that was important in its own right for archaeological analysis. While ecological studies of settlement patterns have continued and are recognized as often, if not always, being a necessary preliminary for social and political interpretations, a growing number of American archaeologists came to view settlement patterns as an important source of information about demographic trends and the social, political, and religious institutions of prehistoric societies. They also came to think of settlement patterns in terms of a hierarchy of levels: activity areas within structures,

structures, associated activity areas around structures, communities, and the distribution of communities across landscapes. Each of these levels was recognized as having been shaped by factors that differ in kind or degree from those that influence other levels. Individual structures reflect family organization, settlements community structure, and spatial distributions the impact of trade, administration, and regional defence. Because of this the combined study of two or more levels is likely to shed more light on archaeological cultures than is the study of only one level (Trigger 1968b; Flannery 1976; Clarke 1977; Kent 1984). Of all the functionalist approaches, settlement archaeology, with its focus on inferring patterns of social behaviour and its rejection of ecological determinism, is the one that most closely approximates social anthropology of the Durkheimian variety.

Willey's research in the Virú Valley inspired intensive surveys of changing settlement patterns in various parts of the world. As the result of a prolonged study in southern Iraq, Robert McC. Adams (1965, 1981; Adams and Nissen 1972) was able to demonstrate that irrigation systems tended to elaborate and collapse as a consequence of political changes rather than being a major cause of these changes. K. C. Chang (1963) has shown continuity in the development of social and political systems in northern China from the beginning of the Neolithic period through the Xia, Shang, and Zhou dynasties, while Makkhan Lal (1984) has traced the interaction between technology and environment in northern India during the period that saw the development of Gangetic civilization. Karl Butzer (1976) demonstrated that overall population pressure could not have played a major role in the rise of ancient Egyptian civilization, which developed most rapidly in the far south, where the exploitation of the smaller natural basins required less effort than did that of the larger and more productive basins farther north. Trigger (1965) used mainly cemetery data to study how changes in technology, the natural environment, trade, and warfare altered the size and distribution of population in Lower Nubia over 4,000 years. Richard E. Blanton (1978) has correlated changing settlement patterns in the Oaxaca area of Mexico with changing configurations of political organization. Finally, while William T. Sanders' detailed study of the Valley of Mexico was designed from an ecological perspective, it has shown that changing forms of political and economic organization, as well as idiosyncratic historical factors, have played a major role in shaping the size and distribution of these settlements (Sanders *et al.* 1979). These studies have challenged simplistic views that population increase or irrigation agriculture alone played a preponderant role in shaping the development of complex societies and that cultural changes invariably occur in a slow, gradual fashion.

Almost from the beginning archaeologists recognized the value of settlement patterns for studying social change at the tribal level as well as the origin and development of civilizations. This thinking received early expression in a unilinear scheme of types of community patterning devised at a seminar on the functional and evolutionary implications of such patterning held under the chairmanship of Richard Beardsley in 1955 (Beardsley *et al.* 1956). As a result of this seminar terms such as free wandering, restricted wandering, central based wandering, and semipermanent sedentary came to be used to describe the settlement and subsistence systems of native North American peoples. Over the years systematic studies of the settlement patterns of particular regions have increased archaeologists' awareness of the regional diversity and complexity of adaptations as well as of the rapidity with which these adaptations sometimes changed (Willey 1956; Ritchie and Funk 1973; B. Smith 1978).

Conclusions

Functionalist interpretations of archaeological data had long been inherent in studies of the relations between cultures and their environments and of how artifacts were made and used. Yet the proliferation and increasing sophistication of such views that represented a significant trend in British and American anthropology, beginning in the 1930s, encouraged archaeologists to view prehistoric cultures as internally differentiated and to some degree integrated ways of life. This in turn promoted a consideration of the internal as well as the external causes of change. At first the examination of internal causes was mainly directed towards ecological factors. Yet, while Taylor and in an even more explicit fashion Clark did much to develop the use of archaeological data for reconstructing prehistoric patterns of life, they made few contributions towards explaining changes in the archaeological record. In contrast, Childe, while developing some very interesting models of

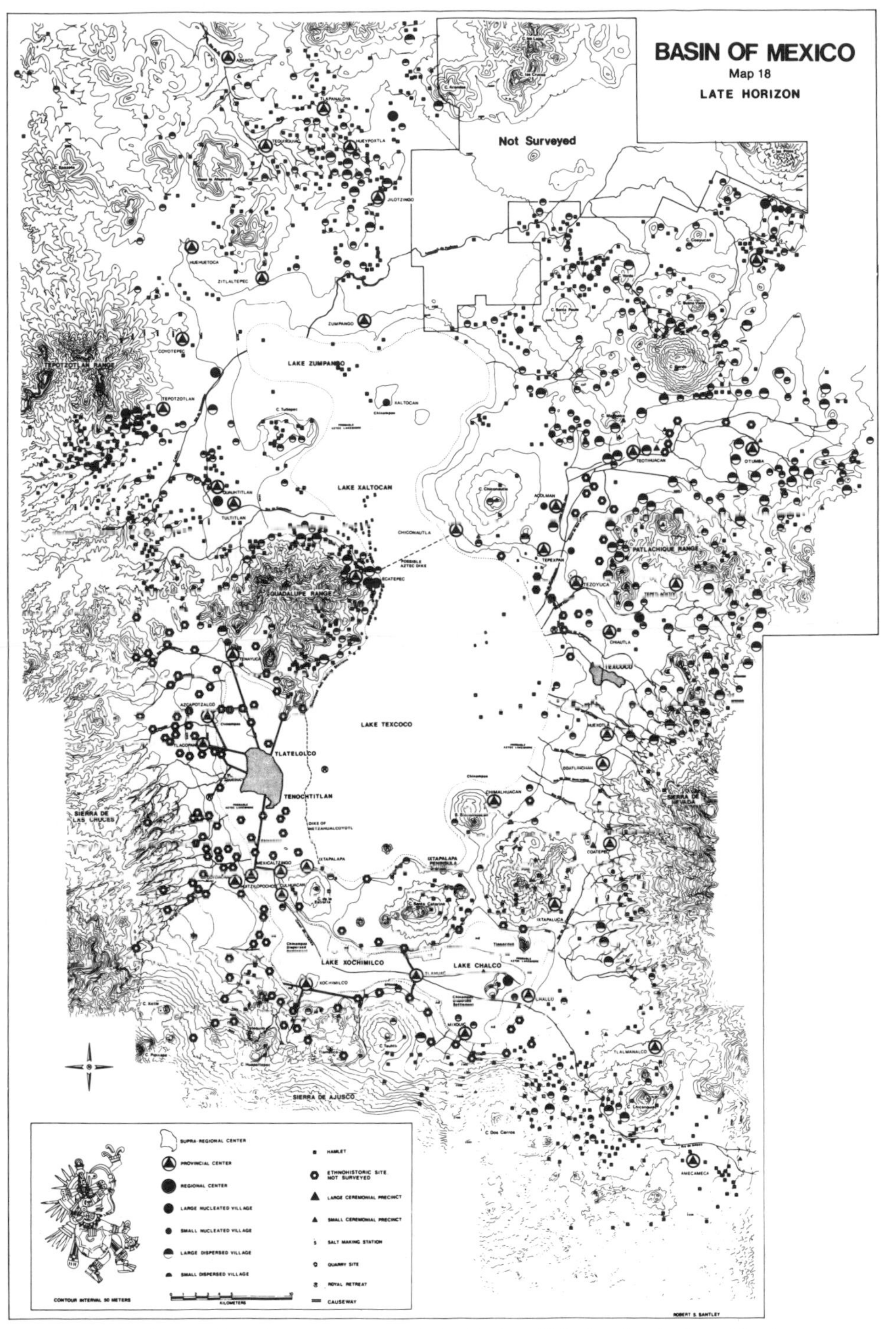

41 Sanders *et al.* settlement pattern of the Basin of Mexico for the Late Horizon

social change, failed to address how these models could be applied in any detail to the study of the archaeological record. Settlement archaeology, by contrast, encouraged the relatively holistic study both of prehistoric cultures at specific points in time and of how these cultures changed. This development of a concern with changes in structural and functional relations over time marked the beginning of a processual, as opposed to a synchronically functional, study of prehistoric cultures.

The development of functional and then processual approaches to archaeological data represented a replacement of the increasingly sterile preoccupation of culture-historical archaeology with ethnicity by a vital new interest in how prehistoric cultures operated and changed. A functionalist orientation was encouraged by the development of social anthropology, which initially was no more concerned with problems of internal social change than earlier diffusionist explanations had been. Growing interest in change was related to social developments after World War II that will be examined in the next chapter.

From an internal point of view culture-historical archaeology was a logical prelude to the systematic study of prehistoric cultures from functional and processual perspectives. The culture-historical approach had revealed the basic framework of cultural distributions in time and space and of intercultural relations that was complemented by a functionalist emphasis on the systematic study of the internal configurations of cultures. Yet, while initially building on traditional culture-historical chronologies, functional and processual approaches soon raised archaeological questions that required refinements in chronology and the understanding of spatial variation (especially intra-site variation) in the archaeological record. American archaeologists strengthened and renewed their long-established ties with anthropology in a search for ethnographic parallels and theoretical concepts that would assist them to interpret their data from a functional or processual point of view. In doing so they reaffirmed a relationship first established in the nineteenth century. European archaeologists tended to remain sceptical of analogies in the absence of some sort of direct historical connection between the cultures being compared and viewed their work as an enrichment of their continuing analysis of archaeological data.

CHAPTER 8

Neo-evolutionism and the New Archaeology

we can predict the transience of the New Archaeology itself – but we should not confuse transience with insignificance.

D. L. CLARKE, *Analytical Archaeologist* (1979), p. 101

The two decades following World War II were an era of unrivalled economic prosperity and unchallenged political hegemony for the United States. Despite the threat of nuclear war, this was a time of great optimism and self-confidence for most middle-class Americans. As had happened in Britain and Western Europe in the middle of the nineteenth century, this self-confidence encouraged a relatively materialistic outlook and a readiness to believe both that there was a pattern to human history and that technological progress was the key to human betterment. In American anthropology these trends were manifested in the revival of an interest in cultural evolutionism. While evolutionism did not become the predominant trend in American anthropology, it greatly increased in popularity in the 1950s and 1960s and exerted a significant influence throughout the discipline.

Neo-evolutionism

The neo-evolutionism that developed in the United States in the 1960s was yet another attempt by anthropologists living in a politically dominant country to 'naturalize' their situation by demonstrating it to be the inevitable outcome of an evolutionary process that allowed human beings to acquire greater control over their environment and greater freedom from nature. Yet neo-evolutionism differed in certain crucial features from the unilinear evolutionism of the nineteenth century. Its ecological, demographic, or technological determinism left no room for the idea that cultural change occurred because gifted individuals used their intelligence and leisure time to devise ways to control nature more effectively and thus improve the quality of human life. Instead neo-evolutionists argued, as diffusionists and social anthropologists had done, that human beings sought to preserve a familiar style of life unless change was forced on them by factors that were beyond their control. This position, which was rationalized in terms of ecosystemics, embodied views about human behaviour being naturally conservative that were far removed from the individual creativity that had been lauded by Spencer or that most nineteenth-century evolutionists had used to explain cultural change. This alteration appears to reflect the difference between an early stage in the development of capitalism, when individual initiative was still highly valued, and a more developed phase dominated by multinational corporations, when the individual is no longer idealized as a major factor bringing about economic growth.

The two principal exponents of neo-evolutionism in the 1950s were the ethnologists Leslie White (1900–75) and Julian Steward (1902–72) (see White 1949, 1959; Steward 1955). White regarded himself as the intellectual heir of L. H. Morgan and of the indigenous, evolutionary tradition of American anthropology. He rejected the historical particularism, psychological reductionism, and belief in free will inherent in Boasian anthropology. In their place he offered the concept of 'General Evolution', which treated progress as a characteristic of culture in general, although not necessarily of every individual culture. White deliberately ignored the influence of environments and of one culture upon another and concentrated on explaining the main line of cultural development, which was marked by the most advanced culture of each successive period regardless of their historical relationship. He argued that this approach was justified because in the long run cultures that failed to keep ahead were superseded and absorbed by more progressive ones. Hence from an evolutionary point of view they are irrelevant.

White defined cultures as elaborate thermodynamic systems. In his early writings he argued that they functioned to make human life more secure and enduring, although later he rejected that view as anthropocentric and claimed that they evolved to serve their own needs (White 1975: 8–13). His perception of cultural change was materialistic and narrowly deterministic. He maintained that cultural systems are composed of techno-economic, social, and ideological components and that 'social systems are . . . determined by technological systems, and philosophies and the arts express experience as it is defined by technology and refracted by social systems' (White 1949: 390–1). He formulated his concept of technological determinism in terms of a 'basic law of evolution' which stated that, all things being equal, culture evolves as the amount of energy harnessed per capita increases, or as the efficiency of putting energy to work is increased. This law is summarized in the formula

$$\text{Culture} = \text{Energy} \times \text{Technology } (C = E \times T).$$

Despite the sweeping claims that White sometimes made for his theories, he stressed that, while they account for the general outlines of cultural development, they cannot be used to infer the specific features of individual cultures (White 1945: 346).

Although White's technological determinism has often been stated to be of Marxist origin, conceptually it has nothing in common with Marxism except a general materialist orientation. Instead, it reflects one of the principal themes of American social-science scholarship, which has been described as privileging the relationship between technology and society at the expense of other kinds of relations, such as those between self and society (Kroker 1984: 12).

Steward championed an alternative multilinear, ecological, and more empirical approach to the study of cultural evolution. He assumed that there were significant regularities in cultural development and that ecological adaptation was crucial for determining the limits of variation in cultural systems. He sought by means of comparative studies to determine the different ways in which cultures had developed in different types of natural environments, believing that they would tend to assume the same forms and follow similar developmental trajectories in similar natural settings. These similarities constituted the 'cultural core', which consisted of those features of a culture that were most closely related to subsistence activities. The core embraced economic, political, and religious patterns that could be empirically determined to have major adaptive significance. Steward argued that the aim of evolutionary anthropology should be to explain the common features of cultures at similar levels of development rather than 'unique, exotic, and non-recurrent particulars' which can be attributed to historical accidents (Steward 1955: 209).

M. D. Sahlins and E. R. Service (1960) tried to reconcile these two approaches by differentiating between general and specific evolution. These were defined as being concerned with progress and adaptation respectively. Although the concept of evolution was thereby dissociated from automatically implying progress, in later studies Sahlins (1968) and Service (1962, 1975) used ethnographic data to construct speculative and highly generalized sequences of unilinear development, employing concepts such as band, tribe, chiefdom, and state. Implicit in their approaches, and in the scheme of political evolution developed by Morton Fried (1967), was the assumption that the greater selective fitness of technologically advanced societies ensured that progress characterized cultural change as a general feature of human history.

The most theoretically sophisticated approach of this sort is Marvin Harris' (1979) cultural materialism. He assigns a privileged role in shaping cultural systems to an array of material conditions, including technology, demography, and economic relations, and seeks to explain all sociocultural phenomena in terms of the relative costs and benefits of alternative strategies, as measured in terms of these criteria. Much of his work has been directed towards trying to explain the origin of food taboos, religious beliefs, and other cultural esoterica in terms of the relations that these customs have to basic economic considerations (Harris 1974, 1977). While overtly less concerned with delineating evolutionary sequences than were Sahlins, Service, and Fried, Harris' approach is no less evolutionary than theirs.

What distinguished the various materialist approaches that developed in American anthropology in the 1960s from the evolutionary schemes of the nineteenth century was their view of causality. White adopted a very narrow form of technological determinism that reflected faith in technology as a source of social progress, while Steward embraced a less restrictive ecological and Harris a still broader economic determinism. Judged by Marxist standards all of these approaches are examples of vulgar materialism, because they view human behaviour as shaped more or less exclusively by non-human constraints. Marxism, by contrast, includes humanly arranged relations of production in the economic base that determines social change.

Already by the middle of the nineteenth century some archaeologists were constructing sequences to describe the development of native cultures in the New World (Wilson 1862). These approaches, which located the main centres of development in Mesoamerica and Peru, did not disappear following the adoption of a culture-historical approach. In *Ancient Civilizations of Mexico and Central America* H. J. Spinden (1928) distinguished three levels of development, Nomadic (hunting and gathering), Archaic (agriculture), and Civilization; while in *Method and Theory in American Archaeology*, Willey and Phillips (1958) assigned all cultures to five stages of increasing complexity: Lithic (big-game hunting), Archaic (intensive collecting), Formative (village agriculture), Classic (early civilizations), and Post-Classic (later prehispanic civilizations). Despite their evolutionary appearance these formulations sought to describe, rather than to account for, cultural change in developmental terms. They also relied as heavily on diffusionist explanations as did other culture-historical formulations.

Yet, with their growing interest in functionalist and processual explanations of the archaeological record, many American archaeologists were predisposed to be receptive to neo-evolutionary concepts, which emphasized regularities in culture. They noted that many of the key variables that White and Steward posited as major causes of cultural change were relatively accessible for archaeological study, unlike the idealist explanations of the Boasians. Because of their lack of direct information concerning human behaviour and beliefs, archaeologists were also less inclined to be critical of the shortcomings of neo-evolutionary theory than were ethnologists. Only a few objected that neo-evolutionism encouraged simplistic explanations and did not rule out adequately the possibility of alternative ones (Lamberg-Karlovsky 1975: 342–3). Neo-evolutionary anthropology intensified and gave new directions to trends already at work in prehistoric archaeology.

One of the first applications of neo-evolutionary theory to archaeology was B. J. Meggers' 'The law of cultural evolution as a practical research tool' (1960). She argued that because of the absence of non-human sources of energy in small-scale societies, White's law, as it applied to them, could be rewritten in the following fashion:

$$\text{Culture} = \text{Environment} \times \text{Technology}.$$

This suggested that any archaeologist who was able to reconstruct the technology and environment of a prehistoric culture should be able on the basis of that information to determine what the key features of the rest of the culture were like. Furthermore, any shortcomings were not the responsibility of archaeology but resulted from the failure of ethnologists to elaborate adequate theories relating technology and environment to the rest of culture. Meggers believed it to be an advantage that archaeologists were 'forced to deal with culture artificially separated from human beings' (Meggers 1955: 129) and that her formulation placed so much emphasis on techno-environmental determinism that it saw no need to use archaeological data to study non-material aspects of cultural systems. Her attitude towards the use of ethnographic analogy resembled that of many nineteenth-century evolutionary anthropologists. Her position was, however, too lacking in direct application to attract significant support among archaeologists. Likewise, White's treatment of technology as an independent variable bringing about change too closely resembled Montelius' view of change occurring as a result of the desire of human beings to control nature more effectively. To a growing number of archaeologists, who were becoming aware of cultural ecology and were anxious to provide a materialist explanation of what factors promoted or discouraged technological innovations, White's views seemed old-fashioned, idealist, and teleological. Nevertheless, some archaeologists admired his deductive approach to understanding cultural change (Binford 1972: 110–11).

The New Archaeology

In 1959 Joseph Caldwell published an article in *Science* titled 'The new American archeology'. In it he surveyed major trends that he saw transforming archaeology. He cited growing interest in ecology and settlement patterns as evidence of a new concern with cultural process. Archaeological cultures were no longer regarded merely as the sum total of their preserved artifact types, each of which can be treated in a stylistic fashion as independent and equally significant. Instead they have to be analysed, as Taylor had proposed, as configurations or even as functionally integrated systems. He also supported the neo-evolutionary belief that behind the infinite variety of cultural facts and specific historical situations is a finite number of general historical processes. Finally he adopted the neo-evolutionary position that not all cultural facts are of equal importance in bringing about change. The primary aim of archaeologists must be to explain changes in archaeological cultures in terms of cultural processes.

Caldwell's paper reveals that during the decade following the publication of Taylor's *A Study of Archeology* the concept of processual change within cultural systems had achieved a new level of importance in American archaeology. While this was encouraged by developments within archaeology, in particular the study of ecology and settlement patterns, it was also promoted by the growing popularity of neo-evolutionary anthropology, with its emphasis on cultural regularities. The essential and enduring elements of the New Archaeology were the collective creation of a considerable number of American archaeologists during the 1950s.

These concepts were popularized among the younger generation of American archaeologists by Lewis Binford, who added new elements to create the approach that since the 1960s has been recognized around the world as the American New Archaeology. Binford engaged in a series of vigorous polemics in which he sought to demonstrate the advantages of the New Archaeology over traditional approaches, which he identified primarily with the modified form of the Midwestern Taxonomic Method practised at the University of Michigan while he had been a graduate student there in the 1950s. The resulting polarization made the New Archaeology appear to be a dramatic break with the past rather than a continuation and intensification of the functionalist and processual trends that had been developing in American and Western European archaeology since the 1930s. Although there was considerable passive support for old-fashioned culture-historical archaeology, many so-called 'traditional' archaeologists were adherents of these recent trends who merely objected to particular facets of Binford's programme. The rapid adoption of the New Archaeology thus reflected the predisposing tendencies at work in the 1950s, while Binford's polemics disguised a considerable degree of consensus about the general direction in which American archaeology should evolve.

Binford outlined the programme of the New Archaeology in two papers: 'Archaeology as anthropology' (1962) and 'Archaeological systematics and the study of culture process' (1965). He identified the goal of archaeology as being the same as that traditionally assigned to anthropology: to explain the full range of similarities and differences in cultural behaviour. He also maintained that archaeological data were particularly useful for studying changes that occurred over long periods of time. These explanations were seen as taking the form of generalizations about systemic change and cultural evolution. As a student of Leslie White, Binford was predisposed to believe that there were strong regularities in human behaviour and that there was little difference between explaining a single instance of social change and a whole class of similar changes. Hence his main concern was to account for cultural similarities rather than differences. Throughout his career he has devoted himself to explaining problems such as increasing complexity in hunter–gatherer societies, the development of agriculture, and to a much lesser degree the evolution of civilization (Binford 1983b).

Like Grahame Clark, Binford viewed cultures as humanity's extrasomatic means of adaptation. Changes in all aspects of cultural systems were therefore interpreted as adaptive responses to alterations in the natural environment or in adjacent and competing cultural systems. Binford described evolution as 'a process operative at the interface of a living system and its field' (1972: 106). This ecosystemic view essentially ruled out human inventiveness and innovation within cultural traditions as independent forces capable of bringing about major changes. It also treated cultures as normally tending towards equilibrium or homeostasis, with change being induced by external factors.

Although Binford viewed cultural change as being initiated by non-cultural or external factors causing perturbations in what would otherwise tend to be homeostatic systems, he insisted, as Clark and Taylor already had done, that it had to be understood in terms of the responses that occurred within cultural systems. He thus shared the tendency, already evident in settlement archaeology, to concentrate on understanding cultural change from an internal point of view. This approach emphasized systemic relations and therefore continuities in change as opposed to the discontinuities brought about by migration and diffusion. Within the general context of neo-evolutionism there was a growing tendency to believe in the capacity of human beings to invent and reinvent new forms of technology, social behaviour, and beliefs and values as these were required by evolving social systems. Steward (1955: 182) had argued that every cultural borrowing might be construed as an 'independent recurrence of cause and effect' and Harris (1968: 377–8) had dismissed diffusion as a 'nonprinciple'. Chang (1962: 190–1) maintained that, if in the course of its development Chinese civilization had been unable to borrow new technological processes from the outside, the Chinese would have invented the same processes or ones of similar economic and social significance. Thus Binford differed from traditional American archaeologists by emphasizing humanity's capacity for innovation at the same time that he agreed with them in viewing undisturbed cultures as normally static.

Like Caldwell, Binford stressed the internal differentiation and systemic integration of cultures. He objected to the established normative view, which regarded cultures as collections of ideas held in common and transmitted over generations by members of particular social groups. In some of his writings his objections to views of culture as a mental phenomenon appear to rule out White's concept of culture as being symbolic in nature, although he otherwise praises White's views (Binford 1972: 105–13). Like Caldwell, he also objected to each item of culture being regarded as equal in significance to all others and the percentage of similarities and differences in artifact types being treated as a measurement of the amount of effective communication between groups. He maintained that traditional archaeology attributed differences between cultures to geographical barriers or resistant value systems, while it viewed ideas as being spread from one culture to another by diffusion and migration. Although this description may have represented accurately the views about cultures held by traditional culture-historical archaeologists working in the midwestern United States or even those of Walter Taylor, it did not take account of the views of a growing number of functionalist archaeologists in the United States or of Clark and Childe in Britain. As early as 1925 Childe had employed a functionalist view of culture to facilitate his culture-historical analyses when he distinguished between ethnic traits, which did not diffuse readily, and technological ones, which did.

Binford argued that cultures were not internally homogeneous. All of them were differentiated at least according to age and sex roles and the degree to which they were internally shared by individuals varied inversely with their complexity. Individuals always participated in cultures differentially, making a total cultural system a set of functionally interrelated roles. Because of this, it was wrong for archaeologists to treat artifacts as equal and comparable traits. Instead they must try to determine the roles they had played within living cultural systems. This necessitated an effort to achieve a relatively holistic view of these systems.

At this point Binford could have attempted, as Willey (1953), Childe (1958a), and various settlement archaeologists had done, to reconstruct social systems. This approach concentrated on delineating patterns of human interaction and determining the functional relationship of cultural traits to social systems. Instead he followed White in viewing cultures as adaptive systems composed of three interrelated subsystems: technology, social organization, and ideology. Thus he supported the view that human behaviour was determined by forces of which human beings are largely unaware and which frequently are located in the natural realm.

Binford argued that material items do not interact within a single subsystem of culture but reflect all three subsystems. Technomic aspects of artifacts reflect how they were used to cope with the environment; sociotechnic ones have their primary context in the social system; and ideotechnic ones relate to the ideological realm. In 1962 he suggested that each type of artifact might be interpreted as relating primarily to one of these classes, but by 1965 he noted that individual artifacts frequently encoded information about all three. A knife might be used for cutting, but its gold handle could denote the upper-class social status of its owner and a symbol engraved on the blade might invoke divine protection for him.

Binford went further than either Clark or Taylor had done in arguing that, because artifacts have primary contexts in all subsystems of culture, formal artifact assemblages and their contexts can yield a systematic and understandable picture of total extinct cultures. He maintained that the archaeologist's primary duty is to explain the relations that are extant in the archaeological record. In particular he repudiated the idea that it was inherently more difficult to reconstruct social organization or religious beliefs than it was to infer economic behaviour. The idea that archaeologists could study any problem that ethnologists could, and over much longer periods of time, won support among many young archaeologists who were frustrated by the artifact-centred, culture-historical approach that

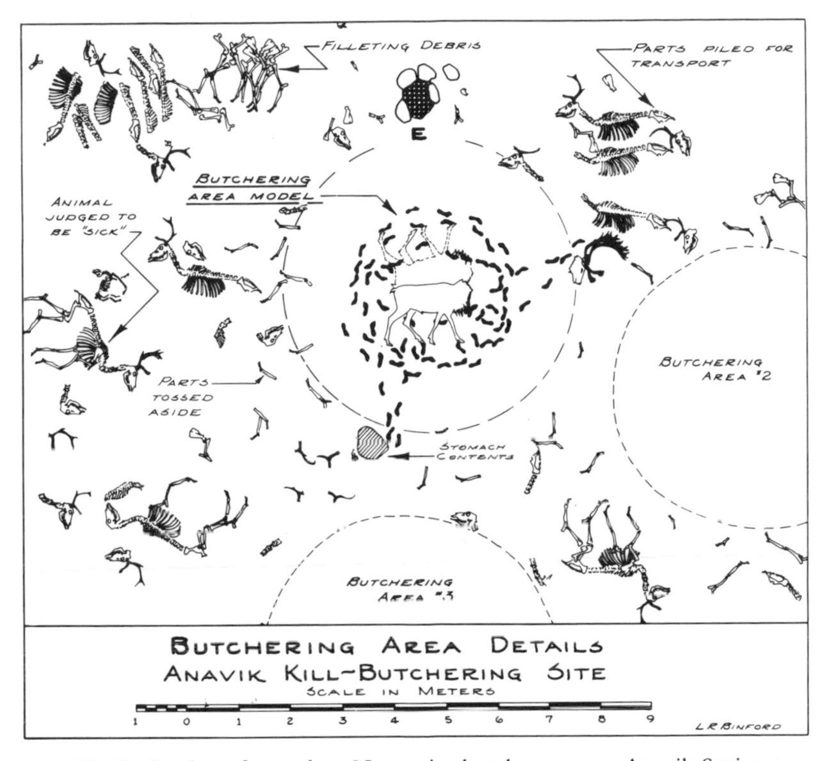

42 Binford's plan of a modern Nunamiut butchery area at Anavik Springs, Alaska, showing where caribou were dismembered and waste products were disposed

still continued to pervade much American archaeology in the early 1960s. They were anxious to demonstrate that ethnologists were wrong when they smugly proclaimed that archaeology was 'doomed always to be the lesser part of anthropology' (Hoebel 1949: 436).

Binford observed that archaeologists had already made significant progress in using knowledge derived from the physical and biological sciences to interpret those aspects of the archaeological record relating to technomic behaviour, especially subsistence patterns and technological practices. On the other hand, anthropologists did not know enough about correlations between social behaviour or beliefs and material culture to infer much sociotechnic or ideotechnic information from the archaeological record. Only after such correlations had been established and archaeologists had acquired a holistic knowledge of the structural and functional characteristics of cultural systems could they begin to investigate problems of evolutionary changes in social systems and ideology. Binford argued that in order to establish such correlations archaeologists must be trained as ethnologists. Only by studying living situations in which behaviour and ideas can be observed in conjunction with material culture was it possible to establish correlations that could be used to infer social behaviour and ideology reliably from the archaeological record. Binford saw this as a promising approach to understanding the past because, as a neo-evolutionist, he believed that there was a high degree of regularity in human behaviour which comparative ethnographic studies could reveal. These regularities could then be used to infer many aspects of prehistoric cultures that were not directly observable in the archaeological record. If human behaviour were less regular than he assumed, such correlations would be fewer in number and less useful for reconstructing prehistoric cultures and understanding change.

Some of the principal early applications of the New Archaeology were attempts to use ceramics to infer the residence patterns of prehistoric communities. It was assumed that, if women made the pottery used by their families, design elements would tend to cluster where knowledge of pottery making was transmitted from mothers to daughters in matrilocal societies but would become randomized in patrilocal ones where female potters from different lineages lived adjacent to one another (Deetz 1965; Whallon 1968; Hill 1970; Longacre 1970). The sex of potters was determined by applying the direct historical method rather than by means of forensic evidence as Tret'yakov had done in the 1930s. In these early studies the alternative possibility that some pottery was professionally made and exchanged over long distances was not examined, nor were the conditions under which broken pottery was discarded (S. Plog 1980). These pioneering efforts by American archaeologists to infer social organization from archaeological evidence therefore did not reach the high standards Binford had set for such work. They also may have provided a misleading impression of the kind of operations that were required by the deductive approach.

Among Binford's principal original contributions at this time was his insistence that the correlations used to infer human behaviour from archaeological data had to be based on the demonstration of a constant articulation of specific variables in a system. Only if a particular behavioural trait could be shown always to correlate with a specific item of material culture, wherever both could be observed, could such behaviour be inferred from the occurrence of that item in the archaeological record. This in turn necessitated a deductive approach in which relations between variables that are archaeologically observable and ones that are not are formulated and tested in a statistically significant number of ethnographic situations in which both variables can be observed. Only by means of such measurement of concomitant variation can regularities be established that are useful for understanding prehistoric cultural systems. Analogies are merely a source of hypotheses to be tested in this manner (Binford 1972: 33–51). Binford championed the positivist view that explanation and prediction are equivalent and that both rest upon the demonstration of a constant articulation of variables. The rigorous application of a positivist approach was seen as eliminating subjective elements and establishing a basis for the objective, scientific interpretation of archaeological data. To achieve this level of rigour, however, archaeologists had to adhere to deductive canons which utilized well-established correlations, as outlined by Carl Hempel (1962, 1965) in his covering-law model of explanation. From this perspective the most useful correlations are those that hold true whenever specific conditions are present. Since then archaeologists have realized that, because of the complexity of human behaviour, most correlations are statistical rather than absolute in nature and that most statistical correlations are of a lower rather than a higher degree of magnitude, a problem that ethnologists engaged in cross-cultural studies have long had to contend with (Textor 1967). Under these circumstances the problem of equifinality, or different causes producing the same effect, becomes increasingly troublesome, as archaeologists engaged in simulation studies have realized (Hodder 1978; Sabloff 1981). Yet Binford has continued to pay much less attention to deductive–statistical than to deductive–nomological explanations (M. Salmon 1982: 120–2).

The extension of the covering-law method to the explanation of cultural change tended to exclude consideration of all but situations of notable regularity. This correlated with Binford and his followers repudiating historical studies, which they equated with chronology, description, and a preoccupation with accidental occurrences

(Binford 1967b: 235; 1968b). This line of reasoning had been introduced to American archaeologists by the ethnologist Clyde Kluckhohn (1940) when he wrote that Mesoamerican archaeologists had to choose between historical studies that sought to recreate unique events in all of their idiosyncratic detail and scientific research that addressed significant trends and uniformities in cultural change. This invidious dichotomy between history and science, which paralleled the distinction that American anthropologists drew between history and evolution, was reinforced by Taylor (1948: 156–7) and Willey and Phillips (1958: 5–6), who regarded culture-historical integration as an objective that was inferior to formulating general rules of cultural behaviour. Binford viewed archaeologists' efforts to explain particular historical events as inductive behaviour that would doom archaeology to remain a particularistic, non-generalizing field. He argued that archaeologists instead must seek to formulate laws of cultural dynamics. While in historical retrospect this position can be seen as reflecting the belief that human history is governed by strong regularities, it deflected archaeological interest from significant aspects of cultural change that do not display such regularities.

Binford also denied the relevance of psychological factors for understanding prehistory. He identified the use of such concepts with Boasian idealism and the culture-historical approach and argued that they had no explanatory value for an ecological interpretation of culture and cultural change. On the contrary, within an ecological framework specific psychological factors could be viewed as an epiphenomenal aspect of human behaviour that arose as a consequence of ecological adaptation. He also argued that archaeologists are poorly trained to function as palaeopsychologists (Binford 1972: 198).

New Archaeologists have continued to condemn explanations of change that invoke either conscious or unconscious psychological factors. Instead they have identified relations between technology and the environment as the key factors determining cultural systems and, through them, human behaviour. In this respect they clearly differ from Marxists who see individual and collective perceptions of self-interest as a major cause of change. On the other hand this rejection of perceptions is shared by many other Western social scientists. It seems to reflect a tendency that has its roots in Christian theology to equate reason and volition with free will. If human behaviour is to be explained it must therefore be shown to be determined by something other than reason. This factor has been variously identified as culture (Tylor, Kroeber), society (Durkheim), subconscious drives (Freud), or ecosystems (Steward).

Systems theory

Binford's ideas quickly attracted a large following among American archaeologists, especially younger ones. At least one senior scholar, Paul Martin (1971), rallied publicly to his support. Binford's work also influenced Colin Renfrew (1979, 1984), an English archaeologist who taught for a time in the United States, and had much in common with the formulations of David Clarke (1968), another Englishman who was, however, independently influenced by the locational analysis and general systems approaches of the New Geography that had developed at Cambridge University (Chorley and Haggett 1967). In America also attempts were soon made to account for cultural change in terms of General Systems Theory. This was a body of concepts that the biologist Ludwig von Bertalanffy began to develop in the 1940s, which sought to delineate the underlying rules that govern the behaviour of entities as diverse as thermostats, digital computers, glaciers, living organisms, and sociocultural systems. It was assumed that all of these could be conceptualized as systems made up of interacting parts and that rules could be formulated that described how significant aspects of any system functioned, regardless of its specific nature (Bertalanffy 1969; Laszlo 1972a, b, c). Systems theory allowed archaeologists to transcend the limitations of traditional social anthropological analyses of static structures by studying not only structure-maintaining but also structure-elaborating (or morphogenetic) processes. Many of the most important of these studies were based on cybernetics, which sought to account for how systems functioned by mapping feedback between their various parts. Negative feedback maintains a system in an essentially steady state in the face of fluctuating external inputs, while positive feedback brings about irreversible changes in the structure of the system. The concept of feedback offered archaeologists a more precise, and potentially quantifiable, mechanism for interrelating the various components of a changing cultural system than did the essentially static social anthropological concept of functional integration (Watson *et al.* 1971: 61–87).

There was, however, no agreement about how feedback was to be measured. It has been identified with goods, energy, or information, and with all three combined. The concept of energy was especially congenial to ecological approaches. In an influential pioneering study Kent Flannery (1968) argued that favourable genetic changes in maize and beans encouraged Mesoamerican hunter–gatherers to reschedule their food procurement patterns in order to increase their dependence on these two plants, thus setting in motion systemic changes that did not stop until maize and beans had become the principal foci of intensive agriculture. Soon after, the concept of information processing became central to a discussion of the development of social hierarchies and complex societies. This theorizing drew upon and helped to elaborate a body of propositions derived from General Systems Theory concerning disproportional growth. These propositions attempted to explain the effects of increasing scale on the evolution of new institutions for collecting information and making decisions (Flannery 1972; Rathje 1975; Johnson 1978, 1981). While archaeologists were rarely able to apply General Systems Theory in a rigorous mathematical fashion, it has provided a model for studying cultural change that gave new meaning to Binford's call to do this in terms of systemic analyses.

The development of an internal view of cultural change was greatly assisted by radiocarbon dating, which was invented by Willard Libby in the late 1940s and immediately applied to dating archaeological material (Libby 1955). This new technique reduced the need for archaeologists to rely on seriation and cross-cultural trait distributions to construct cultural chronologies. It also became possible for the first time to date sites around the world in relationship to one another and to assign calendrical dates rather than only relative ones to prehistoric sites. Archaeologists were thus able to study rates as well as sequences of change. Renfrew's (1973a, 1979) reinterpretation of European prehistory was based almost entirely on calibrated radiocarbon dates, which he used to demonstrate that Neolithic and Bronze Age sites north and west of the Aegean were considerably older than Montelius and Childe had determined on the basis of cross-dating.

Radiocarbon dating had a similar effect on the study of North

American prehistory. There, everywhere except in the Southwest, where calendrical dates for sites back to the beginning of the Christian era had been derived dendrochronologically since the 1920s, radiocarbon chronologies revealed that cultural sequences had developed over longer periods and far more slowly than had previously been believed (cf. Ritchie 1944, 1965). By greatly slowing the rate of cultural change in the eastern United States and Western Europe, radiocarbon dating made it easier for archaeologists to credit the possibility that major changes had come about as a result of internal changes rather than attributing them to diffusion and migration as they had previously done.

Although the New Archaeologists agreed that the main causes of cultural change were not to be found within sociocultural systems or identified with human volition, they did not agree about either the specific causes of change or the degree to which social behaviour was shaped by these factors. Ecological explanations of change continued to be very important, although unicausal theories, such as those that attributed the origins of civilization to the development of complex irrigation systems, were gradually abandoned (Hunt 1972). Ecological factors once again came to be viewed more as a constraint upon human behaviour than as an explanation of the specific forms that human behaviour has taken. At the same time other causal factors were considered. Ester Boserup's *The Conditions of Agricultural Growth* (1965) revived an interest in speculations dating back to the eighteenth century that gradual population increase could be a major independent variable bringing about cultural change. Although her theory had been devised to explain the development of more intensive forms of agriculture, archaeologists applied it to explain the origins of agriculture (P. Smith 1976) and civilization (Young 1972), and finally the totality of cultural change (M. Cohen 1977). While it provided a major stimulus for palaeodemographic studies, the results were rarely sufficiently detailed or comprehensive to permit a substantial test of the theory. In due course archaeologists began to stress the cultural and biological factors that influence the rate of population growth and demographic factors have ceased to be widely regarded as independent causes of change (Cowgill 1975; Binford and Chasko 1976).

Robert Dunnell and some of his students opted for a different sort of systemic approach, that uses biological ('scientific') evolutionary theory to explain cultural as well as biological variability (Dunnell 1980a; Wenke 1981; Rindos 1984). They argue that traditional cultural evolutionism has failed to internalize such key tenets of scientific evolutionism as random variation and natural selection. While admitting that mechanisms of trait transmission are more varied and the stability of the units on which selection operates is less so with respect to cultural than to biological phenomena (both issues that Kroeber [1952] and other anthropologists discussed long ago), they maintain that an approach based on general principles of scientific evolutionism can offer explanations of human behaviour that are superior to those offered by cultural evolutionary approaches. This often involves the radical reformulation of traditional questions. For example, David Rindos (1984: 143) has defined domestication as a mutualistic relation of varying degrees between different species. He does not view the adaptation of plants and animals to human needs as different in nature from the adaptation of human beings to the needs of plants and animals. This approach carries to an extreme the denial that consciousness and intentionality play a significant role in shaping human behaviour.

Although systems theory inspired some highly specific explanations of cultural change, such as Flannery's hypothesis concerning the development of plant domestication in Mesoamerica, in the long run it encouraged archaeologists to note the complex ramifications of cultural processes. This stimulated identification of the numerous interlinking factors that brought about cultural change and led some archaeologists to recognize that even key variables might have played a less important role in shaping cultural systems than they had hitherto believed. This in turn has led many archaeologists to adopt a more inductive approach to explaining causality. It was also recognized that because of the complexity of cultural systems the same factors might have different effects or different ones the same effect depending on individual circumstances. Flannery (1972) suggested that explanations of cultural development should concentrate less on the conditions bringing about cultural change than on the types of systemic changes that could be observed in the archaeological record. He offered, as examples of evolutionary mechanisms, 'promotion' and 'linearization'. Promotion involved established institutions rising in a developing hierarchy of control to assume transformed and more far-reaching roles. Linearization occurred

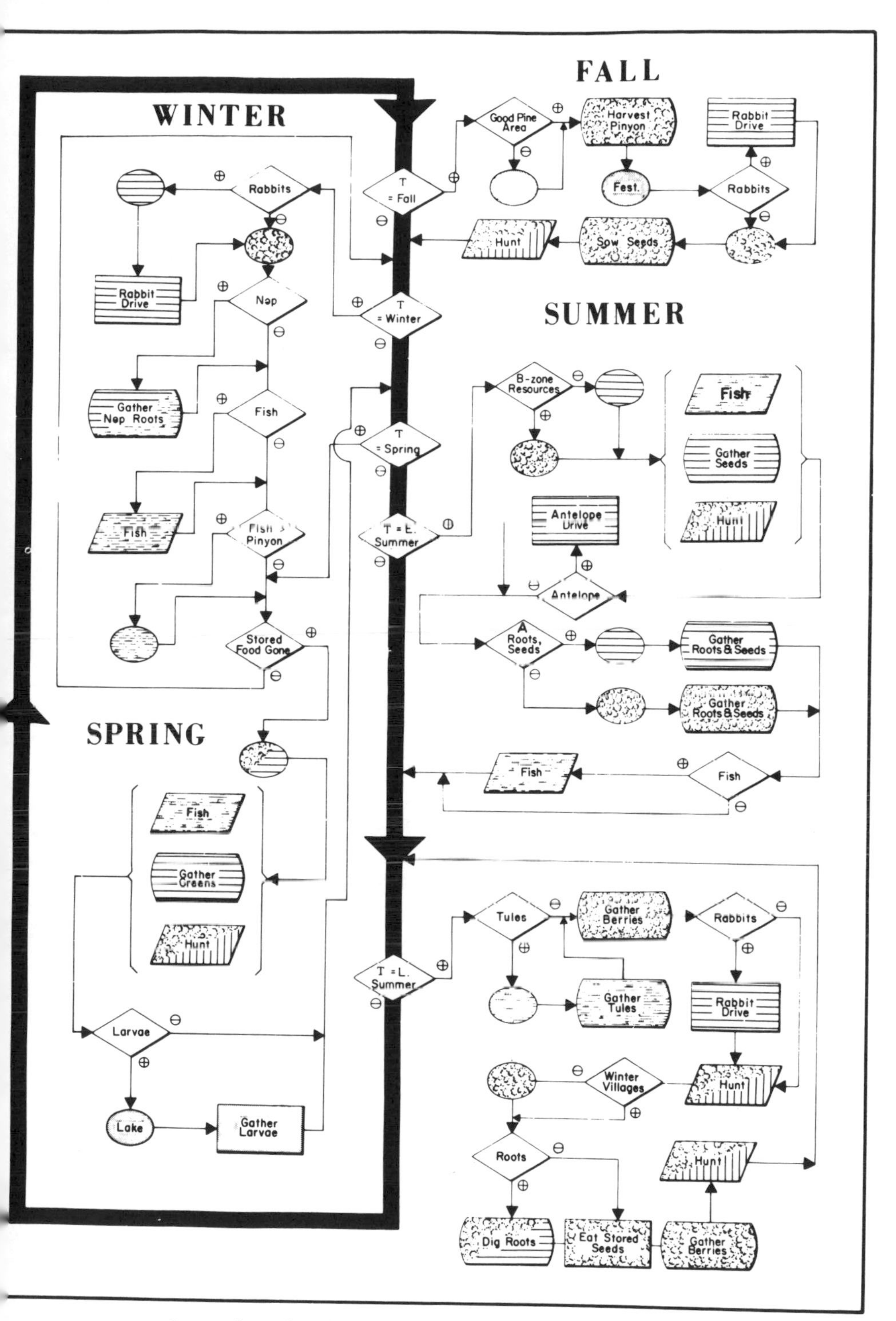

43 System flow chart for Shoshonean Indian subsistence cycle, by D. H. Thomas, 1972

when higher-order controls cut past and eliminated traditional lower-order ones after the latter had failed to function in a more complex setting.

Flannery's approach was extremely valuable for gaining an understanding of change from a social-structural point of view. It also drew attention to a source of constraint on human behaviour that was different from, and seemingly independent of, the ecological constraints that American archaeologists previously had been considering. If social and political systems could only assume a limited number of general forms (a point Childe had already made in *Social Evolution*), these forms restricted the variation that was possible in human behaviour and the routes that cultural change can follow. Yet such limitations do not explain why changes occurred in the first place. In terms of causal factors, a systems approach serves to describe rather than to explain change.

Many archaeologists have concluded that, because a systems approach makes fewer assumptions about causality and is more inductive, it is conceptually superior to theories that assume in advance why change takes place. These archaeologists have been accused of using systems theory in a Boasian fashion to beg the question of causality (Leone 1975). Yet Sanders, Parsons, and Santley (1979: 360) have failed in their efforts to demonstrate that ultimately four or five ecological variables can account for as much as 80 per cent of the variation in the archaeological record.

Archaeologists soon began to move further away from rather than nearer to a consensus about factors governing sociocultural change. Working within a neo-evolutionary tradition, processual archaeologists tried hard to demonstrate that a limited number of ecological and demographic variables played a predominant role in shaping sociocultural systems. Yet the regularity in these systems consistently turned out to be less than neo-evolutionary theory predicted. It was also more difficult than neo-evolutionary theory suggested for archaeologists to infer one aspect of sociocultural systems from known characteristics of another part, especially features of social organization and ideology from knowledge of the economy. Stuart Struever (1968) argued, for example, that the means by which a population derives its subsistence from the environment plays such an important role in shaping the entire cultural system that the nature of settlement patterns can be predicted and hence

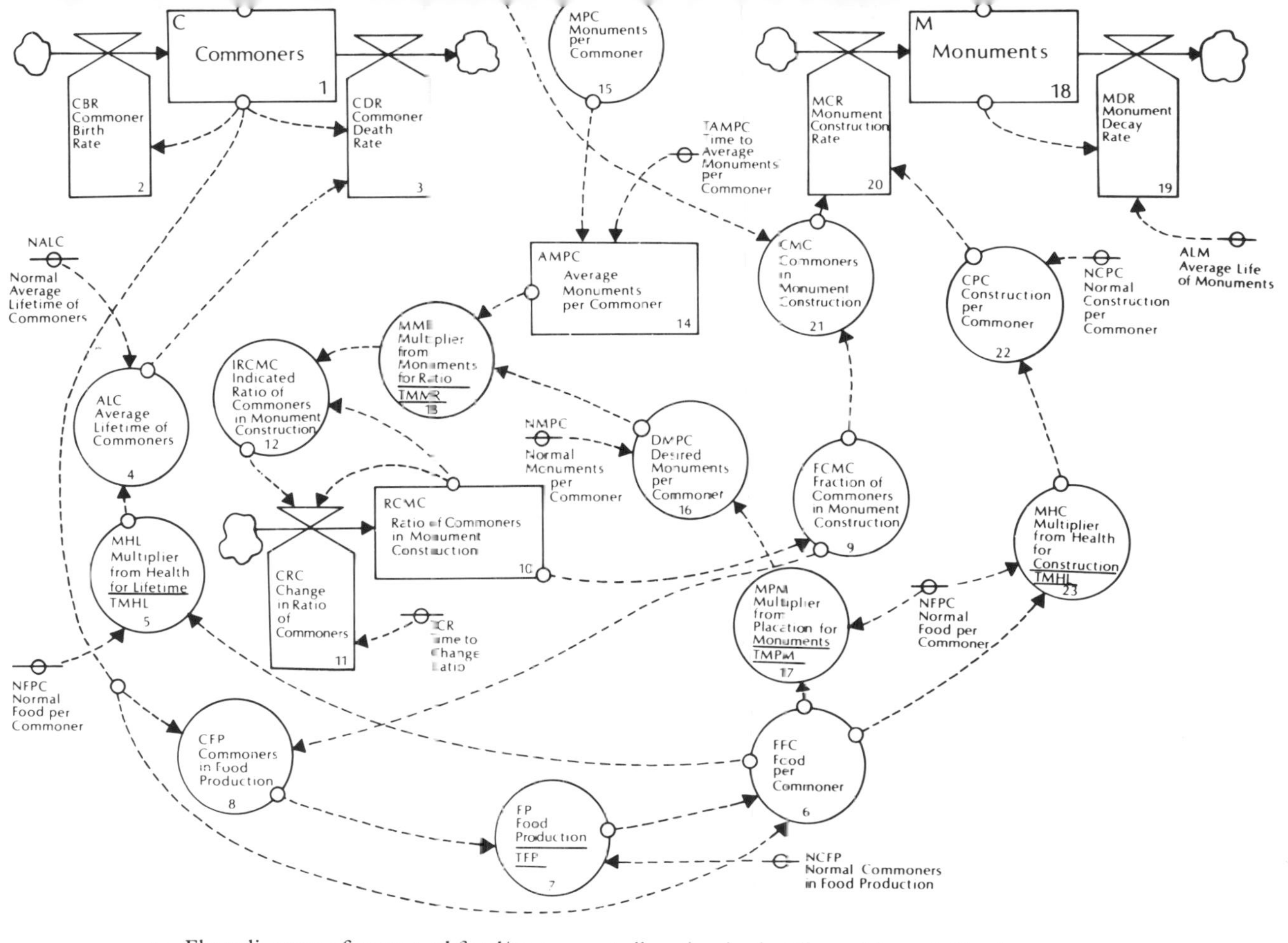

44 Flow diagram of presumed food/monument allocation in the Classic Maya civilization

explained in terms of technology and the natural environment. He viewed settlement patterns as 'an essential corollary of subsistence' and interpreted 'variations between cultures [as] responses to differing adaptive requirements of specific environments' (p. 133–5). He therefore believed that archaeological settlement patterns only served to confirm that relationship. Yet a growing understanding of settlement patterns has indicated that prediction is not so simple and that significant factors other than technology and environment shape their development (Trigger 1968b; Clarke 1977). Under these circumstances an inductive systems approach offered a growing number of archaeologists a methodology that seemed more productive of insights into the causes of variation than did the narrowly deterministic explanations suggested by neo-evolutionists. These archaeologists either implicitly or explicitly rejected the rigidly deductive approach originally advocated by the New Archaeology.

The New Archaeology promoted a more sophisticated and productive view of sampling by revealing the often unconscious biases that had governed traditional archaeological research and the inadequacies of these approaches for understanding prehistoric cultures as systems. Prior to the development of settlement archaeology, the excavations of urban centres had concentrated on ceremonial precincts and palaces, while generally ignoring how ordinary people had lived. Regional investigations often paid little attention to the seasonality of hunter–gatherer sites and ignored low-level sites, such as peasant hamlets, in hierarchical societies. Settlement studies, such as Gordon Willey's systematic investigation of peasant hamlets in the Belize Valley (Willey *et al.* 1965) had already begun to correct these biases. New Archaeologists advocated the use of sampling strategies to guide both surveys and excavations and economize on the time and labour needed to carry out research. Underlying this advocacy was their belief that, because strong regularities were inherent in cultural systems, a small part of a system could be representative of the whole. Now, however, it was no longer a single site, but some portion of a site network that was thought to be typical of the whole.

Various forms of sampling helped archaeologists to recover a more representative selection of the material to be found in large heterogeneous sites. Yet random sampling has come to be seen as an initial excavation strategy that must be supplemented in the later

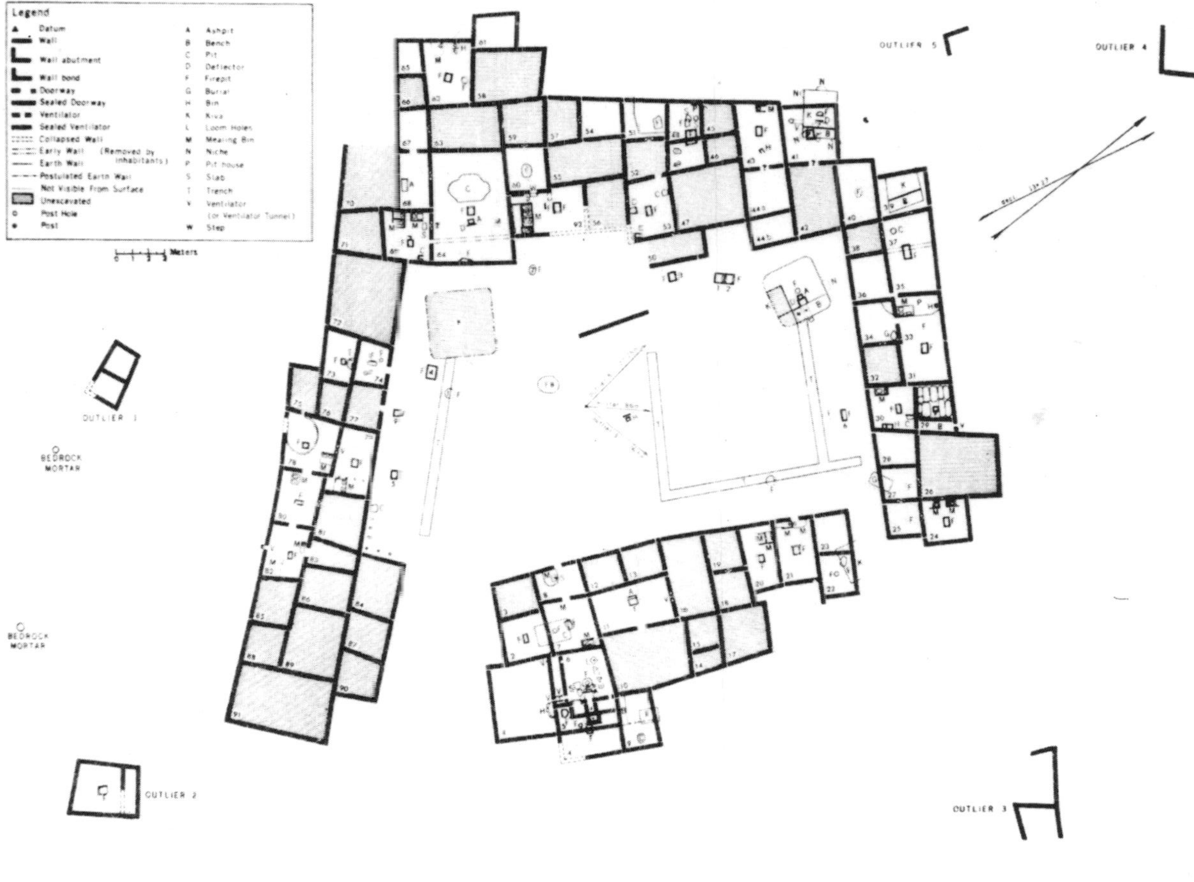

45 Sampling at Broken K Pueblo, J. N. Hill, 1968

stages of research by an increasing number of judgemental decisions about what areas should be excavated (Redman 1986). Studies of early civilizations based upon total regional surveys have provided the data to allow simulated examinations of the representativeness of various sampling strategies. Sanders, Parsons, and Santley's (1979: 491–532) survey of the Valley of Mexico revealed marked diversity in local patterns of development and also the need to study the entire region in order to understand what was happening in its various parts. For example, the massive increase in population and growth of urbanism in the Teotihuacan Valley early in the Christian era can only be understood when it is realized that similar population growth was not occurring elsewhere in the Valley of Mexico, but on the contrary the population of those areas was declining at that time. Robert Adams (1981) has shown similar local diversity in his studies of Mesopotamian settlement patterns. These findings have severely challenged the belief that patterns from one area are necessarily representative of a whole region. As a result it is now agreed that much larger samples than had hitherto been thought necessary are required before they are representative of a whole and that the study of changes over long periods requires something approaching total samples. These changes in views of sampling correlated with the realization that regularities in cultural systems had been overestimated during the initial stages of the New Archaeology.

Anti-historicism

Critics have argued that the New Archaeology represented a revolution in the technical and methodological spheres rather than in archaeological theory (Meltzer 1979). Yet the stand that Binford took against the still influential culture-historical approach in the United States was no less a break with that past in terms of high-level theory than it was methodologically. The questions that must be answered are why did his approach appeal so powerfully to a rising generation of American archaeologists and why, apart from Binford's undeniable charismatic qualities, was he able so quickly to popularize views that until then had only slowly been spreading through American archaeology?

Thomas Patterson (1986a) has argued that the majority of New Archaeologists were recruited from the increasingly powerful and nationalistically oriented middle class that has its base in the central and western parts of the United States rather than from the more internationally inclined east-coast elite that had dominated American economic and intellectual life during the early years following World War II. At the most basic level the nomothetic orientation of the New Archaeology appealed to the tendencies of these Americans to value what was technologically useful at the same time that they remained suspicious of pure science because of what they saw as its elitist tendencies, as well as its suspected disregard for conventional religious beliefs. The contempt for what was not practical also manifested itself in the low respect accorded to historical studies in America (Bronowski 1971: 195), an opinion epitomized in the industrialist Henry Ford's remark that 'History is . . . bunk' (Lowenthal 1985: 244). The low value accorded to history further reflected the 'present-mindedness' of American society, which romantically viewed itself as having prospered by throwing off the shackles of the past, as represented by traditional claims of descent, class, and tradition, and creating a new society rationally designed to serve the interests of the enterprising individual (Kroker 1984: 8). Even though prehistoric archaeology was a branch of anthropology, its culture-historical approach reduced its prestige and led it to be regarded as a dilettantish pursuit by the American public and by other anthropologists.

The New Archaeology followed the lead of the generalizing social sciences, such as economics, political science, sociology, and ethnology by claiming to be able to produce objective, ethically neutral generalizations that were useful for the management of modern societies. This desire to conform to a more prestigious model of scholarly behaviour was reinforced as the National Science Foundation emerged as a major source of funding for archaeological research. It was argued that archaeology could provide information about the nature of long-term interactions between human groups and the environment that would be of value for modern economic planning (Fritz 1973), a view shared even by some archaeologists who rejected the general philosophy and methodology of the New Archaeology (Dymond 1974). The study of prehistoric irrigation systems in Arizona might reveal unsuspected problems associated with modern ones in the same area, while stratified archaeological sites in California were looked to for information about the frequency of major earthquakes that could help to decide whether or not atomic-energy generators should be installed nearby (F. Plog 1982). These suggestions are reminiscent of the practical applications that were used to justify Soviet archaeology in the 1930s and later by Childe (1944b) as a practical reason for public support of archaeological research. In *The Archaeology of Arizona* Paul Martin and Fred Plog (1973: 364–8) argued that generalizations about human reactions to stress derived from ecological studies of prehistoric Arizona might help to explain the behaviour of underprivileged black and hispanic groups living in the ghettos of modern American cities.

This emphasis on the possible practical applications of their research encouraged social scientists to abandon holistic attempts to understand human behaviour, and instead led them to seek solutions to problems conceived in limited technical terms (Wolf 1982: ix). Such research was endowed with further scientific credentials by positivist claims of ethical neutrality. To produce 'relevant' findings that would justify an honoured place for archaeology in a society in which 'technocratic efficiency is considered as the supreme value' (Kolakowski 1976: 229), many American archaeologists saw themselves having to turn away from a historical understanding of the past to create the generalizations about human behaviour that were the hallmark of successful social scientists. It is within this context that we must understand Binford's (1967b: 235) claim that historical interpretation is unsuited to play more than a 'role in the general education of the public'. He was not the first archaeologist to promote the idea that such generalizations were to be regarded as archaeology's supreme achievement. Kidder (1935: 14) had argued that the ultimate goal of archaeological research should be to establish generalizations about human behaviour, while Taylor (1948: 151) and Willey and Phillips (1958: 5–6) saw them as constituting a common anthropological focus for archaeological and ethnological research.

The anti-historical bias of the New Archaeology can also be viewed as an ideological reflection of the increasing economic and political interventionism of the United States on a global scale after World War II. Its emphasis on nomothetic generalizations was accompanied by the obvious implication that the study of any national tradition as an end in itself was of trivial importance. Richard Ford (1973) called into question the legitimacy of 'political archaeology' and of any correlation between archaeology and nationalism, asking archaeologists instead to embrace a 'universal humanism'. By denying the worth of such studies the New Archaeology suggested the unimportance of national traditions themselves and of anything that stood in the way of American economic activity and political influence. The corrosive effects of similar arguments in other fields upon the national traditions of neighbouring Western countries have been well described for this period (G. Grant 1965). In particular, it has been documented how the American promotion after World War II of abstract expressionist art as the dominant international style resulted in the disintegration or trivialization of many national and regional traditions of painting. There is also strong evidence that the promotion of this art style was carried out deliberately and with financial support from the United States government as well as from private foundations (Lord 1974: 198–215; Fuller 1980: 114–15). While New Archaeologists may not have been conscious agents in the promotion of United States political and economic hegemony, their programme appears to have accorded with that policy.

The most striking impact of this anti-historical viewpoint was exhibited in relation to native North American prehistory. By making the explanation of internal changes central to its interpretation of archaeological data, the New Archaeology stressed the creativity of native North Americans to a much greater extent than diffusionist explanations had done and for the first time placed native people on an equal footing in this respect with Europeans and other ethnic groups. Only amateur archaeologists, such as Barry Fell (1976, 1982) R. A. Jairazbhoy (1974, 1976) and Irvan van Sertima (1977), have continued to belittle native people by attributing major elements of their cultural heritage to prehistoric visitors from the Old World. The New Archaeology thus implicitly ended over a century of condescending and often overtly racist interpretations of native prehistory by white archaeologists. Yet from the beginning processual archaeologists ignored the significance of their achievement as a result of their insistence that generalizations were the principal goal of their discipline and by studying ecological adaptation at the expense of historically specific artistic traditions and religious beliefs.

By doing this, New Archaeologists used data concerning the

heritage of native North Americans to formulate generalizations that they claimed were relevant for understanding Euro-American society. This tendency to use data about native North American prehistory as a basis for generalizing about human behaviour suggested that for the most part the significance of native people for archaeologists had not changed. Despite some involvement on behalf of Indians in land-claims cases, most processual archaeologists remained as spiritually alienated from native North Americans as their predecessors had been in the nineteenth century. This alienation has proved increasingly costly to the interests of archaeologists at a time when the native population of North America is rapidly growing and native people are becoming militant in their struggle to control their own social, economic, and political destiny. Efforts by native people to forbid or regulate access to prehistoric sites have resulted in a growing number of legal confrontations between archaeologists and native people and only limited and often ineffectual efforts at accommodation (Meighan 1984). While some native groups, such as the Pueblo of Zuñi, have sponsored their own programmes of archaeological research in an effort to achieve a more detailed and accurate view of their history (E. Adams 1984; Ferguson 1984), most native people have been repelled by the negative attitudes toward them that traditionally have been reflected in interpretations of archaeological data and in particular by the refusal of archaeologists to study the past as a record of native American history and culture.

British archaeologists who were influenced by the New Archaeology did not adopt the anti-historical attitudes of their American counterparts. David Clarke, a highly original thinker who was even more deeply influenced by the systemic approach of the New Geography than by Binford, was rightly critical of the intuitive manner in which many British archaeologists sought to compose 'historical narratives' without first analysing archaeological data in a rigorous manner in order to extract as much behavioural information as possible from them. Yet he did not condemn the historical analysis of archaeological data. After the publication of *Analytical Archaeology* (1968), which brought a host of quantitative methods pioneered by other social and biological sciences to bear on problems of archaeological classification and explaining cultural change, he returned to the study of European prehistory. His later papers dealing with this subject are characterized by a concern for the ecological basis of cultural development, attention to the social milieu in which economic transactions occurred, and a balanced interest in local development and regional networks of interaction. In 'The economic context of trade and industry in barbarian Europe till Roman times' (Clarke 1979: 263–331), which he wrote for *The Cambridge Economic History*, he attempted to summarize the relevant archaeological data in the light of Karl Polanyi's theories concerning the social embeddedness of primitive economies. This paper has been described as 'a great advance on previous work in its discussion of the social functions of artefact-types and its inference of the circulation-systems of which they are the fossilized remains' (Sherratt 1979: 197). His more detailed studies addressed such central issues of European prehistory as a reinterpretation of the social organization and economy of the late Iron Age settlement at Glastonbury (Clarke 1972b) and a survey, taking account of ecological, ethnographic, demographic, and economic, as well as archaeological data to counteract the traditional faunally oriented interpretations of the Mesolithic economics of Europe (Clarke 1979: 206–62). Colin Renfrew (1979) has also devoted his career to studying European prehistory. In addition to a major revision of the continent's chronology, he has used techniques introduced by the New Archaeology to address problems of trade, political development, and changing social organization in prehistoric times.

While American archaeologists, traditional and New, have tended to equate history with the study of chronology and idiosyncratic events, Clarke and Renfrew, who were trained in a European tradition that views prehistory as an extension of historical enquiry into periods that lack written records, were familiar with historiography and therefore recognized the unrealistic nature of the dichotomy that American anthropologists (and formerly British social anthropologists as well) drew between history and science. The British historian E. H. Carr (1967: 117) observed that 'Every historical argument revolves around the question of the priority of causes'. The American archaeologist A. C. Spaulding's (1968) claim that the chief distinction between science and history is the latter's overwhelming dependence on common-sense explanations did a grave injustice to the work of many twentieth-century historians, in whose writings interpretations of an impressionistic sort have been

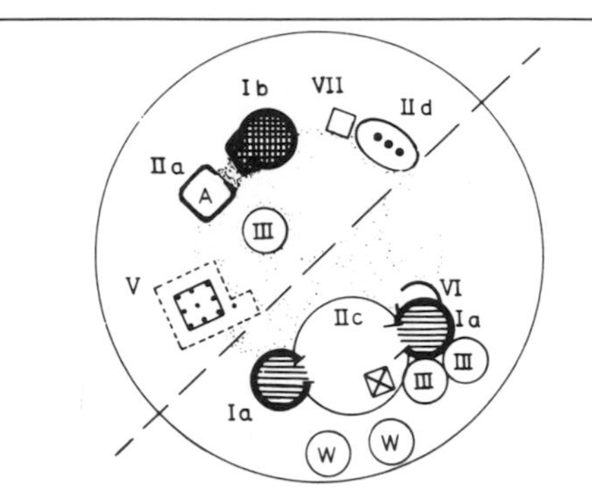

FIG. 21.1. The modular unit – the social and architectural building block of which the settlement is a multiple. The analyses of vertical and horizontal spatial relationships, structural attributes and artefact distributions convergently define a distinct range of structures (I–VII) repeatedly reproduced on the site. Each replication of the unit appears to be a particular transformation of an otherwise standardized set of relationships between each structural category and every other category. The basic division between the pair of major houses (Ia) and their satellites, and the minor house (Ib) and its ancillaries may be tentatively identified with a division between a major familial, multi-role and activity area on one hand and a minor, largely female and domestic area (see Fig. 21.6).

Below: the iconic symbols used to identify the structures in the schematic site models, Figs. 21.2–21.5.

— Ia Major house
— Ib Minor house
— IIa Ancillary hut
— IIb Workshop hut
— IIc Courtyard
— IId Baking hut
— IIe Guard hut
— IIf Annexe hut
— III Workfloor
— IV Clay patch
— V Granaries or Storehouses
— VI Stables
— VII Sties or Kennels
— Waggon stance
.... Palisade or fence

46 Modular housing unit at Glastonbury Iron Age site, as identified by D. L. Clarke

replaced by ones based on solid bodies of social-science theory. While the extent of the role played by chance factors in shaping historical events is a subject for debate, historians agree that individual behaviour is not random and must be viewed in relation to a social and cultural matrix that can be explained, if not predicted, by general rules (Carr 1967: 113–43). Clarke, in particular, was willing in trying to explain complex historical situations to move beyond Binford's Hempelian logico-deductive positivism, which he was aware was already considered outmoded by most philosophers. He also maintained the necessity to compare alternative explanations and that 'speculation is both essential and productive if it obeys the cardinal injunctions that it must predict and that some of those predictions must ultimately be testable' (Clarke 1979: 259). The early work of Clarke and Renfrew has provided strong evidence, as have more recent contributions by other Western European archaeologists (Renfrew and Shennan 1982), that historical interpretation and evolutionary generalization are not antithetical approaches but instead may proceed concurrently and to their mutual advantage in archaeology.

Cataclysmic archaeology

Beginning in the 1970s the cultural-evolutionary paradigm that guided the high-level interpretations of the New Archaeology underwent a major change. Since the late 1950s the optimism and security of the middle classes in the United States had been seriously eroded by a succession of chronic and deepening economic crises that were exacerbated by repeated failures of foreign policy, especially in Vietnam. These events produced a marked decline of faith in the benefits to be derived from technological development. This in turn spawned a proliferation of middle-class protest movements. While these movements consistently have avoided addressing the crucial economic and political problems of American society, they have profoundly altered social values and influenced the social sciences.

The oldest of these is the ecology movement, which views unrestrained technological development as poisoning and gradually destroying the world ecosystem. Its beginnings were signalled by the publication of Rachel Carson's *Silent Spring* (1962). It has since promoted awareness of an immediate danger to public health from a broad array of technological processes and warned that in the long term even more catastrophic consequences may result from the continuing pollution of the environment. The second movement, to promote a conserver society, stresses that certain natural resources essential for industrial processes are available only in finite quantities in nature; hence the world is rapidly reaching a point where further industrial expansion may become impossible. It is predicted that the exhaustion of key resources will result in declining living standards, or even the collapse of civilization. Hitherto it had generally been assumed that new raw materials or sources of energy would be found before old ones became depleted. Paul Ehrlich's *The Population Bomb* (1968) drew attention to yet another cause of anxiety. He argued that if unprecedented population growth were not checked, the results would be disastrous in the near future. As a result of these movements, social scientists and the general public became increasingly sceptical about the benefits of technological progress. As their political and economic insecurity increased, they, like the late nineteenth-century European middle classes, came to view cultural evolution as a source of danger and perhaps ultimately of disaster. Even rapid cultural change was condemned for producing dysfunctional 'future shock' (Toffler 1970).

These shifting attitudes laid the groundwork for a conceptual reorientation of archaeology that was as dramatic as the late nineteenth-century shift from unilinear evolutionism to the culture-historical paradigm had been. The new paradigm marked yet another retreat from the optimistic view of change formulated during the Enlightenment and intensified neo-evolutionism's rejection of the belief that technological innovation was the result of a process of rational self-improvement and the driving force promoting cultural change. Two specific developments in economics and social anthropology served as a catalyst for this shift.

Boserup (1965) had argued that while increasingly labour-intensive modes of agriculture yielded more food per unit of land, they required more labour for each unit of food produced. Therefore only the necessity to support slowly but inevitably increasing population densities would have led groups to adopt such systems. Her thesis was construed as evidence that developments which previous generations of archaeologists had interpreted as desirable results of humanity's ability to solve problems and make life easier and more fulfilling were in fact responses to forces beyond human control. Throughout history these forces had compelled people to work harder, suffer increasing exploitation, and degrade their environments.

The demonstration by Richard Lee and Irven DeVore (1968) that hunter–gatherer economies could support a low population density with less effort than was required by even the least demanding forms of food production not only was interpreted as support for Boserup's position but also led archaeologists to adopt new interpretations of prehistoric hunter–gatherers. Instead of being viewed as living on the brink of starvation, they were portrayed as leisured groups with plenty of spare time to devote to religious or intellectual pursuits. Even relatively conservative archaeologists began to idealize the more egalitarian prehistoric cultures as examples of 'conserving societies' that provided models of how we ourselves should behave in relation to the environment (Cunliffe 1974: 27). Some archaeologists questioned the evidence on which these formulations were based and their general applicability (Bronson 1972; Cowgill 1975; Harris 1979: 87–8). Yet the rapid and relatively unchallenged way in which these studies came to influence the interpretation of archaeological data, often in the absence of adequate measures of prehistoric population size or even of relative population change, suggests the degree to which they accorded with the spirit of the time.

Archaeologists also began to express reservations about conventional neo-evolutionary theories that analysed change as if it occurred in slow, gradual trajectories of the sort that Braidwood and MacNeish had documented in their studies of the origins of agriculture in the Near East and Mesoamerica. Robert Adams (1974: 248–9) pointed out that there were abrupt shifts in the development of early civilizations, sometimes separated by long periods when relatively few changes occurred. Soon after Renfrew (1978) attempted to use catastrophe theory, which had been invented by the French mathematician René Thom, to explain changes in the archaeological record. Catastrophe theory treats the question of how, as the result of particular conjunctions of internal states, a set of fluctuating variables can produce discontinuous effects (Saunders 1980). While it remains to be demonstrated how rigorously Thom's mathematics, which can treat only four variables at once, can be used to explain social behaviour, the concept attracted considerable attention among archaeologists in Britain and America (Renfrew and Cooke 1979). Although Thom and Renfrew were both interested in 'catastrophes' that produced more complex as well as simpler states, the ready acceptance of catastrophe theory as an analogue of social process reflected widespread fears that Western societies might be sliding towards a catastrophe in the conventional as well as the mathematical sense. Finally archaeologists have sought to imbue the concept of discontinuous cultural change with additional scientific prestige by drawing parallels between it and that of punctuated equilibrium being promoted by some evolutionary biologists (S. Gould 1980; Eldredge 1982). These views of cultural change have made archaeologists more aware of the need to distinguish varying rates of change in the archaeological record, sometimes over relatively short periods of time. Gaps are also being recognized in the archaeological record that in the past would have been filled by unwarrantedly projecting known cultures backwards and forwards in time or hypothesizing undiscovered intermediary forms. This has challenged archaeologists to acquire ever greater control over cultural chronologies. It has also reinforced the belief that cultures are more fragile and cultural change more fraught with dangers than archaeologists had believed hitherto.

These new ideas about the nature of cultural change have promoted a pessimistic and even tragic version of cultural evolution that interprets demographic, ecological, and economic factors as constraining change to occur along lines that most human beings do not regard as desirable but which they are unable to control. This eschatological materialism implies that the future is always likely to be worse than the present and that humanity is journeying from a primitive Eden, filled with happy hunter–gatherers, to a hell of thermonuclear annihilation. We have already noted that neo-evolutionism differed from nineteenth-century evolutionism in its rejection of the belief that cultural change occurred as the result of rational and willing action by human beings who sought to acquire greater control over their environment. This new cataclysmic evolutionism also differed from previous disillusionment about progress, which had resulted in diffusionists denying that there was any natural order to human history. Instead of denying that there was such an order, cataclysmic evolutionists stressed a fixed process of change that at best human beings might hope to slow or halt, but which otherwise would result in their ruin (Trigger 1981a). Only a few archaeologists who see trouble ahead for their own society continue to argue that it is possible to learn from the past how to 'adjust and cope' (J. Bradley 1987: 7).

Cataclysmic evolutionism, with its curious resemblances to the medieval view of history, but with God replaced by an evolutionary process that renders human beings the victims of forces beyond their control, seems to be the product of an advanced capitalist society that is not performing to the satisfaction of large numbers of the middle classes. Significantly, neither evolutionary archaeologists nor most of the opponents of environmental pollution, unchecked population growth, and the wastage of natural resources treat these problems as ones that can be resolved by means of concerted economic and political reforms carried out on the national and international levels. Instead they mystify these problems by locating their causes in a general evolutionary framework and seek when possible to ameliorate them in discrete, piecemeal ways. By exculpating leading industrial societies of explicit political responsibility for what is happening, cataclysmic archaeology helps to reaffirm the expansionist goals of American society in the midst of a growing international economic and ecological crisis. It also seeks to promote social solidarity by denying the political origins of social conflict. On the downswing of a long cycle, cataclysmic evolution attributes the shortcomings of a world economy to largely immutable evolutionary forces rather than to specific and alterable political and economic conditions that have evolved under American hegemony. This explanation has attracted a willing audience amongst the insecure middle classes of other Western nations, who are as anxious as are their American counterparts to believe that they are not responsible for the fate that they fear is overtaking them.

While the origin of ideas has no necessary bearing on whether or not they are correct, it is fairly obvious that the high-level evolutionary theories that guided the interpretation of archaeological evidence in the 1970s reflected a serious and prolonged economic, political, and social crisis in which the interests of the dominant middle classes were perceived as deeply threatened. It is also evident that these high-level views influenced the expectations of archaeologists concerning how the archaeological record might best be interpreted. All of this seriously calls into question the objectivity that the New Archaeology claimed on the basis of its positivist methodology.

A number of archaeologists, especially among those doing research or employed in the southwestern United States, have proposed interpretations of the archaeological record that closely approximate the central values of conservative American political ideology. In *The Archaeology of Arizona* Martin and Plog (1973) viewed cultures as adaptive systems and argued that those possessing the greatest amount of random variation were best fitted to survive when confronted by environmental or demographic challenges or competition from neighbouring groups. Dunnell (1980a) and Cordell and Plog (1979) also assume that there is present in every society a broad spectrum of alternative behavioural patterns on which the cultural equivalent of natural selection can operate. This viewpoint emphasizes the adaptive value of individual choice in a manner analogous to economic free-market theories. William Rathje (1975) utilized certain principles concerning disproportional growth to construct a scheme that seeks to account for how expanding early civilizations coped with the problem of processing increasing amounts of information. He proposed that in the early stages increasing complexity was managed by employing greater numbers of officials to process information and make decisions. Later an attempt was made to forestall the growth of bureaucracy beyond economically acceptable limits by resorting to greater standardization. The development of uniform system-wide codes (such as fixed weights and measures) decreased the amount of accounting that was necessary. Still later, efficiencies were attempted by encouraging greater autonomy at lower levels, while the whole society was integrated as a series of economically interdependent regional components. Blanton *et al.* (1981) have applied the basic ideas of this scheme to the evolution of complex societies in highland Mesoamerica. They argue that, while the economies of the earlier Classic civilizations were deeply embedded in the political organizations of the region, later economies were more entrepreneurial and functioned more independently of state control than ever before. The archaeologically attested results of such *laissez-faire* arrangements are said to have been a vast increase in the quality of goods available to most people. Other archaeologists have argued that, on the contrary, in late prehispanic times the economy of the Valley of Mexico was strongly controlled by the Aztecs, who used their military power to centralize lucrative craft production in their capital Tenochtitlan (Parsons *et al.* 1982; Hassig 1985). Peter Wells (1984) has assigned a major role to entrepreneurs coming from outside the established local elites in bringing about social change in Iron Age Europe, thus making this period an exemplar of 'Thatcherite enterprise culture' (Champion 1986).

While these interpretations look like rationalizations of American and British *laissez-faire* idealism, many of them have sought theoretical justification at the highest possible levels. Martin and Plog grounded their discussion in ecological theory and Rathje related his to General Systems Theory. Yet no specific attempts were made to adapt these theories to the archaeological study of human behaviour. The advantage of random variation was presented as a universally valid principle without any attempt to inventory the extent of such diversity empirically or to identify the factors that determine its range. This is a weakness paralleling the lack of concern for factors causing variability in rates of population growth in theories that invoked this factor as an independent cause of cultural change. Nor did the exponents of intracultural diversity take account of the requirements that the necessity for the safe and effective deployment of increasingly powerful technologies might generate for planning and consensus. Likewise Rathje did not consider the possibility that, unlike modern states, the rulers of early civilizations might have limited the interventions of their cumbersome data-processing systems into the affairs of ordinary people to those matters that related directly to securing the goods and services required to achieve their own specific goals. The development of Near Eastern civilization suggests a gradual but continuing increase in bureaucracy and the use of military force rather than the reverse. What is most interesting about their theories is that, despite their potential overt attraction to American archaeologists, who generally tend to be conservative, they have aroused less interest than has cataclysmic evolution. The appeal of explanations that disguise or naturalize stressful economic and political relations seems to be greater than that of ones that express a conservative ideology more directly.

A conservative ideology may, however, be exerting a more powerful influence on interpretations of prehistory with respect to the study of fossil hominids. Under the direct or indirect influence of sociobiology, there is a growing tendency to stress evidence of biological and behavioural differences and to treat these differences as correlated. This in turn leads to growing suspicion of interpretations of the behaviour of Lower Palaeolithic hominids that are based on analogies with modern hunter–gatherer societies. We are informed that the Australopithecines were more like specialized apes and that the technological and behavioural capacities of early *Homo* increasingly appear to have been unlike our own (Cartmill *et al.* 1986: 419). While former tendencies to emphasize the human-like qualities of early hominids are interpreted as an ideological overreaction to Nazism, no attention is paid to the possible ideological basis of currently popular alternative explanations.

Conclusions

Both Soviet (Klejn 1977) and American (Davis 1983: 407) archaeologists have drawn attention to some striking similarities between the New Archaeology and the archaeology created in the Soviet Union in the early 1930s. These parallels are the more interesting because all but a handful of American archaeologists remained almost completely unaware of the strengths and weaknesses of Soviet archaeology until the late 1970s. Both approaches were based on an evolutionary view of cultural change and sought to understand the regularities exhibited by that process. They agreed that these regularities were strong and could be studied by using a materialist framework. Migration and diffusion were played down in favour of trying to explain the changes that occurred within cultural systems over long periods of time. Traditional typological studies that sought to elucidate chronologies and spatial variations in material culture were regarded as old-fashioned and there was a corresponding increase in functional interpretations of archaeological data.

Yet, despite these similarities, there was a marked difference in the high-level theories that guided the interpretation of archaeological data. The New Archaeology embraced various forms of ecological and demographic determinism, which located the major factors bringing about change outside the cultural system and treated human beings as the passive victims of forces that mostly lie beyond their understanding and control. On the other hand, dialectical materialism, while not denying the importance of ecological factors as constraints on human behaviour or minimizing the role they played, especially in the early stages of cultural development, locates the major cause of cultural transformations squarely within the social realm, where it takes the form of competition to control wealth and power between different groups within the same society. Even in its most mechanistic and evolutionary formulations, such as prevailed in the Soviet Union in the 1930s, Marxism accords a central role to human beings pursuing their self-interest as members of social groups. What was most striking about the New Archaeology was its unwillingness to accord human consciousness or volition any role in bringing about cultural change. Marxists could argue that neo-evolutionism's denial of a creative role for human beings reflects the dehumanizing effects of the growth of corporate capitalism, which effectively has destroyed the concept of an economic system built upon individual initiative that was the ideal of the middle classes in the nineteenth century.

Although the New Archaeology advocated studying all aspects of cultural systems, archaeological publications indicate that most New Archaeologists concentrated on subsistence patterns, trade, and to a lesser degree social organization. Binford's own research largely has been concerned with technology and subsistence patterns as they relate to ecological adaptations. Major aspects of human behaviour, such as religious beliefs, aesthetics, and scientific knowledge, received little attention. The scope of the New Archaeology does not appear to have expanded beyond that already embraced by the ecological and settlement-pattern approaches that developed in the 1950s. The fields investigated by the New Archaeology also fall within the lower echelons of Hawkes' hierarchy, although Binford rejected the claim that this hierarchy established inevitable restrictions on the archaeological study of any aspect of human behaviour.

The explanation for this failure to study all aspects of human behaviour lies with the ecological approach. The New Archaeology shared the neo-evolutionary belief that cultural systems were characterized by a high degree of uniformity and that it was possible to account for this uniformity by identifying the ecological constraints that shaped human behaviour. Yet it now appears that, while whole cultural systems can be viewed as constrained to some degree by the nature of their adaptation to the ecosystem, the constraints exercised on the technology and economy are far stronger and more immediately recognizable than are the ones on social organization, and these in turn are greater than are the constraints on specific beliefs and values. Hence the techniques adopted by the New Archaeology work best when dealing with those aspects of culture that are subject to the greatest restraint. The New Archaeologists appear to have erred in assuming that ecological constraints would exert the same degree of influence on all aspects of culture and hence in feeling justified when they ignored alternative factors that shaped the archaeological record. Paul Tolstoy (1969: 558) was correct when he stated that determinists consider worthy of attention only those traits with which their theories appear equipped to deal.

Yet, almost from the beginning, doubts were expressed about the adequacy of this formulation, especially by those who attempted a systemic approach. In the 1970s and 1980s growing awareness of these weaknesses challenged some Western archaeologists, including ones who had played a key role in establishing the New Archaeology, to rethink their basic assumptions about human behaviour and how the archaeological record should be interpreted. This also led a growing number of archaeologists to recognize for the first time that the ideological underpinnings of archaeological interpretations were something other than the mistaken notions of the past and to challenge the positivist pretence of ethical neutrality.

CHAPTER 9

The explanation of diversity

> ... *theoretically informed history and historically informed theory must be joined together to account for populations specifiable in time and space, both as outcomes of significant processes and as their carriers.*
>
> ERIC WOLF, *Europe and the People without History* (1982), p. 21

During the 1970s a growing number of American archaeologists became convinced that there was more diversity in prehistoric cultures than could be accounted for by general evolutionary schemes, such as those of Sahlins and Service, or even by Steward's multilinear evolutionism. There was also a slowly but continuously growing recognition that neo-evolutionism had unduly restricted the questions about the past that archaeologists were prepared to consider important (Leach 1973). In her conclusion to a comparison of the cultural development of the adjacent Mixtec and Zapotec peoples, Joyce Marcus (1983a: 360) observed that 'If we are genuinely interested in understanding individual Mesoamerican cultures, we cannot ignore drift, adaptive divergence, convergence, and parallel evolution while concentrating single-mindedly on advance through stages of sociopolitical organization'. She also stated that 'the familiar variables of agricultural intensification, population growth, warfare, and interregional trade are by themselves insufficient to explain the diversity of Mesoamerican cultures'. Kent Flannery (1983) added that unilinear evolution is inadequate to realize the general anthropological goal of explaining sociocultural differences as well as similarities.

Ethnological critiques, especially those made by anthropologists who are not basically hostile to evolutionary studies, have also undermined the credibility of general evolution. It has been pointed out that neo-evolutionists have delineated tribal groups mainly on the basis of New Guinea big-men societies, which have very different social and political structures from native societies in eastern North America (such as those of the Iroquois) that shared the same mode of production and are generally asserted to be at the same stage of development (Whallon 1982: 156). Morton Fried's (1975) claim that many of the more complex features associated with tribal societies are products of acculturation resulting from contacts with Western peoples, rather than spontaneous internal developments, has led some archaeologists to view this stage with great suspicion (Renfrew 1982a). It has similarly been demonstrated that many features of chiefdoms arose as a result of their political and economic articulation with more advanced societies (Wolf 1982: 96–100). As a result of such observations archaeologists have become increasingly interested in trying to explain the cultural diversity that used to intrigue the historical particularists (Renfrew 1982b). There is growing willingness to admit that human behaviour is shaped by diverse factors and that at least some forms of behaviour may not be recorded in an unambiguous fashion in the archaeological record. While most archaeologists continue to interpret their data from a materialistic, and often more specifically an ecological, perspective (P. Watson 1986: 441), there is also increasing questioning of the extent to which ecological and economic factors play a determining role with respect to human behaviour. These developments have brought about many changes in archaeological analysis and how archaeologists view human nature. Alison Wylie (1985a: 90) has gone so far as to observe that 'there is a strong case to be made that [idiosyncratic variability at a societal or individual level] is the distinctively human and cultural feature of the archaeological subject; hence, it should be the special interest of an anthropological archaeology'. At least some of these trends have involved a revival of interest in topics associated with culture-historical archaeology that were ignored as a result of the development of the New Archaeology.

Intersocietal contact

One of the developments that has characterized this changing perspective has been a tendency to abandon the view that societies or cultures are closed, or tightly bounded, units that can be studied independently of one another and to pay more attention to the role played by external stimuli in bringing about cultural change. Wolf

(1982: ix) has argued that anthropologists, especially under the influence of neo-evolutionism 'seem to have forgotten that human populations construct their cultures in interaction with one another and not in isolation'. He goes on to state that the cultural connections that an older generation of anthropologists studied as diffusion can only be rendered intelligible in systemic terms when they are set into a broader political and economic context.

The study of interaction between societies was never ruled out by the New Archaeology. Binford (1972: 204) strongly approved of Caldwell's (1964) concept of an 'interaction sphere', which he had developed to explain how a Hopewellian burial cult, which involved the interment of goods manufactured from exotic materials with individuals of high status, came to be shared by many prehistoric societies in the American Midwest. Yet growing interest in the development of specific sociocultural systems and the neo evolutionary emphasis on independent invention led many followers of settlement archaeology and the New Archaeology to minimize the importance of intersocietal contact and competition.

In recent years a number of archaeologists working in the Near East have advocated the need to view Mesopotamian civilization as part of a much larger zone in which from early times many cultures influenced one another's development through various forms of political and economic interaction (Lamberg-Karlovsky 1975; Kohl 1978; Alden 1982). There has also been discussion of 'peer polity' interaction in prehistoric Europe (Renfrew and Shennan 1982) and elsewhere (Renfrew and Cherry 1986) and of 'cluster interaction' in Mesoamerica (B. Price 1977). Blanton and his co-authors (1981) have argued that because of the intensity of economic, political, and ritual interaction among the ruling classes throughout Mesoamerica in prehispanic times, the development of any one region, such as the Valley of Mexico, cannot be understood independently of that of neighbouring regions. They therefore propose to treat the whole of Mesoamerica as a single 'macroregional unit' bound together by the interaction of local elites; an approach that places prodigious demands upon the information-gathering capacity of archaeologists. This approach also raises major questions about how the boundaries of macroregions are to be defined. Blanton and his co-authors argue that what is recognized as Mesoamerica was a network of states and chiefdoms united by intensive reciprocal interaction of a political and ritual nature, which can be recognized in the archaeological record. It has long been surmised that economic and ritual influences of Mesoamerican origin also influenced the cultural development of the southwestern United States and eastern North America, although it is not often possible to define the social contexts in which these presumed contacts occurred (Griffin 1980).

It is also recognized that not only goods, persons, and ideas but also whole institutions can spread from one society to another. The introduction of the Christian church as a hierarchical organization with its own trained personnel into Anglo-Saxon England and of Buddhism into Japan, both in the sixth century A.D., left a marked and lasting impact on the economic, social, and political organization of those countries and one that was clearly different from what could be expected if an indigenous state cult had developed. In both cases the imported clerical bureaucracy played a crucial role in strengthening the administration of nascent states (Sansom 1958: 60–81; Trigger 1978a: 216–28). That societies can be influenced by their neighbours in these ways makes their trajectories of development harder to predict than neo-evolutionary archaeologists had assumed (Green and Perlman 1985).

Some archaeologists have attempted to introduce more theoretical rigour into the study of interaction between societies. Carl Lamberg-Karlovsky (1985a) has used the historian Fernand Braudel's concept of the *longue durée* (Stoianovich 1976) to distinguish between gradually cumulative processes and periods dominated by alternating centripetal and centrifugal forces that transformed the social and cultural order and altered relations between the societies of Mesopotamia and the Iranian plateau between 3400 and 1600 B.C. More archaeologists have been attracted by Immanuel Wallerstein's (1974) world-system theory (Kohl 1978, 1979, 1987; Ekholm and Friedman 1979; Blanton *et al.* 1981; Renfrew and Shennan 1982: 58). This approach involves the study of large-scale spatial systems, assuming an interregional division of labour in which peripheral areas supply core ones with raw materials, the core areas are politically and economically dominant, and the economic and social development of all regions is constrained by their changing roles in the system. Kohl has suggested that the world systems of antiquity probably only superficially resembled those of modern times. In particular, he argues that the rankings of cores and peripheries may have been less stable than they are now and that political force may have played a more overt role in regulating them. What is of general importance is the growing realization that societies are not closed systems with respect to neighbouring ones any more than in relation to their natural environment and that the development of a society or culture may be constrained or influenced by the broader social network of which it is a part. There is also increasing recognition that the rules governing these processes are themselves worthy of scientific investigation. The challenge is to broaden not merely a functional but also a systemic analysis to cover processes that used to be explained in terms of diffusion. The studies of economic interaction between a Near Eastern core and European periphery that were begun by Childe in *The Most Ancient East* (1928) anticipated world-system theory in many important aspects and have no doubt predisposed European archaeologists to accept Wallerstein's approach. Childe's ideas in turn were based on patterns of interaction established by Montelius in his diffusionist studies.

These observations have raised additional questions about the concept of sociocultural systems. No one will deny that various social boundaries are defined by reduced levels of interaction. Yet can a hierarchy of levels be distinguished in which individuals are grouped as members of families, families as parts of communities, communities as components of societies, and societies to form larger interaction spheres? Or do individuals participate differentially in patterned interactions at many levels and as members of many different kinds of social groups (R. McGuire 1983)? One must not minimize the importance of brokers and decision-makers, such as chiefs, government officials, and kings, who mediate between different levels of society and thereby effect varying degrees of closure. Yet a detailed analysis of networks of social, political, and economic interaction calls into question the idea that societies or cultures are more significant units of analysis than are numerous larger and smaller categories (cf. Clarke 1968). The social entity to be studied is determined by the problem that is being investigated.

There is also growing interest in the degree to which cultures or societies constitute systems in any rigorous sense. Are they in fact strongly integrated and hence highly selective with respect to innovation or, providing that they fulfil a minimal number of prerequisites to supply enough food, clothing, shelter, reproduction, and child care to ensure their continuity (Aberle *et al.* 1950), is the rest of their content freely variable and hence likely to be influenced by a random selection of ideas picked up from neighbouring cultures? Wolf (1982: 390–1) argues that we cannot 'imagine cultures as integrated totalities . . . [they] are only cultural sets of practices and ideas, put into play by determinate human actors under determinate circumstances'. The latter view of culture as a collection 'of multifarious and often incongruous elements work[ing] together in tolerable harmony' (Hanbury-Tenison 1986: 108) is close to that of historical particularism, especially when we remember that Boas and his students saw the need for some degree of psychological consistency in each culture (Benedict 1934). While few archaeologists have explicitly abandoned the terminology associated with a systemic view of culture, many would no longer agree with Steward that diffusion can do no more than duplicate internal processes of cause and effect. A large number of archaeologists now acknowledge that societies can be altered not only by political and economic pressures from neighbouring groups but also by ideas that are borrowed from adjacent societies, to the extent that the recipient culture may develop in ways that it would not have done in the absence of these external stimuli (Lamberg-Karlovsky 1985a: 58–60). Accompanying this is a growing interest in the roles played by non-economic factors, such as religious beliefs, in bringing about social change. While most archaeologists profess a materialistic orientation, the degree to which ecological adaptation determines cultural systems is increasingly seen not as given in the study of society but as an issue that in due course must be answered empirically.

Changing views of interaction among cultures have reopened the often-debated question of the significance of ethnographic analogies for archaeological interpretation. Evolutionary anthropologists assumed that the earliest recorded descriptions of native cultures revealed what these had been like prior to European contact and that such information could be used without serious question for cross-cultural studies of behavioural variation. For example, the San, or Bushmen, of southern Africa were treated as a paradigmatic hunter–gatherer society. Archaeology is now revealing that many native cultures were vastly altered as a result of European contact before the earliest descriptions of them were recorded by Europeans

(Ramsden 1977; Cordell and Plog 1979; Wilcox and Masse 1981). It is possible that every hunter–gatherer and tribal society in the world was influenced to some degree by contact with technologically more advanced societies prior to ethnographic study (Brasser 1971; Fried 1975; Wobst 1978; Monks 1981: 288; Trigger 1981b). There is growing archaeological and historical evidence that the Bushman way of life has been modified significantly in recent centuries by contacts with European settlers and over a longer period by interaction with their pastoral Bantu and Hottentot neighbours (Schrire 1980, 1984). The impact that these other groups have had on the southern African environment also may have altered Bushman life in many ways. Under such circumstances, it is dangerous for anthropologists to assume that Bushmen, or any other modern hunter–gatherer societies, are necessarily equivalent to Palaeolithic ones. These studies, although revolutionary after a long period dominated by neo-evolutionism, resume a pattern established by Strong (1935) and Wedel (1938), with their archaeological demonstration that the highly mobile equestrian hunting populations found on the Great Plains of North America in the historical period were a relatively recent phenomenon and that in some areas sedentary agriculturalists had preceded them.

The various economic ties that link modern hunter–gatherers to their non-hunter–gatherer neighbours also call into question whether modern and ancient hunter–gatherers (or tribal societies) share the same mode of production and can therefore be treated as societies at the same stage of development. Binford (1983a: 337–56) used northern native groups that have been engaged for generations in trapping and exchanging furs with Europeans as a basis for suggesting certain generalizations about the nature of hunter–gatherer adaptations to high-latitude environments. Some anthropologists believe that because of the inherent flexibility of their adaptation to the boreal forest, the economies of at least some of these groups have not been radically altered by the fur trade (Francis and Morantz 1983: 14–15); others disagree. Only detailed archaeological studies can determine objectively to what extent ethnographic descriptions of hunter–gatherer or tribal agricultural societies provide a representative picture of what these societies were like in prehistoric times (D. Thomas 1974). Until more such investigations have been made, the significance of major cross-cultural studies based on ethnographic data must remain doubtful. It has already been demonstrated that the comparison of societies that have been influenced by European colonization can give a false impression of the degree of variation in cultural phenomena such as kinship terminologies (Eggan 1966: 15–44).

Archaeology thus has an important role to play not only in unravelling the complex history of the past but also in providing a historical perspective for understanding the significance of ethnographic data. A growing number of anthropologists are coming to believe that ethnologists and social anthropologists, whether studying social structure or change, are investigating the results of acculturation because their data are derived from small-scale societies that are being either destroyed or integrated ever more completely into the modern world system. History and archaeology alone can study the evolution of cultures in the past. It is also becoming clear that no society can be properly understood or even classified from a structural point of view without taking account of its relationship with other societies (Wolf 1982; Flannery 1983).

Relations among coexisting societies, especially ones at different levels of development, are once again being viewed as constituting as important a source of change, and therefore as strong an evolutionary force and as legitimate an object of anthropological understanding, as are the ecologically generated changes that have been studied by neo-evolutionary anthropologists. Evolutionary theory should not be concerned only with ecologically stimulated change. It should seek to understand how neighbouring societies have influenced each other's development throughout history (Wolf 1982; McNeill 1986). In particular, anthropologists should try to develop generalizations about how societies, especially those with different types of economies, influence each other. Social anthropologists are already doing this for present-day, small-scale societies that are being drawn into the capitalist world system. Archaeologists are challenged by the formidable task of developing similar generalizations for a vast array of pre-capitalist societies. Alexander and Mohammed (1982) have pioneered this sort of approach by elaborating a frontier model to explain the interaction of hunter–gatherer and early agricultural societies in the Sudan. Golson (1977) has stressed the need to consider competition among different types of hunter–gatherer societies as a major source of change.

A body of evolutionary theory that seeks to explain not only ecologically generated change but also transformations resulting from interactions between different societies necessarily must be exceedingly complex. It is probably unrealistic to think of such a theoretical structure ever being completely elaborated (Trigger 1984e). On the contrary, it will continue to be refined as long as the social sciences make progress in understanding human behaviour. Such a body of theory will also tend to be more eclectic and inductive in its origins than the tenets of the New Archaeology would approve. It will, however, provide a more substantial and realistic basis for understanding cultural change than has neo-evolutionary anthropology with its almost exclusive preoccupation with ecological explanations. It will also move archaeology closer to the general practices of the social sciences, both methodologically and theoretically.

Neo-historicism

At the same time that archaeologists are perceiving the need to broaden the range of their theoretical generalizations, they are considering the possibility that individual societies are so complex, their structures so loose, and the external forces influencing them so eclectic that the precise cause of their development can at best be predicted only partially and for the short term. For many archaeologists the complexity of any human society renders the concept of causality of little value for understanding its origin (Flannery 1972; Rowlands 1982). It is realized that if historians, after generations of intensive research, continue to debate the reasons for the rise and fall of the Roman Empire, it is unrealistic for archaeologists to conclude either too optimistically that the processes they study can be definitively explained by simplistic formulations or too pessimistically that complexity precludes understanding (D. Fischer 1970). This has led to a growing rejection of the positivist view that all explanation must be equivalent to prediction. M. Salmon (1982: 109; see also W. Salmon 1984 and W. Salmon *et al.* 1971) has argued that much of it takes the form of a statistical-relevance model, whereby an event is explained when all factors statistically relevant to its occurrence and non-occurrence are assembled and the appropriate probability values for its occurrence are determined in the light of these factors.

What she does not point out is that this approach is almost identical to the traditional method of historical explanation. Yet historians tend to be more sceptical about the possibility of identifying all relevant factors and recognize that, in the short term, probability values can be assigned to many of them only provisionally and on the basis of common sense (Dray 1957). This does not diminish the value of archaeology for producing generalizations about human behaviour or long-term trends in cultural development. It does suggest, however, that explanations of change in specific societies must be based on detailed knowledge of what happened as well as sound theories, and even then allowances must be made for the intervention of unexpected factors.

The prolonged, and by archaeological standards, sophisticated, debate concerning the collapse of the Classic Maya civilization demonstrates that more data are needed to narrow the range of possible explanations and permit the formulation of more refined research problems (Culbert 1973; Hammond 1977). While increasing theoretical sophistication reduces the range of the unpredictable, it is no more possible for social scientists to retrodict the past in detail than it is for them to predict the future. The explanation of the past is thus seen as being of necessity idiographic, even though general principles must be invoked to support arguments in every possible instance.

Historical knowledge, in the sense of understanding how and why specific societies developed as they did in the past, is essential for explaining the current state of societies around the world. Because only archaeology and documentary history provide the evidence required to delineate cultural development in the past, they are essential for understanding the historical background of the data which all of the other social sciences analyse. The growing realization that this is so is slowly providing the basis for a new and complementary relationship between archaeology and ethnology. In this relationship archaeology does not try to emulate ethnology but, by studying the development of concrete social systems, provides an indispensable basis for producing reliable generalizations about structure and change. Far from being peripheral to the other social sciences, archaeology and history are crucial for understanding them.

Despite these developments, mainstream American processual

archaeology has not begun to see society itself or individual human beings as the source of any significant amount of sociocultural change (for exceptions, see R. Adams 1965; Willey 1986). The latter view, together with a growing emphasis on 'mind' and 'values', is currently represented by a minority but rapidly growing movement in British and American archaeology that variously labels itself symbolic, structural, or critical archaeology (Renfrew 1982c). This movement has largely been inspired by Marxist approaches that date from the late 1960s in French and British anthropology. These have their roots not in orthodox Marxism but in the efforts to combine Marxism and the structuralism of the anthropologists Maurice Godelier, E. Terray, and P. P. Rey and the philosopher L. Althusser; the antipositivism of the Frankfurt School, a para-Marxist movement dating from the 1920s, especially as represented in the writings of Jürgen Habermas (1975) and Herbert Marcuse (1964) and the anarchistic theory of knowledge of Paul Feyerabend (1975); and finally the economic analyses of Claude Meillassoux (1981). Despite their differences in detail, such archaeological works stress the complexity of modes of production, the important role played by human consciousness in bringing about change, the major significance of clashes of interest between men and women or people of different ages in promoting conflict in classless societies, and the inescapable impregnation of all human activities, including scientific research, by ideology. They also share the conviction that Marx and Engels failed to produce a detailed analysis of pre-class societies and that it is the duty of Marxist anthropologists to remedy this defect not by returning to the works of the founders of Marxism but by constructing new Marxist theories of pre-capitalist societies on the basis of current knowledge of these groups (Bloch 1985: 150).

Through these channels a number of important Marxist concepts have been introduced into British and American archaeology as alternatives to the tenets of processual archaeology. Foremost among these is a concern to explain sociocultural change in terms of a general theoretical framework that accords a central role to social relations. Processual archaeology, along with neo-evolutionism, structuralism, cultural materialism, and cultural ecology, are rejected because they unduly reify stability, treat the causes of cultural change as being external to social relations, and regard human beings as passive objects that are moulded by external factors. Ecology is viewed as constraining rather than directing change and new technologies are interpreted both as responses to social and economic change and as a major force bringing it about. Social conflicts arising from contradictory interests are identified as vital and pervasive features of human societies and a major source of change. This view is contrasted with the integrative concerns of functionalism, classical structuralism, and phenomenology, to the great disadvantage of all three.

The new approaches also champion a human-centred view of history. Marxism refuses to explain meaning, symbolism, and social phenomena in terms of non-social determinants in order to provide archaeology with a veneer of conventional social science (Tilley 1984: 144). Instead of treating human behaviour as passively shaped by external forces, Marxist archaeologists stress intentionality and the social production of reality. They also insist on a holistic approach. Ideally, parts of society are always studied in relation to the whole and individual social systems in terms of broader networks of intersocietal relations. Marxist archaeologists seek to explain not only cross-cultural regularities but also the particularities, individual differences, and specific contexts that distinguish one concrete instance of social change from another. In striving to create a unified social science, Marxism ignores the distinctions between history and evolution and between history and science. The study of history is regarded as scientific in nature and as embracing generalization. Finally these approaches insist on the social basis of knowledge. Knowledge and self-consciousness are viewed not as absolutes but as the products of specific societies. The social context of current archaeological research is seen as influencing interpretations of the past. This suggests that certainty of the sort envisioned by positivistically oriented researchers cannot be obtained.

Idealism and neo-Marxism

There are, however, significant differences in the way that crucial issues are treated not only between Marxist-inspired Western archaeologists and Soviet ones but also among different Western Marxist archaeologists. It has traditionally been assumed that a materialist perspective is fundamental to Marxism. Marxist archaeologists such as Antonio Gilman (1984) maintain that the economy plays a dominant role in shaping the social, political, and religious superstructure of any society, although they do not rule out a reciprocal relationship between these two levels. Other archaeologists emphasize reciprocity to such an extent that they deny the primacy of the economic base. Susan Kus (1984) and Peter Gathercole (1984) question the very distinction between base and superstructure, which Gathercole suggests is a reflection of Western society's preoccupation with economics. John Gledhill (1984) claims that Western Marxists generally view non-economic factors as dominant in pre-capitalist societies.

A preoccupation with non-economic phenomena is strikingly evident in the vast amount of attention that is accorded to religion and ideology (Miller and Tilley 1984; Conrad and Demarest 1984). Ideology is described by Kristian Kristiansen (1984) as an active factor in social relations, while Michael Parker Pearson (1984: 61) states, without any reference to their economic function, that tools are as much the products of ideology as is a crown or law code. Some archaeologists discuss ideology within an explicitly materialist context. Thus Kristiansen describes the megalithic religion of Western Europe as an extension of production, while Miller and Tilley (1984: 148) state that ideology is not an autonomous comment but part of efforts to produce, maintain, and resist social changes that relate to the clash of interests between groups. On the other hand M. P. Pearson's (1984: 63) suggestion that ideology can direct economic activity, Mary Braithwaite's (1984: 107) statement that understanding the role of material culture in ritual and prestige practices is a necessary first step in reconstructing other dimensions of changes and patterns represented in the archaeological record, and Christopher Tilley's (1984: 143) approval of Habermas' efforts to elevate the ideological sphere to 'an important explanatory role' must be interpreted as support for an idealist interpretation of human behaviour.

Even more indicative of an idealist position is the recurrent description of ritual as a 'discourse' that is designed to reaffirm existing social relations by making them appear to be part of the natural order or to enhance the power of privileged groups or individuals. Tilley (1984: 143), however, following Marx and Engels closely on this point, reminds us that such views underrate the ability of oppressed individuals to analyse their situations and that ideology is therefore never all-embracing in its control. Instead it becomes part of a dialogue between two or more parties, including exploiters and exploited. Yet he did not go on to observe that it follows from this that the continuity of a ritual suggests that the material needs of all groups of participants were perceived as being satisfied in some manner as a result of it. In his analysis of Neolithic Swedish burial mounds, it would have been more in accord with traditional Marxist procedures to determine what factors in the economy promoted individualism and a breakdown of lineage-based social control than to attribute this change in the first instance to the collapse of legitimation ceremonies (J. Thomas 1987: 422). It also has not been demonstrated that in pre-class societies ritual serves only to enhance group prestige. Much of it appears to have been directed towards disguising and symbolically counteracting the ineffectiveness of a rudimentary technology to cope with natural forces (Godelier 1978: 4–6). It is also not clear that in classless societies social relations as such had to be or were disguised by ideology.

These archaeologists also disagree concerning how much must be known about prehistoric ideologies to establish what role they played. Some argue that specific symbolic meanings and social processes are 'recursively related' and therefore the former must be known in some detail if cultural change is to be explained (Hodder 1984a). Braithwaite (1984: 94) suggests that the exact content of belief systems may be irretrievable archaeologically, although their operation is not. Her 'operation' seems little different from a functionalist approach to ritual and ideology.

Viewed from a cross-cultural perspective, the reconstructions of belief systems so far attempted seem conceptually limited and ethnocentric. On the basis of randomly selected ethnographic analogies, artifacts placed in graves have been described as sacrifices to dead ancestors who had the power to influence the well-being of their descendants. Tilley's (1984) generalized linking of death and destruction with the promotion of fertility, life, and social order is not substantially different from the speculations of James Frazer. There is no evidence of techniques that would allow detailed insights into culturally specific aspects of rituals, except those associated with the direct historical approach and the use of written documents.

Marxists traditionally have assumed that the most influential contradictions that bring about social change are between the means and relations of production. This does not imply technological determinism since the relationship between the means and relations of production is a reflexive one. Marx and Engels assumed that in class societies change took the form of a struggle between different classes to control and exploit the relations of production. Primitive societies were viewed as classless and therefore as ones in which such struggles could not occur. They looked to pre-class societies to prove that the basic institutions of class societies were transient and not grounded in an immutably competitive human nature. This, however, has led to queries whether a specifically Marxist analysis of change in pre-class societies is possible (Gilman 1984: 116). Marxists have accorded adaptive factors a more important role in bringing about cultural change at this stage, which is explained as according with the weaker forces of production. Using such an approach, Engels was able to go far beyond any Darwinian biologist of his time, including Darwin himself, in proposing a materialistic theory of human origins that accorded a primary role to labour in the context of social groups (Trigger 1967b; Woolfson 1982). Engels described the human hand as a product as well as an organ of labour. He suggested that natural selection operating on a rudimentary ability to use tools resulted in bipedalism and then in the expansion of the human brain. This led not only to new and more complex forms of economic behaviour but also to the emergence of language as a more effective instrument of communication and of a new form of consciousness and self-objectification that allowed flexibility and planning to become uniquely important elements of human adapt ations. Thus, by combining Marxist theory with Darwinian biology, Engels deductively formulated a view that it took non-Marxist biologists another 80 years to achieve independently (S. Washburn 1960). Engels' formulation also indicates clearly that, if traditional Marxists assign adaptive factors a major role in bringing about change in small-scale societies, these factors are not seen as operating automatically. Instead they are viewed as bringing about changes in relations of production as a result of decisions consciously made within a social context.

Many French neo-Marxist anthropologists have adopted a different approach to explaining change in classless societies. They have attempted to minimize the differences between classless and class societies and to extend a Marxist analysis of changes in class societies to explain changes in simpler ones. This approach has been adopted by a number of archaeologists. M. P. Pearson (1984) maintains that in pre-class societies 'interest groups' consisting of young and old, men and women, or members of different clans or lineages, struggle in much the same manner as classes do in more advanced ones. He also asserts erroneously that an essential premise of Marxism is that all human beings are motivated by self-interest and seek power to pursue such interests. Tilley (1984) follows Meillassoux and Terray in claiming that exploitative social relations exist in all social formations. Such uniformitarian views of society run contrary to the traditional Marxist claim that human nature is transformed in substantial ways by social change (Fuller 1980: 230–64; Geras 1983). They also tend to undermine the Marxist hope that in the future societies can be created that are not based on exploitation and, what is more important, ignore overwhelming ethnographic evidence that in small-scale societies prestige is acquired and maintained through redistribution and generosity rather than by the hoarding of material wealth (Sahlins 1968).

Marxists had viewed false consciousness as a characteristic of all pre-class and class societies. They maintain that for these societies to operate effectively it is necessary for them to disguise their technological helplessness and to make exploitation appear as altruism. This view, particularly in the form in which it was expounded by Gyorgy Lukács, provided a point of departure for the virulent antipositivism of some members of the Frankfurt School. That in turn has appealed to Western archaeologists rebelling against the strictures of positivism. They refuse to accept that, while the questions that archaeologists pose may be influenced by the milieu in which they live, so long as they have sufficient data and follow sound analytical procedures, the results will be the closest possible approximation of scientific truth, uncontaminated by ideology or personal prejudice. Daniel Miller (1984: 38) asserts that positivism, which he defines as accepting only what can be sensed, tested, and predicted as knowable, seeks to produce technical knowledge that will facilitate the exploitation of human beings by oppressive elites, while Miller and Tilley (1984: 2) claim that it encourages the acceptance of unjust social orders by persuading people that human societies are irresistibly shaped by external pressures. These charges parallel Marcuse's (1964) assertion that positivism always has supported politically reactionary causes, a charge that the Polish philosopher Leszek Kolakowski (1978c: 400–2) has definitively refuted.

An increased understanding of the pervasiveness of ideology has led to growing awareness that not only the questions asked but also the answers that are judged to be acceptable in archaeology are influenced by the general beliefs and attitudes of individual archaeologists and the societies in which they live (Saitta 1983). This is a view shared by many non-Marxists. The latter include Stuart Piggott (1950) and Glyn Daniel (1950), who long ago examined the impact of intellectual fashions, such as rationalism and romanticism, in their histories of archaeology. The new relativism has encouraged analyses that reveal the degree to which archaeological interpretation and popularization have expressed the ideologies of dominant groups in America and elsewhere. It has become fashionable to believe that historical interpretations are 'always produced in the service of class interests' (Leone 1986: 418). This approach has also begun to promote awareness of how private sponsors and government agencies have shaped the development of archaeology through selective support of research (Wilk 1985; Patterson 1986a) and how the sexist biases of archaeologists have influenced their interpretations of the past (Gero 1983; Conkey and Spector 1984). Archaeologists have been reminded that even what they regard as data are mental constructs and hence not independent of frequently unconscious presuppositions (Wylie 1985b: 73). As a result there is a growing belief that archaeological interpretation must be understood in a social, political, and historical context and that archaeologists must pay attention to how societies, or groups within a society, shape the interpretation of the past for their own ends (Leone 1986: 432).

Yet among the relativists there is a sharp disagreement whether archaeological interpretation can ever be more than an expression of ideology and personal opinion or whether knowledge of the social factors that influence it can help archaeologists to transcend these limitations and achieve greater objectivity. Some relativists have claimed that archaeologists have no moral right to interpret the prehistory of other peoples (Hodder 1984b) and that their main duty should be to provide individuals with the means to construct their own views of the past, although it is not clear how this information can be supplied without introducing inherent biases into it.

These extreme views have powerful implications for any theory of knowledge in archaeology. While a growing number of Marxist and non-Marxist archaeologists agree that, because of the complexity of concrete human situations, predictions and explanation cannot be equated, Miller and Tilley (1984: 151) follow B. Hindess and P. Hirst (1975: 1–5) in rejecting any positivist or empiricist conception of knowledge. They claim that statements about the past must be judged exclusively in terms of their internal coherence, 'which can only be criticised in terms of internal conceptual relations and not in terms of externally imposed standards or criteria for "measuring" or "determining" truth or falsity'. Gathercole (1984) and others stress the subjectivity of archaeology by portraying it primarily as an ideological discipline. M. J. Rowlands (1984) sees extreme relativism as a danger threatening archaeology. Kolakowski (1978c: 300) goes much further with respect to the social sciences as a whole when he denounces Lukács' efforts to isolate Marxism from empirical criticism as an irrational as well as an antiscientific development. This trend is carried further when archaeologists such as Miller and Tilley follow scholars of the Frankfurt School in interpreting Marxism as simply another subjective perspective on the human condition. Marx's claim for a special scientific status for his approach is rejected as a vain effort to give his work a 'veneer' of positivist science.

What is not taken into account is that Marx's recognition of the phenomenon of false consciousness was not accompanied by a total rejection of what is now called positivism. Engels noted that while absolute knowledge is unattainable, in trying to approximate it human beings come to possess an increasingly complete and accurate picture of reality as a whole, which is confirmed by the effectiveness of their actions (Kolakowski 1978a: 396). Through G. V. Plekhanov and Lenin this position has become central to Soviet Marxism (Bloch 1985: 95–123; Kolakowski 1978b: 305–527). Extreme relativism, on the other hand, makes definitive claims about what can be known concerning the nature of reality that contradict its own basic position that nothing can be known for certain. It also denies the role of archaeology and the other social sciences as sources of increasing knowledge that can be used to control the natural world and help to shape human destiny. In addition to reflecting growing despair among American intellectuals that scientific knowledge can help to bring about constructive social change, these attacks on positivism and empiricism encourage the belief that all so-called scientific knowledge of human behaviour consists of nothing more than self-serving fantasies. This in the long run can only assist those who seek to discredit the social sciences, and reason generally, as a guide to human action.

The incursion of Marxist concepts into Western archaeology has called into question a number of previous certainties and raised important new debates. Yet those who champion these concepts exhibit an astonishing lack of interest in Soviet archaeology, in the theoretical differences between anthropological and orthodox Marxism, and in the work of Gordon Childe, although Leone (1972: 18) once remarked that one of the reasons Childe was 'the best archaeologist the field has produced is that he possessed and used a powerful paradigm, Marxian materialism'. Many Western archaeologists go out of their way to characterize Soviet archaeology as 'stale' and 'unproductive', without trying to learn what it has accomplished. Their attitude contrasts curiously with the more serious interest in Soviet archaeology displayed by a few conservative British and American archaeologists (Renfrew 1970: 174). This conforms with Kolakowski's (1978c: 524–5) perhaps exaggerated claim that, while Marxist views have permeated the historical sciences and humanities, Marxism as a system has ceased to be an intellectual force in Western society. More specifically he argues that the Frankfurt School and its 'critical theory' are 'not so much a continuation of Marxism in any direction, as an example of its dissolution and paralysis' in the West (ibid. 395). Matthew Spriggs (1984b: 5) recollects that in 1977 French anthropological Marxism seemed to offer archaeologists 'a potentially unifying perspective'. Yet it is now commonly observed that Western Marxism seems to duplicate internally most of the schisms found in the non-Marxist social sciences. In archaeology this clearly has happened because for the most part interpretations are based on selected Marxist principles rather than on Marxism as a philosophical system.

Contextual archaeology

Although Ian Hodder has participated in and even inspired many of the trends noted above, his contextual approach to archaeology stands apart from them in certain respects and is now recognized as the principal challenge and rival paradigm to processual archaeology (Binford 1986, 1987). Basic to contextualism is Hodder's ethnographically well-documented claim that material culture is not merely a reflection of ecological adaptation or sociopolitical organization but also an active element in group relations that can be used to disguise as well as to reflect social relations. Overtly competing groups may use material culture to emphasize their dissimilarities, while an ethnic group wishing to use another's resources may attempt to minimize the material manifestations of such differences. High-status groups actively use material culture to legitimize their authority (Hodder 1982b: 119–22), while in some African cultures calabash and age-graded spear styles, which cut across ethnic boundaries that are marked in terms of other aspects of material culture, signal the general opposition of women and young men to dominant elders (ibid. 58–74). Even tensions within certain extended families have been shown to be expressed and reinforced by variations in pottery decoration (ibid. 122–4). Hodder's view that material culture is used as an active element in social interaction contradicts the carefully developed arguments of processual archaeologists that the relative elaboration of graves within a society accurately mirrors the degree of social differentiation (Saxe 1970; J. Brown 1971; O'Shea 1984). Research by Hodder and his students has shown that complex ideas relating to religion, hygiene, and status rivalry also play significant roles in influencing burial customs (M. Pearson 1982). In some societies simple burials reflect a social ideal of egalitarianism that is not effectively put into practice in everyday life (Huntington and Metcalf 1979: 122). Thus to determine the social significance of burial customs archaeologists have to examine other aspects of the archaeological record, such as settlement patterns. As a result of such research, it may quickly become apparent that a particular society with simple burial customs was not egalitarian in practice and this in turn will reveal the ideological status of these customs.

The contextual approach is based upon the conviction that archaeologists need to examine all possible aspects of an archaeological

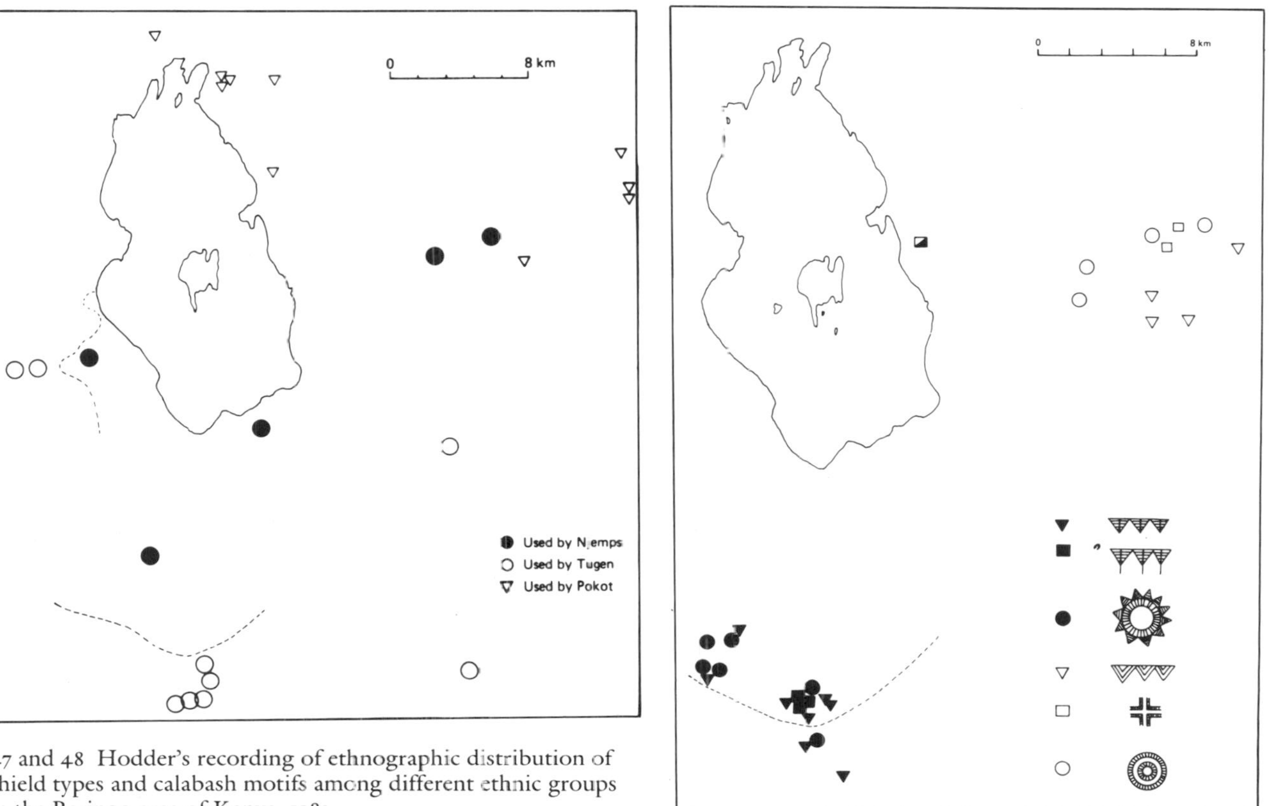

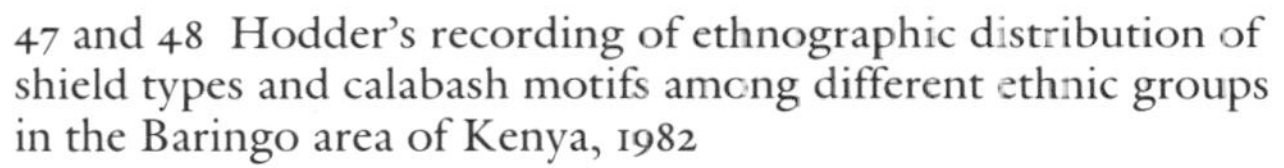

47 and 48 Hodder's recording of ethnographic distribution of shield types and calabash motifs among different ethnic groups in the Baringo area of Kenya, 1982

culture in order to understand the significance of each part of it. It is assumed that in the case cited above the discrepancy between burial and settlement patterns would reveal the ideological colouration of the burials, provided that archaeologists were convinced that burials representing all social classes had been found. By drawing attention to properties of material culture that hitherto had been ignored, Hodder has revealed the dangers inherent in interpretations of archaeological evidence that is analysed in isolation from its broader cultural context. He has also demonstrated material culture to have dynamic symbolic properties that accord better with a Marxist or historical particularist interpretation of culture than they do with a neo-evolutionary one. By arguing that an archaeological culture cannot be interpreted adequately in a piecemeal fashion, Hodder places new demands on archaeologists for a comprehensive internal study of archaeological cultures, which complement the demands of world-system advocates for broader regional coverages. This is very different from the belief of processual archaeologists that a few selected variables can be studied at a single site to answer a specific archaeological problem (Brown and Struever 1973).

Contextual archaeology also rejects the validity of the neo-evolutionary distinction between what is culturally specific and cross-culturally general that was the basis of Steward's dichotomy between science and history. This validates an interest in culturally specific cosmologies, astronomical lore, art styles, religious beliefs, and other topics that lingered on the fringes of processual archaeology in the 1960s and 1970s. As Dunnell (1982a: 521) has observed, the ecological and evolutionary approaches borrowed from the biological sciences were not designed to explain motivational and symbolic systems. Hodder encourages archaeologists once again to take account of the complexities of human phenomena and to realize that universal generalizations do not exhaust the regularities that characterize human behaviour. They are urged to look for order within individual cultures or historically related ones both in terms of specific cultural categories, such as the canons governing artistic productions, and in the way different cultural categories relate to one another (Bradley 1984).

The study of patterning in material culture has been influenced strongly by Claude Lévi-Strauss' structural approach, especially his investigation of the symbolic patterns underlying native American mythology. Basic to this form of analysis is the conviction that where the richness and variability of the archaeological record is too great to be explained only as a response to environmental constraints or stimuli, factors internal to the system must also be considered (Wylie 1982: 41). Ernest Gellner (1985: 149–51) has elegantly contrasted ecology and economics, which study the regularities resulting from a scarcity of resources, and structural approaches, which study the order that human beings impose on those areas of their lives that, because of their symbolic nature, are not subject to any form of scarcity. Yet the relationship of the symbolic order to economic and adaptive forms of behaviour still remains to be defined. It is no longer possible to maintain that symbolic aspects of material culture are merely a passive reflection of more pragmatic behaviour. Yet how can the archaeologist determine in specific cases, except pragmatically, whether the relationship is one of reflection, inversion, or contradiction? Furthermore, linguistic analogies suggest that the relationship between material culture and its symbolic meaning may be essentially arbitrary (Gallay 1986: 197).

Structural archaeologists express admiration for the pioneering work of André Leroi-Gourhan (1968), who documented patterns in the locations and associations of the different animal species represented in Upper Palaeolithic caves in Western Europe and interpreted these as referring to myths dealing with the relations between male and female principles, as well as for Alexander Marshack's (1972) demonstration of seasonal patterns in associated mobiliary art. These works encouraged the discovery and exploration of further patterning in the archaeological record that had been ignored by processual archaeologists, such as the orientation of Neolithic tombs in Sweden (Tilley 1984) and similarities in the patterning of Neolithic tombs and houses in Western Europe (Hodder 1984a). Yet so far no archaeologist has discovered how to get beyond speculation in interpreting the cultural meaning of such regularities for early prehistoric times. Gallay (1986: 198–200, 281) has argued that no way can be found to demonstrate an isometric relation between our ideas about the past and ideas that were actually held in the past.

Archaeologists have had more success in relating the designs of houses and gardens in colonial Virginia and New England to class values and attitudes that are documented in the written records of

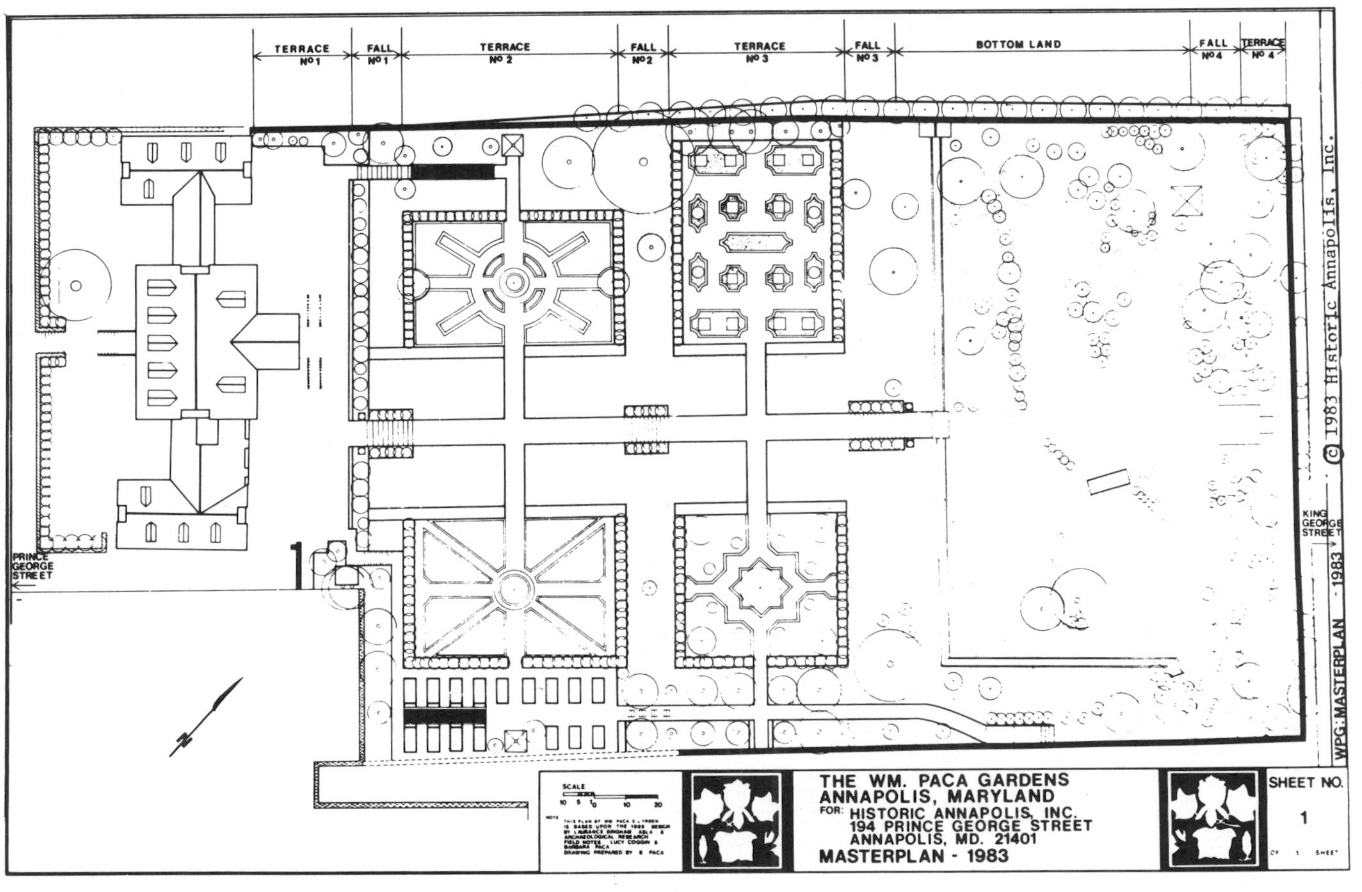

49 Eighteenth-century William Paca Garden, Annapolis, Maryland; the outlines of the garden are archaeologically determined

that period (Glassie 1975; Deetz 1977; Isaac 1982; Leone 1982). This experience is similar to that of art historians who can find order in the themes and styles of Greek statuary as it changed over time. Yet, while they can relate this to a definable, changing aesthetic, they cannot understand the significance of that aesthetic in verbal terms without written records. Hodder (1982b: 192–3; 1982d) has been interested in seeing if cross-cultural regularities can be discovered in attitudes toward dirt or the elaboration of pottery designs. If such regularities could be found, they would probably have a basis in human psychology. They would also indicate patterning in human behaviour that cross-cuts both of the levels (adaptive and stylistic) that Gellner has identified. Such relationships remain, however, problematical.

The study of the symbolic meaning of material remains during recent millennia has been facilitated by the direct historical approach. R. L. Hall (1979) has drawn upon ethnographic and ethnohistorical material concerning native religious beliefs and symbolism collected in eastern North America since the seventeenth century to explain the structure of Adena burial mounds in that region over 1,500 years earlier, as well as why certain classes of artifacts were included in later Middle Woodland burials. George Hamell (1983) has used regularities in historically recorded Iroquoian, Algonkian, and Siouan myths to explain the significance of the inclusion of natural crystals, objects made from marine shell and native copper, and certain other materials in eastern North American burial contexts for over 6,000 years, from late Archaic times into the historical period. Both of these anthropologists offer detailed symbolic explanations of regularities in burial customs for which no cross-cultural generalizations could account. The main problem that is posed by this work is that of verifiability. In the cases of Hall and Hamell, proof rests upon the applicability of analogies drawn between ethnographic and archaeological data that there are sound reasons to believe are historically related. Hamell's evidence is particularly convincing because there is strong proof in the archaeological record of continuity in the use of these materials from their earliest appearance into the historical period. In recent years San ethnography has been used to indicate the shamanistic significance of much southern African rock art and the meaning of specific symbols, such as the eland (Schrire *et al.* 1986: 128). Yet in his study of *Jewish Symbols in the Greco-Roman Period* Erwin Goodenough (1953–68) has demonstrated the fallacy of assuming that continuities in iconography necessarily indicate continuity in mythology, since the significance accorded to representations is as likely to change over time as are the ways beliefs are symbolized (Goff 1963: xxxv). Yet a general continuity in cultural context and in a total symbol system argues strongly in favour of a continuity in meaning (Vastokas 1987).

Hodder, like Childe, further stresses the importance of cultural traditions as factors playing an active role in structuring cultural change. These traditions supply most of the knowledge, beliefs, and values that simultaneously influence economic and social change and are reshaped by that change. They can also play an active role in resisting or promoting specific changes. This corresponds with Marx's observation that 'human beings make their own history . . . not under circumstances chosen by themselves . . . but directly encountered, given, and transmitted from the past' (Kohl 1981b: 112). It is not possible to predict either the content of a cultural tradition in all of its specific detail or the detailed trajectories of cultural change. Yet when these trajectories are known from the archaeological record they increase the archaeologist's ability to account for what has happened in the past.

Both the Marxist-inspired versions of archaeological interpretation and contextual archaeology began as semi-peripheral, and specifically British, critiques of the imperialist pretensions of American processual archaeology. These critiques have been adopted by a growing number of American archaeologists who have become aware of some of the contradictions between rhetoric and reality in their own society as it has grown increasingly reactionary and defensive in recent years. Exposure to Marxist ideas, usually at second or third hand, has helped to reveal the mechanistic strictures of neo-evolutionary theory, which treats human beings as passive instruments rather than the makers of history. There is a growing awareness of the complexity of cultural change, of the need to view this process in its totality, and of the inadequacy of the dichotomy between history and evolution. New interpretations generally have moved in the direction of greater idealism and express growing doubts that anything approaching an objective understanding of the past is possible.

Ironically these developments appear to reflect yet a further stage in the growing despair that it is possible to do anything to change the direction in which American society is moving by those who might like to see it changed. Many of the self-styled Marxists perceive the ideological factors buttressing the structures of capitalism and seem to believe that ideas alone may bring about or prevent social change. Orthodox Marxism claims that such a naive idealism dooms its exponents to political impotence. This trend towards idealism in archaeology may be viewed as a secular equivalent of the increasing preoccupation with religion in middle-class American society in general and therefore as marking a further stage in the disintegration of the self-confidence of this class (Harris 1981). Long ago Engels postulated a positive correlation between the self-confidence of the middle classes and their propensity to adopt a materialist outlook (Marx and Engels 1957: 256–80).

While these idealist archaeologists recognize that a variety of mental, symbolic, and social factors bring about sociocultural change, they are unwilling to accept the Enlightenment view that planning and intentionality also play a significant role in doing so, even if it is admitted that the effects of change are often not the ones that were foreseen. Yet, as Leach (1973: 763–4) has observed, our capacity for 'original speech creativity' is closely linked with non-verbal forms of creativity as well as with human consciousness. This, he added, implies that human beings are not just part of a world governed by 'natural law' but have a unique ability to engage in 'work' (praxis) that allows them to alter their surroundings intentionally. Given that foresight and planning are characteristics of human behaviour, there is no reason why these features should not be assigned a significant role in any account of social change, even though the constraints that channel and select behaviour cannot be ignored. The principal error of Enlightenment philosophers and nineteenth-century unilinear evolutionists was the autonomous role they assigned to human creativity. In the future a major subject of debate may be between materialists who identify the principal endogenous locus of change with relations of production and idealists who identify it with pure intentionality. A dichotomous treatment is not, however, inherent in these concepts.

In North America, prehistoric archaeology as a whole still has not moved far enough away from neo-evolutionism to see itself as constituting, not merely a branch of anthropology, but also a technique for studying the past within a broader discipline of prehistory. The latter position is commonly held in Europe and in the past has been discussed sympathetically by a few American archaeologists such as Irving Rouse (1972). There is growing recognition that the human skeletal evidence studied by physical anthropologists may tell us as much about prehistoric diet as do floral and faunal analyses (Cohen and Armelagos 1984) and even more about band exogamy than does the study of artifact styles (Kennedy 1981). Yet there is little general awareness of the value of combining the study of archaeological data with that of historical linguistics, oral traditions, historical ethnography, and historical records, although it is clear that many archaeological problems can be resolved in this way. In American studies of African prehistory, there is a strong tradition of such interdisciplinary studies (Murdock 1959a; D. McCall 1964). The same is true of Polynesia (Jennings 1979) and Joyce Marcus (1983b) follows J. E. S. Thompson (1898–1975) in arguing the benefits of such an approach for Mayan research. The resistance seems to come from the view, widely held by processual archaeologists, that their discipline must be based as exclusively as possible on the study of material culture. Even though most of them agree that the ultimate goal of archaeology is to understand human behaviour and cultural change, they seek maximum disciplinary autonomy by relying only on universal generalizations about relations between material culture and human behaviour to translate archaeological data into information about such behaviour. This desire to push the interpretative potential of archaeology as far as possible without relying on other disciplines for information about the past is partly justified by the fear that interdisciplinary approaches can degenerate into an exercise in dilettantism. Such concerns do not, however, nullify the value of interdisciplinary research, provided that it is understood that such studies must exploit the historical potential of each discipline to the greatest extent possible, using its own data and methods before comparisons of findings are attempted.

Growing realization that many aspects of past human behaviour can be understood through correlations of a more culturally specific nature eventually should suggest the limitations of a purely archaeological approach and encourage archaeologists to seek to discover how other types of information can be combined with archaeological data to promote a better understanding of the past. The result will be a still broader and more enriched version of contextualism. Implementing this sort of approach requires cultivating a wider range of cultural interests than have been associated with processual archaeology. In their book on the Inca town of Huánuco Pampa, Craig Morris and Donald Thompson (1985: 58–9) are content to describe the *ushnu* or platform in the centre of the town as a structure related to aspects of ceremonial life. While they discuss its use in state ceremonies, they do not note that the *ushnu* was symbolically the place where the powers of heaven and earth met and that control of these powers was a central claim of the state (Gasparini and Margolies 1980: 264–80).

Archaeology as itself

In mainstream Western archaeology there has been a growing awareness of the distinctive qualities of archaeological data and of the need to understand these qualities if archaeology is to provide reliable information about human behaviour. In England this has taken the form of an enhanced awareness of the differences between archaeological and historical methods (Clarke 1968: 12–14) and in America a growing conviction that archaeology is different from ethnology and the other social sciences. The most obvious difference is that prehistoric archaeology is the only social science that has no direct access to information about human behaviour. Unlike economists, political scientists, sociologists, and ethnologists, archaeologists cannot talk to the people they study or observe their activities. Unlike historians they have no written accounts of what human beings thought or did in prehistoric times. That must be inferred as far as this is possible from the remains of what they made and used.

It has long been recognized that the archaeological record normally contains a far from complete sample of the material remains of the past. In 1923, John Myres (1923a: 2) observed that it consisted of the equipment which the people 'of each generation were discarding'. In *Archaeology and Society*, Grahame Clark (1939) examined in great detail factors that influence the preservation of archaeological data. In their initial enthusiasm, New Archaeologists tended to assume that the archaeological record, if adequately interpreted, offered a relatively complete and undistorted picture of the societies that had produced it. Gradually, however, following Robert Ascher (1961: 324), these archaeologists became aware that artifacts were made, used, and frequently discarded in different contexts, not all of which were equally represented in the archaeological record. Archaeological sites were distorted or destroyed by subsequent human activities and natural processes, and finally the recovery of archaeological information was dependent upon the knowledge, interests, and resources of individual archaeologists. Knowing what happened at each of these stages was vital for understanding the limitations and significance of the archaeological record.

The first major step towards formalizing such knowledge was taken by David Clarke in 1973 in a paper entitled 'Archaeology: the loss of innocence' (Clarke 1979: 83–103). He argued that archaeology would remain 'an irresponsible art form' unless a body of theory was systematized that related archaeological remains to human behaviour. The basis for such a systematization was the recognition that archaeologists possessed only an attenuated sample of what they proposed to study. This observation was encapsulated in Clarke's memorable comment that archaeology was 'the discipline with the theory and practice for the recovery of unobservable hominid behaviour patterns from indirect traces in bad samples' (p. 100). The scientific interpretation of archaeological data depends on recognizing that, of the full range of hominid activity patterns and social and environmental processes that occurred in the past, archaeologists have access only to the sample of associated material remains that in turn have been deposited in the archaeological record, survived to be recovered, and actually been recovered. Clarke defined five bodies of theory that archaeologists intuitively employ in their interpretive leaps from excavated data to final report. The first of these was pre-depositional and depositional theory, covering the relations of human activities, social patterns, and environmental factors with each other and with the samples and traces that are deposited in the archaeological record. Post-depositional theory treats the natural and human processes that affect the archaeological record, such as erosion, decay, ground movement, plundering, ploughing, and the reuse of land. Retrieval theory deals with the relations between what survives in the archaeological record and what is recovered. It is largely a theory of sampling, excavation procedures, and flexible response strategies. Analytical theory deals with the operational treatment of recovered data including classification, modelling, testing, and experimental studies. Finally, interpretive theory deals with relations between the archaeological patterns established at the analytical level and directly unobservable ancient behavioural and environmental patterns. Thus interpretive theory infers the processes that pre-depositional theory explains. Clarke believed that the challenge for archaeologists was to develop a corpus of theory appropriate for each of these categories. Only a small portion, mainly relating to the pre-depositional and interpretive levels, could be derived from the social sciences. The rest had to come from the biological and physical sciences. The totality of this theory, together with metaphysical, epistemological, and logical theory relating to archaeological operations, was necessary to create a scientific discipline of archaeology.

In the United States, Michael Schiffer (1976) independently pioneered an analogous but less inclusive approach (in that it did not embrace Clarke's analytical level), which he called 'behavioral archeology'. He proposed that archaeological data consisted of materials in static relations that have been produced by cultural systems and subjected to the operation of non-cultural processes. Because of these two sets of processes the archaeological record is 'a distorted reflection of a past behavioral system' (p. 12). The challenge is for archaeologists to eliminate this distortion in order to gain an accurate understanding of past behaviour. Schiffer was optimistic that this could be done provided that three sets of factors were controlled. The first are 'correlates', which relate material objects or spatial relations in archaeological contexts to specific types of human behaviour. Correlates allow archaeologists to infer how artifacts were made, distributed, used, and recycled, often in exceedingly complex ways, in living societies. If a cultural system were frozen at a specific moment in time, as to some extent happened to the city of Pompeii as a result of being buried under the ash of Mount Vesuvius in A.D. 79, and perfectly preserved, no additional factors would have to be taken into account in order to understand life at that moment. The interpretation of archaeological sites normally, however, requires archaeologists to take account of site-formation processes, which involves determining how material was transferred from a systemic to an archaeological context and what happened to that material in the archaeological record. The first of these are 'cultural formation processes', or C-transforms, which attempt to understand the processes by which items are discarded in the normal operation of a cultural system. Through the detailed study of discard rates, discard locations, loss probabilities, and burial practices, C-transforms can predict the materials that will or will not be deposited by a social system in the archaeological record and thus establish a set of relations that will permit the cultural system to be inferred more accurately from its remains. Ethnographic research on problems of this sort suggests that artifacts and artifact debris are more likely to be abandoned in the localities where they were used in temporary hunter–gatherer sites than in larger and more sedentary ones, where the disposal of waste material was much more highly organized (Murray 1980).

The realization that large numbers of artifacts are found in contexts of disposal rather than those of manufacture or use has stimulated much ethnoarchaeological research that aims to discover regularities in patterns of the disposal of refuse. It has also prompted observations that archaeology may of necessity be primarily a science of garbage. J. A. Moore and A. S. Keene (1983: 17) have pronounced studies of site formation processes to be 'the archaeological agenda for the 1980s'. Other studies seek to determine the transformations that artifacts undergo in the course of usage. Stone tools are likely to be curated and reused much more intensively in sites lacking easy access to sources of raw material than in ones close to such sources (Binford 1983a: 269–86). C-transforms also include post-depositional human activities, such as ploughing and looting, that may distort the archaeological record. This may often happen in predictable ways, such as the greater likelihood that robbers will remove gold objects rather than commonplace ones from graves. Finally non-cultural formation processes, or N-transforms, allow archaeologists to determine the interactions between cultural materials and aspects of the non-cultural environment from which they are recovered. Schiffer argues that by accounting for the ways in which archaeological data functioned in systemic contexts, entered the archaeological record, and were transformed by it, archaeologists should be able to eliminate the 'distortions' caused by formation processes and infer the original systemic context in which the artifacts functioned. This can be done by formulating laws about the relationships between material culture on the one hand and human behaviour and natural forces on the other. These laws include many low-level empirical generalizations. This had led Binford (1983a: 237) to describe Schiffer as being primarily an inductivist.

Binford (1983a: 235) has challenged Schiffer's view by arguing that the archaeological record cannot be 'a distortion of its own reality'. He maintains that the challenge of archaeological interpretation is to understand the 'distorted' material as a significant part of the archaeological record and that most of Schiffer's C-transforms, such as periodically cleaning out hearths, were everyday activities. Yet, since Schiffer seeks to understand processes, it seems unreasonable to suggest that he treats past cultural systems as frozen in time. What Binford does demonstrate is that it is naive to believe that archaeologists can totally purge the archaeological record of the various disorganizing processes that controlled its formation and, having done that, reconstruct the cultural system as Schiffer hopes to do. Schiffer's approach has helped to stimulate much research that has resulted in a more sophisticated understanding of the behavioural significance of archaeological data. Previously factors such as discard rates were barely considered by archaeologists except in assessing the significance of animal bones. It is now increasingly recognized that many cultural processes are so complex and varied and that the chances of equifinality are so great that the neutralization of distorting influences cannot produce a complete interpretation of the archaeological record from a behavioural point of view (von Gernet 1985; P. Watson 1986: 450). As belief in neo-evolutionism wanes and the diversity of human behaviour increasingly is accepted, this limitation tends to be acknowledged as inherent in the data rather than as a methodological weakness. Hence, while archaeologists continue to apply Schiffer's approach profitably, many of them do not expect his full programme to be realized.

Binford (1977, 1981) has also contributed to a growing awareness of the distinctiveness of archaeology from anthropology with his emphasis on middle-range theory. He argues that the dependence of archaeological knowledge of human behaviour in the past on inference rather than direct observation often renders the independence of observations and explanations suspect and leads to the fallacy of 'confirming the consequent' (1981: 29). From this he concludes that archaeologists cannot use the archaeological record or the inferred past to test their premises and assumptions. To develop reliable means for knowing the past they must engage in middle-range research, which consists of actualistic studies designed to control for the relations between the dynamic properties of the past, about which they seek knowledge, and the static material properties common to past and present. As in his earlier work, Binford sees the key for understanding archaeological data from a positivist perspective as lying in the establishment of valid correlations between material culture, which archaeologists can observe, and behaviour, which they cannot. His present formulation clearly distinguishes, however, between general theory, which seeks to explain human behaviour, and middle-range theory, which is concerned with inferring such behaviour from archaeological data. Middle-range theory is therefore of interest exclusively to archaeology, as opposed to general theory, which is the common concern of all the social sciences.

Middle-range theory embraces acts of identification, such as distinguishing different classes of habitations, hide scrapers, or base camps, as well as diagnosing the economic, social, and ideological functions of artifacts. It also includes identifying patterns of human behaviour as these may relate to family organization, village structure, and political relations, although in this case growing respect is shown for the observation made long ago by David Aberle (1968) that concepts that are very useful for ethnographic interpretation may not be well suited for interpreting archaeological data. For example, archaeologists find it easier to deal with behavioural categories, such as matrilocal residence, than with jural concepts, such as matrilineal descent. Middle-range theory also subsumes the study of cultural and natural site-formation processes. It thus embraces the study of regularities in physical processes as well as in cultural behaviour. Much of Binford's (1984) most important research in recent years has involved using arguments about natural site-formation processes to challenge the human origin of many of the patterns observed in the archaeological record for Lower Palaeolithic times. He has shown that many of the data interpreted as evidence of big-game hunting or even major scavenging at that time could be merely natural distributions of bone in incidental association with traces of human activity. While this issue is far from settled, Binford's research has called into question the validity of some long-standing interpretations of early hominid behaviour. He has also demonstrated that, in their support of particular theories about hominid behaviour, archaeologists have failed to consider possible alternatives or to analyse the data sufficiently thoroughly.

Binford's concept of middle-range theory has stimulated an increasing amount of ethnoarchaeological research as well as experiments that duplicate the manufacture and use of prehistoric artifacts. Ruth Tringham (1978) has discussed how these two approaches can be combined to their mutual advantage, thereby carrying forward an argument originally advanced by Sven Nilsson 150 years earlier. Binford's (1978) own work exemplifies the careful application of ethnoarchaeological research to archaeological problems. His desire to understand the behavioural significance of the well documented variability in the Mousterian assemblages of Western Europe led him to carry out fieldwork among modern hunting groups in Alaska. He has since applied what he learned about their economic and spatial behaviour to a whole series of problems relating to Old-World Palaeolithic archaeology (Binford 1983b).

At least two major difficulties have been identified with the use of middle-range theory. The first objection is that ethnoarchaeological studies are 'theory dependent' and 'paradigm relative' (Wylie 1989). Just as in archaeology, what is accepted as a valid correlation is partly influenced by the presuppositions of the investigator. The principal advantage of ethnoarchaeology, or any ethnographic study, is that behaviour is observed, not inferred, hence the opportunities for speculations to multiply are more limited.

A second and related problem is the relevance of middle-range theory for archaeological interpretations. Binford is aware that using present regularities to explain the past involves uniformitarian assumptions and argues that these claims must be warranted by supporting arguments. He suggests, for example, that the ecological and anatomical characteristics of still extant species which ancient human beings exploited are 'enduring objects for which uniformitarian assumptions might be securely warranted' (Binford 1981: 28) and expresses the hope that other domains can be elaborated as research progresses. Other archaeologists see these uniformitarian assumptions as involving as great a leap of faith as those Binford suggests affirm the consequent (P. Watson 1986: 447–8). Uniformitarian assumptions have their dangers. One of these is ignorance of what is happening at the present time. Scientists may misunderstand the past because they fail to take account of long-term processes, as was the case with geology prior to the recognition of plate tectonics and continental drift. Another problem is that social scientists may consider to be universal, characteristics of human behaviour that are specific to a particular stage of cultural development. Marxists, who believe that human nature is substantially altered by evolutionary change, are less willing to invoke universal features of human behaviour than are archaeologists who assume, along with the philosophers of the Enlightenment, that human behaviour remains unaltered by social change. Problems can also rise in applying analogies, because archaeologists are unable to distinguish what is characteristic of humanity in general (or of a particular mode of production) and what is specific only to historically related cultures. Anthropologists remain unable to distinguish on theoretical grounds between analogies, resulting from convergent evolution, and homologies, that owe their similarity to historical relations. Instead, they must do so empirically, using historical or archaeological evidence. The variety of forces bringing about social change also complicates the question of what modern societies can serve as true analogies of prehistoric ones. We have already noted that, while Binford found that the settlement patterns of hunter–gatherers in high latitudes shared many features that distinguished them from hunter–gatherer patterns in warmer climates, all of these northern societies were engaged in trapping and selling furs to Europeans long before they were studied by anthropologists. We do not know whether the common features Binford described represent an ecological adaptation extending back thousands of years or had developed in recent centuries as a consequence of new economic relations. In this case archaeological data about prehistoric settlement patterns are essential to provide insights into the developmental significance of modern behavioural patterns and produce convincing warranting arguments. Yet, despite such cautionary tales, a blanket rejection of uniformitarianism may be far more dangerous for the development of archaeology than its opposite. Despite this problem, middle-range theory is a very useful device for interpreting archaeological data.

A more important limitation appears to be that human behaviour is considerably less uniform than Binford, as a neo-evolutionist,

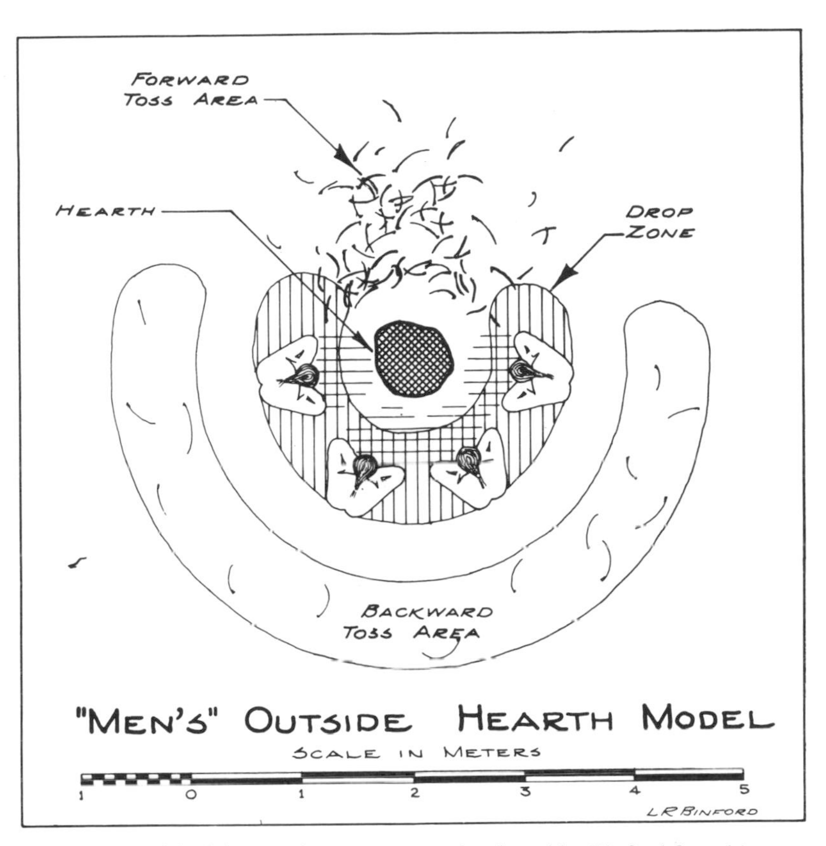

50 Model of drop and toss zones, as developed by Binford from his ethnoarchaeological study of the Nunamiut of Alaska

continues to believe. Much more ethnographic documentation is needed before we can agree with his assertion that all hunter–gatherers use their camp space in much the same way, producing easily recognizable features such as bedding areas, drop zones, toss zones, and aggregate dumping areas, and proceed to interpret all Palaeolithic archaeological sites in terms of models derived from the Bushmen and Nunamiut (Binford 1983b: 144–92). Even if the use of camp space can be proved to be relatively uniform, there are many aspects of human behaviour that cannot be accounted for in terms of universal generalizations, whether these concern behaviour in general or societies at specific levels of development (Watson *et al.* 1984: 264). Hence more culturally specific explanations, such as have been proposed by Hodder and other structuralist archaeologists, are likely to play an important role in explaining archaeological data alongside Binford's middle-range theory (von Gernet and Timmins 1987).

A final, more narrowly empiricist approach advocated by André Leroi-Gourhan (1968) and more recently by Robert Dunnell (1971, 1982b) seeks to separate archaeology from its ties with social anthropology and ethnology, and perhaps with the social sciences generally. It is alleged that this relationship has encouraged a flawed approach to archaeological interpretation, based on ethnographic analogy. Instead the archaeological record must be understood on its own terms. While Dunnell allows that aspects of the archaeological record that represent style rather than function cannot be encompassed by this approach, he believes that it facilitates the study of the evolutionarily significant portions of archaeological data, which are seen as explainable in terms of biophysical variables (cf. Wylie 1985b; Watson 1986: 444–6). Other archaeologists have proposed to explain archaeological data by employing principles derived from sociobiology (Nash and Whitlam 1985), a position that Dunnell (1980a: 60–6) specifically has repudiated. Both approaches require an arbitrary delineation of what is important and not important about human behaviour and also the ignoring of unique features of such behaviour that have developed in the course of biological evolution. More importantly, however, it has not been demonstrated that the empirical data of archaeology can be interpreted behaviourally without recourse to some sort of analogies (P. Watson 1986: 446). However much experimental work is done, for example in the form of use-wear studies, inferences about human behaviour permeate all levels of such research and its application to interpreting archaeological data. The danger is that uncritical common-sense analogies may unwarrantedly replace more disciplined ones based on ethnographic and historical studies. Valid concerns about the dangers of using ethnographic analogies have not succeeded in producing a credible alternative.

There is currently very little interest in the relevance of the formal classifications of artifacts for the study of problems other than chronology and cultural classification. The significance of formal variation for understanding ecological, social, political, ethnic, symbolic, and ideational aspects of prehistoric cultures remains to be established (Gardin 1980; C. Carr 1985). Until these dimensions can be distinguished formally in the archaeological record, a major technique for bridging the gap between the archaeological and behavioural spheres will remain unexploited.

Conclusions

The growing realization that archaeology is methodologically differentiated from the other social sciences because of its inability to observe human behaviour or speech first hand, particularly as represented by Binford's middle-range theory, closely parallels the arguments advanced by Klejn and his associates in the Soviet Union that archaeological data first must be understood in their own right before they can be used to study historical problems. In both cases the question arises whether a body of strictly archaeological theory that is concerned with inferring human behaviour from archaeological data can be more objective than high-level theories that are concerned with explaining human behaviour and are demonstrably influenced by archaeologists' responses to contemporary social issues. That archaeologists around the world, regardless of their political orientation, appear to be able to adopt each other's interpretive innovations while maintaining different high-level views of human behaviour, suggests that to some degree middle-range theory and the operations used to infer human behaviour from archaeological data may be relatively uninfluenced by social biases. Yet the formulation of middle-range theory involves the use of concepts that acquire their significance in social settings. This indicates that the differentiation between middle-range and general theory may not be as great in that respect as many archaeologists believe.

Although a few archaeologists maintain that deterministic forms of evolutionism are 'returning to center stage' (Dunnell in Rindos 1984: ix), most American and Western European ones seem to be increasingly convinced that human behaviour is complex and that accounting for its development requires nothing less than explaining the course of human history in all of its bewildering diversity and specificity. In their more extreme manifestations, these developments are moving in the direction of historical particularism, a doctrine that is in accord with the intellectual obfuscation and despair about effecting constructive change that are currently rampant in American popular culture. Yet most American archaeologists seem unlikely to reject the accomplishments of the last 30 years to embrace a form of neo-Boasianism, even if they judge the neo-evolutionism of the 1960s to be no longer tenable. They appear to be abandoning the idea that only aspects of culture that recur cross-culturally are worth understanding, to be trying to understand specific sequences of development in their historical complexity, and to be abandoning the proposition that prediction is the only form of explanation. At the same time archaeologists are likely to remain concerned with delineating and explaining cross-cultural regularities in human behaviour and to use these explanations, where they are appropriate, to understand specific sequences of development (P. Watson 1986: 442–3). In the future, evolutionary theory probably will be concerned not only with the regularities that societies exhibit as they develop from one level to another but equally with how adjacent interacting societies at different stages of development influence one another. For the first time we will have an evolutionary theory that is able to take account of colonial relations past and present and hence of some of the basic processes that have led to the development of anthropology and prehistoric archaeology. Finally Western archaeologists are likely to become increasingly aware of the relations between individuals and groups who study the past and how they view it, an awareness that should also reveal more clearly to archaeologists the nature of the contemporary Western societies in which they live.

The future perception of causality is harder to predict. There is good reason to believe that, if a respectable emphasis on understanding cross-cultural regularities persists, archaeologists will continue to regard material factors as significant constraints on human behaviour and therefore as major influences shaping cultural development. In all probability there will be less emphasis on specific technological and ecological factors and more on broader economic relations, as well as on constraints on social and political organizations provided by general systems theory. Ideologies, beliefs, and cultural traditions generally will be seen as part of the context in which economic change comes about. What is unclear is the importance that will be accorded to these factors and whether they will be interpreted as operating within the constraints set by economic and social conditions or as promoting major cultural changes in a more independent fashion. It is unlikely there will be unanimity on this topic. It is also uncertain whether concepts, such as planning, intentionality, and foresight, will play a significant role in understanding cultural change within either a materialist or a non-materialist framework, since they are theoretically compatible with both. For them to do so, archaeologists will have to adopt a much more critical role with respect to their social milieu than is currently the case.

Whatever happens, the growing sense of the unity and complementarity of historicism and evolutionism in Western archaeology should allow archaeological explanation to move beyond the vulgar materialism of processual archaeology, the sterile idealism of historical particularism, and the ersatz Marxism of the critical and structuralist approaches. This moderate shift, following a short period when neo-evolutionism was in the ascendant, would contrast with the radical swing from unilinear evolutionism to historical particularism at the end of the nineteenth century and the long periods during which each of these two extreme positions was dominant. If a similar radical swing does not occur today, it is at least partly because archaeologists have learned from experience the unproductiveness of these dichotomous and extreme views of human behaviour. This suggests that a body of procedures for inferring human behaviour has developed within Western archaeology that is now sufficiently mature to influence how it interprets its data, sometimes in opposition to external beliefs and values.

CHAPTER 10

Archaeology and its social context

There simply is not, at the present time, any explicit, objective set of rules or procedures by which the influence of concealed interests upon thought and belief can be established. However, it remains possible in many instances to identify the operation of concealed interests by a subjective, experimental approach.

BARRY BARNES, *Interests and the Growth of Knowledge* (1977), p. 35

We have now reached the point where we can discuss the significance of the history of archaeology for understanding the nature of archaeological interpretation and assess the discipline's relative degree of objectivity or subjectivity. These questions are relevant for determining the role that archaeology can aspire to play in human history. Is it restricted to reflecting society and passively participating in the political movements that transform our lives or can it, as Childe (1946b, 1947b) hoped, play an important part alongside the study of history in creating a more objective 'science of progress' that will help to elucidate major social issues and guide humanity towards a better future?

The goals of archaeology

In recent years there has been much debate concerning the ultimate goal of archaeological research. Strongly positivistic archaeologists, such as Dunnell (1971: 120–1), stress that it must be to explain the archaeological record. Clarke (1968) viewed archaeology more broadly as the potential nucleus of a general science of material culture, past and present, that would complement social and cognitive anthropology. In a similar vein Schiffer (1976: 4) has argued that 'the subject matter of archeology is the relationships between human behavior and material culture in all times and places'. Other archaeologists, however, would restrict this role to historical archaeology

(Deagan 1982: 167) and Binford (1981: 28) objects that it cannot be the central focus for archaeology 'since the archaeological record contains no direct information on this subject whatsoever!' Daniel (1975: 370–6) has argued that to restrict the discipline to the study of material remains would be to cultivate a new artifact-centred antiquarianism. Most archaeologists continue to regard archaeology as a means to study human behaviour and cultural change in the past, although they are far from agreed about what is involved in doing so.

These various definitions of the ultimate goals of archaeology have significant implications for establishing the scope of what are considered to be archaeological activities. Traditionally archaeology has been equated with the recovery, analysis, and interpretation of the material remains of the human past. Yet archaeology has always extended beyond these limits. No one has ever considered replicative experiments as other than archaeological. Although strictly speaking they do not study material from the past, their relevance for archaeological interpretation, and for it alone, is unquestioned. On the other hand, while archaeologists have long relied on ethnographic analogies to interpret archaeological data, only recently has the carrying out of major projects of ethnoarchaeological research in an effort to learn more about relations between material culture and human behaviour been regarded as integral to archaeology (Binford 1978; R. Gould 1978, 1980; P. Watson 1979; Hodder 1982b). It can equally be considered as an ethnographic activity carried out by archaeologists. Schiffer (1976: 8–9) has added to these activities the study of material objects in ongoing cultural systems in an effort to describe and explain present human behaviour (see also Reid *et al.* 1974). This includes research such as William Rathje's (1974) Garbage Project, which employed techniques of archaeological analysis to study changing patterns in the use and disposal of resources within the modern city of Tucson, Arizona. While they admit that archaeological methods and expertise are employed in such analyses, far fewer archaeologists are prepared to view research of this sort as an integral part of their discipline. Most archaeologists continue to regard studying the past as an essential attribute of archaeology.

Yet, while each of the above goals has implications concerning priorities in archaeological research, they are not mutually exclusive.

There is no way in which either the archaeological record or modern material culture can be understood without relating them to human behaviour. Conversely, if archaeologists are to learn more about human behaviour and cultural change in the past, they must seek new and convincing ways to infer such behaviour from archaeological data. It is also only through the study of human behaviour that archaeology can be related to the other social sciences.

Archaeology: history and science

Throughout the course of its development archaeology has had especially close relations with one or the other of two social sciences: history and anthropology. Traditionally the relationship has been closer with history when archaeologists study what they believe to be the remains of their own ancestors or of civilizations for which much written documentation is available and closer to anthropology when they study Palaeolithic times or more recent, technologically less-advanced cultures to which they do not believe their own society is closely related. This distinction has become somewhat blurred in recent years as a growing number of Western European archaeologists have turned to anthropology in an effort to understand local Neolithic, Bronze Age, and Iron Age societies better.

The disciplinary distinction between history and anthropology, as we have seen, had its origins in ideological considerations. Nineteenth-century Europeans regarded themselves as naturally progressive and the native peoples whom they were subjecting to colonial domination as inherently static and hence beyond the pale of historical research. It has taken a long time for these two disciplines even to begin to come to grips with the implications of this bias, which remains surprisingly alive (Trevor-Roper 1966: 9). There is no inherent reason why archaeologists should derive their understanding of human behaviour almost exclusively from anthropology. A special relationship generally is justified on the ground that ethnologists study the same kind of societies as do prehistoric archaeologists and that therefore ethnology is a more fertile source of interpretative analogies than is any other social science. Yet, if archaeologists are to use universal generalizations about human behaviour to explain their data, as processual archaeologists advocate, there is no reason why these generalizations should not come from human geography, economics, political science, sociology, and psychology, as well as from ethnology. It has been argued that most of the disciplinary boundaries that characterize the Western social sciences are arbitrary, to the extent that they often preclude the asking and answering of fundamental questions about the nature and development of modern industrial societies (Wolf 1982: 7–19). By contrast Marxists have maintained a holistic approach to the social sciences as they have developed their critique of capitalist societies.

The discussion about whether archaeology is related more closely to history or to anthropology is closely tied to an equally inconclusive debate about whether the archaeological understanding of human behaviour should take the form of historical explanations or nomothetic generalizations. Since most archaeologists are committed to understanding what has happened in the past, this dispute has centred on the question of whether their primary goal should be to explain individual events in all of their idiographic particularity or to produce evolutionary generalizations about the nature of cultural change. The first option has been supported by culture-historical archaeologists, whose main concern is with the detailed study of specific peoples, cultures, or regions, while the second has been vociferously advocated by processual archaeologists. In practice, archaeologists of both persuasions have sought to formulate not only evolutionary generalizations but also functional ones as a basis for inferring human behaviour from archaeological data.

This debate stems from a false dichotomy between history and science that was introduced into American archaeology by Kluckhohn and Steward, and reinforced by the adoption of neo-evolutionism. The latter encouraged prehistoric archaeologists to believe that human behaviour and cultural change exhibited strong regularities that could be accounted for in terms of evolutionary generalizations, and that doing this constituted scientific explanation. That left history, as a humanistic residual, to account for the 'unique, exotic, and non-recurrent particulars' of cultural change, all matters that neo-evolutionists judged to be of little, if any, scientific importance. As a general rule, this meant that science dealt with ecological adaptation, while history studied the stylistic aspects of culture.

These dichotomies between ecology and style and between

science and history are at best unconvincing. Many anthropologists regard entire cultures as adaptive systems, which leaves no grounds for opposing ecology and style. More importantly, as a result of the declining influence of neo-evolutionism, it has become clear that cultural change is far more diversified than any neo-evolutionary view of parallel or even multilinear evolution has countenanced. While it is informative to know the features that events assigned to a particular class (such as revolutions a, b, and c) have in common, and why this is so, these features rarely exhaust what is of theoretical interest or needs to be explained about such events. Hence, while it may be possible to isolate certain features common to all revolutions, it is not possible to predict all the features of any one revolution from revolutions in general. No matter how much relevant theory is available, the armchair prehistorian cannot produce a detailed reconstruction of the course of history from such understanding alone. It is also clear that at least part of the diversity observed in the archaeological record results from cultures at different levels of development or pursuing different strategies at the same level influencing and constraining each other. The concept of cultures interacting as part of a world system takes us far from the simplistic view that, at least in adaptive terms, cultural borrowing is no different from internal innovation, which was the stock-in-trade of neo-evolutionists.

That in turn suggests that there is no quick and easy way by which archaeologists can create a body of evolutionary theory that will allow them simultaneously to predict or retrodict (predict backwards) the course of human history. Even if it is possible to develop a body of theory that explains how cultural change in general takes place, in the same sense that the synthetic theory of biological evolution explains changes in living species, this will not allow archaeologists to retrodict how specific ways of life changed in prehistoric times. That can only be accomplished by studying the archaeological data relevant to specific sequences of development and trying to explain those sequences in all of their particularistic complexity. These sequences cannot be accounted for without reference to generalizations about human behaviour and cultural processes; but likewise they cannot be explained without taking account of idiosyncratic and hence unpredictable concatenations of influences. Had there been no western hemisphere for Europeans to discover in 1492, or had it contained no gold and silver and populations to mine these metals, there is no doubt that the subsequent economic and political development of Europe would have been very different (Marx 1906: 823–4). It has also become increasingly obvious that, because of this, ethnologists must understand the historical significance of the data that they use to generalize about human behaviour before the significance of these generalizations can be understood. Finally, it is being recognized that to refuse to consider regularities significant if they are not universal ones is to ignore and belittle large and important areas of human experience. If structuralist claims concerning the role played by cultural patterns in moulding human behaviour are even partially correct, such refusal may severely limit the ability of archaeologists to explain why change has taken place. Attempts to understand numerous cultural sequences in all of their idiosyncratic complexity will also lead to the recognition of unsuspected regularities in cultural behaviour that can contribute to a more detailed understanding of evolutionary processes. The elaboration of world-systems theory appears to be a significant move in that direction. All of this indicates the bankruptcy of the traditional dichotomy between history and evolution. Nomothetic generalizations and historical explanations are indissolubly linked processes, neither one of which can make progress without the other or be reduced to the other.

These arguments also suggest some major limitations on the role of covering laws in archaeological explanation. Many evolutionary generalizations may be formulated inductively as a result of detailed efforts to interpret individual cultural sequences and then raised to a higher level of significance after their cross-cultural applicability is noted. Because of the overlapping nature of many competing high-level theories of human behaviour, it often remains unclear which of them best accounts for such empirical generalizations. It may further be argued that the ultimate task of evolutionary theory, and the standard by which it must be judged, is its ability to explain what has happened in the past, as revealed through idiographic studies, rather than to construct hypothetical schemes of development that are invariably too general to predict what actually happened in the past (Murdock 1959b).

For explaining specific historical events or sequences of change, the approaches that Wesley Salmon (1967, 1984; Salmon *et al.* 1971) and Merrilee Salmon (1982) have called 'statistical-relevance' explanation and William Dray (1957) has discussed as 'how possibly' explanations are essential. These should not be viewed as an alternative to deductive explanation since both extensively employ arguments of this sort. An important characteristic of 'how possibly' explanations is the reconstruction of a chain of events, accompanied by an effort to account for these events and the sequence in which they occurred. Explanations ideally should be based on well-established laws of human behaviour, although common sense must often be used as a 'filler' because of the lack of such theory. Many answers to questions that arise as part of 'how possibly' explanations take the form of additional data that eliminate one or more alternative possibilities (Dray 1957: 156–69). The concept of archaeological explanations taking the form of alternative possibilities, some of which eventually may be eliminated by new data, is a corollary of this approach (Chamberlin 1944; G. Isaac 1984). In due course new archaeological findings or research in other fields also may help to provide generalizations that can replace common-sense or empirical solutions to problems.

As the result of a declining preoccupation with neo-evolutionary theory, there has also been in recent years a widening appreciation that a holistic knowledge of what has happened to specific groups of people in the past is a matter of great humanistic as well as scientific interest. Archaeological studies have refuted the idea, sustained if not created by nineteenth-century anthropologists, that non-literate peoples were primitive and unchanging. Scholars in emerging nations in Africa and elsewhere look to archaeology to provide knowledge of their pre-colonial development and treat archaeology as a vital instrument of historical research. In North America, Australia, and other parts of the world where native peoples have been overwhelmed by European settlement, the image of the 'unchanging savage' has been demonstrated, with the help of archaeological data, to have been a myth that developed as part of the process of European colonization. In this context the notion that archaeological data should be used only to formulate and test as an end in themselves a potpourri of general theories about human behaviour and cultural change is increasingly being viewed as not only conceptually inadequate but also neo-colonialist and insulting to the Third World and to native peoples (D. Miller 1980; Langford

1983; Ucko 1983). By ignoring its social responsibilities, archaeology may be dooming itself to irrelevance in the opinion of many people who otherwise might be interested in its findings, as well as encouraging needless hostility (Wiseman 1983).

This humanistic outlook also reinforces the view that it is reasonable to employ a direct historical approach and to use non-archaeological sources of data, such as oral traditions, historical linguistics, and comparative ethnography, in order to produce a more rounded picture of prehistoric cultures and to rule out alternative explanations that archaeological data alone might not be able to exclude. The employment of all possible sources of data and the search for congruence among these data sets may be regarded as an extension of Hodder's contextual approach and an important means of gaining insights into the significance of archaeological findings. This is a point that historical archaeologists make repeatedly with respect to their own work (South 1977a). All of these observations strengthen the conclusion that, when dealing with archaeological (just as with historical) data, prediction and explanation are not identical, as the New Archaeologists maintained they were. The reason for this lies in the complexity of human behaviour, which produces far more complicated situations than are encountered in biology.

It is being recognized that, however useful correlations between material culture and human behaviour may be for inferring such behaviour from the archaeological record, these correlations only indicate what happened in the past; they do not provide explanations of why events happened. Explanations require an operational account of the regularity which links a proposed cause and effect (M. Salmon 1982: 132). In the case of natural constraints on human behaviour, such as may arise from ecological factors, this may involve determining the effect of a specific natural cause and showing how in terms of human physiology or psychology a particular response is required. Yet, because the behaviour of human beings is largely, if not wholly, mediated by cultural factors, thought and intention are a necessary part of understanding it. Archaeological explanations of human responses to environmental challenges, to pressure from neighbouring societies, and to tensions that arise within societies must therefore make sense in terms of what the archaeologist knows about human logic and decision making. M.

Salmon (1982: 132) cites as a rudimentary example of a causal account of the regularity connecting small population size and egalitarian social structure Anthony Forge's (1972) claim that human beings can handle only a limited number of detailed interpersonal relationships. As societies become larger, some form of segmentary organization and more clearly defined patterns of leadership are required.

The problem is that the archaeologist has no direct access to the thoughts of the past, while social scientists disagree quite profoundly about the nature of thought as exhibited in the modern world. Some anthropologists stress the importance of reason in determining human behaviour, especially in practical spheres, such as those that relate to ecological and economic concerns. They make extensive use of rationalist concepts, such as G. K. Zipf's (1949) 'principle of least effort', and emphasize the metaphorical status of religious beliefs, which are notoriously diverse (Gellner 1985; Sperber 1985). On the other hand, relativists stress the variations in patterns of thought from one culture to another and the difficulty of predicting how people behave in one culture from how they are known to behave in another. Childe (1949: 6–7) long ago pointed out that human beings adapt to environments not as they occur in nature but as they perceive them to be. Yet, if perception and reality were too discordant, natural selection would quickly eliminate such societies. The same may be true of some forms of political behaviour. This suggests that, at least with respect to certain practical aspects of human behaviour, some form of universal logic may suffice to explain the general outlines of what happened in the past.

Nevertheless, the problems encountered by economists in trying to understand the nature of economic behaviour in non-Western societies warns against complacency about the ability of archaeologists to infer the nature of decision making in prehistoric ones. Also, because of the human capacity to envision and choose among alternative solutions to problems, it may not be possible to specify causality in archaeologically observable terms, except when dealing statistically with large numbers of cases. This is what Childe (1928: 46) had in mind when he argued that some hunter–gatherer groups threatened by desiccation might alter their way of life, while others might move to less affected environments or even die out. Rather than deny that psychological states are relevant to interpreting archaeological data, archaeologists should pay more attention to assessing the extent to which cultural conditioning rather than universal logic influences human behaviour as it is reflected in the archaeological record, as well as the extent to which alternative models can profitably be constructed that treat culturally conditioned behaviour as a black box.

Relativist critiques

Because archaeology deals with complex phenomena and is not an experimental discipline, it is particularly vulnerable to what is accepted as true at any one time being whatever appears to be most reasonable to each successive generation of archaeologists. They may establish sound correlations, weed out logical inconsistencies, and demonstrate that accepted interpretations do not accord with new data. Yet a historical survey reveals that interpretations are often subtly influenced by social and personal preconceptions of reality that preclude an awareness of the full range of alternative explanations that would allow more comprehensive formal testing and determining the actual limits within which a generalization holds true. In many instances neither adequate data nor strong enough correlations are available to counteract such biases. Under these circumstances the difference between a nomothetic generalization and an informal argument by analogy is by no means clear-cut.

As archaeologists become more aware of the complexity of what they have to explain, they also become more interested in learning how and to what extent their experience of the present influences their interpretations of the past. Many see the milieu in which they work affecting both the questions they ask and the answers that they are predisposed to regard as reasonable. It is perhaps deceptively easy to show that throughout the world the interpretation of archaeological evidence is influenced by specific social, economic, and political conditions, as well as by the tendency for individuals and groups to promote their own interests by representing selfish goals as altruistic ones. It can also be documented that in a very general fashion analogous social situations independently have encouraged similar treatments of archaeological data. In particular in the Western and Third Worlds these interpretations reflect the political and economic concerns of the middle classes, as expressed in various expansive and defensive postures. In addition, archaeological interpretations are influenced directly by gender prejudices, ethnic concerns, the political control of research and publishing, the financing of archaeological activities, generational conflicts among researchers, and the idiosyncratic influences of charismatic archaeologists. They are also influenced by society indirectly through analytical models that are offered by the physical, biological, and to a still greater degree the social sciences, as well as by the continued acceptance of established archaeological explanations, the outmoded character of which has not yet become apparent.

Yet simple correlations between archaeological interpretations and social conditions are encountered only rarely. Most interpretations are not straightforward reflections of such conditions but versions of the past created by archaeologists trying under specific historical circumstances to promote or defend preferred social interests. These interests are varied and each of them can be supported in many different ways. Racial doctrines can be used to promote national unity or to justify colonial aggression. Strongly held religious beliefs can be held responsible for retarding technological progress or hailed as a major factor promoting cultural development. The options that are selected reflect the specific balance of interests in individual cultures and the relationship of particular archaeologists to these interests. Such considerations not only play a major role in shaping variations in archaeological practice but also respond to changing social conditions. The tendency for archaeological interpretation to be influenced by society does not appear to be diminishing as archaeology becomes more theoretically sophisticated, as some archaeologists have suggested it would (Clarke 1979: 154). Instead it appears to remain one of archaeology's permanent features.

At worst this could mean that there is no past to study, not only in the undeniable positivist sense that what we interpret is merely 'the marks of the past in the present' but also in accord with Collingwood's more profound definition of history as a discipline in which one can only relive the past in one's own mind. This implies that there is no way in which the archaeologist or historian can verifiably reconstruct the past as it actually was. Yet Gellner (1985: 134) points out that most archaeologists believe that 'the past was once present, as *the present*, and it was real'. They are convinced that the things people did in the past really happened and that their having happened has played a significant role in shaping the archaeological record that we study. The past therefore had, and in that sense retains, a reality of its own that is independent of the reconstructions and explanations that archaeologists may give of it. Moreover, because the archaeological record, as a product of the past, has been shaped by forces that are independent of our own beliefs, the evidence that it provides at least potentially can act as a constraint upon archaeologists' imaginations. To that extent the study of the past differs from writing a work of fiction. The aim of archaeology can thus be to recover knowledge of what has been forgotten. Yet the crucial questions remain how far we can go in acquiring an objective understanding of the past and how certain we can be of the accuracy of what we believe we know about it, given the propensity of value judgements to colour our interpretations.

In recent years prehistoric archaeology has shifted from a naive positivism to a more far-reaching acceptance of relativism than at any time in the past. After several decades of positivist optimism, a growing number of archaeologists are prepared to believe that they can never achieve an objective historical understanding of the past. Some of the more radical relativists have concluded that because of this they have the right to use archaeological data for any purpose that they wish. They see them as a source of aesthetic pleasure or as providing material for fantasies about the past that offer personal or public satisfaction. This view reduces archaeology to the status of antiquarianism, which treats archaeological data as ends in themselves. There are also those who propose to use archaeological data as propaganda to promote political or social causes, which are usually identified as being of a left-wing or populist variety. Yet the history of archaeology indicates that the political causes that archaeologists have willingly promoted and supported, including Nazism, have as often been harmful to humanity as they have been constructive. Archaeology is currently being used to support some curiously reactionary positions, as evident in the work of Grahame Clark and a few American archaeologists. While some scholars find the intellectual egalitarianism of extreme relativism appealing, it encourages a philosophical nihilism in which not only 'anything goes' but also archaeology can be used to support any cause.

The question that archaeologists face is therefore not whether value judgements influence their interpretations of the past, since they clearly do, but whether they must accept the position of the extreme relativists or whether some containment of this process is possible. Historians of the Ranke school traditionally have drawn a distinction between a relatively stable core of factual data about the past, which is objective and can be expected to expand incrementally as new documents are studied, and the interpretation of these data, which is highly subjective and differs radically from one historian to another. Ranke promoted the view that determining what had really happened in the past was the essence of history and the interpretation of why it had happened little more than an expression of personal opinion. Maurice Mandelbaum (1977), who continues to defend this position, calls this factual core 'history proper'. Yet he has failed to convince philosophers of science that the facts of history are objectively ascertainable. Wylie (1985b: 73) points out that even 'the most straightforward observational experience is actively structured by the observer and acquires significance as evidence . . . only under theory- and "paradigm"-specific interpretation'. In the case of archaeology the situation is even more fraught with difficulties, since, before past human behaviour is explained, it must be inferred from material remains that in turn acquire status as data as a result of theory-influenced and hence at least partly subjective processes of classification. Hence both when classifying material remains and even more when interpreting human behaviour, archaeologists are dealing with something quite different from the objective facts postulated by the Ranke school (Patrik 1985).

Data collection and empirical generalizations

Archaeologists have nevertheless succeeded in creating a large and growing corpus of data and low-level generalizations about the past that over the years has withstood careful scrutiny. Basic to these generalizations are typologies that have been devised for the classification of archaeological finds. It is generally accepted that these typologies are creations of archaeologists rather than reconstructions of categories that were necessarily significant to the makers or users of the material being studied, although claims for such equivalence are sometimes made. These classifications reflect the interests of individual archaeologists in dating, determining the function, and studying the style of archaeological material. Even efforts to classify 'objectively' by searching for 'natural' clusterings of attributes within large data matrices are subjective to the extent that the listing of attributes is based on the archaeologists' knowledge and sense of the significance of the material they are analysing. Yet almost all classifications are seen as revealing non-random patterns of attributes, which in turn provide a test of the usefulness and significance of individual ones.

New classifications are devised as fresh problems arise and old ones are refined and modified over time. Archaeologists in a particular area may vacillate between classifications based on types and on attributes. Serious problems are encountered in the integration of classifications that have been developed by groups of archaeologists working independently of each other in the same region. The classification of artifacts has become more self-conscious as archaeologists have grown more familiar with the evidence of patterning in material culture. A much wider range of artifacts is also being examined than in the past, when pottery and lithics often were the only finds to be studied in detail. One of the clearly positive effects of the structuralist approach is that it calls the attention of archaeologists to many new categories of data about which empirical generalizations can be made. Nevertheless, many classifications have endured over long periods and despite major changes in interpretative fashion. This suggests that they are based to a substantial degree on reasonably objective empirical observations.

Many of the same observations can be made about the delineation of archaeological cultures. Attempts at cultural classification have produced many empirical generalizations about intersite distributions of artifact types that remain valid, even though the understanding of the archaeological culture has altered radically over the years. There have also been, however, what appear to be advances in the understanding of these distributions. So long as archaeologists identified cultures exclusively with ethnic groups there was a tendency to regard the boundaries of both as equivalent and normally clearly demarcated. While these assumptions worked reasonably well with 'tribal' societies, they did not account for the 'openness' of less sedentary hunter-gatherer bands and the cultural differentiation along class lines that characterized hierarchical societies (Trigger 1968a: 16–18). The latter were sometimes conceptualized in terms of separate peasant and elite cultures (Rouse 1965: 9–10). In recent years new notions of material culture as a reflection of various kinds of group interests rather than simply of ethnic identity have encouraged more detailed polythetic analyses of cultural remains (Hodder 1982b), although the techniques for the latter sort of analysis were evolved prior to these new concepts of culture (Clarke 1968).

Over the years great progress has been made in the recovery, identification, and quantification of plant and animal remains, a process much enhanced by the development of flotation as a technique for retrieving data. Trace-element analysis has provided important new information which allows the sources of many materials to be pinpointed and goods that have been exchanged to be distinguished from local copies (for the limitations and complexities of such interpretations, see Gill [1987]). The distributions of various kinds of artifacts are also being plotted in relation to intrasite features with greater regularity. With the help of computers a much broader range of empirical generalizations about many hitherto unstudied or understudied classes of archaeological evidence is now being produced.

Important advances in the dating of archaeological finds also have been made since World War II, largely as a result of the development of physical dating techniques, in particular those employing radiocarbon, thermoluminescence, and potassium-argon ratios. These techniques have revolutionized our understanding of prehistory. Yet this has happened not because these techniques have overturned local relative chronologies based on seriation and stratigraphy but because they have provided new, more reliable, and universally applicable techniques for correlating these sequences with a calendrical chronology, a procedure that in most parts of the world hitherto had been based almost entirely on guesswork. These correlations not only have provided extremely important information about the rates of cultural change in prehistoric times, which archaeologists previously had tended to overestimate, but also have called into question some interregional synchronisms based on typological criteria. While these findings have greatly altered prehistoric chronologies and their accompanying culture-historical interpretations, especially for Europe and North America, the overall effect was less to negate previous relative chronologies for small areas than to add new dimensions to our understanding of them. This too suggests a generally progressive trend in the interpretation of archaeological data.

There is no internal logic that would allow us to predict when new techniques will be introduced. The development of many of them depends upon innovations in the physical and biological sciences and hence upon factors which bear no relationship to archaeology. Yet, once adopted by archaeologists, most technical innovations have spread quickly around the world. The same is true with respect to analytical techniques developed within archaeology, although perhaps to a lesser degree because these are often more culturally specific. This is not to deny that local political and social concerns influence the acceptance and application of new techniques. Long-standing preoccupation with epigraphic, art-historical, and religious subjects has resulted in little interest being shown in the use of scientific techniques to study subsistence patterns in Near Eastern archaeology, which traditionally has been concerned with the historical period and especially with problems relating to biblical history. Yet these techniques are gradually being applied in this area, beginning with the less popular study of prehistoric material (Bar-Yosef and Mazar 1982).

It is also clear that, at least in the short run, progress is not always continuous or irreversible. After 1929 those who shaped the development of Soviet archaeology discouraged an interest in artifact typology and cultural classification on the grounds that 'bourgeois formalism' inhibited a Marxist interpretation of archaeological data. Yet, in recent years, a growing number of Soviet archaeologists have recognized that such studies are essential for developing detailed chronologies and answering cultural-historical problems as an essential preliminary to any behavioural interpretation of prehistory (Bulkin *et al.* 1982). There is currently much interest in the Soviet Union in Clarke's analytical approach to the study of archaeological data (Davis 1983: 418). In Western Europe and North America a growing preoccupation with settlement archaeology and the processual interpretation of archaeological data during the 1950s and 1960s likewise frequently inhibited an interest in formal analyses of archaeological data, even though it is clear that formal comparisons of tool types still have an important role to play in helping to answer questions such as whether there was any historical relationship between the early stages of metallurgy in the Near East and Central Europe (Trigger 1980c; Bradley 1984: 38–40). Yet, while particular techniques and analytical concepts may be ignored temporarily for ideological reasons or because theoretical commitments direct the attention of archaeologists elsewhere, it appears that in the long run methods that are capable of expanding knowledge of the past are adopted by archaeologists wherever they are seen as useful and sufficient resources are available to support them. On these grounds it can be concluded that archaeological methods have long been international in application and cumulative over time. The same can be said of empirical generalizations about patterning in the archaeological record, particularly as they are exhibited in typology and cultural classification.

Internal dialogue

Archaeologists have also made dramatic advances in inferring human behaviour from archaeological data, especially with respect to technology, subsistence, exchange, residence patterns, and some aspects of political organization. This contributes to a more comprehensive and disciplined understanding of what has happened in the past. Many of these advances utilize analytical methods that originate in the physical sciences, such as trace-element analysis to identify the spatial movement of raw materials. Yet Hodder (1984b) has demonstrated that such data are insufficient to reveal the social contexts within which these goods were transported. In cooperation with zoologists, archaeologists have tried through the analysis of the age, size, and sex variations of different animal species to determine how prehistoric herds were managed or what sort of hunting practices were followed. These studies have become of major importance as part of efforts to determine whether early hominids were big-game hunters or merely scavengers (Binford 1984). Likewise the identification of population movements and even patterns of community exogamy relies increasingly on advances in the physical anthropological analysis of human skeletal remains (Kennedy 1981; Molto 1983), while the economic and political interpretation of site distributions employs techniques of spatial analysis that were pioneered in economics and geography (Hodder and Orton 1976).

The behavioural interpretation of archaeological data, whether produced directly by archaeologists or as a result of physical and biological analysis, depends to a considerable degree upon types of research now generally classified as experimental archaeology and ethnoarchaeology. Such research seeks to correlate particular sets of archaeological evidence with specific forms of human behaviour. While both approaches were pioneered by Scandinavian archaeologists in the nineteenth century, they have been greatly elaborated in recent decades. Among the most important consequences of ethnoarchaeological research is a growing understanding of the circumstances under which material remains become incorporated into the archaeological record. If knowing how goods were disposed of does not always permit archaeologists to infer under what circumstances they were made and used, as Schiffer (1976) hoped it would, this knowledge provides archaeologists with a better understanding of the limitations of the archaeological record (von Gernet 1985). In a similar fashion, the study of lithic reduction processes permits archaeologists to infer in what state lithic material was moved from one locale to another and for what purpose it was used in each place (Binford 1983a: 269–86). Likewise, studying where modern hunter–gatherers eat, sleep, process food, and manufacture tools within their camps is seen as helping archaeologists to understand how in Upper Palaeolithic and more recent times hunter–gatherers organized their living space (Binford 1983b: 144–94). Attention is being paid to how experimental and ethnoarchaeological findings can be combined to construct increasingly persuasive algorithms for inferring human behaviour from archaeological data (Tringham 1978).

Archaeologists are also paying increasing attention to understanding the natural processes that play a role in site formation and result in post-depositional alteration of the archaeological record. In East Africa it is important, if archaeologists are to infer early hominid behaviour, to determine what sort of animal bones are present in sites as a result of hominid activity and what sorts were part of the natural background in which Lower Palaeolithic hominids lived. Although archaeologists in the richest and technologically most advanced nations are best equipped to play a leading role in carrying out the detailed research necessary to correlate material remains and human behaviour, advances have been made in many parts of the world and useful findings have spread quickly from one region to another. Hence this aspect of archaeology, like the production of empirical generalizations, is truly international and displays a pattern of growing elaboration.

This internationalism is particularly evident in the convergent trends exhibited by Western and Soviet archaeology since the 1950s, despite their commitment to differing high-level paradigms. From this convergence a number of important lessons can be learned. In the early stages of its development, Soviet archaeology rejected traditional culture-historical approaches and emphasized the interpretation of archaeological data in terms of economic and social behaviour as well as the analysis of social change. Soviet archaeologists pioneered the systematic investigation of settlement archaeology and of modern use-wear analysis. Only recently have they recognized the importance of systematic typology and of processes such as diffusion and migration for explaining the archaeological record. In contrast, since the 1950s, Western archaeologists, who for a long time were concerned almost exclusively with typology, diffusion, and migration as the key elements of the culture-historical approach, have paid growing attention to the societal factors promoting cultural change. Both Soviet and Western archaeologists have displayed a growing interest in ecological interpretations. Each of these elements is of demonstrable importance for achieving a more rounded understanding of the behavioural significance of archaeological data.

It appears that archaeology everywhere has a package of topics that must be investigated if the full range of information about human behaviour is to be extracted from its data. In earlier times, and still today to a lesser extent, different kinds of data are studied selectively by different schools of archaeology. The order in which different modes of analysis are adopted in particular research traditions also seems to be highly variable and to reflect the differing values and political orientations of the various societies to which the archaeologists belong. Yet, as archaeological research develops, it becomes increasingly evident that such selectivity about low- and middle-range theory is unproductive, even if archaeologists disagree about the ultimate use that is to be made of their data. It appears that in the absence of dogmatic ideological controls archaeologists in any particular country eventually will adopt the complete range of analytical concerns, at least so far as these are economically supportable. This suggests the recognition of a corpus of methods for inferring human behaviour in the past that constitutes the ideal, if not the reality, of archaeological research everywhere.

There is also a growing tendency to distinguish the methods and theories that are needed to infer human behaviour from archaeological data from the general theories that are invoked to explain such behaviour. Binford has labelled theoretical propositions of the first sort middle-range theory and argues that it can only be derived by studying the relationship between material culture and human behaviour at the present time. In a similar vein Klejn and some other Soviet archaeologists argue that Marxism, while providing a comprehensive and thoroughly satisfactory explanation of human behaviour and the course of human history, does not supply a methodology for translating archaeological data into information about human behaviour, which in Marxist terms constitutes historical data. They maintain that the archaeological record bears no historical information in a pure form and that the information that it does contain has to be transformed into historical data by following a multi-stage procedure that they call 'theoretical archaeology'. This involves systematically classifying archaeological data and building detailed cultural chronologies, before considering the ethnic, technological, ecological, and social significance of these data, and finally addressing the historical and evolutionary processes that have shaped the archaeological record. Only the latter stage of this process can be equated with historical materialism in the strict sense. The other stages are concerned with overcoming the limitations of archaeological data and using them to create new sources or records in the form of written texts, a major part of which consists of archaeological data interpreted in behavioural terms (Bulkin *et al.* 1982: 284–5). Klejn and his colleagues also imply that, because the operations needed to transform archaeological data into sources of historical and behavioural information are ideologically more neutral than is historical interpretation, it is in this area that Soviet and Western archaeologists can and do cooperate without Soviet ones compromising their ideological integrity. Binford makes similar claims about the ideological neutrality of his middle-range theory, although as a hyper-positivist he would extend these claims to cover general theory also.

It is, however, by no means clear that middle-range efforts to infer human behaviour from archaeological data are wholly or even largely free from the presuppositions that affect general theory and complicate its efforts to explain behaviour. Specific behavioural interpretations frequently turn out to be erroneous or questionable. These problems become especially serious in situations where, because of the complexity of what is being studied, careful arguments linking archaeological data and human behaviour are difficult to develop or apply. Examples are the opposed interpretations of the increasing frequency of high-quality pottery in the Valley of Mexico in late Aztec times as evidence either of state manipulation of the economy or of the success of a free market economy. Binford maintains that this sort of subjectivity can be reduced where well-established middle-range generalizations structure the behavioural interpretation of archaeological data. Yet this approach does not eliminate all possibility of subjective bias.

Some important problems centre on the applicability of uniformitarian principles. Binford (1981: 27–9) has drawn attention to these problems and urged the need to justify the application of middle-range theory to specific archaeological data with warranting arguments, although the nature of these arguments is not specified. While Binford is highly critical of assumptions that the behavioural patterns of early hominids resembled those of modern hunter–gatherers, in work dealing with more recent times his neo-evolutionary faith in strong regularities governing human behaviour leads him to minimize the difficulties involved in interpreting archaeological data. This is evident in his studies of hunter–gatherer use of camp space and hunting territories. Human behaviour is not so regular that convincing generalizations about spatial behaviour can be based upon two or three ethnographic case studies, even if these are very detailed ones. He also does not take account of possible effects of the modern world-system on ethnographic analogies. This has suggested to other archaeologists that the degree of similarity between modern hunter–gatherer societies and Palaeolithic ones is a question for archaeologists to investigate, not something that can be assumed. Finally the Marxist claim that changing modes of production alter human nature, if justified, calls into question the applicability of many generalizations about human behaviour, especially those of a psychological variety. Marxism does not rule out the possibility of human nature, in the sense of some very general, culturally unalterable, species-specific behavioural patterns. Yet it quite properly urges the need for caution in assuming the universality of particular forms of human behaviour. In applying uniformitarian concepts it is essential for archaeologists to try to determine the range of societies to which a particular generalization is applicable. At present, however, doing this remains more art than science.

Yet it is clear that carefully investigated middle-range propositions applied in appropriate cases can help to reduce the subjective elements involved in inferring human behaviour from archaeological data. These propositions do not guarantee interpretations of archaeological evidence against distortions resulting from the interests, values, or fantasies of archaeologists but they do provide a setting in which interpretations are subjected to the maximum degree possible to the constraints imposed by archaeological evidence. Where universal generalizations do not apply, strong arguments are required to demonstrate that correlations between material culture and some culturally specific behavioural pattern or belief are valid. Such demonstrations frequently take the form of the direct historical approach, where evidence of continuity in material culture is seen as justifying the extrapolation of associated aspects of behaviour and beliefs from ethnographic cultures back into prehistoric times. Yet to what extent would it be justified to employ what is known about Chinese scapulimancy in the Shang Dynasty to interpret protohistoric evidence of scapulimancy among the Naskapi of eastern Canada? In part that would depend on what is known about the historical relations between eastern Siberia and North America in terms of scapulimancy and perhaps shamanism in general (Furst 1977; Chang 1983). The use of culturally specific analogies is a field awaiting systematic development and one that is vital if archaeologists are to understand the past in terms of culturally specific as well as general aspects of human behaviour.

Limitations of behavioural inference

We must now consider the limitations of what can be inferred from archaeological evidence concerning prehistoric human behaviour. Archaeologists have long used archaeological data to study technology, subsistence patterns, warfare, and exchange, and since the 1960s they have made significant advances in inferring residence patterns, hierarchical social organization, and some aspects of political organization. To appreciate the progress of archaeology since the 1950s, one has only to compare current inferences about human behaviour in prehistoric times with Childe's gloomy prognostications about what was possible in *The Prehistory of European Society* (1958a), a book written when he fervently wished to learn more about social and political behaviour. Yet surveys of recent advances in archaeology suggest that more progress continues to be made in understanding prehistoric economies than social organization, while relatively few advances have been made in the study of prehistoric ideology. Among the papers dealing with the interpretation of archaeological evidence in the first eight volumes of Schiffer's *Advances in Archaeological Method and Theory* (1978–86) 39 per cent deal with data recovery and chronology, 47 per cent with ecology, demography, and economic behaviour, 8 per cent with social behaviour, and only 6 per cent with ideology, religion, and scientific knowledge. There is also a marked economic bias in recent syntheses of European prehistory (Jarman *et al.* 1982; Dennell 1983; Champion *et al.* 1984; Wells 1984; Barker 1985). This limitation has been repeatedly commented on in recent years and calls have been made to define new and broader goals for archaeology in order to overcome what is seen as the domination of current research by methodological concerns (Moore and Keene 1983).

As early as 1954 Hawkes had postulated that there was an ascending scale of difficulty in interpreting archaeological data in terms of human activities: technology was the easiest category, while economy, social and political organization, and ideology exhibited escalating difficulties. Since then archaeologists have debated whether this hierarchy is inherent in the nature of archaeological data or results from the failure of archaeologists to address relevant interpretative problems. Binford (1972: 93–4) inspired a whole generation of American archaeologists by asserting that it was the result of the methodological shortcomings of archaeologists. He argued that all aspects of sociocultural systems were reflected in the archaeological record. Yet, during the last 25 years, processual archaeologists, including Binford (1978, 1981), have continued to study mainly the lower echelons of Hawkes' hierarchy.

Binford's view of what archaeology can do is linked to his commitment to neo-evolutionism. Neo-evolutionists believe that cultures at the same stage of development have many characteristics in common, especially structural features that have adaptive significance. Only insignificant features, that are mainly stylistic in nature, can profitably be regarded as the random products of historical accidents (Steward 1955). Because of this high level of regularity, it should be relatively easy for archaeologists to formulate a large number of middle-range generalizations that permit them to infer a wide range of human behaviour from archaeological data. Neo-evolutionists also believe, as nineteenth-century unilinear evolutionists did, that, if they can determine what one part of a prehistoric culture, especially its subsistence pattern, was like, they will be able to predict the rest of the system, at least in general terms. These two approaches are seen as constituting an interlocking and mutually verifying methodology for the reconstruction of human behaviour at specific times and places in the past. Yet why have these approaches so far not been more successful in inferring the higher levels of Hawkes' hierarchy?

Childe (1956a: 45–6) argued that it was easier for archaeologists to infer prehistoric technological and economic behaviour on the basis of general principles than it was for them to infer social organization and beliefs because the former are subject to a higher degree of constraint by factors that can be understood in terms of universally applicable natural laws (see also Gallay 1986: 126–37, 182). Archaeologists learn about how artifacts were made through replicative experiments and determine the spread of raw materials by means of trace-element analyses. Likewise, they use principles derived from biology to infer many aspects of subsistence behaviour. On the other hand, the details of kinship organization, political systems, and social values are far more varied and the specific causes of this variability are more difficult to establish. Cultural traditions, which are not insignificant in terms of ecological adaptation, play an especially important role in determining the content of these aspects of culture and they can be altered as a result of cultural contact as well as in response to changing internal factors. Both of these impacts make the content of cultural systems impossible to predict in detail on the basis of general laws alone. Childe (1936: 98) argued that no one could infer the details of British parliamentary government in the nineteenth century from a general understanding of the capitalist mode of production. Although there was a clear connection between the rise of capitalism and the form of power that was exercised in Britain at that time, the development of the British parliament has to be understood in relation to an evolving set of political institutions extending back as far as the medieval period. Problems of equifinality also complicate interpretations as the complexity of behavioural phenomena increases. More recently, detailed ethnoarchaeological studies have been revealing the subtlety and complexity of the correlations between material culture and human behaviour, especially at the social and symbolic levels (Bonnichsen 1973; Hodder 1982b; Hayden and Cannon 1984). It has become evident that in many cases material culture does not reflect human behaviour. Instead the relationship between the two is mediated by conceptual frameworks that often may not be inferable from archaeological data alone. Does this mean, as Hawkes believed, that archaeologists have a far better chance to infer what is generically animal than what is specifically human about prehistoric human behaviour?

Many archaeologists, myself included, believe that the search for sociocultural regularities, of which Binford's middle-range theory is a part, has resulted mainly in the discovery of external constraints on human behaviour. Not surprisingly, many of these are biological, ecological, and technological restrictions acting directly on the economy and social organization. Nevertheless other sorts of constraints have been discovered. General systems theory suggests limitations on the range of variation in social and political structures that do not appear to be of ecological origin, including relations between the multiplication of social units and the elaboration of control hierarchies (G. Johnson 1978, 1981). In general, however, the nature of constraints suggests a model of culture in which lower levels restrict the range of variation possible at still higher ones but do not by themselves determine the forms that higher levels take. This means that, while ecological relations may strongly limit the degree of variation that is possible in economic behaviour, they do not determine all aspects of economic institutions. Likewise the economy may constrain the range of variation in social and political behaviour, and social and political relations may limit the range of variation in religious practices and aesthetics, but neither of these levels is determined wholly by more basic ones. On the contrary, because material constraints are applied less directly, progressively higher levels display an ever larger number of specific features that cannot be accounted for ecologically. Thus, while cultures are influenced by a hierarchy of negative constraints that determine the limits of functional compatibility between levels and hence of their possible variation, each level is semi-autonomous to the extent that all of its properties cannot be derived from those of a lower one (Friedman and Rowlands 1978b: 203). This leaves much scope, especially at the level of social organization and religious beliefs, for other factors, such as cultural traditions and cultural influences of external origin, to play a major role in shaping cultural patterns. It also provides a theoretical basis for Hawkes' hierarchy.

Contextual archaeologists have attempted to counter this model by identifying constraints that apply specifically to the higher levels of Hawkes' hierarchy. These include possible cross-cultural regularities in attitudes towards dirt and correlations between pottery designs and the social status of women (Hodder 1982a: 62–5). Similar efforts have been made in the past to correlate art styles with social organization (J. Fischer 1961) or the psychological characteristics of prehistoric populations (Wallace 1950). It is assumed that the basis for such correlations would be uniformities in human cognitive or psychological processes rather than ecological considerations. Yet so far the search for universal regularities of this sort has not produced substantial results that would be useful for archaeologists. The most important regularities are ones that relate to specific historical traditions and archaeological data pertaining to these traditions appear to be interpreted most effectively by means of some variant of the direct historical approach. This may leave some aspects of the archaeological record eternally beyond the pale of anything more than clever speculation. How can it ever be proved that Leroi-Gourhan was correct, or even moving in the right direction, in associating bison with female principles and horses with male ones in European Palaeolithic cave art? Laming-Emperaire's (1962: 293–4) work did not support the association, while more recent studies of meaning in cave art have offered different, but seemingly equally unprovable, interpretations (Conkey 1982). All of this suggests that, insofar as it refers to the use of universal generalizations, Hawkes' hierarchy of difficulty in archaeological interpretation is essentially correct (Gallay 1986: 154, 182). It also suggests that, because of the lack of deterministic structuring with respect to many aspects of sociocultural phenomena, the capacity of middle-range theory to infer numerous aspects of human behaviour from the archaeological record alone will remain limited.

The achievements of archaeology

In spite of these limitations, archaeologists have been able to infer an increasing range of human behaviour from archaeological data, using either middle-range theory or some variant of the direct historical approach. There is no guarantee that such inferences are not contaminated by subjective factors. Yet the development of new and more rigorous algorithms for inferring behaviour from archaeological data and specifying the appropriateness of ethnographic analogies provides the means for maximizing the constraints of archaeological evidence on such subjective factors. So does the independent utilization of different techniques for inferring the same or closely related behaviour and comparing the results to see whether or not they correspond, as advocated by contextual archaeologists and by anthropologists such as Murdock (1959a). Finally archaeological finds can be corroborated and supplemented by other forms of historical data. If we cannot as archaeologists learn everything about the past, we can at least learn much that is important. To that extent we have proved the accuracy of Daniel Wilson's prediction, when he wrote of his early work on Scottish prehistory: 'We need not despair of learning somewhat of the early Caledonian, of his habits, his thoughts, and even of his faith, when we are able to refer to so many specimens of his handiwork and inventive design' (1863, 1: 486).

There is also good reason to believe that archaeological findings about what human beings have done in the past have irreversibly altered our understanding of human origins and development, at least for those who are prepared to abide by scientific canons of reasoning. Prior to the nineteenth century, evolutionary schemes of human development were seriously entertained alongside creationist views and various cyclical speculations. Each of these was a possible description of human history but there was no scientific evidence that would allow scholars to determine which of these theories offered the best explanation of human origins. Since that time archaeological data have presented solid evidence which indicates that human beings evolved from higher primate stock, most likely in Africa. There is considerable disagreement about the significance of morphological variations among early hominids and which of them were the direct ancestors of modern human beings. Yet it is clear that throughout most of their history human beings and their hominid ancestors subsisted by eating wild plants and animals. By late Lower Palaeolithic times hominids had spread from tropical regions at least into colder temperate climates and by the Middle and Upper Palaeolithic periods some human beings had adapted to living in periglacial conditions. Prior to 40,000 years ago humans had made their way across a narrow stretch of ocean into Australia–New Guinea and by 11,000 years ago they had spread throughout the New World from Bering Strait to Tierra del Fuego. By the end of the last Ice Age, if not earlier, denser and more sedentary collecting populations had developed in richer natural environments in many parts of the world. Food collecting was supplemented by food production, which gradually became the principal source of nourishment in many parts of the Old and New Worlds. There is no suggestion of a historical connection between major zones where plant and animal domestication occurred and steadily growing evidence of continuities within various regions suggests that this was a process that happened independently in many places. The same can be said about the first civilizations, which evolved as some tribal agricultural societies were transformed into hierarchical, class-based ones, dominated by a small elite who used part of the surplus wealth they controlled to produce monumental architecture and works of art that served as status symbols.

It is also clear that many societies did not advance through this sequence. Some remained at the hunter–gatherer stage into modern times, while occasionally agricultural or pastoral societies adopted hunter–gatherer economies. As some cultures grew more complex, relations between neighbouring societies of differing sizes and often with dissimilar economies became more common. Under certain ecological conditions more complex societies were able to dominate and exploit their less evolved neighbours, but in other situations pastoral or swidden agricultural societies maintained their autonomy into modern times.

Historians and social scientists from Arnold Toynbee to Julian Steward have also considered the role played in human history by cyclical processes, such as the rise and fall of civilizations. These questions are notoriously difficult to deal with because of ambiguities in defining the units involved. There is no basis for believing that developmental processes, analogous to the childhood, maturity, and senility of individuals, repeat themselves, especially with respect to societies at different stages of development. On the other hand, the repeated consolidation and disintegration of dynastic power is a widespread phenomenon that is clearly marked in the archaeological record (Steward 1955: 196–206). The duration of these cycles varies greatly from one culture and one period to another even in societies that are judged to be at the same level of sociocultural development, which suggests a complex causality. Such cyclical patterning is worthy of careful study.

While much remains to be learned about the timing and precise nature of cultural stability and change in various parts of the world in prehistoric times, the general picture outlined above is sustained by an immense corpus of evidence collected and analysed by archaeologists. This does not mean that in the future archaeologists may not discover earlier intensive collecting or agricultural societies than those presently known, new civilizations, or even unsuspected connections between different parts of the world. Yet for over a century the general picture of what happened in prehistoric times that results from archaeological discoveries has been refined rather than overturned. The same cannot be said of explanations of why these things happened. Moreover, while the broad outline of prehistory presented in modern textbooks may not differ enormously from some of the speculative evolutionary reconstructions of the nineteenth or even the eighteenth centuries, it does differ in being based on archaeological evidence that is replete with circumstantial detail, both about the nature of individual cultures and about specific sequences of change. These data elaborate what is known about both the particular courses and the general pattern of prehistory.

This does not mean that every specific interpretation of archaeological data is correct. In recent years Binford (1981, 1984; Binford and Stone 1986) has used a combination of taphonomic evidence and knowledge of site-formation processes to call into question a whole series of long-accepted claims about early hominid behaviour. He shows the insubstantial nature of the evidence that big-game animals were hunted at Torralba in Spain and at many other Lower Palaeolithic sites. He also questions the evidence for cannibalism and possibly the use of fire in the Lower Palaeolithic levels at Zhoukoudian and has drawn attention to other studies that have concluded that the alleged traces of Mousterian bear cults in Central European caves can be accounted for as products of natural processes. Whatever the outcome of these debates, Binford has demonstrated that archaeologists frequently make inadequately supported claims about the behavioural significance of the archaeological record and thus promote unsubstantiated views of prehistoric human behaviour (Binford 1981: 293). Nor, in these instances, are the issues only of local or minor significance, since he is suggesting that human beings may have been scavengers rather than big-game hunters through most of the Palaeolithic period.

Yet, while Binford complains about the lack of self-correcting mechanisms in interpreting archaeological data, his questions about the behavioural significance of Palaeolithic sites will generate more middle-range investigations and the search for new and more conclusive evidence, as contending parties seek to resolve the problems he has raised. In a recent survey of late nineteenth- and early twentieth-century controversies about the status of eoliths, Grayson (1986) concludes that such debates and the techniques for resolving them are a long-established aspect of archaeology. The conscious use of experiments and scientific observations to resolve problems of archaeological interpretation can be traced back to the Scandinavian archaeologists of the early nineteenth century and to British archaeologists who were influenced by the experimental approach of the Royal Society of London 100 years earlier.

Our understanding of other aspects of prehistory has been altered significantly as a result of changing ethnographic knowledge. Traditionally evolutionary ethnologists have distinguished between hunter–gatherer bands and agricultural tribes. In recent years it has become evident that the more sedentary collecting societies, such as those that were encountered on the west coast of Canada in the nineteenth century, have more in common, demographically and in terms of social and political organization, with sedentary tribal agricultural societies than they do with big-game hunters (Testart 1982; Price and Brown 1985). This observation has provided a new basis for interpreting the evidence concerning 'Mesolithic' societies in the Old World and 'Archaic' ones in the Americas, which in the past seemed anomalous and difficult to understand. On other occasions new insights came about as a result of archaeological discoveries. Michael Coe's demonstration that the Olmec civilization, which flourished along the Gulf coast of Mexico, dated to the first millennium B.C. called into question the long-held belief that early civilizations developed only in arid regions where irrigation was necessary for agriculture (Coe and Diehl 1980). Since then it has become increasingly obvious that, because of poor preservation and difficulties of research, tropical-forest regions are poorly represented in studies of the development of civilization. Coe's discovery also called into question certain high-level evolutionary theories that had attempted to explain the origin of complex societies (Sanders and Price 1968).

This indicates that erroneous interpretations of what happened in the past can be detected as a result of the discovery of new archaeological evidence, which contradicts previous conclusions; an awareness of new theories of human behaviour, which provide fresh insights into the meaning of archaeological data; and the development of middle-range theory. The deliberate construction and testing of two or more mutually exclusive interpretations of data can enhance this process, a point noted long ago by archaeologists but largely lost sight of as a result of processual archaeology's insistence on the importance of deductive explanations. In combination these procedures increase the capacity for the constraints that are inherent in the evidence to counteract the role played by subjective elements in interpreting archaeological data. All but the most fanatical relativists will see the results of such a process of critical comparison and reinterpretation tending in the direction of a more objective understanding of the behavioural significance of archaeological data.

External dialogue

Explaining why things have happened takes archaeologists beyond their own discipline and compels them to invoke a broad spectrum of social-science theory in an effort to account for the behavioural patterns they have inferred from archaeological data. Yet even those social scientists who can observe human behaviour directly are unable to agree about why people behave as they do, why cultural change occurs, or what is the overall meaning of history. Instead we find both subtly and radically different explanations competing with one another with respect to almost every aspect of human behaviour, with no evidence that one general theory is about to prevail over another. There are many reasons for this. The complexity of factors at work in concrete situations may be consistent with more than one causal theory, allowing individual interpretations of specific situations to diverge significantly (Wylie 1985b: 77). The factors shaping such situations may be sufficiently numerous that it means little to conceive of single ones as exerting a determining influence. The role that individual factors play also may vary according to the variety or strength of those that are involved in a particular situation. Flannery (1972) clearly had this in mind when he argued the futility of trying to explain the origin of complex societies by searching for regularities in the factors that had led to their development. It is also clear that in complex situations of this sort the values and preconceptions of the analyst are relatively free to influence the interpretations of archaeological evidence. These subjective influences may vary from archaeologists trying to project their own ideals of society into the past, as Arthur Evans may have done with his reconstructions of Minoan Crete (Bintliff 1984; Wood 1985), to the vast ideological gap that separates the elitist view of human history recently expounded by Grahame Clark (1983, 1986) from Childe's interpretation of the baleful effects of class exploitation on the technological development and quality of life in the early civilizations. Yet if archaeologists often cannot provide conclusive explanations for events that are clearly documented in the archaeological record, their shortcomings in this respect are no greater than those of other social scientists, who are equally unable to agree about why things happen.

Two sets of factors alter general views of human behaviour. The first is changing social and political circumstances, such as led to the temporary abandonment of racist, and even biological, interpretations of human behaviour throughout the Western countries as a consequence of the defeat of Nazism. At one level this can be interpreted as a more or less wholly subjective process. Yet, inasmuch as beliefs inspire action, they have some selective value in terms of their ability to promote or threaten the survival of the societies that hold them. They must therefore evolve in the direction of a more objective understanding of human behaviour if technologically advanced societies are to survive and flourish (McNeill 1986: 20–1). Even if what is known about the great capacity of scientific and religious interpretations of human behaviour to disguise self-interest as altruism does not inspire any great faith in the automatic ability of an evolving understanding of human behaviour to save humanity, the basic point – that ideas have selective value – remains valid. Because of that, in the long run general views about human behaviour may be subjected to selective modification, rather than changing in a purely random fashion or for entirely idiosyncratic reasons.

The second set of factors that all but hyper-relativists agree can alter interpretations of human behaviour is new factual evidence. By their very nature, general theories of human behaviour are unlikely to be refuted by any one scientific observation. Yet, even at this level, the constraints of cumulative evidence, including that provided by archaeology, have allowed some progress to be made in the general understanding of human behaviour. As a result of over a century of research and interpretations that have vacillated from one extreme to another, it now seems to be accepted that the radical claims of both historical particularism and unilinear evolutionism are no longer credible. More order is observable in cross-cultural perspective than would be the case if each culture were the product of purely fortuitous circumstances. Yet there is sufficient diversity to rule out any simple, strongly deterministic causality (Trigger 1982a). To be sure, individual archaeologists continue to differ about where they stand between these two extremes. Binford upholds a neo-evolutionary faith in the regularity of human behaviour and Dunnell (in Rindos 1984: ix) looks forward to scientific evolution and its uniformities 'returning to center stage'. On the other hand, Hodder's thinking sometimes, but not always, tends in the direction of Boasian particularism. Yet even these positions are considerably more moderate than were the extremes of the 1950s.

Archaeologists remain unable to distinguish, except on the basis of historical and archaeological evidence, between cultural similarities that arise as a result of independent development (analogies) and those that occur as a result of historical connections (homologies) (Binford 1968b: 8–12). Individual features shared by circumpolar hunter–gatherer cultures cannot be assumed to result from independent adaptation to a common environment unless it can be empirically ruled out that they can be traced back to a common origin or have come to be shared as a result of diffusion. Yet parallels in the development of complex societies in distant parts of the world, during periods when cultural connections between these regions appear to have been extremely limited or non-existent, as well as in relationships between neighbouring societies at different levels of development in many parts of the world, suggest cross-cultural regularities that no explanation of human history or behaviour can afford to ignore. On the other hand, it has also become clear, through the study of archaeological as well as ethnographic data, that there are important variations in social organization and cultural patterns among societies at the same level of development in different parts of the world that cannot be accounted for in terms of neo-evolutionary theory. Both historical traditions and diffusion clearly play a role in shaping not only stylistic factors but also significant aspects of economic, social, and political behaviour.

These observations suggest that cultures are not as tightly integrated as evolutionists have believed, in the sense that particular changes in one aspect of a culture are likely to bring about predictable changes in other aspects. Nor does it appear that any one part of the cultural system plays an overwhelmingly predominant role in shaping the whole, contrary to what ecological and technological determinists have claimed. If either of these propositions were true, there would be significantly less cultural variation than can be observed at a single point in time in the ethnographic record or over long periods of time archaeologically.

This does not rule out a materialist approach to the understanding of human history. It appears in keeping with what we know about biological evolution and human origins to assume that social existence has always played a primary role in shaping human consciousness and that the mode of production strongly influences the general character of the social, political, and intellectual processes of life, provided that it is understood that this signifies that the economic base (broadly defined) limits the possibility of variation in other aspects of human behaviour rather than dictates what the nature of that behaviour will be. There is also no reason to deny the reciprocal influence of the superstructure on the base, although the precise nature and extent of this influence remains to be defined and it may vary widely from one society to another. Childe, in particular, has viewed political power and religious beliefs as forces capable of successfully opposing but not initiating major cultural transformations. Finally, a truly materialist approach embraces rather than denies the view that human beings react not to the world as it is but as they perceive it to be, since this incorporates mental phenomena into a materialist framework. This has encouraged Marxism to account for cultural change as the result of a dialectical process involving individual and group interests rather than trying to explain it solely in terms of external constraints of the sort proposed by cultural ecology or systems theory. Yet there clearly is no consensus about these issues nor are there sufficiently strong arguments to narrow the broad spectrum of passionately held opinions that individual social scientists are prepared to defend concerning the forces that shape human history. Many archaeologists, including some who claim to be Marxists, adhere to an idealist position that assigns primary importance to religious beliefs and other ideological factors as the basic forces shaping cultural change.

There is nevertheless reason to believe that in the long run the continuing collection and analysis of archaeological data will result in a better understanding of human behaviour and of the forces that have shaped human history. Evidence is provided by the growing confidence with which archaeologists are able to distinguish between their own varied explanations of what has happened in prehistoric times and alternative popular beliefs for which there is not a scientifically acceptable factual basis (J. White 1974). These popular beliefs attest to the ideological importance of what archaeologists are studying and even more significantly to the growing inability of archaeologists who adhere to even a modicum of scientific method to satisfy certain popular needs. One example is the persistent and widespread resistance to the idea that more advanced cultures have developed as a result of internal processes that can be understood in scientific terms. In the eighteenth and nineteenth centuries some writers sought to support what they saw as the literal truth of biblical accounts by arguing that human beings had originated in the Near East and that primitive cultures had come into existence as a result of degeneration as humanity spread from its place of origin and divine instruction. Some less biblically influenced speculations sought to trace the origin of known civilizations back to mysterious beginnings on lost continents, such as Atlantis and Mu, while in the early twentieth century hyper-diffusionists derived agriculture and civilization from Egypt or Mesopotamia, where they were alleged to have evolved as the result of a historical accident. In recent years, faced with a growing threat of nuclear annihilation, increasing numbers of insecure and secularly oriented members of the educated middle classes have taken comfort in the belief that intelligent beings from another planet have been benevolently guiding human development and will save humanity, or some chosen remnant of it, from an apocalyptic catastrophe (J. Cole 1980; Feder 1984; Eve and Harrold 1986). These extraterrestrial salvationists look to archaeology to provide evidence of interplanetary contacts that will support their arguments, in much the same manner as evolutionists looked to it for support a century ago.

In the eighteenth century, when knowledge of the archaeological record was almost non-existent, degenerationist and evolutionary views stood on an equal footing, both being based on nothing more than speculation about how human societies might have come into being. Under these circumstances, it is not extraordinary that a scholar such as William Stukeley, who was capable of carrying out sound antiquarian research, should have been attracted to what we now regard as the extravagant fantasies of the degenerationist school. Even in the late nineteenth century, a careful scientist such as John William Dawson could cogently object that the archaeological record had been studied in too few parts of the world and that even Western European finds were too little known to be sure that more advanced cultures had not existed alongside Palaeolithic ones throughout human history. In North America, alleged Palaeolithic finds indeed turned out to be the quarry refuse of later, more advanced cultures. Ignoring Dawson's claims was an expression of faith in cultural-evolutionary theories or in the value of limited positive evidence over undiscovered alternatives; it was not a triumph of science. By the 1920s the hyper-diffusionist view of human history, although promoted by reputable ethnologists and physical anthropologists, was overwhelmingly rejected by archaeologists because it did not correspond with the archaeological record as it was by then understood for various parts of the world. Hyper-diffusionist influences were limited to explaining restricted archaeological phenomena, such as the megalithic monuments of Western Europe.

Extraterrestrial salvationism was born and remains an amateur fad with semi-religious connotations. Its always tentative explanations of isolated archaeological finds do not provide a satisfactory alternative interpretation of the archaeological record (von Daniken 1969, 1971). Extreme relativists, such as Barnes and Feyerabend, may argue that the views of the past held by professional archaeologists and extraterrestrial salvationists are cultural alternatives and that philosophers and historians of science have no basis for distinguishing between them in terms of their correctness or scientific status. Archaeologists cannot rule out the possibility that extraterrestrial visitors have influenced the course of human development to some degree, any more than they can exclude the biological existence of purple unicorns. Yet, clumsy, inadequate, and uncertain as our present scientific understandings of cultural change may be, they account for what is observed in the archaeological record in both its totality and individual features, while extraterrestrial salvationism keeps alive only by making speculative and always inconclusive claims about isolated phenomena. It is surely folly, given the available evidence, to claim 'symmetrical' status for these two approaches.

Archaeology has also demonstrated the capacity to entertain multiple working hypotheses and to alter its interpretations in order to account better for growing bodies of archaeological data (Gallay 1986: 288–95). In the early part of the twentieth century, diffusion was invoked to explain evidence of changes in the archaeological record that did not accord with earlier racist views that North American Indians were incapable of cultural change. Yet diffusion by itself continued to imply a certain lack of creativity. The New Archaeology not only accounted for internal changes in archaeological cultures that were becoming increasingly evident as more detailed archaeological research was carried out, but, in order to explain these changes, was led to invoke internal responses that unselfconsciously eliminated the last vestiges of the view that native North Americans were inherently less creative than were Europeans. The influence of less hostile public stereotypes of native people in bringing about these changes should not be underestimated, but neither should the constraint of the archaeological record. Once again, it is the amateur fringe that continues to explain the prehistory of North America in terms of Libyan, Carthaginian, Scandinavian, Black African, and Asian visitors and thus denigrates, we trust unwittingly, native peoples by attributing major elements of their cultural heritage to others (Fell 1976, 1982; for an anthropological explanation of the material referred to in the second book, see Vastokas and Vastokas 1973). In doing so these amateurs rely exclusively on diffusionist canons of archaeological interpretation that long ago were discovered to be inadequate by professional archaeologists. Archaeologists do not deny the importance of diffusion. Nor do they deny that some pastoralists and agriculturalists have become hunter–gatherers in the course of human history. Yet these happenings are now viewed in a broader context, in which other processes, such as ecological adaptation and internal cultural change, are occurring. Simultaneously, an increasingly detailed archaeological record offers growing resistance to faddish and unbalanced explanations of what happened in the past.

Future prospects

Subjective factors clearly influence the interpretation of archaeological data at every level. They are not merely a visible contaminant that can be removed by a commitment to some allegedly morally neutral code of science and more specifically by proper procedures for testing hypotheses, as the more ardent positivists suggest. They sometimes function as a creative element in archaeology insofar as they serve as a major spur to research. Kossinna's commitment to a romantic and highly misleading belief in German ethnic and racial superiority led him to devise new ways of studying significant spatial patterning in archaeological data that archaeologists with very different personal commitments have continued to find useful. On the other hand less creative cycles can be observed in which, at least partially in response to changing social, political, and economic conditions, archaeologists have swung between extreme evolutionary and culture-historical perspectives and between positions that have either emphasized the biological basis of human behaviour or totally ignored it (Cartmill *et al.* 1986).

Yet, if subjective factors intervene at every level in the interpretation of the past, so too does archaeological evidence, which, at least within the bounds of a commitment to scientific methodology, partially constrains and limits what it is possible to believe about the past. Contrary to what some innovators allege, in their desire to portray all previous phases in the development of archaeology as primitive and unstructured, archaeologists have not been unaware of the continuing need to question accepted interpretations of archaeological data. Nor have they failed to utilize new evidence in an attempt to gain a more objective understanding of the past. Since at least the eighteenth century they have sought to devise tests that relate to the behavioural significance of archaeological data. These include replicative experiments, use-wear analysis, and experiments to see whether supposed 'artifacts' are the products of human action, animal activity, or natural forces. Attempts have also been made to assess the validity of ethnographic analogies, although this process has been made especially difficult by the problems involved in distinguishing between cultural analogies and homologies. For as long as this sort of verification has been attempted, archaeologists have engaged in scientific studies.

Accompanying such activities, however, there is always a temptation to leap to conclusions in the absence either of sufficient data or of adequate analysis and proper methods of interpretation. This occurs at every level of archaeological research, although it is perhaps at the highest level, the explanation of behaviour, that the most daring leaps are made. Many archaeologists are eager to draw far-reaching conclusions about the past from their findings even if this requires them to read specific forms of behaviour into their data without adequate linking arguments and to make use of poorly tested explanations of human behaviour. Particularly if interpretations correspond with common sense and the values held by the investigator, archaeologists may be quite unaware of the inadequacies of their work. In the past toleration for this type of laxness resulted to a large degree from a smaller number of researchers trying to cope with large and intractable problems. In pioneer efforts to collect data and reconstruct a broad picture of the past many of the niceties of archaeological research were ignored. This uncontrolled situation allowed interpretations of archaeological data to survive even though their theoretical or factual basis had been discredited. Examples of this are the diffusionist efforts of European archaeologists to locate the origins of culture in the Near East long after the medieval world view was abandoned and the slowness of American archaeologists to see evidence of change in the archaeological record as a refutation of static stereotypes about the North American Indians. Yet the recent trend to examine alternative explanations of the same data and to develop formal arguments in support of these interpretations represents an elaboration, rather than a transcending, of the highest ideals of earlier research. While it is unlikely that scientific procedures can ever wholly eliminate subjective factors from the interpretation of archaeological data, they can significantly enhance the constraints that archaeological evidence exerts upon these interpretations.

Archaeology is best able to contribute to a general understanding of human behaviour in terms of the information that it provides about changes that occur over longer periods of time and which therefore cannot be studied using contemporary social-science data. This temporal perspective compensates to a considerable degree for lack of direct information about perceptions and intentions, which, in the absence of other sources of information about culturally specific aspects of the past, largely reduces archaeology to considering constraints on human behaviour. High-level theories of human behaviour are said to be incapable of direct refutation. Yet, by comparing different archaeological sequences and trying to understand them as evidence of societies changing over time, archaeology discovers diachronic regularities that are significant for evaluating high-level theories. The successful pursuit of such understanding requires not only that care be paid to inferring behaviour from archaeological data but also the elaboration of ever more detailed chronologies. This takes archaeologists back to the first problem that was addressed by their discipline and which it can never outgrow. Only insofar as archaeologists understand the order in which cultural factors change, do they have a basis for beginning to understand the causal relations linking them (Wylie 1985b: 77–8).

To some degree general, or high-level, theories are like languages. It is theoretically possible to express any idea in any language, although the difficulty with which a particular concept may be conveyed will vary greatly from one language to another, depending on the context of its lexicon. Moreover, a message can depart only a short distance from conventional understandings and established norms before it loses intelligibility and relevance to the receiver, however capable a language may be of transmitting the ideas through periphrases and detailed explanations. In the same manner, the difficulty of conceiving of a satisfactory explanation for a particular form of human behaviour will vary according to the general theory that is espoused. In due course growing problems in using a particular general theory to explain human behaviour may lead social scientists, including archaeologists, to abandon that theory on the grounds that it is inefficient by comparison with some alternative one. In this way the constraints of evidence can exert a selective influence over general theories. On the other hand, subjective factors may lead social scientists to continue using a particular high-level theory long after its inefficiency has been demonstrated. Such theories are often modified and upgraded to try to adapt them to new circumstances. Only rarely are high-level theories definitively abandoned.

Yet it is a matter of record that the views of modern societies about how they came into being and change are radically different, not only from the divinely ordered world of the ancient Sumerian scribes but also from the creationist views that predominated in Western society 200 years ago. The findings of archaeology, however subjectively interpreted, have altered humanity's perception of its history, its relationship to nature, and its own nature in ways that are irreversible without the total abandonment of the scientific method. Archaeology is itself a product of social and economic change, but what it has led us to believe about the past is more than a fanciful projection of contemporary social concerns into the past. It is neither separate from society nor a mere reflection of it, but has a role to play in a rational dialogue about the nature of humanity, which a better understanding of the relationship between archaeological practice and its social context will facilitate. By helping to expand our temporal and spatial frames of reference, archaeology has irreversibly altered 'the range and quality of human thought' (Becker 1938: 25).

The fact that archaeology can provide a growing number of insights into what has happened in the past suggests that it may constitute an increasingly effective basis for understanding social change. That in turn indicates that in due course it may also serve as a guide for future development, not in the sense of providing technocratic knowledge to social planners but by helping people to make more informed choices with respect to public policy. In a world that has become too dangerous for humanity to rely on trial and error, archaeologically derived knowledge may even be important for human survival. If archaeology is to serve that purpose, archaeologists must strive against heavy odds to see the past as it was, not as they wish it to have been.

BIBLIOGRAPHICAL ESSAY

The relevance of archaeological history

A chronicle and critique of the historiography of archaeology is presented in Trigger (1985a). The various orientations that have been adopted are surveyed in chapter one of the present volume.

Some of the first histories of archaeology were written either to expose the inadequacies of previous work (Haven 1856) or to popularize new trends (Morlot 1861; reprinted in Trigger 1986a). Most of the early histories were, however, chronicles of archaeological discovery that explained by whom and under what circumstances the most dramatic archaeological finds had been made. One of the most popular and enduring of these works is Ceram[Kurt Marek]'s *Gods, Graves, and Scholars* (1951). The continuing popularity of this genre is indicated by Fagan's best-selling *The Rape of the Nile* (1975); his *Elusive Treasure* (1977), dealing with New World archaeology; Lloyd's *Foundations in the Dust* (1947, 2nd edn 1981); and Bacon's *The Great Archaeologists* (1976). In these books there are few, if any, references to the work of archaeologists such as Gordon Childe or Grahame Clark, who, although they made no spectacular discoveries of archaeological data, have played a major role in shaping a professional understanding of how archaeological data should be interpreted.

A smaller, but now rapidly increasing, number of works have attempted to investigate the intellectual development of archaeology, an effort encouraged but little participated in by Crawford (1932) and Childe (1955). The first major pioneering study was Casson's *The Discovery of Man* (1939). Brief sketches of the early development of prehistoric archaeology that were written about this time include Shorr (1935), Peake (1940), and Childe (1953). A second milestone was Daniel's *A Hundred Years of Archaeology* (1950; 2nd edn. 1975), which traced the development of archaeology in Britain and Western Europe and, together with his earlier study *The Three Ages* (1943), set a new standard for investigating the history of archaeology and the development of archaeological concepts. Daniel (1963a, 1981a, and many other works) continued to write about the development of Western European archaeology until his death in 1986. His first book was followed by M. Miller's (1956) polemical history of Russian and Soviet archaeology, Bibby's *The Testimony of the Spade* (1956), also dealing with the history of European archaeology, and Laming-Emperaire's *Origines de l'archéologie préhistorique en France* (1964). Daniel promoted the writing of a number of regional and national histories of archaeology: Willey and Sabloff's *A History of American Archaeology* (1974), now in a second edition (1980), Klindt-Jensen's *A History of Scandinavian Archaeology* (1975), and Bernal's *A History of Mexican Archaeology* (1980). The periodization employed by Willey and Sabloff was partly suggested by Schwartz's *Conceptions of Kentucky Prehistory* (1967). In 1973 Fitting published a multi-authored study of the history of archaeology in different regions of North America, which, together with many papers in Watson (1985), can be profitably read alongside Willey and Sabloff's more general study. Sklenář (1983) has published a history of archaeological research and interpretation in Central Europe.

The study of national histories of archaeology on a world-wide basis was encouraged by an International Conference on the History of Archaeology held under the sponsorship of the International Union of Prehistoric and Protohistoric Sciences at Aarhus in 1978 (Daniel 1981b). This work was further promoted in a set of fourteen papers published in *World Archaeology* (Trigger and Glover 1981, 1982) and by J. D. Evans *et al.* (1981: 11–70). These publications indicated the importance of broader perspectives for evaluating past as well as current trends in archaeological interpretation. Guidi (1988) provides a valuable survey of the world-wide history of archaeology, with special sections dealing with the history of Italian archaeology.

Various works have attempted to study in detail the development of thought about specific archaeological problems. Silverberg (1968) has documented the history of speculation about the Moundbuilders in the United States, while Piggott (1968) has studied the impact on archaeology of speculations about the druids, and Gräslund (1974, 1976, 1987) has analysed the role played by typology in the early development of Scandinavian archaeology. McKusick (1970) traced the history of a celebrated conflict between national and regional institutions in the United States about the authenticity of some finds made in the nineteenth century; Grayson (1983) has examined in detail the key debates concerning human antiquity in Europe; Meltzer (1983) has clarified the nature of nineteenth-century controversies about the earliest human inhabitants of the New World; Chippindale (1983) has examined changing interpretations of Stonehenge; and Patterson (1986a) has documented how political factors have influenced archaeological research in the

United States. Piggott (1976), Trigger (1978a), and Hudson (1981) have published collections of essays dealing with the history of archaeology in Europe and America.

In recent years there has been a growing emphasis on biographies as an instrument for studying the development of archaeological interpretation. This technique was pioneered in Piggott's (1950) *William Stukeley*. Recent studies of early figures in the history of archaeology include Brongers' (1973) analysis of the work of the Dutch antiquarian C. J. C. Reuvens, Woodbury (1973) on Alfred Kidder, Marsden (1974) on early English barrow diggers, R. H. Cunnington (1975) and Woodbridge (1970) on William Cunnington and Richard Colt Hoare, Hunter (1975) on John Aubrey, M. Thompson (1977) on Pitt-Rivers, and Drower (1985) on Petrie. While most of these studies were written by archaeologists, Killan's (1983) splendid biography of the nineteenth-century Canadian archaeologist David Boyle is by a professional historian. Three books on the life and work of Gordon Childe (McNairn 1980, Trigger 1980a, S. Green 1981), as well as numerous papers (see chapter 5, above), reflect the enormous interest in this archaeologist. Willey (1974a) has edited a valuable set of self-critical reflections by senior archaeologists, a practice continued by Daniel with invited pieces in *Antiquity* and by Robertshaw in his history of African archaeology (1988). MacNeish (1978) and Caton Thompson (1983) have published perceptive intellectual (and in Caton Thompson's case also personal) autobiographies. M. Ash is currently at work on a book-length biography of Daniel Wilson. Some other biographies, such as J. Hawkes' (1982) on Wheeler, and autobiographies (M. Leakey 1984; Daniel 1986) are primarily of personal interest.

A relatively neglected topic is the history of archaeological institutions. Major contributions to this field are Joan Evans' (1956) history of the Society of Antiquaries of London, a collection of papers edited by Bell (1981) dealing mainly with the Society of Antiquaries of Scotland, and Hinsley's (1981) magisterial account of the anthropological work of the Smithsonian Institution prior to 1910. Piggott (1976) examines the emergence of county archaeological societies in Britain in the context of the railway age and the Industrial Revolution.

Brongers (1976) has published the material for a systematic treatment of the history of archaeology in the Netherlands, in the form of a chronologically arranged bibliography. While not a history of thought, this technical report suggests how more rigorous historiography might improve the writing of the history of archaeology. An increasing number of studies employ quantitative techniques developed by historians of science. These include the thematic analysis of papers appearing in archaeological journals (Zubrow 1972, 1980) and the use of citation analysis to establish chains of influence (Sterud 1978). Such painstaking approaches, when prudently applied, permit more rigorous historical analysis than has been common in past histories of archaeology.

Anthologies of historically significant archaeological publications are also of value for those interested in the history of archaeology. Popular collections include J. Hawkes (1963) and, on the New World, Deuel (1967). Heizer (1959) provides a set of outstanding papers of methodological importance. Anthologies dealing with major interpretative issues are Heizer (1962a) and Daniel (1967). Larsen (1985) presents papers dealing with 'Palaeolithic' cultures in North America written in the nineteenth century and Trigger (1986a) a collection dealing with North American studies of coastal shell mounds from the same period. DePratter (1986) has edited an impressive collection of papers relating to the archaeology of the southeastern United States written between 1788 and the present. More regional anthologies of papers dealing with the archaeological study of North America are found in other volumes of *The North American Indian* series, edited by D. H. Thomas and published by Garland Publishing.

Recent studies of the development of anthropology, with the main or sole emphasis on ethnology or social anthropology, are by Harris (1968), Voget (1975), Honigmann (1976), and Evans-Pritchard (1981). Hodgen (1964) and Slotkin (1965) examine the early development of anthropology, the latter with reference to a large number of reprinted texts. Stocking's (1982) essays survey important themes relating to the general development of anthropology, as do his recent study of Victorian anthropology (1987) and his annually published series *History of Anthropology* (Stocking 1983–). Major works examining the development of history as a discipline include H. Barnes (1937), Shotwell (1939), Fitzsimons *et al.* (1954), Gooch (1959), Barraclough (1979), Hexter (1979), Braudel (1980), Breisach (1983), Kenyon (1983), and Levine (1986).

General studies of the nature of scientific analysis that have relevance for discussions of the development of archaeology include Braithwaite (1953), Popper (1959, 1963), Nagel (1961), Kuhn (1962), Smart (1963), Kaplan (1964), Hempel (1965, 1966), W. Salmon (1967, 1984; W. Salmon *et al.* 1971), Meehan (1968), Hesse (1974), and Berstein (1983). Among the major works dealing with problems of historical interpretation, the following have been of special interest to archaeologists: Collingwood (1946, see also 1939), Gardiner (1952, 1974), Dray (1957, 1964), Danto (1965), E. Carr (1967), Walsh (1967), Elton (1969), D. Fischer (1970), C.

Morgan (1973, 1978), McClelland (1975), R. Martin (1977), and Atkinson (1978).

Petrie's *Methods and Aims in Archaeology* (1904), despite its title, discussed methodological problems only. G. Clark (1939), W. Taylor (1948), and Childe (1956a) discussed methodology and the general goals of archaeological research. The positivist concept of processual archaeology is expounded in S. Binford and L. Binford (1968), Clarke (1968), Watson *et al.* (1971, 1984), Schiffer (1976), and anthologies of papers by L. Binford (1972, 1983a), Clarke (1979), and Renfrew (1979, 1984). More recent works questioning or rejecting various aspects of processual archaeology include Gardin (1980), Hodder (1982a), M. Salmon (1982), Gibbon (1984), and Gallay (1986). A complete bibliography of works dealing with archaeological theory published since 1960 would run into many thousands of entries.

In recent years there has been growing interest in how the past and its physical remains are perceived and responded to within the context of popular culture. The most comprehensive discussion of this subject is Lowenthal (1985), although he has little to say about archaeology.

Finally, my efforts to view archaeological interpretation as an expression of the ideology of various fractions of the middle class is not a normative approach, which maintains simplistically that all archaeologists react in the same way to a particular set of social stimuli, as Shanks and Tilley (1987: 31) have alleged. Nor does it contradict their claim that individuals interpret the past to promote their own goals and ideologies. It represents a level of generalization, based on common interests shared by members of the same class, that has long been recognized as legitimate, at least within the Marxist tradition.

Classical archaeology and antiquarianism

There is unfortunately no comprehensive study of the origins of antiquarian research either in Europe or world wide. For an effort to construct an evolutionary sequence of conceptualizations of the past, see Childe (1956b). Ancient Egyptian and Mesopotamian historiography is magisterially discussed by Van Seters (1983) and Redford (1986), as well as more generally by Butterfield (1981). Classical, medieval, and early modern views of the past are surveyed by Casson (1939), Sanford (1944), and Wace (1949), as well as, within the context of broader anthropological concerns, by Hodgen (1964) and Slotkin (1965). Toulmin and Goodfield (1966) and Rossi (1985) examine early challenges to biblical chronology and the changing philosophy of history since the medieval period. Weiss (1969) chronicles the Italian Renaissance's discovery of classical antiquity and Rowe (1965) discusses the Renaissance as it relates to anthropology. Harris (1968: 8–52) surveys Enlightenment concepts as they relate to anthropology and archaeology and Cassirer (1951) and Hampson (1982) provide a general background on the attitudes and values of the Enlightenment. Wang (1985) offers a brief survey of traditional Chinese historiography.

The history of classical archaeology, Egyptology, and Assyriology has been chronicled in many popular works. A selective bibliography of these is found in Daniel (1975: 401–3). For the early development of classical archaeology, see Weiss (1969) and Stoneman (1987), and for more recent times MacKendrick (1960). Leppmann (1970) covers the career of Winckelmann. M. Bernal (1987) discusses in detail, and perhaps too polemically and selectively (he omits even to mention Montelius), certain aspects of the ideological basis of classical studies, in particular their emphasis on the purity and primacy of Greek culture. Fagan (1975) provides a readable account of the development of Egyptology, while Lloyd (1947) chronicles the history of Assyriology. Rudolph (1963), Li (1977), and Chang (1981) trace the early development of antiquarian studies in China, as do Hoffman (1974) and Ikawa-Smith (1982) for Japan.

The development of antiquarian research in Europe north of the Alps is surveyed as part of more general histories by Daniel (1950), Laming-Emperaire (1964), and Sklenář (1983); and for America by Willey and Sabloff (1980). Many specialized studies have examined the early development of antiquarianism in Britain. The historiography of the late medieval and early modern periods has been studied by Walters (1934), Kendrick (1950), and L. Fox (1956). L. Clark (1961), Lynch and Lynch (1968), Marsden (1974, 1984), and Piggott (1976, 1978) survey the development of a scientific approach to prehistoric archaeology prior to 1800. Aubrey's archaeological manuscripts have been reproduced by Fowles (1980, 1982).

The recognition of prehistoric stone tools as being of human manufacture and the role played by the Three-Age theory in the study of prehistory prior to 1800 has been commented on by Heizer (1962b), Daniel (1963a, 1976) and Rodden (1981). Biographical studies that are particularly valuable for illuminating the development of archaeology include Piggott (1950) on Stukeley, Hunter (1975) on Aubrey, and R. H. Cunnington (1975) on William Cunnington. These works do not confirm Crawford's (1932) attribution of a leading role in the development of antiquarian research to increasing numbers of archaeological finds resulting from industrial development.

Among the numerous works examining the early attitudes of Europeans towards the native peoples of the New World are Fairchild (1928), H. Jones (1964), and Chiappelli (1976). Spanish views are discussed by Hanke (1959), Keen (1971), and Pagden (1982), and English and French ones by Pearce (1965), Jaenen (1976), Berkhofer (1978), Vaughan (1979, 1982), Sheehan (1980), and Kupperman (1980). These views explain to a degree the slowness with which archaeology developed in the New World and the explanations that American archaeologists offered of their data in the nineteenth century.

The beginnings of scientific archaeology

The most comprehensive account of this period is Daniel (1950: 29–121). The titling of his chapters suggests that only Palaeolithic studies are to be equated with scientific archaeology, while Scandinavian archaeology was a form of antiquarianism. In fact, the inclusion of developments in Scandinavia and Switzerland after 1840 in chapter 3 (pp. 77–85) shows that Daniel did not hold that view.

While much has been written about the role played by Christian Thomsen in the development of prehistoric archaeology, most accounts overemphasize his application of the Three-Age theory and fail to stress his invention of seriation (e.g. Klindt-Jensen 1975: 49–57). Specialized studies of his work include Heizer (1962b), Daniel (1976), Gräslund (1981), and Rodden (1981). The early development of Scandinavian and Scandinavian-style archaeology is examined by Morlot (1861), Bibby (1956), Gräslund (1974; for an English summary see Gräslund 1976; 1987), Klindt-Jensen (1975, 1976), and Kristiansen (1985). Weiss (1969: 167–79) discusses the development of numismatics prior to the eighteenth century.

The developments in uniformitarian geology that provided a necessary background for the emergence of Palaeolithic archaeology are chronicled in Zittel (1901), Geikie (1905), Gillispie (1951), Chorley *et al.* (1964), Davies (1969), Schneer (1969), and Porter (1977). Similar developments in evolutionary biology are covered by Irvine (1955), Wendt (1955), Barnett (1958), Eiseley (1958), Haber (1959), and Greene (1959).

The establishment of a scientific understanding of human antiquity has been masterfully surveyed by Gruber (1965) and Grayson (1983). The latter's definitive treatment should be consulted for numerous primary and secondary references. The origins of prehistoric archaeology in France are surveyed by Laming-Emperaire (1964). Sackett (1981) examines later developments and, in particular, the influence of Mortillet. Grayson follows the French in equating the development of Palaeolithic archaeology with that of prehistoric archaeology, and excluding Scandinavian-style archaeology as the study of protohistoric times. This terminological difference should not obscure the high degree of similarity between his position and the one adopted in this book.

The early development of archaeology in the United States has been described by Willey and Sabloff (1980: 19–40), while disputes about the Moundbuilders are covered in greater detail by Silverberg (1968). The anthropology of this period is discussed by Bieder (1986). Squier's work is examined by Tax (1975) and the influence of Joseph Henry by W. Washburn (1967). American shell-mound excavations are discussed by Christenson (1985) and Trigger (1986a).

The imperial synthesis

Nineteenth-century United States archaeology is included in this section because it was primarily shaped, as was American anthropology as a whole, by the encounter of dramatically expanding European settlement with the native peoples of central and western North America. General discussions of racial interpretations of human behaviour in the nineteenth century that are relevant for understanding archaeological practice in colonial settings are provided by Harris (1968), Stocking (1968), S. Gould (1981), Stepan (1982), and Bieder (1986). The development of physical anthropology and of racial views concerning the North American Indians has been studied by Glass *et al.* (1959), Glacken (1967), and Horsman (1975, 1981). The debate between polygenists and monogenists is examined in its British context by Stocking (1973) and in its American one by Stanton (1960). The impact of Darwinian evolutionism on racial thinking and the disagreements between Darwin and Wallace concerning the evolutionary status of 'primitive' human groups have been surveyed by Eiseley (1958). Street (1975) describes popular British stereotypes of Africans between 1858 and 1920, while MacGaffey (1966) documents the impact of such stereotypes on African ethnological studies.

Little has been published about Lubbock's archaeological and ethnological writings, although a number of studies may be in progress. This dearth is incommensurate with his influence as a promoter of Darwinian thought on the study of archaeology in colonial settings. His standard biography is Hutchinson (1914).

Willey and Sabloff (1980: 40–82) trace the development of North American archaeology during the middle and late nineteenth century, while Silverberg (1968) chronicles the demise of the Moundbuilder myth. Hinsley (1981) examines the role played by the Smithsonian Institution in the professionalization of native American studies, including archaeology. He also examines the social factors influencing the development of archaeology at the Peabody Museum of Archaeology and Ethnology (Hinsley 1985). McKusick (1970) offers a case study of the competition to interpret archaeological data between amateur and professional archaeologists in the United States, while Meltzer (1983) analyses the role played by archaeologists employed by the United States federal government in the nineteenth-century 'Early Man' controversies. The work of Hinsley and Meltzer, along with that of Grayson, has helped to set new standards in writing the history of archaeology. Trigger (1980b, 1985c, 1986b) examines the role of racism in American archaeology at this time.

Until recently little was available concerning the history of African archaeology apart from that of ancient Egypt (see chapter 2). Fagan (1981) and Posnansky (1982) each provide a brief survey of the history of sub-Saharan archaeology, while M. Hall (1984) and Schrire *et al.* (1986) examine its development in South Africa. Garlake (1973, 1983) provides a thorough account and evaluation of archaeological investigations at Great Zimbabwe and other stone ruins in south-central Africa and of the controversies surrounding them. Robertshaw (1988) has edited a multi-authored survey of the history of African archaeology that will provide definitive coverage of most regions for some time to come. African critiques of early archaeological research are also beginning to appear (Ki-Zerbo 1981; Andah 1985).

The most accessible accounts of the development of New Zealand archaeology are by Sorrenson (1977), Davidson (1979), Gathercole (1981), and Sutton (1985). Gathercole provides references to a number of other studies in New Zealand archaeological newsletters. The history of Australian archaeology has been touched on by McCarthy (1959), Megaw (1966), Mulvaney (1969), and R. Jones (1979) and treated more extensively by Mulvaney (1981), Murray and White (1981), and McBryde (1986). A series of articles dealing with the history of Australian anthropology has been edited by G. McCall (1982). Some valuable comments relating to modern colonial and post-colonial archaeology are found in D. Miller (1980).

Culture-historical archaeology

National consciousness has a long history. Already in the sixteenth and seventeenth centuries it played a significant role in the development of archaeology in northern and western Europe. Political scientists frequently distinguish this early patriotism, which tended to be dynastically focused, from the nationalism that developed in Europe in the wake of industrialization and which has since spread around the world. Gellner (1983) defines the latter as an all-embracing sense of group identity that is promoted by mass media, widespread literacy, and a comprehensive educational system. While this distinction is a useful one, common usage frequently treats earlier forms of patriotism as falling within a broader definition of nationalism.

Harris (1968: 373–92) and Trigger (1978a: 54–74) discuss the development of diffusionism in anthropology and archaeology. Adams *et al.* (1978) trace the separate use of the concepts of diffusion and migration to explain cultural change, although their failure to relate both types of explanation to changing attitudes toward evolutionism is a major drawback. Daniel (1963a: 104–27) discusses hyper-diffusionism and Rouse (1958, 1986) examines the archaeological analysis of migration. Gräslund (1974, 1976) presents the most detailed analysis of Montelius' assumptions and methods, while Bibby (1956: 176–83) and Klindt-Jensen (1975: 84–93) explain them more briefly. Renfrew (1973a) provides a critique of the assumptions underlying Montelius' work.

Kroeber and Kluckhohn (1952) document the origins and history of the anthropological concept of culture. While there is no detailed study of the development of the concept of the archaeological culture, Meinander (1981) ably summarizes what is known about its origins in Europe. The development of this concept in Europe and America is compared in Trigger (1978a: 75–95).

Unfortunately, no detailed evaluation of the important contributions of Kossinna to the development of archaeology has been published in English. The best general summaries are provided in German by Klejn (1974), who presents Kossinna's views and criticizes them from a Marxist perspective, and by Veit (1984), who examines his impact on Western European archaeology. Schwerin von Krosigk (1982) discusses in detail his methods and theories with special reference to his papers deposited at the Christian–Albrechts University in Kiel. Huxley's (1896: 271–328) essay 'The Aryan Question and Prehistoric Man' provides valuable insights into how scholars viewed European prehistory at the end of the nineteenth century. German nationalism is discussed by Kohn (1960) and in a broader European context by Poliakov (1974).

A detailed general account of Childe's work is presented in Trigger (1980a), some aspects of which are modified and up-dated in Trigger (1984b, 1986c). His specific contributions to culture-historical archaeology are discussed in Trigger (1980a: 32–55). S. Green (1981) chronicles his family background, life, and career, while McNairn (1980) reproduces extracts from his writings, together with a commentary. Specialized discussions and evaluations of his work are found in Piggott (1958),

Ravetz (1959), Allen (1967, 1981), Gathercole (1971, 1976, 1982), G. Clark (1976), Trigger (1982b), Tringham (1983), and Ridgway (1985). Myres (1911) is essential background reading to understand Childe's cultural-historical approach.

European archaeology during the period 1880 to 1960 is surveyed by Daniel (1950), Klindt-Jensen (1975), Sklenář (1983), and in many articles cited in these works. American culture-historical archaeology is covered by Willey and Sabloff (1980: 83–129) and by Woodbury's (1973) biography of Kidder, as well as by collections of reprinted articles edited by Wedel (1985) on the Plains and R. Ford (1987) on the Southwest. The weaknesses of this approach were examined by W. Taylor (1948).

Less extensive research has been done on the history of culture-historical archaeology in other countries. The most important collections of studies are edited by Daniel (1981b), Evans *et al.* (1981), and Trigger and Glover (1981, 1982). Chinese archaeology is discussed by R. Pearson (1977), Li (1977), Chang (1981), W. Watson (1981), and Olsen (1987); Japanese archaeology by Ikawa-Smith (1982), Tanaka (1984), and Fawcett (1986); Mexican archaeology by Bernal (1980) and Lorenzo (1981, 1984) and Maya archaeology in particular by Hammond (1983) and Marcus (1983b); South Asian archaeology by Chakrabarti (1981, 1982) and Thapar (1984); Near Eastern archaeology by Masry (1981), Silberman (1982), Bar-Yosef and Mazar (1982), Reid (1985), and Hanbury-Tenison (1986). Silberman discusses the early development of Palestinian archaeology in the context of Great Power rivalries. He is currently working on a follow-up study, *Between the Past and the Present: Archaeology, Ideology, and Nationalism in the Modern Near East* (1988). African archaeology is examined by Fagan (1981), Posnansky (1982), and Nzewunwa (1984). Robertshaw's (1988) history of African archaeology covers the transition from colonial to national archaeology. On the current relation of African archaeology to the study of African history, see D. McCall (1964), Ki-Zerbo (1981), and Ehret and Posnansky (1982).

Major studies dealing with the development of archaeological methods within the culture-historical context are reprinted in Heizer (1959); those relating to stratigraphy are found on pp. 222–343 and those relating to seriation (including the innovative studies of Petrie and Kroeber) are on pp. 376–448. Pitt-Rivers' contributions to the development of excavation techniques are examined by M. Thompson (1977) and Wheeler's by J. Hawkes (1982).

Soviet archaeology

My direct knowledge of Soviet archaeology is limited by my not reading Russian. I believe that I have been able to derive from Russian works in translation and various secondary sources (some sympathetic, some highly antagonistic) a reasonably balanced view of Soviet archaeology. I have not been able to use as effectively as I would wish Gening (1982). He presents a comprehensive account of Soviet archaeology from the mid-1920s into the mid-1930s, as well as thumbnail sketches of the major figures in Soviet archaeology at the end of the book. Soviet scholarly views of primitive societies are discussed by Howe (1976, 1980) and Bloch (1985).

The most detailed history of Russian and Soviet archaeology available in English is M. Miller (1956). It is a highly polemical work written by an *émigré* archaeologist in the early years of the Cold War. It should be carefully compared with briefer and more recent accounts of the history of Soviet archaeology by Russian archaeologists (Klejn 1977; Bulkin *et al.* 1982) as well as various studies of scientific research and cultural policy in the Soviet Union in the 1920s and 1930s: G. Fischer (1967), Graham (1967), S. Cohen (1973), Fitzpatrick (1974), Shapiro (1982), and O'Connor (1983). These works have led me to move further from Miller's interpretations of the 1930s than in Trigger (1984c). Periodizations of the development of Russian and Soviet archaeology have been made by Miller (1956), Gening (1982), Soffer (1985), and Dolitsky (1985).

Archaeology in the Soviet Union in the 1930s and early 1940s is discussed by Tallgren (1936), G. Clark (1936), Field and Prostov (1937), and in a series of papers by Childe (1940b, 1942b, c, d, e, 1943, 1945b, 1952). Major translated Soviet archaeological writings of the early post-war period include rival Soviet (1959) and English (1961) translations of Mongait's *Archaeology in the U.S.S.R.*, M. Thompson's (1967) selected papers on the medieval excavations at Novgorod, Semenov (1964) on use-wear analysis, and various syntheses of Siberian archaeological research: Rudenko (1961, 1970), Michael (1962, 1964), Okladnikov (1965, 1970), and Chernetsov and Moszyńska (1974). Valuable information is also contained in entries from the *Great Soviet Encyclopedia*, especially Artsikhovsky's (1973) essay on 'Archaeology'. Surveys of work done during this period are provided by Field and Price (1949), Combier (1959), Chard (1961, 1963, 1969), Debetz (1961), Frumkin (1962), Boriskovsky (1965), and Klein (1966). Polemical literature includes M. Thompson (1965) and Klejn (1969, 1970). Extracts from Mongait's notorious 'The crisis in bourgeois archaeology' are translated in M. Miller (1956: 147–52).

More recent Soviet archaeological publications to appear in translation include Dolukhanov (1979), Klejn (1982), and a volume of articles on Central Asia in the Bronze Age (Kohl 1981a). Translations of papers by Soviet archaeologists appear regularly in *Soviet Anthropology and Archeology*. Changing Soviet applications of Marxism to the social sciences are discussed by Danilova (1971) and in Gellner (1980). Examinations of the current state of Soviet archaeology include Klejn (1973a, 1973b, 1977), Levitt (1979), Ranov and Davis (1979), Davis (1983), Tringham (1983), Soffer (1983, 1985), and Dolitsky (1985). The most comprehensive statement is Bulkin *et al.* (1982). Discussions of the much-debated concept of culture are reviewed in Bulkin *et al.* (1982), Klejn (1982), and Davis (1983).

Functionalism in Western archaeology

The growing influence of functionalism on archaeology marks the point at which most general histories become anecdotal rather than systematic in their coverage. The exception is Willey and Sabloff (1980: 130–80) for the United States. Some useful material is also found in Daniel (1950: 302–8). A number of detailed studies of this period are currently said to be in progress. Harris (1968: 464–567) traces the early development of social anthropology. Some important essays on this subject are found in Stocking (1984). Information on Durkheim is provided by Alpert (1939), Duvignaud (1965), and Parsons (1968).

The early development of an environmental approach in Scandinavia, Central Europe, and England is discussed by Morlot (1861), Daniel (1950), Bibby (1956), Klindt-Jensen (1975), Goudie (1976), and Moberg (1981). Deuel (1973) provides the most comprehensive account of the history of aerial photography and its impact on environmental research in archaeology. Spate (1968) discusses environmental possibilism. References to studies of Childe's early economic approach are included in the bibliographical note for chapter 5. There has been no detailed evaluation of the contributions of Grahame Clark. He has written a brief intellectual autobiography (Clark 1974) and a critique of his work at Star Carr (Clark 1972). Sieveking (1976), G. Clark (1976) and Chapman (1979) assess his influence and the work of his students. Clark (1988b) reprints his major papers on economic studies of prehistory.

Willey and Sabloff (1980) and Dunnell (1986) provide a detailed chronicle of the development of a functionalist approach in United States archaeology since the mid-1930s. They do not, however, trace the origins of this approach in the American archaeology of the late nineteenth and early twentieth centuries, as do W. Taylor (1948: 73–80) and

Trigger (1978c). J. Bennett (1943) and W. Taylor provide contemporary accounts of the growth of a functionalist approach in the 1940s. Taylor also offers a devastating critique of the culture-historical approach in American archaeology. The development of the ecological approach in American archaeology is described from an autobiographical perspective by Braidwood (1974) and MacNeish (1974, 1978) and the early development of settlement archaeology by Trigger (1967a) and Willey (1974b). An autocritique of some of the early weaknesses of the settlement approach and a discussion of its relation to the New Archaeology are found in Trigger (1984d).

Neo-evolutionism and the New Archaeology

Harris (1968: 634–87) discusses the development of neo-evolutionism. Major statements of this position are found in L. White (1949, 1959), Steward (1955), Sahlins and Service (1960), Service (1962), and Fried (1967). For a spectacular renunciation of neo-evolutionism, see Sahlins (1976). Murdock (1959b) provides an alternative American view of evolutionary processes, which is closer in spirit (although not politically) to Childe's later works.

Willey and Sabloff (1980: 181–210) supply the most detailed discussion of the beginning of the New Archaeology in America. Binford (1972: 1–14) details his own rebellion against the culture-historical approach, specifically the epigonal variant of the Midwestern Taxonomic Method that he encountered at the University of Michigan in the late 1950s. His early writings are reprinted in Binford (1972). The widely shared disenchantment with American culture-historical archaeology is documented in Trigger (1984d: 368–9). The name of the movement is derived from Caldwell (1959), and Deetz (1965) is often considered to be an independent pioneer (Willey and Sabloff 1980: 209). The spread of the New Archaeology into American historical archaeology is chronicled in South (1977a, 1977b). Clarke's contributions are surveyed by colleagues and friends in Clarke (1979). His main writings are found in Clarke (1968, 1979). Renfrew's early essays are reprinted in Renfrew (1979). Many of the most important early papers exemplifying the New Archaeology can be found in Binford and Binford (1968), Leone (1972), Clarke (1972a), Redman (1973), and Renfrew (1973b). The first textbook treatment of the New Archaeology was Watson *et al.* (1971; 2nd edn. 1984), although its impact was already evident in the second edition of Hole and Heizer's (1969) influential general textbook. A widely-read popularization of new scientific techniques was written by David Wilson (1975).

Contrasting views about the novelty of the New Archaeology are found in W. Taylor (1969, 1972) and Binford (1968b). While not diminishing the importance of Binford's contributions, the historical roots of both his ideas and Taylor's are now clearer than when Willey and Sabloff (1980: 188) wrote *A History of American Archaeology*. While Clarke cited Binford in his early works, Binford and his followers initially ignored Clarke and later treated him as a disciple of Binford, a position that ignored the distinctiveness of his early work and the major inspiration that it drew from the Cambridge-based New Geography. Binford (1983a: 69) has since recognized the many fundamental differences between his early work and Clarke's.

The most extensive polemic directed against the New Archaeology is Courbin (1982), who seeks in a Rankean fashion to equate archaeology with the recovery of archaeological data. Brief but equally pugnacious defences of culture-historical archaeology as it was practised in the 1950s include J. Hawkes (1968), A. Hogarth (1972), and Daniel (1975: 370–4). All of these more extreme polemics are by Europeans. In the United States such works are notable by their absence. There the most notable abjuration of the methodological concerns of the New Archaeology in favour of 'doing archaeology' is Flannery (1982). Significantly this piece was written by an archaeologist whose credentials as a processual theorist are impeccable. On the other hand, ringing endorsements from older archaeologists were equally rare in the 1960s and 1970s, the most notable exception being P. Martin (1971). Critical evaluations of the general programme of the New Archaeology were offered by Bayard (1969), R. Watson (1972), Sabloff *et al.* (1973), Dumond (1977), Trigger (1978a: 2–18), Larson (1979), Gandara (1980, 1981), and Gibbon (1984). Criticism of primary reliance upon a deductive approach has been made, among others, by C. Morgan (1973, 1978), Read and LeBlanc (1978), and most powerfully by M. Salmon (1982) and Kelley and Hanen (1988). The antihistoricism of the New Archaeology has been opposed on technical grounds by Sabloff and Willey (1967) and on philosophical and strategic ones by Trigger ([1970] 1978a: 19–36; [1973] 1978a: 37–52). Pinsky (1987) has written a detailed study of the use of ethnographic data by the New Archaeology.

On the use of statistics and other forms of mathematical analysis in archaeology see Hodson *et al.* (1971), Doran and Hodson (1975), Hodder and Orton (1976), D. Thomas (1976, 1978), Cowgill (1977), Hodder (1978), and Sabloff (1981). Discussions of General Systems Theory can be found in Wiener (1961), Buckley (1968), Bertalanffy (1969), Emery (1969), and Laszlo (1972a, b, c). Saunders (1980) offers a general review of catastrophe theory.

The explanation of diversity

The most comprehensive survey of recent trends in American archaeology is the volume edited by Meltzer *et al.* (1986), especially the papers in it by Dunnell, Jennings, Knudson, Leone, and P. Watson. Other surveys include Willey and Sabloff (1980: 248–64) for the 1970s and articles by Dunnell (1979, 1980b, 1981, 1982a, 1983, 1984, 1985), Wylie (1982, 1985a, 1985c), Gibbon (1984), Trigger (1984e), Hodder (1985), Yengoyan (1985), Patterson (1986b), Leone *et al.* (1987), and Earle and Preucel (1987) for more recent trends. Renfrew (1980) and Wiseman (1980a, 1980b) discuss the relationship between humanistic and social science approaches in archaeology. Hodder (1986) provides a definitive statement of the contextual approach.

Major anthropological works casting doubt on neo-evolutionism include Fried (1975), Sahlins (1976), and Wolf (1982); see also Wallerstein (1974). Kolakowski (1978a, b, c) provides a comprehensive history of Marxist thought. The recent influences of Marxism (and so-called Marxism) on anthropology are discussed by Bloch (1985). Easily accessible works exemplifying the more radical anti-positivist tendencies in archaeology include Hodder (1982a, c), Miller and Tilley (1984), and Spriggs (1984a). Trigger (1985d) provides a critique of the latter two publications, while Wylie (1985c) supplies a sympathetic but firm appraisal of the role of critical theory in archaeology. In two recent papers Binford (1986, 1987) has offered an energetic defence of positivism. E. Green (1984) has edited a volume of essays on ethics and values in American archaeology. For an international discussion of this theme, see D. Miller (1980). Hodder (1987) evidences the growing attractions of historical analyses in archaeology. Important studies relating to ethnoarchaeology include Kleindienst and Watson (1956), Jochim (1976), Yellen (1977), Binford (1978), R. Gould (1978, 1980), Tringham (1978), Kramer (1979, 1982), P. Watson (1979), Hodder (1982b), Tooker (1982), and Hayden and Cannon (1984). Ingersoll *et al.* (1977), Coles (1979), and Hayden (1979) provide a selection of works on experimental archaeology. Discussions of the unique properties of archaeological data and how such data can be made relevant to the social sciences are found in Clarke ([1973] 1979: 83–103), Schiffer (1976), Binford (1977, 1981, 1983a, b, 1984), and Bulkin *et al.* (1982).

Archaeology and its social context

Discussions of current trends in archaeology resulting from the declining influence of neo-evolutionism and cultural ecology include Gibbon

(1984), Trigger (1984e), and Gallay (1986). Trends in interpretative methodology are discussed by M. Salmon (1982) and Kelley and Hanen (1988). The most comprehensive illustrations of current trends in archaeology are the fifteen volumes of pre-circulated papers that formed the basis for discussions at the World Archaeology Congress: Southampton 1986. Ucko's (1987) account of that conference is a good reference for the current politicization of Western archaeologists.

REFERENCES

Abbott, C. C. 1881. *Primitive Industry*. Salem, G. A. Bates.

Abercromby, J. 1902. The oldest Bronze-Age ceramic type in Britain. *Journal of the Royal Anthropological Institute* 32: 373–97.

Aberle, D. F. 1968. Comments. In S. R. and L. R. Binford, pp. 353–9.

Aberle, D. F., A. K. Cohen, A. K. Davis, M-J. Levy Jr, and F. X. Sutton. 1950. The functional prerequisites of a society. *Ethics* 60: 100–1.

Abramowicz, A. 1981. Sponte nascitur ollae . . . In G. Daniel, 1981b, pp. 146–9.

Adams, E. C. 1984. Archaeology and the native American: a case at Hopi. In E. L. Green, pp. 236–42.

Adams, R. McC. 1965. *Land Behind Baghdad*. Chicago, University of Chicago Press.

1974. Anthropological perspectives on ancient trade. *Current Anthropology* 15: 239–58.

1981. *Heartland of Cities*. Chicago, University of Chicago Press.

Adams, R. McC. and H. J. Nissen. 1972. *The Uruk Countryside*. Chicago, University of Chicago Press.

Adams, W. Y., D. P. Van Gerven, and R. S. Levy. 1978. The retreat from migrationism. *Annual Review of Anthropology* 7: 483–532.

Alden, J. R. 1982. Trade and politics in proto-Elamite Iran. *Current Anthropology* 23: 613–40.

Alexander, J. and A. Mohammed. 1982. Frontier theory and the Neolithic period in Nubia. In *Nubian Studies*, ed. by J. M. Plumley pp. 34–40. Warminster, Aris and Phillips.

Allen, J. 1967. Aspects of Vere Gordon Childe. *Labour History* 12: 52–9.

1981. Perspectives of a sentimental journey: V. Gordon Childe in Australia 1917–1921. *Australian Archaeology* 12: 1–11.

Alpert, H. 1939. *Emile Durkheim and his Sociology*. New York, Columbia University Press.

Andah, B. W. 1985. No past! no present! no future! Anthropological education and African revolution. Inaugural lecture, Department of Archaeology and Anthropology, University of Ibadan.

Andersson, J. G. 1934. *Children of the Yellow Earth*. London, Kegan Paul.

Andresen, J. M., B. F. Byrd, M. D. Elson, R. H. McGuire, R. M. Mendoza, E. Staski, and J. P. White. 1981. The deer hunters: Star Carr reconsidered. *World Archaeology* 13: 31–46.

Andriolo, K. R. 1979. Kulturkreislehre and the Austrian mind. *Man* 14: 133–44.

References

Artsikhovsky, A. V. 1973. Archaeology. *Great Soviet Encyclopedia* 2: 245–50. New York, Macmillan.

Ascher, R. 1961. Analogy in archaeological interpretation. *Southwestern Journal of Anthropology* 16: 317–25.

Atkinson, R. F. 1978. *Knowledge and Explanation in History: An Introduction to the Philosophy of History*. Ithaca, Cornell University Press.

Atwater, C. 1820. Description of the antiquities discovered in the State of Ohio and other western states. *Archaeologia Americana: Transactions and Collections of the American Antiquarian Society* 1: 105–267.

Bachofen, J. J. 1861. *Das Mutterrecht*. Stuttgart, Krais und Hoffman.

Bacon, E. 1976. *The Great Archaeologists*. London, Secker and Warburg.

Bahn, P. G. 1978. The 'unacceptable face' of the Western European Upper Palaeolithic. *Antiquity* 52: 183–92.

Bailey, A. M. and J. R. Llobera. 1981. *The Asiatic Mode of Production*. London, Routledge & Kegan Paul.

Barker, G. 1985. *Prehistoric Farming*. Cambridge, Cambridge University Press.

Barley, M. W. 1977. ed. *European Towns: Their Archaeology and Early History*. New York, Academic Press.

Barnes, A. S. 1939. The differences between natural and human flaking on prehistoric flint implements. *American Anthropologist* 41: 99–112.

Barnes, B. 1974. *Scientific Knowledge and Sociological Theory*. London, Routledge & Kegan Paul.

1977. *Interests and the Growth of Knowledge*. London, Routledge & Kegan Paul.

Barnes, H. E. 1937. *A History of Historical Writing*. Norman, University of Oklahoma Press.

Barnett, S. A. 1958. ed. *A Century of Darwin*. Cambridge, Massachusetts, Harvard University Press.

Barraclough, G. 1979. *Main Trends in History*. New York, Holmes and Meier.

Bar-Yosef, O. and A. Mazar. 1982. Israeli archaeology. *World Archaeology* 13: 310–25.

Bayard, D. T. 1969. Science, theory, and reality in the 'New Archaeology'. *American Antiquity* 34: 376–84.

Beardsley, R. K., P. Holder, A. D. Krieger, B. J. Meggers, J. B. Rinaldo, and P. Kutsche. 1956. Functional and evolutionary implications of community patterning. *Memoir* (Menasha, Wisconsin, Society for American Archaeology) 11: 129–57.

Beauchamp, W. M. 1900. *Aboriginal Occupation of New York*. Albany, Bulletin of the New York State Museum, 7 (32).

Becker, C. L. 1938. What is historiography? *American Historical Review* 44: 20–8.

Bell, A. S. 1981. ed. *The Scottish Antiquarian Tradition*. Edinburgh, John Donald.

Benedict, R. 1934. *Patterns of Culture*. Boston, Houghton Mifflin.

Bennett, J. W. 1943. Recent developments in the functional interpretation of archaeological data. *American Antiquity* 9: 208–19.

1944. Middle American influences on cultures of the southeastern United States. *Acta Americana* 2: 25–50.

References

Bennett, W. C. 1945. Interpretations of Andean archaeology. *Transactions of the New York Academy of Sciences*, series 2, vol. 7, pp. 95–9.

Bent, J. T. 1892. *The Ruined Cities of Mashonaland*. London, Longmans, Green.

Berkhofer, R. F. Jr. 1978. *The White Man's Indian: Images of the American Indian from Columbus to the Present*. New York, Knopf.

Berlinski, D. 1976. *On Systems Analysis*. Cambridge, Massachusetts, M.I.T. Press.

Bernal, I. 1980. *A History of Mexican Archaeology*. London, Thames and Hudson.

Bernal, M. 1987. *Black Athena: The Afroasiatic Roots of Classical Civilization*, vol. 1, *The Fabrication of Ancient Greece, 1785–1985*. London, Free Association Books.

Berstein, R. J. 1983. *Beyond Objectivism and Relativism*. Philadelphia, University of Pennsylvania Press.

Bertalanffy, L. von. 1969. *General System Theory*. New York, Braziller.

Best, E. 1916. Maori and Maruiwi. *Transactions of the New Zealand Institute* 48: 435–47.

Bibby, G. 1956. *The Testimony of the Spade*. New York, Knopf.

Bieder, R. E. 1975. Albert Gallatin and the survival of Enlightenment thought in nineteenth-century American anthropology. In *Toward a Science of Man: Essays in the History of Anthropology*, ed. by T. H. H. Thoresen, pp. 91–8. The Hague, Mouton.

1986. *Science Encounters the Indian, 1820–1880: The Early Years of American Ethnology*. Norman, University of Oklahoma Press.

Bietak, M. 1979. The present state of Egyptian archaeology. *Journal of Egyptian Archaeology* 65: 156–60.

Binford, L. R. 1962. Archaeology as anthropology. *American Antiquity* 28: 217–25.

1965. Archaeological systematics and the study of culture process. *American Antiquity* 31: 203–10.

1967a. Smudge pits and hide smoking: the use of analogy in archaeological reasoning. *American Antiquity* 32: 1–12.

1967b. Comment. *Current Anthropology* 8: 234–5.

1968a. Some comments on historical versus processual archaeology. *Southwestern Journal of Anthropology* 24: 267–75.

1968b. Archeological perspectives. In S. R. and L. R. Binford, pp. 5–32.

1972. *An Archaeological Perspective*. New York, Seminar Press.

1977. ed. *For Theory Building in Archaeology*. New York, Academic Press.

1978. *Nunamiut Ethnoarchaeology*. New York, Academic Press.

1981. *Bones: Ancient Men and Modern Myths*. New York, Academic Press.

1983a. *Working at Archaeology*. New York, Academic Press.

1983b. *In Pursuit of the Past*. London, Thames and Hudson.

1984. *Faunal Remains from Klasies River Mouth*. New York, Academic Press.

1986. In pursuit of the future. In D. J. Meltzer *et al.*, pp. 459–79.

1987. Data, relativism and archaeological science. *Man* 22: 391–404.

Binford, L. R. and W. J. Chasko Jr. 1976. Nunamiut demographic history: a provocative case. In *Demographic Anthropology*, ed. by E. B. W. Zubrow, pp. 63–143. Albuquerque, University of New Mexico Press.

Binford, L. R. and J. A. Sabloff. 1982. Paradigms, systematics, and archaeology. *Journal of Anthropological Research* 38: 137–53.

Binford, L. R. and N. M. Stone. 1986. Zhoukoudian: a closer look. *Current Anthropology* 27: 453–75.

Binford, S. R. and L. R. Binford. 1968. eds. *New Perspectives in Archeology*. Chicago, Aldine.

Bintliff, J. L. 1984. Structuralism and myth in Minoan studies. *Antiquity* 58: 33–8.

Black, J. L. 1986. *G.-F. Müller and the Imperial Russian Academy*. Montreal, McGill-Queen's University Press.

Blakeslee, D. J. 1987. John Rowzée Peyton and the myth of the Mound Builders. *American Antiquity* 52: 784–92.

Blanton, R. E. 1978. *Monte Albán: Settlement Patterns at the Ancient Zapotec Capital*. New York, Academic Press.

Blanton, R. E., S. A. Kowalewski, G. Feinman, and J. Appel. 1981. *Ancient Mesoamerica: A Comparison of Change in Three Regions*. Cambridge, Cambridge University Press.

Bloch, M. 1985. *Marxism and Anthropology*. Oxford, Oxford University Press.

Boas, F. 1887. Museums of ethnology and their classification. *Science* 9: 587–9.

Böhner, K. 1981. Ludwig Lindenschmit and the Three Age system. In G. Daniel, 1981b, pp. 120–6.

Bonnichsen, R. 1973. Millie's Camp: an experiment in archaeology. *World Archaeology* 4: 277–91.

Bordes, F. H. 1953. Essai de classification des industries 'moustériennes'. *Bulletin de la Société Préhistorique Française* 50: 457–66.

Boriskovsky, P. J. 1965. A propos des récents progrès des études paléolithiques en U.R.S.S. *L'Anthropologie* 69: 5–30.

Boserup, E. 1965. *The Conditions of Agricultural Growth*. London, Allen and Unwin.

Boule, M. 1905. L'Origine des éolithes. *L'Anthropologie* 16: 257–67.

Bradley, J. W. 1987. *Evolution of the Onondaga Iroquois: Accommodating Change, 1500–1655*. Syracuse, Syracuse University Press.

Bradley, R. 1984. *The Social Foundations of Prehistoric Britain*. London, Longman.

Braidwood, R. J. 1974. The Iraq Jarmo Project. In G. R. Willey, pp. 59–83.

Braithwaite, M. 1984. Ritual and prestige in the prehistory of Wessex *c*. 2,200–1,400 BC: a new dimension to the archaeological evidence. In D. Miller and C. Tilley, pp. 93–110.

Braithwaite, R. B. 1953. *Scientific Explanation*. Cambridge, Cambridge University Press.

Brasser, T. J. C. 1971. Group identification along a moving frontier. *Verhandlungen des XXXVIII Internationalen Amerikanistenkongresses* (Munich) 2: 261–5.

Braudel, F. 1980. *On History*. Chicago, University of Chicago Press.

Breisach, E. 1983. *Historiography: Ancient, Medieval, and Modern*. Chicago, University of Chicago Press.

Brongers, J. A. 1973. *1833: Reuvens in Drenthe*. Bussum, Rijksdienst voor het Oudheidkundig Bodemonderzoek.

1976. Material for a history of Dutch archaeology up to 1922. *Berichten van de Rijksdienst voor het Oudheidkundig Bodemonderzoek, Jahrgang* 26: 7–62.

Bronowski, J. 1971. Symposium on technology and social criticism: Introduction – Technology and culture in evolution. *Philosophy of the Social Sciences* 1: 195–206.

Bronson, B. 1972. Farm labor and the evolution of food production. In B. Spooner, pp. 190–218.

Brose, D. S. 1973. The northeastern United States. In J. E. Fitting, pp. 84–115.

Brown, I. W. n.d. Southeastern Indians: ethnohistory, art, and archaeology. In *Indians of the Southeast: A Series*, ed. by P. H. Wood, G. A. Waselkov, and T. Hatley. Lincoln, University of Nebraska Press (in press).

Brown, J. A. 1971. ed. *Approaches to the Social Dimensions of Mortuary Practices*. Washington, Society for American Archaeology, Memoir no. 25.

Brown, J. A. and S. Struever. 1973. The organization of archeological research: an Illinois example. In C. L. Redman, pp. 261–80.

Bruwer, A. J. 1965. *Zimbabwe, Rhodesia's Ancient Greatness*. Johannesburg, Keartland.

Bryson, G. 1945. *Man and Society: The Scottish Inquiry of the Eighteenth Century*. Princeton, Princeton University Press.

Buckley, W. F. 1968. ed. *Modern Systems Research for the Behavioral Scientist: A Sourcebook*. Chicago, Aldine.

Bukharin, N. I. 1931. Theory and practice from the standpoint of dialectical materialism. In *Science at the Cross-Roads*, ed. by N. I. Bukharin *et al.* [articles paginated separately]. London, Kniga.

Bulkin, V. A., L. S. Klejn, and G. S. Lebedev. 1982. Attainments and problems of Soviet archaeology. *World Archaeology* 13: 272–95.

Bulleid, A. H. and H. St. G. Gray. 1911, 1917. *The Glastonbury Lake Village*. 2 vols. Taunton, Glastonbury Antiquarian Society.

Burkitt, M. C. 1928. *South Africa's Past in Stone and Paint*. Cambridge, Cambridge University Press.

Burling, R. 1962. Maximization theories and the study of economic anthropology. *American Anthropologist* 64: 802–21.

Butterfield, H. 1981. *The Origins of History*. New York, Basic Books.

Butzer, K. W. 1976. *Early Hydraulic Civilization in Egypt*. Chicago, University of Chicago Press.

Caldwell, J. R. 1958. *Trend and Tradition in the Prehistory of the Eastern United States*. Menasha, Wisconsin, American Anthropological Association, Memoir no. 88.

1959. The new American archeology. *Science* 129: 303–7.

1964. Interaction spheres in prehistory. In *Hopewellian Studies*, ed. by J. R. Caldwell and R. L. Hall, pp. 133–43. Springfield, Illinois State Museum Scientific Papers no. 12.

Cancian, F. 1966. Maximization as norm, strategy, and theory: a comment on programmatic statements in economic anthropology. *American Anthropologist* 68: 465–70.

Carr, C. 1985. ed. *For Concordance in Archaeological Analysis: Bridging Data Structure, Quantitative Technique, and Theory*. Kansas City, Westport Publishers.

Carr, E. H. 1967. *What is History?* New York, Vintage.

Carrasco, D. 1982. *Quetzalcoatl and the Irony of Empire*. Chicago, University of Chicago Press.

Carson, R. L. 1962. *Silent Spring*. Boston, Houghton Mifflin.

Cartmill, M., D. Pilbeam, and G. Isaac. 1986. One hundred years of paleoanthropology. *American Scientist* 74: 410–20.

Cassirer, E. 1951. *The Philosophy of the Enlightenment*. Princeton, Princeton University Press.

Casson, S. 1939. *The Discovery of Man*. London, Hamish Hamilton.

Caton Thompson, G. 1931. *The Zimbabwe Culture*. Oxford, Oxford University Press.

1983. *Mixed Memoirs*. Gateshead, Paradigm Press.

Ceram, C. W. 1951. *Gods, Graves, and Scholars: The Study of Archaeology*. New York, Knopf.

Chakrabarti, D. K. 1981. Indian archaeology: the first phase, 1784–1861. In G. Daniel, 1981b, pp. 169–85.

1982. The development of archaeology in the Indian subcontinent. *World Archaeology* 13: 326–44.

Chamberlin, T. C. 1944. The method of multiple working hypotheses. *Scientific Monthly* 59: 357–62.

Champion, T. C. 1986. Review of P. Wells, *Farms, Villages and Cities*. *Man* 21: 554.

Champion, T. C., C. S. Gamble, S. J. Shennan, and A. W. R. Whittle. 1984. *Prehistoric Europe*. New York, Academic Press.

Chang, K. C. 1962. China. In *Courses toward Urban Life*, ed. by R. J. Braidwood and G. R. Willey, pp. 177–92. Chicago, Aldine.

1963. *The Archaeology of Ancient China*. New Haven, Yale University Press.

1981. Archaeology and Chinese historiography. *World Archaeology* 13: 156–69.

1983. *Art, Myth, and Ritual: The Path to Political Authority in Ancient China*. Cambridge, Massachusetts, Harvard University Press.

Chapman, R. 1979. 'Analytical Archaeology' and after – Introduction. In D. L. Clarke, pp. 109–43.

Chard, C. S. 1961. New developments in Siberian archaeology. *Asian Perspectives* 5: 118–26.

1963. Soviet scholarship on the prehistory of Asiatic Russia. *Slavic Review* 22: 538–46.

1969. Archaeology in the Soviet Union. *Science* 163: 774–9.

Chernetsov, V. N. and W. Moszyńska. 1974. *Prehistory of Western Siberia*. Montreal, McGill-Queen's University Press.

Chiappelli, F. 1976. *First Images of America: The Impact of the New World on the Old*. Berkeley and Los Angeles, University of California Press.

Childe, V. G. 1925a. *The Dawn of European Civilization*. London, Kegan Paul.

1925b. National art in the Stone Age. *Nature* 116: 195–7.

1926. *The Aryans: A Study of Indo-European Origins*. London, Kegan Paul.
1928. *The Most Ancient East: The Oriental Prelude to European Prehistory*. London, Kegan Paul.
1929. *The Danube in Prehistory*. Oxford, Oxford University Press.
1930. *The Bronze Age*. Cambridge, Cambridge University Press.
1931. *Skara Brae: A Pictish Village in Orkney*. London, Kegan Paul.
1932. Chronology of prehistoric Europe: a review. *Antiquity* 6: 206–12.
1933a. Is prehistory practical? *Antiquity* 7: 410–18.
1933b. Races, peoples and cultures in prehistoric Europe. *History* 18: 193–203.
1934. *New Light on the Most Ancient East: The Oriental Prelude to European Prehistory*. London, Kegan Paul.
1935a. *The Prehistory of Scotland*. London, Kegan Paul.
1935b. Changing methods and aims in prehistory. *Proceedings of the Prehistoric Society* 1: 1–15.
1936. *Man Makes Himself*. London, Watts (pages cited from 4th edn, 1965).
1939. *The Dawn of European Civilization*. 3rd edn. London, Kegan Paul.
1940a. *Prehistoric Communities of the British Isles*. London, Chambers.
1940b. Archaeology in the U.S.S.R. *Nature* 145: 110–11.
1942a. *What Happened in History*. Harmondsworth, Penguin (pages cited from 1st American edn, 1946).
1942b. Prehistory in the U.S.S.R. I. Palaeolithic and Mesolithic, A: Caucasus and Crimea. *Man* 42: 98–100.
1942c. Prehistory in the U.S.S.R. I. Palaeolithic and Mesolithic, B: The Russian Plain. *Man* 42: 100–3.
1942d. Prehistory in the U.S.S.R. II. The Copper Age in South Russia. *Man* 42: 130–6.
1942e. The significance of Soviet archaeology. *Labour Monthly* 24: 341–3.
1942f. The chambered cairns of Rousay. *Antiquaries Journal* 22: 139–42.
1943. Archaeology in the U.S.S.R. The forest zone. *Man* 43: 4–9.
1944a. *Progress and Archaeology*. London, Watts.
1944b. The future of archaeology. *Man* 44: 18–19.
1945a. Directional changes in funerary practices during 50,000 years. *Man* 45: 13–19.
1945b. Archaeology and anthropology [in the USSR]. *Nature* 156: 224–5.
1946a. *Scotland before the Scots*. London, Methuen.
1946b. Archaeology and anthropology. *Southwestern Journal of Anthropology* 2: 243–51.
1947a. *History*. London, Cobbett.
1947b. Archaeology as a social science. *University of London, Institute of Archaeology, Third Annual Report*, pp. 49–60.
1949. *Social Worlds of Knowledge*. London, Oxford University Press.
1950. Cave men's buildings. *Antiquity* 24: 4–11.
1951. *Social Evolution*. New York, Schuman.
1952. Archaeological organization in the USSR. *Anglo-Soviet Journal* 13(3): 23–6.
1953. The constitution of archaeology as a science. In *Science, Medicine and*

History, ed. by E. A. Underwood, pp. 3–15. Oxford, Oxford University Press.

1954. Prehistory. In *The European Inheritance*, ed. by E. Barker, G. Clark, and P. Vaucher, pp. 3–155. Oxford, Oxford University Press.

1955. The significance of lake dwellings in the history of prehistory. *Sibrium* 2(2): 87–91.

1956a. *Piecing Together the Past: The Interpretation of Archaeological Data.* London, Routledge & Kegan Paul.

1956b. *Society and Knowledge: The Growth of Human Traditions.* New York, Harper.

1958a. *The Prehistory of European Society.* Harmondsworth, Penguin.

1958b. Retrospect. *Antiquity* 32: 69–74.

Childe, V. G. and M. C. Burkitt. 1932. A chronological table of prehistory. *Antiquity* 6: 185–205.

Chippindale, C. 1983. *Stonehenge Complete.* London, Thames and Hudson.

Chorley, R. J., A. J. Dunn, and R. P. Beckinsale. 1964. *The History of the Study of Landforms or The Development of Geomorphology*, vol. 1, *Geomorphology before Davis.* London, Methuen.

Chorley, R. J. and P. Haggett. 1967. eds. *Models in Geography.* London, Methuen.

Christenson, A. L. 1985. The identification and study of Indian shell middens in eastern North America: 1643–1861. *North American Archaeologist* 6: 227–44.

Clark, J. G. D. (Grahame). 1932. *The Mesolithic Age in Britain.* Cambridge, Cambridge University Press.

1936. Russian archaeology: the other side of the picture. *Proceedings of the Prehistoric Society* 2: 248–9.

1939. *Archaeology and Society.* London, Methuen.

1940. *Prehistoric England.* London, Batsford.

1942. Bees in antiquity. *Antiquity* 16: 208–15.

1952. *Prehistoric Europe: The Economic Basis.* London, Methuen.

1954. *Excavations at Star Carr.* Cambridge, Cambridge University Press.

1957. *Archaeology and Society.* 3rd edn. London, Methuen.

1972. *Star Carr: A Case Study in Bioarchaeology.* Reading, Massachusetts, Addison-Wesley Modular Publications, McCaleb Module no. 10.

1974. Prehistoric Europe: the economic basis. In Willey, 1974a, pp. 31–57.

1975. *The Earlier Stone Age Settlement of Scandinavia.* Cambridge, Cambridge University Press.

1976. Prehistory since Childe. *Bulletin of the Institute of Archaeology, University of London* 13: 1–21.

1983. *The Identity of Man.* London, Methuen.

1986. *Symbols of Excellence.* Cambridge, Cambridge University Press.

1988a. *Prehistory at Cambridge and Beyond.* Cambridge, Cambridge University Press.

1988b. *Economic Prehistory: Papers on Archaeology.* Cambridge, Cambridge University Press.

Clark, K. M. 1962. *The Gothic Revival.* 3rd edn. London, John Murray.

Clark, L. K. 1961. *Pioneers of Prehistory in England.* London, Sheed and Ward.
Clarke, D. L. 1968. *Analytical Archaeology.* London, Methuen.
1972a. ed. *Models in Archaeology.* London, Methuen.
1972b. A provisional model of an Iron Age society and its settlement system. In D. L. Clarke, 1972a, pp. 801–69.
1977. Spatial information in archaeology. In *Spatial Archaeology*, ed. by. D. L. Clarke, pp. 1–32. New York, Academic Press.
1979. *Analytical Archaeologist.* New York, Academic Press.
Cleere, H. 1984. ed. *Approaches to the Archaeological Heritage.* Cambridge, Cambridge University Press.
Coe, M. D. 1981. Religion and the rise of Mesoamerican states. In *The Transition to Statehood in the New World*, ed. by G. D. Jones and R. R. Kautz, pp. 157–71. Cambridge, Cambridge University Press.
Coe, M. D. and R. A. Diehl. 1980. *In the Land of the Olmec.* 2 vols. Austin, University of Texas Press.
Cohen, M. N. 1977. *The Food Crisis in Prehistory.* New Haven, Yale University Press.
Cohen, M. N. and G. J. Armelagos. 1984. eds. *Paleopathology at the Origins of Agriculture.* New York, Academic Press.
Cohen, S. F. 1973. *Bukharin and the Bolshevik Revolution: A Political Biography.* New York, Knopf.
Cole, F.-C. and T. Deuel. 1937. *Rediscovering Illinois.* Chicago, University of Chicago Press.
Cole, J. R. 1980. Cult archaeology and unscientific method and theory. *Advances in Archaeological Method and Theory* 3: 1–33.
Coles, J. 1979. *Experimental Archaeology.* London, Academic Press.
Collingwood, R. G. 1939. *An Autobiography.* Oxford, Oxford University Press.
1946. *The Idea of History.* Oxford, Oxford University Press.
Colton, H. S. and L. L. Hargrave. 1937. *Handbook of Northern Arizona Pottery Wares.* Flagstaff, Museum of Northern Arizona, Bulletin no. 11.
Combier, J. 1959. Recherches sur l'âge de la Pierre en U.R.S.S. *L'Anthropologie* 63: 160–74.
Conkey, M. W. 1982. Boundedness in art and society. In Hodder, 1982c, pp. 115–28.
Conkey, M. W. and J. D. Spector. 1984. Archaeology and the study of gender. *Advances in Archaeological Method and Theory* 7: 1–38.
Conrad, G. W. 1981. Cultural materialism, split inheritance, and the expansion of ancient Peruvian empires. *American Antiquity* 46: 3–26.
Conrad, G. W. and A. A. Demarest. 1984. *Religion and Empire: The Dynamics of Aztec and Inca Expansionism.* Cambridge, Cambridge University Press.
Cook, S. 1966. The obsolete 'anti-market' mentality: a critique of the substantive approach to economic anthropology. *American Anthropologist* 68: 323–45.
Cordell, L. S. and F. Plog. 1979. Escaping the confines of normative thought: a reevaluation of Puebloan prehistory. *American Antiquity* 44: 405–29.
Courbin, P. 1982. *Qu'est-ce que l'archéologie? Essai sur la nature de la recherche archéologique.* Paris, Payot.

Cowgill, G. L. 1975. On causes and consequences of ancient and modern population changes. *American Anthropologist* 77: 505–25.
1977. The trouble with significance tests and what we can do about it. *American Antiquity* 42: 350–68.
Crawford, O. G. S. 1912. The distribution of Early Bronze Age settlements in Britain. *Geographical Journal* 40: 299–303.
1921. *Man and his Past*. London, Oxford University Press.
1923. Air survey and archaeology. *Geographical Journal* 61: 342–60.
1932. The dialectical process in the history of science. *Sociological Review* 24: 165–73.
Crawford, O. G. S. and A. Keiller. 1928. *Wessex from the Air*. Oxford, Oxford University Press.
Culbert, T. P. 1973. ed. *The Classic Maya Collapse*. Albuquerque, University of New Mexico Press.
Cunliffe, B. 1974. *Iron Age Communities in Britain*. London, Routledge & Kegan Paul.
Cunnington, R. H. 1975. *From Antiquary to Archaeologist*. Princes Risborough, Shire Publications.
Cushing, F. H. 1886. A study of Pueblo pottery as illustrative of Zuñi culture growth. Washington, *Bureau of American Ethnology, Annual Report* 4: 467–521.
Dall, W. H. 1877. On succession in the shell-heaps of the Aleutian Islands. Washington, *United States Geological and Geographic Survey, Contributions to North American Ethnology* 1: 41–91.
Dalton, G. 1961. Economic theory and primitive society. *American Anthropologist* 63: 1–25.
Daniel, G. E. 1943. *The Three Ages: An Essay on Archaeological Method*. Cambridge, Cambridge University Press.
1950. *A Hundred Years of Archaeology*. London, Duckworth.
1958. Editorial. *Antiquity* 32: 65–8.
1963a. *The Idea of Prehistory*. Cleveland, World.
1963b. The personality of Wales. In *Culture and Environment: Essays in Honour of Sir Cyril Fox*, ed. by I. Ll. Foster and L. Alcock, pp. 7–23. London, Routledge & Kegan Paul.
1967. *The Origins and Growth of Archaeology*. Harmondsworth, Penguin.
1975. *A Hundred and Fifty Years of Archaeology*. 2nd edn. London, Duckworth.
1976. Stone, bronze and iron. In J. V. S. Megaw, pp. 35–42.
1981a. *A Short History of Archaeology*. London, Thames and Hudson.
1981b. ed. *Towards a History of Archaeology*. London, Thames and Hudson.
1986. *Some Small Harvest*. London, Thames and Hudson.
Danilova, L. V. 1971. Controversial problems of the theory of precapitalist societies. *Soviet Anthropology and Archeology* 9: 269–328.
Danto, A. C. 1965. *Analytical Philosophy of History*. Cambridge, Cambridge University Press.
Darnton, R. 1984. *The Great Cat Massacre and Other Episodes in French Cultural History*. New York, Basic Books.

Davidson, J. M. 1979. New Zealand. In *The Prehistory of Polynesia*, ed. by J. D. Jennings, pp. 222–48. Cambridge, Massachusetts, Harvard University Press.

Davies, G. L. 1969. *The Earth in Decay: A History of British Geomorphology, 1578–1878*. New York, American Elsevier.

Davis, R. S. 1983. Theoretical issues in contemporary Soviet Paleolithic archaeology. *Annual Review of Anthropology* 12: 403–28.

Dawkins, W. B. 1874. *Cave Hunting: Researches on the Evidence of Caves Respecting the Early Inhabitants of Europe*. London, Macmillan.

Dawson, J. W. 1888. *Fossil Men and their Modern Representatives*. 3rd edn. London, Hodder and Stoughton (1st edn 1880, Montreal, Dawson Brothers).

1901. *Fifty Years of Work in Canada, Scientific and Educational*. London, Ballantyne, Hanson and Company.

Deagan, K. 1982. Avenues of inquiry in historical archaeology. *Advances in Archaeological Method and Theory* 5: 151–77.

Debetz, G. F. 1961. The social life of early Paleolithic man as seen through the work of the Soviet anthropologists. In *Social Life of Early Man*, ed. by S. L. Washburn, pp. 137–49. Chicago, Aldine.

Deetz, J. J. F. 1965. *The Dynamics of Stylistic Change in Arikara Ceramics*. Urbana, University of Illinois Press.

1977. *In Small Things Forgotten*. Garden City, Anchor.

De Laet, S. J. 1957. *Archaeology and its Problems*. New York, Macmillan.

Delâge, D. 1985. *Le pays renversé: Amérindiens et européens en Amérique du nord-est 1600–1664*. Montreal, Boréal Express.

Dennell, R. 1983. *European Economic Prehistory: A New Approach*. New York, Academic Press.

DePratter, C. B. 1986. ed. *The Late Prehistoric Southeast: A Source Book*. New York, Garland.

Deuel, L. 1967. *Conquistadors Without Swords: Archaeologists in the Americas*. New York, St. Martin's Press.

1973. *Flights into Yesterday: The Story of Aerial Archaeology*. Harmondsworth, Penguin.

Devon, Earl of. 1873. Inaugural address to the annual meeting held at Exeter, 1873. *Archaeological Journal* 30: 205–10.

Diehl, R. A. 1983. *Tula: The Toltec Capital of Ancient Mexico*. London, Thames and Hudson.

Dixon, R. B. 1913. Some aspects of North American archeology. *American Anthropologist* 15: 549–77.

1928. *The Building of Cultures*. New York, Scribner's.

Dolitsky, A. B. 1985. Siberian Paleolithic archaeology: approaches and analytic methods. Current Anthropology 26: 361–78.

Dolukhanov, P. M. 1979. *Ecology and Economy in Neolithic Eastern Europe*. London, Duckworth.

Doran, J. E. and F. R. Hodson. 1975. *Mathematics and Computers in Archaeology*. Edinburgh, Edinburgh University Press.

Dragadze, T. 1980. The place of 'ethnos' theory in Soviet anthropology. In E. Gellner, pp. 161–70.

Dray, W. 1957. *Laws and Explanation in History*. Oxford, Oxford University Press.

1964. *Philosophy of History*. Englewood Cliffs, Prentice-Hall.

Drower, M. S. 1985. *Flinders Petrie: A Life in Archaeology*. London, Gollancz.

Duff, R. S. 1950. *The Moa-Hunter Period of Maori Culture*. Wellington, Government Printer.

Dumond, D. E. 1977. Science in archaeology: the saints go marching in. *American Antiquity* 42: 330–49.

Dunn, S. P. 1982. *The Fall and Rise of the Asiatic Mode of Production*. London, Routledge & Kegan Paul.

Dunnell, R. C. 1970. Seriation method and its evaluation. *American Antiquity* 35: 305–19.

1971. *Systematics in Prehistory*. New York, Free Press.

1979. Trends in current Americanist archaeology. *American Journal of Archaeology* 83: 437–49.

1980a. Evolutionary theory and archaeology. *Advances in Archaeological Method and Theory* 3: 35–99.

1980b. Americanist archaeology: the 1979 contribution. *American Journal of Archaeology* 84: 463–78.

1981. Americanist archaeology: the 1980 literature. *American Journal of Archaeology* 85: 429–45.

1982a. Americanist archaeological literature: 1981. *American Journal of Archaeology* 86: 509–29.

1982b. Science, social science, and common sense: the agonizing dilemma of modern archaeology. *Journal of Anthropological Research* 38: 1–25.

1983. A review of the Americanist archaeological literature for 1982. *American Journal of Archaeology* 87: 521–44.

1984. The Americanist literature for 1983: a year of contrasts and challenges. *American Journal of Archaeology* 88: 489–513.

1985. Americanist archaeology in 1984. *American Journal of Archaeology* 89: 585–611.

1986. Five decades of American archaeology. In D. J. Meltzer *et al.*, pp. 23–49.

Durkheim, E. 1893. *De la division du travail social*. Paris, Alcan.

1895. *Les Règles de la méthode sociologique*. Paris, Alcan.

1897. *Le Suicide*. Paris, Alcan.

1912. *Les Formes élémentaires de la vie religieuse*. Paris, Alcan.

Duvignaud, J. 1965. *Durkheim: sa vie, son oeuvre*. Paris, Presses Universitaires de France.

Dymond, D. P. 1974. *Archaeology and History: A Plea for Reconciliation*. London, Thames and Hudson.

Earl, G. W. 1863. On the shell-mounds of Province Wellesley, in the Malay Peninsula. *Transactions of the Ethnological Society of London* 2: 119–29.

Earle, T. K. and R. W. Preucel. 1987. Processual archaeology and the radical critique. *Current Anthropology* 28: 501–38.

Edwards, I. E. S. 1985. *The Pyramids of Egypt*. Revised edn. Harmondsworth, Penguin.

Eggan, F. R. 1966. *The American Indian*. London, Weidenfeld and Nicolson.

Ehret, C. and M. Posnansky. 1982. eds. *The Archaeological and Linguistic Reconstruction of African History*. Berkeley, University of California Press.

Ehrlich, P. R. 1968. *The Population Bomb*. New York, Ballantine.

Eiseley, L. C. 1958. *Darwin's Century: Evolution and the Man Who Discovered It*. Garden City, Doubleday.

Ekholm, K. and J. Friedman. 1979. 'Capital' imperialism and exploitation in ancient world systems. In *Power and Propaganda: A Symposium on Ancient Empires*, ed. by M. T. Larsen, pp. 41–58. Copenhagen, Akademisk Forlag.

Eldredge, N. 1982. La macroévolution. *La Recherche* 13 (133): 616–26.

Elisseeff, D. 1986. *China: Treasures and Splendors*. Paris, Les Editions Arthaud.

Ellegård, A. 1981. Stone Age science in Britain? *Current Anthropology* 22: 99–125.

Elton, G. R. 1969. *The Practice of History*. London, Collins.

Emery, F. E. 1969. ed. *Systems Thinking*. New York, Penguin.

Evans, A. J. 1890. On a late-Celtic urn-field at Aylesford, Kent. *Archaeologia* 52: 315–88.

1896. The 'Eastern Question' in anthropology. *Proceedings of the British Association for the Advancement of Science, 1896*, 906–22.

Evans, Joan. 1956. *A History of the Society of Antiquaries*. London, The Society of Antiquaries.

Evans, John. 1850. On the date of British coins. *The Numismatic Chronicle and Journal of the Numismatic Society* 12: 127–37.

Evans, J. D., B. Cunliffe, and C. Renfrew. 1981. eds. *Antiquity and Man: Essays in Honour of Glyn Daniel*. London, Thames and Hudson.

Evans-Pritchard, E. E. 1940. *The Nuer*. Oxford, Oxford University Press.

1981. *A History of Anthropological Thought*. London, Faber and Faber.

Eve, R. A. and F. B. Harrold. 1986. Creationism, cult archaeology, and other pseudoscientific beliefs. *Youth and Society* 17: 396–421

Fagan, B. M. 1975. *The Rape of the Nile: Tomb Robbers, Tourists, and Archaeologists in Egypt*. New York, Charles Scribner's.

1977. *Elusive Treasure: The Story of Early Archaeologists in the Americas*. New York, Charles Scribner's.

1981. Two hundred and four years of African archaeology. In J. D. Evans *et al.*, pp. 42–51.

Fairbanks, C. H. 1942. The taxonomic position of Stalling's Island, Georgia. *American Antiquity* 7: 223–31.

Fairchild, H. N. 1928. *The Noble Savage: A Study in Romantic Naturalism*. New York, Columbia University Press.

Fawcett, Clare. 1986. The politics of assimilation in Japanese archaeology. *Archaeological Review from Cambridge* 5(1): 43–57.

Feder, K. L. 1984. Irrationality and popular archaeology. *American Antiquity* 49: 525–41.

Fell, B. 1976. *America B.C.: Ancient Settlers in the New World*. New York, Quadrangle.

1982. *Bronze Age America*. Boston, Little, Brown.
Ferguson, T. J. 1984. Archaeological ethics and values in a tribal cultural resource management program at the Pueblo of Zuñi. In E. L. Green, pp. 224–35.
Fewkes, J. W. 1896. The prehistoric culture of Tusayan. *American Anthropologist* 9: 151–73.
Feyerabend, P. K. 1975. *Against Method: Outline of an Anarchistic Theory of Knowledge*. London, NLB.
Field, H. and K. Price. 1949. Recent archaeological discoveries in the Soviet Union. *Southwestern Journal of Anthropology* 5: 17–27.
Field, H. and E. Prostov. 1937. Archaeology in the Soviet Union. *American Anthropologist* 39: 457–90.
Fischer, D. H. 1970. *Historians' Fallacies: Toward a Logic of Historical Thought*. London, Routledge & Kegan Paul.
Fischer, G. 1967. ed. *Science and Ideology in Soviet Society*. New York, Atherton Press.
Fischer, J. L. 1961. Art styles as cultural cognitive maps. *American Anthropologist* 63: 79–93.
Fitting, J. E. 1973. ed. *The Development of North American Archaeology*. Garden City, Anchor Books.
Fitzpatrick, S. 1974. Cultural revolution in Russia 1928–32. *Journal of Contemporary History* 9: 33–51.
Fitzsimons, M. A., A. G. Pundt, and C. E. Nowell. 1954. eds. *The Development of Historiography*. Harrisburg, Stackpole.
Flannery, K. V. 1968. Archeological systems theory and early Mesoamerica. In *Anthropological Archeology in the Americas*, ed. by B. J. Meggers, pp. 67–87. Washington, Anthropological Society of Washington.
1972. The cultural evolution of civilizations. *Annual Review of Ecology and Systematics* 3: 399–426.
1976. ed. *The Early Mesoamerican Village*. New York, Academic Press.
1982. The golden Marshalltown: a parable for the archaeology of the 1980s. *American Anthropologist* 84: 265–78.
1983. Archaeology and ethnology in the context of divergent evolution. In *The Cloud People*, ed. by K. V. Flannery and J. Marcus, pp. 361–2. New York, Academic Press.
Flood, J. 1983. *Archaeology of the Dreamtime*. Sydney, Collins.
Ford, J. A. 1936. *Analysis of Indian Village Site Collections from Louisiana and Mississippi*. New Orleans, Louisiana State Geological Survey, Department of Conservation, Anthropological Study no. 2.
1938. A chronological method applicable to the Southeast. *American Antiquity* 3: 260–4.
Ford, J. A. and G. R. Willey. 1941. An interpretation of the prehistory of the eastern United States. *American Anthropologist* 43: 325–63.
Ford, R. I. 1973. Archeology serving humanity. In C. L. Redman, pp. 83–93.
1987. ed. *The Prehistoric American Southwest: A Sourcebook*. New York, Garland.
Forge, A. 1972. Normative factors in the settlement size of Neolithic cultivators

(New Guinea). In *Man, Settlement and Urbanism*, ed. by P. J. Ucko, R. Tringham and G. W. Dimbleby, pp. 363–76. London, Duckworth.
Fortes, M. 1980. Introduction. In E. Gellner, pp. xix–xxv.
Fowler, D. D. 1987. Uses of the past: archaeology in the service of the state. *American Antiquity* 52: 229–48.
Fowles, J. 1980, 1982. ed. *John Aubrey's Monumenta Britannica*, annotated by R. Legg. Sherborne, Dorset Publishing Company.
Fox, C. 1923. *The Archaeology of the Cambridge Region*. Cambridge, Cambridge University Press.
1932. *The Personality of Britain*. Cardiff, National Museum of Wales.
Fox, L. 1956. ed. *English Historical Scholarship in the Sixteenth and Seventeenth Centuries*. London, Oxford University Press.
Francis, D. and T. Morantz. 1983. *Partners in Furs: A History of the Fur Trade in Eastern James Bay, 1600–1870*. Montreal, McGill-Queen's University Press.
Frick, W. 1934. The teaching of history and prehistory in Germany. *Nature* 133: 298–9.
Fried, M. H. 1967. *The Evolution of Political Society*. New York, Random House.
1975. *The Notion of Tribe*. Menlo Park, Cummings.
Friedman, J. and M. J. Rowlands. 1978a. eds. *The Evolution of Social Systems*. London, Duckworth.
Friedman, J. and M. J. Rowlands. 1978b. Notes towards an epigenetic model of the evolution of 'civilisation'. In J. Friedman and M. J. Rowlands, pp. 201–76.
Fritz, J. M. 1973. Relevance, archeology, and subsistence theory. In C. L. Redman, pp. 59–82.
Frumkin, G. 1962. Archaeology in Soviet Central Asia and its ideological background. *Central Asian Review* 10: 334–42.
Fuller, P. 1980. *Beyond the Crisis in Art*. London, Writers and Readers.
Furst, P. T. 1977. The roots and continuities of shamanism. In *Stone, Bones and Skin*, ed. by A. T. Brodzky *et al.*, pp. 1–28. Toronto, Society for Art Publications.
Gallay, A. 1986. *L'Archéologie demain*. Paris, Belfond.
Gamio, M. 1916. *Forjando Patria (Pro Nacionalismo)*. Mexico, Porrúa Hermanos.
Gandara, M. 1980. La vieja 'Nueva Arqueología' (primera parte). *Boletín de Antropología Americana* 2: 7–45.
1981. La vieja 'Nueva Arqueología' (segunda parte). *Boletín de Antropología Americana* 3: 7–70.
Gardin, J.-C. 1980. *Archaeological Constructs: An Aspect of Theoretical Archaeology*. Cambridge, Cambridge University Press.
Gardiner, P. L. 1952. *The Nature of Historical Explanation*. Oxford, Oxford University Press.
1974. ed. *The Philosophy of History*. London, Oxford University Press.
Garlake, P. S. 1973. *Great Zimbabwe*. London, Thames and Hudson.
1983. Prehistory and ideology in Zimbabwe. In *Past and Present in Zimbabwe*, ed. by J. D. Y. Peet and T. Ranger, pp. 1–19. Manchester, Manchester University Press.

1984. Ken Mufuka and Great Zimbabwe. *Antiquity* 58: 121–3.

Gasparini, G. and L. Margolies. 1980. *Inca Architecture*. Bloomington, Indiana University Press.

Gathercole, P. 1971. 'Patterns in prehistory': an examination of the later thinking of V. Gordon Childe. *World Archaeology* 3: 225–32.

1976. Childe the 'outsider'. *RAIN* 17: 5–6.

1981. New Zealand prehistory before 1950. In Glyn Daniel, 1981b, pp. 159–68.

1982. Gordon Childe: man or myth? *Antiquity* 56: 195–8.

1984. A consideration of ideology. In M. Spriggs, pp. 149–54.

Gayre, R. 1972. *The Origin of Zimbabwean Civilisation*. Salisbury, Galaxie Press.

Geikie, A. 1905. *The Founders of Geology*. 2nd edn. London, Macmillan.

Gellner, E. 1980. ed. *Soviet and Western Anthropology*. London, Duckworth.

1983. *Nations and Nationalism*. Ithaca, Cornell University Press.

1985. *Relativism and the Social Sciences*. Cambridge, Cambridge University Press.

Gening, V. F. 1982. *Ocherki po Istorii Sovetskoy Arkheologii*. Kiev, Naukova Dumka.

Geras, N. 1983. Marx and Human Nature: Refutation of a Legend. London, Verso.

Gero, J. M. 1983. Gender bias in archaeology: a cross-cultural perspective. In *The Socio-Politics of Archaeology*, ed. by J. M. Gero, D. M. Lacy and M. L. Blakey, pp. 51–7. Amherst, University of Massachusetts, Department of Anthropology, Research Report no. 23.

Gibbon, G. 1984. *Anthropological Archaeology*. New York, Columbia University Press.

Gill, D. W. J. 1987. Metru.Menece: an Etruscan painted inscription on a mid-5th-century BC red-figure cup from Populonia. *Antiquity* 61: 82–7.

Gillispie, C. C. 1951. *Genesis and Geology: A Study in the Relations of Scientific Thought, Natural Theology, and Social Opinion in Great Britain, 1790–1850*. Cambridge, Massachusetts, Harvard University Press.

Gilman, A. 1984. Explaining the Upper Palaeolithic revolution. In M. Spriggs, pp. 115–26.

Gjessing, G. 1968. The social responsibility of the social scientist. *Current Anthropology* 9: 397–402.

Glacken, C. J. 1967. *Traces on the Rhodian Shore: Nature and Culture in Western Thought from Ancient Times to the End of the Eighteenth Century*. Berkeley and Los Angeles, University of California Press.

Gladwin, W. and H. S. Gladwin. 1930. *A Method for the Designation of Southwestern Pottery Types*. Globe, Medallion Papers no. 7.

1934. *A Method for Designation of Cultures and their Variations*. Globe, Medallion Papers no. 15.

Glass, H. B., O. Temkin, and W. L. Straus Jr. 1959. eds. *Forerunners of Darwin, 1745–1859*. Baltimore, Johns Hopkins University Press.

Glassie, H. H. 1975. *Folk Housing in Middle Virginia: A Structural Analysis of Historic Artifacts*. Knoxville, University of Tennessee Press.

Gledhill, J. 1984. The transformation of Asiatic formations: the case of late prehispanic Mesoamerica. In M. Spriggs, pp. 135–48.
Gobineau, J.-A., comte de. 1853–5. *Essai sur l'inégalité des races humaines.* 4 vols. Paris, Didot.
Godelier, M. 1978. Economy and religion: an evolutionary optical illusion. In J. Friedman and M. J. Rowlands, pp. 3–11.
Godwin, H. 1933. British Maglemose harpoon sites. *Antiquity* 7: 36–48.
Goff, B. L. 1963. *Symbols of Prehistoric Mesopotamia.* New Haven, Yale University Press.
Golson, J. 1977. *The Ladder of Social Evolution: Archaeology and the Bottom Rungs.* Canberra, Australian Academy of the Humanities.
Gooch, G. P. 1959. *History and Historians in the Nineteenth Century.* Boston, Beacon Press.
Goodenough, E. R. 1953–68. *Jewish Symbols in the Greco-Roman Period.* 13 vols. New York, Pantheon Books.
Goodwin, A. J. H. and C. van Riet Lowe. 1929. *The Stone Age Cultures of South Africa.* Cape Town, Annals of the South African Museum no. 27.
Gopal, L. 1985. Foreword. In Trigger 1985b, pp. i–vi.
Gosden, C. 1985. Gifts and kin in early Iron Age Europe. *Man* 20: 475–93.
Goudie, A. 1976. Geography and prehistory. *Journal of Historical Geography* 2: 197–205.
Gould, R. A. 1978. ed. *Explorations in Ethnoarchaeology.* Albuquerque, University of New Mexico Press.
1980. *Living Archaeology.* Cambridge, Cambridge University Press.
Gould, S. J. 1980. *The Panda's Thumb: More Reflections in Natural History.* New York, Norton.
1981. *The Mismeasure of Man.* New York, Norton.
Gradmann, R. 1906. Beziehung zwischen Pflanzengeographie und Siedlungsgeschichte. *Geographische Zeitschrift* 12: 305–25.
Graham, L. R. 1967. *The Soviet Academy of Sciences and the Communist Party, 1927–1932.* Princeton, Princeton University Press.
Graham-Campbell, J. and D. Kidd. 1980. *The Vikings.* London, British Museum Publications.
Grant, G. 1965. *Lament for a Nation: The Defeat of Canadian Nationalism.* Toronto, McClelland and Stewart.
Grant, M. 1916. *The Passing of the Great Race; or, the Racial Basis of European History.* New York, Scribner's.
Gräslund, B. 1974. *Relativ Datering: Om Kronologisk Metod i Nordisk Arkeologi.* Uppsala, Tor no. 16.
1976. Relative chronology: dating methods in Scandinavian archaeology. *Norwegian Archaeological Review* 9: 69–126.
1981. The background to C. J. Thomsen's Three-Age system. In G. Daniel, 1981b, pp. 45–50.
1987. *The Birth of Prehistoric Chronology.* Cambridge, Cambridge University Press.

Grayson, D. K. 1983. *The Establishment of Human Antiquity*. New York, Academic Press.
1986. Eoliths, archaeological ambiguity, and the generation of 'middle-range' research. In D. J. Meltzer *et al.*, pp. 77–133.
Green, E. L. 1984. ed. *Ethics and Values in Archaeology*. New York, Free Press.
Green, S. 1981. *Prehistorian: A Biography of V. Gordon Childe*. Bradford-on-Avon, Moonraker Press.
Green, S. W. and S. M. Perlman, 1985. eds. *The Archaeology of Frontiers and Boundaries*. New York, Academic Press.
Greene, J. C. 1959. *The Death of Adam*. Ames, Iowa State University Press.
Griffin, J. B. 1980. The Mesoamerican–southeastern U.S. connection. *Early Man* 2(3): 12–18.
Gruber, J. W. 1965. Brixham Cave and the antiquity of man. In *Context and Meaning in Cultural Anthropology*, ed. by M. E. Spiro, pp. 373–402. New York, Free Press.
Guest, E. 1883. *Origines Celticae (a Fragment)*. London, Macmillan.
Guidi, A. 1988. *Storia della Paletnologia*. Rome, Editori Laterza.
Haber, F. C. 1959. *The Age of the World: Moses to Darwin*. Baltimore, Johns Hopkins University Press.
Habermas, J. 1971. *Knowledge and Human Interests*. Boston, Beacon Press.
1975. *Legitimation Crisis*. Boston, Beacon Press.
Hall, M. 1984. The burden of tribalism: the social context of southern African Iron Age studies. *American Antiquity* 49: 455–67.
Hall, R. L. 1979. In search of the ideology of the Adena–Hopewell climax. In *Hopewell Archaeology: The Chillicothe Conference*, ed. by D. S. Brose and N. Greber, pp. 258–65. Kent, Kent State University Press.
Hall, R. N. 1909. *Prehistoric Rhodesia*. London, Unwin.
Hall, R. N. and W. G. Neal. 1902. *The Ancient Ruins of Rhodesia*. London, Methuen.
Hallowell, A. I. 1960. The beginnings of anthropology in America. In *Selected Papers from the American Anthropologist 1880–1920*. ed. by F. de Laguna, pp. 1–90. Evanston, Row, Peterson and Company.
Hamell, G. 1983. Trading in metaphors: the magic of beads. In *Proceedings of the 1982 Glass Trade Bead Conference*, ed. by C. F. Hayes, III, pp. 5–28. Rochester, Rochester Museum and Science Center, Research Records no. 16.
Hammond, N. 1977. ed. *Social Process in Maya Prehistory*. New York, Academic Press.
1983. Lords of the jungle: a prosopography of Maya archaeology. In *Civilization in the Ancient Americas*, ed. by R. M. Leventhal and A. L. Kolata, pp. 3–32. Albuquerque, University of New Mexico Press.
Hampson, N. 1982. *The Enlightenment*. Harmondsworth, Penguin.
Hanbury-Tenison, J. 1986. Hegel in prehistory. *Antiquity* 60: 108–14.
Hanke, L. 1959. *Aristotle and the American Indians*. Chicago, Regnery.
Harrington, M. R. 1924. *An Ancient Village Site of the Shinnecock Indians*. New

York, Anthropological Papers of the American Museum of Natural History, no. 22, pt. 5.

Harris, M. 1968. *The Rise of Anthropological Theory*. New York, Crowell.

1974. *Cows, Pigs, Wars and Witches*. New York, Random House.

1977. *Cannibals and Kings: The Origins of Cultures*. New York, Random House.

1979. *Cultural Materialism: The Struggle for a Science of Culture*. New York, Random House.

1981. *America Now: The Anthropology of a Changing Culture*. New York, Simon and Schuster.

Harrison, R. J. 1980. *The Beaker Folk: Copper Age Archaeology in Western Europe*. London, Thames and Hudson.

Hassig, R. 1985. *Trade, Tribute, and Transportation: The Sixteenth-Century Political Economy of the Valley of Mexico*. Norman, University of Oklahoma Press.

Haven, S. 1856. *Archaeology of the United States*. Washington, Smithsonian Contributions to Knowledge, no. 8(2).

1864. Report of the librarian. *Proceedings of the American Antiquarian Society*, April 1864: 30–52.

Haverfield, F. J. 1912. *The Romanization of Roman Britain*. 2nd edn. Oxford, Oxford University Press.

Hawkes, C. F. 1954. Archeological theory and method: some suggestions from the Old World. *American Anthropologist* 56: 155–68.

Hawkes, J. 1963. ed. *The World of the Past*. 2 vols. New York, Knopf.

1968. The proper study of mankind. *Antiquity* 42: 255–62.

1982. *Mortimer Wheeler: Adventurer in Archaeology*. London, Weidenfeld and Nicolson.

Hayden, B. 1979. ed. *Lithic Use-Wear Analysis*. New York, Academic Press.

Hayden, B. and A. Cannon. 1984. *The Structure of Material Systems: Ethnoarchaeology in the Maya Highlands*. Washington, Society for American Archaeology, Paper no. 3.

Heizer, R. F. 1959. ed. *The Archaeologist at Work: A Source Book in Archaeological Method and Interpretation*. New York, Harper and Row.

1962a. ed. *Man's Discovery of his Past: Literary Landmarks in Archaeology*. Englewood Cliffs, Prentice-Hall.

1962b. The background of Thomsen's Three-Age system. *Technology and Culture* 3: 259–66.

Hellmich, M. 1923. *Die Beseidlung Schlesiens in vor- und frühgeschichtlicher Zeit*. Breslau, Preuss und Jünger.

Hempel, C. G. 1962. Deductive–nomological vs. statistical explanation. In *Scientific Explanation, Space, and Time*, ed. by H. Feigl and G. Maxwell, pp. 98–169. Minneapolis, University of Minnesota Press.

1965. *Aspects of Scientific Explanation*. New York, Free Press.

1966. *Philosophy of Natural Science*. Englewood Cliffs, Prentice-Hall.

Hesse, M. B. 1974. *The Structure of Scientific Inference*. New York, Macmillan.

Hewett, E. L. 1906. *Antiquities of the Jemez Plateau, New Mexico.* Washington, Bureau of American Ethnology, Bulletin no. 32.

Hexter, J. H. 1979. *On Historians.* Cambridge, Massachusetts, Harvard University Press.

Heyden, D. 1981. Caves, gods, and myths: world-view and planning in Teotihuacan. In *Mesoamerican Sites and World-Views*, ed. by E. P. Benson, pp. 1–39. Washington, Dumbarton Oaks.

Higgs, E. S. 1972. ed. *Papers in Economic Prehistory.* Cambridge, Cambridge University Press.

1975. ed. *Palaeoeconomy.* Cambridge, Cambridge University Press.

Hill, J. N. 1970. *Broken K Pueblo: Prehistoric Social Organization in the American Southwest.* Tucson, University of Arizona Press.

Hindess, B. and P. Q. Hirst. 1975. *Pre-Capitalist Modes of Production.* London, Routledge & Kegan Paul.

Hinsley, C. M. Jr. 1981. *Savages and Scientists: The Smithsonian Institution and the Development of American Anthropology 1846–1910.* Washington, Smithsonian Institution Press.

1985. From shell-heaps to stelae: early anthropology at the Peabody Museum. In *Objects and Others: Essays on Museums and Material Culture* (History of Anthropology, 3), ed. by G. W. Stocking Jr, pp. 49–74. Madison, University of Wisconsin Press.

Hobsbawm, E. 1964. ed. *Karl Marx, Pre-Capitalist Economic Formations.* London, Lawrence and Wishart.

Hodder, I. 1978. ed. *Simulation Studies in Archaeology.* Cambridge, Cambridge University Press.

1981. Society, economy and culture: an ethnographic case study amongst the Lozi. In *Pattern of the Past: Studies in Honour of David Clarke*, ed. by I. Hodder, G. Isaac, and N. Hammond, pp. 67–95. Cambridge, Cambridge University Press.

1982a. *The Present Past: An Introduction to Anthropology for Archaeologists.* London, Batsford.

1982b. *Symbols in Action: Ethnoarchaeological Studies of Material Culture.* Cambridge, Cambridge University Press.

1982c. ed. *Symbolic and Structural Archaeology.* Cambridge, Cambridge University Press.

1982d. Sequences of structural change in the Dutch Neolithic. In I. Hodder 1982c, pp. 162–77.

1984a. Burials, houses, women and men in the European Neolithic. In D. Miller and C. Tilley, pp. 51–68.

1984b. Archaeology in 1984. *Antiquity* 58: 25–32.

1985. Postprocessual archaeology. *Advances in Archaeological Method and Theory* 8: 1–26.

1986. *Reading the Past: Current Approaches to Interpretation in Archaeology.* Cambridge, Cambridge University Press.

1987. ed. *Archaeology as Long-term History.* Cambridge, Cambridge University Press.

Hodder, I. and C. Orton. 1976. *Spatial Analysis in Archaeology*. Cambridge, Cambridge University Press.

Hodgen, M. T. 1964. *Early Anthropology in the Sixteenth and Seventeenth Centuries*. Philadelphia, University of Pennsylvania Press.

Hodson, F. R., D. G. Kendall, and P. Tăutu. 1971. eds. *Mathematics in the Archaeological and Historical Sciences*. Edinburgh, Edinburgh University Press.

Hoebel, E. A. 1949. *Man in the Primitive World*. New York, McGraw-Hill.

Hoffman, M. A. 1974. The rise of antiquarianism in Japan and Western Europe. *Arctic Anthropology* 11, supplement: 182–8.

Hogarth, A. C. 1972. Common sense in archaeology. *Antiquity* 46: 301–4.

Hogarth, D. G. 1899. ed. *Authority and Archaeology, Sacred and Profane*. London, John Murray.

Hole, F. and R. F. Heizer. 1969. *An Introduction to Prehistoric Archaeology*. 2nd edn. New York, Holt, Rinehart and Winston.

Holmes, W. H. 1903. Aboriginal pottery of the eastern United States. Washington, *Bureau of American Ethnology, Annual Report* 20: 1–237.

1914. Areas of American culture characterization tentatively outlined as an aid in the study of the antiquities. *American Anthropologist* 16: 413–46.

Honigmann, J. J. 1976. *The Development of Anthropological Ideas*. Homewood, Dorsey.

Hood, D. 1964. *Davidson Black: A Biography*. Toronto, University of Toronto Press.

Hooton, E. A. 1938. *Apes, Men, and Morons*. London, Allen and Unwin.

Horsman, R. 1975. Scientific racism and the American Indian in the mid-nineteenth century. *American Quarterly* 27: 152–68.

1981. *Race and Manifest Destiny: The Origins of American Racial Anglo-Saxonism*. Cambridge, Massachusetts, Harvard University Press.

Howe, J. E. 1976. Pre-agricultural society in Soviet theory and method. *Arctic Anthropology* 13: 84–115.

1980. The Soviet Theories of Primitive History: Forty Years of Speculation on the Origins and Evolution of People and Society. Seattle, PhD thesis, University of Washington.

Hudson, K. 1981. *A Social History of Archaeology: The British Experience*. London, Macmillan.

Hunt, E. 1972. Irrigation and the socio-political organization of Cuicatec cacicazgos. In *The Prehistory of the Tehuacan Valley*, vol. 4, *Chronology and Irrigation*, ed. by F. Johnson, pp. 162–259. Austin, University of Texas Press.

Hunter, M. 1975. *John Aubrey and the Realm of Learning*. London, Duckworth.

Huntington, R. and P. Metcalf. 1979. *Celebrations of Death*. Cambridge, Cambridge University Press.

Hutchinson, H. G. 1914. *Life of Sir John Lubbock, Lord Avebury*. 2 vols. London, Macmillan.

Huxley, T. H. 1896. *Man's Place in Nature and Other Anthropological Essays*. New York, Appleton and Company.

Ihering, H. von. 1895. A civilisacão prehistorica do Brasil meridional. São Paulo, *Revista do Museu Paulista* 1: 34–159.
Ikawa-Smith, F. 1982. Co-traditions in Japanese archaeology. *World Archaeology* 13: 296–309.
Ingersoll, D., J. Yellen, and W. Macdonald. 1977. eds. *Experimental Archaeology*. New York, Columbia University Press.
Irvine, W. 1955. *Apes, Angels, and Victorians*. New York, McGraw-Hill.
Isaac, G. L. 1984. The archaeology of human origins: studies of the Lower Pleistocene in East Africa 1971–1981. In *Advances in World Archaeology*, ed. by F. Wendorf and A. Close, pp. 1–87. New York, Academic Press.
Isaac, R. 1982. *The Transformation of Virginia, 1740–1790*. Chapel Hill, University of North Carolina Press.
Isaacs, J. 1980. ed. *Australian Dreaming: 40,000 Years of Aboriginal History*. Sydney, Lansdowne Press.
Jacobson, J. 1979. Recent developments in South Asian prehistory and protohistory. *Annual Review of Anthropology* 8: 467–502.
Jaenen, C. 1976. *Friend and Foe: Aspects of French-Amerindian Cultural Contact in the Sixteenth and Seventeenth Centuries*. Toronto, McClelland and Stewart.
Jairazbhoy, R. A. 1974, 1976. *The Old World Origins of American Civilization*. 2 vols. Totawa, Rowman and Littlefield.
Jarman, M. R., G. N. Bailey, and H. N. Jarman. 1982. eds. *Early European Agriculture: Its Foundations and Development*. Cambridge, Cambridge University Press.
Jennings, J. D. 1979. ed. *The Prehistory of Polynesia*. Cambridge, Massachusetts, Harvard University Press.
Jochim, M. A. 1976. *Hunter–Gatherer Subsistence and Settlement: A Predictive Model*. New York, Academic Press.
Johnson, G. A. 1978. Information sources and the development of decision-making organizations. In *Social Archeology*, ed. by C. L. Redman *et al.*, pp. 87–112. New York, Academic Press.
1981. Monitoring complex system integration and boundary phenomena with settlement size data. In *Archaeological Approaches to the Study of Complexity*, ed. by S. E. van der Leeuw, pp. 143–88. Amsterdam, Van Giffen Institute.
Johnson, S. 1970. *Johnson's Journey to the Western Islands of Scotland*, ed. by R. W. Chapman. Oxford, Oxford University Press.
Jones, H. M. 1964. *O Strange New World: American Culture, The Formative Years*. New York, Viking Press.
Jones, R. 1979. The fifth continent: problems concerning the human colonization of Australia. *Annual Review of Anthropology* 8: 445–66.
Kaiser, W. 1957. Zur inneren Chronologie der Naqadakultur. *Archaeologia Geographica* 6: 69–77.
Kamenetsky, I. S., B. I. Marshak, and Ya. A. Sher. 1975. *Analiz Arkheologicheskikh Istochnikov*. Leningrad, Nauka.
Kaplan, A. 1964. *The Conduct of Inquiry*. San Francisco, Chandler.
Keen, B. 1971. *The Aztec Image in Western Thought*. New Brunswick, New Jersey, Rutgers University Press.

Kelley, J. H. and M. P. Hanen, 1988. *Archaeology and the Methodology of Science*. Albuquerque, University of New Mexico Press.
Kendall, D. G. 1969. Some problems and methods in statistical archaeology. *World Archaeology* 1: 68–76.
1971. Seriation from abundance matrices. In F. R. Hodson, D. G. Kendall, and P. Tăutu, pp. 215–52.
Kendrick, T. D. 1950. *British Antiquity*. London, Methuen.
Kennedy, B. 1981. *Marriage Patterns in an Archaic Population: A Study of Skeletal Remains from Port au Choix, Newfoundland*. Ottawa, Archaeological Survey of Canada, Mercury Series no. 104.
Kent, S. 1984. *Analyzing Activity Areas: An Ethnoarchaeological Study of the Use of Space*. Albuquerque: University of New Mexico Press.
Kenyon, J. P. 1983. *The History Men*. London, Weidenfeld and Nicolson.
Keur, D. L. 1941. *Big Bead Mesa. Memoir* (Menasha, Wisconsin, Society for American Archaeology) 1.
Kidder, A. V. 1924. *An Introduction to the Study of Southwestern Archaeology*. New Haven, Papers of the Southwestern Expedition, Phillips Academy, no. 1.
1935. *Year Book*, no. 34. Washington, Carnegie Foundation.
1962. *An Introduction to the Study of Southwestern Archaeology, with an Introduction, 'Southwestern Archaeology Today,' by Irving Rouse*. New Haven, Yale University Press.
Killan, G. 1983. *David Boyle: From Artisan to Archaeologist*. Toronto, University of Toronto Press.
Kitchen, K. A. 1982. *Pharaoh Triumphant: The Life and Times of Ramesses II*. Mississauga: Benben Publications.
Ki-Zerbo, J. 1981. ed. *General History of Africa*, vol. I, *Methodology and African Prehistory*. Berkeley and Los Angeles, University of California Press.
Klein, R. G. 1966. Chellean and Acheulean on the territory of the Soviet Union: a critical review of the evidence as presented in the literature. *American Anthropologist* 68(2), pt. 2: 1–45.
Kleindienst, M. R. and P. J. Watson. 1956. 'Action archaeology': the archaeological inventory of a living community. *Anthropology Tomorrow* 5: 75–8.
Klejn, L. S. 1969. Characteristic methods in the current critique of Marxism in archeology. *Soviet Anthropology and Archeology* 7(4): 41–53.
1970. Archaeology in Britain: a Marxist view. *Antiquity* 44: 296–303.
1973a. Marxism, the systemic approach, and archaeology. In Renfrew 1973b, pp. 691–710.
1973b. On major aspects of the interrelationship of archaeology and ethnology. *Current Anthropology* 14: 311–20.
1974. Kossinna im Abstand von vierzig Jahren. *Jahresschrift für mitteldeutsche Vorgeschichte* 58: 7–55.
1977. A panorama of theoretical archaeology. *Current Anthropology* 18: 1–42.
1982. *Archaeological Typology*. Oxford, BAR, International Series, no. 153.
Klemm, G. F. 1843–52. *Allgemeine Cultur-Geschichte der Menschheit*. 10 vols. Leipzig, Teubner.
1854–55. *Allgemeine Kulturwissenschaft*. Leipzig, J. A. Romberg.

Klindt-Jensen, O. 1975. *A History of Scandinavian Archaeology*. London, Thames and Hudson.

1976. The influence of ethnography on early Scandinavian archaeology. In J. V. S. Megaw, pp. 43–8.

Kluckhohn, C. 1940. The conceptual structure in Middle American studies. In *The Maya and their Neighbors*, ed. by C. L. Hay *et al.*, pp. 41–51. New York, Appleton-Century.

Kohl, P. L. 1978. The balance of trade in southwestern Asia in the mid-third millennium B.C. *Current Anthropology* 19: 463–92.

1979. The 'world economy' of West Asia in the third millennium B.C. In *South Asian Archaeology 1977*, ed. by M. Taddei, vol. 1, pp. 55–85. Naples, Istituto Universitario Orientale, Seminario di Studi Asiatici.

1981a. *The Bronze Age Civilization of Central Asia: Recent Soviet Discoveries*. Armonk, New York, Sharpe.

1981b. Materialist approaches in prehistory. *Annual Review of Anthropology* 10: 89–118.

1984. Force, history and the evolutionist paradigm. In M. Spriggs, pp. 127–34.

1987. The ancient economy, transferable technologies, and the Bronze Age world system: a view from the northwestern frontier of the ancient Near East. In *Centre and Periphery in the Ancient World*, ed. by M. J. Rowlands and M. T. Larsen, pp. 13–24. Cambridge, Cambridge University Press.

Kohn, H. 1960. *The Mind of Germany*. New York, Scribner's.

Kolakowski, L. 1976. *La Philosophie positiviste*. Paris, Denoël.

1978a. *Main Currents of Marxism*, vol. 1, *The Founders*. Oxford, Oxford University Press.

1978b. *Main Currents of Marxism*, vol. 2, *The Golden Age*. Oxford, Oxford University Press.

1978c. *Main Currents of Marxism*, vol. 3, *The Breakdown*. Oxford, Oxford University Press.

Kossinna, G. 1911. *Die Herkunft der Germanen*. Leipzig, Kabitzsch.

Kramer, C. 1979. ed. *Ethnoarchaeology: Implications of Ethnography for Archaeology*. New York, Columbia University Press.

1982. *Village Ethnoarchaeology: Rural Iran in Archaeological Perspective*. New York, Academic Press.

Kristiansen, K. 1981. A social history of Danish archaeology (1805–1975). In G. Daniel, 1981b, pp. 20–44.

1984. Ideology and material culture: an archaeological perspective. In M. Spriggs, pp. 72–100.

1985. A short history of Danish archaeology: an analytical perspective. In *Archaeological Formation Processes*, ed. by K. Kristiansen, pp. 12–34. Copenhagen, Nationalmusset.

Kroeber, A. L. 1909. The archaeology of California In *Putnam Anniversary Volume: Anthropological Essays Presented to Frederic W. Putnam in Honor of his 70th Birthday*, ed. by F. Boas *et al.*, pp. 1–42. New York, G. E. Stechert.

1916. Zuñi potsherds. New York, *Anthropological Papers of the American Museum of Natural History* 18(1): 7–37.

1952. *The Nature of Culture*. Chicago, University of Chicago Press.

Kroeber, A. L. and C. Kluckhohn. 1952. *Culture – A Critical Review of Concepts and Definitions*. Cambridge, Massachusetts, Harvard University, Papers of the Peabody Museum of American Archaeology and Ethnology no. 47.

Kroker, A. 1984. *Technology and the Canadian Mind: Innis/McLuhan/Grant*. Montreal, New World Perspectives.

Kruglov, A. P. and G. V. Podgayetsky. 1935. *Rodovoe Obshchestvo Stepei Vostochnoi Evropy*. Leningrad, Izvestiia GAIMK no. 119.

Kubler, G. 1962. *The Shape of Time: Remarks on the History of Things*. New Haven, Yale University Press.

Kuhn, T. S. 1962. *The Structure of Scientific Revolutions*. Chicago, University of Chicago Press.

1970. *The Structure of Scientific Revolutions*. 2nd edn. Chicago, University of Chicago Press.

Kupperman, K. O. 1980. *Settling with the Indians; The Meeting of English and Indian Cultures in America, 1580–1640*. Totowa, New Jersey, Rowman and Littlefield.

Kus, S. 1984. The spirit and its burden: archaeology and symbolic activity. In M. Spriggs, pp. 101–7.

Lal, M. 1984. *Settlement History and Rise of Civilization in Ganga-Yamuna Doab*. Delhi, B.R. Publishing.

Lamberg-Karlovsky, C. C. 1975. Third millennium modes of exchange and modes of production. In *Ancient Civilization and Trade*, ed. by J. A. Sabloff and C. C. Lamberg-Karlovsky, pp. 341–68. Albuquerque, University of New Mexico Press.

1981. Afterword. In Kohl, 1981a, pp. 386–97.

1985a. The longue durée of the ancient Near East. In *De l'Indus aux Balkans, Recueil Jean Deshayes*, ed. by J.-L. Huot, M. Yon, and Y. Calvet, pp. 55–72. Paris, Editions Recherche sur les civilisations.

1985b. The Near Eastern 'breakout' and the Mesopotamian social contract. *Symbols*, spring issue, 8–11, 23–4.

Laming-Emperaire, A. 1962. *La Signification de l'art rupestre paléolithique*. Paris, Picard.

1964. *Origines de l'archéologie préhistorique en France des superstitions médiévales à la découverte de l'homme fossile*. Paris, Picard.

Langford, R. F. 1983. Our heritage – your playground. *Australian Archaeology* 16: 1–6.

Larsen, C. S. 1985. ed. *The Antiquity and Origin of Native North Americans*. New York, Garland.

Larson, P. A. Jr. 1979. Archaeology and science: surviving the preparadigmatic crisis. *Current Anthropology* 20: 230–1.

Laszlo, E. 1972a. *Introduction to Systems Philosophy*. New York, Gordon and Breach.

1972b. ed. *The Relevance of General Systems Theory*. New York, Braziller.

1972c. *The Systems View of the World*. New York, Braziller.

Laufer, B. 1913. Remarks. *American Anthropologist* 15: 573–7.

Leach, E. R. 1973. Concluding address. In C. Renfrew, 1973b, pp. 761–71.
Leakey, L. S. B. 1931. *The Stone Age Cultures of Kenya Colony*. Cambridge, Cambridge University Press.
Leakey, M. 1984. *Disclosing the Past*. New York, Doubleday.
Lee, R. B. and I. DeVore. 1968. eds. *Man the Hunter*. Chicago, Aldine.
Leone, M. P. 1972. ed. *Contemporary Archaeology*. Carbondale, Southern Illinois University Press.
1975. Views of traditional archaeology. *Reviews in Anthropology* 2: 191–9.
1982. Some opinions about recovering mind. *American Antiquity* 47: 742–60.
1984. Interpreting ideology in historical archaeology: using the rules of perspective in the William Paca Garden in Annapolis, Maryland. In D. Miller and C. Tilley, pp. 25–35.
1986. Symbolic, structural, and critical archaeology. In D. J. Meltzer *et al.*, pp. 415–38.
Leone, M. P., P. B. Potter Jr, and P. A. Shackel. 1987. Toward a critical archaeology. *Current Anthropology* 28: 283–302.
Leppmann, W. 1968. *Pompeii in Fact and Fiction*. London, Elek.
1970. *Winckelmann*. New York, Knopf.
Lepsius, C. R. 1880. *Nubische Grammatik, mit einer Einleitung über die Völker und Sprachen Afrika's*. Berlin, Hertz.
Leroi-Gourhan, A. 1968. *The Art of Prehistoric Man in Western Europe*. London, Thames and Hudson.
Levi, P. 1979. *Pausanias: Guide to Greece*. 2 vols. Harmondsworth, Penguin.
Levine, P. 1986. *The Amateur and the Professional: Antiquarians, Historians and Archaeologists in Victorian England, 1838–1886*. Cambridge, Cambridge University Press.
Levitt, J. 1979. A review of experimental traceological research in the USSR. In B. Hayden, pp. 27–38.
Lewis, T. M. N. and M. Kneberg. 1941. *The Prehistory of the Chickamauga Basin in Tennessee*. Knoxville, Tennessee Anthropology Papers, no. 1.
Li, Chi. 1977. *Anyang*. Seattle, University of Washington Press.
Libby, W. F. 1955. *Radiocarbon Dating*. 2nd edn. Chicago, University of Chicago Press.
Linton, R. 1944. North American cooking pots. *American Antiquity* 9: 369–80.
Lloyd, S. H. 1947. *Foundations in the Dust: A Story of Mesopotamian Exploration*. Oxford, Oxford University Press (2nd edn, London, Thames and Hudson, 1981).
Long, E. 1774. *The History of Jamaica*. 3 vols. London, T. Lowndes.
Longacre, W. A. 1970. *Archaeology as Anthropology: A Case Study*. Tucson, University of Arizona Press.
Lord, B. 1974. *The History of Painting in Canada: Toward a People's Art*. Toronto, NC Press.
Lorenzo, J. L. 1981. Archaeology south of the Rio Grande. *World Archaeology* 13: 190–208.
1984. Mexico. In H. Cleere, pp. 89–100.

Lowenthal, D. 1985. *The Past is a Foreign Country*. Cambridge, Cambridge University Press.
Lowther, G. R. 1962. Epistemology and archaeological theory. *Current Anthropology* 3: 495–509.
Lubbock, John [Lord Avebury]. 1865. *Pre-historic Times, as Illustrated by Ancient Remains, and the Manners and Customs of Modern Savages*. London, Williams and Norgate.
1869. *Pre-historic Times*. 2nd edn. London, Williams and Norgate.
1870. *The Origin of Civilisation and the Primitive Condition of Man*. London, Longmans, Green.
Lyell, C. 1863. *The Geological Evidences of the Antiquity of Man, with Remarks on Theories of the Origin of Species by Variation*. London, John Murray.
Lynch, B. D. and T. F. Lynch. 1968. The beginnings of a scientific approach to prehistoric archaeology in 17th and 18th century Britain. *Southwestern Journal of Anthropology* 24: 33–65.
McBryde, I. 1986. Australia's once and future archaeology. *Archaeology in Oceania* 21: 13–28.
McCall, D. F. 1964. *Africa in Time-Perspective*. Boston, Boston University Press.
McCall, G. 1982. ed. *Anthropology in Australia: Essays to Honour 50 Years of 'Mankind'*. Sydney, The Anthropological Society of New South Wales.
McCarthy, F. D. 1959. Methods and scope of Australian archaeology. *Mankind* 5: 297–316.
McClelland, P. D. 1975. *Causal Explanation and Model Building in History, Economics, and the New Economic History*. Ithaca, Cornell University Press.
MacGaffey, W. 1966. Concepts of race in the historiography of northeast Africa. *Journal of African History* 7: 1–17.
McGuire, J. D. 1899. Pipes and smoking customs of the American aborigines, based on material in the U.S. National Museum. Washington, *United States National Museum, Annual Report, 1897*, pt. 1: 351–645.
McGuire, R. H. 1983. Breaking down cultural complexity: inequality and heterogeneity. *Advances in Archaeological Method and Theory* 6: 91–142.
McKay, A. G. 1976. Archaeology and the creative imagination. In *Symposium on New Perspectives in Canadian Archaeology*, ed. by A. G. McKay, pp. 227–34. Ottawa, Royal Society of Canada, Symposium 15.
MacKendrick, P. 1960. *The Mute Stones Speak: The Story of Archaeology in Italy*. New York, St. Martin's Press.
McKern, W. C. 1937. An hypothesis for the Asiatic origin of the Woodland culture pattern. *American Antiquity* 3: 138–43.
1939. The Midwestern Taxonomic Method as an aid to archaeological culture study. *American Antiquity* 4: 301–13.
McKusick, M. 1970. *The Davenport Conspiracy*. Iowa City, University of Iowa.
McLennan, J. F. 1865. *Primitive Marriage*. Edinburgh, Adam and Charles Black.
McNairn, B. 1980. *Method and Theory of V. Gordon Childe*. Edinburgh, Edinburgh University Press.
McNeill, W. H. 1986. *Mythistory and Other Essays*. Chicago, University of Chicago Press.

MacNeish, R. S. 1952. *Iroquois Pottery Types: A Technique for the Study of Iroquois Prehistory*. Ottawa, National Museum of Canada, Bulletin no. 124.

1974. Reflections on my search for the beginnings of agriculture in Mexico. In G. R. Willey, 1974a, pp. 205–34.

1978. *The Science of Archaeology?* North Scituate, Massachusetts, Duxbury Press.

MacWhite, E. 1956. On the interpretation of archaeological evidence in historical and sociological terms. *American Anthropologist* 58: 3–25.

Malinowski, B. 1922. *Argonauts of the Western Pacific*. New York, E. P. Dutton.

Mallows, W. 1985. *The Mystery of the Great Zimbabwe*. London, Robert Hale.

Mandelbaum, M. H. 1977. *The Anatomy of Historical Knowledge*. Baltimore, Johns Hopkins University Press.

Marcus, J. 1983a. A synthesis of the cultural evolution of the Zapotec and Mixtec. In *The Cloud People*, ed. by K. V. Flannery and J. Marcus, pp. 355–60. New York, Academic Press.

1983b. Lowland Maya archaeology at the crossroads. *American Antiquity* 48: 454–88.

Marcuse, H. 1964. *One Dimensional Man*. London, Routledge & Kegan Paul.

Marsden, B. M. 1974. *The Early Barrow-Diggers*. Park Ridge, Noyes Press.

1984. *Pioneers of Prehistory: Leaders and Landmarks in English Archaeology (1500–1900)*. Ormskirk, Hesketh.

Marshack, A. 1972. *The Roots of Civilization*. New York, McGraw-Hill.

Martin, P. S. 1971. The revolution in archaeology. *American Antiquity* 36: 1–8.

Martin, P. S., C. Lloyd, and A. Spoehr. 1938. Archaeological work in the Ackmen–Lowry area, southwestern Colorado, 1937. Chicago, *Field Museum of Natural History, Anthropological Series* 23: 217–304.

Martin, P. S. and F. Plog. 1973. *The Archaeology of Arizona*. Garden City, Natural History Press.

Martin, P. S., G. I. Quimby, and D. Collier. 1947. *Indians Before Columbus*. Chicago, University of Chicago Press.

Martin, P. S. and J. Rinaldo. 1939. Modified Basket Maker sites, Ackmen–Lowry area, southwestern Colorado, 1938. Chicago, *Field Museum of Natural History, Anthropological Series* 23: 305–499.

Martin, R. 1977. *Historical Explanation: Re-enactment and Practical Inference*. Ithaca, Cornell University Press.

Marx, K. 1906. *Capital: A Critique of Political Economy*. New York, The Modern Library, Random House.

Marx, K. and F. Engels. 1957. *On Religion*. Moscow, Progress Publishers.

1962. *Selected Works in Two Volumes*. Moscow, Foreign Languages Publishing House.

Mason, O. T. 1895. *The Origins of Invention*. New York, Scribner.

1896. Influence of environment upon human industries or arts. Washington, *Annual Report of the Smithsonian Institution for 1895*: 639–65.

Masry, A. H. 1981. Traditions of archaeological research in the Near East. *World Archaeology* 13: 222–39.

Masterman, M. 1970. The nature of a paradigm. In *Criticism and the Growth of*

Knowledge, ed. by I. Lakatos and A. Musgrave, pp. 59–89. Cambridge, Cambridge University Press.

Matos Moctezuma, E. 1984. The templo mayor of Tenochtitlan: economics and ideology. In *Ritual Human Sacrifice in Mesoamerica*, ed. by E. H. Boone, pp. 133–64. Washington, Dumbarton Oaks.

Meacham, W. 1977. Continuity and local evolution in the Neolithic of South China: a non-nuclear approach. *Current Anthropology* 18: 419–40.

Meehan, E. J. 1968. *Explanation in Social Science; A System Paradigm*. Homewood, Dorsey Press.

Megaw, J. V. S. 1966. Australian archaeology: how far have we progressed? *Mankind* 6: 306–12.

1976. ed. *To Illustrate the Monuments: Essays on Archaeology Presented to Stuart Piggott*. London, Thames and Hudson.

Meggers, B. J. 1955. The coming of age of American archeology. In *New Interpretations of Aboriginal American Culture History*, ed. by M. T. Newman, pp. 116–29. Washington, Anthropological Society of Washington.

1960. The law of cultural evolution as a practical research tool. In *Essays in the Science of Culture*, ed. by G. E. Dole and R. L. Carneiro, pp. 302–16. New York, Crowell.

Meighan, C. W. 1984. Archaeology: science or sacrilege? In E. L. Green, pp. 208–23.

Meillassoux, C. 1981. *Maidens, Meal and Money: Capitalism and the Domestic Economy*. Cambridge, Cambridge University Press.

Meinander, C. F. 1981. The concept of culture in European archaeological literature. In G. Daniel, 1981b, pp. 100–11.

Meltzer, D. J. 1979. Paradigms and the nature of change in American archaeology. *American Antiquity* 44: 644–57.

1983. The antiquity of man and the development of American archaeology. *Advances in Archaeological Method and Theory* 6: 1–51.

Meltzer, D. J., D. D. Fowler, and J. A. Sabloff. 1986. eds. *American Archaeology Past and Future: A Celebration of the Society for American Archaeology 1935–1985*. Washington, Smithsonian Institution Press.

Meyer, E. 1884–1902. *Geschichte des Alterthums*. 5 vols. Stuttgart, J. G. Cotta.

Michael, H. N. 1962. ed. *Studies in Siberian Ethnogenesis*. Toronto, University of Toronto Press.

1964. *The Archaeology and Geomorphology of Northern Asia: Selected Works*. Toronto, University of Toronto Press.

Miller, D. 1980. Archaeology and development. *Current Anthropology* 21: 709–26.

1984. Modernism and suburbia as material ideology. In D. Miller and C. Tilley, pp. 37–49.

Miller, D. and C. Tilley. 1984. eds. *Ideology, Power and Prehistory*. Cambridge, Cambridge University Press.

Miller, M. O. 1956. *Archaeology in the U.S.S.R.* London, Atlantic Press.

Millon, R., R. B. Drewitt, and G. L. Cowgill. 1973. *Urbanization at Teotihuacán, Mexico*, vol. 1, *The Teotihuacán Map*. Austin, University of Texas Press.

Mills, W. C. 1902. Excavations of the Adena mound. *Ohio Archaeological and Historical Quarterly* 10: 452–79.
Moberg, C.-A. 1981. From artefacts to timetables to maps (to mankind?): regional traditions in archaeological research in Scandinavia. *World Archaeology* 13: 209–21.
Molto, J. E. 1983. *Biological Relationships of Southern Ontario Woodland Peoples: The Evidence of Discontinuous Cranial Morphology*. Ottawa, Archaeological Survey of Canada, Mercury Series no. 117.
Mongait, A. L. 1959. *Archaeology in the U.S.S.R.* Moscow, Foreign Languages Publishing House.
1961. *Archaeology in the USSR*. trans. by M. W. Thompson. Harmondsworth, Penguin.
Monks, G. G. 1981. Seasonality studies. *Advances in Archaeological Method and Theory* 4: 177–240.
Montané, J. C. 1980. *Marxismo y Arqueología*. Mexico, Ediciones de Cultura Popular.
Montelius, O. 1899. *Der Orient und Europa*. Stockholm, Königl. Akademie der schönen Wissenschaften, Geschichte und Alterthumskunde.
1903. *Die typologische Methode: Die älteren Kulturperioden im Orient und in Europa*, vol. 1. Stockholm, Selbstverlag.
Moore, C. B. 1892. Certain shell heaps of the St. John's River, Florida, hitherto unexplored. *American Naturalist* 26: 912–22.
Moore, J. A. and A. S. Keene. 1983. *Archaeological Hammers and Theories*. New York, Academic Press.
Moorehead, W. K. 1909. A study of primitive culture in Ohio. In *Putnam Anniversary Volume: Anthropological Essays Presented to Frederic W. Putnam in Honor of his 70th Birthday*, ed. by F. Boas *et al.*, pp. 137–50. New York, Stechert.
1910. *The Stone Age in North America*. 2 vols. Boston, Houghton Mifflin.
Moret, A. and G. Davy. 1926. *From Tribe to Empire: Social Organization among Primitives and in the Ancient East*. London, Kegan Paul.
Morgan, C. G. 1973. Archaeology and explanation. *World Archaeology* 4: 259–76.
1978. Comment on D. W. Read and S. A. LeBlanc, 'Descriptive statements, covering laws, and theories in archaeology'. *Current Anthropology* 19: 325–6.
Morgan, L. H. 1876. Montezuma's dinner. *North American Review* 122: 256–308.
1877. *Ancient Society*. New York, Holt.
Morlot, A. 1861. General views on archaeology. Washington, *Annual Report of the Smithsonian Institution for 1860*: 284–343.
Morris, C. and D. E. Thompson. 1985. *Huánuco Pampa: An Inca City and its Hinterland*. London, Thames and Hudson.
Mortillet, G. de. 1897. *Formation de la nation française*. Paris, Alcan.
Morton, S. G. 1839. *Crania Americana*. Philadelphia, Dobson.
1844. *Crania Aegyptiaca*. Philadelphia, Penington.
Much, M. 1907. *Die Trugspiegelung orientalischer Kultur in den vorgeschichtlichen Zeitaltern nord- und mittel-Europas*. Jena, Costenoble.

Mufuka, K. 1983. *Dzimbahwe Life and Politics in the Golden Age, 1100–1500 AD*. Harare, Harare Publishing House.

Mulvaney, D. J. 1969. *The Prehistory of Australia*. London, Thames and Hudson.

1981. Gum leaves on the Golden Bough: Australia's Palaeolithic survivals discovered. In J. Evans *et al.* pp. 52–64.

Mulvaney, D. J. and J. P. White. 1987. eds. *Australians to 1788*. Broadway, New South Wales, Fairfax, Syme and Weldon.

Murdock, G. P. 1949. *Social Structure*. New York, Macmillan.

1959a. *Africa, Its Peoples and their Culture History*. New York, McGraw-Hill.

1959b. Evolution in social organization. In *Evolution and Anthropology: A Centennial Appraisal*, ed. by B. Meggers, pp. 126–43. Washington, Anthropological Society of Washington.

Murdock, G. P., C. S. Ford, A. E. Hudson, R. Kennedy, L. W. Simmons, and J. H. Whiting. 1938. *Outline of Cultural Materials*. New Haven, Institute of Human Relations.

Murray, P. 1980. Discard location: the ethnographic data. *American Antiquity* 45: 490–502.

Murray, T. and J. P. White. 1981. Cambridge in the bush? Archaeology in Australia and New Guinea. *World Archaeology* 13: 255–63.

Myres, J. L. 1911. *The Dawn of History*. London, Williams and Norgate.

1923a. Primitive man, in geological time. In *Cambridge Ancient History*, vol. 1, ed. by J. B. Bury, S. A. Cook, and F. E. Adcock, pp. 1–56. Cambridge, Cambridge University Press.

1923b. Neolithic and Bronze Age cultures. Ibid., pp. 57–111.

Nagel, E. 1961. *The Structure of Science: Problems in the Logic of Scientific Explanation*. New York, Harcourt, Brace and World.

Nash, R. J. and R. G. Whitlam. 1985. Future-oriented archaeology. *Canadian Journal of Archaeology* 9: 95–108.

Nelson, N.C. 1916. Chronology of the Tano ruins, New Mexico. *American Anthropologist* 18: 159–80.

Nilsson, S. 1868. *The Primitive Inhabitants of Scandinavia*. 3rd. edn, trans. by J. Lubbock. London, Longmans, Green.

Nott, J. C. and G. R. Gliddon. 1854. *Types of Mankind*. Philadelphia, Lippincott, Grambo.

Nzewunwa, N. 1984. Nigeria. In H. Cleere, pp. 101–8.

Obermaier, H. 1916. *El Hombre Fósil*. Madrid, Museo Nacional de Ciencias Naturales.

O'Connor, T. E. 1983. *The Politics of Soviet Culture, Anatolii Lunacharskii*. Ann Arbor, University Microfilms International Research Press.

Odum, E. P. 1953. *Fundamentals of Ecology*. Philadelphia, Saunders.

Okladnikov, A. P. 1965. *The Soviet Far East in Antiquity*. Toronto, University of Toronto Press.

1970. *Yakutia Before Its Incorporation into the Russian State*. Montreal, McGill-Queen's University Press.

O'Laverty, J. 1857. Relative antiquity of stone and bronze weapons. *Ulster Journal of Archaeology* 5: 122–7.

Oldfield, E. 1852. Introductory address. *Archaeological Journal* 9: 1–6.
Olsen, J. W. 1987. The practice of archaeology in China today. *Antiquity* 61: 282–90.
Orme, B. 1973. Archaeology and ethnology. In Renfrew, 1973b, pp. 481–92.
Orton, C. 1980. *Mathematics in Archaeology*. London, Collins.
O'Shea, J. M. 1984. *Mortuary Variability: An Archaeological Investigation*. New York, Academic Press.
Osgood, C. B. 1951. Culture: its empirical and non-empirical character. *Southwestern Journal of Anthropology* 7: 202–14.
Owen, A. L. 1962. *The Famous Druids: A Survey of Three Centuries of English Literature on the Druids*. Oxford, Oxford University Press.
Owen, O. F. 1858. The archaeology of the county of Surrey. *Surrey Archaeological Collections* 1: 1–13.
Paddayya, K. 1983. Myths about the New Archaeology. *Saeculum* 34: 70–104.
Pagden, A. 1982. *The Fall of Natural Man*. Cambridge, Cambridge University Press.
Paine, R. 1983. Israel and totemic time? *Royal Anthropological Institute News* 59: 19–22.
Pande, G. C. 1985. *An Approach to Indian Culture and Civilization*. Varanasi, Monograph of the Department of Ancient Indian History, Culture and Archaeology no. 15.
Parker, A. C. 1907. *Excavations in an Erie Indian Village and Burial Site at Ripley, Chautauqua County, New York*. Albany, New York State Museum, Bulletin no. 117.
1916. The origin of the Iroquois as suggested by their archaeology. *American Anthropologist* 18: 479–507.
1920. *The Archaeological History of New York*. Albany, New York State Museum, Bulletins nos. 235–8.
Parsons, J. R., E. Brumfiel, M. H. Parsons, and D. J. Wilson. 1982. *Prehispanic Settlement Patterns in the Southern Valley of Mexico: The Chalco–Xochimilco Region*. Ann Arbor, University of Michigan, Memoirs of the Museum of Anthropology no. 14.
Parsons, T. 1968. Durkheim, Emile. *International Encyclopedia of the Social Sciences*, ed. by D. L. Sills, vol. 4, pp. 311–20. New York, Macmillan and Free Press.
Patrik, L. E. 1985. Is there an archaeological record? *Advances in Archaeological Method and Theory* 8: 27–62.
Patterson, T. C. 1986a. The last sixty years: toward a social history of Americanist archaeology in the United States. *American Anthropologist* 88: 7–26.
1986b. Some postwar theoretical trends in U.S. archaeology. *Culture* 6: 43–54.
Peake, H. J. E. 1922. *The Bronze Age and the Celtic World*. London, Benn.
1940. The study of prehistoric times. *Journal of the Royal Anthropological Institute* 70: 103–46.
Peake, H. J. E. and H. J. Fleure. 1927. *The Corridors of Time*, vol. 3, *Peasants and Potters*. Oxford, Oxford University Press.

Pearce, R. H. 1965. *Savagism and Civilization: A Study of the Indian and the American Mind*. Baltimore, Johns Hopkins University Press.

Pearson, M. P. 1982. Mortuary practices, society and ideology: an ethnoarchaeological study. In I. Hodder, 1982c, pp. 99–113.

1984. Social change, ideology and the archaeological record. In M. Spriggs, pp. 59–71.

Pearson, R. J. 1977. The social aims of Chinese archaeology. *Antiquity* 51: 8–10.

Perry, W. J. 1923. *The Children of the Sun*. London, Methuen.

1924. *The Growth of Civilization*. London, Methuen.

Petrie, W. M. F. 1901. *Diospolis Parva*. London, Egypt Exploration Fund.

1904. *Methods and Aims in Archaeology*. London, Macmillan.

1939. *The Making of Egypt*. London, Sheldon.

Petrova-Averkieva, Yu. 1980. Historicism in Soviet ethnographic science. In E. Gellner, pp. 19–27.

Piggott, S. 1950. *William Stukeley: An Eighteenth-Century Antiquary*. Oxford, Oxford University Press.

1958. Vere Gordon Childe, 1892–1957. *Proceedings of the British Academy* 44: 305–12.

1959. *Approach to Archaeology*. Cambridge, Massachusetts, Harvard University Press.

1968. *The Druids*. London, Thames and Hudson.

1976. *Ruins in a Landscape: Essays in Antiquarianism*. Edinburgh, Edinburgh University Press.

1978. *Antiquity Depicted: Aspects of Archaeological Illustration*. London, Thames and Hudson.

1985. *William Stukeley: An Eighteenth-Century Antiquary*, rev. edn. London, Thames and Hudson.

Pinsky, V. 1987. Ethnography and the New Archaeology: A Critical Study of Disciplinary Change in American Archaeology. PhD dissertation, Department of Archaeology, Cambridge University.

Pitt-Rivers, A. H. L.-F. 1906. *The Evolution of Culture and Other Essays*. Oxford, Oxford University Press.

Plog, F. 1982. Can the centuries-long experience of the Hohokam . . . be ignored? *Early Man 4(4)*: 24–5.

Plog, S. 1980. *Stylistic Variation in Prehistoric Ceramics: Design Analysis in the American Southwest*. Cambridge, Cambridge University Press.

Polanyi, K. 1944. *The Great Transformation*. New York, Farrar and Rinehart.

1966. *Dahomey and the Slave Trade: An Analysis of an Archaic Economy*. Seattle, University of Washington Press.

Polanyi, K., C. M. Arensberg, and H. W. Pearson. 1957. *Trade and Market in the Early Empires*. Glencoe, Free Press.

Poliakov, L. 1974. *The Aryan Myth: A History of Racist and Nationalist Ideas in Europe*. New York, Basic Books.

Popper, K. R. 1959. *The Logic of Scientific Discovery*. New York, Basic Books.

1963. *Conjectures and Refutations*. London, Routledge & Kegan Paul.

Porter, R. 1977. *The Making of Geology: Earth Science in Britain 1660–1815*. Cambridge, Cambridge University Press.

Posnansky, M. 1976. Archaeology as a university discipline – Ghana, 1967–71. *Proceedings of the Panafrican Congress of Prehistory*, pp. 329–31.

1982. African archaeology comes of age. *World Archaeology* 13: 345–58.

Prescott, W. H. 1843. *History of the Conquest of Mexico*. New York, Harper.

1847. *History of the Conquest of Peru*. New York, Harper and Brothers.

Price, B. J. 1977. Shifts in production and organization: a cluster-interaction model. *Current Anthropology* 18: 209–33.

Price, T. D. and J. A. Brown. 1985. eds. *Prehistoric Hunter–Gatherers: The Emergence of Cultural Complexity*. New York, Academic Press.

Prichard, J. C. 1813. *Researches into the Physical History of Man*. London, John and Arthur Arch.

Priest, J. 1833. *American Antiquities, and Discoveries in the West*. Albany, Hoffman and White.

Pumpelly, R. 1908. ed. *Explorations in Turkestan*. 2 vols. Washington, Carnegie Institution.

Raab, L. M. and A. C. Goodyear. 1984. Middle-range theory in archaeology: a critical review of origins and applications. *American Antiquity* 49: 255–68.

Radcliffe-Brown, A. R. 1922. *The Andaman Islanders*. Cambridge, Cambridge University Press.

Raglan, F. R. R. S. 1939. *How Came Civilization?* London, Methuen.

Ramsden, P. G. 1977. *A Refinement of Some Aspects of Huron Ceramic Analysis*. Ottawa, Archaeological Survey of Canada, Mercury Series no. 63.

Randall-MacIver, D. 1906. *Mediaeval Rhodesia*. London, Macmillan.

Ranov, V. A. and R. S. Davis. 1979. Toward a new outline of the Soviet Central Asian Paleolithic. *Current Anthropology* 20: 249–70.

Rathje, W. L. 1974. The Garbage Project: a new way of looking at the problems of archaeology. *Archaeology* 27: 236–41.

1975. The last tango in Mayapán: a tentative trajectory of production–distribution systems. In *Ancient Civilization and Trade*, ed. by J. A. Sabloff and C. C. Lamberg-Karlovsky, pp. 409–48. Albuquerque, University of New Mexico Press.

Ratzel, F. 1882–91. *Anthropogeographie*. Stuttgart, Engelhorn.

1896–8. *The History of Mankind*. trans. by A. J. Butler. 3 vols. London, Macmillan.

Ravetz, A. 1959. Notes on the work of V. Gordon Childe. *The New Reasoner* 10: 55–66.

Read, D. W. and S. A. LeBlanc. 1978. Descriptive statements, covering laws, and theories in archaeology. *Current Anthropology* 19: 307–35.

Redford, D. B. 1986. *Pharaonic King-Lists, Annals and Day Books: A Contribution to the Study of the Egyptian Sense of History*. Mississauga, Benben Publications.

Redman, C. L. 1973. ed. *Research and Theory in Current Archeology*. New York, Wiley.

1986. *Qsar es-Seghir: An Archaeological View of Medieval Life*. New York, Academic Press.
Reid, D. 1985. Indigenous Egyptology: the decolonization of a profession. *Journal of the American Oriental Society* 105: 233–46.
Reid, J. J., W. L. Rathje, and M. B. Schiffer. 1974. Expanding archaeology. *American Antiquity* 39: 125–6.
Reinach, S. 1893. *Le Mirage oriental*. Paris, G. Masson.
1903. L'Art et la magie: à propos des peintures et des gravures de l'âge du renne. *L'Anthropologie* 14: 257–66.
Renfrew, A. C. 1970. Reply. *Current Anthropology* 11: 173–4.
1973a. *Before Civilization: The Radiocarbon Revolution and Prehistoric Europe*. London, Cape.
1973b. ed. *The Explanation of Culture Change: Models in Prehistory*. London, Duckworth.
1978. Trajectory discontinuity and morphogenesis. *American Antiquity* 43: 203–22.
1979. *Problems in European Prehistory*. Cambridge, Cambridge University Press.
1980. The great tradition versus the great divide: archaeology as anthropology? *American Journal of Archaeology* 84: 287–98.
1982a. Socio-economic change in ranked societies. In A. C. Renfrew and S. Shennan, pp. 1–8.
1982b. Explanation revisited. In *Theory and Explanation in Archaeology*, ed. by A. C. Renfrew, M. J. Rowlands, and B. A. Segraves, pp. 5–23. New York, Academic Press.
1982c. Towards an Archaeology of Mind (inaugural lecture). Cambridge, Cambridge University Press.
1984. *Approaches to Social Archaeology*. Edinburgh, Edinburgh University Press.
Renfrew, A. C. and J. F. Cherry. 1986. eds. *Peer Polity Interaction and Socio-Political Change*. Cambridge, Cambridge University Press.
Renfrew, A. C. and K. L. Cooke. 1979. eds. *Transformations: Mathematical Approaches to Culture Change*. New York, Academic Press.
Renfrew, A. C. and S. Shennan. 1982. eds. *Ranking, Resource and Exchange: Aspects of the Archaeology of Early European Society*. Cambridge, Cambridge University Press.
Ribes, R. 1966. Pièces de la période archaïque trouvées vers 1700 dans la région de Bécancour. *Cahiers d'archéologie québecoise* 2(1): 22–34.
Ridgway, D. 1985. V. Gordon Childe a venticinque anni dalla morte. In *Studi di Paletnologia in Onore di Salvatore M. Puglisi*, ed. by M. Liverani, A. Palmieri, and R. Peroni, pp. 3–11. Rome, Università di Roma.
Rindos, D. 1984. *The Origins of Agriculture: An Evolutionary Perspective*. New York, Academic Press.
Ritchie, W. A. 1944. *The Pre-Iroquoian Occupations of New York State*. Rochester, Rochester Museum of Arts and Sciences, Memoir no. 1.
1965. *The Archaeology of New York State*. Garden City, Natural History Press.

Ritchie, W. A. and R. E. Funk. 1973. *Aboriginal Settlement Patterns in the Northeast*. Albany, New York State Museum and Science Service, Memoir no. 20.

Rivers, W. H. R. 1914. *The History of Melanesian Society*. Cambridge, Cambridge University Press.

Robertshaw, P. T. 1988. *History of African Archaeology*. London, Currey.

Rodden, J. 1981. The development of the Three Age System: archaeology's first paradigm. In G. Daniel, 1981b, pp. 51–68.

Rosen, L. 1980. The excavation of American Indian burial sites: a problem of law and professional responsibility. *American Anthropologist* 82: 5–27.

Rossi, P. 1985. *The Dark Abyss of Time: The History of the Earth and the History of Nations from Hooke to Vico*. Chicago, University of Chicago Press.

Rouse, I. B. 1939. *Prehistory in Haiti: A Study in Method*. New Haven, Yale University Publications in Anthropology no. 21.

1953. The strategy of culture history. In *Anthropology Today*, ed. by A. L. Kroeber, pp. 57–76. Chicago, University of Chicago Press.

1958. The inference of migrations from anthropological evidence. In *Migrations in New World Culture History*, ed. by R. H. Thompson, pp. 63–8. Tucson, University of Arizona, Social Science Bulletin no. 27.

1965. The place of 'peoples' in prehistoric research. *Journal of the Royal Anthropological Institute* 95: 1–15.

1972. *Introduction to Prehistory*. New York, McGraw-Hill.

1986. *Migrations in Prehistory: Inferring Population Movement from Cultural Remains*. New Haven, Yale University Press.

Rowe, J. H. 1965. The renaissance foundations of anthropology. *American Anthropologist* 67: 1–20.

Rowlands, M. J. 1982. Processual archaeology as historical social science. In *Theory and Explanation in Archaeology*, ed. by A. C. Renfrew, M. J. Rowlands, and B. A. Segraves, pp. 155–74. New York, Academic Press.

1984. Objectivity and subjectivity in archaeology. In M. Spriggs, pp. 108–13.

Rudenko, S. I. 1961. *The Ancient Culture of the Bering Sea and the Eskimo Problem*. Toronto, University of Toronto Press.

1970. *Frozen Tombs of Siberia: The Pazyryk Burials of Iron Age Horsemen*. Berkeley, University of California Press.

Rudolph, R. C. 1963. Preliminary notes on Sung archaeology. *Journal of Asian Studies* 22: 169–77.

Sabloff, J. A. 1981. ed. *Simulations in Archaeology*. Albuquerque, University of New Mexico Press.

Sabloff, J. A., T. W. Beale, and A. M. Kurland Jr. 1973. Recent developments in archaeology. *Annals of the American Academy of Political and Social Science* 408: 103–18.

Sabloff, J. A. and G. R. Willey. 1967. The collapse of Maya civilization in the southern lowlands: a consideration of history and process. *Southwestern Journal of Anthropology* 23: 311–36.

Sackett, J. R. 1981. From de Mortillet to Bordes: a century of French Palaeolithic research. In G. Daniel, 1981b, pp. 85–99.

Sahlins, M. D. 1968. *Tribesmen*. Englewood Cliffs, Prentice-Hall.
1976. *Culture and Practical Reason*. Chicago, University of Chicago Press.
Sahlins, M. D. and E. R. Service. 1960. eds. *Evolution and Culture*. Ann Arbor, University of Michigan Press.
Saitta, D. J. 1983. The poverty of philosophy in archaeology. In J. A. Moore and A. S. Keene, pp. 299–304.
Salmon, M. H. 1982. *Philosophy and Archaeology*. New York, Academic Press.
Salmon, W. C. 1967. *The Foundations of Scientific Inference*. Pittsburgh, University of Pittsburgh Press.
1984. *Scientific Explanation and the Causal Structure of the World*. Princeton, Princeton University Press.
Salmon, W. C., R. C. Jeffrey, and J. Greeno. 1971. *Statistical Explanation and Statistical Relevance*. Pittsburgh, Pittsburgh University Press.
Sanders, W. T., J. R. Parsons, and R. S. Santley. 1979. *The Basin of Mexico: Ecological Processes in the Evolution of a Civilization*. New York, Academic Press.
Sanders, W. T. and B. J. Price. 1968. *Mesoamerica: The Evolution of a Civilization*. New York, Random House.
Sanford, E. M. 1944. The study of ancient history in the middle ages. *Journal of the History of Ideas* 5: 21–43.
Sansom, G. 1958. *A History of Japan to 1334* Stanford, Stanford University Press.
Saunders, P. T. 1980. *An Introduction to Catastrophe Theory*. Cambridge, Cambridge University Press.
Saxe, A. A. 1970. Social Dimensions of Mortuary Practices. PhD dissertation, University of Michigan.
Schiffer, M. B. 1976. *Behavioral Archeology*. New York, Academic Press.
1978–86. ed. *Advances in Archaeological Method and Theory*, vols. 1–9. New York, Academic Press.
Schliz, A. 1906. Der schnurkeramische Kulturkreis und seine Stellung zu der anderen neolithischen Kulturformen in Sudwestdeutschland. *Zeitschrift für Ethnologie* 38: 312–45.
Schneer, C. J. 1969. ed. *Toward a History of Geology*. Cambridge, Massachusetts, M.I.T. Press.
Schneider, L. 1967. ed. *The Scottish Moralists on Human Nature and Society*. Chicago, University of Chicago Press.
Schofield, J. F. 1948. *Primitive Pottery: An Introduction to South African Ceramics, Prehistoric and Protohistoric*. Cape Town, South African Archaeological Society, Handbook Series no. 3.
Schrire, C. 1980. An inquiry into the evolutionary status and apparent identity of San hunter–gatherers. *Human Ecology* 8: 9–32.
1984. ed. *Past and Present in Hunter Gatherer Studies*. New York, Academic Press.
Schrire, C., J. Deacon, M. Hall, and D. Lewis-Williams. 1986. Burkitt's milestone. *Antiquity* 60: 123–31.
Schuyler, R. L. 1971. The history of American archaeology: an examination of procedure. *American Antiquity* 36: 383–409.

Schwartz, D. W. 1967. *Conceptions of Kentucky Prehistory: A Case Study in the History of Archeology*. Lexington, University of Kentucky Press.

1981. The foundations of northern Rio Grande archaeology. *Archaeological Society of New Mexico Anthropological Papers* 6: 251–73.

Schwerin von Krosigk, H. 1982. *Gustav Kossinna: Der Nachlass-Versuch einer Analyse*. Neumünster, Karl Wachholtz.

Seligman, C. G. 1930. *Races of Africa*. London, Butterworth.

Semenov, S. A. 1964. *Prehistoric Technology*. London, Cory, Adams and Mackay.

Semenov, Yu. I. 1980. The theory of socio-economic formations and world history. In E. Gellner, pp. 29–58.

Service, E. R. 1962. *Primitive Social Organization*. New York, Random House.

1975. *Origins of the State and Civilization*. New York, Norton.

Shanks, M. and C. Tilley. 1987. *Re-Constructing Archaeology: Theory and Practice*. Cambridge, Cambridge University Press.

Shapiro, J. 1982. *A History of the Communist Academy, 1918–1936*. Ann Arbor, University Microfilms International.

Sheehan, B. W. 1980. *Savagism and Civility: Indians and Englishmen in Colonial Virginia*. New York, Cambridge University Press.

Sheehy, J. 1980. *The Rediscovery of Ireland's Past: The Celtic Revival, 1830–1930*. London, Thames and Hudson.

Sherratt, A. G. 1979. Problems in European prehistory. In D. L. Clarke, pp. 193–206.

Shetrone, H. C. 1920. The culture problem in Ohio archaeology. *American Anthropologist* 22: 144–72.

Shorr, P. 1935. The genesis of prehistorical research. *Isis* 23: 425–43.

Shotwell, J. T. 1939. *The History of History*. New York, Columbia University Press.

Sieveking, G. 1976. Progress in economic and social archaeology. In *Problems in Economic and Social Archaeology*, ed. by G. Sieveking, I. H. Longworth, and K. E. Wilson, pp. xv–xxvi. London, Duckworth.

Silberman, N. A. 1982. *Digging for God and Country*. New York, Knopf.

1988. *Between the Past and the Present: Archaeology, Ideology, and Nationalism in the Modern Near East*. New York, Holt, Rinehart and Winston.

Silverberg, R. 1968. *Mound Builders of Ancient America*. Greenwich, New York Graphic Society.

Skinner, H. D. 1921. Culture areas in New Zealand. *Journal of the Polynesian Society* 30: 71–8.

Sklenář, K. 1983. *Archaeology in Central Europe: The First 500 Years*. Leicester, Leicester University Press.

Slobodin, R. 1978. *W. H. R. Rivers*. New York, Columbia University Press.

Slotkin, J. S. 1965. ed. *Readings in Early Anthropology*. New York, Viking Fund Publications in Anthropology no. 40.

Smart, J. J. C. 1963. *Philosophy and Scientific Realism*. London, Routledge & Kegan Paul.

Smith, B. D. 1978. ed. *Mississippian Settlement Patterns*. New York, Academic Press.

Smith, G. E. 1923. *The Ancient Egyptians and the Origin of Civilization*. London, Harper.

1933. *The Diffusion of Culture*. London, Watts.

Smith, H. I. 1910. *The Prehistoric Ethnology of a Kentucky Site*. New York, Anthropological Papers of the American Museum of Natural History no. 6, pt. 2.

Smith, P. E. L. 1976. *Food Production and Its Consequences*. Menlo Park, Cummings.

Smith, P. E. L. and T. C. Young Jr. 1972. The evolution of early agriculture and culture in Greater Mesopotamia: a trial model. In B. Spooner, pp. 1–59.

Smith, S. P. 1913, 1915. *The Lore of the Whare Wananga*. Wellington, The Polynesian Society.

Smith, W. S. 1958. *The Art and Architecture of Ancient Egypt*. Baltimore, Penguin.

Snow, D. R. 1980. *The Archaeology of New England*. New York, Academic Press.

Soffer, O. 1983. Politics of the Paleolithic in the USSR: a case of paradigms lost. In *The Socio-Politics of Archaeology*, ed. by J. M. Gero, D. M. Lacy, and M. Blakey, pp. 91–105. Amherst, Department of Anthropology, University of Massachusetts, Research Report no. 23.

1985. *The Upper Paleolithic of the Central Russian Plain*. New York, Academic Press.

Sollas, W. J. 1911, 1924. *Ancient Hunters and their Modern Representatives*. London, Macmillan. 2nd edn 1924.

Sorrenson, M. P. K. 1977. The whence of the Maori: some nineteenth century exercises in scientific method. *Journal of the Polynesian Society* 86: 449–78.

South, S. A. 1977a. *Method and Theory in Historical Archaeology*. New York, Academic Press.

1977b. ed. *Research Strategies in Historical Archaeology*. New York, Academic Press.

Spate, O. H. K. 1968. Environmentalism. In *International Encyclopedia of the Social Sciences*, ed. by D. L. Sills, vol. 5, pp. 93–7. New York, Macmillan and Free Press.

Spaulding, A. C. 1946. Northeastern archaeology and general trends in the northern forest zone. In *Man in Northeastern North America*, ed. by F. Johnson, pp. 143–67. Andover, Robert S. Peabody Foundation for Archaeology, Papers no. 3.

1953. Statistical techniques for the discovery of artifact types. *American Antiquity* 18: 305–13.

1960. The dimensions of archaeology. In *Essays in the Science of Culture in Honor of Leslie A. White*, ed. by G. E. Dole and R. L. Carneiro, pp. 437–56. New York, Crowell.

1968. Explanation in archeology. In S. R. Binford and L. R. Binford, pp. 33–9.

Spencer, W. B. 1901. *Guide to the Australian Ethnographical Collection in the National Museum of Victoria*. Melbourne, Government Printer.

Spencer, W. B. and F. J. Gillen. 1899. *The Native Tribes of Central Australia*. London, Macmillan.

Sperber, D. 1985. *On Anthropological Knowledge*. Cambridge, Cambridge University Press.

Spier, L. 1917. *An Outline for a Chronology of Zuñi Ruins*. New York, Anthropological Papers of the American Museum of Natural History no. 18, pt. 3.

Spinden, H. J. 1928. *Ancient Civilizations of Mexico and Central America*. New York, American Museum of Natural History, Handbook Series no. 3.

Spooner, B. 1972. ed. *Population Growth: Anthropological Implications*. Cambridge, Massachusetts, M.I.T. Press.

Spriggs, M. 1984a. ed. *Marxist Perspectives in Archaeology*. Cambridge, Cambridge University Press.

1984b. Another way of telling: Marxist perspectives in archaeology. In M. Spriggs, 1984a, pp. 1–9.

Squier, E. G. and E. H. Davis. 1848. *Ancient Monuments of the Mississippi Valley*. Washington, Smithsonian Contributions to Knowledge no. 1.

Stanton, W. 1960. *The Leopard's Spots: Scientific Attitudes toward Race in America, 1815–59*. Chicago, University of Chicago Press.

Steiger, W. L. 1971. Analytical archaeology? *Mankind* 8: 67–70.

Stepan, N. 1982. *The Idea of Race in Science: Great Britain 1800–1900*. Hamden, Connecticut, Archon Books.

Sterud, E. L. 1973. A paradigmatic view of prehistory. In A. C. Renfrew, 1973b, pp. 3–17.

1978. Changing aims of Americanist archaeology: a citations analysis of *American Antiquity* 1946–1975. *American Antiquity* 43: 294–302.

Steward, J. H. 1937a. *Ancient Caves of the Great Salt Lake Region*. Washington, Bureau of American Ethnology, Bulletin no. 116.

1937b. Ecological aspects of southwestern society. *Anthropos* 32: 87–104.

1953. Evolution and process. In *Anthropology Today*, ed. by A. L. Kroeber, pp. 313–26. Chicago, University of Chicago Press.

1955. *Theory of Culture Change*. Urbana, University of Illinois Press.

Steward, J. H. and F. M. Setzler. 1938. Function and configuration in archaeology. *American Antiquity* 4: 4–10.

Stocking, G. W. Jr. 1968. *Race, Culture, and Evolution: Essays in the History of Anthropology*. New York, Free Press.

1973. From chronology to ethnology: James Cowles Prichard and British anthropology 1800–1850. In J. C. Prichard, *Researches into the Physical History of Man*, ed. by G. W. Stocking Jr, pp. ix–cx. Chicago, University of Chicago Press.

1982. *Race, Culture, and Evolution: Essays in the History of Anthropology*. 2nd edn. Chicago, University of Chicago Press.

1983– ed. *History of Anthropology*. Madison, University of Wisconsin Press.

1984. ed. *Functionalism Historicized: Essays on British Social Anthropology* (*History of Anthropology*, vol. 2). Madison, University of Wisconsin Press.

1987. *Victorian Anthropology*. New York, Free Press.

Stoianovich, T. 1976. *French Historical Method: The Annales Paradigm*. Ithaca, Cornell University Press.

Stoneman, R. 1987. *Land of Lost Gods: The Search for Classical Greece*. Norman, University of Oklahoma Press.

Street, B. V. 1975. *The Savage in Literature: Representations of 'Primitive' Society in English Fiction, 1858–1920*. London, Routledge & Kegan Paul.

Strong, W. D. 1935. *An Introduction to Nebraska Archeology*. Washington, Smithsonian Miscellaneous Collections no. 93 (10).

1936. Anthropological theory and archaeological fact. In *Essays in Anthropology Presented to A. L. Kroeber*, ed. by R. H. Lowie, pp. 359–70. Berkeley, University of California Press.

Struever, S. 1968. Problems, methods and organization: a disparity in the growth of archeology. In *Anthropological Archeology in the Americas*, ed. by B. J. Meggers, pp. 131–51. Washington, Anthropological Society of Washington.

Sutton, D. G. 1985. The whence of the Moriori. *New Zealand Journal of History* 19: 3–13.

Swayze, N. 1960. *The Man Hunters*. Toronto, Clarke, Irwin.

Tallgren, A. M. 1936. Archaeological studies in Soviet Russia. *Eurasia Septentrionalis Antiqua* 10: 129–70.

1937. The method of prehistoric archaeology. *Antiquity* 11: 152–61.

Tanaka, M. 1984. Japan. In H. Cleere, pp. 82–8.

Tansley, A. G. 1935. The use and abuse of vegetation concepts and terms. *Ecology* 16: 284–307.

Tardits, C. 1981. ed. *Contribution de la recherche ethnologique à l'histoire des civilisations du Cameroun*. 2 vols. Paris, Editions du CNRS.

Tax, T. G. 1975. E. George Squier and the mounds, 1845–1850. In *Toward a Science of Man: Essays in the History of Anthropology*, ed. by T. H. H. Thoresen, pp. 99–124. The Hague, Mouton.

Taylor, S. 1982. Zimbabwe ruin row splits department. *The Times*, August 21.

Taylor, W. W. 1948. *A Study of Archeology*. *Memoir* (Menasha, Wisconsin, American Anthropological Association) 69. (Pages cited from the 1967 reprint, Southern Illinois University Press, Carbondale.)

1969. Review of S. R. and L. R. Binford, eds., *New Perspectives in Archeology*. *Science* 165: 382–4.

1972. Old wine and new skins: a contemporary parable. In M. P. Leone, pp. 28–33.

Testart, A. 1982. *Les chasseurs–cueilleurs ou l'origine des inégalités*. Paris, Société d'Ethnographie, Mémoire no. 26.

Teviotdale, D. 1932. The material culture of the moa-hunters in Murihiku. *Journal of the Polynesian Society* 41: 81–120.

Textor, R. B. 1967. *A Cross-Cultural Summary*. New Haven, HRAF Press.

Thapar, B. K. 1984. India. In H. Cleere, pp. 63–72.

Thom, R. 1975. *Structural Stability and Morphogenesis*. Reading, Massachusetts, Benjamin.

Thomas, C. 1894. *Report on the Mound Explorations of the Bureau of Ethnology*. Washington, Bureau of American Ethnology, Annual Report, 12: 3–742.

1898. *Introduction to the Study of North American Archaeology*. Cincinnati, Clarke.

Thomas, D. H. 1974. An archaeological perspective on Shoshonean bands. *American Anthropologist* 76: 11–23.

1976. *Figuring Anthropology: First Principles of Probability and Statistics*. New York, Holt, Rinehart and Winston.

1978. The awful truth about statistics in archaeology. *American Antiquity* 43: 231–44.

Thomas, J. 1987. Relations of production and social change in the Neolithic of north-west Europe. *Man* 22: 405–30.

Thompson, M. W. 1965. Marxism and culture. *Antiquity* 39: 108–16.

1967. *Novgorod the Great*. London, Evelyn, Adams and Mackay.

1977. *General Pitt-Rivers: Evolution and Archaeology in the Nineteenth Century*. Bradford-on-Avon, Moonraker Press.

Thomson, D. F. 1939. The seasonal factor in human culture. *Proceedings of the Prehistoric Society* 10: 209–21.

Thomson, G. 1949. Review of V. G. Childe, *History*. *The Modern Quarterly* N. S. 4: 266–9.

Thruston, G. P. 1890. *The Antiquities of Tennessee*. Cincinnati, Clarke.

Thwaites, R. G. 1896–1901. *The Jesuit Relations and Allied Documents*. 73 vols. Cleveland, Burrows Brothers.

Tilley, C. 1984. Ideology and the legitimation of power in the Middle Neolithic of southern Sweden. In D. Miller and C. Tilley, pp. 111–46.

Toffler, A. 1970. *Future Shock*. New York, Random House.

Tolstoy, P. 1969. Review of W. Sanders and B. Price, *Mesoamerica*. *American Anthropologist* 71: 554–8.

Tooker, E. 1982. ed. *Ethnography by Archaeologists*. Washington, The American Ethnological Society.

Toulmin, S. E. 1970. Does the distinction between normal and revolutionary science hold water? In *Criticism and the Growth of Knowledge*, ed. by I. Lakatos and A. Musgrave, pp. 39–47. Cambridge, Cambridge University Press.

Toulmin, S. E. and J. Goodfield. 1966. *The Discovery of Time*. New York, Harper and Row.

Trevelyan, G. M. 1952. *Illustrated English Social History*, vol. 4, *The Nineteenth Century*. London, Longmans, Green.

'Trevelyan'. 1857. Letters on Irish antiquities by a Cornish man. *Ulster Journal of Archaeology* 5: 150–2, 185–7, 336–42.

Trevor-Roper, H. R. 1966. *The Rise of Christian Europe*. 2nd edn. London, Thames and Hudson.

Trigger, B. G. 1965. *History and Settlement in Lower Nubia*. New Haven, Yale University Publications in Anthropology no. 69.

1966. Sir John William Dawson: a faithful anthropologist. *Anthropologica* 8: 351–9.

1967a. Settlement Archaeology – its goals and promise. *American Antiquity* 32: 149–60.

1967b. Engels on the part played by labour in the transition from ape to man: an anticipation of contemporary anthropological theory. *Canadian Review of Sociology and Anthropology* 4: 165–76.

1968a. *Beyond History: The Methods of Prehistory*. New York, Holt, Rinehart and Winston.

1968b. The determinants of settlement patterns. In *Settlement Archaeology*, ed. by K. C. Chang, pp. 53–78. Palo Alto, National Press.

1969. The personality of the Sudan. In *East African History*, ed. by D. F. McCall, N. R. Bennett, and J. Butler, pp. 74–106. New York, Praeger.

1978a. *Time and Traditions: Essays in Archaeological Interpretation*. Edinburgh, Edinburgh University Press.

1978b. The strategy of Iroquoian prehistory. In *Archaeological Essays in Honor of Irving B. Rouse*, ed. by R. C. Dunnell and E. S. Hall Jr, pp. 275–310. The Hague, Mouton.

1978c. William J. Wintemberg: Iroquoian archaeologist. In *Essays in Northeastern Anthropology in Memory of Marian E. White*, ed. by W. E. Engelbrecht and D. K. Grayson, pp. 5–21. Rindge, Occasional Publications in Northeastern Anthropology no. 5.

1980a. *Gordon Childe: Revolutions in Archaeology*. London, Thames and Hudson.

1980b. Archaeology and the image of the American Indian. *American Antiquity* 45: 662–76.

1980c. Review of A. C. Renfrew, *Problems in European Prehistory*. *Antiquity* 54: 76–7.

1981a. Anglo-American archaeology. *World Archaeology* 13: 138–55.

1981b. Archaeology and the ethnographic present. *Anthropologica* 23: 3–17.

1982a. Archaeological analysis and concepts of causality. *Culture* 2(2): 31–42.

1982b. If Childe were alive today. *Bulletin of the Institute of Archaeology, University of London* 19: 1–20.

1984a. Alternative archaeologies: nationalist, colonialist, imperialist. *Man* 19: 355–70.

1984b. Childe and Soviet archaeology. *Australian Archaeology* 18: 1–16.

1984c. Marxism and archaeology. In *On Marxian Perspectives in Anthropology*, ed. by J. Maquet and N. Daniels, pp. 59–97. Malibu, Undena.

1984d. History and Settlement in Lower Nubia in the perspective of fifteen years. In *Meroitistische Forschungen 1980*, ed. by F. Hintze. *Meroitica* 7: 367–80.

1984e. Archaeology at the crossroads: what's new? *Annual Review of Anthropology* 13: 275–300.

1985a. Writing the history of archaeology: a survey of trends. In G. W. Stocking Jr, *History of Anthropology* 3: 218–35. Madison, University of Wisconsin Press.

1985b. *Archaeology as Historical Science*. Varanasi, Banaras Hindu University, Department of Ancient Indian History, Culture and Archaeology, Monograph no. 14.

1985c. The past as power: anthropology and the North American Indian. In

Who Owns the Past? ed. by I. McBryde, pp. 11–40. Melbourne, Oxford University Press.

1985d. Marxism in archaeology: real or spurious? *Reviews in Anthropology* 12: 114–23.

1986a. ed. *Native Shell Mounds of North America: Early Studies*. New York, Garland.

1986b. Prehistoric archaeology and American society. In D. J. Meltzer *et al.*, pp. 187–215.

1986c. The role of technology in V. Gordon Childe's archaeology. *Norwegian Archaeological Review* 19: 1–14.

1988. History and contemporary American archaeology: a critical analysis. In *Archaeological Thought in America*, ed. by C. C. Lamberg-Karlovsky and P. L. Kohl, pp. 19–34. Cambridge, Cambridge University Press.

Trigger, B. G. and I. Glover. 1981–82. eds. Regional Traditions of Archaeological Research, I. II. *World Archaeology* 13(2); 13(3).

Tringham, R. 1978. Experimentation, ethnoarchaeology, and the leapfrogs in archaeological methodology. In R. A. Gould, pp. 169–99.

1983. V. Gordon Childe 25 years after: his relevance for the archaeology of the eighties. *Journal of Field Archaeology* 10: 85–100.

Tuck, J. A. 1971. *Onondaga Iroquois Prehistory: A Study in Settlement Archaeology*. Syracuse, Syracuse University Press.

Tylor, E. B. 1865. *Researches into the Early History of Mankind and the Development of Civilization*. London, John Murray.

1871. *Primitive Culture*. London, John Murray.

Ucko, P. J. 1983. Australian academic archaeology: aboriginal transformation of its aims and practices. *Australian Archaeology* 16: 11–26.

1987. *Academic Freedom and Apartheid: The Story of the World Archaeological Congress*. London, Duckworth.

Ucko, P. J. and A. Rosenfeld. 1967. *Palaeolithic Cave Art*. London, Weidenfeld and Nicolson.

Uhle, M. 1907. The Emeryville shellmound. *University of California Publications in American Archaeology and Ethnology* 7: 1–107.

Van Sertima, I. 1977. *They Came Before Columbus: The African Presence in Ancient America*. New York, Random House.

Van Seters, J. 1983. *In Search of History: Historiography in the Ancient World and the Origins of Biblical History*. New Haven, Yale University Press.

Vansina, J. 1985. *Oral Tradition as History*. Madison, University of Wisconsin Press.

Van Trong. 1979. New knowledge on Dong-s'on culture from archaeological discoveries these twenty years ago. In *Recent Discoveries and New Views on Some Archaeological Problems in Vietnam*, pp. 1–8. Hanoi, Institute of Archaeology.

Vastokas, J. M. 1987. Native art as art history: meaning and time from unwritten sources. *Journal of Canadian Studies* 21(4): 7–36.

Vastokas, J. M. and R. K. Vastokas. 1973. *Sacred Art of the Algonkians: A Study of the Peterborough Petroglyphs*. Peterborough, Mansard Press.

Vaughan, A. T. 1979. *New England Frontier: Puritans and Indians, 1620–1675*. 2nd edn. New York, Norton.
1982. From white man to red skin: changing Anglo-American perceptions of the American Indian. *American Historical Review* 87: 917–53.
Veit, U. 1984. Gustaf Kossinna und V. Gordon Childe: Ansätze zu einer theoretischen Grundlegung der Vorgeschichte. *Saeculum* 35: 326–64.
Vita-Finzi, C. and E. S. Higgs. 1970. Prehistoric economy in the Mount Carmel area of Palestine: site catchment analysis. *Proceedings of the Prehistoric Society* 36: 1–37.
Voget, F. W. 1975. *A History of Ethnology*. New York, Holt, Rinehart and Winston.
von Daniken, E. 1969. *Chariots of the Gods?* New York, Putnam.
1971. *Gods from Outer Space*. New York, Putnam.
von Gernet, A. D. 1985. *Analysis of Intrasite Artifact Spatial Distributions: The Draper Site Smoking Pipes*. London, Ontario, Museum of Indian Archaeology, Research Report no. 16.
von Gernet, A. and P. Timmins. 1987. Pipes and parakeets: constructing meaning in an Early Iroquoian context. In *Archaeology as Long-Term History*, ed. by I. Hodder, pp. 31–42. Cambridge, Cambridge University Press.
von Haast, J. 1871. Moas and moa hunters. *Transactions of the New Zealand Institute* 4: 66–107.
1874. Researches and excavations carried out in and near the Moa-bone Point Cave, Sumner Road in the year 1874. *Transactions of the New Zealand Institute* 7: 54–85.
Wace, A. J. B. 1949. The Greeks and Romans as archaeologists. *Société royale d'archéologie d'Alexandrie, Bulletin* 38: 21–35.
Wahle, E. 1915. Urwald und offenes Land in ihrer Bedeutung für die Kulturentwickelung. *Archiv für Anthropologie*, N.S. 13: 404–13.
Walker, S. T. 1883. The aborigines of Florida. Washington, *Annual Report of the Smithsonian Institution for 1881*: 677–80.
Wallace, A. F. C. 1950. A possible technique for recognizing psychological characteristics of the ancient Maya from an analysis of their art. *The American Imago* 7: 239–58.
Wallerstein, I. 1974. *The Modern World-System*, vol. 1. New York, Academic Press.
Walsh, W. H. 1967. *An Introduction to Philosophy of History*. 3rd edn. London, Hutchinson University Library.
Walters, H. B. 1934. *The English Antiquaries of the Sixteenth, Seventeenth and Eighteenth Centuries*. London, Walters.
Wang, Gungwu. 1985. Loving the ancient in China. In *Who Owns the Past?* ed. by I. McBryde, pp. 175–95. Melbourne, Oxford University Press.
Waring, A. J. Jr. and P. Holder. 1945. A prehistoric ceremonial complex in the southeastern United States. *American Anthropologist* 47: 1–34.
Warren, S. H. 1905. On the origin of 'eolithic' flints by natural causes, especially by the foundering of drifts. *Journal of the Royal Anthropological Institute* 35: 337–64.

Washburn, S. L. 1960. Tools and human evolution. *Scientific American* 203(3): 62–75.

Washburn, W. E. 1967. Joseph Henry's conception of the purpose of the Smithsonian Institution. In *A Cabinet of Curiosities*, ed. by W. M. Whitehill, pp. 106–66. Charlottesville, Press of the University of Virginia.

Watson, P. J. 1979. *Archaeological Ethnography in Western Iran*. Viking Fund Publications in Anthropology no. 57. Tucson, University of Arizona Press.

1985. ed. Golden Anniversary Issue. *American Antiquity* 50(2).

1986. Archaeological interpretation, 1985. In J. Meltzer *et al.*, pp. 439–57.

Watson, P. J., S. A. LeBlanc, and C. L. Redman. 1971. *Explanation in Archeology: An Explicitly Scientific Approach*. New York, Columbia University Press.

1984. *Archeological Explanation: The Scientific Method in Archeology*. New York, Columbia University Press.

Watson, R. A. 1972. The 'New Archaeology' of the 1960s. *Antiquity* 46: 210–15.

Watson, W. 1981. The progress of archaeology in China. In J. D. Evans *et al.*, pp. 65–70.

Webb, W. S. and W. D. Funkhouser. 1928. *Ancient Life in Kentucky*. Frankfurt, Kentucky Geological Survey.

Wedel, W. R. 1938. *The Direct-Historical Approach in Pawnee Archeology*. Washington, Smithsonian Miscellaneous Collections no. 97(7).

1941. *Environment and Native Subsistence Economies in the Central Great Plains*. Washington, Smithsonian Miscellaneous Collections no. 101(3).

1985. ed. *A Plains Archaeology Source Book: Selected Papers of the Nebraska State Historical Society*. New York, Garland.

Weiss, R. 1969. *The Renaissance Discovery of Classical Antiquity*. Oxford, Basil Blackwell.

Wells, P. S. 1984. *Farms, Villages, and Cities: Commerce and Urban Origins in Late Prehistoric Europe*. Ithaca, Cornell University Press.

Wendt, H. 1955. *In Search of Adam*. Boston, Houghton Mifflin.

Wenke, R. J. 1981. Explaining the evolution of cultural complexity: a review. *Advances in Archaeological Method and Theory* 4: 79–127.

Whallon, R. Jr. 1968. Investigations of late prehistoric social organization in New York State. In S. R. and L. R. Binford, pp. 223–44.

1982. Comments on 'explanation'. In A. C. Renfrew and S. Shennan, pp. 155–8.

Wheeler, R. E. M. 1954. *Archaeology from the Earth*. Oxford, Oxford University Press.

White, C. 1799. *An Account of the Regular Gradation in Man, and in Different Animals and Vegetables*. London, Diley.

White, J. P. 1974. *The Past is Human*. Sydney, Angus and Robertson.

White, J. P. and J. F. O'Connell. 1982. *A Prehistory of Australia, New Guinea and Sahul*. Sydney, Academic Press.

White, L. A. 1945. 'Diffusion vs. evolution': an anti-evolutionist fallacy. *American Anthropologist* 47: 339–56.

1949. *The Science of Culture*. New York, Farrar, Straus.

1959. *The Evolution of Culture*. New York, McGraw-Hill.
1975. *The Concept of Cultural Systems*. New York, Columbia University Press.
Wiener, N. 1961. *Cybernetics*. 2nd edn. Cambridge, Massachusetts, M.I.T. Press.
Wilcox, D. R. and W. B. Masse. 1981. eds. *The Protohistoric Period in the North American Southwest, AD 1450–1700*. Tempe, Arizona State University, Anthropological Research Paper no. 24.
Wilk, R. R. 1985. The ancient Maya and the political present. *Journal of Anthropological Research* 41: 307–26.
Willey, G. R. 1948. A functional analysis of 'horizon styles' in Peruvian archaeology. In *A Reappraisal of Peruvian Archaeology*, ed. by W. C. Bennett, pp. 8–15. *Memoir* (Menasha, Wisconsin, Society for American Archaeology) 4.
1953. *Prehistoric Settlement Patterns in the Virú Valley, Peru*. Washington, Bureau of American Ethnology, Bulletin no. 155.
1956. ed. *Prehistoric Settlement Patterns in the New World*. New York, Viking Fund Publications in Anthropology no. 23.
1974a. ed. *Archaeological Researches in Retrospect*. Cambridge, Winthrop.
1974b. The Virú Valley settlement pattern study. In G. R. Willey, 1974a, pp. 147–76.
1985. Ancient Chinese–New World and Near Eastern ideological traditions: some observations. *Symbols*, spring issue, 14–17, 22–3.
1986. The Classic Maya sociopolitical order: a study in coherence and in stability. In *Research and Reflections in Archaeology and History: Essays in Honor of Doris Stone*, ed. by E. W. Andrews V, pp. 189–98. Tulane, Middle American Research Institute.
Willey, G. R., W. R. Bullard Jr, J. B. Glass, and J. C. Gifford. 1965. *Prehistoric Maya Settlements in the Belize Valley*. Cambridge, Papers of the Peabody Museum of Archaeology and Ethnology no. 54.
Willey, G. R. and P. Phillips. 1958. *Method and Theory in American Archaeology*. Chicago, University of Chicago Press.
Willey, G. R. and J. A. Sabloff. 1974. *A History of American Archaeology*. London, Thames and Hudson.
1980. *A History of American Archaeology*. 2nd edn. San Francisco, Freeman.
Wilson, D. 1851. *The Archaeology and Prehistoric Annals of Scotland*. Edinburgh, Sutherland and Knox.
1862. *Prehistoric Man: Researches into the Origin of Civilization in the Old and the New World*. London, Macmillan.
1863. *The Prehistoric Annals of Scotland*. 2nd edn. London, Macmillan.
1876. *Prehistoric Man*. 3rd edn. London, Macmillan.
Wilson, D. 1975. *Atoms of Time Past*. London, Allen Lane.
Wilson, D. M. 1976. ed. *The Archaeology of Anglo-Saxon England*. London, Methuen.
Wilson, J. A. 1964. *Signs and Wonders upon Pharaoh*. Chicago, University of Chicago Press.
Wiseman, J. 1980a. Archaeology in the future: an evolving discipline. *American Journal of Archaeology* 84: 279–85.
1980b. Archaeology as archaeology. *Journal of Field Archaeology* 7: 149–51.

1983. Conflicts in archaeology: education and practice. *Journal of Field Archaeology* 10: 1–9.

Wissler, C. 1914. Material cultures of the North American Indians. *American Anthropologist* 16: 447–505.

Wobst, H. M. 1978. The archaeo-ethnology of hunter–gatherers or the tyranny of the ethnographic record in archaeology. *American Antiquity* 43: 303–9.

Wolf, E. R. 1982. *Europe and the People without History*. Berkeley, University of California Press.

Wood, M. 1985. *In Search of the Trojan War*. London, BBC Publications.

Woodbridge, K. 1970. *Landscape and Antiquity: Aspects of English Culture at Stourhead, 1718–1838*. Oxford, Oxford University Press.

Woodbury, R. B. 1973. *Alfred V. Kidder*. New York, Columbia University Press.

Woolfson, C. 1982. *The Labour Theory of Culture*. London, Routledge & Kegan Paul.

Woolley, C. L. 1950. *Ur of the Chaldees*. Harmondsworth, Penguin (1st edn., 1929).

Worsaae, J. J. A. 1849. *The Primeval Antiquities of Denmark*. trans. by W. J. Thoms. London, Parker.

Wylie, M. A. 1982. Epistemological issues raised by a structuralist archaeology. In I. Hodder, 1982c, pp. 39–46.

1985a. The reaction against analogy. *Advances in Archaeological Method and Theory* 8: 63–111.

1985b. Facts of the record and facts of the past: Mandelbaum on the anatomy of history 'proper'. *International Studies in Philosophy* 17: 71–85.

1985c. Putting Shakertown back together: critical theory in archaeology. *Journal of Anthropological Archaeology* 4: 133–47.

1989. The dilemma of interpretation. In *Critical Traditions in Contemporary Archaeology*, ed. by V. Pinsky and A. Wylie. Cambridge, Cambridge University Press.

Wyman, J. 1875. *Fresh-Water Shell Mounds of the St. John's River, Florida*. Salem, Memoirs of the Peabody Academy of Science no. 4.

Yellen, J. E. 1977. *Archaeological Approaches to the Present: Models for Reconstructing the Past*. New York, Academic Press.

Yengoyan, A. A. 1985. Digging for symbols: the archaeology of everyday material culture. *Proceedings of the Prehistoric Society* 51: 329–34.

Young, T. C. Jr. 1972. Population densities and early Mesopotamian urbanism. In *Man, Settlement and Urbanism*, ed. by P. J. Ucko, R. Tringham, and G. W. Dimbleby, pp. 827–42. London, Duckworth.

Zipf, G. K. 1949. *Human Behavior and the Principle of Least Effort*. Cambridge, Massachusetts, Addison-Wesley.

Zittel, K. A. von. 1901. *History of Geology and Palaeontology to the End of the Nineteenth Century*. London, Scott.

Zubrow, E. 1972. Environment, subsistence, and society: the changing archaeological perspective. *Annual Review of Anthropology* 1: 179–206.

1980. International trends in theoretical archaeology. *Norwegian Archaeological Review* 13: 14–23.

INDEX

Index

Index

Index

Index

Index

Index

Index

Index

Index

Index

Index

Index

Index

Index

Index

Index

Index